MW00779315

THE CONTAINMENT

THE CONTAINMENT

Detroit, the Supreme Court, and the Battle
for Racial Justice in the North

MICHELLE ADAMS

FARRAR, STRAUS AND GIROUX | NEW YORK

Farrar, Straus and Giroux
120 Broadway, New York 10271

Maps and table courtesy of Myles Zhang.

Library of Congress Cataloging-in-Publication Data
Names: Adams, Michelle, 1963– author.
Title: The containment : Detroit, the Supreme Court, and the battle for racial justice
  in the North / Michelle Adams.
Other titles: Detroit, the Supreme Court, and the battle for racial justice in the North
Description: First edition. | New York : Farrar, Straus and Giroux, 2025. | Includes
  bibliographical references and index.
Identifiers: LCCN 2024023855 | ISBN 9780374250423 (hardcover)
Subjects: LCSH: Discrimination in education—Law and legislation—Michigan—Detroit—
  History. | Busing for school integration—Law and legislation—Michigan—Detroit—History. |
  Milliken, William G., 1922– —Trials, litigation, etc. | Bradley, Ronald—Trials, litigation, etc. |
  National Association for the Advancement of Colored People. Detroit Branch—Trials,
  litigation, etc. | African Americans—Civil rights—Michigan—Detroit—Social conditions—
  20th century. | Detroit (Mich.). Board of Education. | Detroit (Mich.) —History—20th century.
Classification: LCC KF228.M55 A33 2025 | DDC 344.73/0798—dc23/eng/20241007
LC record available at https://lccn.loc.gov/2024023855

Designed by Gretchen Achilles

Our books may be purchased in bulk for promotional, educational,
or business use. Please contact your local bookseller or the Macmillan Corporate
and Premium Sales Department at 1-800-221-7945, extension 5442, or by email at
MacmillanSpecialMarkets@macmillan.com.

www.fsgbooks.com
Follow us on social media at @fsgbooks

1 3 5 7 9 10 8 6 4 2

For Bernard and Frederica

I would unite with anybody to do right and with
nobody to do wrong.

—FREDERICK DOUGLASS

America is woven of many strands; I would
recognize them and let it so remain . . . Our fate is
to become one, and yet many.

—RALPH ELLISON, *Invisible Man*

CONTENTS

NOTE ON THE TEXT

For purposes of consistency with quotations from historical sources, "black" has been left lowercased throughout the text.

CAST OF CHARACTERS
IN ORDER OF APPEARANCE

JOHN ROBERTS – Chief justice of the U.S. Supreme Court (2005–present); wrote majority opinion in *Parents Involved in Community Schools v. Seattle School District*.

ANTHONY KENNEDY – Associate justice of the U.S. Supreme Court (1988–2018); as a member of Roberts Court, joined portions of the majority opinion in *Parents Involved*.

ANTONIN SCALIA – Associate justice of the U.S. Supreme Court (1986–2016); as a member of Roberts Court, joined majority in *Parents Involved*.

STEPHEN BREYER – Associate justice of the U.S. Supreme Court (1994–2022); as a member of the Roberts Court, wrote eloquent dissenting opinion in *Parents Involved*.

THURGOOD MARSHALL – Associate justice of the U. S. Supreme Court (1967–91) and its first African American member; as chief of the NAACP Legal Defense and Educational Fund, argued *Brown v. Board of Education*; as a member of the Burger Court, wrote prophetic dissent in *Milliken v. Bradley*.

ALBERT B. CLEAGE JR. – Minister; black nationalist, political organizer; challenged the Detroit Board of Education at the "Clash in Midtown"; community control advocate.

REMUS ROBINSON – Physician; first black member of the Detroit Board of Education; school integration advocate.

ABRAHAM L. ZWERDLING – Lawyer; chair of the Detroit Board of Education; school integration advocate.

GEORGE ROMNEY – Michigan governor until 1969, when he resigned to become Secretary of Housing and Urban Development under President Richard Nixon.

COLEMAN YOUNG – Political activist and Michigan state senator; later became Detroit's first black mayor.

NORMAN DRACHLER – Superintendent of Detroit Public Schools; school integration advocate.

ANDREW PERDUE – Lawyer; member of the Detroit Board of Education; community control advocate.

JUNE SHAGALOFF ALEXANDER – Community organizer extraordinaire; NAACP national education director; along with Robert L. Carter, key player in the NAACP's drive to bring *Brown* north.

ROBERT L. CARTER – General counsel of the NAACP; along with June Shagaloff Alexander, key player in the NAACP's drive to bring *Brown* north.

ROY WILKINS – NAACP executive director; authorized the NAACP's drive to bring *Brown* north.

PAUL ZUBER – Attorney; civil rights activist; litigated *Taylor v. Board of Education of New Rochelle*.

WILLIAM G. MILLIKEN – Michigan governor following George Romney's resignation; named defendant in the *Milliken* case.

WILLIAM TAYLOR – Lawyer and school desegregation expert; provided legal advice to his friend Abraham Zwerdling.

PATRICK McDONALD – Attorney, member (and later chair) of the Detroit Board of Education; opposed high school integration plan.

CITIZENS COMMITTEE FOR BETTER EDUCATION (CCBE) – Organization of white Detroiters who fought school desegregation efforts.

LOUIS LUCAS – Respected civil rights attorney; lead counsel for the plaintiffs in the *Milliken* case.

VERDA BRADLEY – Mother of the named plaintiffs, Ronald and Richard Bradley, who attended Detroit public schools.

FRANK J. KELLEY – Michigan state attorney general; defendant in the *Milliken* case.

STEPHEN J. ROTH – Federal trial court judge; presided over the *Milliken* case.

PAUL DIMOND – Young attorney who worked on the trial team representing the plaintiffs in the *Milliken* case.

GEORGE BUSHNELL JR. – Attorney for the Detroit Board of Education.

NATHANIEL R. JONES – Succeeded Robert Carter as general counsel of the NAACP.

J. "NICK" HAROLD FLANNERY – Civil rights lawyer who worked on the trial team representing the plaintiffs in the *Milliken* case.

ALEXANDER RITCHIE – Detroiter and lawyer for the CCBE.

ABRAHAM RIBICOFF – Liberal Democrat and United States senator; school integration advocate.

WARREN E. BURGER – Chief Justice of the U.S. Supreme Court (1969–86); wrote majority opinion in *Milliken v. Bradley.*

LEWIS F. POWELL JR. – Associate justice of the U.S. Supreme Court (1972–87); as a member of Burger Court, joined the majority in *Milliken.*

ROBERT GREEN – Detroiter and professor; expert in educational psychology and school desegregation.

DAMON KEITH – Federal trial court judge; presided over *Davis v. School District of the City of Pontiac.*

IRENE MCCABE – Mother and community organizer; staunchly opposed to busing.

WILLIAM SAXTON – Attorney for the suburban school districts.

EARL WARREN – Chief Justice of the U.S. Supreme Court (1953–69); wrote *Brown v. Board of Education* opinion.

HARRY BLACKMUN – Associate justice of the U.S. Supreme Court (1970–94); as a member of Burger Court, joined the majority in *Milliken*.

WILLIAM H. REHNQUIST – Associate justice of the U.S. Supreme Court (1972–86); as a member of Burger Court, joined the majority in *Milliken*; chief justice (1986–2005).

POTTER STEWART – Associate justice of the U.S. Supreme Court (1958–81); as a member of Burger Court, joined the majority in *Milliken*.

ROBERT BORK – U.S. solicitor general who argued on behalf of the United States government in the *Milliken* case.

ROBERT E. DEMASCIO – Federal trial court judge; later presided over the *Milliken* case.

PROLOGUE

On December 4, 2006, I attended an oral argument at the U.S. Supreme Court in Washington, D.C., as a newly admitted member of the Supreme Court Bar. It was my first visit to the high court, but I wasn't a civilian. As a civil rights lawyer and constitutional law professor for more than ten years, I, along with another professor, had submitted an "amicus curiae" brief in a school desegregation case that would be heard that day. ("Amicus curiae" means "friend of the court.") Writing on behalf of the National Parent Teacher Association, we argued that a racially integrated education was an absolute imperative for all children. "In a multiracial setting, all children are provided the best opportunity to master necessary academic skills, to engage in critical thinking, to achieve comfort with members of other races and ethnic groups, and to aspire to their highest potential," the brief confidently asserted. With my work for the NPTA complete, I felt a sense of satisfaction. I had played a small role in what promised to be one of the most important cases of my generation. The case would answer a core constitutional question: What does *Brown v. Board of Education* really mean? Did *Brown* just ban the kind of "dual" school systems that were once ubiquitous in the South: overtly racially separate schools for whites and blacks? Or did *Brown* stand for the proposition that, given the myriad harms of segregation, Americans of different races should be educated together rather than apart, *even if* it meant assigning students on the basis of race to accomplish that goal?

For me, attending this oral argument was not just professional—it was deeply personal. My father, who had died several years before that December morning, had been a criminal defense lawyer in Detroit, Michigan, for more than forty years. He was one of only two black men to graduate from the Detroit College of Law in 1957.[1] That he became a lawyer at that time bordered on the astonishing. A full ten years later, American law schools were producing only about two hundred black lawyers annually.[2] In 1989—when I graduated from law school—American law schools weren't exactly minting black lawyers (in the year in which I graduated there were only about 6,300 black students enrolled in law school *nationwide*).[3] So the fact that I had become a lawyer, just as he had, was a big deal. But it was an even bigger deal that I was now a law professor sitting in the Supreme Court.

To me, my father was a larger-than-life figure. I remember him once lying on a counsel table in open court to illustrate a point during one of my frequent trips downtown to watch him work. "Everyone deserves a good defense," he often told me. And he provided it. My father defended several generations of Detroiters in the city's bustling criminal courts. He was a well-respected lawyer, a pillar of the community. But as I sat in the high court waiting for argument to begin in a case in which I had submitted a brief, it was clear that I had opportunities that simply weren't available to him. He would have been bursting with pride.

The majesty of the setting matched the importance of the case to be heard that day: *Parents Involved in Community Schools v. Seattle School District No. 1. Parents Involved* was about two public school districts: one in Seattle, Washington, and one in Louisville, Kentucky. Both school districts had used race to achieve more racial integration in their respective school systems, and now that policy was under attack.[4]

The trouble was what had happened to the interpretation of *Brown* in the decades since the decision—and the two diverging ways that the ruling was now understood. The first understanding emphasized the harm that segregation created; *Brown* said "separate is inherently unequal" and that racial separation "generates a feeling of inferiority . . . unlikely ever to be undone." Such a harm created a duty on school authorities to desegregate. Following this view, Seattle and Louisville considered race when assigning students to schools because they believed they had a duty to fulfill *Brown*'s promise of integration. But in the second understanding of *Brown*, a primary point of the ruling was that it was unconstitutional for school districts to assign students to schools on the basis of race. Period. On this view, the harm was created when the government *classified* students on the basis of race. In this view of *Brown*, the school districts could not consider race *even in the service of integration.* Now the Supreme Court and its relatively new chief justice, John Roberts, would have to resolve this question: Could school districts use race to reduce segregation in the schools, or did the decision actually limit their ability to intervene along racial lines? The chief justice distilled the issue: "The parties . . . debate which side is more faithful to the heritage of *Brown*."[5] So the question was: Which vision of *Brown*—perhaps the most important constitutional case of the twentieth century—would prevail?

So there I sat, pen poised, head up, attention rapt. The clock struck ten.

The justices appeared from behind the drapes and moved quickly to their seats. The lawyer representing the group of children who had challenged Seattle's school assignment plan began: "Mr. Chief Justice, and may it please the Court." Almost immediately Justice Anthony Kennedy asked a hypothetical question. The justice invited the lawyer to imagine that school authorities were attempting to determine where to build a new school. Kennedy: "There are three sites. One of them would be all one race. Site two would be all the other race. Site three would be a diversity of races. Can the school board with . . . the intent to have diversity pick site number 3?"[6] The lawyer didn't answer the question directly: "Justice Kennedy, I think the answer turns on the reason that the schools have the racial compositions that they do."[7] The racial makeup of the three sites differed because of "residential housing segregation" and "the board wants to have diversity," the justice clarified.[8] The lawyer soon explained that in his view, seeking racial diversity in schools should not be allowed "absent past discrimination."[9] The response implied that "residential housing segregation" and past discrimination were discordant, unrelated phenomena. But if that were the case, why were the areas around the new school sites—in Justice Kennedy's words—"segregated" in the first place?

Later, Justice Antonin Scalia interrupted counsel for the school districts to offer his view of the correct definition of "segregation": "You refer to some of the schools as segregated . . . That's not what I understand by segregated . . . I mean, you know, if you belong to a country club that . . . has 15 percent black members, I would not consider that a segregated country club."[10] The justice continued: "What you are complaining about is not segregation in any reasonable sense of the word. You're complaining about a lack of racial balance." "We are not complaining about segregation resulting from purposeful discrimination," the lawyer conceded.[11] "That's the only meaning of segregation" was Justice Scalia's curt reply.[12] All I could think was: *The school districts are going to lose this case.* Of that I was sure.

Justice Scalia's comments suggested that "segregation" had a specific, technical meaning. From this perspective, the only definition of "segregation" was racial separation directly traceable to purposeful governmental discrimination. Everything else was mere "racial imbalance," which was entirely unobjectionable under constitutional law. Lack of "racial balance" certainly couldn't justify the school districts' use of racial classifications. The justice's remarks held two further assumptions. The first was that "segregation," *if* it still existed, was rare and rapidly vanishing. The country club scenario was far more likely. The second was that the cause of the remaining racial separation—the racial imbalance—so readily observable in places like schools and neighborhoods was unknown and perhaps unknowable. After all, who knew why there was an 85–15 racial split at the country club? It was a mystery, one that perhaps only Sherlock Holmes could solve.

Justice Kennedy's hypothetical question suggested that *Parents Involved*, a school segregation case, also raised significant questions about housing segregation. It did. The core of the question in *Parents Involved* was whether school authorities—cognizant of background conditions that created racially segregated schools such as residential segregation—could take race-based action to overcome those conditions. But the school districts ran right into a wall at the Supreme Court: *What you are complaining about is not segregation in any reasonable sense of the word.*

In subsequent years, the court would set the cause of racial justice back still further, curtailing the enforcement of voting rights and the use of affirmative action in university admissions. The *Brown* court's use of the Fourteenth Amendment and its guarantee of "equal protection" to promote equality would be turned on its head. After attending the *Parents Involved* oral argument, I wasn't surprised.

As I reflected on Justice Scalia's comments in *Parents Involved*, I thought of an earlier school segregation case from 1974 called *Milliken v. Bradley*. It arose in my hometown of Detroit. Every year, I'd teach the case in my constitutional law class and attempt to explain why it was so incredibly important. And every year I failed. I'd explain that the Detroit branch of the NAACP brought a lawsuit against state and local school officials alleging that—as a result of official government policy—students in the Detroit public schools were segregated on the basis of race. The case was a triumph for the NAACP; it proved that Detroit's schools were unconstitutionally segregated. It *won* its case against the state and local government. Because of *Brown*, the victory meant that black students in Detroit were entitled to attend integrated schools. But there was a big problem: there weren't enough white students in Detroit to have meaningful integration, and a Detroit-only integration plan would further incentivize whites to leave the city. Recognizing these difficulties, the trial judge in the case ordered that students in nearby suburban—and largely white—school districts be included in a sweeping plan to integrate Detroit's schools. The trial judge believed that what came to be called a "metropolitan remedy" was both appropriate and required. In this, *Brown* was his guiding light.[13]

I had special feelings for Detroit, but in many ways the city wasn't unique. The racial composition of the Detroit metropolitan area was distressingly familiar. There was even a name for the phenomenon: "chocolate city, vanilla suburbs."[14] The term was popularized by "Chocolate City," a 1975 hit song by the legendary funk band Parliament. The song celebrated the shifting demographics of the nation's capital—"God bless [Washington, D.C.] and its vanilla suburbs"—and "name-checked" several other majority black cities.[15] And, just as the urban-suburban racial divide that characterized the Detroit metropolitan area was prototypical, its causes were equally ubiquitous: racially restrictive covenants, redlining, racial steering, blockbusting, mortgage lending discrimination, racially segregated public housing, urban renewal, exclusionary zoning, white violence. For these reasons, it was hard to overstate the importance of the trial judge's ruling. If metropolitan "cross-district" desegregation could be ordered in Detroit, it conceivably could be ordered anywhere.

But when the *Milliken* case reached the Supreme Court, the judge's plan was overturned. In a 5–4 decision, the justices ruled that the trial judge had gone too far and that suburban school districts that had not formally engaged in racial discrimination could not be included in a larger integration plan. Because of *Brown*, students had a right not to be confined to racially segregated schools. Due to *Milliken*, however, for most black students in the North, the rights protected under *Brown* were meaningless. *Brown* had been violated. Black schoolchildren had *won* the case. But it didn't matter. What mattered more were the interests of the suburban school districts, and they wanted nothing to do with integrating Detroit's schools. Emphasizing suburban innocence, the importance of local control, and a deeply blinkered view of even the most recent history, *Milliken* signaled that the country's serious efforts at school integration had come to an end. As difficult as *Brown* was to implement, it did change the political landscape. After *Brown*, the defaults shifted. *Brown* put southern segregationists on the defensive. *Brown* altered the nature of the national conversation and moved us closer to racial equality. But *Milliken* had exactly the opposite effect. It suggested that the default position was actually much closer to "separate but [un]equal."

Most of the time, my students didn't really understand why *Milliken* was so important, and I couldn't communicate my complex feelings about the case. For me, *Milliken* also triggered something deeply personal. I was born in Detroit in 1963. Both my parents were born there as well, children of the Great Migration. Their parents, along with millions of others, came to Detroit, Chicago, New York, Philadelphia, and a host of other northern and western cities to escape southern Jim Crow. My grandparents (and other Detroit-bound blacks) hoped that the city's booming auto industry would provide better opportunities for them and their children. It did. When my parents got married in 1962, my father already owned a home in southwest Detroit, one that he had paid for entirely in cash.

By the late 1960s, my parents were part of Detroit's thriving black middle class. They were living the American dream and wanted—like so many other Americans, then as now—to move on up. But my parents knew the suburbs were effectively closed to them. That Detroit's suburbs were off-limits for blacks was hardly a secret. Just two years before my parents married, Michigan's mean suburban black population stood at a paltry 2.1 percent.[16] Most white realtors wouldn't show prospective black home-buyers listings in suburban neighborhoods. And, even if blacks somehow managed to purchase a home outside the city, the fear of white violence was real. In June 1967, whites repeatedly attacked an interracial couple, Carado and Ruby Bailey, after they had moved into a suburban Warren, Michigan, subdivision.[17] The event was widely reported. Several days after the move-in, the *Detroit Free Press* noted that "police with riot guns Tuesday night swept 200 jeering people away from a Negro home in Warren that was under siege by white demonstrators for the third consecutive night."[18] Several months later, someone burned a cross in the family's front yard.[19] By some accounts, the harassment continued for years. In 1968, a Michigan Civil Rights Commission official reported that "our experience has been that nearly all attempts by black families to move to Detroit suburbs have been met with harassment."[20] My parents read both of the city's two major daily papers, the liberal-leaning *Detroit Free Press* (morning) and the more conservative *Detroit News* (evening), avidly. I don't know for sure whether they were aware of what had happened to the Baileys. But what I do know is that they dreamed of building a home in northwest Detroit, in a community called Palmer Woods.

Home to white auto executives and industry magnates in the 1920s and 1930s, Palmer Woods was one of the most beautiful areas in the entire city. Although the neighborhood was located within Detroit, you would never know it. The community teemed with English Tudors and other early twentieth-century mansions set back on large, irregular lots. The impressive houses, windy streets, and massive trees gave the area a suburban, parklike feel. But in 1967, Palmer Woods was still almost entirely white.[21] The color line that separated Detroit's neighborhoods (and that between the city and the suburbs) was rigid. Ultimately, my parents bought a corner lot in the area, right off Woodward Avenue (Detroit's "Main Street"). But the lot where their dream home in Palmer Woods would one day be situated wasn't easily obtained. In late 1967—and just a few months after

the deadliest and most violent civil disorder of the 1960s[22]—a white intermediary purchased the land and then assigned the deed to my parents.[23]
How my parents obtained the intermediary and what he charged for his
services is unknown. But what I distinctly remember is my mother telling
me that they couldn't have bought the land without him.

1967 was an important year for my parents for another reason. Both of
them had attended the city's public schools. My father was a proud graduate of Northwestern High School; my mother attended Southwestern
High. But they made a different choice for me. In the fall of 1967, they
enrolled me in Roeper City and Country School, a small private school in
the tony suburb of Bloomfield Hills. The precise reason for their choice
has been lost in the mists of time, although the fact that Roeper was the
very first private school in the state of Michigan to integrate its student
body might have had something to do with it.[24] Perhaps they were reacting to the recent civil disorder. They were likely aware that President
Lyndon Johnson had established the "blue ribbon" Kerner Commission
to study—even while the Detroit riot was still raging—the causes of and
potential solutions for urban civil unrest.[25] Or they might have been responding to information they gleaned from the *Detroit Free Press*. In
February 1967, the paper reported on a U.S. Commission on Civil Rights
study concluding that the Detroit public schools were deeply racially segregated.[26] More than 70 percent of black elementary school students in
Detroit attended schools that were at least 90 percent black; 65 percent of
the city's white grade school students attended schools that were at least
90 percent white. That same report found that "school segregation . . . had
detrimental effects on the social development of the children involved."[27]

In September, the *Detroit Free Press* reported on a recent study of
black Detroiters that might have shed some light on my parents' decision-
making process. The study suggested that, notwithstanding high levels of
discontent, most black Detroiters still continued to believe in the American
dream.[28] A key finding was that black Detroiters were strong supporters of
education. They were optimistic about their children's "chances of reaching professional or technical career levels."[29] The question was whether
this objective could be obtained in Detroit's schools. Black Detroiters'
hope for their children "throws considerable stress upon the whole urban

system and upon the educational resources that are expected to create such mobility," the study warned.[30] Perhaps this was why, only very recently out of diapers, I found myself attending a distant suburban private school in the fall of 1967.

Growing up, I didn't know how I'd come to call Palmer Woods home. Nor was I aware of the changes gripping the Detroit public schools. The school bus held no negative connotations for me. I rode the bus to the predominantly white school every day for nearly fourteen years—beginning at the age of three. The Roeper School was founded by noted progressive educators George and Annemarie Roeper, who had come to the United States in the late 1930s as refugees fleeing the Nazi regime (Annemarie was Jewish).[31] I doubt the irony of the fact that I attended a private school located in the suburbs where I likely could not have enrolled in public school—because of residential segregation—was lost on my parents. Although I was one of few black children, I felt at home. Roeper is where I grew up. The teachers and administrators knew me and my parents well. They not only cared about my education, but they genuinely believed I had something vital and unique to contribute to the world. But as I matured, I began to ask questions. Why were there so few black children at Roeper or on any of the opposing sports teams we played? Why were there so few black families in my classmates' suburban neighborhoods? In the city of Detroit and in the Jeffries housing projects, the public housing development where I frequently visited my beloved grandaunt Melinda, there were plenty of black families. I wondered why.

I graduated from high school in 1981. Uncharacteristically, my father cried as he and my mother dropped me off at Brown University in Providence, Rhode Island, that fall. I'd never seen him do that before and it made a big impression. By 1981, the American auto industry was in deep trouble and the country was in recession. In Detroit, the city's car factories were closing and its manufacturing jobs were disappearing. It felt like every time I read the daily papers or watched the local news the story was always the same: Detroit's rising violent crime rate. Perhaps this explained my father's tears as we said our goodbyes. He had good reason to fear that I might not ever return to the city. Thousands of others had made that choice. In 1950, Detroit was the nation's fifth-largest city with a population of more than 1.8 million people.[32] By 1980, the number was just above 1.2 million and falling.[33] My family and I had gained tremendously from living in Detroit, and we lost something of incalculable value as the city declined. I take great pride in my parents' accomplishments and in the community from which we hailed. But, even at eighteen, this pride was tinged with a sense of loss.

And so every time I taught *Milliken*, I looked at my poorly drawn map of Michigan on the board and my thoughts wandered back to my childhood. Images flooded my mind: black skeet shooters, the Eastern Market, Dutch Girl doughnuts, Hudson's Thanksgiving Day parade on Woodward Avenue, the hair salon on Livernois Avenue, rhubarb bushes and massive sunflowers on city lots, black milkmen, the pea-green Cadillac in which my father taught me to drive. I smelled the scent of my grandfather's sweet pipe smoke and my grandmother's ripe green switches plucked clean for when I misbehaved. I heard Stevie Wonder's funky dance tune, "You Haven't Done Nothin'," and my grandmother singing Bible verses. The laughter of my family and my parents' friends—black lawyers, judges, doctors, nurses, schoolteachers, and administrators, with some well-earned money in their pockets and a job to go to on Monday morning— rang in my ears. When my students raised their hands and asked their questions about *Milliken*, I could never really explain why the case was so important. But it was and it still is: more than any other single case, *Milliken v. Bradley* is where the promise of *Brown v. Board of Education* ended.

During the Jim Crow era, black children were confined to all-black schools. In 1954, *Brown* said that kind of overt discrimination was unconstitutional. Then, the second *Brown* case, decided in 1955,[34] and a handful of crucial follow-on cases decided several years later, actually enforced that right. Finally, black children would be treated as full and equal citizens of the United States. *Brown* and its progeny provided a meaningful remedy for black children who had experienced grievous mistreatment for generations at the hands of the state: desegregation.

Today, desegregation is perceived largely as a southern phenomenon— the *Brown* cases concerned southern and border states—that failed. Americans' collective memory is that we tried to desegregate in the South and it didn't work; perhaps it should never even have been tried. It is true that many whites were extraordinarily hostile to desegregation because it meant exactly that: destroying segregation. Segregation had always been about containment; about keeping blacks in their (lower) place—educational, residential, physical, occupational, social, psychological. But now, blacks were appearing in places they weren't supposed to be, such as in white public schools. Whites attempted to stop this by attacking black children, particularly the early desegregation pioneers like Elizabeth Eckford and the rest of the Little Rock Nine. Everyone knows (or they should) that whites engaged in grotesque acts of harassment and violence in an effort to stop black students from breaking the color line. These were defensive, pro-segregation moves.

But history has more than one story to tell. What most Americans don't know is that school desegregation *as a social policy* was a resounding success for *both* black and white students. First, desegregation shifted important educational resources to black students that had long been denied; in effect, it was a very effective form of wealth and social capital redistribution. Second, by requiring that blacks and whites be educated together starting in the earliest grades, desegregation helped destroy the deeply embedded cultural belief system that underpinned those unspeakable acts at Central High and elsewhere: white supremacy. Viewed from this perspective, the one-two punch of the *Brown* remedy—desegregation—was actually quite radical. At the core of the desegregation story is *both* reactionary white rage—Little Rock—and the possibility that we might as a nation transcend it. This was the promise of *Brown*.

══════

When the court issued its opinion in *Parents Involved*, the outcome was just as I feared: the school systems' integration plans were struck down. Justice Stephen Breyer wrote a lengthy and eloquent dissent in which he claimed that *Brown* was under attack. He argued that *Brown* held out the "promise of true racial equality—not as a matter of fine words on paper, but as a matter of everyday life in the Nation's cities and schools. It was about the nature of a democracy that must work for all Americans."[35]

Justice Breyer reminded the court that *Brown* "sought one law, one Nation, one people, not simply as a matter of legal principle but in terms of how we actually live."[36] He was saying that when you strip away all of the technical legal doctrine, *Brown* was about the promise that one day we could live together as one nation rather than two. *Brown* was about uniting our country rather than dividing it.

What Justice Breyer didn't say was that there had been an extraordinary struggle over whether *Brown's* promise would become a reality involving thousands of people: activists, lawyers, judges, ministers, parents, children, community organizers, school board officials, state and federal legislators, governors, and the president of the United States. What Justice Breyer didn't say was that that struggle was nationwide not regional; that if you wanted to understand what happened to *Brown* you needed to take a trip to Detroit. And what Justice Breyer didn't say was that *Brown's* promise was broken long before I attended my first oral argument at the U.S. Supreme Court.

This is the story of how that happened.

PART I

SOUL FORCE

1

CLASH IN MIDTOWN

On Tuesday morning, June 13, 1967, President Lyndon Johnson and Thurgood Marshall strolled to a podium in the Rose Garden. Marshall stood slightly behind Johnson, with his right hand in his pocket as Johnson spoke deliberately into twin microphones under a blistering sun. As the press corps looked on, Johnson announced that he wanted Marshall to serve as an associate justice on the Supreme Court, and he asked the Senate to confirm his nomination. The president didn't mention Marshall's race. He didn't need to. The importance of the nomination was plain. Marshall had already broken the race barrier two years earlier when Johnson asked him to become the nation's first black solicitor general. ("I want the top lawyer in the United States representing me before the Supreme Court to be a Negro, and be a damn good lawyer that's done it before.")[1] As the reporters snapped their pictures, the president not so subtly reminded the nation about the importance of *Brown v. Board of Education* and Marshall's role in the case: "He has already earned his place in history."[2] Now it was time to take the next step. Two months later, Marshall was confirmed by the Senate in a 69–11 vote and would take his seat as the ninety-sixth justice of the U.S. Supreme Court.

On the very same day that Johnson announced his historic court pick, Reverend Albert Cleage Jr. entered the School Center Building at the corner of Woodward and Putnam Avenues in Midtown Detroit. Passing through the art deco building's two-story-tall, intricately carved archway, Cleage was headed to speak at a Detroit Board of Education meeting. Wayne State University, Cleage's alma mater, was steps away. So, too, was one of famed architect Cass Gilbert's masterpieces, the main branch of the Detroit Public Library.[3] (Gilbert also designed the U. S. Supreme Court building.) And just across Woodward at the Detroit Institute of Arts, Diego Rivera's four-thousand-thirty-square-foot mural, *Detroit Industry*, celebrated the struggle and dignity of the workingman.[4]

Cleage had come to the School Center to do battle—not for integration but for black schools. In his hands was a report prepared by his group, the Inner City Parents Council, detailing the vast disparities between black and white students' achievement levels and dropout rates. In many respects, the report was unremarkable. Black Detroiters had long protested both overt and covert race discrimination in the city's public schools.[5] Anyone remotely familiar with Detroit's schools already knew that black and white students weren't getting an equal education. That the Detroit Board of Education was failing to educate black children was a fairly anodyne observation. Where the report broke new ground was in its assessment of how and why that was the case. The central thesis of *Brown v. Board of Education*, decided in 1954, was that racially segregated schools harmed black children. This was summed up in one of the decision's most famous passages: "To separate them from others of similar age and qualifications solely because of their race generates a feeling of inferiority as to their status in the community that may affect their hearts and minds in a way unlikely ever to be undone."[6] According to *Brown*, the racial separateness itself created harm, the "feeling of inferiority."

The report took a different view. It asserted that Detroit's "failure to educate inner city children stems from the schools' deliberate and systematic destruction of the Afro-American child's self-image and racial pride."[7] From this perspective, the fact that Detroit's schools were largely racially segregated wasn't the problem that needed to be solved. Racial separateness wasn't the source of the harm. White control of black schools was. The presence of even the most talented and committed white teachers and principals, "white power symbols," signaled to black students that they were intellectually inferior and powerless to control their circumstances. This negative messaging sapped black students of the will to learn and set them up to fail. White administrators and racially biased textbooks, the report charged, robbed black children of "any motivation to learn and to develop because he sees nothing around him to make learning and self development . . . an avenue of escape from the conditions in which he lives or an instrument by which he can change these conditions."[8]

The Inner City Parents Council believed that black schools were an essential bulwark against the effects of white supremacy, which permeated almost every element of black life in the city of Detroit: "They do not own the stores where they buy. They do not control the banks which cash their checks. They do not own the apartment houses in which they live. They do not control the political structure which dominates their communities," the report asserted.[9] Only black-controlled schools could counteract the "influences of a white community which constantly threaten to engulf and destroy him."[10] So the group's demand was plain: "Black schools for black children."

At just after 4:00 p.m., the board president began the meeting and called on Cleage to present his report. Cleage didn't mince words. He demanded that the board "reply to the charges indicating what is to be done about the urgency of the problems listed."[11] Dr. Remus Robinson, the first black member of the Detroit Board of Education, wasn't in the mood. A staunch integrationist, he had frequently been the subject of Cleage's criticisms; back in 1962, Cleage had published an article asserting that "Dr. Robinson does not represent the Negro community which elected him to office."[12] Robinson, for his part, thought Cleage's ideas skirted dangerously close to racism. Now he accused Cleage—who demanded all-black schools and rejected integration at the meeting—of adopting "the kind of thinking that has been at the root of the problems you have defined."[13] "I reject the implied suggestion that the all-Negro schools of the South are superior to Detroit schools," Robinson declared.[14] Backing Robinson up was Abraham Zwerdling, a noted white labor lawyer and lifetime member of the NAACP who was next in line to be board president. He pounded on the table, ordering Cleage to be quiet.[15] But Cleage just got louder. "I'm talking!"

he shouted.[16] "This is a big liberal here, but he doesn't want to listen to a black man."[17] Cleage certainly hadn't changed Zwerdling's mind. The board "would not turn its back" on the goal of integration, he proclaimed.[18] This, then, was the central question over which they clashed: Who would control the city's schools? The black community or white administrators? To Cleage, this critical question of control trumped any imperative to integrate the schools.

The day after the meeting, the *Detroit Free Press* ran an article about the gathering, "Outbursts Mar School Meeting," calling it "unusual" and "emotional."[19] The "table-pounding shouting match" between Cleage and Zwerdling made the meeting newsworthy.[20] But it was notable for another reason: the meeting provided an almost perfect distillation of two iconic, rival philosophies of social change, each intended to improve black students' education. The Inner City Parents Council's report and Cleage's testimony at the meeting reflected the first of these, which had taken certain segments of the black community by storm: black nationalism.[21]

Cleage shared a deep ideological kinship with Malcolm X, the most important black nationalist of the twentieth century. The two men were well acquainted, having spoken on numerous occasions. Back in 1963, Malcolm X delivered his famous "Message to the Grass Roots" at the King Solomon Baptist Church in northwest Detroit. (Cleage was in attendance.) Electrifying the boisterous crowd, Malcolm exhorted blacks to "close ranks" to defeat their common white enemy. "Whoever heard of a revolution where they lock arms—as Reverend Cleage was pointing out beautifully— singing 'We Shall Overcome,'" Malcolm exclaimed. "You don't do that in a revolution. You don't do any singing, you're too busy swinging."[22] Cleage praised the speech unequivocally. "I can think of no basic matter upon which we disagreed," he later stated.[23] Just a few months before the June 1967 board of education meeting, Cleage gave a speech praising the late civil rights leader. One of Malcolm's central teachings, the reverend said, was that integration was both "impossible and undesirable."[24] From this perspective, school desegregation—which *Brown v. Board of Education* and several follow-on cases required (at least in the South)—was unnecessary. Malcolm's view, which Cleage endorsed, was that "we are going to control our own communities. We are going to stop worrying about being separate."[25] This was a new front in the debate over the question of school integration: a strike on the principles laid out in *Brown*, but one that came from black nationalists rather than white segregationists.

The Inner City Parents Council wasn't the only organization that made a proposal for improving public education to the Detroit Board of Education on that mid-June afternoon. The Detroit Urban League (DUL) made the other. The DUL was formed in 1916 to assist Detroit's black community, particularly blacks migrating from the South.[26] The DUL was a traditional civil rights organization that, in words of noted University of Michigan historian Sidney Fine, "pressed the city government to deal with such matters as housing, employment, and police-community relations even though it did not take to the streets."[27] The DUL (along with the NAACP) represented the other iconic philosophy intended to advance black educational opportunity: racial integration.[28] Where Cleage and the Inner City Parents Council expressly rejected integration as a means to improve black students' education, the DUL embraced it. *Brown v. Board of Education* was its touchstone. Given that, the fact that the DUL emphasized its commitment to "quality integrated education" at the meeting was no surprise.[29] The group made several proposals to the board of which two stood out: establishing "magnet" schools with unique, high-quality programs attractive to students throughout the city, and developing an "educational park" that would—much like a university—educate thousands of students simultaneously at one multiple-acre site.[30] But what did magnet schools and education parks have to do with "quality integrated education"? The short answer was everything because Detroit was highly residentially segregated.

And so behind the "table-pounding shouting match" were two rival philosophies about how best to achieve racial justice: racial integration and black nationalism. The two philosophies yielded two different sets of proposals aimed at enhancing black students' educational opportunities. These two iconic philosophies had been extensively debated on the national stage by civil rights leaders such as Martin Luther King Jr., Malcolm X, Bayard Rustin, and Stokely Carmichael (later known as Kwame Ture). Now they would frame the local debate about the direction of Detroit's public schools.

By the time Cleage entered the School Center Building on that June afternoon, protest and agitating for social change were part of his DNA. Just
under six feet tall, with penetrating gray eyes and a ruddy complexion,
Cleage was a "race man"[31] who could easily pass for white[32]—and the great-
grandson of a white slave owner. Cleage's Christian faith along with his
belief that all black Americans shared a common culture of racial oppression would become the core of a belief system he called Black Christian
Nationalism.[33] And on June 13, 1967, Cleage was its chief proponent.

A former standout student at Oberlin's divinity school—he once received an A+++ on a term paper—Cleage had been ordained in 1943.[34]
Almost from the start, he had been interested in the intersection of religion and the education of black youngsters. He led a church youth group
in high school and acted as unofficial youth pastor during his time as an undergraduate at the College of the City of Detroit (now Wayne State University). Later, he created youth programs as a minister, and his emphasis
on children led him to become active in reforming the public schools.

Cleage was a pastor at several churches, including the interracial
Church for the Fellowship of All Peoples in San Francisco, before coming
to Detroit to work at St. Mark's United Presbyterian Community Church
at Twelfth and Atkinson in the northwest section of the city.[35] On Sunday,
he would preach against American materialism and advocate support for
the underprivileged.[36] During the week, he whipped up membership
for the NAACP (before he began to criticize it).[37] His political activism
angered his superiors, and he left St. Mark's to form his own church in
1953.[38] By 1957, Cleage's church had a name—Central Congregational—
and it would become a hotbed of political organizing.[39]

During the 1960s, Cleage delivered a series of sermons that fused the
central tenets of black nationalism with Christianity. On Easter Sunday
1967, Cleage dedicated a new mural in the front of his church, an eighteen-
foot-high black Madonna and child. During his sermon, Cleage asked his
congregation to stop worshipping a white Jesus.[40] In place of a white deity,
he called on his flock to build a church that would give black people "faith
in their power to free themselves from bondage, to control their own des-

tiny, and to rebuild the Nation—beginning with those individual followers of a Black Messiah who are ready to break the servile identification of the oppressed with their oppressor."[41] This was Black Christian Nationalism, and Cleage formally changed the church's name to the Shrine of the Black Madonna to reflect his call for a new black theology.[42] Cleage's intellectual contribution to black theology was significant. One scholar characterized him as a key figure—along with Martin Luther King Jr., Malcolm X, and the celebrated theologian James Cone—in developing a distinctive black theology during this period.[43]

Cleage's Black Christian Nationalism reinterpreted Christian texts and dogma, flipping the defaults: Jesus was a black man, and blacks were God's chosen people.[44] Not only that, Cleage argued, Jesus was also a revolutionary sent by God to liberate black people "from the oppression, brutality, and exploitation of the white gentile world."[45] This philosophy was no doubt influenced by men like Stokely Carmichael and other young militants of the civil rights movement who criticized mainstream civil rights leadership as ineffectual, if not collaborationist. While Cleage largely agreed with their prescriptions—self-determination, black control of the black community, the unique beauty of black culture, the unattainability and undesirability of integration—he was impatient with the youngsters: "Stokely hasn't said one word that was not completely implicit in everything Malcolm X taught,"[46] he said in 1967. Carmichael, who had coined the term "black power" after Malcolm X was assassinated, defined it as "a call for black people in this country to unite, to recognize their heritage, to build a sense of community. It is a call for black people to begin to define their own goals, to lead their own organizations and to support those organizations."[47] The young militants' popularity only proved what Cleage thought obvious: the mainstream civil rights movement's philosophy had failed—"the NAACP is washed up, through, finished."[48]

Black Christian Nationalism offered a complete prescription for the liberation of black people by "addressing the psychological, physical, social, economic, and political needs of the black community."[49] Cleage imagined a black "nation within a nation," a world where blacks owned and patronized their own bookstores, food co-ops, media production facilities, legal clinics, nurseries, and farms.[50] He was particularly hostile to integration and individualism; they tended to undermine the racial separateness and commitment to community necessary to build and sustain the black nation. Community control of the public schools was a core objective of Black Christian Nationalism, and to those like Cleage, a natural extension of black power.[51] Writing in 1967, Stokely Carmichael confirmed the connection when he urged black parents to seek control of "the public schools in their community: hiring and firing of teachers, selection of teaching materials, determination of standards, etc."[52] This perspective would come to shape Cleage's views on the stewardship of Detroit's schools, in ways that would have a lasting impact far beyond Detroit.

Cleage even went so far as to run for statewide office himself. He served as the Michigan state chairman of the Freedom Now Party, a short-lived, all-black political party with national aspirations.[53] The party was formed in 1963 by trailblazing civil rights lawyer Conrad Lynn and William Worthy, a radical foreign correspondent who once lost his passport for defying a travel ban to China during the Cold War.[54] Convinced that neither the Republicans nor the Democrats were capable of representing the interests of black voters, the founders of the Freedom Now Party sought to develop an independent slate of black candidates unbeholden to the white power structure who would run for political office up and down the ballot. Speaking at a street corner meeting in Harlem during the summer of 1963, Worthy told those assembled to support the Freedom Now Party: "We may not win many offices, but with one out of ten Americans a Negro . . . we can make our voice heard in the land."[55] Cleage became the party's nominee for governor of Michigan in the fall of 1964.[56] In the end, he drew fewer than 20,000 votes. The winner: Republican George Romney, with 1,642,302 votes. Cleage went on to run for several other elected offices,[57] but lost every contest.[58] The 1966 school board election, where Cleage and Remus Robinson met head-on, was particularly tough. In a field of five, the minister came in dead last. A *Detroit News* article told the tale: "Chief School Critic Trampled; Robinson Leads Board Race."[59]

Less than a year later, Cleage and Robinson—with Zwerdling looking on—were again contesting how Detroit's schools should be run. That fight would rock the city of Detroit and set in motion a chain of events that ended at the doorstep of the U.S. Supreme Court.[60]

A little more than a month after the clash in Midtown, Detroit's racial tensions shot up higher than ever. Early on the morning of July 23, 1967, the Detroit police raided a "blind pig," an after-hours drinking establishment at the corner of Twelfth Street and Clairmount, about a mile away from the Shrine of the Black Madonna. It was supposed to be a routine operation; the police had raided the same bar twice before, once as recently as June 30. But everything went wrong from the start. The raid began later than usual; the crowd inside the bar was larger than the police anticipated; a rear exit was blocked so the arrestees were marched out the front door, where a restless crowd had already assembled; the paddy wagons were delayed; and it was unspeakably hot. When an onlooker shouted, "Black Power, don't let them take our people away; look what they are doing to our people . . . ,"[61] the worst riot of the 1960s was underway.[62] By the time order was restored on Thursday, July 27, forty-three people were dead, at least eleven hundred had been injured, and more than seven thousand were in jail.[63]

Detroit looked like a war zone. Almost five hundred fires had to be extinguished; the city only narrowly averted a Dresden-style firestorm.[64] More than twenty-five hundred stores were burned or looted.[65] Whole city blocks were devastated, and millions of dollars of property were destroyed. The smell of smoke was everywhere. An iconic photo taken at the time shows a small boy dressed neatly in a striped shirt and jumper, hair freshly cut, hands clasped, face blank, standing in the charred remains of what was once his home.[66] The city would never be the same.

But what caused the unrest? Speaking from the White House on July 27, President Johnson refused to characterize the events in Detroit as a civil rights protest; looting, arson, plunder, and pillage were crime and violence through and through.[67] Johnson told the nation that the rioters were criminals, not freedom fighters. Announcing the formation of the Kerner Commission to study the unrest, the president called for an end to the violence and urged the country to pray for racial peace on that upcoming Sunday.[68] Everyone had a theory about the rioters' motivations. Ronald Reagan, then the governor of California, called the black rioters "savages."[69]

Many Detroit-area whites thought they were motivated by "greed, laziness, and criminality."[70] Cleage thought the events on Twelfth Street were only the latest chapter in the long-running black struggle for freedom. "A whole new world is being born," the minister exclaimed.[71] Later, he suggested the rioters never intended to destroy black businesses and homes, while at the same time applauding the removal of businesses that were exploiting the black community.[72]

The only problem was that the facts didn't bear him out. Young blacks destroyed white and black stores alike.[73] The rioters burned the businesses that served them and their own neighbors' homes.[74] Sidney Fine, who wrote perhaps the defining history of the Detroit riot, estimated that almost 30 percent of stores that were destroyed were black-owned.[75] In truth, the best explanation of the rioters' motivations is that they were frustrated and angry at police conduct and much more. They vented their rage by looting businesses and burning buildings somewhat arbitrarily, even as a majority of middle-class blacks and particularly members of Detroit's black leadership saw them as criminals whose actions undermined efforts to achieve racial justice by working within the system.[76]

Later, Pulitzer Prize–winning historian Heather Ann Thompson would characterize the July 1967 conflagration not as a riot but as "an act of both rage and rebellion."[77] But rage and rebellion against what? Thompson ticked off a variety of maladies: "grinding poverty," lack of access to "good housing stock" and "strong schools," and police brutality, all of which helped ignite Detroit's civil unrest.[78] But these weren't independent, wholly isolated phenomena. When it released its report, the Kerner Commission indicted white America—white racism—and its greatest handmaidens: pervasive discrimination and segregation within the city, black ghettos that concentrated poverty and disadvantage, and white abandonment of the city via exodus to the suburbs.[79] And undergirding them all was residential segregation. Writing a generation earlier, a young Thurgood Marshall had reached a similar conclusion. In a June 1944 letter to the executive director of the American Civil Liberties Union, Marshall declared that residential segregation was at the root of "all of the evils of segregation which exists today."[80]

Remarkably, Michigan governor George Romney appeared to agree. Speaking just after order was restored, the Republican governor offered a surprisingly thoughtful analysis of what had gone wrong.[81] His lengthy laundry list of causes for the riot cited "well-intentioned urban renewal programs" that had "displaced ghetto Negroes from their homes" and "produced even greater overcrowding in the already incendiary Twelfth Street area."[82] He implicitly chastised whites for thinking "they could escape the problems of the ghetto by moving to the suburbs."[83] Most startling was Romney's assessment of how housing contributed to the riot. "We must have open housing on a statewide basis," he began.[84] But what did "open housing" mean? One answer was the eradication of rules—even those enacted without a specific racist intent—that made it difficult, if not impossible, for blacks to escape the ghetto. The governor asserted, "Zoning that creates either large-scale economic or racial segregation should be eliminated."[85] Next up was the real estate industry. Romney continued, "We must compel real estate agents to show all listed properties, report all offers, abstain from any effort based on race or religion to influence the property owner in the listing and sale of property."[86] The governor's comments suggested that he already saw the country's racial tensions as being embodied in its housing patterns—and, therefore, in its schools.

———

Cleage predicted that the disorder, the fires, the looting would drive whites out of Detroit. He was right. The riot accelerated a process of white flight that had been underway since 1950.[87] Coleman Young, who would become the city's first black and longest-serving mayor, worried about what whites might take when they left.[88] As he described it, "The riot put Detroit on the fast track to economic desolation, mugging the city and making off with incalculable value in jobs, earnings taxes, corporate taxes, retail dollars, sales taxes, mortgages, interest, property taxes, development dollars, investment dollars," and all the rest.[89] But Cleage saw the departure of whites as an opportunity for black self-determination. Finally, blacks could seize the reins of city government—including control of the schools.

2

SYMPATHY, KNOWLEDGE, AND THE TRUTH

In the years leading up to the civil unrest in 1967, Detroit's schools underwent a significant transition. In 1950, the Detroit school board was solidly dominated by members who were, as described by the Detroit school system's most preeminent historian Jeffrey Mirel, "quite conservative in their politics and especially conservative in relation to school finance."[1] But the board's composition shifted as the city's demographics transformed and a loose coalition of liberal, labor, and civil rights groups pushed for educational change. The coalition wanted more money for Detroit's schools and less racial discrimination. And it wanted more grassroots community involvement in school decision-making.[2] At first, the coalition was unsuccessful, but by the mid-1950s it began to get results.[3] A key moment was the school board election of 1955, when Detroiters elected Remus Robinson, a prominent surgeon and graduate of the University of Michigan medical school, to serve on the board of education. Robinson became the first black official elected citywide.[4] Robinson joined the board with several new members who were "solidly middle class and, while definitely not left wing, were more open to liberal and labor influences than any other group of board members in the history of Detroit."[5] In the following year, Samuel Brownell—who as U.S. commissioner of education had urged southern school districts to comply with *Brown*—became Detroit's school superintendent.

During this period, the board—under pressure from black Detroiters—took some tentative steps to address racial discrimination in the Detroit school system. It increased the number and quality of schools in black neighborhoods, and it dramatically expanded the number of black teachers and other personnel in the system.[6]

But the stubborn reality was that, despite these moves, Detroit was still running a separate and unequal school system.[7] In January 1962, a group of several hundred parents sued the Detroit Board of Education in federal court, alleging that it had maintained a racially segregated and unequal school system since 1910.[8] That case, *Sherrill School Parents Committee v. the Board of Education of the City of Detroit*,[9] was notable for several reasons. First, the case was an early test of *Brown v. Board of Education*'s strength outside of a southern or border state jurisdiction. "The policies and practices of the defendant Board [created and maintained] a school system under which Negro children were segregated in and confined to public schools located in . . . all Negro areas and suffered not only from the social and psychological results of racial segregation but from the effect of a second rate education arising out of inadequate and unequal school and teaching facilities," the plaintiffs argued.[10]

Sherrill was also significant because Albert Cleage was the Parents Committee's chair and a driving force behind the suit.[11] The minister saw himself as standing up for the grassroots: the black parents who were protesting, picketing, and boycotting against separate and unequal education and taking their fight for desegregation right to the Detroit Board of Education.[12] The Detroit branch of the NAACP did not support the lawsuit—at least initially.[13] (Cleage's repeated personal attacks on Remus Robinson, still the only black member of the board, might have been one reason why the Detroit branch hesitated to join the lawsuit.)[14] Writing in his own weekly newspaper, the black nationalist–oriented *Illustrated News*, Cleage excoriated the organization for its reticence: "The failure of the Detroit branch to sponsor the Sherrill School Bias Suit as part of the national NAACP attack upon segregation in the North was a major policy blunder."[15] The Detroit branch's lack of support for the *Sherrill* lawsuit "betray[s] the best interests of the Negro community." "Throughout the city, NAACP [Detroit branch] members are asking 'Why should we continue to support an organization which is afraid to fight when the chips are down.'" The Detroit branch did eventually support the lawsuit.[16] And, as a direct result of *Sherrill*, in late February 1962, it formed a citywide advisory committee on school desegregation.[17] The press release announcing the formation of the advisory committee suggested that the organization would push the Detroit Board of Education on desegregation: "'Every step should be taken, within the scope of school board authority, to effect the highest measure of racial school desegregation possible.'"

Cleage's tactical support of desegregation in the early 1960s was real. "My primary interest has always been the best possible education for black children. We used the Sherrill case because it was the tactic of the time," the minister later stated.[18] As University of Michigan historian Angela D. Dillard confirmed, at "this point in his career, the solution Cleage was putting forth was still based on equity as integration."[19] But it didn't last. Per Dillard: by the late 1960s, Cleage "would reorient himself toward the quest for equity as community control in which Black parents controlled education for Black students taught by Black teachers."[20]

The board's reaction to the *Sherrill* case was instructive—it categorically denied any segregation in the school system.[21] Incensed, Remus Robinson, still the board's only black member, publicly broke ranks with the board's lawyers when they asked that the case be dismissed.[22] A few months after the case was filed, the school board's own blue-ribbon committee on equal educational opportunities released the results of an exhaustive two-year study.[23] The study made clear that black students indeed had cause for complaint. When the study was released, the committee's chair, Nathan J. Kaufman, a white state court judge and former union activist,[24] bluntly told the press: "Where you have segregated housing, you have segregated schools . . . segregation in our schools is a fact."[25] The *Sherrill* case never came to trial, but it wasn't because the lawsuit lacked merit. Instead, as Mirel explained it, "the parents dropped the suit following a major change in the composition of the school board."[26]

On July 1, 1965, an "unassailable liberal majority" took control of the seven-member Detroit school board.[27] The four-member liberal majority, which included Abraham Zwerdling and Remus Robinson, were deeply committed to school integration. So, too, was Norman Drachler, who succeeded Brownell as school superintendent in 1966. (Mirel called him "the most liberal superintendent the city had yet seen.")[28] The liberals seemed poised to integrate and improve the Detroit public schools in short order.[29] But it didn't turn out that way.

For one thing, Detroit's schools faced demographic and economic problems that were beyond the power and capacity of any school board to solve. The racial composition of Detroit's schools—and the city itself—was rapidly changing. In 1963, the Detroit school system became majority black for the very first time as young white families departed for the suburbs.[30] This demographic shift had several important consequences. First, as the white school-age population in the city declined, the remaining white Detroiters became even more hesitant to vote for tax increases to fund the schools.[31] Second, most of the white families who left Detroit were middle and upper income, which had a devastating financial impact on the city's schools. Then, as now, a substantial portion of school funding came from local property taxes; the more valuable the house, the higher the tax base available to fund the local schools.[32] As white families left the city, property values fell, depressing tax revenues available to fund public education. On top of that, the Detroit school system was now faced with historically high enrollments of children with the greatest needs (in the 1967–68 school year, almost 60 percent of Detroit's students were low income).[33]

Second, the liberal, pro-integration board had the misfortune of inheriting a deeply segregated and unequal school system—and actually caring about it—just as black anger at the blatantly discriminatory system was reaching a fever pitch. In late 1965, the Detroit branch of the NAACP, the nation's largest local branch, charged that black students had few vocational and scholarship opportunities and little or no access to advanced placement tests, and were not encouraged to take college prep courses.[34]

Black Detroiters repeatedly demonstrated against inequality in Detroit's schools. In early 1966, black students took the lead. On April 7, more than 2,300 students walked out of Northern High School in the New Center area of the city. The vast majority of Northern students were black.[35] The ostensible reason for the protest was the principal's refusal to allow a school newspaper to publish a student editorial.[36] But the students weren't just protesting in support of free speech. The editorial in question had been written by a member of Northern's senior class and an honors student, Charles Colding. His charge: the Detroit school system was undereducating black students. "We simply do not feel that such a drastic difference in classroom achievement, such as the one between [predominantly white] Redford and Northern, should be allowed to exist," Colding asserted.[37] A day later, the *Detroit Free Press* summarized the student's critique: "The 46-year-old school has a narrow curriculum, low academic standards and inadequate physical facilities."[38] The president of Northern's student council, seventeen-year-old William Hill, agreed: "When I was transferred here from Mumford it was immediately apparent that conditions at Northern were inferior."[39] "The lighting is bad and sections of the roof needs repairs. The curriculum here is narrower than that at either Cass Tech or Mumford," he added.[40]

Other student leaders of the walkout spoke more generally about the importance of education. Michael Batchelor, a senior who hoped to study radiology at Henry Ford Junior College, told the *Detroit Free Press*: "Generally, people say Negroes don't care about education, but this isn't true. Right now the Negro needs an education, and he needs it bad. This is the most important aspect of our lives."[41] He explained how an unequal educational system harmed black students: "We feel that we can't compete with other kids from better high schools when we get in college. It's not native intelligence that will stop us, but education."[42] Judy Walker, a junior who also spearheaded the boycott, aspired to become a police officer. The first step toward a career in law enforcement was a high school diploma; she would be the first in her family to reach that milestone. Her parents, who had migrated from the South, never finished high school. Their experience was foundational to her. "My parents always tell me to work hard and get the good grades. Mother tells me that I have to make it," she explained.[43] Walker was focused on moving forward, not back: "Negroes must do something to get ahead. They can't stay behind."[44]

The action at Northern ultimately ended when the board agreed to reassign the principal, and to create two committees, one to study the problems at Northern and another—the High School Study Commission—to evaluate the conditions at other high schools in the system. The student boycott at Northern had a ripple effect across the system, as students at as many as eleven other high schools threatened sympathy walkouts.[45] The committee formed to study the deficiencies at Northern later vindicated all of the student protesters' allegations.[46]

Just after the Northern boycott was settled, dozens of students at Southeastern High School on Detroit's east side also walked out. One student carried a sign that read: "Stop Inferior Education."[47] The protests weren't confined to the city's high schools. Parents also protested inferior education at Higginbotham Elementary, on the city's far northwest side, just across the border from suburban Ferndale, Michigan.[48] In June 1966, a citizens' committee on equal educational opportunity released a report analyzing citywide achievement scores. The report found that, on average, black students' reading ability was between one and two grades below that of white students.[49] A few months later, the *Detroit Free Press* ran a four-part "undercover" exposé written by a reporter who worked as a substitute teacher for a week at a black middle school. The most critical problem the reporter identified was teacher attitudes; many teachers had low expectations of black students and did not believe they wanted to be educated.[50]

Against this background, the board undertook, as Mirel described it, "a series of bold policy initiatives," including adding even more black personnel to the school system, adopting multicultural study materials, and eliminating blatantly racist textbooks from the school curriculum.[51] (Detroit led the nation in challenging publishers' portrayals of blacks in their textbooks at that time.)[52] But it wasn't nearly enough because, as Cleage and the Inner City Parents Council accurately asserted, the Detroit public schools were failing black students. And there was plenty of evidence beyond Cleage's report, including black Detroiters' widespread protests and a variety of other studies, to support this assertion. As criticism mounted, it was clear that the board's well-meaning actions were too little, too late.

Pressure on the board hardly relented in the lead-up to the civil unrest in 1967. In early April 1967, the *Detroit Free Press* reported on the

National Education Association's (NEA) investigation of Detroit's public schools. The NEA concluded that "economic and racial segregation" pervaded the system.[53] The organization pointed an accusatory finger at the school administration. It had made no serious attempt "to end segregation induced by neighborhood racial patterns."[54] Then there was the money. In mid-April, the paper informed Detroiters that the school system had submitted a $225.5 million budget request to county tax officials for the upcoming 1967–68 school year.[55] Detroit school officials were nervous. The budget was based upon the then existing state aid formula, which was subject to change. (The cost of public education in most states including Michigan—then and now—was divided among federal, state, and local sources, with states and localities providing the lion's share of the money.)[56] In June, Cleage and Robinson loudly debated the school system's future at the clash in Midtown—and soon after the city erupted.

As the dust settled after the unrest, it was clear that education would continue to be a key site of concern and contention. In August, Superintendent Drachler appeared before a U.S. Senate education subcommittee, pleading for more federal money for Detroit schools.[57] Of the five largest cities in the United States, Detroit's children received the smallest amount of school funding per child. The riot had forced Drachler's hand. "Last month's [H]olocaust has deeply affected both the Negro and white middle classes of Detroit. They need reassurance before they will agree not to flee our city," the superintendent told the senators.[58] He feared that Detroit would become the "pauper school system of our metropolitan area."[59] What was more, Detroit's schools stood to lose "$500,000 in taxes because of property destroyed during the riots."[60] But Drachler's entreaties didn't work. In the previous school year, Detroit had received $11.2 million of federal money under the Elementary and Secondary Education Act of 1965, a federal statute designed to address educational inequality.[61] But for the upcoming year, the federal government would reduce that number to $8 million. And the state wasn't going to bail out Detroit's schools, either. As the *Detroit Free Press* reported, "While state aid to schools was increased by $34 per student last year . . . this year Detroit will receive only $9 more per youngster, in [the] face of more students, rising costs and higher teacher salaries."[62]

It didn't get much better in September. Detroit schools had been scheduled to open for the 1967–68 school year on Wednesday, September 6, 1967. But on Thursday, September 7, they were still closed. The reason: ongoing labor-management negotiations—"no contract, no work"—between the Detroit Federation of Teachers and the Detroit Board of Education.[63] The impasse was resolved only after a thirteen-day strike, with the teachers winning substantial salary increases.[64] It wasn't clear where the money for the new raises was going to come from. "The settlement, whose cost is estimated at $18.7 million over the two years, would push the schools into deficit financing," the paper noted.[65] In late September, the Detroit schools received yet another blow, as 6,100 fewer students enrolled than the system had been expecting.[66] This meant a $1.7 million hit, in the form of reduced state aid, to the school system's operating budget. What caused the defections? The teacher strike and the delayed school start certainly didn't help. "There's been a sizable movement of people from this community this summer," a school spokesperson added.[67]

―――――

Cleage protested against—and was deeply angry about—Detroit's discriminatory and unequal public schools. In this, he was just like many black Detroiters. But if that was the case, what made his protest, and his criticism, notable? The answer was that while Cleage was in violent agreement with more traditional civil rights organizations such as the Detroit Urban League and the Detroit branch of the NAACP that the Detroit public schools discriminated against black students, they were (often) in violent disagreement about the solution. Cleage was important because he was one of the prime movers, if not the most important figure, behind the community control movement in Detroit's schools.[68]

In the late 1960s, the core debate among those who wanted to improve educational opportunity for black students was between community control and integration. This was how Mirel explained it: "By 1967, the civil rights movement was torn by the struggle between an older generation of integrationists and a younger, more militant generation of separatists. Gaining control of the schools was a central issue in that debate."[69] Community control of the schools appealed to many blacks who were frustrated with white leadership that continually failed to disestablish separate and un-equal schools. As William Grant, the *Detroit Free Press*'s award-winning education reporter, put it, "Negro groups fear and distrust school boards because they represent the white establishment that has denied their children quality education."[70] Community control of the schools, in De-troit and elsewhere, was a way to claw back power from white authorities who were hurting black children.

Community control was an indictment of white leadership. In effect, community control advocates said: give us control of the schools and we will educate black children. If the schools were to remain racially segregated, black teachers, black administrators, and particularly black parents ought to run them. Perhaps if the community really committed to its schools and truly believed in them, the students could succeed. It was an idea with an impeccable pedigree. W. E. B. Du Bois responded to some of the same concerns in 1935: "Other things being equal, the mixed school is the broader, more natural basis for the education of all youth. It gives wider contacts; it inspires greater self-confidence; and suppresses the inferiority complex. But other things seldom are equal, and in that case, Sympathy, Knowledge, and the Truth, outweigh all that the mixed school can offer."[71]

The community control debate was national in scope. Just a few weeks before the Detroit riot, the New York City schools' superintendent se-lected the predominantly black Ocean Hill–Brownsville section of Brook-lyn to be one of three experimental community control districts.[72] The New York City teachers' union opposed the experiment. While the union's leadership had a liberal, if not radical, reputation, the mostly white rank and file feared a loss of centralized power over curriculum and work rules, particularly those that protected against involuntary transfers to major-ity black schools.[73] In 1968, the teachers walked off the job in a series of strikes that divided the city.[74] As one scholar put it, the crisis at Ocean Hill–Brownsville "caused a serious rift among the city's liberals," fracturing a coalition that had pushed for labor protections and wage increases for black and Puerto Rican New Yorkers just a few years before.[75]

In April 1969, the state of New York adopted a law that enhanced com-munity participation by creating more than thirty local school districts within the city of New York.[76] But the law left important powers such as administration of the city's high schools and control of the local boards' budgets in the hands of New York City's central board of education. This disappointed many community control advocates. Among them was Reverend C. Herbert Oliver, chairman of the Ocean Hill–Brownsville experimental governing board. "We denounced the decentralization law [for not providing complete community control] at the time," he later stated.[77] Commenting on New York's effort in 1980, noted psychologist and educator Kenneth Clark, a national authority on integration and author of a report on school segregation's destructive effect that was cited in *Brown v. Board of Education*,[78] was pointed: "I don't care how much the new structure has given people a sense of control over their own destiny . . . The schools are no better and no worse than they were a decade ago. In terms of the basic objective, decentralization did not make a damn bit of difference."[79]

In Detroit, Cleage was pressing the case for community control in the *Michigan Chronicle*, an influential and heavily circulated black newspaper. In his Message to the Nation column, Cleage offered a ferocious takedown of white teachers in black schools. "Most [white teachers] think of our children as little savages," the minister declared.[80] He demanded that the board of education and school administrators be held accountable to the black community. It would never be possible for black students to get a proper education in white-dominated schools. The black community could not continue "to stand idly by, letting the white man mess [black children] up year after year after year. Every black parent, every black community resident, every black community organization must be ready to back up our militant black students and militant black teachers," he thundered.[81] And Cleage touted his group, the Inner City Parents Council, for its role in confronting the board with critical information about Detroit's schools at the clash in Midtown.[82]

Cleage wrote often, repeatedly calling for administrative accountability and black self-determination.[83] But he wasn't just writing op-eds. Cleage was pushing community control on other fronts as well. Just after the riot, he formed the Citywide Action Citizens Committee, which brought together many of the city's leading black nationalists.[84] In 1968, the group hosted several well-attended community control conferences.[85] The Inner

City Parents Council continued to agitate for the removal of white principals in black schools.[86] And then in November 1968, Andrew W. Perdue, running as a community control advocate, was elected to the Detroit Board of Education with Cleage's vociferous support. Perdue, a 1949 graduate of Wayne State University Law School, didn't have it easy. There were few jobs for black lawyers in Detroit in the late 1940s. So after graduating from law school, Perdue worked the midnight shift at the main branch of the Detroit Post Office for seven years in order to make ends meet prior to establishing a private practice.[87]

Perdue was committed to community control.[88] In March of 1969, and in response to community petitions, Perdue and another black member of the board of education, Reverend Darneau Stewart, voted to change the name of McMichael Junior High to Malcolm X Junior High.[89] Remus Robinson, the only other black member of the Detroit Board of Education, abstained. In late April 1969, each of the board's seven members issued a statement providing his "current impressions" of community control of the schools.[90] Perdue and Stewart said they favored community control. "Power is the name of the game," Perdue stated. "Without power there is a feeling of self-debasement," he added. Robinson wasn't on the same page. He wanted evidence that community control would provide educational benefits before any such proposal could be adopted. During a Detroit Board of Education meeting in mid-May 1969, Perdue urged the board to "increase meaningful community participation in the school system."[91] Writing that same month, Cleage was effusive in his praise: "Our hat is off to Attorney Perdue. Let's all get behind him now and support his heroic efforts to secure for us the power to properly educate our Black children."[92]

Cleage was one of the first and most prominent community leaders to push for community control of Detroit's schools. But his views were out of step with those of most of Detroit's blacks, who largely favored integration. Social scientists analyzing public opinion surveys and other contemporaneous evidence found that in 1967, black Detroiters "expressed massive commitment to the goal of integration."[93] That same analysis yielded a notable finding: "66% of the black respondents said they would support potentially violent demonstrations designed to achieve integration."[94] That was pretty strong support. Why were a supermajority of Detroit's blacks so committed to integration?

In early 1967, the U.S. Commission on Civil Rights published a book-length report titled *Racial Isolation in the Public Schools*—at President Johnson's request—that might have explained why.[95] First, the commission found an extremely high degree of racial separation in the schools, both North and South.[96] In fact, "in the North, the proportion of Negro children in majority Negro schools often equals or exceeds the national average."[97] Consistent with this finding, the commission noted that in "Detroit, Mich., 72 percent of the Negro elementary school students are in 90 percent or more Negro schools."[98] Not only did blacks and whites attend largely separate schools, but there were substantial disparities in economic, social and educational attainment as well.[99] "Racial isolation in the schools tends to lower students' achievement, restrict their aspirations, and impair their sense of being able to affect their own destiny," the commission found.[100] Unsurprisingly, it concluded that the causes of racial isolation were complex. The commission pointed to a variety of interdependent factors, including residential segregation perpetrated by private and public actors; school assignment according to geographical zoning, which was residential segregation's "force multiplier"; racially discriminatory school construction and site selection policies; and (only very recently repealed) laws that required—in the North—racially segregated schools.

Racial isolation in the public schools was widespread and deep-seated, its causes many. What was the fix? According to Johnson's commission, here's what it *wasn't*: providing more money for compensatory education programs in racially isolated schools. After reviewing more than twenty compensatory education programs in large cities, the commission found that "in most instances . . . the data did not show significant gains in achievement."[101] What remedy for racial isolation, then, stood the best chance for producing significant gains in achievement? Properly designed and executed school desegregation programs.[102] In 1967, black Detroiters were very enthusiastic about integration. The best explanation for this is that they had reached the same conclusion as the U.S. Commission on Civil Rights: "Negro children suffer serious harm when their education takes place in public schools which are racially segregated, *whatever the source of such segregation may be*."[103] They favored integration because they believed it would help their children escape segregated and unequal schools. At the same time, the appeal of community control was on the rise—as much out of a pragmatic recognition that the path to integration was arduous as out of separatist ideology.

This shed light on the NAACP's nuanced stance on community control. As two commentators put it, the group's approach attempted to reconcile "its traditional commitment to integration with the growing interest in [community control] in the black community."[104] The NAACP's leaders thought the best way to achieve educational equality was through desegregation, but it demanded that the schools be accountable to black parents, which echoed the language of community control. In 1968, June Shagaloff, the NAACP's national education director, firmly asserted that "decision-making by parents is the only hope, now, of assuring teacher-administrator accountability for pupil achievement."[105] So the organization's official position was that it supported community control as a means of ensuring accountability, but only if school systems adopting a more responsive governance structure also pursued desegregation. The Detroit chapter of the NAACP was on the same page as its parent organization. Speaking to the Detroit school board in April 1969, Amos A. Wilder, a member of the chapter's education committee, pointed to both aims: "We cannot permit the continuation of an education system that is not accountable to the community it purports to serve . . . Nor will we continue to tolerate the twin evils of segregation and domination by the insensitive majority."[106]

One question was whether the two goals were compatible rather than contradictory. From Cleage's perspective, the whole idea of community control was to get whites *out* of black schools, to take the schools back from white educators who had undervalued and miseducated black youth. From this perspective, integration and community control were fatally incompatible. Then there was the question of whether community control inadvertently helped whites who deserved no assistance. The concept of community control cut both ways; it took racial segregation, of the schools and the neighborhoods, as a given. Most white Detroiters wanted to "control" their communities, too. Local control of admissions and transfer decisions would mean few, if any, blacks in their schools. Cleage appeared untroubled that his strenuous advocacy of community control might have provided segregation-preferring whites with an "unearned assist": "We have no objection to whites controlling white schools. I can understand that, and I hope they can understand blacks controlling black schools," he stated in May 1970.[107]

The reality was that some form of community control of Detroit's schools was inevitable given Cleage's nonstop advocacy, the ongoing conflict in Ocean Hill–Brownsville, which effectively nationalized the community control debate, the various crises then confronting Detroit's schools, and the school system's inability to raise the money necessary to meet its challenges. But it was unclear how changing the Detroit school system's governance structure alone would solve its problems. Community control was attractive because it provided the allure of change when few other politically viable alternatives existed. It offered change on the cheap. Or, as Mirel put it, "At a time when the school system faced growing budget deficits and stood little chance of winning millage [property tax] increases, redistributing power seemed like a solution that could placate angry citizens without additional expenditures"—and that, similarly, would ask little of the Detroit area's white residents.[108]

3

SLAY THE DRAGON

In the late 1960s, Detroit's public schools were both racially separate and unequal. But Detroit wasn't an outlier, an extreme case. Instead, Detroit was "Exhibit A" of a much larger phenomenon. President Johnson's letter asking the U.S. Commission on Civil Rights to investigate school segregation recognized the nationwide scope of the problem.[1] He wrote: "Although we have made substantial progress in ending formal segregation of schools, racial isolation in the schools persists—both in the North and the South—because of housing patterns, school districting, economic stratification and population movements."[2] Johnson mentioned that "formal segregation" was mostly eradicated. By this he appeared to be referring to classic, southern-style Jim Crow, under which the public schools had been racially segregated de jure, or "by law." By "racial isolation" he meant schools that were racially monolithic, but whose racial composition couldn't be traced to a state law or local ordinance mandating such. In some instances, including Detroit, the racial composition of these schools mirrored those in the South prior to *Brown*, where individual schools comprised either overwhelmingly black or overwhelmingly white student enrollments. So how did northern schools come to look the way they did? Was this "racial isolation" synonymous with Jim Crow segregation? From a legal point of view, the answer was no if it was caused only by private acts—such as families freely choosing to live in one neighborhood or another. But if racial isolation could be traced directly to some type of governmental action such as "school districting," then perhaps it was more like classic Jim Crow. (Or maybe some mix of the two was at play.) The president's letter acknowledged the complicated question of racial isolation's "origin story": "The problems are more subtle and complex than those presented by segregation imposed by law."[3]

The NAACP had been intensely interested in this question for many years. In June 1959, Robert L. Carter, general counsel of the NAACP, wrote Roy Wilkins, the organization's executive director, urging him to undertake a significant program to challenge school segregation in the North.[4] Carter was no stranger to school desegregation litigation. A graduate of both the Howard and Columbia law schools with refined tastes—the ballet, the opera, and a good game of bridge were among his favorites—Carter was a brilliant lawyer.[5] But his enjoyment of the fine arts and his reserved, introspective personality belied a fierce attachment to the cause of black empowerment. He described himself as, and undoubtedly was, "the most radical of the NAACP's national leadership."[6]

Earlier, as Thurgood Marshall's chief deputy at the NAACP Legal Defense and Educational Fund, Inc. (LDF), Carter had been deeply involved in all of the organization's efforts including the legal drive to eradicate state-mandated segregation in public education. (LDF was originally incorporated in 1940 as the tax-exempt litigation subsidiary of the NAACP; it was, in effect, the NAACP's law firm.)[7] Carter tried unequal teacher salary equalization cases in the South and was the chief architect of the legal strategy that resulted in *Brown v. Board of Education*.[8] Assessing his role as second-in-command of LDF, one commentator stated: "Put simply, every endeavor that LDF undertook during its most pivotal era [the *Brown* era] bears Carter's imprint."[9] Carter subsequently became the NAACP's first general counsel in 1957 after the LDF and the NAACP formally severed direct connections in the face of a southern-instigated Internal Revenue Service probe.[10]

With the LDF focused on enforcing *Brown* in the South, Carter saw a large role for the NAACP in northern school desegregation cases.[11] From the start, he imagined a campaign that would mix affirmative litigation, strong local branch involvement, and aggressive community activism. In his letter to Wilkins, he argued, "I believe that this is an issue which the

National Office should take over as a part of its program; that it should undertake to investigate the problem throughout the North, help organize various communities and undertake a program aimed at stimulating community activity and pressure for better education facilities for Negroes and for integration."[12] Carter believed that the problem of northern school desegregation rivaled that in the South and that the NAACP could make significant inroads above the Mason-Dixon Line. He explained, "It [northern segregation] is indeed even more crucial than the southern question, because with a program and organization we can do much more to alleviate the difficulties than is possible in the South."[13] Carter's letter carried more than a hint of optimism. He wrote, "I may be wrong, but I have a conviction that this is a field in which use of our resources will do more than any other single issue to solidify support for the NAACP."[14] A few months before he wrote Wilkins, Carter confidently predicted segregation's demise: "Segregation as a way of life in the United States is dead. It may well take many years to bury it, but it is dead."[15]

What might have been the source of Carter's optimism? The facts on the ground in the South could not have cheered him. Southern schools were desegregating at a frustratingly slow pace, if at all. But in Washington, the Supreme Court was expanding *Brown*'s reach by applying it in other contexts. In 1955 and 1956, the court cited *Brown* in a series of cases that struck down state mandated segregation in public accommodations, such as beaches, buses, and golf courses.[16] Then in *Cooper v. Aaron* (1958), following the Little Rock school integration crisis, the Supreme Court reprimanded Arkansas state officials for their failure to comply with *Brown v. Board of Education*. (Arkansas state officials had argued that because they weren't parties to the case—no Arkansas school district had been named in the *Brown* litigation—they were free to ignore the *Brown* precedent.)[17] In ringing, triumphant tones, the court reaffirmed its role as the supreme arbiter of constitutional meaning and warned that *Brown* would not be undermined by recalcitrance and intimidation ("the constitutional rights of [black children] are not to be sacrificed or yielded to the violence and disorder which have followed upon the actions of [Arkansas]").[18] So perhaps *Brown* could be extended, its force multiplied. Carter wrote: "Although not mandated by law, [northern school segregation] was a fact of life for the great majority of black children. This was one of the most frightening issues facing blacks in northern urban areas and offered fertile ground for developing and expanding the interpretation of the *Brown* mandate."[19]

Wilkins agreed with his general counsel's recommendation, although his enthusiasm for a full-fledged campaign that would "take *Brown* North" was more qualified. For one, he was concerned about what impact a northern campaign might have on ongoing desegregation efforts in the South, a problem he described as "monumental."[20] Wilkins thought the issue the NAACP faced went well beyond how best to litigate court cases. The question now was how to win the war over public opinion: "We all know that the desegregation battle has entered the stage where it is a contest of ideas rather than a legal contest."[21] And then there was the difficulty of litigating northern cases in the absence of Supreme Court guidance. After *Cooper v. Aaron*, the court did not decide another major southern school segregation case until 1968.[22] And the court did not speak directly to northern (and western) school segregation until 1973.[23] Consequently, Wilkins's consent was cautiously provided: "We ought to lay down pretty carefully memorandum of procedure and also engineer in our own staff a pilot project giving our northern branches blanket instructions to launch this activity."[24]

Carter had just the person to fulfill Wilkins's request. In his letter seeking his superior's approval for the northern campaign, he reminded his boss of the organization's secret weapon. Carter wrote, "In the event that you agree with me that the National Office should undertake this program and develop it, you have in June Shagaloff a person who has a great deal of experience in this field and she would be a logical person to formulate and direct such a program."[25] Called the "Johnny Appleseed of northern school desegregation" because of her work organizing myriad black communities to fight school segregation, Shagaloff was a community organizer on steroids.[26]

Shagaloff—a white woman—was an NAACP baby. She first began working at the organization as an intern while she was still an undergraduate at NYU, majoring in sociology. Thurgood Marshall himself hired Shagaloff immediately upon her graduation in 1951. (She would refer to him as "Mr. Marshall" for the remainder of her life.) Marshall wanted a community organizer so that the NAACP could "translate a legal decision to real change in a community."[27] Shagaloff was game, but she was concerned about her lack of experience. "I said to him, but I don't know anything, and I didn't know anything." Marshall told her, "You'll learn."[28] And she did.

Her first two assignments were in the North. In Amityville, Long Island, she and Constance Baker Motley—LDF's foremost trial and appellate litigator (she argued ten cases before the U.S. Supreme Court, winning nine) and later the first black woman to become a federal judge—fought the city's determination to build a new junior high school in the middle of the black community.[29] Instead, they advocated that the school be located where both black and white students could easily attend.[30] They succeeded, with Shagaloff combing school district records and finding substantial evidence of "intent to segregate, the intent to separate white and Black students in the school district."[31] Motley presented the evidence, the school board selected a different site, and the case was withdrawn. This was one of Shagaloff's first lessons: government actors in the North had intentionally segregated black children and there was plenty of evidence to prove it, *if* one had the resources and the will to uncover it.

This mattered. In the South, segregation was enforced by the positive law: statutes, legal codes, regulations. These laws were hardly mysterious. Their intent and their effect was to segregate. This was what de jure segregation was. But what if racial segregation in the North could be traced to the *intentional acts* of government? If so, northern segregation wasn't de facto—natural, accidental, customary—at all. Technically, "de facto" meant "in fact, in deed, actually."[32] The key point was that de facto segregation—caused by nongovernmental actors—was constitutionally invisible. Conversely, segregation that was imposed by law, either by statute *or* by the intentional acts of government officials, was de jure segregation. And either flavor of de jure segregation violated *Brown*. In 2014, Shagaloff looked back at her first assignment and stated in amazement: "This is a northern school district, in New York State where this is prohibited by law, where no one had challenged the existence of a Black elementary school or white elementary school until the issue of site selection for a new school was proposed. And it was just amazing in the school records the intent—all of the evidence—of the intent to segregate."[33]

Her second assignment took her to Cairo, Illinois, to help desegregate the city's public schools. It was in Cairo that she first began to act as a community organizer. In Cairo, just as in the Deep South, Shagaloff observed that everything was segregated, "lunch counters, hospitals, public libraries, schools, soda fountains . . . whatever institution existed was segregated."[34] But she got to work. Operating from the local NAACP branch as her base, she met with black parents and community leaders, made recommendations, and coordinated protests. The situation on the ground was turbulent and violent. A seasoned observer characterized southern Illinois, including Cairo, as a "hotbed of the Ku Klux Klan."[35] A local NAACP member's home was bombed; a few days later, the authorities arrested Shagaloff and several other NAACP officials for "conspiracy to harm children by creating a volatile situation in the schools."[36] Shagaloff, an out-of-stater, could not post the property bond required for release.

Flying to the rescue of his young colleague, Marshall sat with the local police chief, telling him stories for hours. (Shagaloff remembered him as a less sympathetic version of Chief Gillespie, the Rod Steiger character from *In the Heat of the Night*; "he was white of course, he was fat, he was sloppy, uneducated."[37]) Marshall, ever the raconteur, convinced the police chief to release her.[38] The NAACP filed suit in federal court and the schools were ultimately desegregated.[39] This was Shagaloff's second lesson: how closely parts of the North resembled the South, and relatedly, how dangerous her line of work could be.

After her death in March 2022, *The New York Times* assessed Shagaloff's extraordinary life.[40] The paper noted that she played an underappreciated role in the "nationwide fight for school integration," and that her racial ambiguity sometimes led her to be barred "from certain whites-only public spaces."[41] With dark wavy hair, an olive complexion, and full lips, she was frequently mistaken for a black woman. Shagaloff experienced—not hypothetically or at a remove, but personally—the status reduction, rank discrimination, and everyday humiliations that came with breathing while black. She told an interviewer, "I grew up with two racial identities, from September to June I was a white child, and from June to September I was a child of color, to people who didn't know me or my family. And I just could not understand, since I was the same person, how people could treat me so differently."[42] Later, reflecting on her early influences, she mentioned James Baldwin's *The Fire Next Time*: "James Baldwin wrote that 'color is not a personal reality. It's a political reality.'"[43] But perhaps that meant the political reality could be changed.

The reference to James Baldwin was probably not accidental. As it turned out, she and Baldwin (she called him "Jimmy") would become good friends. In December 1962, she threw a New Year's Eve party for him at her New York apartment.[44] Then on August 28, 1963, she and Baldwin attended the March on Washington for Jobs and Freedom together. Their presence that day was memorialized in a now-iconic photo of them seated together and dressed for the occasion. Baldwin sported a thin-lapelled jacket, crisp white shirt, and narrow tie; aviator sunglasses protected him against the glare of the late summer sun. Shagaloff wore a light-colored, collarless, short-sleeved dress, accessorized with a Bakelite necklace. Her hair was cut fashionably short. Together they epitomized a kind of casual, midcentury cool.

Beyond the captivating fashion statement, the picture tells another story. It displays a relationship, more common today but much less so then, between an obviously brilliant black gay man and a progressive, politically committed (today we might say "woke") white woman. It was easy to see what Shagaloff saw in Baldwin. At the time the picture was taken, he was a national celebrity (Baldwin was on the cover of *Time* magazine on May 17, 1963) and was already being recognized as the "Bard" of the black freedom struggle. Calling him a "prophet," one biographer stated that by 1963, Baldwin had "become the most articulate witness of the nation's agony."[45] But what did Baldwin see in Shagaloff? His distrust of white liberals was well-known—and to a large extent justified.[46] Why pal around with her? She wasn't a celebrity. She wasn't a writer. She wasn't an artist. She wasn't even a lawyer. The attraction must have lay elsewhere. One possibility might have been that Baldwin simply valued her dedication to the struggle. Perhaps the relationship testified to the work Shagaloff was already doing and would continue to do.

In 2018, I spoke to Shagaloff about the drive to bring *Brown* north.[47] Then a spry ninety-year-old, her memory was sharp. Looking back on her multifaceted career as a community organizer, activist, and equal education advocate, she was more than a little circumspect. Shagaloff candidly admitted that she had not achieved as much as she hoped. I confessed that she was a hero to many (including me), and in particular that she helped pave the way for blacks to enter every walk of life, including law teaching. She responded simply: "Yes, but it wasn't enough."

━━━━━

After Cairo, many of the NAACP's local branches in the North contacted the national office seeking assistance in desegregating their local public schools.[48] Shagaloff answered the call. In late 1952 through 1953, she was in New Jersey, Pennsylvania, Brooklyn, and the Bronx, advising local NAACP leaders and the black community about desegregation, and preparing them for the pressures associated with bringing a lawsuit.[49] The northern school districts' techniques for creating and then maintaining racial segregation were starting to have a familiar ring: assigning students to separate schools on the basis of their race, zoning schools so that only students from particular—and segregated neighborhoods—could attend them, intentionally siting the construction of new schools to maximize rather than to reduce school segregation.[50] But at this point, the organization's approach to northern school segregation was still ad hoc; it had not yet made an official commitment to a formal strategy.

Responding to Wilkins's request for a "memorandum of procedure" on how the organization might take *Brown* North, in late August 1959, Shagaloff drafted a four-page, single-spaced multipoint plan of attack. The number-one problem was housing: "De facto segregated public schools result primarily from segregated housing."[51] But she thought the organization was equal to the task. Shagaloff imagined that NAACP branches, community groups, and local leaders, backed by imaginative lawyers at the national office who knew how to win, could take northern segregation down.[52] Her memo pointed toward the importance of working at the local level, which was wise. *Brown* had had a generative impact on northern activists, spurring them to push even harder for desegregation.[53] Throughout the North, community activists—many of them mothers of school-age children—were demanding in no uncertain terms that the public schools be desegregated. The call for desegregation was bubbling up from the streets. The historian Thomas J. Sugrue described the scope and import of this movement: "Blacks in hundreds of northern cities and towns . . . pushed school boards to implement *Brown* through boycotts, demonstrations, and litigation. What *Brown* meant—particularly in the North—was legally and politically up for grabs."[54] Crucially, it was black activists—not white liberals, not white judges, not the national office of the NAACP—who set the agenda.[55] Armed with *Brown*, the northern activists were going to slay the dragon.

The northern activists were happy to take the NAACP's help, but they showed that they could get the job done even without it. In early 1961, activists notched a win in New Rochelle, New York, a suburb to the north of New York City. In *Taylor v. Board of Education of New Rochelle*,[56] a federal trial court ruled that the city had intentionally gerrymandered school attendance lines to "confine Negro pupils within the Lincoln district, while allowing whites living in the same area to attend a school which was not predominantly Negro in composition."[57] The case was litigated by a young black attorney, Paul Zuber, who was unaffiliated with (and often hostile to) the NAACP.

Zuber was more militant and outspoken than most of the NAACP's leadership. During this period, he was quoted as saying (affecting a southern accent), "Down home, our bigots come in white sheets. Up here, they come in Brooks Brothers suits and ties."[58] He would become a frequent thorn in the organization's side. Carter, for one, hardly viewed Zuber as a "lawyer's lawyer." Of Zuber he once remarked, "[He] has a knack for rushing into these situations [northern school desegregation cases] without sufficient thought or planning."[59] But Carter also recognized (and perhaps admired) Zuber's ability to communicate: "He makes headlines because he is emotionally in tune with the times."[60]

In a carefully reasoned opinion, the federal court in *Taylor* keyed its decision to the idea that *Brown* stated a national, rather than a regional, rule. "De jure" segregation included, per the *Brown* decision, southern state laws that mandated racially separate schools as well as "gerrymandering of school district lines and transferring of white children as in the instant case."[61] The federal court would not allow the school district to conceal its intentionally discriminatory acts behind a "de facto" label.[62] This was a big deal. The Supreme Court had yet to address *Brown*'s potential application in the North and the West, where state and local law did not expressly mandate racially segregated schools. Given that, it was quite possible to argue that *Brown* simply didn't apply outside of the South. *Taylor* rejected that view. As the U.S. Commission on Civil Rights described it, *Taylor* said it was clear—to one lower federal court at least—that *Brown* "applies to racial segregation in the North and West resulting from official action, as well as to segregation in the South."[63] Holding that New Rochelle had violated *Brown*, the federal court ordered the city to present a desegregation plan consistent with its opinion.[64]

It was hard to overestimate the impact of the *Taylor* decision. One observer likened it to a "hurtling rocket" that "exploded into the consciousness of Negroes throughout the urban North and Midwest."[65] The U.S. Commission on Civil Rights thought the case a landmark, perhaps the most important school desegregation decision since *Cooper v. Aaron*.[66] A quarter century later, the city formally acknowledged the ruling's importance when it installed a plaque in a downtown park. It read, "This tablet honors all who participated in this struggle for equality in education and commemorates the 25th anniversary of the landmark Taylor vs. Board of Education of New Rochelle decision of 1961, a milestone in the search for unity in the midst of our diversity."[67]

Yet the NAACP still had not adopted an official policy with respect to northern school desegregation cases. Writing during the lead-up to the *Taylor* decision in October 1960, Carter expressed frustration with the national office's inability to take a firm position on the northern litigation. He wrote, "To say that I am distressed is an understatement. After at least five years of unpleasantness with this type of situation . . . we still have failed to formulate any definitive policy or program on northern school desegregation."[68] He continued: "The northern problem will not wait . . . Our branches and Negroes have become restive with the situation."[69]

Then, in July 1961, as the Freedom Riders were escalating their campaign against segregation in interstate bus travel across the South, the NAACP held its fifty-second annual convention at the Sheraton Hotel in downtown Philadelphia. Even the very venue pointed to ongoing discrimination in the North. Like every other major Philadelphia hotel at the time, the Sheraton refused to hire blacks for higher-status, public-facing roles such as waiter or bartender, but was happy to assign them to lower-level positions such as housekeeper, elevator operator, or porter.[70]

On Thursday evening July 13, with baseball great Jackie Robinson presiding, Thurgood Marshall gave the eighth annual Freedom Fund Report Dinner address in the hotel's grand ballroom.[71] Unsurprisingly, most of Marshall's comments relating to public education focused on the situation in the South. But one part of his speech pertained to northern segregation: "The past year has also brought into focus the segregation by custom in the North," Marshall said.[72] This statement reinforced the idea that there was a significant regional dichotomy between northern and southern segregation. Marshall's use of the word "custom"—did this mean public action, private action, or some mix of the two—showed just how difficult the road ahead would be for those trying to take down northern segregation. From there, Marshall pivoted to Paul Zuber, whom he praised vociferously. Zuber's "courageous action . . . almost single-handedly challenged the entire power structure of New Rochelle," he stated.[73] After noting the import of the *Taylor* case, Marshall observed that litigation and social protest movements often have synergistic effects: "[*Taylor*] has inspired many other northern communities to fight segregated schools."[74]

Two days after Marshall's address, the convention delegates took action. Tipping their hat to the activists in New Rochelle ("the battle waged by parents of children in the city of New Rochelle, New York, is typical of the struggle for integrated education throughout the entire country and is to be commended"), the delegates adopted a resolution expressly calling for the elimination of segregation in northern schools.[75] Urging increased branch involvement, the resolution put the problem of northern segregation at the front and center of the NAACP's agenda. This was the NAACP's official declaration of war on northern school segregation.

It was the delegates—rather than the higher-ups—who demanded immediate engagement in the North. The delegates were drawn from the organization's vast membership base. That base represented a large cross section of the African American community, "not only professors, lawyers and teachers, but postmen, maids and bus drivers."[76] And it reflected the extraordinary impact of the second Great Migration on the population of the urban North. Between 1940 and 1980, approximately five million black southerners moved to the North and West, mostly to the big cities.[77] This demographic change profoundly influenced the membership of the NAACP.[78] As one close observer of the NAACP's history put it, "While Southerners were still the majority of the Association's members, they were no longer as dominant as they had been in the past . . . These changes would produce new political demands to which the Wilkins leadership, including his board and staff, would have to adjust in order to retain power."[79]

With a resolution in their back pocket authorizing an "all-out attack" on northern school segregation, Carter and Shagaloff got to work.[80] In early 1962, the duo toured ten cities on the West Coast, surveying the extent of school segregation in areas distant from the Deep South. What they found was not encouraging. School segregation was a national, deeply entrenched problem.[81] Assessing the state of public school desegregation in the North and West the following year, Shagaloff wrote: "In every community where the NAACP has carefully examined the historical development of school attendance patterns, it has been evident in case after case that considerations of color alone, to the extent housing segregation permitted, have determined the basic organization of the public school system."[82] Throughout the 1960s, she crisscrossed the country countless times and worked with hundreds of NAACP branches, gathering information, providing counseling and technical assistance, meeting with state commissioners of education, speaking at conferences, developing desegregation plans, and mobilizing NAACP members to take action.[83] Ultimately, the NAACP's northern campaign—organized by Shagaloff—would reach more than two hundred school systems.[84]

Black folks were in open revolt over the segregated nature of the public schools. In New York City, a movement started by nine black mothers in Harlem in 1956 led to a citywide boycott of the public schools in 1964 that drew nearly half a million participants, almost double the size of the March on Washington the previous year.[85] What did the boycotters want: a comprehensive plan to desegregate New York City's public schools.[86] In Los Angeles, black parents and students picketed all-white high schools and elementary schools, and in the summer of 1963, one thousand protesters marched on the headquarters of the Los Angeles Board of Education.[87] Cleveland, too, had a citywide boycott of its district schools in 1964, drawing an estimated sixty thousand black students.[88]

In Seattle, black activists organized a prolonged school boycott in 1966, in which students cut public school and attended community-based Freedom Schools.[89] It was during that same year that the NAACP filed a lawsuit against the Seattle school board alleging unconstitutional segregation within the city's school system.[90] Although there was never a court determination that the city had engaged in intentional racial segregation, the lawsuit succeeded in prodding the school board to move toward integration. As Justice Breyer later explained it in his dissent in the *Parents Involved* case, "The parties settled after the school district pledged to undertake a desegregation plan."[91] But the lack of a judicial determination—that the city school board had in fact engaged in unconstitutional segregation— made all the difference to Chief Justice Roberts. In *Parents Involved*, the chief justice wrote that "the Seattle public schools have not shown that they were ever segregated by law, and were not subject to court-ordered desegregation decrees."[92] Because of this, the city could not justify its voluntary affirmative action plan as a measure intended to remediate the effects of past intentional discrimination. Of course just because there had never been a *judicial determination* that Seattle had engaged in de jure segregation didn't mean it hadn't.

When they failed to see results, black parents escalated their tactics. In Boston, when a citywide boycott of the public schools failed to inspire white leadership to integrate,[93] the parents organized "Operation Exodus" and began busing black students into white school districts themselves.[94] In Chicago, activists regularly protested the city's segregated schools and demanded the resignation of the school superintendent.[95] On October 22, 1963, more than 220,000 students boycotted the city's public schools, with many attending community-led Freedom Schools.[96] In 1965, when the city still failed to deliver on their demands, hundreds of activists engaged in nonviolent civil disobedience at the Board of Education headquarters and were arrested.[97] Only then did the Chicago school superintendent finally resign.[98]

At the same time, the NAACP was upping its game. In 1962, the NAACP sponsored or filed ten suits challenging northern-style segregation.[99] One community activist in particular was certainly aware of the NAACP's northern legal campaign: Albert Cleage. In early 1962, he had castigated the Detroit branch of the NAACP for refusing to support the *Sherrill* lawsuit even though it "offered every advantage sought by the National NAACP."[100] Why was this? Cleage answered the question in all caps: the *Sherrill* suit challenged all forms of "RACIAL SEGREGATION AND DISCRIMINATION PRACTICED BY THE DETROIT BOARD OF EDUCATION ENYWHERE [*sic*] AND EVERYWHERE IN THE CITY OF DETROIT."

In May 1963, the NAACP announced that it was entering a new phase of its drive to eliminate northern-style segregation, and expanded its campaign to twenty-five states.[101] Earlier in the year, however, the organization had suffered a setback in *Bell v. School City of Gary, Indiana*.[102] *Bell* highlighted a debate over nomenclature that revealed a core conflict in the desegregation of northern schools. At the time of the lawsuit, there were eight different school districts within the city of Gary. School authorities, like so many others then and now, assigned students to particular schools based on where they lived. This was the ubiquitous "neighborhood school rule," which allowed residential segregation to "flow through" to the schools. This was how the *Bell* court characterized one of the plaintiffs' key assertions: "In 1953, there was a change in the line between the Emerson and Roosevelt Districts from Twentieth Avenue to Nineteenth Avenue which affected the students from grades seven through twelve who lived in the area affected by the boundary change. The plaintiffs contend that this shift was made in order to put all of the students in these grades from the Dorrie Miller housing project, which is occupied by Negroes, in the Roosevelt School, a predominantly Negro school, rather than the Emerson School which is a predominantly white school, for the purpose of segregating the races."[103]

Claiming to be "color blind, so far as the races are concerned," Gary school authorities vehemently denied the allegation.[104] The plaintiffs hadn't shown that the defendants drew school district lines with the specific intent to segregate the schools. There was no evidence to that effect, the city school board asserted, and it maintained "no records on the basis of race or color."[105] But perhaps no such records were necessary if school authorities possessed even a passing knowledge of the city's neighborhood-level racial demographics.

The plaintiffs and the court actually agreed that the neighborhood school rule predictably led to racially identifiable schools. "With the use of the neighborhood school districts in any school system with a large and expanding percentage of Negro population, it is almost inevitable that a racial imbalance will result in certain schools," the court observed.[106] Where they differed was on whether that created a problem of constitutional magnitude. The court thought Gary's schools were "racially imbalanced."

In contrast, the plaintiffs believed those very same schools were "segregated" by virtue of the neighborhood school rule. From their perspective, "actual segregation of the races in the Gary schools exists because a large percentage of the Negro children are required to attend schools that are totally or predominantly Negro in composition."[107] The plaintiffs argued that the defendant was required to integrate those schools, regardless of motive or intent.[108] But what made the plaintiffs believe they were entitled to a court order requiring school authorities to integrate? One answer was that "separate but equal" was hardly unknown in Gary. Indiana had permitted localities to adopt a "separate but equal" policy for their public schools if they so chose.[109] Gary accepted the invitation. The city explicitly segregated two schools, Pulaski-East and Pulaski-West, "in accordance with the separate but equal policy, then permitted by Indiana law."[110] After the state repealed the "separate but equal" by choice law in 1949, it passed a new law formally prohibiting racially separate schools throughout the state. Only then did Gary integrate Pulaski-East and Pulaski-West.[111]

Second, most of the city's school district boundary lines were drawn when the separate but equal by choice law was still in effect. This was how the *Bell* court explained it: "[In 1906] Gary was originally laid out in eight school districts and, as the school population demanded, one large school was built in each of the eight districts. Each of these schools handled the education of the public school population within its area, from kindergarten through high school."[112] This was a perfect description of the neighborhood school rule. And there was absolutely no reason to believe that Gary's neighborhoods were racially integrated in the early twentieth century. Basing student school assignments on neighborhood didn't expressly discriminate on the basis of race. But against a background of widespread residential segregation, such a system guaranteed predictable racial outcomes. But that didn't matter to the court. "The problem in Gary is not one of segregated schools but rather one of segregated housing," it concluded.[113]

Behind the dueling characterizations of Gary's schools—"segregated" versus "racially imbalanced"—was a stark division in outlooks. The plaintiffs' argument suggested that segregated schools and segregated housing were linked; each reinforced the other, and as such they both caused harm to black schoolchildren. The court's perspective was quite different; though it acknowledged that the schools reflected the surrounding population, it remained agnostic on *why*. "Either by choice or design, the Negro population of Gary is concentrated in the so-called central area, and as a result the schools in that area are populated by Negro students,"[114] the court observed. This was a curious sentence, suggesting that systemic racial segregation might just as well be a matter of private preference. Alternatively, it might be a matter of "design," an even more spurious description. Didn't design suggest some sort of plan? And if so, whose plan? The court seemed uninterested in the answer. The capper was the passive construction: "As a result the schools in that area are populated by Negro students."[115] In this, the court seemed to suggest that school segregation somehow just happened. In fact, though, Gary required students who lived in the Central District to attend school there, and only there. And, as the *Bell* court conveniently ignored, those school district lines had been drawn under the previous "separate but equal" by choice regime. At the very least, the city knowingly perpetuated a racially discriminatory system. But in *Bell*, that wasn't enough.

As *Bell* and *Taylor* suggested, the challenge for local officials, activists, and families during this time was that the case law was inconsistent. It did not provide clear guidance to those on the ground. As Sugrue put it, "Between 1961 and 1973, lower courts issued a welter of contradictory decisions. In the narrowest of rulings, courts found that northern school districts could not be held culpable for patterns of racial 'imbalance' in schools that resulted from segregated housing patterns. In the broadest of rulings, courts ruled that districts needed to devise far-reaching plans to achieve a desegregated student body."[116]

Against this background of divergent rulings—and sustained white backlash against integration—the black community continued to press their case for integration through both social mobilization and the courts.[117] Zuber, Shagaloff and Carter, and Marshall certainly didn't always see eye to eye. But they agreed that litigation and social protest were mutually reinforcing.[118]

Carter, for his part, had his eye on a big prize: Detroit. In late June 1965, the general counsel gave a talk at a Detroit-area desegregation workshop.[119] Carter observed that, since the beginning of the century, large numbers of blacks had migrated to Detroit and the other great cities of the North. They received a frosty reception. Overcrowding, slums, and ghetto life were what defined most northern blacks' experience.[120] But the situation wasn't static. As blacks moved in, whites moved out. Carter stated: "While [blacks were] crowded into the central city, there has been a steady movement of the whites to the suburbs which has thus far successfully barred Negro penetration, thereby erecting a rising wall of separation between the black central city and the surrounding white suburbia."[121] Blacks were trapped "in the ghetto by barriers," which, in turn, had a deleterious effect on the public schools.[122] And at the very center of the problem was the neighborhood school. He continued, "In light of the rigid patterns of residential segregation, the neighborhood school necessarily means separate Negro and white schools. This in turn means that these schools reinforce and perpetuate the Negro's inferior status."[123]

It was around this time that Carter began planning a "major assault" on school segregation in the city of Detroit.[124] Looking back at this period in his autobiography, he wrote: "The Detroit school district encompassed the majority of blacks in the city. It was surrounded by school districts in the suburbs that were virtually all white. We sought on constitutional grounds to enlarge the Detroit school district to include the surrounding white districts as a means of eliminating racial segregation of the Detroit schools."[125] It was an ambitious objective. Ultimately, a not-insignificant number of federal judges would come around to Carter's way of thinking, unfortunately not the ones who mattered the most.

4

THE HOUSING-SCHOOLS NEXUS

In early 1968 James Del Rio, a black businessman (and soon to be lawyer) with a deep background in real estate, introduced a bill in the Michigan House of Representatives to reorganize the Detroit Public School District.[1] The bill was a direct response to calls from Cleage and others for community control over Detroit's schools.[2] Del Rio, a Democrat representing Detroit's Twenty-Fourth House District on the city's near west side,[3] believed that the current school board was "too large to be workable," and that "the product they're turning out is worse and worse every year."[4] So the bill divided the Detroit public school system into sixteen independent school districts, each with its own separate tax base and elected school board.[5] The Del Rio bill made no pretense of equity among districts. Tax revenues accessed in a particular district could be used only in that district, even though per capita wealth and population varied dramatically among them. But Del Rio was more concerned with giving neighborhoods control of their local schools than with the resources those neighborhoods would then have at their disposal. Perhaps most important, the new districts were drawn to encompass existing black neighborhoods, effectively ensuring that residential segregation would be mirrored in the schools.[6] In effect, Del Rio's bill provided for the total breakup of the Detroit public school system.

Del Rio and Cleage were well acquainted. In 1963, they both served on the Detroit Council for Human Rights, which helped bring Martin Luther King Jr. to Detroit in June of that year for the "Walk to Freedom March."[7] In a contemporaneous article, the *Detroit Free Press* called the Detroit March—a precursor to the March on Washington later that summer—"the largest civil rights demonstration in the nation's history."[8] And they often supported the same causes, which brought them into contact. Del Rio endorsed Cleage's call for black legislators to stage a one-day work stoppage in protest of Congress's refusal to seat ethically challenged Harlem Democrat Adam Clayton Powell Jr.[9] Both publicly favored a change to voting rules for Detroit City Council elections intended to increase the number of blacks elected to that body.[10] But unlike Cleage, Del Rio had once strenuously advocated for city-suburban integration.

In August of 1963 and as the chairman of the housing committee of the Detroit Council for Human Rights, he championed an integration plan that would have moved black Detroiters into the city's suburbs.[11] Reporting on the plan, the *Detroit Free Press* explained that the council would provide black Detroiters with information on about five thousand suburban homes that had been repossessed by the federal government because of "Federal Housing Administration and Veterans Administration foreclosures."[12] At a meeting with suburban officials in connection with the proposed plan, he stated: "Housing segregation is the biggest problem facing the Negro in the North . . . We know the way school boundaries are set up we must desegregate housing to desegregate schools."[13] "Put Negroes in suburbia, and the white people won't panic. There'll be no place else to run," he stated later.[14]

But if Del Rio's school bill really doubled down on residential segregation by configuring the new school districts along racial lines, why did he propose it, given his earlier advocacy of city-suburban integration? For the state legislator the answer was simple: the school reorganization proposal didn't create segregation in the first instance; it was the preexisting racially separate neighborhoods that did that work. Responding to his critics, Del Rio argued that his bill would have no effect on segregation already extant in Detroit's schools. "How can you force segregation? We already have it. It's governed by real estate. Not by the schools," he declared.[15] So Del Rio understood the symbiotic relationship between schools and housing. There was a nexus between the two, with each form of segregation aiding and abetting the other. Given that, it would be very difficult to desegregate one without desegregating the other.

Before his bill came up for a vote, a tragic event occurred, one that would raise—paradoxically—the tantalizing possibility of addressing both housing segregation and its next of kin, segregation in the public schools.

At roughly 5:55 p.m. on April 4, 1968, Dr. Martin Luther King Jr. stepped outside room 306 at the Lorraine Motel in Memphis, Tennessee, to speak to his aides in the parking lot below.[16] King was a frequent visitor of the motel (room 306 was unofficially dubbed the "King-Abernathy" suite). The motel was well-known in the black community. It had been listed in *The Negro Motorist Green Book*, a guide to accommodations that served blacks in otherwise segregated locales (Aretha Franklin, Otis Redding, and Nat King Cole were among its guests).[17] King was talking to Ben Branch, a musician who was to play at a rally later that evening.[18] That was when, as Walter Cronkite later gravely told the nation, a "bullet exploded in his face."[19] Earl Caldwell of *The New York Times*—the first black reporter the paper had ever assigned to cover King—was the only journalist at the Lorraine Hotel at the time.[20] According to Caldwell, the shot that struck King "was more of a blast, like a giant firecracker or a bomb."[21] As the reporter described the scene on the balcony, Ralph Abernathy was "leaning over [King] as though he were trying to talk with him. The blood. The wound was as big as your fist. His eyes. They were open but they had such a strange look. Eyes that were not seeing anything."[22] King died of his wounds shortly thereafter.

Although most associated with the fight against southern Jim Crow, King had been a key voice on housing segregation and northern Jim Crow. Fresh off the success of the Selma campaign and the passage of the Voting Rights Act, in September 1965, he and the Southern Christian Leadership Conference (SCLC) announced that the next phase of their fight for racial equality would take place in Chicago.[23] King and the SCLC shifted their focus to the north for a variety of reasons. First, they were increasingly aware that their success in the South would not automatically "trickle up" to northern blacks. Black activists had already been struggling for years to achieve equality in northern public schools. Their efforts had hardly yielded a knockout blow. Northern whites weren't going to change voluntarily. They would have to be pushed. Hard. Next, King and the SCLC wanted to demonstrate that tactical nonviolence could be effectively applied in a northern locale, particularly after the riots in Harlem and Philadelphia in the summer of 1964 and in Watts in August 1965.[24] If King could succeed in the North on his own terms, it would provide a nonviolent alternative to some northern blacks who were increasingly viewing violence as a legitimate means of effectuating social change.[25] But most importantly, King wanted to shift a regional movement to a national one. Racial discrimination appeared in different local guises, but it was a countrywide problem.[26] Against this background, King told an interviewer, "While I have been working mainly in the South and my organization is a southern-based organization, more and more I feel the problem is so national in its scope that I will have to do more work in the North than I have in the past."[27] The Chicago Freedom Movement was the result.

In January 1966, King and his family moved to a squalid apartment at 1550 South Hamlin Avenue in North Lawndale on Chicago's West Side to begin phase one of the Chicago campaign.[28] He hoped that his actions there could be replicated: "If we can break the backbone of discrimination in Chicago, we can do it in all the cities in the country."[29] The city was an attractive target. It was deeply segregated and had strong, well-organized local civil rights organizations with which to partner. It also had Richard J. Daley, a mayor with the power to produce social change.[30] Dismissing warnings that Chicago might be more difficult to conquer than Selma (Bayard Rustin cautioned: "You've got problems . . . which you don't have in the little southern communities that you are accustomed to . . . You're going to be wiped out"), King plunged ahead.[31]

Initially, his goals were broad, if not inchoate. The starting point would be a war on the slums, which one of King's key lieutenants called "a system of internal colonialism."[32] The Chicago Freedom Movement was taking aim at the northern ghetto. King's thinking was becoming more radical and consequently even more threatening. He was moving toward the idea that an unfettered capitalist system inexorably led to exploitation of those at the bottom, which is where blacks had been all along.[33] The black ghetto facilitated exploitation because it locked blacks in a specific place, making them ripe for the picking.[34]

Exactly how the Chicago Freedom Movement would eradicate such a deeply entrenched system was yet to be determined. In early 1966, Andrew Young admitted, "We haven't gotten things under control. The strategy [for Chicago] hasn't emerged yet, but now we know what we're dealing with and eventually we'll come up with the answers."[35] King agreed. Speaking at a press conference at the Sahara motel in Chicago in January 1966, he acknowledged that "we are in no position [now] to know what form massive action might take in Chicago."[36] Guaranteeing voting rights in the South had been extraordinary difficult. But it was still a single issue with clear adversaries—openly racist governmental officials—who were prone to making catastrophic mistakes in front of television cameras. Everything about this campaign made it harder from the jump: a large northern city, a more sophisticated opponent, and a powerful Democratic political machine that ensured loyalty by doling out elected offices, patronage jobs, and cash to strategic sectors of the black community.[37]

But the biggest difficulty was the nature of the northern problem itself. As one scholar adroitly put it, "In contrast to the South, there was no [classic] de jure discrimination in Chicago, and thus there was no critical, obvious target symbolizing injustice in the way that a southern court house did. How did one root out injustice when it was built into the very structure of society, when virtually every Chicago institution bore a measure of responsibility for it?"[38] It was a good question. In the South, racial segregation was required by law in virtually every facet of life. Separate water fountains, perhaps the most iconic symbol of southern Jim Crow, provided a good example. If southern blacks dared a sip of water from a white fountain, they faced potential criminal sanctions and the full enforcement power of the state government: arrest, prosecution, imprisonment.[39] In the South, the government's role in maintaining racial segregation was readily observable. In the North, government had every-thing to do with the fact that de facto racial segregation was pervasive. It was just that it was much harder to see the government's fingerprints above the Mason-Dixon Line. The difficulty northern activists faced was showing that the government—what lawyers called "state action"—created and maintained racial segregation just as in the South. Because of this, the Chicago Freedom Moment needed a more specific goal, one that was at least theoretically obtainable.

Ultimately, the movement narrowed its goal to the eradication of housing discrimination and segregation.[40] Just a few years earlier, the U.S. Commission on Civil Rights had called Chicago the "most residentially segregated city in America."[41] There would be no slums without housing discrimination, so the movement went right at the cause. The number-one offenders were the real estate industry, the brokers, the real estate boards, and the lenders. The real estate industry was a "ghetto maker and ghetto keeper," a local fair housing expert said at the time.[42] By late June 1966, the movement's goal was to make Chicago an "open city."[43] King also believed that an energetic open housing movement—one that excited activists and put thousands of boots on the streets—could have synergistic effects on President Johnson's newly proposed fair housing legislation.[44] (The SCLC officially called on Congress to enact federal fair housing legislation in April 1966.) The Chicago Freedom Movement "was an attempt to get the nation to make housing segregation illegal," Jesse Jackson stated.[45]

Throughout the summer of 1966, movement activists engaged in var-ious forms of direct action. White realtors routinely denied blacks service, while whites were assisted. The movement tested this, held vigils, and boldly marched into white neighborhoods. They were exposing systematic and pervasive housing discrimination throughout the city. The response was swift and violent. Seething white mobs stoned marchers, smashed windshields, and torched parked cars. At a march in early August, King was "felled" by a rock.[46] There are conflicting accounts of where the rock hit him—the *Chicago Tribune* indicated that he was struck in the back of the neck, while *The New York Times* stated he was hit in the head.[47] He staggered, but moved on. Someone from the crowd threw a knife at the minister, narrowly missing him, wounding a nearby white protester instead.[48] From their homes, whites yelled, "Cannibals," "Savages," and, "Go home, niggers."[49] Remarkably, King told a reporter that he had "never seen as much hatred and hostility on the part of so many people."[50] That statement alone proved Pulitzer Prize–winning historian Taylor Branch's thesis. Chicago, he wrote, "nationalized race, complementing the impact of Watts. Without it King would be confined to posterity more as a regional figure. The violence against northern demonstrators cracked a beguiling, cultivated conceit that bigotry was the province of backward Southerners, treatable by enlightened but firm instruction."[51]

Crucially, the violence against demonstrators in Chicago was committed by private individuals. In the South, the police had often done the deed. This made it possible to interpret the clash in the northern city as between two legitimate, but competing, visions. On one side were blacks' private property rights, the ability to buy a home in the neighborhood of one's choice unencumbered by race. On the other was the freedom to choose one's friends and associates and to live among like-minded neighbors. This certainly wasn't the best interpretation of the events on the ground, but it gave those already so inclined an out. A reporter's question was illustrative. On August 21, 1966, *Meet the Press* aired a special ninety-minute episode focusing on civil rights. Richard Valeriani of NBC News asked King, "In regard to your present movement, in regard to housing, is it not conceivable to you that a majority of white Americans does not want a Negro for a neighbor? And if that's so . . . should the majority preference be respected?"[52] The question implied the answer. It suggested that whites' desire to exclude blacks from their neighborhoods represented the anodyne will of the majority, one entirely different from white southerners' peculiar fetish for racially separate water fountains. King pounced. "It may be true that in the South that many more people did not want Negroes to eat at lunch counters, did not want Negroes to have access to motels and hotels and restaurants. But this did not stop the nation from having its conscience so aroused that it brought into being civil rights laws as a result of our movement to end this."[53] He took a breath and continued, "The same thing must happen in housing."[54]

As the historian David Garrow put it, "Chicago authorities wanted the protests stopped before additional mob violence occurred," so Daley ultimately agreed to negotiate.[55] In exchange for ending the marches, King and the Chicago Freedom Movement came away from the bargaining table with the Summit Agreement. The agreement contained several provisions, the most important of which were the city's promise to enforce an existing antidiscrimination ordinance and to urge the state to pass a fair housing law. The city also committed to nondiscrimination in public housing assignments, placing, per the agreement, "families in the best available housing without regard to the racial character of the neighborhood."[56] The Chicago Real Estate Board, in "a significant departure from its traditional position," agreed to abide by applicable law and cease its opposition to fair housing.[57] No timetables or deadlines were set, however, and the agreement lacked any enforcement mechanisms.[58] The historian Kevin Boyle summed it up this way: "Daley had given them everything— and nothing at all: no guarantees, no timetables, not a single assurance beyond his word that he would fulfill the promises he'd just made."[59] Many local activists were furious. One remarked, "We feel the poor Negro has been sold out by this agreement."[60]

The initial consensus was that the Chicago Freedom Movement was a failure, with the mayor having outmaneuvered the minister.[61] It did not have the immediate synergistic effect on Johnson's proposed fair housing legislation that King had hoped.[62] If anything, the movement generated white backlash in the North, making the prospects for the immediate passage of fair housing legislation less, rather than more, likely. For another, although Johnson proposed (and personally favored) fair housing legislation in 1966, he didn't exploit his considerable political skills to get the bill passed. Per the journalist Jonathan Eig, "Black editorial writers blamed President Johnson for caving in to the real estate lobby and failing to fight for his fair-housing legislation."[63] With Johnson standing on the sidelines, a fair housing measure passed the House, but it was filibustered to death in the Senate and died in September.[64] The bill died again in 1967.

The following year was different. At the beginning of 1968, Johnson was fully committed to the bill's passage, and a key Republican senator changed his position on the legislation, voting in favor of it.[65] But its prospects of passage were still deeply precarious. By most accounts, it was still on track to die by filibuster. But on March 1, 1968, the Kerner Commission released its findings on the causes of the civil disorders that had affected many cities throughout the United States, including Detroit. The commission's report hit Congress like a bombshell. Coming in at more than four hundred pages, it was easy to see why. Broad in geographical and historical scope, and examining virtually every facet of ghetto life—employment, family structure, crime, health conditions, consumer practices, media representation, environmental factors—it was a stunningly comprehensive indictment of American racism.[66]

The Kerner Commission report was most famous for the admonition: "Our nation is moving toward two societies, one black, one white—separate and unequal."[67] But it was the report's conclusions about the relationship among housing segregation, school segregation, and the black ghetto that got Congress's notice as the fair housing legislation was being considered.[68] The schools were segregated *because of* housing discrimination. This was the housing-schools nexus. The commission wrote, "Racial isolation in the urban public schools is the result principally of residential segregation and widespread employment of the 'neighborhood school' policy, which transfers segregation from housing to education."[69] That wasn't all. Housing discrimination not only delivered school segregation, it also created and entrenched the black ghetto. The commission observed, "[Residential] discrimination prevents access to many nonslum areas, particularly the suburbs, and has a detrimental effect on ghetto housing itself."[70] All of this contributed to the commission's recommendation that the federal government enact a comprehensive fair housing law. Not later, but now. Because there was "no substitute" for such legislation, it recommended enactment of an open housing bill "at the earliest possible date."[71]

Eleven days after the commission released its report, the Senate passed a fair housing bill. The commission's report undoubtedly influenced the Senate's action.[72] But the legislation still wasn't out of the woods. The bill went from the Senate over to the House for reconciliation, where it was expected to languish if not die altogether.[73]

But then, on April 4, 1968, as Taylor Branch so evocatively put it, King's "sojourn on earth went blank."[74] King's assassination touched off a wave of riots across the country. More than one hundred cities large and small exploded, including Washington, D.C., Chicago, Baltimore, Cincinnati, and Pittsburgh.[75] Detroit, still recovering from the previous year's convulsions, was also on the list. D.C. was particularly hard hit. Federal troops guarded the White House and the Capitol; thousands of them occupied the city for more than a week.[76] Before it was over, thirteen people had died in the city and more than nine hundred business were damaged.[77]

Reacting to the civil discord that threatened to engulf the country, President Johnson sent a letter to House Speaker John McCormack on Friday, April 5, 1968, urging passage of the stalled fair housing bill.[78] Effective fair housing legislation meant prohibiting racial discrimination in real estate transactions and disestablishing the residential segregation that had come to define the nation's metropolitan areas. Johnson wrote, "Last night, America was shocked by a senseless act of violence. A man who devoted his life to the nonviolent achievement of rights that most Americans take for granted was killed by an assassin's bullet."[79] Johnson continued, "I ask you to bring this bill to a vote in the House of Representatives at the earliest possible moment. The time for action is now."[80]

Johnson's impatience likely stemmed from the fact that, under pressure from the Chicago Freedom Movement, he had first proposed fair housing legislation more than two years earlier. Calling for federal legislation barring race discrimination in housing before Congress in 1966, Johnson skillfully connected all the dots. Housing discrimination, he argued, was a crucial link in a suffocating web of black disadvantage: "It is self-evident that the problems we are struggling with form a complicated chain of discrimination and lost opportunities," he wrote in a special message to Congress.[81] Johnson emphasized how social and economic chances were interrelated—a rung on the ladder to the American dream. He continued, "Employment is often dependent on education, education on neighborhood schools and housing, housing on income, and income on employment."[82] The force of his logic suggested that housing discrimination could not remain unaddressed. "We have learned by now the folly of looking for any single crucial link in the chain that binds the ghetto. All the links—poverty, lack of education, underemployment and now discrimination in housing—must be attacked together."[83]

On April 6, 1968, *The New York Times* reported that King's assassination had likely changed the political realities on the ground: "Congressional leaders said that Dr. King's murder could assure passage next week of a landmark civil rights bill."[84] Just one day after King's funeral on April 10, 1968, the House of Representatives passed the Fair Housing Act by a vote of 250 to 171.[85] President Johnson quickly signed the bill into law. King's assassination was the necessary impetus.[86] As a leading scholar of residential segregation put it, "In the end, it took a martyr's blood finally to outlaw discrimination in housing."[87] The Chicago Freedom Movement played a role in the statute's enactment, too. After King's death, Johnson framed federal fair housing legislation as essential to honor and continue the minister's work.[88] King's campaign for fair housing in Chicago, and the work of the black activists there, bolstered the credibility of Johnson's argument immeasurably.[89] King believed that direct action in Chicago would have a synergistic effect on federal fair housing legislation. It did. He just didn't live to see it.

———

Del Rio's bill reached the floor of the Michigan State House of Representatives for a vote on April 10, 1968—the very same day that the U.S. House of Representatives passed the federal Fair Housing Act.[90] But Del Rio's bill met with a different outcome. It wasn't that the representatives were unsympathetic to the idea of community control. Representative Jackie Vaughn III of Detroit's Twenty-Third House District[91] was a supporter of the idea: "Self-determination is an important concept. We're committed to this concept," he stated.[92] Daisy L. Elliott, a black Democrat representing

Detroit's Twenty-Second House District on the city's lower west side,[93] noted approvingly that the Detroit Board of Education had taken actions consistent with community control. The board had moved to "provide for maximum local participation and accountability, as well as the maximum community involvement necessary for the effective operation of school units."[94] Like the NAACP, the representatives thought community control enhanced accountability—and was perfectly consistent with integration, as the goal of each was quality education. "I think we can achieve both" black self-determination and integration, Vaughn asserted.[95]

But they voted "no" on the bill because it would deliver segregated *and* unequal schools. "To bring a district bill of this nature is an insult to one's intelligence, when it specifically states that the school tax base will be based upon the ability of those people in that particular district [only]," Vaughn thundered.[96] Explaining her "no" vote, Representative Elliott exposed the limitations of community control and intentionally under-resourced communities: "The boundaries proposed would create inadequately financed school districts, unequal pupil-teacher ratios, discrepancies between school capacity and potential enrollments, unalterably segregated schools, and the ghettoizing of families on the basis of socioeconomic characteristics."[97]

David S. Holmes Jr., a black Democrat representing Detroit's Tenth House District,[98] linked school and residential segregation. He argued that if the state legislature really wanted to improve Detroit's schools, it needed to regulate realtors, brokers, and banks, not school administrators: "The industry that has caused segregation basically—the real estate people—cause all the problems of separation of races in Detroit and I think hitting at the Board of Education is the wrong place to hit . . ."[99] "I think if we're going to try to do anything, we ought to [target] the real-estate industry."[100] The lawmaker's comments suggested that eradicating housing segregation would necessarily impact the racial composition of the public schools. In tying the two forms of segregation together, Holmes's statements implicitly—if not explicitly—supported the actions of his federal colleagues in Washington, D.C. Rosetta A. Ferguson, a black Democrat representing Detroit's Ninth District,[101] made the housing-schools nexus argument succinctly: "I voted no because I am completely opposed to discrimination or segregation in any form. Mr. Speaker and Members, equal education will be gained from equal housing which is the key to quality education."[102]

Ultimately, Del Rio's school reorganization bill went down to defeat in the Michigan State House of Representatives by a 59–45 vote. But as social scientists George R. La Noue and Bruce L. R. Smith correctly observed, the fact that Del Rio's bill had been affirmatively reported out of the House Education Committee marked a significant shift signaling "a change in the politics of school [reorganization]. The arena for decision-making had shifted from the Detroit school system to the [state] legislature, and the community control concept had found surprising support."[103]

Community control of the schools wasn't a fleeting issue; it wasn't going to just disappear. In fact, between February 1968 and the early spring of 1969, several school reorganization bills were introduced in the Michigan State legislature.[104] In late March 1969, the House Education Committee held a hearing on community control of the schools, at which both Del Rio and Cleage testified on behalf of Del Rio's bill, which had been reintroduced. Del Rio criticized Detroit's centralized school system, which was "responsible for more riots than all the white racism in America."[105] For his part, Cleage warned the committee that "All Inner City schools are in a complete state of chaos and conflict."[106] But their advocacy failed to move the needle. None of the school reorganization bills, including Del Rio's, garnered enough support to become law. According to William Grant, the *Detroit Free Press* education reporter and a close observer of the Detroit Public Schools, at that moment "legislative discussion of [school reorganization] seemed to be dead."[107]

But then an ambitious state senator named Coleman A. Young got involved. The fifty-year-old Detroit politician's story would end up closely entwined with the city's desegregation battles. Young was an early firebrand. As a young man he worked on the line at Ford Motor, but was fired and blacklisted for his involvement in union and civil rights activism. A member of the famed Tuskegee Airmen during World War II (the first

African American military aviators in the U.S. Armed Forces), he played a key role in the Freeman Field Mutiny, in which more than one hundred African American officers were arrested for resisting segregation.[108] Under the pseudonym Captain Midnight he wrote articles in the black press about the Army's treatment of black soldiers.[109] After the war, Young continued to push for racial and economic equality as a union organizer, until he was forced out of the United Automobile Workers–Congress of Industrial Organizations by leaders looking to shore up their anti-Communist credentials.[110] Believing that the NAACP's agenda was "a little too genteel for our designs," Young helped organize the National Negro Labor Council, a left-wing organization committed to economic liberation.[111] The Labor Council achieved a string of successes, including persuading several national retailers to hire black workers. But it later disbanded after United States attorney general Herbert Brownell labeled it a subversive organization. Young burned the membership rolls.[112]

It was not until 1952, however, that Young made his name in Detroit. Testifying before the House Un-American Activities Committee, Young turned the hearing into a dissertation on white supremacy, defying his questioners with sarcastic retorts, and repeatedly refusing to answer whether or not he was a member of the Communist Party.[113] A leading conservative newspaper assailed Young, describing him as "possibly the most hostile, adroit and evasive witness ever to confront" the committee.[114] Young wouldn't have disagreed with that assessment. His testimony bristled with antagonism:

> MR. FRANK S. TAVENNER (Committee Counsel): You told us you were the executive secretary of the National Negro Congress.
> MR. YOUNG: That word is "Negro," not "Niggra."
> MR. TAVENNER: I said, "Negro." I think you are mistaken.
> MR. YOUNG: I hope I am. Speak more clearly.[115]

Young's performance—the sheer audaciousness of it—made him a hero in black Detroit. As he modestly put it, "The hearings were as big as the damn World Series in Detroit, and they were broadcast live on radio."[116] Over the next decade, Young continued to advocate for leftist causes, worked odd jobs, and was hounded by the FBI. Ultimately, he came to the realization that "the only thing capable of pulling me out of my despair was a good jolt of politics."[117] Young ran for the Detroit Common Council in 1960 and lost. But his criticism of the Detroit Police Department's racist practices struck a nerve.[118] Believing he had an issue that he could "carry to the community,"[119] in 1964 he entered the race for state senate. This time he won.

Young now represented black Detroiters in the fourth senatorial district, the city's lower east side.[120] By 1968, as he contemplated a lifelong career in politics, he had begun to shift away from the open radicalism of his youth and developed, as one scholar described it, "a hard shell of pragmatism."[121] So on April 14, 1969, Young introduced his own school reorganization bill in the Michigan State Senate. In addition to being the chief spokesman for the Democrats in the senate and the leader of the black legislators, Young was a strong proponent of community control.[122] The *Michigan Chronicle* suggested that Young believed that "giving parents an authoritative voice in school matters opens up [an] avenue for the legitimate redress of student grievances and lessens frustration they feel with a bureaucratic and insensitive system."[123] The objective was to "end unrest in Detroit schools." But he understood that the legislature would never approve a bill like Del Rio's, one that effectively destroyed the Detroit Board of Education and created sixteen wholly independent school districts, each with just as much power and authority as any other school district in the state. He therefore proposed a compromise that accommodated a variety of constituencies.

On the one hand, his bill responded to the demand for community control by authorizing the Detroit Board of Education to divide the school system into a minimum of seven new regional districts, each with its own nine-member board. The *Detroit Free Press* concluded that this would "give blacks comprising 60 percent of the Detroit System's enrollment a bigger voice in decision-making."[124] While Young's bill mandated minimum and maximum enrollments for each new district, it left the location of the new districts to the board's discretion. This would turn out to have fateful implications.

Under Young's plan, the new regional boards would exercise classic

Board of Education powers over such matters as budget, curriculum, testing, teacher discipline, retention, and promotion. In addition, one member of each regional board would serve on an enlarged central board of education, the newly reconfigured central Detroit Board of Education. At the same time, the regional boards' decisions would be subject to override by the newly configured central board. So, even as Young's bill responded to the demands for community control, it also provided a check on that control: under the bill the central board would retain substantial policymaking authority. In truth, Young's bill was quite moderate, as the *Detroit Free Press* noted. It characterized the bill as "unlikely to produce major changes in the operation of the system."[125] Nevertheless, Young believed it was the strongest bill that could be achieved under the circumstances.[126] Finally, while the regional boards would have lots of power, they would be prohibited from violating or renegotiating collective-bargaining agreements. That meant the Detroit Federation of Teachers got something, too. Having skillfully navigated these different constituencies, Young faced little opposition in either house. His bill passed by large margins, and Governor William G. Milliken signed it into law on August 11, 1969.[127]

Cleage's role in the school reorganization movement in Detroit was foundational. He and his constituency pushed community control all the way from the School Center Building in Midtown Detroit to the state house in Lansing. Del Rio was unable to transform his school reorganization bills—which Cleage championed—into law. But Young, an adroit politician who took a more moderate approach, succeeded. The result was a bill that *required* the Detroit school system to reorganize. And, like the other school reorganization bills that came before it, Young's bill was silent on desegregation.[128] So the bill that passed left a great mystery ahead: How, exactly, would the Detroit school board, which had the discretion to implement the bill's objectives, exercise that power? Meanwhile, the issue that had motivated Dr. King to take his drive to eradicate Jim Crow north—residential segregation—had hardly receded. Just one day before Young introduced his school reorganization bill, William Grant published an article in the *Detroit Free Press* titled "Detroit vs. Suburban Schools:

Parents Dilemma."[129] The article reported that large numbers of white parents were dissatisfied with Detroit's schools and were departing for the suburbs. But this wasn't an option for black parents, who were limited in "where they [could] go" because of, as Grant euphemistically put it, "integrated housing patterns."[130] But what that really meant was that blacks were prohibited from living in the suburbs. Segregated housing and segregated schools continued to be entwined.

5

SOUL FORCE

I n August 1969, the day after Young's bill became law, the Detroit school board held its next regularly scheduled meeting. Abraham Zwerdling, the board's famously pro-integration president, released a public statement tepidly supporting the act. Clearly holding his nose, he wrote, "We will do our best to try to make this statute work."[1] Zwerdling's lack of enthusiasm for school reorganization was palpable, but he recognized that the state had invested the board with wide discretion to create the new regions, and he wasn't going to waste the opportunity. "In dividing these districts of the City of Detroit in regions, we are going to keep [integrated quality education] in mind," he stated.[2] Young's bill neither required nor prohibited integration. No one who followed the debate in the statehouse thought it was an integration law. But that didn't matter. The legislature had invested the board with discretion, and Zwerdling was going to use it as he saw fit.

By the time he issued a longer and more formal statement the next month, however, Zwerdling had clearly already begun to wrestle with the impossibilities of the task assigned to the board. Young's bill required it to create "regions *within* the existing School District of Detroit," he wrote "rather than crossing the boundaries into the suburbs."[3] Whatever the bill's intentions, this design clashed with his long-standing zeal to achieve racially integrated schools. In his statement, Zwerdling referenced nebulous schemes designed to prevent such integration—what he called "the vast conspiracy of silence concerning the artificial barriers at the city limits which prevent children of Detroit, Grosse Pointe, Dearborn, and other surrounding suburbs from sharing a common school experience."[4] But conspiracy to commit what crime? And who exactly was responsible? He pointed to "surrounding suburbs," "artificial barriers," and "vast expressways"—each the product of government. Government provided highway funds. Government created zoning regulations. Government licensed real estate brokers. Government decided where and how to build public housing. Government regulated banks and insurance companies. Government authorized "slum" clearance. Government incorporated suburban areas. And, of course, government also ran the public school system.

For Zwerdling, the problem wasn't confined solely to individual acts of discrimination; it was larger than that and demanded a more comprehensive remedy. Thus, he asserted that "the Legislature and the Governor [must] face up to the fact that we cannot truly achieve an integrated, open society unless we redistrict the greater metropolitan area."[5]

Why was a white man like Zwerdling so committed to integration? His biography provided one hint. Zwerdling's father was an Austro-Hungarian Jew who came to New York City in 1900, speaking little English. He worked in a garment factory.[6] Zwerdling remembered his father as a striver, someone who studied at night by candlelight and moved to Ann Arbor simply because someone offered him a job there. Ultimately, his father became a successful furrier and put all three of his sons through the University of Michigan Law School. Zwerdling's public school experience was foundational, providing a lasting lesson in the value of integrated education. "When I went to high school in Ann Arbor," he told a reporter, "there was only one high school. Everybody in town went there—black and white, rich and poor. That was an American school. I don't think of white schools and black schools. I'm only concerned about American schools."[7]

Zwerdling's invocation of the "American school" stood out. The reference to a school that served an entire city and by virtue of that every walk of life, might have been more than sentimental. He was very likely aware that various desegregation advocates, scholars, educators, urban planners, federal officials, architects, and philanthropists were searching for a solution to school segregation that would be effective in both the North and

South.[8] The "education parks" championed by the Detroit Urban League back in 1967 were among the solutions they proposed. The central idea was to sever entirely the connection between schools and housing, thereby undermining the impact of residential segregation on the schools. The model was the public university. Proponents of education parks imagined huge parklike campuses spread over fifty or a hundred acres and serving thousands of students in multiple grades. They stressed the importance of locating the parks on the periphery of cities, accessible to urban and suburban residents alike.[9] Recognizing that middle-class whites had more school (and housing) choices than blacks, they believed that one way to solve the problem of "white flight" was to provide a peerless educational experience. In effect, education parks were an early version of the magnet school, on steroids. They would have state-of-the-art libraries, computers, facilities, and programming, and top-notch teachers and counselors with significant experience and certification in their fields.[10]

Zwerdling might well have associated his high school ("an American school") and education parks in his mind. One leading proponent likened them to "a defensible modern version of the common school, perhaps the only form in which that traditionally American institution can be maintained in an urban society."[11] President Johnson's education commissioner, Harold Howe II, was an enthusiastic supporter. In a 1966 speech, "The City Is a Teacher," Howe made his case. "We are particularly interested in finding one or two great American cities that are adventurous enough to join us in planning the educational park of the future," he urged.[12] The commissioner understood that such parks threatened the hyperlocal provision of education, loved by so many Americans. "While such a park would deny the neighborhood school, it would express the vitality, the imagination, and the cultural mix that every vigorous city exemplifies. Students in such a facility would attend a genuine city school in the deepest sense . . . rather than going to school in one section of the city which is untouched by the broader influences of metropolitan life as a whole."[13] Most importantly, the education park would reduce segregation. "Building programs for the future [education parks] could be planed [sic] so that new schools break up, rather than continue, segregation of both the racial and economic sort," Howe stressed.[14]

But they would not be cheap. One estimate put the costs for one large park at $50 million, although significant economies of scale were expected. The U.S. Commission on Civil Rights thought the idea promising, and the federal government funded several feasibility studies.[15] Education parks were contemplated in at least eighty-five cities, including Syracuse, Pittsburgh, and New York.[16] A proposed federal bill, The Equal Educational Opportunity Act of 1967, even included more than $5 billion in appropriations for education parks and other metropolitan desegregation measures.[17] But it was not to be. Correctly perceiving the bill as a major threat to de facto segregation, Republican Congressmen excoriated it on the House floor. "I have here in my hand a document which can only be referred to as 'radical,'" declared Representative Paul Fino of New York.[18] "[It] would set up a multibillion dollar effort to force racial balance in the nation's schools."[19] Exactly. Conservative columnists Rowland Evans and Robert Novak were also ringing alarm bells. Ignoring the fact that education parks were at the cutting edge of social policy in 1966, they characterized them as running "counter to modern, sophisticated thinking about how to solve the education problem in the Negro ghettos."[20] They were also skeptical that federal money should be spent on "Negro schools" at all. After all, if the problem was "the quality of the student's home life," no amount of federal education money could solve it.[21] The bill was never enacted. As one scholar observed, "Most education park proposals remained just that: ideas on paper, never moving to brick and mortar."[22]

———

Zwerdling's political inclinations provided another clue about his commitment to integration. During their clash at the School Center Building in June 1967, Cleage accurately called Zwerdling a "big liberal."[23] Although "liberalism" as a political philosophy had a variety of meanings, what Cleage likely meant by the term was someone with socially progressive views who believed that government should play an active role in assisting those who had been left out and left behind. On this view, it was government's job to increase social welfare not just for the few, but for the many, including workers, the poor, and immigrants. By the late 1960s, this brand of liberalism was inexorably tied to racial integration. President Lyndon Johnson's famous "Great Society" speech, delivered at the University of Michigan in May 1964, epitomized this idea. In the speech, Johnson laid out his vision for the future, introducing a wildly ambitious domestic program that would touch almost every aspect of American life. Johnson described a postwar country rich not just in material resources and military might, but also in its ability to care for all its citizens no matter their color or station. This was the United States as a superpower whose greatness depended "on abundance and liberty for all. It demands an end to poverty and racial injustice, to which we are totally committed in our time."[24]

That commitment, even among liberals, was a recent one. During the early part of the twentieth century, most white Americans were overtly racist, with a majority of whites agreeing as late as 1942 that blacks were intellectually inferior.[25] World War II was a key turning point. Throughout the war, influential liberal publications criticized the state of American race relations in no uncertain terms. In 1943, *The Nation* warned, "We cannot fight fascism abroad while turning a blind eye to fascism at home."[26] Then came Gunnar Myrdal's celebrated examination of race relations, *An American Dilemma*. Myrdal depicted racism as a stain on the national character, inconsistent with the American or liberal creed, terms that Myrdal often used interchangeably.[27] The liberal creed—of fairness, dignity of the individual, justice, commitment to the rule of law, equality of opportunity— was, Myrdal argued, what made America great.

Even as the book was being hailed, some critics warned that Myrdal's focus on reforming white racial attitudes alone would not solve what was known as the "Negro problem." In reviewing the book just after its publication in 1944, Ralph Ellison wrote, "The solution of the problem of the American Negro and democracy lies only partially in the white man's free will. Its full solution will lie in the creation of a democracy in which the Negro will be free to define himself for what he is and, within the large framework of a democracy, for what he desires to be."[28] Still, *Dilemma* was the single most important piece of social science research published about African Americans during the World War II and postwar era. In the North, the book was read widely by the liberal elite, summarized in major newspapers, taught in universities and colleges, and relied upon by government agencies, commissions, police departments.[29]

In 1954, the Supreme Court cited *Dilemma* in *Brown v. Board of Education*, a decision that epitomized the postwar liberal mindset.[30] Then, in the late summer of 1963, King stood on the steps of the Lincoln Memorial to deliver the greatest speech of the era, and perhaps the century. After being introduced as the "moral leader of our nation," King told the interracial participants of the March on Washington for Jobs and Freedom that blacks were architects of their own freedom struggle. The path ahead would not be easy. "We must forever conduct our struggle on the high plane of dignity and discipline," he warned.[31] "Again and again, we must rise to the majestic heights of meeting physical force with soul force," King continued.[32]

The phrase "soul force" stemmed from Gandhi's concept of satyagraha. As a young student at Crozier Theological Seminary, King attended a lecture given by Mordecai Johnson, who had recently returned from India.[33] As David Garrow described it, the Howard University president spoke of "how the nonviolent *satyagraha* of Mohandas K. Gandhi had brought about revolutionary changes in Indian society." King read "extensively on Gandhi," and made a pilgrimage to India in 1959.[34] Gandhi described satyagraha as a form of nonviolent resistance that necessarily involved self-sacrifice. In 1961, he wrote that there were some "occasions, generally rare, when . . . certain laws [are] so unjust as to render obedience to them a dishonor. [The individual] then openly and civilly breaks them and quietly suffers the penalty for their breach."[35] For Gandhi, fighting unjust laws *couldn't* mean inflicting physical harm on an opponent, precisely because humans were fallible. "What appears to be truth to one may appear to be error to the other," he wrote.[36] So for Gandhi, satyagraha was the process of vindicating "truth not by infliction of suffering on the opponent but on one's self." Sometimes Gandhi referred to the root meaning of satyagraha as "truth-force." Other times he called it "soul-force."[37] As one commentator noted, satyagraha as it was "ordinarily understood, accordingly means resisting evil through soul force or nonviolence."[38]

In uttering the phrase "soul force," King certainly meant to communicate the idea that blacks should rely on "creative protest" rather than "physical violence" to destroy Jim Crow. But his words held another implication as well: whites were also part of King's dream. "The marvelous new militancy which has engulfed the Negro community must not lead us to distrust of all white people, for many of our white brothers, as evidenced by their presence here today, have come to realize that their destiny is tied up with our destiny. They have come to realize that their freedom is inextricably bound to our freedom," King said.[39] As he looked out over the reflecting pool with applause ringing in his ears, King distilled the argument to its essence: "We cannot walk alone."[40] One interpretation of King's words was that only an integrated, nonviolent "peace army"—whose defining characteristic was "soul force"—was strong enough to win blacks the full measure of American citizenship.[41] Perhaps for King, "soul force" meant a commitment on the part of Americans of all stripes to the nonviolent destruction of Jim Crow.

King's integration philosophy was deeply tied to his abhorrence of segregation. Late in 1962, he provided a full-throated defense of his position in a speech titled, "The Ethical Demands for Integration." The speech was full of King's typical eloquence: "The hour is late; the clock of destiny is ticking out; we must act now before it is too late."[42] But at its core, it was a broadside attack against segregation. He characterized racial segregation as a uniquely powerful form of social leprosy, one that annihilated blacks' character, psyche, and personhood. Calling it a "tragedy," he said segregation "treats men as means rather than ends, and thereby reduces them to things rather than persons."[43] King emphasized the importance of individual freedom. Individuals who were truly free made important decisions about their lives. "What shall I do, where shall I live, how much shall I earn?" But segregation, which trapped blacks in inferior schools, neighborhoods, and jobs not of their choosing, destroyed the ability to engage in such higher-order decision-making.

King depicted segregation as destroying both the soul and opportunity. But what was the remedy? Desegregation obviously was necessary. But King thought the mere removal of previous legal and social prohibitions was insufficient. His vision was more radical. Desegregation opened the door, but King was focused on what was on the other side. He described integration as "the positive acceptance of desegregation and the welcomed participation of Negroes into the total range of human activities. Integration is genuine intergroup, interpersonal doing."[44] It was easy to lampoon that kind of language as just so much misplaced kumbaya, as Malcolm X had done several weeks before the March ("An integrated cup of coffee isn't sufficient pay for four hundred years of slave labor").[45] Nationalists believed the shared experience of racial discrimination was the glue that irrevocably bound black folk to the black nation.

King, by contrast, believed that race was a social construct that prevented individuals from seeing their similarities. There was no superior race. There was no inferior race. "There is no basic difference in the racial groups of our world," he argued. In God's eyes, only the individual mattered, and "'whiteness' and 'blackness' pass away." So his push for integration made sense; it was grounded in his belief that all individuals shared a common humanity and common potential, which was curtailed in black people by white supremacy. For him, integration meant more than just tolerance. It demanded the true acceptance of blacks within a single "beloved community" where each individual had "the opportunity to fulfill [her] total capacity untrammeled by any artificial hindrance or barrier."[46]

The only problem was one King himself conceded. He wrote, "We must admit that the ultimate solution to the race problem lies in the willingness of men to obey the unenforceable."[47] At the time King thought desegregation mandates readily achievable—but, as King allowed, the law could do only so much. Whites' voluntary acceptance of blacks in their neighborhoods, schools, and families necessitated the eradication of irrational prejudice and a profound change of heart. It required whites to view blacks with compassion and kinship instead of fear and loathing. It required them to cast off bigoted beliefs held for generations, to look past the race of the person to "the content of their character." King's acknowledgment that achieving true integration would be difficult, coupled with his concern about whites' "dark and demonic responses" to civil rights laws, suggested more than a passing agreement with Malcolm's perspective.[48] In 1972, James Baldwin observed that "by the time each met his death, there was practically no difference between them."[49] At King's death in 1968, he had evolved into an anti-poverty, anti-war, anti-imperialist, truth-telling revolutionary, and a fairly pessimistic one at that.[50] King, however, never renounced nonviolence.[51]

Still, it was King's more utopian vision of a "beloved community" that continued to exert a pull on Americans of all stripes. By the time Zwerdling took his place as the head of the Detroit Board of Education in 1969, there had been a sea change in the racial attitudes of many whites, particularly among those who called themselves liberals. They now aligned with the ideals espoused by King and defined themselves as racial egalitarians. But the success of King's dream hinged on whether whites were willing to do more than simply admit blacks were human beings—they would need to take action consistent with this self-image.

———

In early November 1969, the Michigan Civil Rights Commission released a position statement on the implementation of Young's school reorganization law. The commission homed in on a central difficulty: in implementing the law, the board had to promote "equal educational opportunity." But what did that mean? This was the commission's answer: the board was obligated to prevent and "eliminate segregation of children and staff on account of race or color."[52] This meant that the board wasn't free to double down on extant residential segregation. And it provided the board with a helpful hint on how it might steer clear of constitutional prohibitions: draw the new regional district boundaries "to encompass a student population which reflects as nearly as possible the racial mix of the entire . . . district student population."[53] In other words, create integrated rather than segregated regions. Young's bill put decentralization ahead of integration; the Michigan Civil Rights Commission was pushing back.

Meanwhile, Zwerdling was weighing the same problem. After Young's bill passed, he reached out to his old friend and civil rights expert William Taylor for advice on how the board might implement it. In his autobiography, Taylor recalled Zwerdling's concern. The school board president wanted to give "power to black parents."[54] But to do so "he would have to draw lines that would result in racially isolated schools."[55] So Zwerdling sensed a tension, between empowering black parents on the one hand and disestablishing racial segregation in the schools under *Brown*, on the other. But Zwerdling was head of a northern rather than a southern school system. Perhaps in that context there was no conflict between the two goals. And even if there was a conflict, did the northern context make it reconcilable? Taylor, like Zwerdling a Jewish liberal with an elite law school education, had gone to work for Thurgood Marshall almost immediately upon graduation from Yale Law School in 1954. Arriving at LDF just after the first *Brown* decision came down, Taylor worked for several years on a key question now deeply interesting to Zwerdling: What did the *Brown* ruling actually require school authorities to do?[56]

This was hardly a straightforward matter—and understanding Zwerdling's options requires a look back at the original *Brown* decision itself. *Brown* said de jure segregation in the South was unconstitutional because it violated one of the Fourteenth Amendment's central commands, that "no state shall . . . deny to any person within its jurisdiction the equal protection of the laws."[57] Two key concepts were embedded in this language. First was the "no state shall" mandate. From these words, the court developed the "state action" doctrine, which functioned much like a car's ignition key; without it the vehicle was useless. The Fourteenth Amendment's obligations—including the equal protection guarantee—could only be activated if there was "state action." But what did "state action" mean? The short answer was that the Fourteenth Amendment only constrained the actions of the government. It placed no obligations on private behavior— at least that was how the court had interpreted it since 1883, when it struck down the federal Civil Rights Act of 1875 prohibiting race discrimination in privately owned public accommodations.[58]

While simply stated, the "state action" doctrine was deceptively tricky. The Supreme Court assumed a hard-and-fast wall—an inviolable chasm— between the public and the private. But what if such a demarcation was illusory? Government action, particularly in the North, often reflected a mix of both. What if a school official required all students living in a particular community to attend school in that neighborhood? This was the "neighborhood school rule." If the neighborhood was segregated because of private choices (or some mix of custom and law as was the case with racially restrictive covenants), then the school official's action amplified and incorporated private racially discriminatory conduct. Was that state action? Ultimately Supreme Court doctrine suggested that the answer to this question was yes, where school authorities intentionally used "neighborhood residential patterns" to separate the races within the schools.[59]

This led to a second major question. Even if all school authorities' acts were technically state action, not all of those actions violated the Fourteenth Amendment's equal protection clause. What did "equal protection of the laws" mean? Traditionally, the equal protection guarantee was meant to root out government action that impermissibly divided people into classes or groups. Of course, the government has always done that kind of classification. Tax schedules, business regulations, licensing schemes, and countless other laws have treated various classes of people very differently. These rules have rarely raised equal protection concerns because the government could typically supply a minimally sufficient justification—a "rational basis"—for the classification scheme.

Sometimes, however, the government classified on the basis of race. Did that change the analysis? Even before *Brown*, the Supreme Court had held that race-based classifications that "curtail the civil rights of a single racial group" presumptively violated equal protection principles.[60] That rule was announced in the infamous *Korematsu* case where the government used race to justify a grotesque system of discriminatory treatment, the exclusion (and ultimately the internment) of more than one hundred thousand persons of Japanese descent from the West Coast during World War II. According to the court's decision, the government needed an especially compelling reason, such as protecting vital national security interests, to relocate and incarcerate Japanese Americans—a reason that the court found the government did in this case have.[61] But what if the government's classification scheme purported to provide the races with separate, yet equal, treatment? Was such a scheme more like the run-of-the-mill governmental classifications that had always been upheld? Or did such schemes raise special concerns? This was where *Brown v. Board of Education*, decided in 1954, came in.

The question before the court in *Brown* was whether state statutes that required the races to be separately educated violated the equal protection clause. The question was harder than it looked. If the racially separate schools were substantially equal in terms of facilities, length of school year, teacher qualifications, and the like (as the plaintiffs stipulated in the *Brown* case), then perhaps there was no equal protection violation. Maybe "equal protection of the laws" just meant substantial equality in racially separate government provided facilities and services. From this perspective, "separate but equal" was fully *consistent* with equality.

This had been the lynchpin of the Supreme Court's infamous ruling in the *Plessy v. Ferguson* case. Decided in 1896, *Plessy* flatly ignored the social meaning of a Louisiana state law that required "equal but separate accommodations for the white and colored races."[62] As the court's lone dissenter, Justice John Marshall Harlan, confidently asserted, everyone knew the law's true purpose was to subordinate blacks. But the court averted its eyes from what everyone could see and rejected the view that state-mandated segregation in public accommodations formed the building blocks of a race-based caste system. The state law didn't reflect equality, as the court myopically suggested. Instead, as Harlan argued, it created a class of untouchables, a group of people so "inferior and degraded that they cannot be allowed to sit in public coaches occupied by white citizens."[63]

In *Brown*, the court stepped away from *Plessy*. Seeing the importance of education and the psychological harm to black children banished to what were in practice inferior schools, the justices now affirmed that "separate but equal" could not be a model of equality. In fact, it didn't matter if white and black students attended functionally "equal" schools with the same textbooks, quality teachers, and extracurriculars. The racial separation made all the difference. "Separate but equal" violated the equal protection clause (in the field of public education at least), because segregation caused black children substantial harm and undermined equal educational opportunity.[64]

Brown was unquestionably a momentous decision, but it was also open to varying interpretations. To the extent that one believed that segregation weaponized white supremacy, the court's emphasis on the long-lasting and debilitating harms associated with state-enforced racial separation suggested that the case was anchored by an "anti-caste" foundation. From this perspective, equality meant that government acts that perpetuated white supremacy—all of them—were impermissible. On this view, *Brown* finally affirmed Justice Harlan's prophetic dissent, "There is no caste here."[65]

On the other hand, perhaps equality meant something much narrower and more constrained. Justice Harlan's dissent in *Plessy* was also famous for its admonition that our "Constitution is color-blind, and neither knows nor tolerates classes among citizens."[66] Maybe the singular problem with the state statutes at issue in *Brown* was that they weren't "color-blind." There was language in the decision that supported this vision of *Brown*. The court said that segregation's destructive impact on black children was "greater when it has the sanction of the law."[67] Perhaps *Brown* stood for the proposition that only laws that expressly classified on the basis of race ran afoul of the equal protection clause. If this was what *Brown* meant, then maybe de facto segregation was consistent with, rather than a violation of, the equal protection clause.

In 1955, the court issued a second decision in *Brown v. Board of Education (Brown II)*.[68] The question in *Brown II* was what southern school authorities needed to do to cure the constitutional violation that the court in *Brown I* had recognized. *Brown II* was famous for an oxymoron: that school authorities must admit black children "to public schools on a racially nondiscriminatory basis with *all deliberate speed*."[69] The phrase "deliberate speed" was oxymoronic. Did it mean that school authorities had to admit children to the public schools on a "racially nondiscriminatory basis" the very next day? The next year? The next decade? The decision was light on specifics, providing little guidance to southern school systems (or to the lower federal courts that were tasked with superintending desegregation). Then, with the notable exception of *Cooper v. Aaron* (the case upbraiding state officials for resisting desegregation in Little Rock), the court effectively retired from the field of school desegregation for more than a decade.

It wasn't until 1968 that the Supreme Court told southern school authorities definitively that they had an affirmative obligation—even in the absence of litigation—to eliminate all remnants of the prior de jure system. This was a big deal because the plaintiffs didn't need to sue school authorities in order to activate this duty. The school authorities' responsibility was to transition from a "state-imposed dual system to a unitary, nonracial system," plain and simple.[70] But that decision, *Green v. County School Board of New Kent County*,[71] came in a case concerning a rural school district in Virginia with little residential segregation. In October 1969, the court discarded the "all deliberate speed" standard in a case called *Alexander v. Holmes*.[72] In *Alexander*, the Supreme Court ruled that the "obligation of every school district is to terminate dual school systems at once and to operate now and hereafter only unitary schools."[73] Translation: "time's up." Both decisions implied that the federal courts could order southern school districts to bus children in order to comply with *Brown*, although neither expressly authorized the courts to mandate busing. The decision that explicitly authorized busing—*Swann v. Charlotte Mecklenburg Board of Education*[74]—lay many months in the future at the time Zwerdling reached out to his old friend in 1969. In short, the court had said comparatively little about school desegregation *even in the South*—and the practical problem Zwerdling faced—whether the board was legally required to integrate northern schools and if so how—was much more subtle.

In states like Michigan, there were no laws requiring that black students be educated in separate schools. In fact, just the opposite was true. Michigan state law had prohibited segregation in public education since 1842.[75] Yet the schools in Detroit were still racially segregated. Did *Brown* have any application in the Motor City? The Supreme Court had not yet said a word about what equality meant in the North. This was the void into which Taylor stepped.

What was the answer? Taylor was a good lawyer who had read the relevant precedents. He wrote that the lower courts agreed that "public school segregation is forbidden whenever it is the result of intentional government action, whether in the South or the North and whether by law or administrative practice."[76] So what did equality mean in the North? At a minimum, it meant that public school officials were prohibited from taking acts *intended to segregate the public schools*. So the Detroit school board could not deliberately draw the new regional boundaries to confine black children to particular schools. That was the same as de jure segregation, outlawed as a violation of the equal protection clause in *Brown*.

This told Zwerdling one thing not to do, but it hardly indicated a plan of action. The lower courts offered only limited guidance. The Supreme

Court's decision in *Green v. County School Board of New Kent County* stood for the proposition that southern school authorities had an obligation not just to stop discriminating, but affirmatively to desegregate.[77] Did the same rule apply in the North? Was Detroit *required* under the Constitution to desegregate where the races were segregated as a matter of fact, but not law? Taylor told Zwerdling that issue was "far from being finally resolved."[78] There was a split of authority in the lower courts. Latching onto *Brown's* reasoning that segregation causes significant harm to black children, some courts had ruled that school districts had a duty to reduce even de facto segregation.[79]

But other lower courts—like the one in *Bell v. School City of Gary, Indiana*—said school districts had no obligation whatsoever when it came to de facto segregation.[80] A recent federal appellate court case governing Michigan and several nearby states, *Deal v. Cincinnati Board of Education*, was consistent with this view. In *Deal*, the federal court ruled that the Cincinnati school district's neighborhood plan to determine pupil placement did not violate the equal protection clause because the school district "did not cause" any underlying residential segregation.[81] In answering whether there was "a constitutional duty on the part of the board to balance the races in the Cincinnati public schools where the imbalance was not caused by any act of discrimination on its part," the court said no.[82] Under these circumstances, the court put the burden of integration on black parents rather than school authorities. Blacks had "the choice of attending a mixed school if they so desire[d]"[83]—all they had to do was move.

But Taylor rightly distinguished Cincinnati from Detroit. The question in *Deal* was whether the school district's *failure* to address racial imbalances in the schools against the background of residential segregation violated the equal protection clause and thus required desegregation. The answer was no, unless the plaintiffs could show "racial bias"—meaning choice of the neighborhood school rule with a specific intent to segregate—on the part of school authorities.[84] But the situation in Detroit was meaningfully different. As Taylor pointed out, Young's bill *required* "affirmative action" on the part of Zwerdling and the Detroit Board of Education.[85] And the Detroit Board—now required under state law to redistrict—was barred from taking any act that increased segregation.[86] Taylor underlined his conclusion for emphasis: "Even if the law prohibits only de jure segregation and even if Detroit is presently in compliance with the law, in drawing regional school district lines, the Detroit board must not act in a way which will increase or facilitate an increase in racial segregation in public school attendance."[87]

With the benefit of Taylor's advice, Zwerdling knew that it would be difficult to argue that drawing racially homogeneous regions was constitutionally "neutral." And then there was his own oft-professed desire to integrate Detroit's schools. But achieving that goal wasn't going to be easy, particularly if Zwerdling also wanted to guarantee black control over some of the regional districts—as so many of school reorganization's strongest supporters intended. Action "by the central board to overcome *de facto* segregation would make it impossible to have racially homogenous districts," Taylor warned.[88] And this would have a "knock-on" effect, likely rendering "the notion of community participation or control almost meaningless because a great many parents would then not reside or vote in the districts where these children actually attended school."[89]

Taylor's counsel suggested that the board couldn't have it both ways. It was going to have to choose. If the board was really serious about integration, it needed to draw regional lines (and create student assignment policies) to promote that goal, rather than to deliver black control over black regions. Now it was up to the seven-member board, led by Zwerdling and controlled by four liberals (inclusive of Zwerdling), to enact such a plan.

6

DEMOCRACY'S FINEST HOUR

On Tuesday, April 7, 1970, Zwerdling called the regular meeting of the Detroit Board of Education to order at the School Center Building. The meeting was anything but typical. The *Detroit Free Press* described the scene: "Angry parents had filled to overflowing the school board's meeting room."[1] "Hundreds more milled around the outside of the School Center Building . . . unable to get in," the story continued.[2] The scene was one of utter pandemonium.

The word was out. Just two days before the meeting, the *Detroit Free Press* and *The Detroit News* had broken a major story concerning the city's public school system. The essence of both stories was this: the board was planning to vote on a proposal that would integrate many of the city's high schools. The conservative *Detroit News* ran the story on the front page of its Sunday edition, warning that integration of Detroit's high schools "by drastically changing the areas from which their pupils will be drawn will be voted on this week by the Detroit Board of Education."[3] The *Detroit Free Press* characterized the plan's core effect: "The changes would be to put more whites into predominantly black schools and more blacks into predominantly white schools."[4] For the very first time in its history, the board would be requiring white students to attend black schools in black neighborhoods.[5] And, unlike any other major school district in the nation, the board would be changing the racial composition of a substantial number of its high schools voluntarily and not in response to a court order.

Following his consultation with Taylor, Zwerdling had settled on an initial plan to implement Young's school reorganization bill. Up to January 1970, Zwerdling's idea was to follow the letter (although not the spirit) of Young's law by drawing racially heterogeneous regions: "If we drew boundaries that separated blacks into one region and whites into another there would never be any chance of changing things," he explained to a reporter. "We would have frozen the city into segregation."[6] Instead, he wanted to maximize the *possibility* for integration by drawing integrated regions. Zwerdling thought racial integration was necessary in a changing city. He explained his philosophy this way: "If we are going to live together in this city, we are going to have to like [the idea of a balanced, integrated high school]; and we are going to have to work together to make it work."[7] But possibility wasn't the same thing as probability. The difficulty with his initial approach was that integrated schools weren't going to magically appear just because the regions themselves were racially heterogeneous. The reason was because there was a significant gap between the number of black children in the city's schools and the number of black adults eligible to cast votes for the new regions' leadership. And it was each region's leadership that either would—or would not—implement racial diversity. As journalist William Grant explained it, "Although 65 per cent of Detroit public school students were black, only 44 per cent of the city's electorate was black. If the regions were fully integrated—with each region's racial mix duplicating the mix of the city as a whole—they all would have black student majorities and black voter minorities."[8] This was hardly a recipe for black control.

Then, in late January 1970, Remus Robinson was hospitalized with cancer. He was not to recover. A consistent pro-integration vote, Robinson's absence changed the internal politics of the board. Suddenly, the seven-member board effectively had six members and it appeared evenly split on integration. But, as it turned out, the pro-integration "swing" vote came from an unlikely source: Andrew Perdue, the black lawyer and community control advocate who had been elected with Cleage's support.[9]

In March, Perdue signaled that he might be open to voting with the liberals even though his support of community control never wavered. In a lengthy statement, released in mid-March, he clarified his views. Perdue believed in community control because of the extraordinary damage that whites—unaccountable to the black community—had done to black children.[10] "White America has historically exercised an almost absolute control . . . of public school education for black students, and a complete control of curriculum and textbooks. This monopoly has resulted in black Americans being the most poorly educated, the most seriously impaired and the most deliberately misinterpreted of all the major ethnic groups being served by the public schools of this nation," he seethed.[11] From this perspective, community control helped stop the bleeding.

Given the depth of this commitment, Perdue's openness to integration appeared strange, at first. But it made perfect sense given his focus on the welfare of black children. Perdue saw integration as a worthwhile goal, precisely because segregation had such a deleterious effect not just on the black middle class but on the children of the black masses. The "fact that the barriers imposed by segregation have been over come by some of the more talented, the more determined, and the more fortunate, would hardly seem to recommend it to thousands of disadvantaged youngsters for whom segregation has already demonstrated [its] capacity to cripple rather than to challenge," he argued.[12] Besides, he wrote, "Wherever possible the Detroit Board of Education must achieve the maximum amount of integration—this is the law of the land."[13]

What Perdue appeared to fear the most was the worst of both worlds: racially segregated schools over which whites exercised "monopoly" control. In this, he thought the board was heading in the wrong direction. Perdue wrote: "No plan to date . . . has been devised by the Board or presented to the Board [that would] change the racial composition of hardly any school in the system."[14] In effect, he was telling the board its integration plan hadn't gone far enough. It wasn't sufficient to create racially mixed districts, and hope for the best—not at least as white voters in those districts were highly unlikely to elect regional board members who favored integration. So Perdue's vote had a price. If the liberal board members were truly serious about integration, they needed to change student feeder policies so that sufficient numbers of black and white children would flow into particular schools by mandate, not discretion.[15]

Of all people, it was Cleage's man Perdue who was throwing down the gauntlet. He was going to stiffen Zwerdling's resolve. Either create a real integration plan that altered student feeder patterns—meaning school attendance boundaries—or pack the regions with large numbers of black voters so as to guarantee black control.[16] It was one or the other.

Seeking to achieve majority support, Superintendent Drachler presented a plan to six of the seven board members at a private meeting on March 31, 1970. The plan had two components. First, it divided the city into seven new educational regions, each with student enrollments and voting age populations that complied with Young's law. Each of the board's new regions contained both black and white schools and roughly reflected the racial mix of the school district as a whole.[17] This new regional plan didn't mandate that even a single school be integrated. But by drawing heterogeneous regions, the board preserved the ability of the regional boards to desegregate individual schools later on down the line. So the first component of the plan directly implemented Young's law and created integrated *regions*.

The second component changed student feeder patterns within five of the new regions. It was a desegregation plan that would unquestionably alter the racial composition of certain Detroit high schools. This component created integrated *schools*. The desegregation portion of the plan was historic. Per Grant: "It was the first time the board had integrated both ways, requiring whites to go to black schools as well as the reverse."[18] At several white high schools located on the city's northeast and northwest sides—Redford, Cody, and Denby—the black population would increase substantially, from as low as 3 percent to anywhere from 30 percent to more than 50 percent.[19]

At the same time, the plan was also quite modest. It would affect a small fraction of students—roughly nine thousand out of a system with almost three hundred thousand.[20] It would be implemented over a three-year period.[21] And it would apply only to about half of the city's high schools; it had no application whatsoever to any of its elementary or middle schools. The plan was so modest that Coleman Young later memorably referred to it as a "chicken shit integration plan."[22] But the plan was acceptable to Zwerdling, two other board members, and, crucially, Perdue.[23] (Robinson was too sick to attend the meeting.) Patrick A. McDonald and James A.

Hathaway, both white lawyers, opposed it. But the integrationists had their majority. Now all the board had to do was vote on the plan, which it ultimately did at its regularly scheduled meeting on Tuesday, April 7, 1970.

But before the vote could be taken, McDonald—a staunch opponent of the integration plan with political ambitions and one of Zwerdling's most ferocious adversaries—leaked a copy of the plan to the press.[24] The Sunday papers now had a big story. And that was when the phones started to ring off the hook at the board of education offices in the School Center Building, and "all hell broke loose."[25]

━━━

On Monday, April 6, 1970—and one day before the Detroit Board was set to meet—white Detroit-area parents and students exploded. As *The Detroit News* reported it, picketing parents effectively closed two high schools on the west side of the city. One hundred parents protested at Murphy Junior High on the city's northwest side and two-thirds of the students boycotted classes. Also on the northwest side, there were picket lines at Hubert Elementary with three-quarters of the students staying home.[26] At Redford, students marched with signs bearing statements such as "We like it the way it is," which accurately captured the zeitgeist.[27] At the School Center Building, the board's call logs burst with statements in opposition to integration.[28] "This will cause a lot of people to move," one parent warned.[29] "You're going to end up with a black Detroit and white suburbs."[30] Other callers pledged resistance. One wanted the board to know that she would "keep children out of school if she has to," which was a common sentiment.[31] Another Detroiter's telegram to Remus Robinson provided a single terse statement: "Don't kill the city of Detroit."[32]

That evening, angry white Detroiters formed a group, the Citizens Committee for Better Schools, to fight the board.[33] Edward Zaleski, a forty-four-year-old police officer and the group's chairman, told the *Detroit Free Press* that his group had approximately three thousand members (*The Detroit News* put the number at five thousand), and had already raised more than $1,000 to resist the plan.[34] Acknowledging the difficulty of the road ahead, Zaleski admitted that, "It will be a tough fight."[35] But his group was in it for the long haul: "We are prepared to fight this thing all year, or ten years if necessary," he added.[36]

But all of this was just a warm-up for the main event. On Tuesday, April 7, 1970, and in advance of the meeting, several hundred white Detroiters— many of whom had been organized the previous evening by the Citizens Committee for Better Schools—descended on the School Center Building. Zaleski was there. He knew how to get his message across: "We will go all the way to the U.S. Supreme Court to fight this plan," he yelled.[37] Some of the protesters carried signs opposing the board's actions. ("This idea is rated X," "No, no, she won't go.")[38] Others threatened to leave. One sign read: "We moved from the suburbs to Detroit for Redford Hi-Cooley means back to the suburbs."[39] Of the sign, a protester remarked, "Boy, if the board goes through with its plan, white people will move to the suburbs like nothing you've ever seen before."[40]

The second-floor boardroom's capacity was two hundred and fifty. A picture taken at the time shows a crush of parents, pushing and pulling against one another, seeking entrance to the meeting, a handmade protest sign reflected in the window of the entry door. The hallway and all available space outside the meeting room were jammed. Before the meeting began, McDonald reminded the restless crowd that the public had more than one way to voice its displeasure with the board. Just review state law, he told them; public officials were subject to a recall vote if their actions displeased their constituents.[41]

Just beyond the second-floor boardroom's glass doors, parents who had been denied entry chanted, "Hell no, we won't go." Some of them tried to break the glass. At one point, a few of the protesters managed to open the locked entry doors before the police pushed them back outside.[42] Zwerdling tried to maintain control of the meeting by taking the high road. "We can proceed if everybody has a certain amount of forbearance and patience to have a democratic discussion of this matter," he announced.[43] McDonald voiced the concerns of the crowd. "There are hundreds of people who wanted to speak here and you have denied them the right to speak by only allowing 170 to 200 people in this room," he declared.[44]

Attempting to keep the meeting from descending into chaos, Zwerdling shifted the focus to Superintendent Drachler. The public knew only what the papers had reported, while Drachler was prepared to describe both the high school integration plan and the new regional map in detail. Zwerdling still thought it possible to have a rational discussion and perhaps to change some minds along the way. "Until you have had a presentation of the proposal by the Superintendent you do not have the facts completely before you," he pleaded with the audience.[45] "It would seem to me that no matter what your viewpoint is on the subject, for or against, that it would be intelligent and sensible to proceed by first finding out what the proposal is, and let the Superintendent do that."[46]

It is doubtful that Drachler's presentation changed many minds. More than two dozen individuals spoke before the board that day. The vast majority—including white homeowners who wanted to keep their schools as they were and advocates for black community control—testified against the integration plan. Many of them referenced earlier meetings or previous calls or telegrams to the board. Some spoke from prepared remarks. They were there to voice positions they already held. John Webster Jr., representing the Inner City Parents Council and several other black organizations, was Cleage's man at the meeting. Webster wasn't there to make a "fancy presentation," and he kept his comments short and to the point.[47] He told the board that Cleage and the organizations he represented were "unalterably opposed to the plan presented."[48] Sounding very much like Cleage himself, he said Zwerdling's plan posed an existential threat to the black community and had to be defeated. He condemned the board in the fiercest of terms: "So-called integration is not only destructive of the best interests of black people, in fact it is a form of genocide from our point of view, but it also suggests an acceptance of the white man's declaration of white superiority and black inferiority."[49]

Henry Dodge of the Northwest Detroit Council of Civic and Consumer Associations issued a stern warning: "We are not going to plead with you, gentlemen," he said. "We are not going to beg you, gentlemen. We are going to tell you that if you are going to implement this plan, you are going to have trouble such as you have never seen before."[50] Zwerdling had inadvertently left Dodge off the speakers' list, an oversight for which he apologized. Dodge then stated: "I am glad, Mr. Chairman, that you are capable of making mistakes."[51] "The first mistake was when I got this unpaid job—that was the first mistake," Zwerdling replied.[52] But what were his others? One might have been his naive belief that the regional boards would work toward integration. Or perhaps, as the historian Jeffrey Mirel argued, Zwerdling's integration plan was doomed to fail because it was too extreme a "strategy . . . that far exceeded the requirements of [Young's school reorganization] law."[53] Or maybe the opposite was true: as Coleman Young later charged, perhaps the plan didn't go far enough. Instead of hesitant half steps, maybe the board should have mandated racial integration throughout Detroit's school system, including in the elementary and middle schools.

Then again, some of his mistakes might have been strategic. After Remus Robinson (who was sure to cast a pro-integration vote) became ill, Zwerdling delayed the board's vote for several weeks in the hope that he would recover. The delay tactics made it seem as if he was trying to manipulate the vote, which of course he was.[54] Then, there was the surprise. The board's decision to change the high school feeder patterns was never debated. The meeting at which the board settled on the final integration plan was secret. The public only discovered the rough contours of the plan because McDonald leaked it to the press, just a few short days before the board was set to vote. None of these maneuvers enhanced the plan's likelihood of success.[55]

Still, all these really boiled down to one problem: Zwerdling had taken an extraordinarily difficult job. Any meaningful school integration plan needed to disestablish the relationship between home values and segregated schools and bridge the urban-suburban racial divide. And those tasks were far above Zwerdling's (or any single individual's) ability to control. So the vexing problems remained. Several of the white speakers at the April 7 board meeting mentioned how access to particular schools factored into their decision to purchase a home. Some extolled the virtues of the neighborhood school and argued that the board's plan would ensure its demise (you are "destroy[ing] the concept of neighborhood high schools."[56]) Others pressed the idea that purchasing a home in a certain neighborhood created a vested right to attend a particular school. One speaker cautioned the board that its actions could prove costly. "We believe, too, that people bought the real estate and their homes in the belief that their children could attend schools within an approximate area of their homes," the speaker explained.[57] "They do say now that if they cannot do so, they will get out and move. We, in Detroit, have seen too many people already moving."[58] This was a thinly veiled threat: if the board frustrated white homeowners' settled expectations in the name of integration, they would leave.

Who were these whites who were so angered by a modest integration plan that they threatened to leave the city altogether? By 1970, most of Detroit's whites lived in the northwest and northeast edges of the city in neighborhoods like Osborn (for Poles and Germans), Regent Park (for Poles, Italians, and Germans), Warrendale (for Poles and Germans), and Cornerstone Village (for Belgians, Germans, and English), which all bordered the city limits.[59] These neighborhoods were on average 99 percent white with median family incomes around $13,000.[60] Many residents worked in the River Rouge, Jefferson Avenue Assembly, and Dodge Main auto plants located in Dearborn, Jefferson Chalmers, and Hamtramck. The whites who remained in these neighborhoods made between 10 and 20 percent less than those who had left these same neighborhoods in Detroit for suburban Oakland and Macomb Counties after the city's population hit its peak in 1950.[61] Those whites who began leaving Detroit after World War II were on average two to five years younger and quite often headed to places like the ethnic white suburbs of St. Clair County if they were more working-class or Oakland County if they were slightly wealthier and closer to management professions.[62]

In comparison, most blacks lived in the central sections of Detroit surrounding Downtown and Midtown. These neighborhoods like North End, Islandview, and Dexter Linwood (the epicenter of the civil unrest in July 1967) were on average 95 percent black with median family incomes less than $9,000.[63] In contrast to Detroit's white neighborhoods, where on average around 5 percent lived in poverty, these black neighborhoods had poverty rates ranging between 15 and 30 percent.[64] In general, median family income was about $4,000 higher for Detroit whites than for Detroit blacks. But even more importantly, white Detroit families at that time had more wealth than most black Detroit families. One of the biggest reasons why was Detroit home values. The average value of a home in the white neighborhood of Brightmoor near the city limits was around $18,000. But the average value of a home in a black neighborhood like North End near the city center was $12,000.[65] This difference was significant, but it tended to understate the wealth differential between the two races. While less than 30 percent of blacks owned their own home in Detroit, up to 60 percent of Detroit whites were homeowners. So the key difference was between the majority of white homeowners and the majority of black renters.

Were these whites all just unmitigated racists? Many were. In 1967, 30 percent of whites surveyed in Detroit favored school segregation.[66] They wanted white schools for white children. By 1971, that number had climbed by several percentage points.[67] As two grandparents who opposed sending their grandchildren to a predominantly black school put it in their call to the board, "There are a lot of colored at Pershing."[68]

At the same time, some white Detroiters expressed favorable attitudes toward public school integration (to survey takers, at least).[69] But the cost of realizing that preference was actually quite high. The expense came not just in adjusting to the new, integrated school environment. The essentially all-white nature of the schools was actually part of what buyers purchased when they bought homes in essentially all-white neighborhoods. This "white school premium" was part of the cost of the house; it was "capital-ized" in the value of the property. This was the subtext of many speakers' remarks on April 7 ("now, when I purchased my home, the first thing I did was look into the school situation"[70]). But the board's plan threatened to take that value away.

Then as now, house prices were set by racially constrained markets. Many pro-integration (or integration-neutral) whites might have believed that other white families valued integration less than they did, and that given lower black buying power the market for their homes at current prices would collapse if many of their white neighbors moved.[71] For them, Zwerdling's plan created a conundrum. They could stay in the city with the hope that their home values would not decline too much. This risk might have been worth it to whites who—like Zwerdling—were ideologi-cally committed to integration. But for many, in the absence of some way to stabilize housing prices during the period of racial transition (or to disconnect schools from housing altogether), it was economically (although not morally) rational to oppose Zwerdling's plan, or to move. Some white people objected to Zwerdling's plan not on explicit racial animus, but upon predictions about what other white families—whose actions were guided by animus—might do.[72] (One study of white Detroiters, however, found that whites "underestimate[d] the willingness of their white neighbors to accept close interracial contact.")[73] Those families' actions had an impact on the value of their own homes, because housing was a market good. This was the difficulty that those who favored integration, like Zwerdling, faced. Public school integration necessarily implicated housing. And, for many, the family home was the single largest source of wealth. Segregation didn't just lock blacks into desperately unequal schools and neighborhoods. It coerced whites, too, bribing them to ignore their better angels and get out while they still could.

Not everyone who spoke on April 7 excoriated the board. Speaking on behalf of the Detroit Urban League, Francis Kornegay praised the board's work effusively. The DUL knew the board was under fire and was attempting to prop it up by expressing "confidence in the . . . tremendous task that it has been struggling with for months."[74] It favored integration for instrumental reasons. The DUL thought the board's plan would provide more of Detroit's children with a "quality educational opportunity" and raise "the entire educational level in the city of Detroit."[75] But most of all, it supported the board because of *Brown v. Board of Education*. Referring to the case, Kornegay said: "Through the adoption of this plan, and we hope that it is adopted today without delay, the Board of Education will come closer to the fulfillment of the U.S. Supreme Court mandate of May 17, 1954."[76] The DUL was practically down on its knees, pleading with the people of Detroit to support the board so that *Brown* could have a chance before the opportunity to desegregate slipped away for good. Kornegay beseeched the board: "Show united strength [so] that today will be democracy's finest hour."[77]

If there was one moment of calm during the turbulent meeting, it came just after one of the board members called the question in preparation for the final vote. Just then, the board's secretary asked if he could read a statement from Remus Robinson supporting the integration plan. He had written it from his bed in Ford Hospital. Zwerdling approved the request and the board secretary proceeded to read his statement into the record:

To my fellow Board Members . . .

I have been a member of the Detroit Board of Education since April, 1955. During these past 15 years, I have tried—to the best of my ability—to serve fairly the needs of all children from all segments of Detroit's population. I have believed—and have tried to act always from that belief—that every youngster in the city of Detroit deserves to find in our schools the unprejudiced opportunity to develop his talents in such a way as to become a self-motivated, productive citizen in a democratic, pluralistic society. I have consistently supported and in many instances initiated efforts by the Board of Education to provide quality, integrated education because I believe that this is essential to a strong America, to an harmonious community, and to the equality of educational opportunity for all our students.

I am deeply troubled by the forces within society—both black and white—which would continue to foist segregated regional patterns upon future generations of Americans. I cannot, with a clear conscience, submit to these doctrines.

I, therefore, support the proposed plan as providing the best opportunity for quality, integrated education for our students and for effecting the most cooperation among the various racial, religious, and ethnic populations in our city. I believe this plan can work; I believe it is fair; I believe it is in the best interests of the total community.

I also support the proposed plan for reassigning certain high school feeder patterns. This plan will enable more black and white students to attend senior high school together; it will also enable more citizens of the future to recognize—from firsthand experience—that in pluralism there is strength, that in democracy there is hope, and that in equal opportunity there is the possibility for all men to rise to the level of their best talents.[78]

The motion upon which the board voted, which included both the proposal for new regions and the high school integration plan—passed by a vote of four to two. But it was the high school integration plan that captured the public's attention and stimulated the enmity of many, as the *Detroit Free Press* the next morning confirmed. *Pupil Integration Plan Okd*, the front page blared in large bold-faced font.[79] The very first paragraph of William Grant's article distilled the long, raucous meeting to its essence: "The Detroit Board of Education Tuesday voted, 4 to 2, to adopt a plan which will radically change the racial composition of 11 of the city's 22 public high schools."[80]

Later, in explaining his vote, Zwerdling said: "We have heard the urging . . . for a return to a divided society, but we cannot in conscience go along with it."[81]

A resident of Osborn in northeast Detroit was one of the many individuals who called the board in advance of the April 7 meeting to register her disagreement with desegregation. She wondered why is "the Board of Education even considering this plan for the high schools? President Nixon said you don't have to integrate."[82] The Osborn resident wasn't just imagining Nixon's position. Less than two weeks before her call, the president had released his "Statement About Desegregation of Elementary and Secondary Schools," which spelled out his administration's policy on school desegregation.[83] In it, Nixon was attempting to shift public sentiment away from integration and narrow the high court's options when and if it reached the question of whether *Brown* applied in the North. "I have to move the Court now, before the decision, by mobilizing public opinion," he told his aides.[84]

In early 1970, public opinion on integration was actually in flux. Some opinion polls suggested that almost half of all Americans thought school integration was proceeding too quickly.[85] But other surveys painted a more complicated picture. A survey taken in February suggested that almost 60 percent of Americans agreed with the statement that "integration of schools has been the law since 1954 and it was about time to enforce the law."[86] A majority of those sampled said that desegregation would not occur until "some higher authority orders it," and expressed admiration of the *Brown* decision.[87] And 40 percent thought the Nixon administration's position on desegregation was "too wishy washy."[88] On balance, the polling suggested that a majority of Americans accepted *Brown* as the law of the land and that many of them wanted it enforced "without any further delay."[89] Americans might have accepted *Brown*, but the same didn't hold true for busing. A poll taken in March 1970 asked the following question: "One way to integrate the schools is to bus children from one area to another. Suppose it could be worked out so that there was no more busing of school children than there is now in each community and in each state— would you favor or oppose using busing to achieve integrated schools?" Seventy-three percent of the survey respondents were opposed to busing.[90] But the public's view of busing was largely formed in the absence of any explicit high court pronouncement on the issue.

Nixon's position on school desegregation at this moment could fairly be summed up as "just this, and no further." Narrowly elected in the fall of 1968, he inherited the *Brown* cases and the court's emerging, tentative steps toward filling out that doctrine. The president was willing to accept the court's pronouncements with respect to southern schools, particularly because this allowed him to shift the blame for enforcing the desegregation mandate in the South to the federal courts.[91] But Nixon's grudging acceptance of desegregation in the South did not extend to the North, where he thought racial imbalances unconnected to government action.[92] Just a few weeks before the board's April 7 meeting, Nixon told his advisers, "If the Supreme Court goes as far as *de facto* racial balance, all hell will break loose. I'll have to speak in a sound way, on that fine line, representing the decent body of opinion, rejecting extremism on both sides. You know . . . [a presidential statement] could influence the next Supreme Court decision."[93]

Nixon presented de jure and de facto segregation as entirely unrelated phenomena. "There is a fundamental distinction between so-called de jure and de facto segregation," the president wrote in his statement.[94] "De jure segregation arises *by law or by the deliberate act of school officials* and is unconstitutional."[95] Nixon's characterization of de jure segregation did include more than just classic *Brown v. Board of Education* southern-style segregation. The "by law or" construction was broad enough to capture some northern school segregation, but only just a little. For instance, did de jure segregation include student assignment policies that effectively incorporated residential segregation into the schools? President Nixon thought not: "De facto segregation results from residential housing patterns and does not violate the Constitution."[96] He rejected busing to achieve "racial balance," and his administration would not use enforcement tools of the executive branch to achieve those aims. This, then, was the open question that had yet to be considered by the Supreme Court: What was the status of school segregation in the North? Was it de facto? De jure? Or some combination of both? It was a question of enormous import, particularly given the evolving state of public opinion at that time. If northern schools were de jure segregated just as they had been in the South, then school districts in every corner of the country had a duty to integrate their student bodies.

Nixon already had his answer. There was no duty in the North to integrate. The title of a contemporaneous *Wall Street Journal* article reporting on the statement was informative: "Nixon Declares U.S. Won't Demand End of De Facto School Segregation."[97] The *Journal's* assessment of the president's motivations was clear-eyed: the statement will "please Southern and suburban whites who feared having to bus their children across town to school in the ghetto."[98] Nixon's solution for the lingering inequality that admittedly plagued black schools ("it is unquestionably true that most black schools . . . are in fact inferior to most white schools"[99]) was money. In his statement, the president promised $1.5 billion over the next two fiscal years (diverted from other domestic funding sources) to assist in equalizing black schools.[100] Carl T. Rowan, perhaps the nation's most prominent black columnist, wasn't having any of it. He wrote: "Rereading President Nixon's treatise on school desegregation and his promise of massive aid to ghetto schools, I must conclude someone sold Mr. Nixon an old thesis that if you 'give them a lollipop they'll stop trying to go to our schools.'"[101]

7

MONEY IS POWER AND IT WORKS

On the same day as the board was meeting to approve the integration plan, Detroit high school students were already vigorously debating its merits. At Redford High School in northwest Detroit, students at the predominantly white school held an assembly to discuss, as *The Detroit News* put it, "the explosive question of changing enrollment boundaries to achieve school integration."[1] Emotions ran high. Coy Burgess, one of the school's few black students, recognized that desegregation was a form of resource redistribution. "This high school has high standards. Why can't we share them?" he asked.[2] A black English teacher, Mrs. Claudia Traverse, attempted to recharacterize the debate. The issue wasn't busing. "You have created a monster called segregation," she announced to the assembly. "The real issue here is not transportation," she added.[3] Some students booed her remarks. But at least one white student was persuaded. Describing the student as a "short haired blonde in a mini-skirt," *The Detroit News* reported that "in a voice quivering with emotion, she sobbed: 'Support redistricting. Don't desert the city of Detroit.'"[4]

But if Zwerdling thought it was all going to blow over once the board adopted the integration plan, he was sadly mistaken. On the following day, Wednesday, April 8, 1970, large numbers of white students stayed home from Osborn High School to protest the board's action, cutting school attendance by half.[5] Disgusted by the boycott, members of Osborn's black student population retaliated by staging their own walkout. Meanwhile, as the *Detroit Free Press* described it, three hundred and fifty white students from nearby Denby were marching against integration. They left school midmorning, headed for Osborn, about two miles away. The police believed they had an "explosive situation"; they feared a confrontation between Osborn's remaining black students and the white Denby students who were headed their way. So police in riot gear diverted the white students to Osborn's athletic field just east of the school. *The Detroit News* painted a picture of a potentially harrowing situation. "Police averted a possible battle yesterday between 1,000 white students from Denby and half that many black students from Osborn. A barricade of 50 helmeted policemen stood shoulder to shoulder across Seven Mile at Annott to restrain a shouting, jeering throng of youths who had marched two miles to Osborn."[6] The police arrested fourteen students.[7]

On Thursday, April 9, fighting broke out between blacks and whites at Pershing High School.[8] Students protesting the integration plan walked out, demonstrated, or participated in disruptions at ten other schools.[9] There were at least three bomb scares. In response, Detroit police commissioner Patrick V. Murphy urged the city's parents to "remain calm, to seek legal redress of their grievances and to influence their children to avoid violence, threats, disrupting their schools and to attend classes as scheduled."[10]

And it wasn't just white students who were protesting integration. Two hundred fifty black students at all-black Barbour Junior High School on the city's lower east side boycotted classes on Friday, April 10.[11] The school's white principal, Jack Reiter, thought the action was counterproductive. He told the students that they were "playing into the hands of white separatists."[12] Ignoring the principal's plea, the students walked out anyway. The *Detroit Free Press* contextualized the black students' action. Historically, Barbour's rising ninth graders attended Kettering High School, a relatively new school that was, as the *Detroit Free Press* described it, "well equipped."[13] But under the board's integration plan, those same students would now attend Denby High School, which was thirty years older than Kettering and 97 percent white. Denby had been a center of white anti-integration agitation, which the paper noted: "An angry atmosphere at Denby [was] . . . demonstrated all week by white students and parents in the far northeast Detroit Denby district."[14] The paper cited a student who defended the walkout in what it characterized as "black separatist terms." The student remarked, "We don't want to go to any white school, man."[15] By early 1970, there was little doubt that some blacks had moved away from an integrationist ideology and toward a more nationalist orientation. This shift played a role in the boycott. But just as important, if not more so, was the undeniable fact of angry white resistance against integration and the "ill-hidden fear" of white violence that backed it up.[16] The *Detroit Free Press* explained it this way: "Since the school board plan was announced, most black students and parents have been silent, leaving the publicity stage to unhappy white students and parents in northeast and northwest Detroit. The black feelings that emerged Friday [the walkout at Barbour and demonstrations at two other middle schools, Post and Cerveny] were in part a reaction to that white resistance."[17] Detroit's white community was speaking to black Detroiters with undeniable clarity. The cost of integration was going to be high, just as it had been in the South. Was it really worth the price? Ernest Myers, a Barbour ninth grader, wondered whether "we might possibly do better staying at Kettering than going to Denby just because everybody won't be fighting every day."[18] Voicing what the *Detroit Free Press* described as "the overriding theme of the day," Barbour student Kervoicer Tate added, "They don't want us out there anyway."[19]

But even as the board was contemplating the highly controversial high school integration plan, students at the city's only truly integrated high school were struggling to get the board's attention. The racial breakdown at Western High School, on the city's lower west side, was atypical: approximately 40 percent black, just over 45 percent white, and around 15 percent Hispanic.[20] (A sign in the school's lunchroom read, "At Western we live brotherhood.")[21] The school needed more funds for additional remedial programs, an upgraded counseling program, more vocational courses, an enhanced curriculum, and improved physical facilities.[22] At the board's regular meeting on March 24, 1970, Western students and a variety of community groups asked the board for the resources necessary to fund the improvements. Andre King, a black senior who served as the school's student body president, told the board: "Here we have a school where there is not forced integration."[23] He added, "Here you have a chance to show people that integration can work and that you can get things done if you work through the system."[24] On April 14—one week after the board adopted the high school integration plan—Western students renewed their concerns in a letter to the board. (The letter appeared to reflect broad student sentiment as it was signed, "The Western High School Student Body.") In one remarkable passage, the students reminded the board that integration required more than rezoning and changing student assignment patterns. Instead, the objective was quality, integrated education. And that took money:

> Western High and the Western High School community is unique. It is unique because it is the most naturally integrated school in the city. It is not a segregated school, but an integrated one. This should be very important to you because you, right now, are attempting to perpetuate something that has existed at our school for years, and has actually worked. You have implied that, through decentralization, you are setting into perpetual motion a plan that will improve the quality of education in our public school system. Yet, in your recent attempts to legislate integration, you have neglected and even forgotten the school in which natural integration has been working for years. The improvement of education requires much more than decentralization of [sic] redistricting. It requires, also, more and better facilities and things which will help the school to function, not at the minimum level, but at maximum capacity. This, in relation to Western High School, you have failed to provide.[25]

Later in the letter, the students reminded the board that it had repeatedly ignored their pleas: "For the past five years we have been handing to you these, or similar proposals, and you have taken no action."[26] It was a stunning indictment even as the board was struggling to justify—in the court of public opinion—the high school integration plan it had approved on April 7, 1970. In mid-May, more than one thousand Western students marched peacefully to the School Center Building to meet with the board and voice their demands. In late May 1970, the board approved a $515,000 spending package to fund improvements at Western, which the students had sought for years.[27]

As the negotiations with the Western students were playing out, the board was taking to the airwaves in an attempt to calm the public and control the bad publicity around the high school integration plan. On Thursday, April 9, CBS's Detroit affiliate WJBK-TV preempted the popular 8:00 p.m. "Jim Nabors Hour" for a live "call-in" show with Zwerdling, Drachler, and James A. Hathaway, who, along with McDonald, had voted against the integration plan. By 7:30 p.m., CBS's phone lines were jammed, as twenty-five operators filtered questions from almost a thousand callers. Hathaway gloated, remarking that "the Board got a lesson in public relations."[28] Zwerdling responded that the board wasn't forcing anyone to do anything. It was simply adhering to "the law of the land, which says we must have integration."[29] But just a day earlier, Zwerdling had been spitting fire. Striking a defiant tone, he told the *Detroit Free Press*, "Here we are, at a time when the President of the United States and most others are saying we should give up on integration. But the school board in the nation's fourth-largest school system is going ahead and saying 'nuts' to all of them."[30] What changed his tone?

Perhaps it was the activity at the state house in Lansing. Reacting to the integration plan, Representative E. D. O'Brien, a white Detroit Democrat, told the press: "Members of the Board are saying that they don't care what the House does . . . Well, they'd better care."[31] The statement was prescient. As Zwerdling, Drachler, and Hathaway were preparing for the call-in, the Michigan House of Representatives (the lower house of the Michigan state legislature) passed by a significant margin a bill sponsored by O'Brien. The bill scrapped the board's school reorganization plan, and required it to increase the number of regional districts and draw new district boundary lines so that "students [must] attend the high school nearest their home."[32] And the bill gave the public veto power over the board; it provided for a referendum on any plan the board ultimately adopted.[33]

In requiring the board to reorganize in a way that incorporated the neighborhood school—in a city that was rife with residential segregation—the bill was clearly an anti-integration measure. "We have nullified the action taken by the Detroit Board of Education . . . We have returned to a basic concept of a neighborhood school system," O'Brien stated.[34] Every black member of Detroit's legislative delegation voted against the bill (or abstained). One of them stated in defeat, "Today you voted to nullify the

Bill of Rights, the Constitution and rulings of the U.S. Supreme Court."[35] White legislators from across the state, urban, suburban, and rural, had closed ranks to stop integration.[36] It was on to the Michigan State Senate (the upper house of the Michigan state legislature.)

The very next day, the executive director of the NAACP got personally involved. On Friday, April 10, Roy Wilkins wired all of the organization's branches in Michigan requesting their assistance in preserving the board's integration plan.[37] He praised the Detroit school officials. "Detroit Board of Education and Superintendent of Schools have adopted carefully developed, educationally sound plan to achieve decentralization together with desegregation of high schools," he wrote.[38] But now that plan was at risk. "As you know, Michigan state legislature is acting swiftly to kill the new decentralization-desegregation plan of Detroit public schools."[39] He contextualized the events in Detroit by stressing that what happened there would have "significant national implications."[40] Given that, he asked for the branches' full support in mounting "a vigorous campaign to offset legislative opposition."[41] Three days later, Wilkins, along with national education director June Shagaloff, trained his sights on Norman Drachler.[42]

In the wire to the superintendent, Wilkins emphasized that the national NAACP "warmly support[ed]" the April 7 plan.[43] It represented a "vastly improved educational system for all students," and was based on evidence that "racially desegregated schools are a basic and integral part of quality education for every student, black and white, rich and poor."[44] The telegram addressed to the Detroit school system's chief executive contained perhaps a bit of flattery, too: "Big city school systems throughout the country need to look at Detroit."[45]

By the time he sent the two telegrams, Wilkins, a St. Louis native, had worked at the NAACP for almost forty years. He had served in a variety of capacities: assistant secretary, editor of *The Crisis*, executive secretary, and finally as the organization's executive director.[46] An insider's insider, Wilkins excelled at lobbying, strategizing, and consensus building. He preferred litigation to direct action. He was comfortable in the halls of power, less so with confrontation, although he did acknowledge that militancy could be strategically useful. He praised Malcolm X's "powerful language" which created "in white minds the specter of what an aroused, black vengeance squad might do. The white folks began to think it would be better to deal with me . . . than to worry about the Muslims."[47] Wilkins wasn't the most charismatic or inspirational civil rights leader of the day. He wasn't a philosopher. He wasn't going to win any awards for "best boss." His biographer, Yvonne Ryan, noted that he was "difficult, complex, and often petty and demanding with colleagues and peers."[48] But he despised segregation because it was the foundation of a caste system.[49]

Wilkins favored integration because he believed blacks had few other viable options. He described his approach to eradicating racial inequality this way: "The Negro has to be a superb diplomat and a great strategist. He has to parlay what actual power he has along with the good will of the white majority. He has to devise and pursue those philosophies and activities which will least alienate the white majority opinion. And that doesn't mean that the Negro has to indulge in bootlicking. But he must gain the sympathy of the large majority of the American public. He must also seek to make identification with the American tradition."[50]

Wilkins was frequently called an "Uncle Tom" and worse.[51] But his résumé was inconsistent with the sellout label. Just after he arrived in New York to work at the NAACP in 1931, he volunteered for a dangerous assignment. A labor union had discovered that the federal government was paying black workers starvation wages to shore up dams and levees in the Mississippi Delta.[52] The Army Corps of Engineers denied the charges. The workers needed protective legislation, but the Senate investigation into the allegations was going nowhere. An eyewitness account would help move the investigation forward. Wilkins offered to travel to the area—undercover—to corroborate the claims. He explained the mission: "They made 10 cents an hour. I lived in the [work] camps and earned 10 cents an hour. We tried to sneak pictures of the work. You didn't say you were from the NAACP. It would have meant being lynched."[53] He survived the experience and then wrote about it in a report titled "Mississippi Slave Labor." After his death, *The New York Times* credited Wilkins's report with "bringing Congressional action that improved wage and working conditions for blacks in the levee labor camps."[54] The experience was seminal. In his autobiography Wilkins wrote, "If we could bring a few dimes to Mississippi, perhaps we could one day bring freedom."[55]

The executive director's appeal didn't stop the Michigan State Senate. Though it didn't immediately take up the House's bill, it went one better and repealed Young's law altogether.[56] Assessing the meaning of the Senate's action, the *Detroit Free Press* wrote: "The repeal . . . was another expression of legislative rebellion over Detroit Board of Education decisions . . . to set up seven regional districts and to advance racial integration."[57] It was now crystal clear that there were more than enough votes in the Michigan state legislature to kill the board's integration plan.

But the state's Republican governor, William Milliken, wasn't ready to sign a bill into law that would overturn the board's action. At a news conference the day after the board's April 7 meeting, the governor suggested that it had gone "beyond the question of decentralization" and acted inappropriately when it approved the high school integration plan.[58] And he drew a line in the sand when it came to busing, which "poses a very serious problem for black students and white students alike. Some very serious questions can be raised about the desirability of moving students about for integration."[59] At the same time, he sounded a note of caution. Perhaps the board might reconsider its decision. Milliken told a reporter that the board was "struggling" and expressed some hope that it might "[adjust its] course" after more hearings and "new information comes into the picture."[60]

═══

The board was facing pressure from the Detroit community as well as from above. On Monday, May 4, 1970, Aubrey J. Short, a white chemical engineer at General Motors and the permanent chairman of the Citizens Committee for Better Education (CCBE), stood in front of the School Center Building along with forty placard-waving women.[61] (By early May, the group formerly known as the Citizens Committee for Better Schools was identified by the press as the Citizens Committee for Better Education, "a coalition of homeowner groups in the northwest and northeast areas" of Detroit.)[62] The group had moved beyond the protest phase. It was there to kick off a campaign to recall the four members of the Detroit Board of Education—Abraham Zwerdling, Darneau Stewart, Andrew Perdue, and

Peter Grylls—who had voted in favor of the high school integration plan.[63] Short told William Grant that the April 7 decision "was the spark that ignited the citizen protest" because it would send children "into distant and alien neighborhoods."[64] Short's children were directly affected by the April 7 plan. Because of the board's action, his children would now attend Kettering High, a black high school, instead of Denby High, which at the time was almost all white.[65] For the members of the CCBE, immediate action seemed necessary. Sure, the state legislature was on their side, but the governor hadn't yet signed a bill negating the integration plan. What's more, the board was defiant. It vowed to move ahead with the "attendance area changes regardless of what the Legislature does."[66] Something had to be done about a board that was sticking to its guns on integration. At least for now, white Detroiters would not simply move to the suburbs—they were going to stay and fight.

The day after the CCBE announced its recall campaign, June Shagaloff briefed Wilkins on the situation in Detroit. She praised the board. From her perspective as the organization's national education director, the board could certainly have done worse; "the basic approach in Detroit contrasts sharply with the decentralization approach in New York City which, in my view, further establishes racial and class concentration in the schools," she wrote to Wilkins.[67] To Shagaloff, the story was one of a school administration that was deeply committed to integration, notwithstanding intense white opposition.[68] And it was not acting entirely on its own, even if the Detroit branch of the NAACP found itself a bit isolated. "Virtually the only voice in the Negro community for desegregation was the NAACP," Shagaloff wrote.[69] The Metropolitan Detroit Council of Churches released a statement recognizing the board's moral leadership and supporting its action.[70] The council, referencing *Brown*, thought the board had little choice but to pursue integration ("it had to adopt the decentralization plan in keeping with the school desegregation ruling of the United States Supreme Court."[71]) The UAW and several other groups publicly commended the board for its courage in taking a major step toward the goal of integrated education.[72]

The press wasn't helping, however. The *Detroit Free Press*'s editorial page, highlighting some of the board's strategic missteps, only grudgingly endorsed the integration plan.[73] Unsurprisingly, *The Detroit News* was even less enthusiastic. The *News*'s editorial emphasized that the integration plan was likely to result in "an exodus of white and black middle-class families seeking the security of suburban and private school standards."[74] The statement implied that black middle-class families had equal access to the suburbs, which they did not. It also assumed that white and black middle-class families had the same resources and were equally well situated to pay private school tuition, which they were not. The editorial's discussion of race was paradoxical. On the one hand, the paper assured its readership that the "majority of the families in the affected areas are not bigots."[75] But on the other, it warned that the board's challenge in keeping those families was significant because "they may be apprehensive about the racial aspects of the new school boundaries."[76]

On April 18, 1970, the *Michigan Chronicle* published an editorial voicing its strong support for the board.[77] "The Board members who voted for the new school plan have demonstrated a strong and courageous leadership badly needed in our time," the paper asserted.[78] In providing its endorsement, the *Chronicle* was hardly turning its back on community control, although it interpreted the concept more broadly than Cleage and others: "Getting control of an all-black school or an all-black neighborhood is not in itself an unworthy goal, it is just too limited. It is about time blacks had more to say about those things which happen outside the all-black neighborhood, but which affect black people."[79] But it was too little, too late. Sensing that the battle was already lost, Shagaloff wrote: "The Superintendent of Schools believes that the new bill [prohibiting desegregation] will be passed by the Michigan legislature. The situation is very grave and terribly disheartening."[80]

The Detroit branch of the NAACP and the *Michigan Chronicle* were in the board's corner, but that sentiment was not universal. On the same day that it published its editorial supporting the board, the *Chronicle* also reported the results of a survey it had conducted finding that the board's "decision calling for implementation of student bussing plan to bring about racial balance in the city's high schools is split about 50–50 [among blacks]."[81] Then there was Cleage. Unsurprisingly, he strongly opposed the plan. And he wasn't just talking about it, he was taking action. On Friday,

May 8, 1970, Cleage, the Inner City Parents Council, and two other groups affiliated with the Shrine of the Black Madonna joined the CCBE in demanding that the four board members who had voted in favor of the integration plan—including Andrew Perdue—be recalled.[82] In explaining his stance, Cleage struck familiar tones. He interpreted black support for the board through a nationalist lens. Blacks favored the integration plan because "they did not want to side with the white homeowners," Cleage argued.[83] The *Detroit Free Press* article reporting on black support for the recall drive intimated that Cleage's action might undermine a personal relationship. The paper noted, "Perdue has been an attorney for militant black organizations and a good friend of Cleage."[84]

Recalling a board member wasn't easy. It had never happened in Detroit or in any other major city.[85] The CCBE needed more than one hundred thousand signatures just to get the recall question on the August primary ballot. At first, no one took the recall effort seriously. But its campaign swept the city like a brushfire. By late May, the group had seventy thousand signatures and serious momentum.[86] On top of everything else, Zwerdling and the other liberals now had real reason to be concerned about their jobs.

Then on June 14, 1970, Remus Robinson died. Robinson's passing was front-page news in Detroit. His was a lifetime of greatest hits: two-time winner of the Negro National Amateur Golf Championship; the first black person elected to the Detroit Board of Education; NAACP Detroit Branch Distinguished Service Award; Detroit Medical Society Physician of the Year; surgeon-in-chief at Parkside Hospital, successor to Dunbar Hospital, the city's first black hospital.[87]

What might he have been thinking during those final days? Robinson had a lifetime of battles to look back on. In assessing his life, the *Detroit Free Press* observed that he drew fire from many quarters during his time on the board: "Many whites despised him for his pro-integration stand. In later years, however, he was equally hated by many black militants for his unwillingness to support black separatism and nationalism."[88] But if Robinson died with any regrets, it was hard to imagine that these battles were among them. Commitment to integration was core to the man. It is far more likely that he would have thanked the paper for highlighting the challenges he faced.

But perhaps Cleage and the whites who hated him didn't even cross his mind during that time. Those fights had been going on for years; they were old news. Maybe Robinson was thinking about a letter he received from a black eighth grader just a few weeks after the board's tumultuous meeting on April 7. The middle schooler, Linda Gail Johnson, wrote in part:

> I know the [high school integration] plan was to provide an equal education for Blacks and Whites, but you see how we are separated that is all it boils down to, racial discrimination.
>
> I want an equal education just like the white students are getting. I want to be able to go to school and be able to do anything they can do. I know we are not getting an equal education. How can we?!! As long as we stay separated we are not going to get anywhere in this world.
>
> Say we waited until another 25 years pass without passing that plan. What would the schools be like? It would be a mess, there would be nothing but fear and hate between the blacks and whites.
>
> There might be fights at the beginning, but after awhile it would cool down.
>
> It's a good plan keep it regardless to what the people say. If you give people more time to think about it the whites will come running with their money. They would probably do anything to keep the blacks out of their schools, and to keep from sending their children a long ways off. Remember money is power and it works.
>
> I am for the plan 99%, but 1% of the problem is transportation, but I know transportation can be worked out for I am a child of hope and ambition. There is no such word as the word can't to me. I know everything is going to be all right.
>
> I believe the Decentralization Plan is a start for a bright and new future.[89]

Somehow the youngster's perceptive letter managed to contain just about everything that attracted some and yet repelled others about the integration philosophy. The letter took it as a given that racial separation was a form of race discrimination and that blacks could not receive equal educational opportunities in segregated schools ("As long as we stay separated we are not going to get anywhere in this world.") Her fundamental assumption was that racial separation was a problem, and that the board's integration plan would solve it. Above all, she wanted an "equal education."

All of this would have been music to Robinson and Zwerdling's ears and anathema to Cleage. Cleage might have challenged her by asking, "Equal to what?" After all, equality was relative, and could only be established by assessing black status and attainment *in relationship* to similarly situated whites. But why should what whites had be the measure? Why look outside as opposed to within? Black teachers were perfectly capable and indeed far better situated to educate black children than were white teachers. The student thought that whites would ultimately accede to integration ("after awhile it would cool down"). This was one justification for asking black children to internalize the heavy cost of integration and bear the brunt of white hostility. Integrationists carried with them the hopeful belief that whites would change when they came into closer contact with blacks. They hoped the two groups would move forward together. This was certainly Zwerdling's view. But Cleage thought waiting for whites to change—wishing that they would recognize blacks' obvious humanity—was beyond folly; it was absurd.

Then there was the money. On this, the student was elliptical. At first blush, she seemed to be making an observation, pedestrian in nationalist circles, that whites would resist integration at all costs ("They would probably do anything to keep the blacks out of their schools, and to keep from sending their children a long ways off.") But did she perhaps mean something entirely different and more hopeful: that the *threat* of integration would incentivize whites to spend money on public education? That was a possibility, too. In any case, the student certainly had one thing right: "Money is power and it works."

8

RIGHT THING TO LOSE

The state legislature had reacted immediately to the board's high school integration plan. The House and Senate bills that emerged in the wake of the board's action were different, but they shared a single important characteristic: they were intended to prevent black and white students from attending the same Detroit high schools.[1] But no bill could become law unless the governor signed it. Governor Milliken—with a statewide election upcoming in the fall—was in a tough spot. The Traverse City Republican was relatively new to the office, having served as Michigan's lieutenant governor under the leadership of Governor George Romney until Romney resigned in early 1969 to join the Nixon administration as Secretary of Housing and Urban Development.[2] The Michigan gubernatorial election was scheduled for November 3, 1970. This meant that Milliken had to face Michigan voters in just a few short months in order to retain his position. (Milliken ultimately prevailed in a close contest against Democrat Sander Levin that fall, but by fewer than 45,000 votes out of more than 2,650,000 cast.[3]) The *Detroit Free Press* characterized the governor's precarious position this way: "Whatever the governor did, he could anger hundreds of thousands of emotionally charged voters."[4] At the state capital in Lansing, Milliken let it be known that he was open to signing a bill that would overturn the board's action, but only if it was favored by a majority of the Detroit legislative delegation, which was evenly divided between blacks and whites.[5]

Enter Coleman Young. He was furious with the board. One report had him walking the halls of the state house muttering to himself "and [the board] thought they could get away with this in an election year."[6] Young wasn't angry just because it was his law that was on the chopping block due to the board's unexpected approach to implementing it. He thought the board had committed malpractice. It had jeopardized black control of black schools in the service of obtaining what Young—and many members of the Detroit's black community—viewed as a largely symbolic "chicken shit" integration plan.[7] Indeed, Young's law never contemplated integrating Detroit's high schools. The modest integration plan was the board's idea, not his. The *Michigan Chronicle* noted: "Young explained that desegregation of schools was not the intent of Act 244, merely decentralization."[8]

But even if the high school integration plan was weak tea, Young wouldn't let his white colleagues off the hook, either. Calling the state senators who voted to repeal his bill "white bigots," he told the *Detroit Free Press* "this is capitulation to blind prejudice."[9] Young thought them "willing to go to any lengths . . . to defy the U.S. Supreme Court."[10] Young was even more pointed in his criticism in the pages of the *Michigan Chronicle*.[11] The repeal was an "attempt by bigots to defy the law of the land and keep the schools lily white."[12] He added: "Are you telling blacks of our state that you will go to any extent, even the extent of injuring the educational chances of your own children, to maintain white supremacy?"[13]

In stark contrast, much of Detroit's white community thought the board's integration plan was a very big deal indeed. Actual integration was in the eye of the beholder. On the one hand, the plan didn't affect that many students, applied to only half of the city's high schools and none of its middle or elementary schools. On the other hand, the plan did apply to half of the city's high schools and required—for the first time ever—that white students attend black schools in black neighborhoods. And the plan was voluntary. It was not the result of court order. The board members who approved the integration plan did so for a variety of rationales. But one of them was the belief that *Brown v. Board of Education* required the segregated school district to desegregate. The board had made many mistakes and political miscalculations. But believing that *Brown* applied "up north" and that it had an obligation to disestablish segregation wasn't one of them.

Coleman Young was nothing if not a fixer. He knew integration was a nonstarter. So what, if anything, could be saved? The answer was the decentralization plan.[14] So he set to work developing a new bill that would at least give blacks control of their schools—which was the core of what he had wanted all along.[15] "They had the votes to kill the whole thing outright. We had to try and salvage something," Young stated.[16] Better half a loaf than none.

Then there was the recall. Believing that the CCBE would scuttle the recall drive if the state acted, many state officials wanted a bill that would shorten the pro-integration board members' terms. They were concerned that a prolonged recall fight could kick off a replay of the summer of 1967.[17] The prospect of more civil unrest was more than a fanciful possibility. Young was worried, too. "I hate to see the racial confrontation of a recall, if we can cool it," he told *The New York Times*.[18]

Young worked all the angles to put a new bill together. Over a period of three months, he negotiated with black legislators and white conservatives, consulted with the speaker of the house, and held off any action by the conference committee that might have harmonized the Senate and House bills. The result was a bill that disciplined the board in three ways. First, it effectively prohibited implementation of the board's integration plan.[19] This prohibition was unpopular with Detroit's black legislative delegation. Young told them to support it anyway "because the anti-integration clause will last only as long as it takes to get this thing into court."[20] He had every reason to believe that his bill would indeed be challenged in court. The Detroit branch of the NAACP had said as much when its executive secretary testified in support of the board before the state House education committee in early May ("we fully intend to fight any plan approved by the legislature that would directly or indirectly, overtly or covertly be contrary to the spirit and letter of the Supreme Court decision on desegregation"[21]). In a July 1970 article in the *Detroit Free Press* examining the state legislature's negotiations, William Grant wrote that "Young hopes . . . the courts will strike down the anti-integration section."[22] He could not have known then just how much his faith in the judiciary would be tested.

Next, Young's bill reorganized the Detroit public school system by creating eight new educational regions, the boundaries of which—

crucially—would be drawn either by the legislature or by gubernatorial commission, but not by the Detroit Board of Education. Each new region would have its own five-member board, directly elected by the voters residing in that region. One board member from each of the eight new regions would sit on a newly reconstituted and larger central board of education. This meant that the new thirteen-member central board would now be dominated by regional board members, ensuring that the central board could never impose an integration plan on an unwilling constituency.[23] Elections to fill the new regional and central board positions would take place in the fall. The bill also directed these new school boards to adopt attendance policies that gave preference "to those students residing nearest the school."[24] In effect, the bill doubled down on residential segregation by requiring the new school boards to assign students to their neighborhood schools.

Finally, Young's new bill attempted to take the recall issue off the table by shortening the terms of Zwerdling, Stewart, and Grylls, three of the four board members who had voted in favor of the high school integration plan. (Young's first bill had extended their terms beyond the normal expiration date of December 31, 1970; Young's second bill reinstated the normal expiration date.)[25] Zwerdling would be out of a job at the end of the year whether he was recalled or not. Of the provision that effectively removed the board members, one Detroit legislator remarked: "We gave them three heads on a platter . . . That ought to be enough."[26]

Three months of hard work paid off, as both the House and Senate passed Young's bill by overwhelming margins. No fewer than three newspaper articles referred to the bill as a "compromise," which it was.[27] Zwerdling's "chicken shit" high school integration plan had ignited the passions of white Detroiters. Their political power meant that plan was dead as a doornail. Or, as William Grant put it, the state legislators "were spurred into action by widespread opposition by whites in northeast and northwest Detroit to the school board's April 7 decision to change the attendance areas . . . to increase integration."[28] Because the board had then added an integration plan to the decentralization plan it was required to carry out by Young's first bill, the two were inexorably linked. This meant the two plans might very well go down together. Young's second bill—

"Young's compromise"—made sure that didn't happen: decentralization at least would continue.

The Detroit branch of the NAACP did not take the legislative override lightly. It characterized the state's action as a direct threat to city control, one that undermined the ability of the Detroit Board of Education to make core educational decisions. The irony of the NAACP arguing in favor of local control could not have been lost on anyone. Dr. Jesse Goodwin, chairman of the education committee, stated: "We take issue with the wisdom of allowing . . . suburban legislators, who are not accountable to Detroit residents and who have traditionally been very apathetic about the city's financial status, to participate in internal matters traditionally reserved for local governing units."[29] The national organization readily agreed with the Detroit branch's assessment. On July 3, 1970, the delegates to the sixty-first annual meeting of the NAACP unanimously passed a resolution promising to seek "immediate legal redress" if the legislature's action became state law.[30]

Undeterred, on July 7, 1970, Governor William Milliken signed Public Act 48, "Young's compromise," into law.[31] A few weeks earlier, the *Detroit Free Press* had reported Zwerdling's sharp assessment of the genesis of the law the governor would ultimately sign: "If we are to be defeated, let there be no mistake about what the issue is. The issue is whether the school board will move to improve racial balance in the high schools or not."[32] As for the CCBE, it wasn't changing course. It made no plans to call off the recall effort. Aubrey Short told a reporter, "A lot of people have decided they don't like the board of education. If they have changed their minds, then they can vote against the recall on election day."[33]

═══

On August 4, 1970, Detroiters recalled board president Abraham Zwerdling and board members Darneau Stewart, Andrew Perdue, and Peter F. Grylls, all of whom had voted in favor of the integration plan. The recall, which carried by a margin of 60 percent, was historic, as the *Detroit Free Press* noted: "The recall is unprecedented in the 128-year history of the

Detroit school system and is believed to be the first time that a majority of a major city school board has been removed by recall."[34] Support for the recall broke decisively along racial lines.[35] Blacks opposed the recall just about as much as whites favored it.[36] But a passion-gap between the races helped explain the outcome. Notwithstanding Cleage's efforts, an overwhelming majority of Detroit's blacks still favored integration.[37] But that number was declining as large numbers of black Detroiters—in the face of sustained white resistance—reached the pragmatic conclusion that achieving integration would be extraordinarily difficult.[38] Integration was losing its position as a top-priority goal. Detroit-area whites, on the other hand, were deeply invested in the recall issue. They saw it as a uniquely powerful way to register their opposition to racial integration.[39] (Superintendent Drachler later characterized the recall of the board members as a "rejection of the national policy of integration.")[40] The unusually heavy turnout in white neighborhoods, with as many as 90 percent of whites voting in favor of the recall in areas where the board's integration plan would have required their children to attend black schools, made all the difference.[41]

On the same day the city went to the polls to determine the fate of the liberal board members, the gubernatorial commission that had been tasked under Young's compromise with drawing district boundary lines for the eight newly created regions, released its map. Under Young's law, the regional boundaries had to be "compact, contiguous and as nearly equal in population as possible."[42] The commission complied with these requirements. But it made no attempt whatsoever to draw regional boundaries to facilitate integration.[43] It drew each region so that black voters and white voters would each have political control over four regions. The commission's chairman told the press implausibly, "race was not an issue in our decision."[44] Tom Turner, the president of the Detroit branch of the NAACP, had a very different view. He thought the commission had "ghettoized" education in Detroit. "The establishment of political boundaries along racial lines is the first step to the establishment of education along racial lines," Turner stated.[45]

This wasn't the only problem with the commission's map. While the eight new regions were evenly divided between the two racial groups as a matter of political control—with black and white *voters* comprising a numerical majority in an equal number of regions—*black students* were a majority in six.[46] Noting that the aims of the community control movement had largely been frustrated, one scholar observed that the percentage of black students under white control was approximately "40 percent of the total black enrollments."[47] This meant that the new regional map offered the worst of both worlds: zero integration and white political control over two regions where black students predominated. It was exactly the result that Perdue had hoped to avoid.

In early November, pursuant to "Young's compromise," Detroiters went to the polls to elect a slate of school board officials for the newly created eight regional boards and several vacancies on the restructured Central Board of Education. The election was a triumph for the CCBE, as candidates allied with the organization won a dozen regional board seats with high vote totals.[48] Big changes were in store for the newly expanded Central Board of Education, too. It was now dominated by white, anti-integration conservatives; it had the smallest proportion of blacks in almost a generation.[49] The central board's new president was none other than Patrick McDonald, the board member who had leaked the integration plan to the press.[50] Candidates for regional board seats aligned with the community control movement, meanwhile, were soundly defeated at the polls. There were twenty-two such candidates, including one with a particularly high profile: Albert Cleage. He and all the others, save one, were defeated.[51] In analyzing the election results, the *Detroit Free Press* noted that black influence on the Detroit school system had "grown steadily" since 1955 when Remus Robinson joined the board as its first black member.[52] Now it was moving in the opposite direction. Per education reporter William Grant: "Detroit voters have elected the city's most conservative board of education in at least six years and have sharply reduced black representation on the board."[53] Recognizing that he could no longer count on support from the newly transformed board, Superintendent Drachler announced his resignation effective at the end of the school year.[54] Pro-integration liberals had controlled the Detroit school board since 1965. Now they were gone.[55]

Abraham Zwerdling died in 1987. The *Detroit Free Press* published his obituary under the title, "*School Board President Stuck to His Ideals.*" The obituary characterized Zwerdling as a tireless champion of the rights of workers and minorities. Melvin Glasser remembered his friend and former colleague as a man of principle. Of his plans to integrate Detroit's schools, Zwerdling once told Glasser, "I'm not sure I can win this, but it's the right thing to lose."[56]

PART II

THE CONTAINMENT

9

UP FOR GRABS

On Tuesday morning, August 18, 1970, two weeks after the recall election, Louis Lucas entered the grand, block-long federal courthouse at 231 West Lafayette Boulevard in downtown Detroit. Lucas, a white attorney, was a native of New Orleans. He had served as an assistant U.S. attorney and helped form the first integrated law firm in Memphis. Though still in his thirties, he was already a highly skilled litigator. One paper described him as "one of the nation's best-known and most sought-after school-desegregation lawyers."[1] Now he worked with the NAACP.[2] The lawyer was headed to the clerk's office on the first floor to file a complaint in a case challenging the constitutionality of Public Act 48, "Young's compromise." The case was titled *Bradley v. Milliken*.

The plaintiffs in the case were the Detroit branch of the NAACP and a group of Detroit families, parents, and their children who attended Detroit public schools. The complaint listed the individual plaintiffs' names alphabetically; Ronald and Richard Bradley, and their mother, Verda (sometimes spelled "Virda"), were listed first. The case was filed as a "class action." Later, the court would rule that the plaintiff class included "all school children of the City of Detroit and all Detroit resident parents who have children of school age."[3] "Milliken" referred to William Milliken, the state governor. The complaint also named two other state officials as defendants as well as the entity responsible for providing education throughout the state: Frank J. Kelley, the state attorney general; John W. Porter, the state school superintendent; and the Michigan State Board of Education. As for the city, the complaint also named as defendants the Detroit Board of Education, the various board members, and Norman Drachler, Detroit's school superintendent.[4] The clerk accepted the complaint, stamped it filed, and gave it a docket number: Civil Action 35257. Lucas paid the fifteen-dollar filing fee and the clerk issued a summons informing the defendants that they had been sued. The case was randomly assigned to federal district court judge Stephen J. Roth.

Earlier in the summer, Verda Bradley had approached the Detroit branch of the NAACP to see if the organization could assist her. Her son Ronald, aged six, was a kindergartener at Clinton Elementary at 8145 Chalfonte Street in northwest Detroit. (Her older son, Richard, attended Murphy Junior High School at 23901 Fenkell Avenue.) Clinton had changed dramatically as white families left the neighborhood for the suburbs. The school, now vastly predominantly black, was horribly overcrowded and so poorly resourced that it lacked toilet paper.[5] As a lunch-hour aide and a school parent who participated in the Chalfonte Community Council, the Clinton School Advisory Board, and the PTA, she knew the school intimately.[6] Bradley's assessment of Clinton's failings was blunt: "We did not have things in the school that we had before it became all black . . . When schools become all black the Board of Education seems to forget about black schools."[7] "We had 1,500 students in a school that was made for 500 students," she added.[8] Bradley elaborated on Clinton's decline in an interview for *The Crisis*, the NAACP's official publication: "There used to be a little truck that came around 5 or 6 o'clock every morning to sweep away the snow in the school-yard. But when the white people left, they ran out of money."[9] Working within the system hadn't yielded results, so Bradley changed tactics. She and her husband, Chester, weren't able "to get any satisfaction from the Board of Education so we went to the NAACP for help."[10] The timing was propitious. "They told us that they were preparing the suit and we decided to join it."[11]

The daughter of a family friend, Bernice Reese, characterized Bradley as a longtime advocate: "I remember Momma Bradley was always fighting for something, beautiful lady who knew her rights."[12] She showed initiative early on. As a teenager, Bradley moved to Detroit during World War II to work in the city's booming auto industry. Part of the Great Migration, she possessed, as *The Crisis* put it, "the typical black migrant's dream that she would prosper well in the North where industrial jobs were plentiful and segregation was not a legal nightmare."[13] She found a cottage on Greenlawn Avenue in northwest Detroit, right across the street from Clinton Elementary, in a neighborhood that boasted more than a few white families.[14] As a child in the South, she had always attended segregated schools.[15]

One way to think about Bradley's motivation to join the lawsuit was that she saw it as an opportunity to leverage whites' social and economic power for the benefit of her child and other black children. She believed— correctly—that even the liberal Detroit Board of Education would be more responsive to the needs of schools with a substantial white population. In an interview with education reporter William Grant in the *Detroit Free Press*, she'd confessed her ambition: "I want to see the schools better."[16] About Bradley, Grant wrote: "[She] believes that Clinton Elementary has been ignored by school authorities because it is virtually all black. She sees school integration, even by busing, as a way of changing things and providing a better education for her son."[17]

So Bradley viewed integration instrumentally, as a means to an end. It was a way to achieve school quality and address the concerns that first brought her to the Detroit branch.[18] This was a strategic view of integration, one that was often underappreciated. Black nationalists often derided integrationists for lacking self-esteem and a strong connection to the black community. "Self-hatred is the inevitable corollary of the dream of integration," Cleage once stated.[19] But this characterization didn't fit Bradley, who cared deeply about her family and her community. Her comments suggested a more pragmatic reason to crave integrated schools: that was where the money was. As Michigan senator Phillip A. Hart, who had been the floor manager of the 1965 Voting Rights Act, would write in late 1971, "Many blacks are convinced that money follows whites—that black children do not get the same deal that whites do unless they are going to school with white children. And let us face it, there is about 100 years of history to back up that belief."[20] Speaking to reporters about her participation in the case in 2004, Bradley explained: "They thought we were just trying to get in the schools with whites. We were just trying to be . . . equal."[21]

Other named plaintiffs spoke of the importance of racial integration in fostering intergroup cooperation. Ray Litt, an electrical contractor and chairman of the Palmer Park Precinct Community Relations Committee—and the only white plaintiff—joined the case because "I have a concern for an integrated society."[22] His daughters attended Vandenberg Elementary School on the city's west side. They were in the minority there and had had a good experience. "Our own school is a good school . . . and I think the experience that my own kids are having there should be the kind of experience shared by all people all over the metropolitan area," Litt told the *Detroit Free Press*. "We cannot live in a separate society," he later stated.[23] But he also appreciated Bradley's pragmatic argument, telling a reporter, "The politics of our society usually dictate the resources in our society usually go where the white folks are."[24]

Another of the named plaintiffs, Blanche Goings, had grown up in Alabama and felt the constant humiliation of life under Jim Crow. She recalled the sting of segregation. "I can remember 40 years ago standing on the highway and watching the little yellow bus stop to pick up three white kids to take them to a school closer than the school I had to walk to."[25] She thought the current administration was moving backward rather than forward: "Now when that bus is going to stop for me President Nixon says he's going to put an end to it." Goings's daughter Jeanne, also named in the suit, attended the prestigious Cass Tech High School, and that was by design: "I tried to maneuver my own children into integrated situations and that is one reason Jeanne is going to Cass." Goings echoed many of Litt's concerns. She remarked, "I want to see children grow up together because they have to live together."[26] Litt and Goings's comments were grounded in the idea that educating the two races together would encourage students to see their commonalities rather than their differences, easing the enmity between the races.

—————

Given that state law had quashed Zwerdling's high school integration plan, it was unsurprising that the complaint sought relief from the governor, other state officials, and state agencies. But the complaint also named the

Detroit Board of Education and various local school officials as defendants, which seemed strange. Zwerdling and the liberals had lost their positions precisely *because* they were trying to integrate the Detroit public schools.

Initially, the board welcomed the suit. In July 1970, as the recall fight raged and with the liberal members of the school board tenuously hanging onto power, Superintendent Drachler reached out to the NAACP—surreptitiously—for assistance in challenging the state law.[27] Drachler arranged a secret meeting between his deputies and NAACP officials in New York to strategize. At the meeting, school officials took the position that suing the board would be unfair and counterproductive. Better to focus on the state law. Striking down the state law would free the board to take even more aggressive steps toward integrating the schools.[28]

But Lucas pushed back on this idea. As he pointed out, Young's compromise couldn't be looked at in a vacuum. Paul Dimond, a talented young lawyer who was part of the NAACP litigation team, described Lucas's concern: "The case against Act 48 might well depend on proof and findings of preexisting illegal school segregation," and that could draw in the board.[29] Lucas wanted to leave the door open to a more ambitious change. As he told an interviewer, "If the Board were so dedicated to desegregation, why wouldn't it want the plaintiffs to seek a sweeping desegregation order rather than have a fight every time the school board wants to desegregate another 3,000 of its 290,000 pupils? Why not solve the whole problem at once."[30] Naming the board as a defendant would ensure, as Dimond recalled Lucas's way of thinking, "actual desegregation."[31]

George Bushnell Jr., the board's lawyer (and the son of a Michigan Supreme Court Justice), was adamantly against naming the board as a defendant. Even Tom Turner, the president of the Detroit branch of the NAACP, had to be convinced.[32] Ultimately, however, the NAACP did decide to include the board as one of the parties it was suing. As Lucas's boss, NAACP general counsel Nathaniel R. Jones, would later explain in a memo, the recall changed his thinking. He candidly told his own boss, Roy Wilkins: "In reaching my decision, I had to bear in mind that our friends were no longer on the Board."[33] Furthermore, he pointed out, the board had overseen earlier policies that fostered segregation and inequality. "I would be guilty of malpractice and the NAACP open to censure and even removal from the case as not effectively representing a class if we failed to lay before the Court the full history of the policy and practices the liberal members on the Board are attempting to correct," he wrote. "The only way that this could be done, after recall, was by having the body corporate before the Court."[34]

A civil rights activist with a careful, measured style, Jones was born in 1926 in Youngstown, Ohio, to two Virginia transplants.[35] As a young child, Jones lived in a racially mixed neighborhood and attended the James Hillman school, which was integrated "with a mere sprinkling of black students."[36] Hillman was academically strong. But the all-black school near where he lived for a time with his father after his parents divorced was poorly resourced. Jones soon began using his mother's address in order to attend Hillman Junior High. He remarked, "The inconvenience of sharing the bus pass with my mother was well worth it, given the difference between the schools."[37] That Jones was allowed to attend Hillman did not mean he was treated equally there. For one thing, Hillman had no black staff whatsoever, including custodians. Reflecting on his "theoretically nonsegregated" education, Jones recalled, "I became conscious at a young age of the limits of permissible interaction between the races."[38]

Jones was first introduced to black lawyers at a local YMCA forum in the late 1930s. He recalled "a number of impressive-looking black men in vested suits" who brought "inspiring messages of hope to our local leaders and community members."[39] Their discussion of racial discrimination prompted him to wonder if the racial prejudice he observed was pure happenstance or whether it was somehow institutionalized.[40] It was during this period—the late 1930s and early 1940s—that young Nate Jones became a civil rights activist. His actions were varied and prolific. He organized to end segregation at the city's swimming pools, pushed the National Amateur Baseball Federation to allow teams with black ballplayers to participate in its tournament, demanded to be enrolled in the Army Air Corps flight training program (which had capped the number of black cadets it would accept), threatened his college with legal action for discriminating against black vets, advocated on behalf of black women denied access to nurse training programs, sued a local restaurant for race discrimination, and participated in sit-ins and other direct nonviolent actions at restaurants, catering halls, and skating rinks that refused to serve blacks. And this was all before Jones enrolled in the Youngstown College Law School in 1951.[41] Jones, who would later become a federal court of appeals judge (just one rung below the Supreme Court), was often described in reserved if not milquetoast terms as "conscientious" and "competent." But his was a résumé that a great many activists would envy.

In 1961, Jones became an assistant U.S. attorney, still a rare accomplishment for a black lawyer.[42] In 1967, his boss, Merle McCurdy, the first black U.S. attorney for the Northern District of Ohio, recommended Jones for a job that would require a move to Washington, D.C.: assistant general counsel to President Johnson's National Advisory Commission on Civil Disorders, more commonly known as the Kerner Commission.[43] Jones accepted the position. Of the commission's findings Jones later stated, "It was painfully clear that the dry rot resulting from decades of disparities, neglect, and educational deficits would require drastic intervention."[44] In 1969, Roy Wilkins offered Jones the position of general counsel of the NAACP. Jones agonized over the decision. The position would require his family to relocate to New York, and it entailed a substantial reduction in salary. When he sought guidance, a friend told him, "An offer such as that is a Call. One doesn't reject a Call. You have a duty to accept it. If you don't like it after working at it for a while, you can always walk away. If you don't accept it, you will forever wonder about your decision."[45] Jones took the job. Later, he would sign off on the NAACP's attempt to make desegregating the Detroit schools a matter of immediate national import.

━━━━

The complaint that Lucas filed in the federal courthouse on that Tuesday morning met all the rules necessary to maintain a federal case. It gave notice to the defendants of the plaintiffs' claims. And it explained why the plaintiffs believed the federal court had jurisdiction (i.e., the ability to hear and decide the claims presented). But like all good complaints, it did much more than that. Behind the technical legal language—jurisdiction, class action, injunctive relief—the complaint told two stories.

The first story focused on Young's compromise. In this part of the complaint, the plaintiffs alleged that the state violated the equal protection clause of the Fourteenth Amendment when it voided the board's high school integration plan. The lawyers knew that at the very least they had to plead that the government (the "state action" requirement) had deprived the plaintiffs of equal protection of the laws (the equality mandate) to make this claim stick.

Was there "state action?" That was easy. Act 48, Young's compromise, was passed by the state legislature and signed into law by the state's governor. But what about equal protection? *Brown* stood for the proposition that, if the state of Michigan passed a law *requiring* separate schools for black and white children, such an action would violate the equal protection clause. Was Young's compromise the same or different? On the one hand, the state law didn't expressly *require* Detroit's schools to be racially segregated as had been the case in the South. On the other hand, the complaint claimed that Young's compromise was "enacted with the express intent of preventing the desegregation of the [Detroit public school] system."[46] No one argued that phrasing the law as a prohibition (you may not desegregate), rather than as an affirmative command (you must segregate), made a material difference. And even President Nixon had conceded that de jure segregation included "deliberate act(s) of school officials," which presumably included other government officials including state legislators as well.[47]

The state legislators didn't spell out discriminatory intentions in the text of the state law, of course. But the complaint made several allegations suggesting that discrimination was their true purpose. First, Young's compromise pertained to Detroit alone, "where the bulk of Negro school children in the State of Michigan are concentrated." Similarly, the law affected only the Detroit Board of Education, prohibiting it from assigning students and establishing attendance zones, while every other school district in the state was free to take such action.[48] Finally, the complaint asserted that Young's compromise violated the Fourteenth Amendment because it constituted a "reversal by the State of Michigan of action taken by the Detroit School Board which action was consistent with and mandated by the Constitution of the United States."[49] That sentence wasn't a picture of clarity. But what the complaint seemed to be getting at was that the high school integration plan was the board's attempt to comply with *Brown*. And the state would not let that attempt—however modest—stand. It swooped in and killed the board's integration plan before it could go into effect. It was as if the state had issued a direct command: the schools in Detroit shall now and forever remain segregated. So the complaint's first story was about the state of Michigan's successful attempt to quash school integration in Detroit.

The document also told a second story, one that preceded the board's action on April 7. Racial segregation of students, faculty, and staff, the complaint alleged, was the board's official policy. School authorities used a wide variety of mechanisms to create and maintain that scheme. The complaint asserted that "the racially discriminatory policy . . . included assigning students, designing attendance zones for elementary junior and senior high schools, establishing feeder patterns to secondary schools, planning future public educational facilities, constructing new schools, and utilizing or building upon the existing racially discriminatory pattern in both public and private housing."[50] Through these techniques, the Detroit school board was running a "dual" school system—one for blacks and one for whites—just like the southern systems the Supreme Court had castigated in *Brown v. Board of Education*. That meant that Detroit's schools actually were de jure segregated, which *Brown* had said violated the equal protection clause of the Fourteenth Amendment. If the assertions in the complaint were true, school authorities in Detroit had violated the United States Constitution.

So the complaint alleged two types of de jure segregation: the state's gutting of the board's modest integration plan, and the board's long-standing official policy of segregating Detroit's schools. As the initial document in a federal lawsuit, the complaint not only outlined the plaintiffs' claims, but also asked the court to provide a remedy for the constitutional violations it identified. So what did the plaintiffs want? First, they wanted the board's modest integration plan reinstated and put into effect at the beginning of the upcoming (1970–71) academic year.[51] This remedy spoke to the complaint's first story.

The complaint also sought a court order preventing the defendants from segregating the schools.[52] No more assigning students to one-race schools. Stop constructing new schools in the heart of residentially segregated neighborhoods. Cease the practice of allocating black faculty, staff, and administrators only to all-black schools. All of this spoke to the complaint's second story, that the Detroit public schools were de jure segregated. Supreme Court doctrine required that a "dual" school system transition to a "unitary" school system "in which racial discrimination would be eliminated root and branch."[53] And this was exactly what the plaintiffs demanded in their complaint. The complaint asked the court to require the defendants to eliminate "the racial identity of every school in the system and to maintain now and hereafter a unitary, nonracial school system . . . [using] all methods of integration of schools including rezoning, pairing, grouping, school consolidation, use of satellite zones and transportation."[54] Finally, it was worth noting that the complaint sought "injunctive relief," such as a court order requiring the defendants to stop engaging in segregation, rather than money damages.[55] This mattered because in the federal system, most cases seeking monetary relief were eligible to be tried by a jury; those seeking an injunctive remedy were not.[56] Were the *Bradley* case to be tried, Judge Roth would be the ultimate decision-maker.

Though the *Bradley* complaint included the Detroit Board of Education, it was silent on the dozens of nearby suburban school districts that comprised the rest of the Detroit metropolitan area. This was the case for at least two reasons. First and foremost, the lawyers believed that the state of Michigan bore the lion's share of the responsibility for the plaintiffs' harms. As Dimond later emphasized in an email message to me in early 2019, "The State of Michigan was the PRIMARY and LEAD defendant. Under Michigan law, it was also our . . . view that the State of Michigan [was] the responsible party under the 14th amendment prohibition that 'No State . . . shall deny to any person within its jurisdiction the equal protection of the laws.'"[57] To that end, the plaintiffs sued the governor, the state attorney general, the state school superintendent, and the State Board of Education—all state-level entities or officials—as well as the Detroit Board of Education. (As a technical matter, the Detroit Board of Education was also a state-level agency under Michigan law.) This was why no suburban school districts were named as defendants in the complaint.

Later, former Detroit Board of Education member John Mogk expressed frustration that the plaintiffs' complaint ignored the suburbs. I interviewed Mogk in 2018.[58] During our conversation, he asked, "Why didn't he [Nate Jones] include the suburbs when he filed the case?"[59] Part of the answer was that the plaintiffs' trial team did not believe the suburbs (or their school districts) were necessary parties. Dimond put it this way: "There was case law suggesting that school districts have no constitutional right to a hearing and need not be made parties if they are not necessary for providing relief. In our preliminary thinking, the state board [of education] could provide all necessary relief, including supervision of transfers across school district lines."[60] If, in fact, all power derived from the state, naming the suburban school districts in the complaint might have had a perverse effect, suggesting they had more power than they actually possessed.[61] They weren't mini-sovereigns. It was true that cities, towns, and suburbs (and school districts) had an independent legal character. This meant that they could sue and be sued in their own right. Those units of government also enjoyed some separate powers. For instance, school districts sometimes had the ability to impose taxes and issue bonds.[62] But the powers those smaller units of government exercised were limited to the ones granted by the state. Cities, towns, suburbs, and school districts were creatures of the state; their power derived from the states in which they were located.[63] This meant they could only exercise power that was delegated to them by the state. And the states (and their subordinate units) were obligated to comply with the Constitution.[64] The plaintiffs' theory was that, if the state violated the equal protection clause, subunits of the state could be ordered to be part of the remedy.

Second, before any metropolitan remedy that might implicate the suburbs could be obtained, the plaintiffs first had to establish liability. This meant that the plaintiffs had to satisfy a court of law that the defendants named in the complaint had violated a legal obligation—like the Fourteenth Amendment of the United States Constitution. The complaint was silent on the suburbs because at this early stage, the lawyers were keenly focused on proving that the defendants named in the complaint had violated the law. They were putting first things first: prove their case first and worry about any potential suburban remedy later. Or, as Dimond put it, "As to appropriate remedies, neither Jones nor the NAACP had a clear idea at the outset."[65] Doctrinal uncertainty contributed to this. *Brown v.*

Board of Education II did contain some tantalizing language suggesting that federal courts had the power to consider "revision of school districts and attendance areas into compact units to achieve a system of determining admission to the public schools on a nonracial basis."[66] But the plaintiffs' counsel worried that this language was too slender a hook to bring multiple suburban school districts within the court's jurisdiction.[67] The real elephant in the room was this: If *Brown* applied in the North, did it require truly meaningful integration with substantial numbers of (out of district) whites? Or would elimination of the state and city mechanisms that caused segregation and adoption of a Detroit-only integration plan that involved Detroit's remaining white population be enough?

The *Detroit Free Press* was willing to look down that road. In an editorial titled "Law Holds for Detroit as Well as for Dixie," published just three days after the complaint was filed, the paper predicted—correctly—that *Brown* would apply in Detroit.[68] But it also foresaw that any remedy exempting the suburbs would be pyrrhic. "It is also true that integration in Detroit itself is of limited significance," the paper warned, "while the suburbs can throw up their defenses at Eight Mile Road and limit integration to those in the city."[69] J. "Nick" Harold Flannery, a civil rights lawyer who would later join the plaintiffs' litigation team, sent Nate Jones a provocative letter agreeing with the editorial and recommending a remedy that would include the metropolitan area.[70] A Detroit-only desegregation suit would make the situation on the ground worse, not better, he believed: "I'm suggesting that a conventional desegregation suit in a system the size of Detroit will absorb resources like the Pyramids and that its principal effect will be to accelerate white flights to Warren [a Detroit suburb] and similar havens."[71] But, he confessed, "In candor, I think that we may well lose on that issue through the Supreme Court."[72] In the end, the team decided to leave the suburbs—and any request for metropolitan relief—out of the complaint.

When the *Bradley v. Milliken* complaint was filed in late summer 1970, much had yet to be decided. During the previous decade, Shagaloff and Carter had thrown everything they had at northern-style segregation, without winning the war. As one of Carter's most trusted lieutenants put it, "Multiple components of the white power structure—from the politicians to the courts to the unions and school boards—as well as white majority voters" fought them to a draw.[73] But they hadn't lost, either. The Supreme Court had not yet spoken to the issue of *Brown*'s application in the North, and lower court precedent pointed in a variety of directions. *Brown* was still "up for grabs."

Seen from this perspective, the Detroit litigation presented a tantalizing opportunity. It was a chance, finally, to slay the dragon in one of the largest northern school districts in the country, one in which the state had brazenly attempted to reinstate segregation. A win in Detroit could be used elsewhere. As a member of the Detroit Board of Education trial team put it, one of the plaintiffs' goals was to "advance the state of the law so that facts such as those present in Detroit would become a sufficient basis for findings of de jure segregation in other districts."[74] But with great opportunities came great challenges, not the least of which was whether a meaningful desegregation remedy could be achieved in a school district that was already more than 60 percent African American.[75] There were many pitfalls on the road ahead.

———

When the plaintiffs drew Stephen Roth as the judge in their case, they were getting someone of intelligence and sensitivity. But Roth was also a man of his time, with the kind of preexisting racial attitudes that sadly reflected it. Indeed, he'd been known to "use pejorative racial epithets in private conversation."[76] But his mind wasn't closed. Roth began the litigation as a deep skeptic of the plaintiffs' claims. By the time of his death, however, the judge was one of the nation's strongest defenders of *Brown*'s promise. Roth was capable of evolution, but that didn't mean he was destined to evolve. Instead, he changed in response to the facts, facts that were brilliantly marshaled by the NAACP over the course of an historic forty-one-day trial.

In the fall of 1970, with all eyes on the Bradley case, Judge Roth sat for an interview with William Grant, the *Detroit Free Press*'s education reporter.[77] An official court portrait revealed Roth as a man in late middle age, with slightly long, graying hair combed smoothly over the sides and front. Chin resting on his right hand, eyes focused down and to the left to a point beyond the camera, Roth appeared deep in contemplation. His prominent eyebrows, strong nose, and wide forehead recalled a certain type of aging "tough guy" movie star of the era: William Holden, Robert Mitchum, Ernest Borgnine. Kicking back in a swivel chair as he lit a Cuesta-Rey Caravelle cigar, Roth struck a conciliatory tone with the journalist. "I hope I am in the position of being able to render some service to the community by helping solve this problem. But if people turn on me . . . well, that's just part of the job."[78] At this moment, Roth imagined himself Detroit's peacemaker.

Roth's biography told a classic twentieth-century American immigrant story: a young child comes to the United States speaking no English and then rises to one of the most esteemed positions in his profession. Born in the village of Sajószöged, Hungary, in 1908 to a family of modest means, Roth immigrated to the United States as a small child. Young Istvan (Stephen) sailed aboard the *Kronprinzessin Cecilie*, along with his mother, Johanna, and his older sister, Elizabeth, in steerage.[79] The family settled in the north end of Flint, Michigan, at the corner of Leith and St. John in 1913.[80] Their neighborhood (near the Buick plant where Roth's father worked) wasn't the nicest, a fact that might have led him to empathize with others who were less fortunate. An old friend remarked later about the *Bradley* case, "I know [Roth] must have gone through the tortures of hell trying to do what's right . . . That's a sensitive person, very conscientious."[81]

Roth worked hard, graduating in just two and a half years from a racially mixed public high school in Flint. After graduation, his mission was to accumulate enough funds to put himself through college. And he did, by working as a bank teller, and then as a spot welder and metal finisher in the Buick, Chevrolet, and Fisher plants in Flint.[82] Roth graduated from the University of Notre Dame in 1931, working this time as a cook and a dishwasher in a boardinghouse to earn additional money. He sold his car to pay tuition.[83] His was not a life of silver spoons. Four years later, he graduated from the University of Michigan Law School, and his life as a lawyer was underway.[84]

Roth's professional life was characterized by periods of private practice, punctuated by frequent forays into politics. A lifelong Democrat, he first campaigned for public office right out of law school (Flint City Council) and lost. But in 1940, he was elected, this time to the office of Genesee County prosecutor. In that position he prosecuted and won a case—by some accounts the first ever in the state—protecting the rights of a black man who had been refused service in a restaurant.[85] Still, Roth was never considered a liberal. Throughout his career as a politician and then later on the bench, Roth was "a deliberate man within the Democratic party's conservative wing."[86] He served as a state court judge in Genesee County for ten years. Then in 1962, President John F. Kennedy appointed him to the federal district court for the Eastern District of Michigan. He would serve as a federal trial judge for the rest of his life.

10

TAKING ON NORTHERN JIM CROW

t 11:15 a.m. on Thursday, August 27, 1970, with school set to
open on September 8, Judge Roth held the very first hearing in
the *Bradley v. Milliken* case. The hearing concerned a request
that the plaintiffs had made of the judge: that he order the defendants to
stop implementing Public Act 48 and require them to reinstate the April 7
high school integration plan—all before the start of the upcoming school
year.

At this early stage of the case, Roth was unsympathetic, if not hostile,
to the plaintiffs' attorneys. Paul Dimond described the judge at this point
as "impatient."[1] Jones concurred and characterized him as reacting with
"considerable irritation."[2] William Grant agreed with the plaintiffs' assessment of Roth's early skepticism. In an article titled *Roth's Views Did Dramatic Turnabout*, the reporter wrote that early on the judge "suggested
that 'the outsiders' [NAACP] should leave Detroit alone 'so it can solve its
own problems.'"[3] Roth warned the attorneys, "I would think it unlikely you
could persuade the court to move with instant dispatch. I am not comput-
erized. I am not automated, so you can't expect pushbutton relief here . . .
I'm not going to move hastily."[4] Nothing had yet convinced him that Detroit was running a "dual system of schools, either de jure or de facto."[5] If
anything, Roth believed the Detroit Board of Education had behaved in
an exemplary fashion: "To the contrary, the evidence before the court indicates that there has been a conscious, deliberate, progressive, and continu-

ous attempt to promote and advance integration of both pupils and faculty. This has occurred without the sanction of an injunction."[6]

So on September 3, 1970, Judge Roth denied the plaintiffs' request to restore the April 7 integration plan.[7] Bristling with disappointment, Nathaniel Jones issued a terse formal statement that threw down the gauntlet. It began, "Today's denial of the application by Negro school children in Detroit, and the Detroit NAACP Branch for [an order] against the recent action by the Michigan Legislature, will be appealed immediately to the U.S. Court of Appeals for the Sixth Circuit."[8] Calling Roth's determination "unsupportable in law," Jones continued, "we deeply regret that the rights of black children are once again ignored in a decision that is out of harmony with the whole trend of removing racial bars to equal educational opportunities."[9] The plaintiffs had lost round one. But the case was far from over.

On October 13, 1970, the federal judiciary gave the NAACP just what it wanted. The United States Court of Appeals for the Sixth Circuit, sitting in Cincinnati, ruled that Act 48 was unconstitutional. Judge Roth had gotten it wrong, and the Sixth Circuit was going to correct him. The appeals court wrote, "State action in any form, whether by statute, act of the executive department of a State or local government . . . will not be permitted to impede, delay, or frustrate proceedings to protect the rights guaranteed to members of all races under the Fourteenth Amendment."[10]

The NAACP's decision to appeal Roth's ruling was vindicated. What happened in Michigan looked too much like southern intransigence to let it slide. Responding to the assistant attorney general at oral argument in the Sixth Circuit, Lucas had said, "I must confess to a certain feeling of déjà vu . . . I can't tell whether I've been listening to Michigan's attorney general or Mississippi's attorney general."[11] The appeals court agreed. (One of the judges reportedly chuckled at Lucas's remark.)[12] But this was still the same court that had decided the *Deal* case just four years before—the same court that said, as the Sixth Circuit put it, that there was no obligation "to bus white and Negro children away from districts of their residence" to achieve racial balance.[13] How was that possible? It did what many courts do when they don't want to explicitly overturn a recent precedent: it made a distinction. The Detroit Board of Education took "affirmative steps on its own initiative" to achieve integration.[14] And that was precisely what the state wanted to stop: "This action was thwarted, or at least delayed, by an act of the State Legislature. No comparable situation was presented in *Deal*."[15] So the Sixth Circuit struck down the state law.[16] "The District Judge is directed to give no effect to . . . Act 48, because of its unconstitutionality," the appellate court wrote.[17] Young's compromise was dead.

The Sixth Circuit had answered the relatively easy question of whether Young's compromise violated the Constitution. The answer was yes. The *Detroit Free Press* summarized the appellate court's ruling: "In effect, the judges said state legislators do not have authority to overrule local school boards seeking to increase integration."[18] But because the complaint told two stories, not just one, the case wasn't over. Harder questions remained. Per the Sixth Circuit: "We conclude the [other] issues presented in this case, involving the public school system of a large city, can best be determined only after a full evidentiary hearing."[19] This meant that there would still have to be a trial in the federal district court on the question of whether Detroit had already been operating a Jim Crow "separate and unequal" school system. For this reason, the appellate court remanded the case to Judge Roth. It was unlikely to be a quick and uncomplicated affair.

The NAACP took a victory lap. Tom Turner, president of the Detroit branch, framed the win from a larger perspective, implicitly recognizing the contribution of black activists. The final sentence of his press release attempted to "thread the needle" between the NAACP's historic commitment to integration and the rising calls for black power: "The NAACP intends to stay in the vanguard of those forces who militantly struggle through the democratic process to secure integration in American life."[20] For Zwerdling, now off the board because of the recall, it was a moment of sweet vindication: "The U.S. Court of Appeals has confirmed our understanding of the law. The April 1970 action of the board was taken because it was morally and legally right."[21] Jones stated simply: "We have succeeded in freeing the Detroit Board of Education of the shackles placed by the legislature. It is expected that in due course the April 7th plan will be effectuated."[22]

One could certainly have read the court of appeals ruling as requiring the board of education to implement the April 7 plan by the earliest possible date. This was not Judge Roth's interpretation. In early November 1970, he gave the board significant latitude to submit a variety of different desegregation plans, as long as they achieved roughly the same amount of integration as the April 7 plan, and could be implemented by the first day of the upcoming spring semester.[23] The options varied widely. One of them, a magnet school plan designed by conservative Patrick McDonald, now the president of the board of education, dispensed with any requirement that the high schools integrate; it made integration entirely voluntary.

But many white parents failed to appreciate the judge's flexibility. On November 14, 1970, the board held a rare Saturday meeting to publicly preview the plans it intended to submit to Judge Roth. Braving rain and snow, six hundred angry white parents, some carrying antibusing signs, showed up to harangue the board. Some of the parents' signs carried choice words for Judge Roth. One read: "I smell something Rothen."[24] Another stated that "I'd rather fight Roth than switch schools."[25] Yet another described Roth as a "cruel animal."[26] Some members of the crowd openly advocated defying federal court orders.[27] "Tell Judge Roth that this is his decision and he can enforce it," Ross Christie, of a Gratiot-Chalmers homeowners group, declared.[28] Harry Salsinger, covering the meeting for *The Detroit News*, wrote that "speaker after speaker repeated, 'Our children will go to a neighborhood school or not at all.'"[29] The few who spoke in favor of the April 7 plan were loudly booed. Ultimately, the board of education submitted three plans to Judge Roth: the April 7 plan, the magnet school plan, and a part-time curricular plan with specialized courses intended to attract a biracial enrollment.

On December 3, 1970, Judge Roth approved McDonald's magnet school plan. Each magnet school would serve two of the city's eight geographically defined educational regions and provide specialized educational subjects (vocational studies, business, the arts, and the sciences), thereby attracting, at least theoretically, a more racially diverse student body.[30] But the proposal was entirely voluntary, in contrast to the April 7 plan, which expressly required race mixing in specific high schools. At the time, magnet schools were a new educational innovation. Observers had reason to believe that they might help integrate some school systems. Typically regarded as the nation's first magnet school that was designed expressly to integrate, the McCarver Elementary School in Tacoma, Washington, had opened in 1968.[31] It was intended to be "good enough to pull in white students from the more affluent neighborhoods."[32] And it did. But Tacoma, unlike Detroit, had never been sued for violating the principles enunciated in *Brown*. In contrast, McDonald offered a magnet school plan *as a remedy* for what an appeals court held was a constitutional violation. In the South, that kind of remedy would not fly. As the Supreme Court had recently held in the *Green v. New Kent County* case, the use of purely voluntary, "freedom of choice" plans alone could not satisfy school districts' obligations under *Brown*.[33]

In his order, Roth attempted to cast himself as a neutral decision-maker tasked with making a difficult decision against the background of timeless truths. He began portentously: "Child-raising, that is, education, is the first and largest industry of every species, including man . . . A school system is but one, and perhaps the most important, way in which the human society discharges its responsibility to its young, to itself and to its survival."[34] But then he got down to brass tacks. Integration was important, but quality education trumped that goal in significance. From Roth's perspective, a voluntary program made sense. But the April 7 integration plan was "forced-feeding."[35] His supposition was that obtaining quality, integrated education in Detroit could not be achieved without voluntary white participation. The judge wrote: "If to integrate is 'to combine to form a more complete, harmonious or coordinated entity,' then the [magnet] plan we have chosen is . . . most likely to be productive. It places the emphasis not on 'desegregation' (representing the legal right of blacks), but on 'integration' (an ideal of social acceptability)."[36] And his skepticism of the plaintiffs' case had not yet abated: "We cannot at this point proceed on the assumption that plaintiffs will succeed in proving their claim, in the hearing on the merits, that the Detroit school is a segregated school system, de jure or de facto."[37]

From Roth, the new board of education got everything it asked for and then some. He gave the board additional time to implement the voluntary magnet plan, and postponed the start of the trial until "sometime in early spring 1971."[38] Roth's generosity surprised one school board member. Stunned, he admitted, "We never expected the judge to accept a voluntary plan. We thought Roth would disregard McDonald's plan."[39] Cornelius Golightly, who had been appointed to fill Remus Robinson's seat after his death, was incredulous.[40] "If the court wanted an integration plan with a lot of form and no substance, then this was the plan. It will cost nothing and it will do nothing," he told the *Detroit Free Press*.[41] Golightly later became the first black president of the Detroit Board of Education.[42]

Explaining his decision at an unusual in-chamber news conference, Roth tipped his hand. He scolded the NAACP's lawyers, accusing them of carpetbagging: "[You] outsiders . . . should go away and let Detroit solve its own problems."[43] The difficulty with Roth's statement was that Verda Bradley was hardly an opportunist. Her interests were local, specific to her family. She was a Detroiter trying to solve a Detroit problem: the inequities at Clinton Elementary and the segregation of the city's public schools. Roth was openly hostile to the plaintiffs' case. He had, according to Dimond, "laid bare his ideology."[44]

There were now a few months to wait before the trial began in the spring of 1971. In the meantime, the CCBE pursued a bid to get formally involved in the case. Newly victorious after the recall election, the group had moved to "intervene" as a defendant in the *Bradley v. Milliken* litigation when the plaintiffs first filed the lawsuit.[45] (Outside parties may intervene in ongoing federal litigation in order to protect their interests—be joined as official parties to the lawsuit—if they meet certain requirements under federal court rules.) In its legal papers, CCBE said its purpose was "to promote quality education and preserve the neighborhood school as an integral principle of education in the Detroit Metropolitan Area."[46] This was true. But what the organization's papers neglected to mention was that, in practice, it represented *white parents* whose children attended the Detroit public schools.

At the hearing on CCBE's motion, Alexander Ritchie, the organization's lawyer, told the court that it was his clients' "profound conviction that the Detroit System as it has been operated in the past and as it is being operated today is not, and has never been a segregated school system."[47] CCBE agreed with the defendants that they had not committed any constitutional violation. On that front, there was no need to intervene, as the group's interests were already being represented by the defendants' attorneys. But CCBE's legal position went beyond what the defendants were arguing. Its view was that the plaintiffs' claims threatened white parents in a very specific and constitutionally relevant way. "Intervening defendants now assert that they have a constitutional right under the 14th amendment to attend the school nearest their home without the necessity that the school be racially balanced in accordance with the demands of the plaintiffs," the organization asserted.[48]

This was a curious argument given that there was (and is) no constitutionally protected right to attend one's neighborhood school. Notwithstanding that, the group's participation made it clear that white Detroiters were going to make their voices heard. Perhaps most importantly, the organization was looking ahead to what type of relief the court would order were it to find for the the plaintiffs. CCBE sought to be included in the lawsuit as a defendant because it was adamantly opposed to "enforced busing throughout the Detroit school system."[49]

Initially, Judge Roth denied CCBE's motion to intervene.[50] At the hearing on CCBE's motion it appeared that the judge's concern was keeping the case from running off the rails. "If you are permitted to intervene as a party here . . . what is to prevent a lot of other people [state and local taxpayers, school building contractors, labor unions] from asking to come in?" Roth mused.[51] But then, on March 22, 1971, he changed his mind. Just before the trial was set to begin, Judge Roth entered an order that would have a profound impact on the case. Roth allowed CCBE to intervene as a defendant as long as it did not "in any serious way interfere with the presentation or production of the case on behalf of the principal defendant."[52] The stage was set for the trial.

———

The trial began at 9:40 a.m. on Tuesday, April 6, 1971. The plaintiffs' task was to show that Detroit's public schools were segregated in violation of the Fourteenth Amendment. Lucas's opening statement framed the issues for the court. He began, "This case originated with respect to the plaintiffs and their counsel in terms of the act of the legislature impeding certain efforts of the Detroit Board to desegregate some of its schools."[53] But then Lucas pivoted to the complaint's second story about preexisting segregation—which made sense. After all, the Sixth Circuit Court of Appeals had already invalidated Young's compromise: "In the trial of the case on the merits, the District Judge is directed to give no effect to . . . Act 48."[54]

Lucas continued, telling the court that "there existed in the school system of the city of Detroit, a pattern which inescapably led to the conclusion that there was purposeful segregation of the schools, elementary, junior, senior high, that the faculties have been purposefully segregated."[55] The NAACP attorney was previewing the plaintiffs' argument. They sought to show that the Detroit Board of Education—intentionally, purposefully, deliberately—used a variety of techniques to segregate the schools: student and faculty assignments, transportation policies, school construction and site selection determinations, and more.[56] How would the plaintiffs prove that the defendants used these mechanisms *intentionally* to segregate the schools? Lucas appeared to concede that there wasn't much direct evidence of intent—but the circumstantial evidence was a mile high. "It's not merely a case of a few incidents," Lucas asserted, "but it all adds up to a segregated pattern in terms of result, and we submit in terms of intent."[57] So this would be the plaintiffs' case. Piece by piece, brick by brick, they would build a wall of evidence that led to but one conclusion: the Detroit public schools were de jure—not de facto—segregated. Lucas told the court that the Detroit case was "a classic 14th amendment lawsuit and will be presented to the court in that manner."[58] Few could have missed the lawyer's meaning. The quintessential "classic 14th amendment lawsuit" in the school context was, of course, *Brown*. The statement suggested that, notwithstanding the regional difference, the two cases were inexorably linked. And if the state action challenged in *Brown* was a violation of the Fourteenth Amendment, so, too, was the state action challenged in the Detroit case.

There was one more thing: housing. Lucas continued, "In addition, we will show that the Board by its [school] construction policy has consciously

utilized the pattern of racial residential segregation in the city of Detroit"
to segregate the schools.[59] Like the Kerner Commission, the *Bradley*
plaintiffs believed that residential segregation caused school segregation.
The relationship between the two kinds of segregation was complex. It was
both synergistic (school and housing segregation taken together created a
uniquely devastating harm) and symbiotic (each one abetted the other).
If this was the case, then the *causes of residential segregation* had to be
probed. This raised extraordinary litigation difficulties. The challenge was
that residential segregation had multiple overlapping causes. There were
any number of actors who weren't before Judge Roth—brokers, insurance
companies, banks, title companies, city housing officials, white families
who threatened violence if blacks moved into their neighborhoods and the
police force that protected them, and myriad federal actors—who were
responsible for residential segregation in Detroit. Some of these actors
were bound by the Constitution because they were "state actors": the police, city housing officials. But others were private actors, such as white
families, brokers, insurance companies. The Constitution didn't constrain
their actions.

So the plaintiffs had several challenges. The first was figuring out how
to tell such a complex story. How, exactly, did all of the pieces fit together?
Was residential segregation a static condition or did its effects, such as
the boundaries within which the racial constraints operated, change over
time?

The second task was connecting Detroit's residential segregation
story—which included both public and private players—to the actions of
the defendants the plaintiffs *had sued*. This was exactly where the federal
appellate court in *Deal* had stumbled. In *Deal*, the Sixth Circuit Court of
Appeals said, "Because of factors in the private housing market . . . the
imposition of the neighborhood concept on existing residential patterns
in Cincinnati creates some schools which are predominantly or wholly of
one race or another. Appellants insist that this situation . . . presents the
same separation and hence the same constitutional violation condemned
in *Brown*. *We do not accept this contention*."[60] Later, Nick Flannery, now
a member of the plaintiffs' trial team, spoke to this very challenge. He
told the court that "the dichotomy between so-called de facto and de

jure school segregation is simplistic to the point of naivete, that school segregation cannot be separated from the policies of public and private discrimination in housing, and the dynamics of those policies."[61]

Finally, the plaintiffs had to deal with *Deal*. Perhaps residential segregation had overlapping causes and multiple protagonists, public and private. But in many instances, the government itself discriminated on the basis of race in housing. Not only that, it also sanctioned, assisted, furthered, bankrolled, enabled, and enforced private racial discrimination in the real estate market. Then the school authorities, by use of the neighborhood school rule and other techniques, intentionally swallowed these discriminatory acts whole. The question was where their culpability began.

The defendants enjoyed a safe harbor as long as everyone agreed that the racial cast of Detroit's neighborhoods was entirely voluntary. "Can it be said that this limitation [the neighborhood school rule] shares the arbitrary, invidious characteristics of a racially restrictive system? We think not," the Sixth Circuit had concluded in *Deal*.[62] From this perspective, there was no "state action," much less a violation of the Constitution. The defendants' argument, which Dimond helpfully summarized, was that "school authorities imposed no racial restrictions on school assignments because families freely chose the neighborhood in which they wished to live and send their children to school."[63]

The plaintiffs had to pierce this fantasy, which was at the core of how northern Jim Crow actually operated. As Dimond put it, "If we could show that the housing segregation resulted from racial discrimination . . . then we might be able to [prove] that school authorities should not get off scot-free by arguing that they only incorporated residential segregation through an allegedly neutral system of neighborhood pupil assignments."[64] The plaintiffs' job was to strip the bark off neutrality, voluntariness, and choice. They had to show that intentional racial segregation was, in effect, the Detroit public school system's *official policy*.

Earlier northern school segregation cases, such as *Deal*, *Taylor*, and *Bell*, had challenged some of the very same discriminatory techniques that the Detroit school system employed. But the *Bradley* case was remarkable in some ways. What made it so was the plaintiffs' overarching commitment to probing the relationship between schools and housing. The Kerner

Commission had observed that most inner-city schools were highly segregated and pointed the finger directly at housing: "Racial isolation in the urban public schools results largely from residential segregation."[65] This observation showed the true scope of the Detroit litigation: by exposing the intimate and interdependent relationship between schools and housing, the plaintiffs effectively put the *entire structure of northern segregation on trial*.

If the plaintiffs could prevail in Detroit, in one of the nation's largest school systems, then perhaps they could succeed anywhere in the country. Would the Detroit litigation finally "cash in" on the valiant efforts of the countless activists who had pushed for school desegregation in the North? It would take forty-one days to try the constitutional violation (ten full days of which focused on residential segregation in the Detroit area), thousands of hours of preparation, countless exhibits, witnesses, and depositions, and a small stable of experts to find out.

=====

On April 19, 1971, and just after the *Bradley v. Milliken* trial had gotten underway, the United States Senate began debate on legislation that had the potential to dramatically reshape the nation's metropolitan areas, North and South. The proposed legislation spoke directly to the complex problem with which the trial team in the Detroit case—and the Kerner Commission before it—struggled.

In his proposed amendment to an education funding bill, the liberal Connecticut Democrat Abraham Ribicoff had nothing less than the eradication of American apartheid in his sights.[66] Writing in *The New York Times*, Tom Wicker called the proposal "the first serious attack on racial division in America."[67] The proposal was nothing if not ambitious. Create a nationwide school integration program. Check. Destroy the misleading de jure / de facto distinction. Check. Focus on the metropolitan area rather than the school district as the appropriate target of federal desegregation efforts. Check. Front-burner residential segregation as a key driver of school segregation. Check. Employ Congress's "heavy artillery," the threat of cutting off federal funds for noncompliance with integration mandates. Check. Leave room for state and local preferences and experimentation in meeting federal integration goals. Check.

And that wasn't all. The senator paired the integration bill with a companion proposal that directly targeted suburban residential segregation. Ribicoff wanted to prevent federal facilities from locating (or federal contractors from doing business) in any community unless it provided adequate low- and middle-income housing for government workers.[68] Federal money would be available to help communities construct the housing, which was the carrot. The ability to cancel the private contracts of firms that moved to errant communities or prevent federal facilities from relocating to such localities, was the stick.[69] Journalist Tom Wicker titled his column praising the Connecticut senator's effort "Mr. Ribicoff Comes Through."[70] Noted black columnist William Raspberry was less complimentary. "Mere integration isn't likely to solve any of the problems now confronting blacks," he warned.[71] But he nevertheless offered qualified support for the senator's efforts. "But to the degree that the Ribicoff proposals go toward giving blacks a choice about where they will live and educate their children, they are very much worthwhile. That alone may be reason enough to enact them."[72]

The core of Ribicoff's proposal was straightforward. In exchange for federal education money, state and local educational agencies were required to submit a plan detailing how they would integrate the public schools.[73] Ribicoff was talking big money: twenty to twenty-five *billion* dollars during the implementation phase of the program.[74] But this big, fat, juicy carrot wasn't the only inducement. There was also a stick. "Any [school] district . . . refusing to participate should lose all of its Federal funds and states which continue to provide their own funds to such a district should lose Federal education monies allocated to them," Ribicoff warned.[75] In effect, the bill said: you give us integration, we give you federal money. The proposal bribed white suburbanites to integrate their schools. At the same time, it stressed the importance of local control, experimentation, and flexibility. The bill emphasized the participation of local stakeholders, parents, teachers, and students drawn from both "minority and majority population groups."[76] These multiracial groups would consult with local educational authorities to develop a plan that would "reduce and eliminate minority group isolation in our public schools, whatever the cause of such isolation."[77] "A plan developed at the local level is much more likely to be supported by those in the community than one imposed by authorities from Washington or another city," Ribicoff stated later.[78]

Under the proposal, localities could use, and the federal government would fund, a variety of devices to enhance integration. These methods included magnet schools; redrawing school boundaries; creating unified school districts; pairing majority white schools and school districts with majority minority schools and school districts; and, of course, busing.[79] But it was up to the localities to choose the means through which they fulfilled the federal mandate. The bill also provided funding for the "soft costs" necessary to make integration work at the granular level: counselors and training to assist children and teachers of all races to adjust to a desegregated environment, in-school education programs, extracurriculars, public education efforts, community activities, and cooperative exchanges. The purpose of these mechanisms was to ease the transition from racial isolation to racial integration, to break down racial enmity on all sides.[80] Finally, the proposal suggested a particularly exciting cutting-edge technique for achieving racial diversity: education parks. (One of the bill's proponents cited an article by Thomas Pettigrew describing them as an "elegantly effective" solution to the problem of school segregation.)[81] Even education park enthusiasts conceded that they were expensive. Ribicoff was offering to pay for them and all the rest.

The bill conditioned receipt of federal money on coming into compliance with the federal government's preferred policy outcome. This was how joint federal-state spending programs typically worked. Less typical was Ribicoff's target. His proposal dispensed with normal state and local jurisdictional boundaries. Village, town, city, and county boundaries were irrelevant. School district lines were immaterial. The senator explained his hostility to school district lines: "We need to understand that the traditional units of government with which we deal in education—school districts—are part of the racial isolation problem, not its solution."[82] Ribicoff thought school district lines operated as fences. "It is precisely because of the existence of such boundaries and supports lent to such boundaries by other official or private action, that the majority race has been able successfully to isolate itself from minorities," he wrote.[83] These fences had to be unlocked, their gates thrown open. The only way to do so was by transcending "existing school district boundaries."[84]

Instead of the school district, the proposal's unit of measurement was the "standard metropolitan statistical area," or "SMSA." Developed by the Census Bureau, SMSAs typically contained numerous jurisdictions that were economically and socially linked. In 1970, the Detroit SMSA contained dozens of cities and towns (including Detroit, Warren, Dearborn, and other suburbs), stretched across three counties (Wayne, Oakland, and Macomb), and counted more than four million people, just under half of the state's total population.[85] Ribicoff's proposal treated areas like the Detroit SMSA as a single community for the purposes of education. This was the most important part of the bill. And it was radical.

Under the proposal, the Detroit SMSA would effectively have had a *single metropolitan school system*. Under the standard model, suburbanites' property taxes paid for no small portion of their children's neighborhood school. This model of education funding placed a premium on local residency and encouraged suburban residents to hoard resources. Why pay for a nonresident's child to be educated, particularly if that child was black? Now federal money would work to pull suburbanites' preferences in the other direction. It was as if Ribicoff were saying to them: "You want segregation? Fine. Reach into your pocket and pay for it because we won't." The integration goal he set wasn't extraordinarily aggressive. Ribicoff wanted each school in a given SMSA to roughly reflect the minority concentration of the SMSA as a whole. The schools didn't need to mirror the area's demographics exactly. Far from it. Fifty percent would do. So, if the SMSA's proportion of minority students was one-quarter, twelve and one-half percent at the individual school level was just fine.[86] Localities had twelve years to achieve this goal: two years for planning and a ten-year implementation period.[87]

One scholar of northern segregation wrote: "Looking back on Ribicoff's proposal, it boggles the twenty-first-century mind. Try to imagine the integration of every school system within a twelve-year span. It sounds fantastical, too good to be true."[88] The Minnesota senator Walter Mondale introduced Ribicoff's proposal: "The pending amendment to this measure by the Senator from Connecticut is, in my opinion, the most courageous and perhaps most hopeful single effort that I have seen to deal with the problem of the large ghetto and need to approach it from a metropolitan standpoint."[89] But the nation never found out if Ribicoff's bill overpromised and underdelivered. The country could only wonder if it was just an audacious fantasy, a piece of ill-conceived social engineering of the highest order. The nation would never know because Ribicoff's bill died on the floor of the U.S. Senate.

With Congress failing to advance desegregation in the North, the ball was even more in the judiciary's court. Ribicoff expressed doubt that the Supreme Court could succeed where Congress had failed. Just before the Senate voted on his proposal he stated: "I do not know what the Supreme Court will do in the future, but it would be tragic if the Supreme Court were not to strike down segregation in the North."[90] But if he was going down, he would go down swinging. So he lobbied the high court directly from the floor of the United States Senate: "The Supreme Court says that de jure segregation is wrong. I think that they must say that de facto segregation is also wrong."[91]

11

ANOTHER BRICK IN THE WALL

Containment. If there was one word, one idea, one theory that defined the plaintiffs' case, it was "containment." The concept of the containment was the fixed star in their evidentiary constellation. This was how the plaintiffs' attorney Nick Flannery previewed the concept to Judge Roth: "The principle [is] that racial containment of black persons in Detroit, as in many of our major metropolitan areas, is not a fortuitous phenomenon but it is in fact a result of private and public housing discrimination which permeated our generation and those before it and, your Honor, further there is an interlocking relationship between the racial composition of schools and discrimination with respect to housing opportunities."[1]

But what did Flannery's statement really mean? The dictionary defines "containment" as the act of "controlling or limiting something or someone harmful."[2] It was impossible to understand the plaintiffs' containment theory without appreciating the extent to which blacks were viewed not just as harm-causing agents, but as contagions to be quarantined and avoided at all costs. The plaintiffs' theory was that white Detroiters were engaged in a constant rearguard action of containing, controlling, and stonewalling, of separating themselves from African Americans.

The containment idea surfaced throughout the trial. One witness

defined "containment" as in essence "the very careful and deliberate pre-
vention of blacks or any other particular minority from being able to move
freely in a given community."[3] Another witness provided a slightly more
expansive characterization, one that directly implicated the real estate industry. He told the court: "When the areas in which black families have
already been permitted to reside no longer supply enough houses for the
housing demand in the black community, well then, block by block, square
mile by square mile, the periphery of the areas in which black people reside is expanded, and the white families residing therein are induced to
move and to sell their homes to black families."[4] Did the containment just
operate within the four corners of the city of Detroit? Hardly. Yet another
witness stated, "Containment of black persons in Detroit is operating not
only in the portions of Detroit that remain white in residency, but also in
the surrounding [suburban] areas."[5] Was the containment just a series of
random, unconnected acts? Not a chance. Instead, it was *policy*. As the
plaintiffs' young attorney Paul Dimond argued (somewhat rhetorically):
"Your Honor, if the defendant were willing to stipulate to the policy of
containment practiced by both the public school officials and the public
officials in charge of housing and various agencies and private persons and
residential patterns, our whole point is that hand in hand this policy of
containment has denied Fourteenth Amendment rights."[6]

The idea was to put as much geographical space as possible—to erect
impermeable buffer zones—between the races. And when blacks spilled
over one wall and escaped one zone, whites would erect yet another barrier
and move farther out. The process was dynamic, meaning it involved multiple parties. It was historic, meaning it had been going on for a very long
time. It was common, meaning it characterized not just Detroit but most,
if not all, major cities in metropolitan areas. And it had never stopped. This
was how the ghetto was built. It was as if blacks and whites were playing a
series of repeated "cat and mouse" games.[7] But these weren't really games
at all, because the stakes were too high. How, exactly, did the containment
concept relate to the plaintiffs' trial burden? Dimond: "Our theory of the
case [would] . . . be built around the theme that school authorities worked
hand in glove with other community actors to contain blacks in separate
schools and to protect whites, for as long as possible, from having to attend

school with any substantial number of minority children."[8] In order to do that, "the specific links between housing and school segregation . . . would have to be developed as the trial progressed."[9]

Judge Roth got his first taste of containment on April 6, 1971, the first day of trial. A leading treatise on trial techniques noted that "in the courtroom as well, a picture was indeed worth a thousand words. If a picture was so useful, so too could be a map."[10] If there was one exhibit that changed the course of the *Milliken* trial, it was this: a ten-by-twenty-foot map of Detroit which the plaintiffs' trial team placed to Judge Roth's right, just above the heads of defense counsel. They intentionally positioned it directly in Roth's line of sight so that he often stared at it "when contemplating an issue or looking away from a witness."[11] Beginning with the most recent official census data and extending back thirty years (1970, 1960, 1950, and 1940), the map used four separate overlays to depict the extent and scope of residential segregation in the city of Detroit. The map told the story—pictorially—of how the "cat and mouse" game played out over a generation and a half.[12]

Later, one of the defendants' lawyers would concede, "It was the smartest thing the NAACP did in the case. Who could look at that map for four months and not realize that Detroit was segregated?"[13] Dimond agreed. In 2022, he told me that "the best thing we did as trial counsel was start with the evidence of pervasive housing discrimination throughout metropolitan Detroit causing an expanding black core always surrounded by an expanding white ring, with this primary color line of containment fast approaching the boundaries of the Detroit School District. This harsh reality—mapped before his eyes—visibly converted Judge Roth by day ten of the violation hearing."[14]

What caused the containment? The answer was that there was no single cause. There was no lone "smoking gun," no easy explanation. Whites used many methods and techniques to contain blacks within certain areas of Detroit. The map, with its layered overlays of census data, represented a kind of archaeological dig into Detroit's residential history. Similarly, the housing case that the plaintiffs' counsel would present (the first ten days of the trial) was like a tapestry—composed of many invisible threads, which when woven together yielded a striking, unified design. The discriminatory

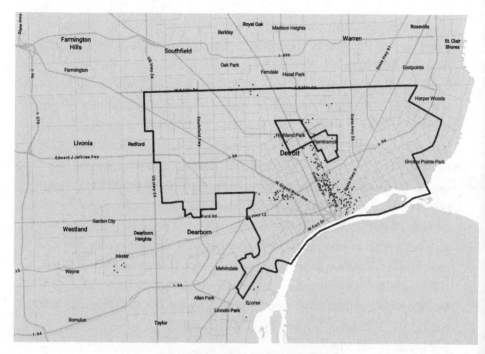

Black population of Detroit, 1940

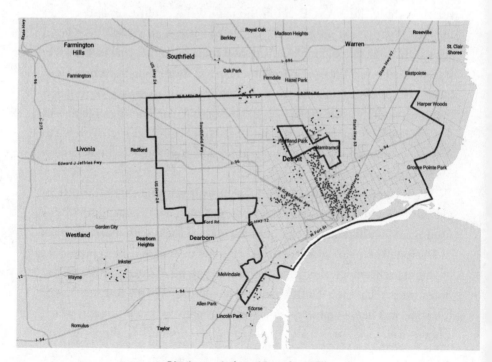

Black population of Detroit, 1950

EACH DOT REPRESENTS ONE HUNDRED BLACK RESIDENTS.

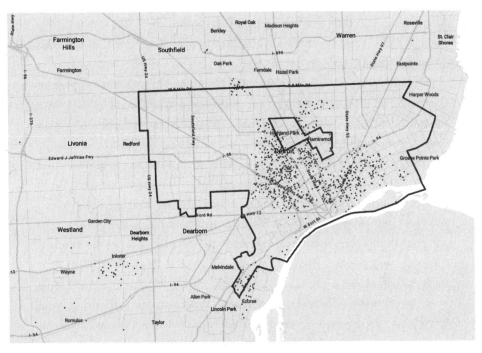

Black population of Detroit, 1960

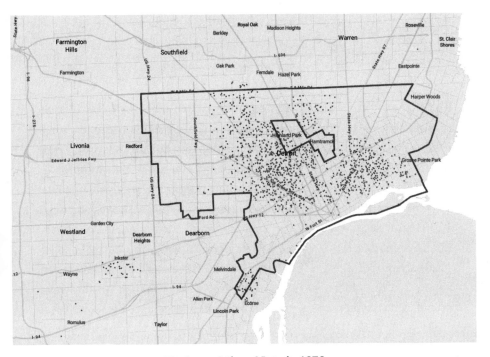

Black population of Detroit, 1970

methods and techniques that caused segregation were the threads. The plaintiffs' job was to demonstrate how, when woven together, those threads created the containment.

Later, education reporter William Grant would call this portion of the trial "an elaborate housing discrimination case," which "attorneys for the NAACP . . . say is the best ever presented in a school integration case."[15] And it almost didn't happen. Believing that the housing evidence was unnecessary, Roth had pressured the board to stipulate to the fact that Detroit's housing was racially segregated.[16] Why the pressure? Because at that point, Roth didn't see the relationship between housing and schools. As Grant described it, "Judge Roth, believing that the case was being unnecessarily prolonged, tried to convince the board's counsel to stipulate the existence of segregation in housing, which at that point he considered irrelevant."[17] Had it done so, the plaintiffs' housing case would never have been so extensive. The board's refusal to do so was almost certainly an "own goal." As it would turn out, the housing evidence had a catalytic effect on the judge's thinking, exposing him to detailed information about residential segregation in *both* the city and the suburbs. The housing case almost certainly changed the nature of the desegregation order Roth ultimately imposed.

The plaintiffs tapped Richard Marks, assistant director of the Detroit Commission on Community Relations, to explain the containment process.[18] (The agency was created in the 1940s to investigate and resolve race discrimination claims in housing, employment, education, and law enforcement.) Rising from his seat and approaching the map, Marks launched into a synthesis of thirty years of Detroit's residential history. It wasn't pretty. In 1940, Marks said, the census "clearly showed major areas of concentration as being black . . . as a central city population group but with some major areas of dispersion."[19] He continued, "Historically blacks have lived within . . . the older city bounded by Livernois, bounded on the west, bounded by Connor on the east and bounded in general by Six Mile on the North."[20] Ten years later, he said, "the basic containment pattern, non-whites in the city, began to emerge very clearly."[21]

Translation: between 1940 and 1950, Detroit's black population doubled, but there was nowhere to go.[22] Black Detroiters were stuck, hemmed in, corralled. Later, noted sociologist Karl Taeuber would confirm that Detroit's experience was hardly exceptional. He testified that "racial residential segregation . . . prevails in the North and in the South, among industrial cities, among resort cities, university towns, large cities, smaller cities. In effect it was a universal pattern . . . There were some changes between 1940 and 1960, but for the most part by this point in our history all cities were highly segregated."[23]

Marks noted that by 1950, "restrictive covenants have now been declared unenforceable."[24] These covenants were race-based deed restrictions. Lawyers often said these types of covenants "ran with the land," meaning they restricted the use or sale of the property in perpetuity and could not be negotiated away. But the obvious question was who would enforce the covenants. It would have been one thing if whites effectuated covenants through peer pressure, such as by ostracizing a neighbor who threatened to sell her home to a black family. This might have been immoral, but it would not have amounted to state action. But covenants were enforced by the state courts via injunction. And they *were* state actors. The covenants were private agreements. But did judicial enforcement convert them, in effect, to public acts to which the Constitution applied? The question that reached the Supreme Court in 1948 was whether judicial enforcement of racially restrictive covenants violated the equal protection clause.[25] In *Shelley v. Kraemer*, the court said the answer to that question was yes.[26] The case had a strong Michigan connection. One of the restrictive covenant cases consolidated for review by the Supreme Court in *Shelley*—*Sipes v. McGhee*—had originated in Detroit.[27] Robert C. Weaver's 1948 magisterial study of urban housing, *The Negro Ghetto*, emphasized the ubiquitous nature of racially restrictive covenants in Detroit.[28] Weaver, who would later become the very first Secretary of Housing and Urban Development, wrote: "Covenants and other devices in [Detroit] . . . eliminate Negroes from most of the land and houses in the city."[29]

By prohibiting state court injunctions, *Shelley* took the teeth out of racial covenants. (Later, the Fair Housing Act would prohibit their use even if no effort was made to enforce them.)[30] But by midcentury, much of the damage in Detroit and other cities already had been done. In effect, the covenants acted as racialized zoning codes, excluding blacks from occupying housing in three-quarters of the city of Detroit.[31] Later testimony suggested that it was even worse than that. On the second day of the trial, Allen E. Priestley, the vice president of the largest title company in Detroit, told the court that "from 1910 through February 15, 1950, *almost all new subdivisions throughout Metropolitan Detroit* [including the suburbs] contained restrictions and covenants against ownership and occupancy by Negroes."[32]

It was hard to overestimate the importance of this statement. This meant that blacks were trapped in the older sections of the city even as Detroit, the fastest-growing city in the country, dramatically expanded.[33] Whites could move out of Detroit, but racially restrictive covenants in the suburbs made it nearly impossible for blacks to do the same.[34] Racially restrictive covenants were ubiquitous, and their aftereffects lingered long after the Supreme Court nullified them. Priestley made another notable admission along these lines. "The racial restrictions contained in deeds continued to be reported by Burton Abstract & Title Company in its abstracts and title insurance policies until December 16, 1969."[35] The date was a head-scratcher. It was more than a year and a half *after* the Fair Housing Act was enacted—and more than twenty years after the *Shelley* decision. "Of course it was not our business to enforce these restrictions," Priestley stated later.[36] "We merely reported to the potential buyer that such a restriction had been placed on the title in the past and left it up to the buyer to decide what to do," was Priestley's self-serving defense. The United States Department of Justice wasn't buying what Priestley was selling. Burton only stopped the practice after it received a written request from DOJ indicating that the company was in violation of the federal law.[37]

Burton Abstract wasn't the only laggard when it came to racially restrictive covenants. Martin Sloane, the chief of the housing section at the U.S. Commission on Civil Rights and witness for the plaintiffs, pointed his finger at the federal government and in particular at the Federal Housing

Administration.[38] Established in 1934, the FHA revolutionized homeownership by insuring millions of mortgages that met its new standards. (It was hard to imagine the post–World War II housing boom without the agency.)[39] Prior to the FHA, consumers faced significant barriers to homeownership, such as large down payments and balloon mortgages.[40] The FHA made it much easier—particularly for first-time homebuyers—to enter the market by providing federal insurance for mortgage loans. In effect, the FHA told private lenders: "Go ahead and write the loan on the terms we specifiy. If the buyer defaults, the federal government will pay the lender and take possession of the home."[41] But FHA insurance was available only to federally approved mortgage lenders. And the loans had to meet certain requirements, including using racial covenants.[42]

Sloane explained how the agency actively promoted residential segregation. For years, its underwriting manual recommended that racially restrictive covenants be included in deeds to ensure against "incompatible racial elements" and "adverse influences," meaning "occupancy of properties except by the race for which they were intended."[43] In this, the federal government amplified racially restrictive covenants' destructive power. It was as if racially restrictive covenants were patient zero and the feds were flying the sick patient to every city in the country and introducing her to all the locals—for free. That was bad enough. But then Sloane made a startling remark. *Shelley*, which unambiguously prohibited court enforcement of racially restrictive covenants, was decided in 1948. The FHA, which was aware of the Supreme Court ruling, simply ignored it. Instead, the agency waited until nearly two years after the decision was handed down to "change its policy from one of encouraging racially restrictive covenants to one of refusing to insure mortgagors on properties which carried racially restrictive covenants."[44] Later, on cross-examination, Sloane was asked why it took the FHA so long to change its policy in the wake of *Shelley v. Kraemer*. "This is not unusual," he replied.[45] Sloane continued, "They take too long, I think, but a change of policy you can appreciate is a radical one from one of actively promoting and pushing racial covenants to one of . . . refusing to insure any mortgage to a racial covenant. It's a radical turn."[46]

Sloane wasn't kidding. Shifting away from its commitment to racial discrimination was a sea change for the agency. Sloane told the court the ugly truth about the federal government's love affair with segregation: "FHA in its early days was perhaps the most active exponent of racial discrimination and racial segregation in housing."[47] And it wasn't just the FHA. Sloane called out a veritable laundry list of federal agencies that were committed to racial discrimination: the Veterans Administration, the Federal Public Housing Agency, the Home Loan Bank Board, the Comptroller of the Currency, the Federal Reserve Board, and the Federal Deposit Insurance Corporation, the FDIC.[48] Dimond observed that "these federal agencies had been involved in approximately 80 percent of the housing built in the United States since the mid-1930s."[49]

———

Richard Marks continued his excavation of the containment. The pre- and post–World War II periods were ones of intense racial competition over housing resources within the city of Detroit. Blacks usually came out on the wrong end of the stick. The plaintiffs' witness reminded the court that Detroit had been "The Arsenal of Democracy" during the war.[50] Huge numbers of workers streamed into the city to build military armaments. The goal was "500 planes a day."[51] Then, at war's end, thousands of veterans returned home. Detroit's housing need was great. Housing production ramped up. Marks told the court, "There was extensive vacant land, so much so that [from] 1945 to 1955, approximately 200,000 homes were built in Detroit west of Livernois, north of Six Mile and east of Connor." Two hundred thousand was a big number, but virtually none of this housing was made available to blacks. "Only in three areas could blacks buy new houses. Those are areas of established occupancy, Eight Mile–Wyoming, and the Sojourner Truth area, or what is called the Dog's Leg section of Detroit, far southwest. So that out of the two hundred thousand new homes built in that ten-year period, blacks occupied perhaps one percent of those or were able to purchase one percent of them," Marks explained.[52] It was a staggering admission.

Public housing was a flash point for black-white conflict in Detroit. Marks testified that the World War II period was one "of extensive community controversy over the placement of . . . public housing."[53] The historian

Thomas Sugrue later confirmed Marks's observation in his classic examination of midcentury Detroit, *The Origins of the Urban Crisis: Race and Inequality in Postwar Detroit*. "Proposals to construct public housing in or near white areas [was] the most contentious political issue of the 1940s and early 1950s in Detroit," the historian wrote.[54] The crisis at the Sojourner Truth housing project exemplified this conflict.

Believing its location to be uncontroversial, government officials announced plans to construct a two-hundred-unit housing project named after Sojourner Truth in the Seven Mile–Fenelon neighborhood in northeast Detroit. Government officials designated the project for black occupancy because, as Sugrue put it, of "its proximity to an already existing concentration of blacks."[55] This was consistent with Detroit Housing Commission (and FHA) policy. The commission's official minutes stated: "The Detroit Housing Commission will in no way change the racial characteristics of any neighborhood in Detroit to occupancy standards of housing projects under its jurisdiction . . . It is the opinion of the commission that any attempted change in the racial pattern of any area in Detroit will result in violent opposition to the housing program."[56] The commission adopted this policy expressly at the behest of the mayor and the city legislature. Public housing in Detroit was officially segregated. As another of the plaintiffs' witnesses confirmed, Detroit (and the federal government's) policy was to develop housing projects "for white tenants or black tenants only during this period."[57]

Nearby white residents formed the Seven Mile–Fenelon Improvement Association to oppose the project.[58] (Later, a city administrator with extensive experience in Detroit community relations would testify that "our investigations revealed that there are many [white] neighborhood associations [like Seven Mile–Fenelon] who had a major portion of their purpose the exclusion of black families from their area for the protection of their area from undesirables, to use a common term, from moving into the area.")[59] One white resident wrote that the project would "jeopardize the safety of many of our white girls" and "ruin the neighborhood."[60] Meanwhile, with blacks facing a particularly acute housing shortage, civil rights groups had little choice but to accept segregated public housing. In the 1930s, Detroit's white leaders had issued an ultimatum: "Either [you] have a segregated project, or [you] won't have any. So make up your minds."[61]

Under pressure, government officials flip-flopped. At first, they caved to whites' demands and designated Sojourner Truth as a white project. But the NAACP, the national office of the Urban League, and others pressured the officials to reverse their decision.[62] The campaign succeeded, and the officials reinstated the project's initial designation.[63] On the eve of the project's opening, the Klan burned a cross near the project. The next day, February 28, 1942, by some accounts twelve hundred whites massed to keep blacks from moving in. As the move-in proceeded, fighting erupted.[64] There was a strong police presence at the project—several hundred officers were on duty—but they failed to protect blacks from white violence.[65] There were scores of injuries, and more than two hundred people were arrested before police were able to restore order. Virtually all of the arrestees were black, as were most of those hospitalized.[66] Ultimately, blacks did move into the Sojourner Truth project, but it took a small army to do it. As the historian and Detroit expert Richard W. Thomas described it, "Twelve hundred state homeguard troops, three hundred state police, and eight hundred Detroit police escorted them to the housing project. The troops remained on guard in the neighborhood for several weeks."[67]

Assessing the impact of the Sojourner Truth incident, Sugrue wrote, "White community groups learned to use the threat of imminent violence as a political tool to gain leverage in housing debates. City officials, desperately hoping to avoid racial bloodshed, had no choice but to take seriously the specter of civil disorder."[68] Marks testified that violence was a key technique that whites used to maintain the containment: "But any time that a black family sought to move beyond that new defined psychological and brick line . . . whenever a black family tried to move in, there was violence."[69] And the court didn't just need to take Marks's word for it. Another Detroit official stated for the record, "I personally witnessed many incidents where [white] crowds would gather on the lawn and stones would be thrown, policemen were assaulted and injured. I saw a home and talked to a family that was firebombed in the middle of the night. One night back in the fall of 1962, eight different houses were vandalized in one night and a crowd of some 300 to 500 people congregated in this one particular block."[70]

Segregation in public housing didn't just affect those who lived in particular housing projects. Public housing projects also helped turn black neighborhoods into ghettos. Local authorities, armed with federal housing money, built extremely high-density, multiple-unit public housing projects either within or directly adjacent to black areas.[71] Public housing was "sticky." Once the apartment buildings were constructed, they had an anchoring effect, concentrating the poorest blacks with the greatest needs in shoddily built, poorly designed structures in areas with the least opportunity. Large numbers of multibedroom units skewed adult-child ratios. In turn, high numbers of adolescents with less adult supervision meant more vandalism and crime.[72] It was not a recipe for success. A former member of the Detroit Housing Commission testified that "We have learned from the past, that it is not best for the people or the city to have these large high-rise constructions in public housing. Too many instances they're not the best thing for the children who reside there."[73] He added, "They become crime traps."[74] Blacks with the greatest resources left the chronically underfunded projects, further isolating the black poor.

Segregated public housing also had a deleterious effect on the schools. A Michigan Civil Rights Commission official later told the court: "The present pattern of public housing sites approved by the Detroit Common Council had and will reinforce not only residential segregation but school segregation."[75] The situation was unlikely to change anytime soon. Martin Sloane noted in his testimony that the federal government produced approximately eight hundred thousand units of low-income housing by the early 1970s.[76] He was not optimistic that those units could soon be integrated: "The patterns of such housing in the various cities in which they are located are so clear that it would take a monumental effort to reverse these patterns, black families know the housing projects that they are supposed to be living in; white families know the housing project they were supposed to be living in because the patterns of rigid racial segregation were established over a thirty-year period and [are] very difficult to reverse."[77]

Referring back to the overlays, Marks noted that in 1960, the containment line had moved outward a bit, but the big action occurred between 1960 and 1970. He told the court that by "1970, breakthroughs really were occurring, so much so that it gave people in our city great hope that we were ending restrictions in the housing market, that people were being viewed as people, able to compete and buy housing."[78] But such hopes were premature. The containment lines became more malleable in part because whites were leaving the city. "It was a great movement of whites to the suburbs, a great loss of white population by the central city" that had allowed blacks to climb out of the ghetto, Marks told the court.[79] The new containment line was the jurisdictional boundary of Detroit itself: "So that all we saw happening was simply the relaxation of a previous line-restricting barrier and at least the beginnings of a new line forming roughly [just north of Eight Mile Road near] . . . Greenfield [Road]."[80] By this, Marks meant the suburbs.

Marks had one more tale to tell before he stepped down. It came courtesy of CCBE's lawyer, Alexander Ritchie, who cross-examined him late in the day.

> MR. RITCHIE: Now, in your own words, exactly what do you mean by the policy of containment of blacks within the residential areas of the city of Detroit?
>
> MR. MARKS: Well, when a piece of property is not freely available to any person who has the desire to purchase, the money to purchase, and [there is] a willing seller, we would view that as an example of individual restriction, that's a refusal to consummate a deal on a piece of property that is available on the market with a person who is desirous of purchasing.
>
> When that pattern . . . exists throughout a total area, we call that containment. It is just as effective a barrier as if a wall were built in the community.
>
> As a matter of fact, in the 8 Mile and Wyoming section when Negroes first moved into that area, the builder who had title to some property west of where Negroes were living actually put up a cement wall . . . which for years was a symbol in our city of the way in which the Negro was an undesired neighbor.[81]

Marks was referring to what Detroiters often called the "wailing wall," the "Eight Mile wall," or the "Birwood wall."[82] The wall was perhaps the most prominent symbol of the containment in the entire Detroit metropolitan area. Located in the Eight Mile–Wyoming area in northwest Detroit, the wall was massive. Rising to a height of six feet, it was one foot thick and spanned a distance of one-half mile.[83] With capped concrete pylons connecting each of the wall's sections, it had the ominous look of a prison barricade. The story behind the wall was somewhat obscure. But what it attested to was the federal government's official policy of racial apartheid.

Early in the twentieth century, African Americans had managed to establish a small enclave in northwest Detroit in the Eight Mile–Wyoming area. By the 1930s, the area, which was still largely rural, had several thousand black inhabitants.[84] Blacks built the community themselves with little governmental assistance. In fact, the area was "redlined." During that period, the federal Home Owners Loan Corporation (HOLC) surveyed more than two hundred cities purporting to assess the risk of investing in real estate in those cities' various neighborhoods.[85] The agency drew "residential security" maps, which gave each portion of a surveyed city a color-coded grade. Black areas always failed. As Sugrue put it, the Eight Mile–Wyoming area, like "every other black section of Detroit . . . was marked 'D' [meaning hazardous or high investment risk] or 'red' on the Home Owners Loan Corporation appraisal maps of Detroit, flagging the area as unsuitable for federal loans and subsidies."[86] Excluded from federal housing assistance, black homeowners were forced to rely on private credit markets. Several scholars described the effect of "residential Jim Crowism": "Exorbitant interest rates, dangerous balloon payments, and/or 'rent-to-own' arrangements that meant the loss of one's home after missing a single payment."[87] Redlining systematically disadvantaged black neighborhoods in Detroit and throughout the nation.

By the early 1940s, the Eight Mile–Wyoming black enclave was at risk. As whites continued to migrate toward the outskirts of the city, it sat directly in the path of development.[88] Now, a developer wanted to build an all-white subdivision immediately to the west of the black settlement.[89] The developer also wanted something else: federal housing assistance. So the developer and the federal government cut a deal. As Sugrue told it, "The developer worked out a compromise with the FHA, garnering loans and mortgage guarantees in exchange for the construction of [the wall], running for a half-mile on the property line separating the black and white neighborhoods."[90] It didn't take much imagination to understand how a thick, concrete barrier between the two neighborhoods stigmatized and humiliated black families, just as the "whites only" signs did in the South. On one side of the wall, the all-white subdivision would have access to the full panoply of federal housing assistance. On the other was the redlined black community. The wall symbolized white supremacy—and enacted it. The segregation wall still sits there today.

Black residents of the Eight Mile–Wyoming community didn't take the wall lying down. They campaigned strenuously for federal housing assistance.[91] Finally, after struggling for several years they won a partial victory in 1944.[92] Government officials agreed to provide FHA subsidies for single-family home construction in the neighborhood—along with six hundred units of temporary war housing, meaning public housing.[93] Ultimately, the area became a bastion of black homeownership.[94] But the Eight Mile–Wyoming struggle was the exception that proved the rule. Even as black community groups won their battle, Sugrue wrote, "The discriminatory lending policies of the FHA remained intact."[95]

Like an artist contemplating an oversized blank canvas, the plaintiffs' trial team was trying to build a complete picture of the containment, piece by piece, story by story, witness by witness. Karl Taeuber confirmed that Detroit (and most other American cities) was highly segregated.[96] It didn't happen by chance. It wasn't a choice blacks were making. Nor was blacks' economic status the culprit. Instead, the cause was race discrimination. "I believe that this is the major factor accounting for the kind of segregation that occurs," he testified, "not just in the present but also in the past, because the structure of the city is well-established now."[97] Roth was startled by Taeuber's testimony that, according to one report, black/white segregation was more than double that of other ethnic groups. Dimond recalled that as Roth "turned to his right, he confronted the huge map showing the stark *racial* division in Detroit."[98] Dimond continued, "It would have been difficult for any [judge] listening to this testimony to overlook the extent of the racial segregation and the probability that the condition would long endure because it resulted primarily from racial discrimination, not 'ethnic choice' . . . experienced by many immigrant groups."[99]

The trial team needed a witness who could explain the real estate industry's role in creating the containment. And they got it when they put John Humphrey on the stand. Humphrey was a black real estate broker who had lived in Detroit since 1938. With more than twenty years of experience in the field, first as a salesman and then as an officer of the Detroit Real Estate Brokers Association, he was well qualified to provide a panoramic view of the city's real estate industry. The first set of questions Humphrey was asked might have caught a casual observer off guard. Paul Dimond asked him: "Are you a realtor?" Humphrey responded, "I am not a realtor."[100] But how could a former officer of a real estate brokers association not identify as a "realtor"? It made no sense. Except that it did. The Detroit Real Estate Brokers Association was for black real estate "brokers." In Detroit, a "realtor"—a salesperson who performed exactly the same functions as a real estate broker—was white. Humphrey testified, "When I joined the Real Estate Brokers Association, the realtors was a white organization that did not allow black membership at that time."[101]

So before Humphrey even got to the substance of his testimony, he had already identified a significant problem affecting both Detroit and its suburbs. Right up through 1971, there were effectively two race-based real estate associations in Detroit: the historically black Detroit Real Estate Brokers Association, and the Detroit Real Estate Board, which was the white organization. By the time of trial, the Detroit Real Estate Board was allowing black brokers to join the organization. But the moment was clearly one of transition. The reality was that most black brokers and most white realtors were still operating through two separate professional associations. This didn't just mean that the two associations might have hosted separate Christmas parties. The two organizations effectively served two separate markets. This had enormous practical ramifications on the operation of the Detroit metropolitan area real estate market.

The two real estate organizations signaled that Detroit area white realtors effectively functioned as a cartel.[102] Members might share listings with other members of their respective associations, but black brokers weren't going to get white listings or anything else the white realtors organization had to offer. This meant that black brokers, who represented a largely black clientele, never even knew about and thus could not show houses in white areas. They were "boxed out" of the white-neighborhood market. Humphrey testified to that effect. Dimond asked him, "Have you had difficulty getting listings in white areas?" Humphrey responded succinctly, "Yes."[103]

White realtors also refused to "co-broke," meaning share listings and split commissions with black brokers on sales in white areas.[104] White realtors used racial coding systems or otherwise marked listings as "white" or "black" to ensure that black buyers were not shown houses in white neighborhoods. Humphrey's testimony confirmed the listing coding system, "The X and XX would denote the race. The X is white; the XX is black."[105] The white realtors' actions weren't just customary. They were coordinated, endorsed, sanctioned. The all-white Detroit Real Estate Board's official policy up through 1962 was that "the realtor should not be instrumental in introducing into a neighborhood a character of property or use which will clearly be detrimental to property values in the neighborhood."[106] This was a euphemistic way of admonishing white realtors for giving black buyers access to white neighborhoods.

Not only was this the official policy of the white Detroit Real Estate Board, but it was also reinforced by Michigan state law. Approximately midway through the housing part of the plaintiffs' case, the plaintiffs' counsel introduced two key pieces of evidence into the record. The first was Michigan's real estate license law. In order to sell real estate in Michigan, a salesperson had to be licensed to do so under state law. The second was a set of rules dating from 1946, promulgated by a state commission with purview over corporations, securities, and real estate. The commission rules stated that all real estate professionals "ought to observe a code of ethics." The rules continued, "This commission subscribes to the code of ethics which has been adopted by the National Association of Real Estate Boards."[107] And what did that code of ethics say? That "a realtor should never be instrumental in introducing into a neighborhood a character of property or occupancy members of *any race or nationality* or any individuals whose presence will clearly be detrimental to property values in that neighborhood."[108]

These pieces of evidence established a crucial link between the public and the private, between the regulatory authority of the state of Michigan and the seemingly disparate and uncoordinated acts of discrimination undertaken by the real estate industry. Real estate salespersons had to be licensed and observe a code of ethics. While Michigan did not expressly *require* salespersons to adopt the National Association of Real Estate Boards' pro-segregation code, the state certainly preferred it. In practice, the hundreds of thousands (if not millions) of acts of "private" real estate discrimination were directly endorsed by the state of Michigan. So when white realtors refused to show prospective black buyers homes in white neighborhoods, did those acts amount to de facto segregation? Or were they de jure?

Nor was that the end of Michigan's support of racist real estate practices. In 1960, the state commission that had recommended the pro-segregation code of ethics moved to change its ways. It adopted a rule declaring that any licensed real estate professional who discriminated on the basis of race was engaged in "unfair dealing," potentially subjecting the agent to disciplinary action.[109] But three years later, the Michigan State Supreme Court ruled that the commission lacked the power to adopt that rule.[110] This was ironic. The commission lacked the power to discipline real estate professionals for racial discrimination. But it most certainly did possess the power to strongly recommend that those same real estate professionals maintain and perpetuate residential segregation. Of that decision, Dimond later wrote that it denied "blacks equal protection by authorizing state-licensed real estate brokers to enforce by covert means . . . overt racial restrictions."[111]

Lacking access to the white realtors' listings, black brokers could not "break" the white cartel. But they did try. In 1952, Humphrey sold a house to a black family on Riopelle Street in northeast Detroit. The neighbors made their displeasure known by breaking all the windows in the house and harassing the family. The city responded by providing round-the-clock police protection, but it wasn't enough. Humphrey testified, "While the policeman was there, they threw snakes in the basement and frightened the people to the point that they—the lady had a nervous breakdown and had to move out."[112] Snakes in the basement was bad enough, but Humphrey's story was really just beginning.

DIMOND: Were you involved in these incidents?

HUMPHREY: Only to the extent that I made the sale of the property and visited the area when this harassment was going.

DIMOND: During your visits, was any harassment directed at you?

HUMPHREY: Yes, sir. Police officers, plainclothes, in the presence of neighbors stopped me and yanked the door open from both sides—grabbed me on the shoulder, pulled me out and told me to put my hands up.

And I said, "Well, what is this all about?" You know, I knew they knew who I was.

He said, "Put your hands up."

I said, "If you want to search me, you take me to the station."

And he grabbed for his gun. And I think I come as close to getting shot as I have been in my life. I think that's the closest time I've been to getting shot in my life.

I stuck them up in a hurry and he patted me—and all type of harassment.

This was typical because of the fact that I was in the area where this incident happened and I happen to have been the real estate man who made the sale.

DIMOND: . . . was this a white area?

HUMPHREY: It was all white prior to this.[113]

Humphrey confirmed a variety of other techniques white realtors used to prevent black buyers from gaining access to white neighborhoods: exaggerating a home's defects, charging higher sale prices, failing to advertise listings in the black-read *Michigan Chronicle*, refusing to submit black buyers' offers, representing that a home was off the market when in fact it was still for sale.

At the close of Humphrey's testimony, George Bushnell Jr., the board's lawyer, pushed the court to disallow it. He argued, "If the court please, I would move to strike all of Mr. Humphrey's testimony. It's a tale of horror; a tale of degradation and dehumanization. I am tremendously sympathetic to it but it does not have one thing to do with the defendant Board of Education . . . I move to strike it."[114]

Roth wasn't buying. "Objection is overruled and the motion to strike is overruled."[115]

———

A certain geographic tension emerged in the course of the presentation of the plaintiffs' housing case. The lawsuit alleged race discrimination in the Detroit public schools. But economically, Detroit was deeply intertwined with many nearby southeastern Michigan suburbs. The city and neighboring suburbs, and their housing markets, were effectively a single metropolitan region—at least for some. Much of the testimony elicited from the witnesses during the housing portion of the case reflected that fact. For instance, the court was informed of studies demonstrating that blacks were deeply interested in obtaining suburban housing but that "fear and custom exclude black families from purchasing such property;"[116] that the all-white Detroit Real Estate Board operated in both Detroit and suburban areas,[117] but that the all-black Detroit Real Estate Brokers Association's members had no access to their listings; that large numbers of blacks worked in Warren but very few could live there;[118] that the U.S. Department of Housing and Urban Development (HUD) had found that the reason why so few minorities lived in Warren, Dearborn, Grosse Pointe, Ferndale, and other suburban locales was because of racial discrimination; that vandalism, harassment, and intimidation deterred blacks from attempting suburban moves; and that black pioneers who did manage to obtain suburban housing faced similar treatment once they got there. By 1970, the containment line had effectively moved to the Detroit city line, trapping blacks within the city while allowing whites to escape to the suburbs. It would be hard to put the housing genie back in the Detroit-only bottle, as Roth's response to the state defendants' "continuing objection to the relevancy of the whole housing question" demonstrated.[119] "Well, we previously transgressed the city lines and I see no reason why we can't do it again. I think both sides have gone into matters outside the city limits with respect to housing."[120]

Attorneys for the defendants argued that *all* of the housing testimony was irrelevant. This was a school case, not a housing case, they fumed. The Detroit school board could not be held responsible for discriminatory actions in the housing sphere that "happened" to cause segregation in the schools. Now they were doubly frustrated as witnesses testified about activity that took place outside the city of Detroit. Their fallback argument was that even if some of the housing testimony was relevant to the school case, any evidence going to housing discrimination *outside* the city of Detroit should be struck. The argument fell on deaf ears. Roth let all of the evidence come in. The board's refusal to stipulate that Detroit was residentially segregated was coming back to haunt it.

The plaintiffs' housing evidence was overwhelming, and everyone knew it. And that contributed to people on all sides beginning to assume the case might have to address the metropolitan area as a whole. Consider the position of CCBE, which represented white families living in the northwest and northeast areas of the city. If the plaintiffs won, the court would be required to order a desegregation remedy. But a Detroit-only desegregation remedy wasn't in the interests of the organization. It wanted all of white Detroit to know it. On April 25, 1971, William Grant reported in the *Detroit Free Press* that the group had left "thousands of leaflets . . . on doorsteps in the city's predominantly white neighborhoods" warning of citywide busing and majority black schools if the NAACP prevailed in the *Bradley* lawsuit.[121] Nothing less than "the destruction of our Detroit" was at stake. And there was something else: white fear of declining home values. Whites refusing to participate in a Detroit-only desegregation remedy might well leave the city. And if many white families had the same idea simultaneously, white homeowners risked the possibility of selling their homes into a declining market. The CCBE leaflets highlighted this risk: "To protect our neighborhood schools and *our investments in our homes* we need contributions immediately."[122]

Surveying the situation, at least one very important member of CCBE began to have a heretical thought: the group had gone to court to oppose government-mandated integration, but if integration had to happen, maybe it was better if it happened over a wider area, not a smaller one. Including the suburbs in any remedy Roth might order offered the possibility of risk minimization *for whites*. As the number of whites in any potential desegregation remedy grew, the effect of that remedy on any particular white family was reduced. Perhaps this reasoning was why

CCBE counsel Alexander Ritchie had a "come to Jesus" moment so early in the housing case.

Alexander Buchan Ritchie was a native Detroiter who, at the time of the trial, had lived on the same Detroit street for more than thirty years.[123] After graduating from Wayne State University Law School in 1949, he worked for an insurance company before discovering his true love: trial work. The lawyer had strong ties to Detroit's public schools. He was a member of the Arthur School PTA, and his wife Gladys taught at Robinson Elementary in the Jefferson Chalmers area of Detroit. Ritchie was involved in the all-white CCBE from its inception, serving on its board and attending its early meetings.[124] He ably represented the group during the recall drive. Aubrey Short, the CCBE's chairman, once called him "the most brilliant attorney I ever met."[125] Ritchie served as CCBE's counsel for little pay. If he was a closet integrationist, he hid it well.

If there was one place where Ritchie's transition began, it was on his cross-examination of Martin Sloane, the chief of the housing section at the U.S. Commission on Civil Rights. He proposed to Sloane "that a decree by this court desegregating the remaining balance of that school district which you see presented before you, would be on its face a study in futility."[126] Then, a few moments later, he posed an actual question: Would a Detroit-only desegregation plan cause "a mass exodus of the remaining white citizens into the suburbs?"[127] This was what CCBE really cared about. Sloane hemmed and hawed, never really answering the question directly. But perhaps Ritchie was appealing to a different audience.

Roth's interest was piqued: "Mr. Sloane, I'm interested in pursuing Mr. Ritchie's thought, if you will forgive me for injecting the question here."[128] Roth's mind was working; he seemed to be thinking and sharing his thoughts in open court. He began, "I'd like to pursue Mr. Ritchie's question. This is a suit alleging segregation in the school system in the City of Detroit. If you have an opinion, I'd like to have it."[129]

Now the importance of the large map of the Detroit metropolitan area that the plaintiffs' counsel had so carefully positioned in Roth's line of sight became clear. "Do you have an opinion as to what would happen to . . . [the white areas as depicted on the map]?" Roth asked.[130] He clarified: "Would they, as Mr. Ritchie suggests, lead really to an abandonment in large numbers by white folks so that when you ended up with the city you'd have a city that was no more integrated than it was when you started. Do you have an opinion on that?"[131]

Sloane finally began to formulate an answer. There might be a tipping point, "say 35, 40 or 50 percent blacks, suddenly the entire school system . . . will turn completely black."[132] But then he hedged, suggesting that "this is a matter of conjecture."[133] Sloane's expertise was national, so he was hesitant to provide specifics about Detroit. He felt more comfortable talking about Washington, D.C., where he lived. Sloane noted that achieving integration in the D.C. school system would be very difficult given that it was more than 90 percent black. But then he offered this key insight: "But if you think in terms of the metropolitan area as a whole, the problem becomes a good deal less difficult."[134] He continued, "You have to talk in terms of metropolitan wide desegregation, residentially as well as in education. And it is, in fact, I think an exercise in futility to think in terms of integrating a school system which is already so predominantly black as to make racial integration an impossibility. It is, however, not an impossibility if you talk in terms of the metropolitan area as a whole."[135]

If there was one "aha" moment during the trial, this was it. Roth jumped in immediately, musing, "Well, I don't know whether fortunately or unfortunately this lawsuit is limited to the City of Detroit and the school system, that we're only concerned with the city itself and we're not talking about the metropolitan area."[136] But the seed had been planted in what was once unfertile soil. Now there was reason to doubt that meaningful desegregation could be achieved without including the suburbs. The irony, of course, was that it was CCBE—not the plaintiffs—who first injected this line of inquiry into the case. It was the fourth day of the trial.

Just before Sloane stepped down, Flannery confirmed the plaintiffs' openness to Ritchie's approach. He told the court: "If this record should disclose that school children in the City of Detroit cannot be afforded equal protection of the laws, equal educational opportunity, measured against the requirement of equal protection laws, we have the State as a defendant in this action."[137] In other words, Flannery seemed to be suggesting that having the state of Michigan—not just the Detroit Board of Education—as a defendant in the lawsuit opened the possibility of using the suburbs to create a meaningful remedy. "We are not prepared to concede, your honor, that a metropolitan solution would not be viable or would be inappropriate."[138] Flannery's sea of double negatives confirmed that, while the plaintiffs might be willing to go along with metropolitan relief, they weren't aggressively pushing it. But from then on, according to Dimond, the metropolitan issue "hung over the case."[139]

By the time the plaintiffs' housing case ended in late April 1971, there had been two fundamental changes. First, CCBE—whom exactly no one would have characterized as integrationist—had morphed into a pro-metropolitan desegregation group. The turn was born of self-interest, but the shift obtained nonetheless. (Although Ritchie later became a true believer.) On April 22, 1971, William Grant confirmed the group's metamorphosis: "Ritchie has been laying the foundation in the trial in Detroit for a motion to have U.S. District Judge Stephen J. Roth consider including suburban school systems in any future integration plan."[140] Second, the elaborate housing case with its focus on the containment changed Roth. Dimond characterized Roth as having undergone a "dramatic conversion" in response to the housing evidence.[141] Grant added: "Judge Roth, in any private discussion of the case, would walk across his chambers to the shelf where he kept his papers on the case and . . . read statistics on Detroit's diminishing white population [introduced during the housing portion of the case]. He considered these . . . data to be the keys to understanding the case."[142]

12

GARBAGE IN, GARBAGE OUT

O n April 20, 1971, just as the housing portion of the *Bradley* case was nearing its conclusion, the U.S. Supreme Court issued its most important school desegregation decision since *Green v. New Kent County*, which had been decided in 1968. The case was called *Swann v. Charlotte-Mecklenburg Board of Education*. *Green* had arisen in a southern rural county. *Swann* was also a southern case, but it was meaningfully different. The result of a consolidation in 1960, Charlotte-Mecklenburg was a city-county school district in North Carolina with thousands of students, dozens of schools, and a large, residentially concentrated black population.[1] *Swann* was set in a major metropolitan area, one that looked a lot like many others throughout the country. Because of this, it held tantalizing possibilities for school desegregation cases in the North.

The issue in *Swann* was how much power did the federal courts really have to force school districts to desegregate? The answer was: a lot. Judge James B. McMillan, the federal trial court judge, having found that the Charlotte-Mecklenburg school system was unconstitutionally segregated, required significant alterations of school attendance zones, that each school in the district roughly mirror the racial breakdown of the district as a whole, and that more than thirteen thousand children be bused, all to effectuate desegregation.[2] McMillan pushed back on the idea that black schools just happened to be located in black residential areas, and that school segregation had a single cause. The judge wrote: the "facts are that the present location of white schools in white areas and of black schools in black areas is the result of a varied group of elements of public and private action, all deriving their basic strength originally from public law or state or local governmental action."[3] State law requiring the legal separation of races in education was just one of the culprits. The others would have been familiar to anyone who sat in the courtroom during the first several days of the *Bradley v. Milliken* trial. McMillan continued: "These elements include among others . . . racial restrictions in deeds to land; zoning ordinances; city planning; urban renewal; location of public low rent housing."[4] For all of this, the judge concluded the government was responsible: "There is so much state action embedded in and shaping these events that the resulting segregation is not innocent or '*de facto*,' and the resulting schools are not 'unitary' or desegregated," he wrote.[5]

Chief Justice Warren Burger, writing for the court, upheld McMillan's order almost in its entirety. The court ruled that federal district judges had the power to racially gerrymander school zones, to require (at least initially) that schools achieve a specific racial balance, and, most importantly, to mandate busing to achieve desegregation. *Swann* was where the court greenlit busing, and it made the case a landmark.[6] Future Supreme Court justice Lewis F. Powell Jr., then still in private practice, authored an amicus "friend of the court" brief in *Swann* on behalf of the Commonwealth of Virginia. Powell warned that whites would flee if the court made racial balance a constitutional requirement. The "effort to attain racial balance promotes resegregation and movement to suburbia," he wrote. It was a preview of things to come.[7]

The *Swann* opinion spoke with less clarity on the question of residential segregation. Suggesting, ominously, that one case "can carry only a limited amount of baggage," the court declined to reach the question of "whether a showing that school segregation is a consequence of other types of state action, without any discriminatory action by the school authorities, is a constitutional violation requiring remedial action by a school desegregation decree."[8] Nevertheless, the court ruled—with more clarity than ever before—that federal trial courts had broad remedial authority in school desegregation cases. This was what really mattered. The court's opinion also contained crucial language linking school siting decisions to neighborhood- and metropolitan-level segregation. Burger wrote: "People gravitate toward school facilities, just as schools are located in response to the needs of the people. The location of schools may thus influence the patterns of residential development of a metropolitan area and have important impact on composition of inner-city neighborhoods."[9]

Responding to the court's ruling in *Swann*, Roy Wilkins said the case "toppled" the neighborhood school "from its perch as the determinant of desegregation policy."[10] The plaintiffs' counsel also liked what they saw. Lou Lucas told William Grant, "The decision removes any question that the local court has a full range of remedy."[11] Ritchie, the CCBE lawyer, concurred. Not surprisingly, he had hoped that the court would prohibit busing to achieve desegregation. Now, after *Swann*, he understood the technique was firmly within Judge Roth's arsenal should he find a constitutional violation.

Swann put Nixon on the defensive. He had openly lobbied Burger for a different result. Nixon met with Burger and John Ehrlichman, the president's chief domestic adviser, over breakfast on December 18, 1970. At the time, the *Swann* case was still under consideration.[12] At the meeting, Nixon reminded Burger of the huge significance of the "school cases." They also discussed "forced integration" and northern school desegregation. For any district or court of appeals judge, this conversation would have violated the American Bar Association's Code of Judicial Conduct, which prohibited judges from discussing any "pending or impending proceeding" in the absence of all the parties. But the ABA's Code of Judicial Conduct did not apply to Supreme Court justices.[13] Nixon had hoped that "Burger and the majority of the Court would follow his lead."[14] That didn't happen. At least not yet.

At a news conference shortly after *Swann* came down, a reporter posed the following question to the president: "Do you believe that busing should be used as a technique to overcome racial segregation based on housing patterns in the North?"[15] Referencing his March 1970 statement on the schools, Nixon doubled down on his opposition to "busing for the purpose of achieving racial balance," and voiced his "support of the neigh-borhood school."[16] The president acknowledged that *Swann* took a differ-ent approach. Nixon pledged that the executive branch would abide by the Supreme Court's rule, but only the narrowest possible interpretation of it. In so doing, he glossed over the strong similarity between the Charlotte-Mecklenburg school district and many major metropolitan areas in the North.

But then Nixon turned, offering a reading of the case that confined it to the South. He framed *Swann*: "The Court explicitly did not deal . . . with the problem of de facto segregation as it exists in the North."[17] But he suggested that it might in short order. As he had the year before in his official statement on school segregation, Nixon was selling the idea that northern segregation was the result "not of what a governmental body did, but housing patterns coming from individual decisions."[18] But no reason-able person sitting in Judge Roth's courtroom would have explained the containment as the result of nongovernmental, "individual decisions." To do so would have done violence to the complex tale the plaintiffs' lawyers so ably told. In this way, one could see the de jure / de facto distinction as a fight between two different stories. In one story, the dynamics of northern segregation—with housing and school segregation interdependent—was byzantine, multiparty, and complicated; it involved state actors. The other story was simplistic, one-dimensional. Under this narrative, southern ve-nality was reflected in its laws. Those laws required blacks and whites to be separately educated, and for that the South needed to atone. Federal court intrusion into local educational matters was appropriate, at least for a while, because the region was clearly and obviously guilty of denying blacks equal educational opportunity. According to this story, the North was innocent. Nixon finished his answer to the reporter's question this way: "Where it is de jure we comply with the Court. Where it is de facto, *until the Court speaks* . . . my view [remains the same]."[19]

Later, in early July 1971, June Shagaloff Alexander[20] spoke at the NAACP's annual convention in Minneapolis. She expressed concern about the Nixon administration's willingness to enforce *Swann*: "The Nixon Ad-ministration has consistently failed to provide leadership for the country in ending segregated schools in the South—and we still are not clear which way they're going."[21] She didn't sugarcoat the situation above the Mason-Dixon Line, either, characterizing it as "bleak." Nevertheless, the education director hadn't given up hope. Shagaloff Alexander ended her address with a statement intended to rally the troops: "And in 1971, the threshold of a new decade, when so much is still possible, we are not about to give up now!"[22]

———

On April 29, 1971, the tenth day of the *Bradley v. Milliken* trial, the court transitioned to hearing evidence on the school portion of the case. In response to a question regarding the status of settlement negotiations, Ritchie launched into a lengthy monologue. Referencing the map, the lawyer candidly admitted the city was segregated. He told the court, "The white citizens of Detroit recognize the significance of this map."[23] "I don't think I can stand here on their behalf and argue that we do not have a segregated city," he continued.[24]

A hush fell over the courtroom. CCBE had admitted Detroit was segregated. "If there hadn't been an Alex Ritchie in this case, we would have had to invent one," Dimond later told the press.[25]

Notwithstanding Ritchie's admission, he wasn't recommending that the case be settled or folding his hand. On the contrary, his argument was that *even if* the city was residentially segregated, the school board still could not be held liable for a constitutional violation. The fact that this was a northern school desegregation case made all the difference. "We take the position, joining our brother representing the school board, that whatever the situation in the school is it is not a result of a de jure system of segregation but is merely the result of the so-called neighborhood patterns of living in the city [de facto segregation] which have no materiality as far as the definition of segregation, the legal definition."[26]

But then, perhaps recognizing the implications of his admission, Ritchie hedged his bets. "It is quite possible for any litigant to lose a case," he observed.[27] If the court was going to rule in the plaintiffs' favor, he needed to try to sculpt the eventual remedy. In a remarkable statement, Ritchie invited Roth to think outside the box. Noting that he had had several open meetings with white Detroiters, he told the court, "There is a feeling that this court should consider extending its jurisdiction to the surrounding school districts, namely, those of the suburban communities which surround the city of Detroit."[28] Next, Ritchie suggested including the suburbs would allay white Detroit's fears: "If the suburban school districts were made parties . . . [and the order included] their systems, their pupils, their teachers and their facilities, I think that the people that I represent would abide by such an order."[29] He concluded by suggesting that a spoonful of sugar would make the medicine go down: "I think they may object to it, but I think they would appreciate it in seeing that the court in equity had joined all of the other white citizens and it would be my reaction they would abide such an order."[30]

Ritchie spoke for CCBE and other white Detroiters. It was unclear if suburban whites would reach the same conclusion. Maybe he was just a good lawyer, advocating zealously for his specific clients—white Detroiters. But there was good reason to believe that he had a real change of heart over the course of the trial. Ritchie wasn't just acknowledging that the suburbs were part of a solution to Detroit's problems. By mid-1972, he was publicly touting the plaintiffs' argument that black families had been deliberately herded into certain neighborhoods and schools away from white families and were now owed a remedy. Remarking on the plaintiffs' housing evidence, he told the press: "I have lived in Detroit all my life, and I never would have believed these things are true. I am astonished."[31] On the suburbs, his comments were pointed. They were protected, "so latticed up," that a metropolitan remedy was the only "solution and the judge knows it."[32] Pointing to Warren, where only a few black families lived, Ritchie stated: "How can you say that we have an integrated society. We have to start moving to break down the barriers."[33]

The lawyer also expressed concern about the impact on his city of a Detroit-only desegregation plan: "Detroit whites will just move to the suburbs. What will that have achieved?" he asked.[34] Later, he would tell white audiences, "What makes you think you are any different from the South?

Over a thousand school districts in the South have been integrated. Are you committed to separation of the races in Michigan; but not in the rest of the country?"[35]

═══════

The housing portion of the plaintiffs' case was impressive in its scope and presentation. It was also unusual. (Lucas later reportedly told an interviewer that the NAACP lawyers "were convinced they had presented the most thoroughly documented housing case ever made in a school desegregation case.")[36] The next portion of the plaintiffs' case, while important, was more consistent with the kind of proofs one expected to see in a case alleging unconstitutional school segregation. Although the plaintiffs' task was more conventional, it wasn't easy. As was true in the housing portion of the case, there was no single piece of evidence that conclusively demonstrated the defendants' liability. Instead, the plaintiffs' counsel built their school case against the defendants witness by witness, one piece of evidence at a time.

The plaintiffs' first witness was Dr. Robert Green, a black professor who was an expert in educational psychology and school desegregation.[37] He had been a full professor at Michigan State University and the director of the university's Center for Urban Affairs all before the age of forty, and boasted an impressive CV.[38] But he was more than a well-qualified academician. His civil rights pedigree was impeccable. Just after he was hired as an assistant professor at Michigan State, he took a yearlong leave of absence to work with King and the SCLC. "Brother Green, you ought to join us in the struggle," the reverend had told him.[39] Later King would boast: "Robert L. Green is the only PhD who has left a university to come to work for me."[40] Working with the SCLC, the young professor developed education initiatives, encouraged terrified southern blacks to register to vote, and helped others file discrimination complaints with the United States Department of Justice.[41]

He understood, based on firsthand experience, the threat of white violence against civil rights activists. Green detailed a harrowing incident in his memoir. Green, King, and several others were traveling in Mississippi by car when the driver stopped at a light near a Texaco gas station. James Belk, a white service station employee, approached the vehicle. He pulled a pistol out his pocket, put it to King's head, and yelled: "Martin Luther King! I will blow your brains out!"[42] King, unfazed, replied, "Brother, I love you." Belk lowered the weapon and retreated.[43] Green was in James Meredith's hospital room after Meredith was shot while attempting a solitary march from Memphis, Tennessee, to Jackson, Mississippi—the March Against Fear—in order to stimulate black voter registration. Green helped organize the resumption of the March, this time with King and other major civil rights organizations and activists participating. On June 14, 1966, the March, now several thousand strong, arrived in Grenada, Mississippi. Green borrowed a small American flag from a local black child and moved toward a Confederate monument in the town square. He scaled it, placing the flag in a crevice just above a large relief of Jefferson Davis, the president of the Confederacy. A photo captured the moment. It depicted Green standing on the ledge of the massive, four-sided monument, looking back defiantly over his right shoulder at the crowd assembled below. Just a few feet away, a young boy straddled the shoulders of a man with a slightly receding hairline (his father perhaps) and a smile on his face. The boy looked on in wonder. The image of Neil Armstrong planting an American flag on the moon came to mind.[44]

Dimond described the purpose of the professor's testimony as showing that "school authorities intentionally identified schools as black or white."[45] This was consistent with the plaintiffs' litigation burden. In proving de jure segregation, the plaintiffs needed to show intentional or purposeful segregation. They did not need to demonstrate that the defendants harbored ill will, malice, or animus toward black children[46]—only whether, as the plaintiffs' briefs put it, "public school officials have made a series of educational policy decisions which were based wholly or in part on considerations of the race of students or teachers."[47] Their obligation was to demonstrate that the school authorities acted "with reasonable foreseeable knowledge" that their actions would cause racial segregation.[48]

As the reader knows, *Brown v. Board of Education* recognized that school segregation's harms were of constitutional magnitude. Those harms were twofold. First, the court ruled that school segregation denied black schoolchildren equal educational opportunity. The states were not required to provide public education. But where they chose to do so, the

Fourteenth Amendment's equal protection clause obligated them to provide such a valuable public benefit to blacks on an equal basis. Second, the court ruled that segregation generated "a feeling of inferiority as to their status in the community that may affect their hearts and minds in a way unlikely ever to be undone."[49] By this, the court meant that segregation violated the Constitution because it stigmatized and subordinated a racial group.

This portion of the court's holding recognized, implicitly if not explicitly, that segregation had a particular and deleterious social meaning. Its overriding purpose was to shame and humiliate blacks. But segregation wasn't just a system of rules and procedures that policed the black body, where blacks could or could not sit, could or could not enter, could or could not be educated. That system also attempted to discipline blacks' minds, their collective psyche. Segregation taught blacks to see themselves as less than, as disempowered, to school their expectations. (In many respects, black nationalism, with its emphasis on the unique beauty of black art, music, and culture, served as a crucial corrective to the "mind harms" embedded within the system of segregation.) In this way, segregation was a core building block of a caste system.

Brown acknowledged, at least in part, what segregation did to black people. But it addressed only one side of the white supremacy equation. What *Brown* didn't speak to was the false inflation of self-worth, the irrational exuberance in one's own self-esteem, that segregation engendered in whites. Green spoke to this, telling the court: "There is a body of data that supports the point of view that school segregation in general is very harmful and very damaging not only to black youngsters, but to white youngsters as well."[50]

Surely, if segregation created "a feeling of inferiority" in black youngsters, the corollary must also be true. Segregation invited whites to believe they were superior to blacks because, as Green put it, "all they know about people of color is what they hear in the homes over dinner, what they might hear whispered at a church social function."[51] So superior they might feel that they need not deign to interact with blacks, even in perhaps the most important of all public spaces, the public schools. This assumption of superiority was an unearned status benefit, one that perverted both the white psyche and white culture. And it was a benefit that many whites guarded jealously. This had wide-ranging and extraordinarily destructive ramifications, as Green explained.

Green focused on the unique role that public schools could play in counteracting whites' bigoted beliefs. He asserted that the public schools were not neutral bystanders when it came to deconstructing white supremacy. Instead, Green offered a binary. The schools either reinforced racist attitudes or helped to modify them. Detroit public schools did the former. There was no middle ground, because "racial segregation in the United States carries with it a strong connotation of racial inferiority and one should not assume that this is any different in an educational setting."[52] This was true because of unequal resource allocation, because the segregated schools were located in segregated neighborhoods, and because black children perceived black schools as inferior—which was "systematically reinforced by the greater society." And it was also true because of black achievement outcomes.

Green outlined how segregation negatively affected black students' academic achievement levels. One data point in particular caught Judge Roth's attention. The judge interrupted Lucas's direct examination:

JUDGE ROTH: Am I to understand that you are satisfied, based on your own experience and studies and that of other experts in the field, that, generally speaking, there is no achievement difference, scholastically speaking, between black and white children at the entry level?

DR. GREEN: That in general there is a body of data that supports the point of view that the discrepancy between black and white students at the entry level tends to be minimal, very small.[53]

A few moments later, Dr. Green contextualized his statement emphasizing the importance of socioeconomic status.

DR. GREEN: Sir, I said that socioeconomic status does play a role here, and if we take a youngster from a very essentially poor background, let's say poor educational background, who is three and a half years of age, and we'll compare that youngster with another three and a half year old from an affluent background, the differences are larger. But, if we control that factor, if we take black and white youngsters from essentially the same background, the differences would be very minimal. Again, if we place a black youngster in a segregated school system and a white youngster in a segregated school system, then the difference would be reinforced and would begin to emerge and become very dramatic."[54]

Roth's question suggested that he might have believed that blacks and whites started the educational process from wildly different positions. If so, subsequent academic achievement scores might simply reflect the initial "going in" disparities. Instead, it was the other way around, with the achievement disparities increasing over time. Green provided the Detroit data. It was sobering: "The schools that are over 90 percent black are approximately six months below at fourth grade, below the schools that are less than 10 percent black or over 90 percent white. At the sixth grade the schools that are over 90 percent black are a full year behind the schools that are predominately white . . . At the eighth grade the schools that are over 90 percent black are over a year and a half or over 1.5 years behind."[55] Green thought desegregation could mitigate these differences. The "data readily suggests that busing youngsters, black youngsters to white schools and white youngsters to predominantly black schools, can, in fact, positively facilitate academic achievement."[56]

As an expert in educational psychology and school desegregation, Dr. Green was undoubtedly aware of the recently released Coleman Report (formally titled "The Equality of Educational Opportunity Study"), which supported his testimony. Dr. James Coleman, a noted Johns Hopkins sociologist, conducted the study for the United States Department of Health, Education, and Welfare in 1966. It was destined to become a classic in the field. Clocking in at more than seven hundred pages and assessing hundreds of thousands of surveys from four thousand public schools nationwide, the report was one of the largest social science studies ever conducted.[57] Analyzing a massive data set, it confirmed that public schools were highly racially segregated. The report also provided extensive documentation of a substantial black-white achievement gap.[58] That the schools were segregated and that a racial achievement gap existed weren't particularly surprising. Most observers believed that inequality in school funding explained the racial disparity in academic achievement levels. As one researcher who worked on the study put it, "What the government really expected was that the South was discriminating by having lousy schools for poor and minority kids."[59] Coleman's report broke new ground by refuting that expectation. There were "some definite and systematic" differences between black and white schools, the report stated.[60] Blacks often got the short end of the stick when it came to school facilities, curricular and extracurricular offerings, science labs, schools meeting accreditation standards, and teacher quality.[61] But black schools weren't always inferior. Or, as Coleman put it, "There is not a wholly consistent pattern—that is, minorities are not at a disadvantage in every item listed—but that there are nevertheless some definite and systematic . . . differences."[62]

So what was causing the disparity in academic achievement? Here was Coleman's conclusion: the crucial factors were the student's own social class and the composition of the student body.[63] Per Coleman's report: "One implication stands out above all: That schools bring little influence to bear on a child's achievement that is independent of his background and general social context." The sociologist continued: "The inequalities imposed on children by their home, neighborhood, and peer environment are carried along to become the inequalities with which they confront adult life at the end of school."[64] Even Harold Howe II, the U.S. commissioner of education, called this finding "unexpected."[65]

The differences in school quality mattered, but they weren't the prime driver of racial disparities in student achievement, Coleman asserted. Black students performed better academically when they were surrounded by students from stronger educational backgrounds. And, on average, white students had stronger educational backgrounds than black students. Students who had access to reading material in the home, who traveled, and whose parents had higher levels of education exerted a positive upward pull on their peers' educational outcomes.[66] Coleman put it this way: "The apparent beneficial effect of a student body with a high proportion of white students comes not from the racial composition per se, but from the better educational background and higher educational aspirations that are, on average, found among white students."[67]

Acknowledging this reality was tricky. It was easy to hear a slur in the statement. Perhaps white students were just smarter, more academically capable, than black students. Maybe there was some inherent incapacity in black students (or in the black family), some intellectual deficit, that made it difficult for them to compete with whites or to succeed at the highest levels. So the conclusion had to be contextualized by acknowledging what segregation actually did in real life. Segregation systematically advantaged whites and disadvantaged blacks, in education and across myriad other domains. That was its purpose. From this perspective, it would have been surprising if white students *didn't* have stronger educational backgrounds than blacks.

The relationship between segregation and the racial achievement gap was complex. It involved more than one cause. School segregation was where race *and* class fatally intersected. Per Coleman's report: "The racial and socio-economic composition of a classroom is an important and determining factor in educational achievement."[68] Later studies confirmed this finding.[69] The problem was twofold. First, segregating children from impoverished backgrounds—concentrating them in high-poverty schools— exerted a negative pull on student achievement. One social scientist described the class piece of the equation this way: "Children in [segregated high-poverty] schools tend to be less healthy, to have weaker preschool experiences, to have only one parent, to move frequently and have unstable educational experiences . . . to have friends and classmates with lower levels of achievement."[70] And this didn't even include the inequalities often found in the schools these children attended (fewer challenging courses, narrower curricula, less experienced teachers, and the like).[71] These and other disadvantages accumulated one on top of the other, creating a downward pull that depressed student achievement.

But race was in the mix, too, creating additional mischief. For one, black children were generally much poorer than white children. Additionally, they were often residentially segregated in less well-resourced neighborhoods. Finally, the neighborhood school rule and other mechanisms ensured that residential segregation—which was predicated on race discrimination—carried over into the public schools. Race compounded and amplified the effects of poverty concentration. Racial segregation and socioeconomic segregation couldn't easily be disentangled. As another prominent social scientist, Sean F. Reardon, later concluded: "Racial segregation—particularly racial economic segregation—exacerbates already unequal educational opportunities stemming from large racial disparities in family resources, neighborhood conditions, and early childhood education."[72] But if black students were included in white schools and classrooms, they could gain access to the advantages those students had accumulated, *by virtue of the segregated system.* "One key to systematically reducing racial *school* segregation is reducing racial *residential* segregation, particularly between-district residential segregation," Reardon added.[73]

Coleman's view was that "It appears that a pupil's achievement is strongly related to the educational backgrounds and aspirations of the other students in the school."[74] But did this mean that money *never* mattered? No. Later research showed that when money was spent *wisely*— such as on early childhood programs, reducing class sizes, increasing the length of the school year, and raising teacher salaries—additional funding moved the needle on learning outcomes and students' economic success.[75]

——

A larger philosophical question lurked behind Green's testimony. What was the purpose of public education? Cleage thought public education was intended primarily to transmit the "three Rs." He believed that white-run public schools in Detroit had failed black students in this task. The only solution to this problem was to cede power to black parents so they could provide the necessary control and oversight to help black students succeed. Green agreed that a core function of public education was to transmit the three Rs. But he believed public education had a larger purpose as well: "I feel very strongly about the role that education can play in humanizing young people, in humanizing this nation, and a very significant part of this humanization process is learning to live with and to respect each other,"[76] Green said.

Green's testimony suggested that all-white schools were transmitting messages of white supremacy, messages that were very difficult to unlearn. If they wanted to do otherwise, the schools had to be integrated, starting in the earliest grades. One could hear echoes of *Brown v. Board of Education* in Green's testimony. Although *Brown* was open to conflicting interpretations, one leading understanding of the case was that it was grounded in the importance of integration. In *Brown*, the court said that education was the "foundation of good citizenship" and thus must be open to all on an equal basis.[77] In this way, *Brown* suggested that integration was a desirable social goal because integrated schools produced better educational results for black schoolchildren, and/or because integration increased social welfare more generally.

Segregated schools replicated themselves, too. They produced whites who, when faced with demands for integration or greater black participation in public school administration, were already primed to leave. As Green said, some of that impact had been felt already. He told the court, "All the whites have fled. Northwest Detroit has fled to Oak Park, Livonia, Bloomfield Hills."[78] Green believed that, had Detroit's schools done their job correctly, whites wouldn't have had one foot out the door. "I see that flight being significantly related to what we have not done in our public schools. If we did a headcount we would find a good number of those residents today, and another good example, the fact that blacks can't buy houses in Warren is a failure of the Detroit Public School System. Livonia was sticks and woods when I was a kid. That suburban community was built because the Detroit Public School System did not perform its functions. It was built because we had all white elementary schools, all white junior high schools and all white high schools."[79]

What Green seemed to be getting at was that if children were educated in a racially monolithic environment, there was little reason to believe that segregation would ever be eliminated. The system would self-perpetuate.

Green argued that segregated city schools led inexorably to segregated suburban schools. Segregation begat segregation. Garbage in, garbage out. His testimony was based on the more commonly accepted rationale for integration than that emphasized by Verda Bradley. Bradley pushed integration as an instrumental vehicle to obtain access to whites' resources. She was interested in improving her son's education at Clinton Elementary. Green's approach was instrumental as well. But it focused on the idea that, by coming together in the same geographic space—ideally the public schools—blacks and whites might have positive, if not society-changing, interactions. Perhaps being educated together would lead them to appreciate their shared humanity. Integration might reduce, if not eliminate, racist and stereotypical views. Integration, and perhaps only integration, could stop the cycle.

Green's supposition had a lengthy and respected provenance. Writing in 1954 (the same year *Brown* was decided), psychologist Gordon Allport popularized the "contact hypothesis." In *The Nature of Prejudice*, Allport argued that intergroup contact could diminish racial stereotypes and prejudice.[80] He wrote: "The trend of evidence clearly indicates that white people who live side by side with Negroes of the same general economic class in public housing projects are on the whole more friendly, less fearful, and less stereotyped in their views than white people who live in segregated arrangements."[81] Later research conclusively demonstrated that Allport's conclusion was correct: intergroup contact improves intergroup relations.[82] But integration alone wasn't enough. All integration did was create the *possibility* for stereotype reduction and related aims. Simply throwing everyone in the same school wasn't going to solve such an entrenched problem. The prevalence of tracking was one reason why. Allport cautioned, "We must not assume that integrated housing automatically solves the problem of prejudice. At most we can say that it creates a condition where friendly contacts and accurate social perceptions can occur."[83]

The nature of the contact, and the conditions under which that contact occurred, mattered. Allport thought "equal status contact between majority and minority groups in the pursuit of common goals" was a necessary precondition for stereotype reduction.[84] But even equal status "one-offs," such as interactions between blacks and whites in stores or restaurants, typically weren't enough to move the needle. In order to change minds, people of different races needed to do things together and develop a common bond. A good example was a multiracial athletic team. Athletic teams had communal and durable objectives; pursuit of the sport, the thrill of competition, the joy of vanquishing a respected opponent. As Allport put it: "The cooperative striving for the goal . . . engenders [interracial] solidarity."[85] He added two additional elements to the mix. Allport reasoned that the two groups needed to work cooperatively instead of competitively in order to ensure prejudice reduction.[86] The athletic team fit the bill here, too. Finally, the entire process needed external support, such as from the law, in order to succeed. Allport put it this way: "The establishment of a legal norm creates a public conscience and a standard for expected behavior that check *overt* signs of prejudice."[87] Later research suggested that the relationship between intergroup contact and prejudice reduction was so robust that Allport's conditions were not even essential for intergroup contact to do its work. Their presence, however, greatly "enhance[d] the tendency for positive contact outcomes to emerge."[88]

This was all well and good. But it was ephemeral and a little effete. Who cared what some social scientist thought about race relations? For that matter, what difference did Green's testimony make? As an African American who had obtained a PhD in educational psychology in 1963—making him a rarity, then or now—wasn't he the very prototype of the "pointy-headed intellectual"? He was hardly the man on the street. Why credit his testimony if it was so atypical?

The first answer was that Green was an "expert" witness. At the time, regular or "lay" witnesses could provide their opinions in federal court, but only when it was necessary for a jury to understand their testimony. In contrast, the professor was allowed to give his opinion about segregation, the racial achievement gap, the Detroit school system, and related issues because he possessed special knowledge and expertise that the average lay person was not expected to have.[89]

Still, wasn't it more likely that Cleage rather than Green represented the views of the black majority? The answer came from Green himself.

Responding to a question about whether blacks opposed busing, Green reframed the question. The issue wasn't really busing, it was equity and fairness: "There has been some opposition from black parents, not with regard to busing per se, but to what happens once the youngsters reach that particular school."[90] If there was to be busing to promote integration, it had to be "a two-way process" that would "meaningfully benefit both the black and white youngsters."[91] Still, Green's position remained easy to caricature. Decades later, Justice Clarence Thomas would do just that by conflating diversity or integration with "classroom aesthetics" and suggesting that "there is nothing 'pressing' or 'necessary' about obtaining whatever educational benefits might flow from racial diversity."[92]

But Green's testimony wasn't so easily dismissed. First, he was a Detroit native. His ties to the city and to its people were deep and abiding. His parents, two brothers, a sister, and dozens of other relatives lived in Detroit. Choking back emotion, the professor spoke of his love of Detroit and how its schools had failed. Second, Green had attended the city's public schools—Dwyer and Moore Elementary, Sherrard Intermediate, and Northern High.[93] He wasn't a disinterested academic. This was how he explained his educational experience: "I went to the Detroit public schools for 12 years and I never knew any white youngster. I attended class with very few, maybe one, two or three. Therefore, when I became an undergraduate student for a brief period of time at Wayne State and a longer period of time at San Francisco State College, I was lacking in a kind of past informal relationship that should have occurred in the classroom that would have allowed me to develop the kind of healthy attitude about whites that I should have."[94] He continued: "The only thing I knew about white people is what my father told me about whites in terms of his experience in Georgia. My father saw whites lynch black people. My father left the South at 17 because he saw a youngster split down the middle and burned at Haddock County, Georgia."[95]

Later, Green learned to view whites as individuals. He testified: "There are white people who don't like black people. There are white people who sit on the fence, and there are white people who were very supportive of the concerns of blacks, but I would never have gotten that from my experiences at Sherrard Intermediate School and Northern High School in Detroit."[96]

What difference did it make that Green encountered so few whites in his K–12 experience? Did it really matter? Perhaps not if the purpose of education was to equip students to live and work solely among their own racial group. But Green's studies and professional work had taken him far beyond the single-race society of his youth—and he saw what this potential could mean for any American, black or white or otherwise.

13

TEN BUSES

S howing that Detroit school officials and the state of Michigan intentionally segregated the city's public schools was core to the plaintiffs' case—and it would consume more than two dozen days of the trial. It was tedious. It was systematic. And, at times, it was mind-numbingly boring. At one point, after several exhibits had been introduced, Roth exclaimed: "The record should reflect that I am still awake."[1]

But it got the job done. A host of witnesses showed just how carefully school segregation had been established and maintained. There were parents, school administrators, and board members. There were professors, a variety of experts, statisticians, and state and local education officials. All assembled to prove that the defendants violated the Constitution—and the rule established in *Brown*—by intentionally segregating Detroit's public schools.

The plaintiffs called on several black mothers who described how in June 1970—and before the recall election—they were informed that their children would be moved from overcrowded black schools to majority white schools near their homes. But then, once the recall happened and just before school started, their children were reassigned to black schools distant from their homes.[2]

One of them, Inez Kimble, stated that her child was initially assigned to Pulaski Elementary, which was located, as Kimble testified, in an "all-white" neighborhood that she described as "very nice in atmosphere."[3]

In contrast, the black school that replaced it in the fall was encircled by houses that "had the windows knocked out, and all around the place is nothing but abandoned houses."[4] Kimble testified that the reassignment was based on race, and that she protested the assignment to both the Detroit and the state Boards of Education.[5] Describing her motivations, Kimble told the court, "It is not the matter of distance and we are not against busing, it's just segregation that we are against. We wanted to try to get so the white and blacks can get to know the black ways and they can get to know the white ways and so they can grow up and not be like the older generation. They can have love in their heart."[6]

Gordon Foster, a desegregation expert, detailed a cornucopia of techniques that Detroit school authorities could use to maintain purposeful segregation. Linking to the argument the plaintiffs had developed during the housing portion of the case, the expert warned that these mechanisms "tend to further racial isolation" and "increase containment of minority groups."[7] It wasn't just that these techniques intensified the "containment of minority groups." It was that the devices depended upon high levels of residential segregation—the containment—for their success.

Numerous principals, superintendents, board members, and other school officials proceeded to explain *how* the Detroit school board took exactly the actions the expert outlined to segregate the city's schools. They told the court how black children were bused past nearby white schools to majority black schools, how school attendance zones and school feeder patterns were manipulated or "gerrymandered" to maintain segregation, and how schools were constructed at specific locations to perpetuate segregation. They described how white students were allowed to transfer out of black schools for "racial reasons," and how whites living in racially transitioning areas were allowed to "opt-out" of integration by the use of optional attendance zones. The plaintiffs also put on evidence demonstrating that the school system's teaching, administrative, and supervisory staff was racially segregated.

Notwithstanding the plethora of detail, the plaintiffs continued to hold Judge Roth's attention. The judge overruled the defendants' myriad objections, much like a third base coach waving his runner home. The following colloquy was representative. Bushnell: "I trust the court will understand that I do make my objections for the record." Roth: "You have a standing objection; you have continuing objections, and then you have particularized objections." Bushnell: "Yes, sir."[8]

Later, as the trial wound down, Roth telegraphed just how much his thinking had evolved: "If the court in this case finds that the situation calls for some other judicial action then the School Board ought to be preparing themselves to meet that eventuality. But the state defendants too. I don't think that the [s]tate defendants should hide, put their heads in the sand and avoid considering what may happen if certain developments already made plain in this case take shape."[9]

With respect to the state of Michigan, the court heard from a highly credentialed consultant with expertise in urban education, delivery of educational services, and race- and class-based educational disparities. He testified that in Michigan education was a state function, that the state was responsible for a large share of each district's education funding, and that there was no valid educational rationale for educating one group of children in Detroit and another in the suburbs.[10] The expert said school district lines were "drawn somewhat arbitrarily" and were "usually influenced by history rather than an educational consideration for the child."[11]

The plaintiffs examined a high-level state education official who spoke to how the state discriminated against Detroit's students. Detroit parents paid state taxes, but they weren't getting the same benefits. Lucas asked the state official, "If a child lives in [Detroit] and lives more than a mile and half from the school to which he is assigned he may not receive the state [transportation] aid because it is unfunded at the present time?" The official responded, "That is correct." Lucas's next question was this: "But if he lives the same distance away and lives [in the suburbs] . . . then he could receive state aid?" "That is correct," the official replied.[12] The court heard how the state education aid allocation formula systematically advantaged suburban schools.[13] In Michigan, money for the public schools came from two main sources, direct state aid and taxes generated from the property located in the particular school district. Both sources of funds were subject to an allocation formula—set by the state—which treated the city and suburban school districts very differently. As Dimond explained it, "Detroit families tax themselves much higher on a much lower tax base but could spend only a smaller percentage of their local tax dollars on schooling—generating fewer local dollars per pupil than many of their more favored suburban neighbors."[14] And the plaintiffs put copious evidence before the court about the state law that had set the whole litigation in motion: Act 48, which effectively overturned the modest integration plan the Detroit school board had adopted on April 7, 1970.

Toward the end of the trial, the plaintiffs sought to introduce into evidence the minutes of a July 1, 1969, Detroit Board of Education meeting. After some back and forth among the lawyers, the judge stated: "All right. The exhibit may be received."[15]

Even in a case with thousands of exhibits, this one stood out. The minutes included Abraham Zwerdling's inaugural address as the board's president. It was a classic exposition of his worldview: "I believe that the American Dream can be realized—but only in an integrated, open society."[16] He called out Cleage and his brethren: "The harsh realities of life strengthen the self-defeating forces of black separatism in education which are so suspiciously acceptable to white conservatives," he wrote.[17] And he asked key rhetorical questions: "Why is there so much talk of dividing up the School District of Detroit and not a breath of a suggestion that we redistrict to achieve integration by crossing city boundaries?"[18]

Roth admitted the entire address into evidence. But the plaintiffs wanted to draw the judge's attention to a very specific part of the board president's speech. Lucas recited a passage that was particularly useful for the plaintiffs' case: "The State Legislature has full power to pass legislation mandating the reorganization of school districts across the city and even county boundaries."[19] This statement reminded the court that the state could, if it so chose, mandate the reorganization of school districts across city and county boundaries.[20] Zwerdling suggested one way that might be achieved: the state could create a school district that "would embrace the Martin Luther King and Southeastern High Schools and their constellations together with the Grosse Pointe School District and St. Clair Shores School District. That would mean a school district of 56,000 children, which is the type of region we are talking about within the City of Detroit. In that instance the school district would be 59.5% white and 40.5% black, so it would have balance from that standpoint."[21] Combining

ABOVE Thurgood Marshall (left)
and President Lyndon B. Johnson
(right) in the Oval Office, 1967
(White House Photo Office)

RIGHT Albert Cleage in his church,
the Shrine of the Black Madonna,
in 1968 (Bettmann / Getty Images)

ABOVE Remus Robinson (left) and Louise Grace (right) on April 12, 1955, the day Robinson was sworn in as the first African American member of the Detroit Board of Education (Detroit Federation of Teachers)

RIGHT Abraham Zwerdling as a young lawyer in 1949 (*Ann Arbor News*)

BELOW State senator Coleman Young in an undated photo (Bentley Historical Library, University of Michigan)

ABOVE June Shagaloff, community organizer extraordinaire, in 1962 (Bancroft Library, University of California, Berkeley)

BELOW LEFT NAACP general counsel Robert Carter in 1963 (*The New York Times* / Getty Images)

BELOW RIGHT NAACP executive director Roy Wilkins at Cobo Hall in Detroit in 1972 (Bettmann / Getty Images)

ABOVE Louis Lucas, lead counsel for the *Milliken* plaintiffs, circa 1972 (*Detroit Free Press*)

LEFT Governor William Milliken at a news conference in 1974 (UPI)

BELOW Verda and Ronald Bradley, named plaintiffs in the *Milliken* case, circa 1980 (*Detroit Free Press*)

ABOVE Michigan attorney general Frank Kelley (right) and assistant attorney general Eugene Krasicky (left) at the United States Supreme Court in 1973 in connection with *Milliken v. Bradley* (Associated Press)

BELOW LEFT Nathaniel R. Jones, general counsel of the NAACP, at a press conference in 1971 (Librado Romero / *The New York Times* / Redux)

BELOW RIGHT Judge Stephen Roth in a press photo from 1972 (The Historical Society for the United States District Court for the Eastern District of Michigan)

LEFT Alexander Ritchie, counsel for the CCBE, circa 1972 (*Detroit Free Press*)

BELOW Children in front of the segregation wall in Detroit, 1941 (John Vachon / Library of Congress)

TOP Changing of the guard: outgoing chief justice Earl Warren (left), President Richard Nixon (center), and incoming chief justice Warren Burger (right) outside the United States Supreme Court on June 25, 1969 (Marion S. Trikosko / Universal Images Group via Getty Images)

ABOVE LEFT Judge Damon Keith in an undated photo (The Historical Society for the United States District Court for the Eastern District of Michigan)

ABOVE RIGHT Irene McCabe in 1971 (Associated Press)

ABOVE President Richard Nixon (center) presents Lewis Powell (left) and William Rehnquist (right) with their commissions as associate justices of the United States Supreme Court on December 22, 1971. (Richard Nixon Foundation)

BELOW The Burger Court in 1973 (The United States Supreme Court)

the Martin Luther King area with the Grosse Pointe area would create economic balance as well, Zwerdling added. It was food for thought.

———

By the close of the plaintiffs' case, as Dimond put it, "the voluminous evidence spelled 'intentional segregation.'"[22] When the trial shifted to the defendants, Bushnell and the board tried to stop the bleeding by emphasizing the Detroit school board's good deeds. (They cited the April 7 plan as one.) Meanwhile, in early June, Ritchie repeated his preference for a metropolitan plan by arguing that Roth should "expand the scope of [any] order into other [suburban] districts."[23]

Then, in mid-July, the CCBE lawyer made good on all his talk. Ritchie filed a motion with the court requesting that more than eighty suburban school districts in southeastern Michigan be added as parties to the *Bradley v. Milliken* lawsuit.[24] Ritchie based his motion on two federal rules. The first allowed federal courts to join a party to a lawsuit "on motion or on its own . . . at any time."[25] The second required federal courts to join a party to a lawsuit if "in his absence complete relief cannot be accorded among those already parties."[26] Although the motion was short, it contained some notable assertions. It described the suburban school districts pointedly as "white segregated school districts." In addition, the motion characterized them as "agents of the state of Michigan."[27] Ritchie later put some "meat on the bones" of this assertion, arguing that under Michigan state law "education of children is a state function and that the [suburban] district[s] themselves are merely instrumentalities of the state."[28] For good measure, he added, "the lines which confine the school districts of the City of Detroit [are] . . . historical artifacts . . . which have no functional relationship to the broad purpose of educating all of the children."[29] Perhaps most interestingly, Ritchie's motion asserted that leaving those "white segregated school districts" on the sidelines would "impose an unconstitutional burden on the intervening defendant [CCBE]"—meaning white Detroiters.[30] If the motion succeeded it would ensure that *all* Detroit-area whites, whether city or suburban, would have skin in the game. The lawyer was zealously protecting his clients, Detroit's white population. Making virtually all whites residing in southeastern Michigan parties to the case immeasurably strengthened his clients' hand. It linked whites' fate across jurisdictional boundaries and, crucially, provided urban whites with access to the substantial political clout white suburbanites enjoyed.

Ritchie believed that the defendants were likely to lose the case, which was the basis of his claim that complete relief could not be provided without the suburban districts' inclusion. At a hearing on the motion, he told the court: "An objective analysis of the proofs which have come in . . . [suggests] a judgment of this Court which would result in an integration order."[31] Ritchie was focused like a laser on the scope of that potential order, which he argued could not be "confined within the geographical boundaries of the Detroit School System."[32] Ritchie argued that the number of whites in the city of Detroit was rapidly declining. But in order to have "a school district which was conceived of as an integrated school district," white students were necessary.[33] The court had already heard a significant amount of testimony during presentation of the plaintiffs' case about the suburbs, much of which negated claims of white innocence.

The court had heard earlier from sociologist Karl Taeuber, who testified that it was unlikely that individual choice explained why black professionals (who presumably could afford more expensive housing) did not live in the suburbs. Real estate broker (not realtor) John Humphrey told the court about his experiences attempting to purchase a personal residence in two suburban locations in 1968.[34] In Bloomfield Hills, a realtor attempted to discourage Humphrey from buying a prospective property by emphasizing the negative: "I don't know why you'd want to buy this house because it floods every time it rains . . . It's in bad shape, bad location." In Southfield, another realtor told Humphrey that the sales price of a house was $20,000 more than the listed price.[35] A former Detroit Urban League official explained how he "sought to purchase a home in Grosse Pointe, and we have met with some difficulty there."[36] The court entered into evidence an official policy statement adopted by the Michigan Civil Rights Commission in the spring of 1970, which read: "Recent studies show while black families have the same housing desires as white families and the housing desired by both is almost exclusively being built in the suburban areas where discrimination, fear and custom exclude black families from purchasing such property."[37] Judge Roth heard about instances of "vandalism, harassment and intimidation" when Carado and Ruby Bailey attempted to move into Warren in June 1967.[38] And this was all during the early housing phase of the trial, before the plaintiffs demonstrated how the state of Michigan favored the suburbs—and disfavored Detroit—with respect to state education and transportation aid.

Lucas, opposing CCBE's motion, said the suburban school districts were unnecessary. From the plaintiffs' perspective, the responsible parties were already in the dock: the state defendants. This "court has power to order relief beyond the confines of the present geographical boundaries of the city of Detroit but . . . the Court does not need additional parties in order to grant that relief. The State Board of Education is the parent of these districts," he asserted.[39] It was an important point on which the plaintiffs refused to cede even an inch. "The Fourteenth Amendment speaks to the state and state action is what the case is all about," Lucas told the court.[40]

Assistant attorney general Eugene Krasicky, representing the state defendants, amplified Ritchie's argument. "If this court is going to adopt a metropolitan plan these parties [the suburban school districts] should have a right to be here and they should have a right to protest and they should have the full measure of their rights with every right of due process of law."[41] The suburban school districts had rights—rights to be heard—which were so important that they demanded federal court protection. Krasicky's and Lucas's views were diametrically opposed. The plaintiffs believed that the question of whether the suburban school districts should be included, as well as any other metropolitan issues, went to the question of what relief should be ordered. But the question of whether the defendants had violated the Constitution by segregating Detroit's schools came first. As Dimond put it, we "argued that [Ritchie's] motion related to relief and should be deferred pending the liability ruling."[42] Roth took the various arguments under advisement and adjourned the hearing.

By July 30, 1971, the liability phase of the case was over. The plaintiffs anticipated victory. On that day, Paul Dimond wrote Nate Jones: "We look forward to a favorable decision in Detroit. In any event that case will be a landmark or a benchmark. I am convinced that Lou did a great job, and that the case was presented in a compelling fashion."[43]

―――――

Detroit was not the only Michigan city where school segregation was being challenged. Located in Oakland County in southeastern Michigan and roughly twenty-five miles from Detroit, Pontiac was the state's fourteenth-largest city.[44] A 1960 promotional film produced by Pontiac business leaders and city officials touted the city's growth and promise.[45] The civic boosters showcased a small Midwestern city that punched above its weight class when it came to manufacturing. "Pontiac is primarily known as an industrial city, the birthplace of a famous automobile [the Pontiac brand of cars made by General Motors]. Here the plants . . . turn out products that serve the nation and parts that go into the manufacture of automobiles and trucks," the narrator intoned.[46] The filmmakers depicted a harmonious, racially diverse, working-class city with "some of the finest schools in our nation . . . where our children learn to live together as good useful citizens."[47] The portrayal did not match the reality. During the very same year that the film was released, the Pontiac Board of Education reaffirmed its commitment to the "neighborhood school concept," mandating that all students in the Pontiac school district "should attend the school which services the attendance area in which they live."[48]

On May 28, 1971, and as the plaintiffs' counsel were presenting their case to Judge Roth in downtown Detroit, the United States Court of Appeals for the Sixth Circuit handed down an opinion in *Davis v. School District of the City of Pontiac*, a case concerning segregation in the Pontiac School District.[49] Back in February 1970, the federal trial judge in the case, Damon Keith, had ruled that the Pontiac school system was unconstitutionally segregated.[50] Keith was something of a legend in his hometown of Detroit: Thurgood Marshall protégé, chair of the NAACP Detroit branch membership committee, a Wayne County commissioner, chair of the Detroit Housing Commission, cochair of the Michigan Civil Rights Commission, founder of one of Detroit's first black law firms, second black Michigander in history to be appointed a federal district court judge

(Wade H. McCree Jr. was the first).[51] At his death in 2019, Michigan governor Gretchen Whitmer called Keith "a civil rights icon."[52]

In no uncertain terms, Keith ordered Pontiac school officials to integrate the school system: "Such integration shall be accomplished by the revising of boundary lines for attendance purposes, as well as by busing so as to achieve maximum racial integration."[53] The day after Keith issued the ruling requiring Pontiac's schools to integrate, Remus Robinson sent him a congratulatory telegram ("beautiful, man beautiful").[54] But much of the rest of Keith's correspondence file wasn't as laudatory. One unsigned postcard read, "What makes you think that people who have not been to downtown Detroit [since the 1967 riots] are going to let their kids mingle with the niggers via bus line?"[55]

Facing a requirement that it integrate the school system by the fall, the school district appealed. The appellate court stayed (halted) the implementation of Judge Keith's order until it could issue its decision. Ultimately, though, the school district lost. Pontiac would have to adopt new boundaries and busing that year. Wade H. McCree Jr., only the third black man to serve as a federal court judge in American history, wrote the opinion for the appellate court.[56] He would later become Jimmy Carter's solicitor general, and defend busing to achieve desegregation in federal court.[57] Judge McCree wasn't shy about expressing his views on race. A lawyer once made the great mistake of suggesting that the judge was incapable of giving a white litigant a fair shake. McCree responded: "The ultimate of arrogance is achieved when a white person thinks another white person can make a judgment without being influenced by race, and a black person cannot."[58]

The appellate court upheld the lower court, ruling that there was substantial evidence to support its findings of purposeful segregation. Importantly, the court made a distinction between the circumstances in Pontiac and in *Deal*, the Cincinnati case, upon which the Pontiac school district had attempted to rely. *Deal*, the Sixth Circuit said, concerned whether there was an affirmative obligation on a school district to eradicate segregation where it had done nothing to stimulate it.[59] The answer to that question was no. But *Deal* did not govern the present situation. The court ruled that there was plenty of evidence—racially motivated school construction, racial gerrymandering of attendance zones in conjunction with the use of neighborhood schools, placement of black teachers and administrators only in black schools—to support the finding that Pontiac had, in fact, "intended to foster segregation."[60]

And it wasn't just what the school district had done. What it hadn't done mattered, too. Judge Keith had ruled that "when the power to act is available, failure to take the necessary steps so as to negate or alleviate a situation which is harmful is as wrong as is the taking of affirmative steps to advance that situation. Sins of omission can be as serious as sins of commission."[61] What Keith seemed to be saying was that a school system's consistent failure to desegregate where it was also affirmatively segregating, was one more brick in the wall. In this context, the *failure to desegregate* was one more piece of evidence going to discriminatory intent. And intent was the sine qua non of proving de jure segregation in a northern school district. In upholding Judge Keith's ruling in its entirety, the Sixth Circuit approved this approach to establishing a constitutional violation. The plaintiffs in *Bradley v. Milliken* noted this prominently in a brief they submitted to Judge Roth.[62] The *Davis* decision was the first time a federal *appellate* court ruled that a northern school district was de jure segregated because of the actions of local public school officials.[63] It was a ruling that northern civil rights activists had been looking for since at least the late 1950s.

It also demonstrated the importance of black lawyers and judges. It goes without saying that the lawyer who challenged Judge McCree was wrong. Indeed, the idea that black judges lacked the necessary objectivity to preside over cases dealing with race was not only insulting and absurd, but perhaps exactly backward: for McCree and Keith, their race was their superpower. It allowed them to see what white judges often missed, or, like Roth, had to be painstakingly educated to accept. Keith reflected on the importance of the Sixth Circuit's affirmance: "I felt comforted when the court of appeals unanimously affirmed me and said I had made the case for distinguishing Pontiac from the Cincinnati case. It would have been easy to go the other way. If I didn't want to bite the bullet, I could have said, 'Look, I'm bound by the Circuit's decision in the Cincinnati case [*Deal*] and this is no different.' That would have been easier and less controversial. You wouldn't have had the turmoil. Wouldn't have had the bombing of buses, the picketing of schools . . . But it wouldn't have been the right thing."[64]

Keith's statement, which suggested that there was more than one legally supportable outcome in the *Davis* case, also revealed something vital about judging a case. Sometimes judges have to pick between two (or more) legally supportable outcomes. Good judging involves a mix of skills and characteristics; it is as much an art as a science. So how did Keith know *how* to do "the right thing?" One factor might have been his life experience. Just a few short years before Keith decided the *Davis* case, he recalled an instance of police harassment: "They saw me, they stopped, and they got out of the car. They asked, 'Who are you?' I told them my name. Told them I was a lawyer. They patted me down anyhow. It was humiliating."[65] Brainpower and mental clock speed obviously were necessary for good judging, but those qualities weren't sufficient. Character, acumen, empathy, life experience, emotional intelligence, bravery, and an appreciation of history all mattered, too. Being a good judge was hard. Being a great one was even harder.

The U.S. Supreme Court declined to review the Sixth Circuit's order in the Pontiac case. So the appellate ruling in the *Davis* case stood, and that meant that Pontiac school officials were going to have implement Judge Keith's order, with its busing mandate. They didn't have much time. The beginning of the 1971–72 school year was just a few short months away.

Meanwhile, in Detroit, the plaintiffs' counsel could breathe a sigh of relief. With McCree backing up Keith, *Deal* was looking less and less like a roadblock for the plaintiffs. They just needed to do what they were already doing. They needed to convince Judge Roth that the school officials in Detroit had engaged in the same kinds of behavior as the school officials in Pontiac. They were well on their way.

═══════

At around 10:00 p.m. on Monday, August 30, 1971, just a few days before Judge Keith's busing order was to go into effect, a series of explosions rocked an unguarded, eleven-acre bus depot at 650 North Saginaw in Pontiac. Fifty-seven buses had been parked in the lot. Ten of them were destroyed. The bombing was later determined to have been caused by dynamite placed near fuel tanks.[66] Fortunately, no one was injured. The cost to the city in property damage was about $50,000. Later, five former Ku Klux Klan members would be found guilty of conspiring to interfere with the execution of a court-ordered desegregation plan and other charges in connection with the bombing.[67] Included among the five was "Grand Dragon" Robert Miles, the Klan's leader in Michigan.

The key evidence that led to the Klan members' conviction was provided by an unpaid FBI informant, a thirty-seven-year-old Pontiac firefighter and father of six named Jerome Lauinger. *The Detroit News* provided a clue as to his motivation. Lauinger had been "stung as a child by both anti-Semitic and anti-German bigotry."[68] The firefighter described his infiltration of the Klan and subsequent testimony against the defendants as "my down payment on democracy."[69]

Tensions in the city had been growing all summer. On August 14, 1971, the *Detroit Free Press* reported that a local organization calling itself the National Action Group, a Pontiac homeowners association, strenuously opposed Judge Keith's integration plan.[70] *The New York Times* later characterized NAG as "the center of the white opposition to busing" in Pontiac.[71] The group had been busy. It was actively lobbying elected officials—NAG sent more than 650 antibusing messages to politicians in Washington—and planned a court suit and rally to prevent busing. The group's spokesperson was a telegenic thirty-six-year-old white mother of three named Irene McCabe.

The next day, McCabe was pictured in the same paper speaking at the NAG-sponsored rally. Marchers carried signs reading "Thanks Mr. Nixon, we have one friend on our side" and "Integration yes, busing no."[72] McCabe recommended a boycott: "The law does not require you to send your children to kindergarten, but the school district gets state aid if they attend."[73] "If you keep them home, we can hurt the school district financially," she added.[74] She told the crowd to stay within the bounds of the law in order to achieve their aims. But if that didn't work, all bets were off. "Let's see what we can do within the law," she told them, "before we do anything else."[75] Responding to NAG's aggressiveness, William Waterman, a lawyer who represented the plaintiffs in the *Davis* case, blamed political leaders for fanning the flames of hatred. He told the *Detroit Free Press*, "Of course, with Nixon's conduct of late, and Alabama Governor George Wallace's actions, these people are inspired to defy court orders."[76] This "could promote civil disorder or even Civil War," he added.[77] One day before the bus bombing, a local legislator had urged Pontiac parents to defy the federal court order.[78]

A detailed profile in the *Detroit Free Press* showed the extent to which McCabe had become a local celebrity.[79] The story depicted a classic middle American, one who was "proud of her Greek heritage, and equally proud of her American citizenry."[80] The piece provided a narrative about McCabe that would stick: the wife of a Postal Service supervisor who had been reluctantly drawn into political action. "It took a mini-riot . . . to get her involved," the paper noted breathlessly.[81] With her blond hair swept back off her face in a classic early seventies style—think Goldie Hawn—McCabe was the woman next door with, as another local paper stated, "enough sex appeal to lead militant whites on an epic anti-busing crusade."[82] "Her clothes looked K-Mart, her hair looked Clairol, and her accent had Kentucky bourbon on its breath," the paper concluded.[83]

Speaking to the *Detroit Free Press*, McCabe painted herself as an innocent victim of reverse racism. McCabe told the paper, "If you're a colored child, and you run to the NAACP if you don't like the way things are going, knowing someone will take your cause to the courts, you can get away with anything."[84] (One could only wonder how Verda Bradley would have reacted to this statement.) McCabe believed the situation was very different for white children. "But the white kids, the white kids are used and abused. The administrators were gutless wonders."[85] Someone had to step in. Of one thing she was absolutely certain. There was no segregation in Pontiac. Keith was all wrong. "I know it's a lie when Judge Damon Keith says we have legal segregation," she told the paper.[86] "We have an open housing law in Pontiac, and that's all you need."[87]

On September 1, 1971, NAG was in Judge Keith's courtroom asking him to stop the use of buses to achieve racial balance in Pontiac. The group believed that busing would harm the "basic rights of children."[88] Perhaps unsurprisingly, NAG's argument fell on deaf ears. Keith dismissed the suit, stating, "This case will not be settled in the streets of Pontiac."[89] The buses would roll the following Tuesday.

In November 2015, I had an opportunity to interview Judge Keith at a conference at the Duke University School of Law.[90] At the age of ninety-three, the judge had lost some of his mobility; he responded to my questions from a wheelchair. But Keith was still sharp.[91] Reflecting on the Pontiac case, Judge Keith told me, "It was awful. They threatened to kill me." Indeed, near the start of the school year, the FBI informed Judge Keith that the Ku Klux Klan was planning to "execute" him. Robert Miles denied it: "Judge Keith has done more for Klan recruitment in Michigan than anyone. It would be like killing the goose who laid the golden egg."[92]

One day before school was set to begin, McCabe led a two-mile anti-busing protest march, which culminated at a junior high school. The march received national attention. Howard K. Smith, reporting on *ABC Evening News*, told his viewers, "And in Pontiac, Michigan, where ten school buses were dynamited last week, the tensions are growing by the hour."[93] Smith shifted to Jim Kincaid, who was on the ground in Pontiac. His dispatch focused almost entirely on the white antibusing demonstrators. There was no mention of Judge Keith's findings, which formed the basis of his order. It was as if the "court ordered plan" had appeared from outer space; it was being imposed from on high. A casual viewer would never have guessed that Keith's busing order affected only about one-third of the school system's students, or that average busing distances were just two and one-half miles.

The *ABC Evening News* film clip showed large numbers of whites waving flags, carrying placards, and marching. Blacks were nowhere to be found. This was hardly accidental. McCabe was particularly adept at framing the busing issue for the press. As the historian Matthew F. Delmont later wrote, McCabe "successfully leveraged the characteristics of television news—its emphasis on newsworthy events and crisis, its selective use of historical context, its nominal political neutrality, and its emphasis on the production of drama and narrative—to make her case against 'busing.'"[94] The *ABC Evening News* segment showed that skill set in action. McCabe was the heroine of the segment, identified on-screen as "Irene

McCabe, Housewife." She told the cheering crowd: "My daughter will not be on that bus. She will not be in a parochial school. She will be home. United we stand, divided we fall." It was the first of four straight days of national news coverage of the situation in Pontiac.[95] Later, at another NAG rally, McCabe would remark, "This is our civil rights movement."

The wall-to-wall news coverage amplified NAG's message exponentially, even though the group itself never boasted more than a few thousand local members.[96] In the 1960s, the television networks used their huge megaphones to help the civil rights movement. Of the press and its effect on the movement, John Lewis once remarked: "If it hadn't been for the media—the print media and television—the civil rights movement would have been like a bird without wings, a choir without a song."[97] But for every action there was a reaction. By the early 1970s, the news media had largely shifted gears to focus on the "real" Americans: the silent majority and antibusing whites.[98]

All eyes were on Pontiac when school opened on Tuesday, September 7, 1971. The mood was one of apprehension, if not dread. Judge Keith was in his chambers early that morning. Facing death threats, he later told his biographers that "federal marshals had been driving by my house for days."[99] Looking back, he said, "It was so much worse than I thought it would be. I didn't know there would be such hatred."[100]

Meanwhile, the buses themselves took center stage. The *Detroit Free Press* ran a front-page picture of a solid row of Pontiac school buses, noting their local provenance. "Those Pontiac-made school buses—GM has built 21 specifically for Pontiac itself in the past two weeks—have suddenly become symbols of danger and evil to many residents of the city," the paper noted.[101] Pontiac was, after all, a factory town, dominated by three GM plants (Pontiac Motors, GM Truck & Coach, and Fisher Body). McCabe, her back to the camera, was pictured just below the armada of buses.

Whatever new conflagration was expected, it did not come to pass. For one, half of Pontiac's 21,300 school population—most of the absentees were white—simply stayed home.[102] Ultimately, the school district lost about 11 percent of its student population during the 1971–72 school year—mostly whites.[103] That's not to say the day was a picture of racial harmony. Early in the morning, several women attempted to keep the buses from running by chaining themselves to a bus yard gate. Others yelled, as journalist William Serrin described it, "'Nigger, Nigger' at black children and teachers."[104] There were three bomb threats, and the *Detroit Free Press* reported that "several white students were assaulted by blacks near Central High School."[105] But it was clear that school officials had feared much worse. They breathed a collective sigh of relief as "the large-scale violence predicted by many parents and politicians has not materialized in Pontiac."[106]

One reason large-scale violence was mitigated was because of the PTA. Lucille McNaughton, a member of a biracial integration committee, said, "The vast majority in Pontiac are in the middle. They want to do what's right, but they're not sure what that is. We feel if we stress the positive we can counteract some of the bad publicity and really give our children a better education."[107] By the end of the first week, school enrollment had increased, and school officials reported that court-ordered busing was proceeding "generally well."[108]

NAG had one more major offensive up its sleeve. One week after school opened, the group picketed two GM plants—Fisher Body and Pontiac. Large numbers of workers refused to cross NAG's picket lines, and factory production ground to a halt, at least for a time.[109] McCabe considered the action a success. *The New York Times* reported that "Mrs. McCabe hoped to demonstrate that her antibusing group had the support of white workers and they were willing to support her organization, even against the wishes of the union or General Motors."[110] By late September, the group declared victory even as busing continued in Pontiac, and something like normalcy characterized the school system. On September 23, 1971, Walter Cronkite reported on the *CBS Evening News* that NAG was ending its two-and-a-half-week boycott of the Pontiac public schools. "The leader, Mrs. Irene McCabe, said the protesters feel they have demonstrated the depth of community opposition to busing and will now concentrate their fight in the courts."[111] Cronkite continued, "To continue the boycott, in Mrs. McCabe's words would 'only injure the children.'"[112]

Even if McCabe was unable to prevent Judge Keith's order from taking effect in Pontiac, NAG still won the war. As Delmont explained it, the media-savvy McCabe was the public "face of 'antibusing' politics in the early

1970s."[113] And it was the white antibusing activists who, having won control over the public discourse about desegregation, ultimately prevailed. It was an important shift. The issue was no longer white racism as operationalized through school segregation. Instead, it was how the government was upending white expectations and destroying neighborhood schools, which were sacrosanct. And this was communicated through one simple word: "busing." As the historian concluded: "Framing school desegregation as being about 'busing' rather than unconstitutional racial discrimination privileged white parents' fears over legal evidence. Ultimately, 'busing' failed to more fully desegregate public schools because school officials, politicians, courts, and the news media valued the desires of white parents more than the rights of black students."[114]

14

ACCIDENT OF GEOGRAPHY

O n September 27, 1971, Roth announced his "Ruling on Issue of Segregation" at a housekeeping conference among the counsel in the *Bradley* case with surprisingly little fanfare.[1] The informality of the announcement belied its importance. It was obvious, on the very first read, that the order had the potential to upend public education in southeastern Michigan.

The judge's ruling also demonstrated just how successful the plaintiffs' lawyers had been at educating Roth. The decision began with several pages of statistical data outlining city and suburban demographic trends, which initially seemed unremarkable. But what the data showed was that, after reaching a peak in 1950, Detroit's overall population was declining, while the suburban population had exploded, increasing by nearly two million since 1940. At the same time, the city's black population—and particularly its black school-age population—was increasing. Detroit was rapidly becoming both smaller and blacker, while whites were fleeing to the suburbs.[2]

Roth built to a crescendo: "In 1992 [Detroit public schools] will be virtually 100% [black] if the present trends continue."[3] Next he provided another dose of key information: The areas surrounding eight predominantly black high schools in Detroit had significant problems that impeded the educational process, including high infant mortality, crime, poverty, pupil turnover, and tuberculosis rates.[4] The implication was that Detroit's schools were both separate and unequal, although the judge had yet to point a finger.

Then came the ruling's two most interesting paragraphs. They reflected what Roth had learned from the plaintiffs' housing case. Crucially, these observations preceded any discussion of the techniques the defendants used to segregate Detroit's schools. It was as if the judge were telling the reader: "We can't understand this school segregation case without investigating residential segregation. Each is dependent on the other." "The City of Detroit is a community generally divided by racial lines," he began.[5] This statement was uncontroversial. It was something even a casual observer would have recognized. But then, in the next few sentences, he placed Detroit within a metropolitan context. The city did not exist alone like an iceberg, unconnected to other nearby cities and towns. "Residential segregation within the city and throughout the larger metropolitan area is substantial, pervasive and of long standing. Black citizens are located in separate and distinct areas within the city and are not generally to be found in the suburbs."[6] These observations suggested not just that blacks were segregated within the city limits, but that they could not gain access to suburbs, either. It was highly likely that the plaintiffs' containment theory had informed Roth's thinking.

If blacks were segregated, the next question was what had caused that condition. Perhaps they'd self-segregated. Maybe blacks just wanted to live among themselves. The judge shot that idea down: "While the racially unrestricted choice of black persons and economic factors may have played some part in the development of this pattern of residential segregation, it is, in the main, the result of past and present practices and customs of racial discrimination, *both public and private*, which have and do restrict the housing opportunities of black people. On the record there can be no other finding."[7]

Synthesizing what he learned during the trial, the judge focused on how multiple actors bore collective responsibility for Detroit's ills: "Governmental actions and inaction at all levels, federal, state and local, have combined, with those of private organizations, such as loaning institutions and real estate associations and brokerage firms, to establish and to maintain the pattern of residential segregation throughout the Detroit metropolitan area."[8] The problem was that the federal government was not a defendant. Nor were multiple other responsible parties—other governmental actors, realtors, banks, insurance agents, title companies, and the rest. It seemed strange to charge state and local officials for the acts of parties not before the court. Roth spoke to that, too: "While it would be unfair to charge the present defendants with what other governmental officers or agencies have done, it can be said that the actions or the failure to act by the responsible school authorities, both city and state, were linked to that of these other governmental units."[9]

This was the idea that the defendants *had* knowingly incorporated others' bad acts into their school decisions. Their school segregation techniques built on—and would have been unsuccessful without—the foundation created by the containment. The two were linked, interwoven, inextricable. They were like coffee and cream, peanut butter and jelly, Ginger Rogers and Fred Astaire. Racially restrictive covenants, FHA segregationist policies, segregated public housing, segregated real estate salespersons associations, redlining, an actual segregation wall, the snakes in the basement: all of it was incorporated into the defendants' acts. And for this, the defendants *were* responsible: "The Board's building upon housing segregation violates the Fourteenth Amendment," Roth wrote.[10]

Roth had come a long way during the litigation. He had changed. Now he found his voice: "When we speak of governmental action we should not view the different agencies as a collection of unrelated units. Perhaps the most that can be said is that all of them, including the school authorities, are, in part, responsible for the segregated condition which exists."[11] The state and local defendants—alone—were not entirely responsible for the segregated conditions in Detroit schools. "The principal causes undeniably have been population movement and housing patterns," the judge acknowledged.[12] But he held the defendants liable anyway based on the "substantial role" they had played in "promoting segregation."

Roth pointed to the symbiotic relationship between housing and schools. He was riffing on *Swann*, which the Supreme Court had decided just a few months earlier: "And we note that just as there is an interaction between residential patterns and the racial composition of the schools, so there is a corresponding effect on the residential pattern by the racial composition of the schools."[13] It wasn't just that residential segregation caused school segregation. The converse was also true. The discriminatory actions of school officials could change the complexion of residential areas, of metropolitan Detroit itself. This was the true importance of the plaintiffs' housing evidence. It had elevated and nationalized what was otherwise a relatively technical school segregation case set in an aging, rust belt city. *Bradley v. Milliken* was about how northern segregation was created, maintained, and perpetuated.

In the remainder of the decision, Judge Roth detailed the defendants' segregation techniques. It read like a litany of school segregation's "greatest hits." Roth found that the Detroit school board had intentionally segregated the city's schools. It accomplished this by: using optional attendance zones that "allow white youngsters to escape identifiably 'black' schools,"[14] busing "black pupils past or away from closer white schools with available space to black schools,"[15] racially gerrymandering student attendance and school feeder zones so as "to contain black students,"[16] and by selecting sites for and then constructing more than two dozen new schools in a manner that "negates opportunities to integrate, 'contains' the black population and perpetuates and compounds school segregation."[17] Roth acknowledged a wide variety of actions the board had taken, including the April 7 plan, "to lessen the impact of the forces of segregation" and "advance the cause of integration."[18] But those actions, while laudable, did not disturb his finding of de jure segregation against the board.

The state of Michigan, Roth wrote, had also violated the Constitution. The judge began by noting the state's myriad powers and responsibilities with respect to education. Under state law, "leadership and general supervision over all public education is vested in the State Board of Education."[19] The scope of the state's powers with respect to education was vast. Here was how Judge Roth described those powers: "The duties of the State . . . include, but are not limited to, specifying the number of hours necessary to constitute a school day; approval until 1962 of school sites; approval of school construction plans; accreditation of schools; approval of loans based on state aid funds; review of suspensions and expulsions of individual students for misconduct; . . . authority over transportation routes and disbursement of transportation funds; teacher certification and the like."[20] And, in addition, the state had "plenary power" to create, reorganize, or dissolve school districts within the state at will.[21]

The Fourteenth Amendment was directed at the states. The amendment prohibited the state of Michigan from denying to any person "equal protection of the laws." Against that background, Judge Roth ruled that the "responsibility for providing educational opportunity to all children on constitutional terms is ultimately that of the state."[22] True, the state had delegated some of the responsibility to administer the Detroit public school system to the Detroit Board of Education. But the state could not delegate away its constitutional responsibilities. Instead, the judge ruled that the "constitutional obligation toward the individual schoolchildren" was shared between the Detroit school board and the state of Michigan.[23] Roth held that Michigan had *acted directly to control and maintain the pattern of segregation in the Detroit schools.*"[24]

So what exactly did the state do? First, through Act 48—Young's compromise, which catalyzed the litigation—the state acted "to impede, delay and minimize racial integration in Detroit schools."[25] Next, until 1962, the state approved all school siting decisions.[26] This meant that the state approved the location of all new schools sited in Detroit up through 1962—virtually all of which were segregated. The state also approved school construction plans.[27] Roth noted that thirteen primary schools had been constructed in Detroit since 1959, and that fourteen new schools opened for use in the city in the 1970–71 school year.

School construction in Detroit was race based, as was demonstrated during the trial. On May 7, Lou Lucas asked desegregation expert Gordon Foster: "From your examination of the pattern of construction in the school system, 1960 to 1970, do you have an opinion as to the effect of that pattern of construction on segregation in the Detroit School System?"[28] Foster replied, "My opinion is that construction practices were followed in such a way as to increase segregation. I say this because of the large number of schools that were opened that were either all black or all white or with a disproportionate number of one race or the other upon opening."[29] But the state's involvement didn't stop there. Roth found that the state provided transportation money for students in "many neighboring, mostly white, suburban districts," but not to students in Detroit "regardless of their poverty or distance from the school to which they were assigned."[30] It enforced bonding and state aid schemes that meant that suburban districts were able "to make far larger per pupil expenditures despite less tax effort."[31] His conclusion: the state's "funding limitations . . . created and perpetuated systematic educational inequalities."[32]

Toward the end of the opinion, Roth pivoted and spoke directly to Detroit's black population. The judge wrote: "We need not minimize the effect of the actions of federal, state and local governmental officers and agencies . . . to observe that blacks, like ethnic groups in the past, have tended to separate from the larger group and associate together. The ghetto is at once both a place of confinement and a refuge. There is enough blame for everyone to share."[33] It was perhaps a surprising statement after a lengthy trial showing how actively black Detroit residents had been excluded. Whatever one thought of community control advocates like Albert Cleage, they were attempting to make lemonade out of lemons. It was whites who had planted the lemon trees.

But the statement was also empathetic, painting the ghetto as both a prison and a shelter from white venality. It showed Roth, perhaps now a bit wiser than when the litigation began, reaching for the mantle of peacemaker. Dimond believed that the judge was asking "the black community in Detroit to join with him in an unprecedented effort to challenge segregation for all of the children rather than accept either white domination or community control of segregated schools."[34] Roth believed in the system, and he was asking Detroit's blacks to believe in it, too. The question was whether that faith would be rewarded.

Having ruled on liability, Roth turned to the remedy. The segregation ruling was silent on metropolitan relief. Instead, it simply indicated that the judge would ask the parties to submit proposed desegregation plans. But then, at a scheduling conference on October 4, 1971, Roth expressed "serious reservations" about a Detroit-only desegregation plan. "Perhaps only a plan which encompasses all or some of the greater Detroit metropolitan area can hope to succeed in giving our children the kind of education they are entitled to constitutionally," the judge mused.[35] Roth hadn't yet made up his mind ("the options are [still] completely open"), but he was getting there.[36] One thing was certain: he believed that the

Detroit metropolitan area's racial cast was no accident. "We note here that the metropolitan area is like a giant jigsaw puzzle, with the school districts cut into irregular pieces, but with the picture quite plainly that of racial segregation."[37]

Wanting to see all the possibilities, Roth asked the Detroit Board of Education to submit a city-only desegregation proposal and the state defendants to provide a metropolitan desegregation plan.[38] CCBE, of course, favored city-suburban desegregation. "Early in the trial, your Honor, I introduced . . . the idea that the only salutary solution to the academic and educational problems in Detroit would be a metropolitan plan," Ritchie reminded the court.[39] The lawyer reiterated that a metropolitan plan would be acceptable to CCBE, and noted that "with the approval of my clients I came here today with a rudimentary metropolitan plan." Ritchie offered to submit a more fully developed version of the plan and Roth agreed.

Finally, there was the issue of CCBE's motion to join the suburban school districts. Roth wasn't yet ready to make a decision. "With respect to remarks you gentlemen have made about other school districts, I am not going to make any definitive ruling at this time. We haven't come to that pass yet," Roth stated.[40] "As you well know it is overwhelming to consider joining 50, 60, or 80 other parties to this lawsuit, each of which is composed of superintendents and boards," the judge continued.[41] This remark suggested that the judge was inclined to deny CCBE's motion. But then Roth pivoted, indicating that the number of parties in the lawsuit likely would expand: "On the other hand I do not propose to stop the voice of anybody who is apt to be affected by the plan. So this is a matter of mechanics. When the time comes . . . we will . . . make a decision that we believe will be a fair one and yet will permit us to [achieve] some remedial effects and perhaps [put] into effect some plans for desegregation."[42] Dimond characterized this as a judicial "invitation" to the suburban school districts to make their own motion to intervene in the lawsuit.[43] Whether the suburban school districts came in via CCBE's motion or via their own appeared to be, as the judge put it, "a matter of mechanics."[44] But what this really meant was that Roth was increasingly likely to order metropolitan relief.

The NAACP was exultant. Reacting to Roth's order, Nathaniel Jones held a press conference in Detroit: "When we met with you reporters over a year ago at the inception of this lawsuit, we declared that in bringing it, our faith in the legal system was being put to a test. We were attempting to make the system work for the black children of Detroit."[45] He continued, "Well, today, another link in the chain of justice was forged with the decision of Judge Steven Roth, in the Detroit School case."[46]

Jones underscored the national importance of the ruling. "That decision, which declares the rights of the black children—and the responsibilities of both the Detroit Board of Education and the State of Michigan—is a reaffirmation of the strength and vitality of the Constitution," he stated.[47] Judge Roth's ruling was proof positive that working within the system could lead to black equality. "The plaintiffs, by going to court, were giving the system a chance to work. And their faith in the system has been vindicated."[48]

Reaching out to the defendants, he asked them to do the same. "Now, it is incumbent upon those whom we challenged in this lawsuit, to display an equal degree of faith and trust in our courts and the legal system," Jones said.[49] Perhaps recognizing just how arduous the road ahead would be, he pleaded with the defendants to "join hands and hearts with us, in an attempt to assist the court in working out a meaningful solution to the problem of education in this community."[50]

Although Roth ruled that the state and the city had violated the Constitution—it was a liability holding—his opinion was totally silent on what the appropriate remedy for the constitutional violation might be. But that didn't mute the reaction in the suburbs. In fact, suburban furor was amplified by the actions of the CCBE, as *The Detroit News* confirmed. On October 1, it ran a story about the reaction to Roth's ruling in Livonia, which included this observation: "Many suburban parents panicked when they learned of [CCBE's] motion to enjoin 85 suburban school districts in Wayne, Macomb, and Oakland counties to the Detroit suit. Roth has not yet ruled on the motion."[51] Suburban parents weren't going to take Roth's decision, and the troubling possibilities it raised, lying down.

Two days after Roth released the segregation ruling, *The Detroit News* reported that "two suburban housewives" had organized a meeting in Taylor to build opposition against any plan "for bussing children out of the Taylor School District."[52] Five hundred people attended the meeting, where petitions urging state officials to block cross-district busing were circulated. Antibusing forces were on the march in southeastern Michigan. An antibusing Warren group called "Save Our Children" announced a boycott of the schools. (One report had the absentee rate on the day of the boycott at approximately 30 percent.)[53] The chairman of the group, Phillip Lee, stated ominously: "This is not just a guess—I know there will be violence."[54] Another Warren group, "The Silent Majority," planned an antibusing rally. An organization called "Citizens Against Busing" pushed for a constitutional amendment against busing.[55] The group counted chapters in Taylor, Lincoln Park, Garden City, Southgate, Wayne, and Westland. Even NAG got into the act. In response to Roth's ruling, the organization offered to coordinate suburban antibusing efforts.[56] The group said it was sponsoring an antibusing rally for the people of Wayne, Oakland, and Macomb Counties, areas that might be affected by a metropolitan desegregation order. *The New York Times* reported that NAG was calling for a statewide school boycott in late October to protest busing.[57] Unsurprisingly, Irene McCabe gave the press a juicy quote: "We have known it was coming all along . . . That's why we have been fighting so hard. But, before, people just didn't believe us. They were like the people of Pontiac when we watched what happened down South and thought it would never happen here."[58]

Liberal organizations like the Detroit Urban League, meanwhile, were firmly behind Roth. Francis A. Kornegay, the organization's executive director, praised the decision: "The flag in Judge Roth's ruling, the flag of equal justice, hangs high over Detroit."[59] The *Detroit Free Press* reported that both Detroit's black congressmen, John Conyers and Charles Diggs, favored "busing across municipal lines in the Detroit area."[60] "Until such time as there is an alternative developed to the neighborhood school concept, which by its very nature—because of housing patterns and so on—is making racist institutions out of our schools, I support busing," Diggs said.[61] The Michigan Civil Rights Commission hailed the ruling. In a letter to the State Board of Education, officials wrote: "Judge Roth describes the reality that black youth have been illegally confined to segregated, inferior schools within the Detroit school district, and have suffered from state-imposed financial limitations.[62]

Prominent religious leaders also hailed the decision. Not for the last time would they provide crucial moral leadership during a period of extraordinary political turmoil. The Rabbinical Commission of Detroit issued a statement to all the synagogues in metropolitan Detroit, supporting "busing children between school districts or within the same school district if no better solution can be found."[63] It also urged members of the Jewish community to "follow the law on this matter, whatever it should prove to be."

On Sunday, October 3, 1971, Reverend Robert Marshall of the suburban and largely white Birmingham Unitarian Church preached a stem-winder titled "In Defense of Busing." The sermon touched on a wide variety of topics including Irene McCabe and the showdown in Pontiac, housing segregation, and *Brown*. But the key argument he made to his parishioners was why busing was the "issue of our times and life."[64] He told his congregation that we are at "one of those risky watershed moments when lesser considerations give way to basic decisions, no matter what we might wish."[65] The minister was asking his parishioners what kind of nation they wanted to have. But his was not a bland, universalistic call for goodwill. Instead, Marshall argued that the fates of blacks and whites, the city and the suburbs, were tied. As he told it, the price of suburban protectionism was extraordinarily high, imperiling whites' own self-interest. "Today the only way white America can keep the children of black America from equal treatment before the law is by destroying their own legal system. Only if we are willing to see our system used whimsically and selectively—a dangerous road—only if we are willing to eliminate the features of the Constitution which protect whites, can we keep those features from protecting blacks."[66]

Roth's findings that the defendants had committed serious constitutional violations in Detroit were difficult to dispute. Indeed, they were *never* disturbed on appeal. If one accepted those findings, then it required extraordinary contortions to explain why a metropolitan remedy, which gave the victims of that conduct the best chance of redress, should be rejected before it was tried. What Marshall seemed to be saying was that those kinds of contortions had negative spillover effects. They didn't stay hermetically sealed within one case. They were contagious. They had a tendency to undermine faith in the equal application of the rule of law.

"So now either all America will have a genuine and a real and bona fide law and order," Marshall continued, "or no one will. Either all kids will be safe—or none. Either all kids will be fed and clothed decently and have good schools and a fair chance, either all schools will receive equitable and comparable tax support—or there will be no schools. Either the total society will regard all children as assets for the future, or there will be no future."[67] It wasn't the cheeriest sermon. But looking back, it's hard to argue that he was wrong about the decision's huge stakes.

Some of the support for Roth's decision was more surprising. In the wake of the ruling, many of the state's top Democratic leaders endorsed busing, and the Democratic State Central Committee issued a probusing resolution titled *Statement on Quality Education* that was "almost unparalleled in states with major desegregation cases," one commentator wrote later.[68] Busing "is an imperfect answer," the statement read in part.[69] "But it is an answer for today. We accept the decisions of the courts and Congress. We accept busing as an instrument for immediate implementation of the courts' rulings. We accept busing as an imperfect and temporary mechanism to help erase the imbalances of our educational system."[70]

One of the resolution's most prominent supporters was Michigan state attorney general Frank J. Kelley. Kelley, of course, was also a defendant in the *Bradley v. Milliken* litigation. Although he would later assert that he was "smeared as being in favor of cross-district school busing," both *The Detroit News* and the *Detroit Free Press* reported that he and several other leading Democrats endorsed the resolution.[71] Though he never attained higher office, Kelley—who would go on to become the state's and the nation's longest-serving attorney general in history[72]—had serious political ambitions. One scholar later theorized that Kelley signed the resolution endorsing busing "reluctantly" so as to protect himself in the Democratic senatorial primary, which would be decided by more liberal voters.[73] He could worry about pivoting to the center once he had secured the nomination.

Michigan's two U.S. senators, meanwhile, split on the issue. Michigan's junior senator, Robert P. Griffin, a Republican, decried "forced busing," and in October 1971 proposed a constitutional amendment to ban busing for the purposes of desegregation. In a speech on the floor of the United States Senate in support of the proposal, the Republican sounded a theme of white innocence: "Whatever the sins of their fathers, unreasonable punishment ought not be imposed upon the children of a new generation who are guilty of nothing but being born black or white."[74] The proposed amendment read: "This Constitution shall not be construed to require that pupils be assigned or transported to public schools on the basis of their race, color, religion or national origin."[75] *The Detroit News* reported that the proposal had dim prospects of advancing in the Senate,[76] but described it as strategic: "It is a politically popular move and could help Griffin in his uphill battle to retain his Senate seat in the 1972 elections," *The Detroit News* observed.[77]

The state's senior U.S. senator, Democrat Phil Hart, by contrast, spoke in favor of busing at the annual "Phil Hart Day" dinner in suburban Mount Clemens. "Whatever tensions and inconveniences we may feel in the desegregation process now, they'll be nothing to the tensions we will endure after 20 years of doing little or nothing," he told the group.[78] It was a gutsy position. Several days later, as the historian David Riddle explained it, "Roseville-NAG voted to mount a recall campaign against Hart, who had polled overwhelmingly in those precincts in the last election. The recall campaign fizzled, but Hart's attempt to reason with Macomb County Democrats over the busing question also failed."[79]

Amid all this political back and forth, pressure on Roth intensified. Just a few days after Hart's appearance, *The Detroit News* reported that the FBI was investigating threats of violence made against Judge Roth, and that "'routine extra security precautions' are being taken for Roth's protection."[80]

———

On November 3, 1971, Governor Milliken gave a speech, televised statewide, to announce that the state would immediately appeal Judge Roth's ruling.[81] (The Detroit school board, now dominated by conservatives, also voted to appeal shortly thereafter.)[82] In it, Milliken denied that the state had any liability for segregation in Detroit's schools: "I don't believe that the State Board of Education, the Attorney General, or the Governor have intentionally caused segregation."[83]

The governor provided a primer on school desegregation law, explaining the de jure / de facto distinction. "After examining the evidence, the judges have been making findings that segregated education does, in fact, exist either by accident of geography or housing patterns, or by design and by action of school and other officials. If segregation exists by accident of geography or pre-existing housing patterns it is called 'de facto' segregation. If accomplished by design in actions of school or State officials, it is called 'de jure' or 'intentional' segregation."[84] A court could only order a busing remedy where it had found intentional or de jure segregation, the governor added.

There were at least two problems with Milliken's statement. First, it ignored the government's role in creating housing segregation, which the plaintiffs proved conclusively during the first several days of trial. Second, it drew a rigid dichotomy between the "accident of geography or housing patterns" and school officials' actions. But Roth had seen how state and local school officials knowingly *incorporated* housing segregation—much of which could be traced to official government policy—into their actions. School and housing segregation were linked, interdependent phenomena. After the plaintiffs' housing case, the phrase "by accident of geography or housing patterns" was absurd. It hid the truth. It expressed an alternative reality. The United States Court of Appeals for the Sixth Circuit ultimately dismissed the appeal in late February 1972.[85]

One day after the governor's speech, U.S. congressman William Broomfield, a Republican representing Royal Oak, Michigan, jumped into the fray by introducing an amendment to an education bill. "Mr. Chairman," he began, "my amendment would postpone the effectiveness of any U. S. district court order requiring the forced busing of children to achieve racial balance until all appeals to that order have been exhausted."[86] The congressman was clearly referring to the recent rulings in Pontiac and Detroit. Pointing to a recent decision by the chief justice, Broomfield suggested that those rulings were "unprecedented," and thus were illegitimate interpretations of constitutional law: "Only last September, Chief Justice Warren Burger said some federal judges were misreading the Court's April decision on busing [*Swann*] by ordering more than the law requires."[87]

Indeed, as recently as a few weeks earlier, in the course of a subsequent opinion, Burger had expressed discomfort with some lower courts' interpretation of *Swann*.[88] "Nothing could be plainer, or so I had thought, than Swann's disapproval of the 71%–29% racial composition found in the Swann case as the controlling factor in assignment of pupils, simply because that was the racial composition of the whole school system," the chief justice scolded.[89] His point was that *Swann* did not require that every single school in a school system reflect the racial balance of the system as a whole. In effect, Burger was signaling his growing discomfort with busing, which wasn't a great sign for advocates seeking to apply *Swann* in the North. At the same time, as *The New York Times* put it, Burger made the observation in an opinion in which he "refused to stay the enforcement of a lower court's decision that ordered extensive busing to achieve racial balance."[90] It was status quo ante, for now.

Congressman Gerald Ford, representing a mostly white district in western Michigan, provided Broomfield with a helpful assist: "The amendment merely holds the status quo in a school district until final judgment has been made by the United States Supreme Court. I think that is fairness. That is equity. We ought to approve it."[91] Michigan congressman Lucien Nedzi informed the House that he and a majority of the state's Democratic delegation would support the amendment.

There were any number of problems with Broomfield's proposal. But the most serious was that it apparently was unconstitutional. The *Alexander v. Holmes* decision in 1969 had interred once and for all *Brown v. Board of Education II*'s embrace of gradualism.[92] "All deliberate speed" had given way to "Time's up." Then, in *Swann*, in 1971, the court explicitly authorized federal courts to order busing as a remedy for de jure segregation. Against this background, it was hard to see the legal argument for postponing a remedy that the Supreme Court had authorized—particularly after a lower court had found a constitutional violation.

On the House floor, first-term congresswoman Shirley Chisholm ripped into Broomfield and other proponents of the bill. Elected to the House of Representatives in 1968 representing Brooklyn's Twelfth Congressional

District, Chisholm was the first black woman ever to serve in Congress.[93] In 1972, she would become a trailblazer yet again when she became the first woman (and the first black person) to seek the Democratic presidential nomination. But before she entered politics, Chisholm had been a nursery school teacher and administrator and an educational consultant; she held a master's degree in early childhood education from Columbia University. Few members of Congress knew more than she did about what racism meant for students. Now, opposing the amendment, she spoke with unbridled ferocity: "Where have you been these many years? The black and Spanish-speaking children in the southern and western parts of the United States have been bussed right past the white schools in your communities in order to go to the dilapidated buildings reserved for them to acquire some kind of education. Where have your voices been for those children through all those years?"[94]

Chisholm had no patience for the white innocence argument favored by politicians like Milliken and Griffin—men who wrapped white bias in a cloak of blamelessness and pushed the view that northern segregation was caused by an "accident of geography."

"You know, let me bring it right down front to you," she told her colleagues.[95] "The fact of the matter is racism is so inherent in the bloodstream of this country that you cannot see beyond a particular limit. You are only concerned when whites are affected . . . Come out from behind your mask and tell it like it really is."[96] Chisholm built to a crescendo: "There is a chance this evening to come out from behind your mask. Forget they are white children. Forget they are black children. Forget they are Spanish-speaking children. Just remember one thing: They are America's children."[97]

Her words were fire. But they failed to move the majority of her colleagues. The House passed the amendment by a large margin. In June 1972, President Nixon signed an education bill into law that included Broomfield's proposal.[98]

=====

On November 8, 1971, the Detroit NAACP Executive Board issued a statement ripping Milliken's address. In effect it called Milliken, widely considered a moderate Republican, a racist. "Unfortunately, Governor Milliken has chosen to join forces with the racist inspired and supported 'antibusing' movement."[99] He had been captured by the segregationists, the NAACP Board thought. The governor had told the people of Michigan that "children black or white don't learn by riding buses."[100]

That argument, which would be repeated again and again, was an obvious straw man. Everyone knew that busing was only a means of transportation, one that the state had financed for years. The issue wasn't the buses, it was the color of the children riding them. "The actions by the governor and state legislature make it abundantly clear that the rampant racism demonstrated in the deep South during the late fifties and sixties over school desegregation has surfaced in the State of Michigan," the board wrote.[101]

But perhaps the worst part of the governor's speech, to the Detroit NAACP, was its hypocrisy. Milliken portrayed himself as some sort of civil rights activist: "No Governor is more deeply and fervently committed than I am to the cause of human rights, of equal rights, in such vital areas as housing, job opportunities and education," he boasted.[102]

The NAACP would have none of it: "The Governor continues to applaud himself on his great concern for human rights, while at the same time places himself on record as opposed to any meaningful ways for obtaining these 'human rights' for black children."[103] Coleman Young agreed. Just a few days earlier, Young had sharply criticized Milliken's decision to appeal, telling the *Detroit Free Press* that the governor was a "modern-day equivalent of George Wallace standing in the courthouse door."[104] Young wasn't finished: "The governor has wet his finger and put it to the political winds and decided, as has [President] Nixon and [U.S. Sen. Robert] Griffin and certain Democrats that racism is the political horse to be ridden in 1972."[105] The senator's comments were worth parsing.

On the one hand, Young appeared to be grandstanding. On this view, these were incendiary words directed (mostly) at members of the other party seemingly for political gain. After all, it was *his very own bill*— "Young's compromise"—that had violated the Constitution. From this perspective, it was hard to take Young's bombast seriously. But there was a strong countervailing view: Young had always thought the portion of his bill that invalidated Zwerdling's high school integration plan was unconstitutional. Indeed, he had urged other black legislators to support his bill notwithstanding that fact—better half a loaf than none at all—always with the hope that the federal courts would do the right thing.

Nate Jones, meanwhile, with a bit of irony, interpreted Milliken's comments as a compliment. "An unintentional, but unmistakable tribute has been paid to the NAACP," he wrote in a memo to his executive staff.[106] The governor's speech proved the value of the *Bradley* litigation, Jones wrote. The fact "that he was moved to make it, highlights the significance of the case."[107] And, appeal or not, there was more to come. *Bradley* was a blueprint for northern school litigation. "You will be hearing much more about the Detroit case," the general counsel predicted.[108]

In late December 1971, Roy Wilkins sent Judge Roth a remarkable letter.[109] He wrote with hesitation. After all, the NAACP was the plaintiff in a major case that was currently pending before the judge. Roth had yet to issue his remedial decision. But Wilkins didn't let that stop him. Citing "the public interest that has developed in the wake of" the segregation decision, the NAACP's executive director said he felt compelled to write because of the decision's "manifest significance." The ruling was "impressive," "courageous," and "replete with historical truths," Wilkins enthused. With that kind of language, it was hard to argue that the NAACP chief wasn't trying to "butter up" the judge. But then, he referenced *Brown*. "In my view, your decision may well come to be seen as momentous in the same way as that rendered in Brown vs. Topeka," Wilkins wrote.[110] Maybe this was just his way of "working the ref." Yet it was hard to imagine Wilkins name-dropping *Brown* at the drop of a hat. That decision was too momentous. The judge replied just after Christmas: "It was most appropriate that your kind letter should reach me at this time of the year, when we rekindle our hope that peace may yet come to mankind."[111] Roth thanked Wilkins for writing, notwithstanding the potential impropriety of communication between a judge and a party with the case before him. Wilkins's letter moved the judge. Roth admired the NAACP head and he let him know it. The judge wrote, "It is my prayer that in the remainder of my participation in the Detroit school case I may be able to see as keenly and stand as firmly as you have on so many trying occasions."[112]

The plaintiffs in the *Bradley v. Milliken* case had convinced a highly skeptical trial judge that Detroit's deep residential segregation was the result of systematic racial discrimination—the containment. Although it was less obvious than the "whites only" signs that had dominated the southern landscape, much of that discrimination was the result of official government policy just the same. This had extraordinary implications. First, it undermined the 1966 *Deal* decision, which had attributed school segregation to nongovernmental forces: "Because of factors in the private housing market, disparities in job opportunities, and other outside influences (as well as positive free choice by some Negroes), the imposition of the neighborhood concept on existing residential patterns in Cincinnati creates some schools which are predominantly or wholly of one race or another."[113] But after the *Bradley* trial, *Deal's* innocent "outside influences" explanation didn't wash. Next, the scope of the containment evidence, suggesting that the racial complexion of Detroit's suburbs was also largely the result of governmental discrimination, undercut the narrative of innocence that cloaked the white suburbs. This, too, militated toward a metropolitan remedy. Judge Roth had much to consider as he contemplated the shape and scope of his remedial order.

15

SOMETHING WE COMFORTABLY TELL OURSELVES

As black Detroiters awaited a remedy from Judge Roth, their attitudes about integration were already rapidly evolving. In October 1971, the *Detroit Free Press* ran an article titled "Blacks Skeptical of School Busing."[1] The piece surveyed black Detroiters' views of metropolitan desegregation in light of Judge Roth's recent segregation ruling. The article reported that most blacks were "thoughtfully cautious" about a potential city-suburban desegregation plan, believing that it might offer an opportunity "for better education for their children."[2] But that support was deeply qualified. It existed only to the extent that "the suburban schools have anything better to offer and if their children are not made targets of racial hatred." The article suggested that although both blacks and whites harbored reservations about busing, their concerns were meaningfully different. "Some black parents and other blacks flatly oppose city-suburban busing, but not for the same reasons, or with the same degree of emotionalism, as some white suburban opponents," the piece observed. Whites' reasons for opposing city-suburban busing were left unspecified.

A December 1971 survey found that while black Detroiters still overwhelmingly preferred integrated schools, they believed that qualified teachers were "the key factor in attaining quality education."[3] That same study suggested that about two-thirds of survey participants, particularly those with young children, were disinclined "to have their children attend school at a distance for the sake of going to an integrated school."[4] Several months later, another *Detroit Free Press* piece on the busing debate sounded some of the same themes.[5] Dorothy Riley, a black school librarian whose two children attended Duffield Elementary School in southeast Detroit, opposed busing her children to the suburbs: "Younger kids are at the mercy of white kids," she said.[6] A Detroit father of a six-year-old girl seconded Riley's fear: "I can see that my child would get a better education [in the suburbs]—but I don't want her on a bus for two hours.[7] Even though she is bored where she is, I don't want her bused into a hostile area."[8] "If they don't want my kids out there, why should I send them?" Elizabeth Miller added, "It's like running right into the devil—moving into an all-white neighborhood where they're trying to run away from us."[9] As recently as 1967, black Detroiters' support for integration had been rock solid. But now the cracks were beginning to show.

Even as some black Detroiters hesitated about cross-district integration, other members of the Detroit metropolitan area embraced that possibility. In early October 1971, Jack Shea, a thirty-two-year-old white insurance salesman of suburban Royal Oak, founded Citizens for Suburban Responsibility. The *Detroit Free Press* reported on one of the pro-cross-district-busing group's early meetings, which boasted about 125 attendees, mostly white, many of whom were parents.[10] The group, which was centered in the Birmingham–Bloomfield Hills area, passed a resolution supporting cross-district busing in the event that Judge Roth were to order it. At least one attendee understood the relationship between schools and housing: "It's time to stress open housing in the suburbs," a man from suburban Rochester stated.[11] "It's time to open these neighborhoods completely to blacks," he added.[12] Later that month, the group placed a three-quarter-page ad in the *Detroit Free Press* titled *Bring Us Together*. In it, the organization extoled the importance of city-suburban unity.[13] "The issue is whether our children will learn to live together or learn to hate separately," the ad warned.[14] "Busing is one possible method for achieving quality education," it added.[15] Reverend Robert Marshall, minister of the

Birmingham Unitarian Church and author of the fiery pro-integration sermon, was identified along with Shea as one of the group's cochairmen. "I hate busing but I hate segregation more," Marshall stated later.[16]

But joining such a group sometimes came at a cost. *The Detroit News* described how whites disciplined other whites for supporting integration. One member of the Citizens for Suburban Responsibility who lived in Clarkston—and who used a pseudonym with the paper because she feared reprisal—described threatening phone calls, the harassment of her children, her neighbors' refusal to speak to her, and how her house and her husband's car were vandalized, all because she refused to sign an antibusing petition. She seriously considered moving. "I guess I was forced to join," the Clarkston resident stated.[17] "I thought I was all alone out here. I didn't think anyone else felt like we did about the need for integration. But now that I've found this group [CSR], I don't feel so all alone anymore."[18]

Then, on March 24, 1972, the *Detroit Free Press* published an article titled "New Group Gives Backing to Busing."[19] The piece discussed the formation of the Metropolitan Coalition for Peaceful Integration, an umbrella group with "a score of powerful organizations." The paper wasn't exaggerating. The coalition included the Episcopal Diocese of Michigan, the Catholic Archdiocese of Detroit, the Detroit Federation of Teachers, the League of Women Voters, the Jewish Community Council of Metropolitan Detroit, and the Metropolitan Detroit Council of Churches, among others. Several reports pegged the number of groups in the organization at thirty or more.[20]

The coalition's purpose was to provide the necessary backup, in the community and on the ground, when and if Judge Roth issued a metropolitan desegregation order. "We aim to make whatever plan is ordered a successful plan," Maxine Rose, the coalition's operations coordinator told the *Detroit Free Press*.[21] On its "to do" list were the creation of a speakers' bureau, hosting public forums, distributing literature, and developing a publicity campaign. Rose previewed an ambitious agenda: "We're planning a massive, massive effort to shatter myths about the crazy things that people think are going to happen if we bus children."[22] She continued, "All of the organizations and people involved are contributing funds or services . . . to help us put together material that will be factual."[23]

The Detroit News described one of the coalition's proposals: "Plans are for a Detroit and a suburban mother to work as a pair, each meeting the school bus at her neighborhood school and assuming responsibility for the other's child while in her neighborhood. If the partner's child becomes ill at school, the mother would take the child to her home until the parents could arrange to pick him up."[24] (Fathers, apparently, would not play this role.) Elwood Hain, a white professor at Wayne State University Law School and the group's founder and cochairman, explained the coalition's motivation. The group believed in integration, full stop. This expressly included busing if the court required it. "In metropolitan America it must mean that," Hain told the press.[25] The professor put a uniquely Detroit spin on the group's position: "In the Motor City it is preposterous to object to using our technology to solve our problems."[26]

At around the same time that the Metropolitan Coalition for Peaceful Integration was forming, President Nixon addressed the nation about busing. Speaking on March 16, 1972, he reminded the country of his long-standing views—"my own position is well-known: I am opposed to busing for the purpose of achieving racial balance in our schools"—and he then zeroed in on the guilty party: the federal judiciary.[27] "The reason action is so urgent is because of a number of recent decisions of the lower federal courts," Nixon stated.[28] The president didn't name Judge Roth. He didn't have to.

Nixon also appeared to be referring to a recent federal ruling that required the consolidation of the Richmond, Virginia, school district with nearby white counties.[29] The bottom line was that the city of Richmond hadn't complied with *Brown* and it engaged in "passive resistance" through the late 1960s.[30] The city used freedom of choice plans and other forms of subterfuge to prevent desegregation. As a result, in 1971 federal judge Robert Merhige issued a desegregation order in a long-running case, *Bradley v. School Board of City of Richmond*. (Listed alphabetically, a Bradley was the first named plaintiff in both the Richmond and Detroit cases; the two Bradleys were unrelated.) The judge's ruling required more than twenty thousand Richmond students to be bused to facilitate integration.[31] But the order came too late. Thousands of whites had already fled to all-white schools in Henrico and Chesterfield Counties, just outside the city.[32] Merhige's intracity busing order only further accelerated this process.[33] So, in early 1972, he ordered the merger of the Richmond, Henrico, and Chesterfield school systems. The consolidated school system would have had approximately 100,000 students, one-third of them black.[34] "The proof here overwhelmingly establishes that the school division lines between Richmond and the counties coincide with no natural obstacles to speak of and do in fact work to confine blacks on a consistent, wholesale basis within the city, where they reside in segregated neighborhoods," the judge wrote.[35] It was as if Merhige were saying to the region's whites, "You can run, but you can't hide." Several days later, thousands of Richmond area residents embarked on a motorcade to Washington, D.C., to protest the judge's ruling.[36] It was highly likely Nixon meant Merhige *and* Roth when he declared, "These courts have gone too far." Something had to be done.

Nixon told the nation that amending the Constitution to prohibit busing had a "fatal flaw—it takes too long."[37] While there was some appetite on Capitol Hill in early 1972 for an antibusing amendment, the reality was that it was extremely difficult to amend the Constitution, which usually required attaining supermajority support for the proposed amendment in both houses of Congress *and* the states.

So the president seized on the next best thing: a moratorium. With that, he told the nation that he would send proposed legislation to Congress calling for "an immediate halt to all new busing orders by Federal courts."[38] Additionally (and ominously), he directed the Justice Department to intervene in desegregation cases "where the lower courts have gone beyond the Supreme Court requirements in ordering busing."[39] If it hadn't been clear before, it certainly was now. The executive branch was signaling its intent to side with defendants rather than plaintiffs in school desegregation cases. A robust moratorium proved unfeasible in Congress, however, and Nixon's proposed moratorium never became law. Ultimately, however, the president signed off on Broomfield's amendment—which had drawn serious fire from Shirley Chisholm—a far weaker freeze than he desired. The amendment prohibited court-ordered busing "for the purposes of achieving [racial] balance" until all appeals had been exhausted.[40] But it did not apply to most busing orders, those issued by a court as a component of a desegregation plan after a finding of a constitutional violation.[41]

During the speech, Nixon also announced his support for the Equal Educational Opportunities Act of 1972. The proposed measure would provide $2.5 billion to improve "the education of children from poor families."[42] The proposal wouldn't break the budget. As one paper noted, "The $2.5 billion which he promised . . . will consist entirely of funds the administration previously had earmarked for similar purposes."[43] In emphasizing that the federal funds would be used to upgrade "the schools in the central cities" so that the "children who go there will have just as good a chance to get quality education as do the children who go to the schools in the suburbs," the president tipped his hand.[44] This was a proposal to more adequately fund racially separate schools. Nixon proposed rewarding segregated school districts with federal dollars. It was a commitment to *Plessy v. Ferguson*.

But for some listeners Nixon hadn't gone far enough. One of these was Irene McCabe. The day before the president's speech, McCabe left Pontiac headed for Washington, D.C.—on foot. The goal of her protest march was nothing less than a constitutional amendment prohibiting busing. The distance was approximately six hundred miles, a trek that would take well over a month to complete. But McCabe, along with "five other mothers from the National Action Group," as the press identified them, was ready.[45] As the group left Pontiac, a Dixieland band played "Goodnight, Irene." Cheered on by a small crowd, some of them sang "Walk on, Irene, Walk on, Irene, 'til busing is a dream." McCabe danced the first few steps.[46]

The walk would be grueling; the marchers expected to cover upward of twenty miles per day. McCabe didn't mind. "When your physical body is worn out and your strength is gone, your convictions carry you through," she told a reporter. She predicted that 250,000 antibusing activists would meet her in Washington when she arrived there at the end of April.[47] In Taylor, Michigan, on the second night of her march, McCabe gathered with her supporters to watch the president's address.[48] Hoping that Nixon would push for the antibusing constitutional amendment she desired, her dissatisfaction was palpable. "All we have is this great flood of rhetoric," she told the press. "We're going to choke on rhetoric and I'm very disappointed because I love this president," McCabe complained. Determined to continue the march all the way to D.C., she hoped Nixon's position might yet evolve. She told the press that public opinion—and the pressure created by her march—would force the president to back the amendment.[49]

Other listeners were displeased with Nixon's speech, but for different reasons. The Reverend Jesse Jackson called the speech the "most dangerous speech that I have heard in this century."[50] "Beware of any issue that George Wallace and Richard Nixon agree on," the reverend warned.[51] Jackson sounded an alarm bell about the fall election, too. If Nixon were to prevail in November, "it will give Wallace authority in the White House." New York's liberal mayor John Lindsay, who, having switched parties, was now a candidate for the Democratic nomination, characterized the president's proposals as a "cave-in" to Wallace.[52] And it wasn't just Jackson and Lindsay pushing the Wallace-Nixon connection. A southern newspaper, the Louisville *Courier-Journal*, noticed it as well. Observing that Nixon had embraced Wallace's views, the paper argued that racial segregation had hardly disappeared. Instead, it had mutated to meet new realities. As the *Journal* put it, "White Americans have discovered that the *reality* of segregation may be preserved without the embarrassment of blatantly discriminatory laws. That's certainly been the case in many Northern states and cities, which have never endorsed the crass honesty of the white South."[53] "Let the Courts Speak," the paper implored.[54] Congress and the president couldn't be trusted to continue "our journey toward racial justice and equality."

Nate Jones was apoplectic. Responding to the president's proposals, he threw down the gauntlet. "If that moratorium that President Nixon has recommended is enacted into law, your NAACP will go into court before the ink is dry to challenge this immoral, unconstitutional, politically dishonest, transparent attempt by the president and the mob of constitutional rapists he leads."[55] A common complaint was that the NAACP was timid, milquetoast. But the general counsel's language showed that the organization knew how to bare its teeth. Busing wasn't the real question. It was a "synthetic" issue, Jones asserted. Busing was the rhetorical equivalent of a "head fake" in basketball; it was offered for its ability to confuse and mislead. The real concern was "resegregation and denying Negro children their constitutional rights to an equal education."[56] "We will fight," Jones vowed.

———

By March 1972, Roth was prepared to rule on the suburban school systems' inclusion in the *Bradley* case. On March 15, 1972, he allowed forty-three suburban school systems located in Detroit's "tri-county" or metropolitan area, Wayne, Oakland, and Macomb Counties, and a suburban white citizens group, to intervene in the suit.[57] Why only forty-three suburban school districts? The answer was that the decision was strategic. As Dimond explained it, "Other suburban districts, on advice of their counsel, refrained from participating on two grounds: first, their interest in opposing *any* cross-district pupil assignments would actually be represented by the suburban intervenors; and, second, the entire case might have to be retried because of their considered absence."[58] (Roth continued to defer ruling on CCBE's earlier motion, that numerous suburban school districts be added as parties, to "await further developments in this proceeding.")

Meanwhile, the Detroit Board of Education switched its position on the remedy. As *The Detroit News* reported, "The Detroit Board of Education made a formal decision to back a metropolitan plan as preferable to a citywide desegregation plan."[59] This likely occurred because the board saw the writing on the wall: Roth was going to reject a Detroit-only plan. Better to have a say in shaping whatever metropolitan plan the judge would ultimately produce. James A. Hathaway, the president of Detroit's central board of education, told *The Detroit News*: "I think we are switching our focus from the negative . . . to taking a positive role in telling the court what the Detroit Board feels is necessary for quality, integrated education."[60] This meant that only the state defendants remained committed to a Detroit-only plan. *The Detroit News* put it this way: "Admitting the new [suburban] defendants will even the odds somewhat against Eugene Krasicky, assistant state attorney general, who was the only lawyer in the case actively opposing a metropolitan desegregation plan."[61] The intervenors stood united in their complete opposition to any metropolitan desegregation order. What they wanted was a chance to convince the court that "they should become part of a corrective school plan only after all, or some of them, have been proven guilty of . . . de jure segregation."[62] The NAACP remained steadfast in its opposition to intervention. The suburban school districts' interests were already adequately represented by the state, it believed, which *had* engaged in de jure segregation.[63]

Roth permitted intervention but with a significant caveat: he placed strict conditions on the suburban school systems' participation in the lawsuit. He wanted their views on "the legal propriety or impropriety of considering a metropolitan plan," and asked them to "review any plan or plans for the desegregation of the so-called larger Detroit Metropolitan area."[64] But the judge wasn't going to retry the case. This meant that the intervening suburban school districts would not be allowed to raise any challenge at all to Roth's earlier finding of liability. Their interests were, as *The Detroit News* put it, "'subordinate' to that of the original defendants."[65] The suburban districts' inclusion in the case clearly tipped Roth's hand, indicating that the eventual desegregation order would extend beyond the jurisdictional boundaries of the city of Detroit.

Perhaps not surprisingly, then, on March 28, 1972, and after several days of hearings, Roth ruled that a Detroit-only desegregation plan could not remedy the constitutional violations he had found the previous year. Earlier, Roth had claimed wide-ranging authority—stemming directly from Supreme Court doctrine—to redress constitutional harms. "In addressing itself to this task the Supreme Court has said [in *Swann*] that the 'scope of a district court's equitable powers to remedy past wrongs is broad, for breadth and flexibility are inherent in equitable remedies,'" the judge had written.[66]

Now he cashed that check. Because the Detroit school system was already more than 60 percent black, a city-only desegregation plan would not achieve "the greatest possible degree of actual school desegregation," as *Green* and *Swann* required.[67] But Roth wasn't just concerned about the current state of play. He worried that a Detroit-only plan would "change a school system which is now Black and White to one that would be perceived as Black, thereby increasing the flight of Whites from the city and the system, thereby increasing the Black student population."[68] The judge's *own actions* might make an already rapidly deteriorating situation worse. (On March 28, 1972, Roth also began a series of hearings on the nature and scope of the proposed metropolitan plans.)

In retrospect, what was most striking about the ruling was the dialogue between Judge Roth and Judge Merhige, the federal judge in the Richmond trial. Just a few months earlier, in *Bradley v. Richmond*, Merhige had ordered the merger of city and suburban school districts to effectuate desegregation. The judge said, in effect, that suburban localities could not fence out blacks. State law could not give them that power. Roth, in turn, cited Merhige's decision expansively (two full block quotes) to support his conclusion. Roth thought the same concern obtained in Detroit. He wrote, "The state, however, cannot escape its constitutional duty to desegregate the public schools of the city of Detroit by pleading local authority. As Judge Merhige pointed out in Bradley v. Richmond."[69] The two judges were vibrating on the same wavelength. Roth was going to look beyond the city limits to desegregate Detroit's schools. The suburbs were in. Reacting to the order, Alexander Ritchie told the *Detroit Free Press*, "Just say I am happy, very happy."[70] It was around this time that the *Detroit Free Press* took note of Ritchie's transformation. In an article titled "Detroiter Switched His Stand," William Grant characterized the lawyer as an "advocate of integration."[71] Grant also reported something else of note: Ritchie's turnabout had deeply influenced Roth. "Many of the other attorneys in the case believe that the simple homespun honesty of Alexander Buchan Ritchie had more impact on Judge Roth than most of the other things he heard during a four-month trial."[72]

William L. Taylor, now the director of the Center for National Policy Review at Catholic University Law School in Washington, D.C., took notice. He instantly grasped the extraordinary potential of the two rulings. In a paper for the National Policy Conference on Education for Blacks, written just a few days after Judge Roth issued his decision, he heralded the rulings, which marked "a new and important phase of the struggle for equal educational opportunity."[73] The two cases were mutually reinforcing; they were broadly applicable throughout the country because so many metropolitan areas were similarly segregated. In effect, they were northern and southern variations on the same theme. To Taylor, the essential elements of both the Richmond and the Detroit cases "were state responsibility for public education, the containment of black people in the central city by policies of housing discrimination, and the lack of justification for maintaining separate districts in a single metropolitan community where such districting resulted in segregated schools."[74] In this, Richmond and Detroit were hardly outliers. Instead, they were prototypical examples of most metropolitan areas in the United States. Taylor noted that the moment was one of great possibility. But it was also one of great peril given population trends and the growth of suburbia, which was largely closed to blacks. The wild card was what might happen once either or both of those cases reached the high court in Washington, D.C.: "Brown v. Board of Education may become a historical anachronism unless its principles are interpreted broadly enough to encompass metropolitan relief."[75]

William Grant agreed. The journalist had reported on the case since its inception, and his deep familiarity with the lawsuit (and relevant legal doctrine) showed. On May 5, 1972, the *Detroit Free Press* published an article by Grant titled "Subdivisions Aren't 'Sovereign': Roth Case Based on Legal Precedents."[76] In the piece, Grant stressed that the plaintiffs had shown how the suburbs were on the hook, too. "The black students from the old Royal Oak Township school system, for example, were bused across district lines to black schools in Detroit because Royal Oak Township did not have its own high school and none of the surrounding white school systems would take the black students," he wrote.[77] Grant was onto the fact that Americans told themselves two very different stories about racial segregation: a southern story and a northern story. But the two story idea was a fallacy. Instead, there was a single story. Grant told his readers that what happened in Royal Oak Township "is something we comfortably tell ourselves was done only in the legally segregated school systems of the South. But it was done here as well."[78]

Of course, Roth had not made any findings against specific suburban school systems. But there was legal doctrine available, which Grant discussed in detail, suggesting that such findings were unnecessary. Grant informed the public about a lower court case decided in 1962 called *Allen v. County Board of Prince Edward County*. In that case, a federal trial court noted that "the United States Constitution recognizes no governing units except the federal government and the states. A contrary position would allow the state to evade its constitutional responsibility by carve-outs of small units."[79] And he mentioned *Reynolds v. Sims*, a 1964 Supreme Court landmark dealing with reapportionment, the process by which legislative seats are redistributed based on population shifts. The "pull quote" from *Reynolds*: "Political subdivisions of States—counties, cities or whatever—never were and never have been considered as sovereign entities."[80]

Then there was *Brown v. Board of Education II*, where the court instructed lower federal courts that they could consider "problems related to . . . revision of school districts and attendance areas" when determining whether school authorities had complied with *Brown*'s mandate.[81] Judge Merhige's recent decision, consolidating city and suburban school districts in Richmond, was just the frosting on the cake. Against that background, Grant provided this assessment of the current state of play: the "legal groundwork has been laid and the Supreme Court would not have to step very far beyond the decisions already handed down to allow school integration in the nation's cities to reach into the suburbs as well."[82] It was an important reminder that, when it came to school desegregation, much was still undecided. *Brown*'s reach, at least for the moment, was still unlimited.

———

In its new stance, the Detroit Board of Education submitted a metropolitan plan that was notably expansive.[83] *The Detroit News* characterized Detroit's plan as creating a "superdistrict." The Detroit board argued that the desegregation area should be expanded to include as many schools in upper middle-class communities as possible.[84] The board wanted not just an increased black-white racial mix, but socioeconomic integration, too. It emphasized this argument in its papers. "The Board takes the position that the presence of a predominance of middle class students in the classroom increases the chance for improved achievement by the poor and does not impede the achievement of the middle class students."[85] This was consistent with the findings of the Coleman Report.

So a plan that simply traversed Detroit's borders wasn't enough. From the board's perspective, a proposal that targeted only white working-class communities near Detroit, such as Ferndale, Roseville, and Wyandotte, would be a disaster. The board feared that this would "suggest to the typical resident of these blue collar suburbs, that he is being forced to allow his children to participate in this process not because he is white and suburban while the City is black, but rather because he doesn't have the money to move to Birmingham."[86] Such a plan would also send the wrong message to more affluent whites who often purported to support integration in the abstract. It would signal that they could escape the plan's effects by moving to Bloomfield Hills or other more well-to-do enclaves.[87] Capture the most affluent school districts, the board believed, and a reduction in white flight *and* white hostility to integration would follow. So the Detroit Board of Education wanted a desegregation plan that would cover a large geographic area. It was emphatic that a superdistrict be created: "It is imperative that the . . . desegregation plan include essentially all Wayne, Oakland, and Macomb counties, the tri-county area making up the metropolitan Detroit area."[88]

In support of its metropolitan plan, the Detroit board sought to show that relatively lengthy bus rides were not unusual for students in the Detroit metropolitan area. To that end, the board examined two high school students who attended the Roeper City and Country School in Bloomfield Hills.[89] (I graduated from Roeper in 1981.) Stephen James Scott was black. Richard Mark Shapero was white. Both tenth graders lived in Detroit. They testified that they routinely rode the bus forty-five minutes or more to attend the private school. The length of the ride did not prevent either of them from taking part in extracurricular activities. The buses were full, carrying between fifty and sixty students of various ages between the city and the suburb. Shapero, who had entered Roeper when he was barely out of diapers, had started riding the bus when he was in kindergarten. Scott described how the bus picked him up on Woodward Avenue, then "it proceeds north but it goes on Second to pick up girls, then it goes over to Hamilton to pick up three students further north, then it goes into Palmer Woods."[90] Ultimately, the bus swung back over to Woodward Avenue at Seven Mile Road—near where I boarded the bus to Roeper each school day after my parents moved to their dream house—and then proceeded north all the way to Bloomfield Hills. Busing was already a way of life for some, such as myself; why couldn't it be for many more?

CCBE's proposed metropolitan plan also spoke to the importance of socioeconomic diversity. Citing the Coleman Report, the proposal submitted by the group observed: "There no longer are enough children from middle-class families inside the city of Detroit to bring about the sort of socioeconomic mix needed to promote the academic achievement among children from poor families that must be promoted if one is serious about providing all children with an equal educational opportunity."[91] The author of CCBE's proposed plan was Richard Moreshead, an education professor at the University of Michigan-Dearborn. The professor had "skin in the game." His two daughters attended the Detroit public school system. And, his experience was deeply relevant. He chaired the education department, and had taught previously in both the Detroit and Grosse Pointe public schools.[92] Responding to a question at the metropolitan hearings about why he had rejected a small-scale plan, Moreshead was succinct: "It was my view Mr. Ritchie that unless a plan is broad enough to incorporate sufficient area to curtail white flight, any plan will then lead to resegregation of a school district and increased racial isolation, both of blacks and whites."[93]

The state defendants weren't exactly excited about metropolitan desegregation. On March 21, 1972, they had filed a brief with the court challenging the propriety of any such plan. The state defendants argued that "it is not open to question that the state of Michigan has never practiced racial separation pursuant to state constitution, statute, rule or regulation."[94] This, of course, was irrelevant, as the plaintiffs had challenged and proven "northern-style" de jure segregation on the part of the state. The remainder of their brief asserted that neither they nor the court had the power to alter school district boundaries, and that a metropolitan desegregation plan would have a deleterious effect on certain bond obligations and teacher contracts. None of these arguments were availing, as Judge Roth rejected a Detroit-only desegregation plan a week later. Dimond's assessment at this juncture: "The state defendants refused to express their preference for any plan and avoided assisting the court in resolving the complex issues before it."[95]

William Saxton, who represented most of the suburban systems, attempted to argue that desegregation did not produce quality educational outcomes for either race.[96] Saxton's argument was that, if there was no discernible evidence that desegregation provided specific educational benefits—which, inconveniently for him, there was—then that remedy was not justified. In so doing, he attempted to tap into the political zeitgeist of the day. Saxton: "I have assumed, your honor . . . [that] . . . our primary concern should not be putting children on the bus to give them a ride; our primary concern should be are we going to give them a quality education."[97] This was Lucas's swift reply: "That is a straw man raised by counsel, and he injects the new political curse word of busing. The objective here is not busing, but desegregation of the schools, ending the racial segregation of the schools and the community. And how the children get to school is merely a matter of providing the transportation if it is too far to walk."[98] What Saxton was really trying to do was push the narrowest possible interpretation of *Brown v. Board of Education*: that *Brown*, as he described it, just required "removing any legal or other barriers which preclude one from attending a school district on account of their race."[99] The actual desegregation of the schools wasn't required.

That cramped reading of *Brown* was prescient. It sounded very much like the understanding of *Brown* Chief Justice Roberts would employ almost two generations later in the school segregation case whose oral arguments I would attend in 2006: *Parents Involved in Community Schools v. Seattle School District*. There, the chief justice suggested that *Brown's* central meaning was that school districts could not "determine admission to a public school on a racial basis."[100] From this perspective, *Brown* simply prohibited school districts from using racial classifications in student assignments, and nothing more. It was an interpretation of the iconic case with which Saxton would have agreed enthusiastically.

In any event, Roth shut Saxton down: "You were trying to equate segregation with failure to provide quality education, a position that I cannot agree with. I keep reminding you that we are on the road to desegregation which I believe is compelled by the evidence and the law . . . Your quarrel appears to be with the Supreme Court of the United States [*Brown*]."[101] "It is as simple as this. They [higher courts] say when you find segregation you have to go about the business of desegregating. That is what I'm trying to do," the judge added.[102]

Refusing to accept Roth's earlier ruling that had rejected a Detroit-only desegregation plan, Saxton pressed a jurisdictional argument. In an interview, the lawyer succinctly stated his position: "The violation is limited to Detroit, and the solution must be found there."[103] This assertion worried the plaintiffs. Back in September of 1970, Nick Flannery had advised Nate Jones to "consider metropolitan relief."[104] The plaintiffs had "punted" on that issue at the time, preoccupied with the difficult question of establishing liability—and proving that *Brown* was violated—in a northern locale. The reality was that they lacked, as the plaintiffs' attorney Paul Dimond put it, "a clear idea at the outset" of what the appropriate remedy might be should they succeed. They hadn't wanted to put the cart before the horse. But now the question of metropolitan relief was front and center; it could no longer be evaded. Dimond conceded that the plaintiffs were on their back foot. With respect to metropolitan desegregation, their "legal vision was not clear," he admitted.[105] But it needed to be.

So the plaintiffs shifted into "hurry up" offense mode, augmenting the evidence produced at trial regarding segregation throughout the Detroit metropolitan area, and the state's responsibility for new school construction and the statewide provision of education. To this metropolitan proof they added "state board computer printouts showing the massive program of new construction of all-white schools in the suburbs since 1950," and "current statistics on the racial composition of student body and staff in the suburban schools."[106] The plaintiffs' hope was that all of this evidence taken together "would demonstrate that the 'containment' violation did not end at the boundaries of the Detroit school district."

On April 14, 1972, Judge Roth brought the metropolitan hearings to a close. He thanked all the lawyers: "It is always a pleasure for any trial judge to have top professionals conducting hearings such as this, and that is what I've had in this case," he told them.[107] Now, with the benefit of the hearings, the judge faced the difficult task of determining the nature and scope of a metropolitan desegregation plan.

———

On Saturday evening, April 15, 1972, as Roth was gearing up to issue a metropolitan desegregation order, around three thousand Democratic loyalists dined on roast beef at Detroit's downtown Cobo Hall as several candidates for the Democratic presidential nomination—George McGovern, Hubert Humphrey, and Edmund Muskie—addressed the crowd.[108] The *Detroit Free Press* reported that all three senators "denied that busing would be a major issue in the presidential campaign."[109] But a fourth Democratic candidate, famously pro-segregation Alabama governor George Wallace, was not invited to the event because he had refused to take a unity pledge, promising to support the eventual Democratic nominee should he fail to capture the nomination.

Instead, on that same night, Wallace kicked off the Michigan leg of his campaign at a raucous rally at the Michigan State Fair. He was fresh off a second-place showing in Wisconsin's Democratic primary. Located just south of Eight Mile Road (the dividing line between the city and the northern suburbs), the fifty-acre site hosted the longest-running state fair in the United States[110]—an event that, at its peak in 1966, attracted more than 1.2 million visitors.[111] There, Wallace drew a crowd of ten thousand, which officials struggled to control. They had to close the venue well before Wallace delivered his remarks.[112] The paper reported that many onlookers "were pressed against the doors in a vain effort to hear." Wallace gave his speech twice to accommodate all his supporters. Unlike his rivals, he most certainly believed that busing would be an important issue.[113]

On May 9, 1972, Wallace attended a rally at a youth center in Dearborn. Located on Detroit's southwest border, the city was a hotbed of antibusing resistance. (A contemporaneous picture showed Dearborn mayor Orville Hubbard and Irene McCabe with hands clasped as they marched to protest busing).[114] The candidate thought Michigan was in the bag. "There's been a lot of talk about how the Democratic establishment could stop Wallace, but it's too late to do any stopping. You already know what's going to happen on May 16," he told the crowd.[115] The overwhelmingly white, working-class group was on his side and Wallace knew it. "I'm just putting the hay down where the goats can get it," he declared.[116] Denouncing busing as the "most asinine, cruel thing I've ever heard of," he worked them into a frenzy.[117]

Wallace had similar results in Muskegon, Grand Rapids, and Lansing. He was a front-runner in Michigan, and *Bradley v. Milliken* was a big reason why. Confirming that busing dominated Michigan's upcoming primary, the *Detroit Free Press* summed up the state of play just days before the election. "At the root of that aroused anger among voters is the well-founded expectation that U.S. Judge Stephen J. Roth of Detroit will soon order an integration plan for metropolitan Detroit that would require the busing of many white and black children from Detroit to the suburbs and the suburbs to Detroit."[118]

Then, on Monday, May 15—just one day before Michigan's presidential primary—Arthur Bremer, a twenty-one-year-old from Milwaukee, shot Wallace at a campaign stop in Maryland.[119] Critically injured, the Alabama governor survived, but he would never walk again.[120] Wallace's plight only seemed to excite Michigan Democrats' enthusiasm further. With voters turning out in record numbers, he won the state's Democratic primary. Republican crossovers accounted for much of Wallace's strength, but at least one statistician believed that he persuaded enough Democrats to prevail on their ballots alone.[121] Wallace carried the Maryland primary that day as well. Michigan-area papers described his victory breathlessly. Wallace's win was "smashing"; he carried the state in a "landslide." One paper exclaimed: "Defying union and Democratic party leaders alike, a record flood-tide of primary election voters has swept Alabama Gov. George Wallace" to victory.[122]

As voters were going to the polls in Michigan, Barbara Walters moderated a timely debate on NBC's popular *The Today Show*.[123] In the studio that day were Irene McCabe and Alma Stallworth, a black Democrat and a first-term member of the Michigan House of Representatives from Detroit. Walters, who would become the first female cohost of the program shortly thereafter, was a talented interviewer.[124] But her introduction to the segment showed just how successful McCabe and other antibusing activists had become in controlling the narrative. Describing busing as an issue that does not seem to have "party lines," Walters characterized Michigan as the epicenter of the dispute. (There was a large "shadow map" of the state of Michigan projected just below the *Today Show* logo, directly behind the panelists.) Pontiac was the eye of the storm. In that city "there were big and sometimes violent antibusing demonstrations last fall," Walters stated in her trademark lisp. Then she shifted seamlessly to McCabe. "And a Pontiac housewife, Mrs. Irene McCabe, walked her way to national recognition this spring when she and half a dozen other women hiked on foot all the way to Washington to express their indignation over busing to achieve racial balance in the schools. This was a forty-one-day walk. It ended with an audience with the top assistant to President Nixon, John Ehrlichman."[125]

Walter's introduction showed how successful the anti-integration faction had already been in framing the debate. First, there was no mention of desegregation. The newscaster referred to the two sides as "probusing" and "antibusing." But busing was a time-honored way of transporting children to school, not an end in itself. Labeling the issue "busing" rather than "desegregation" was a key move, one the national media now adopted and amplified. It allowed whites to oppose integration without appearing to be openly racist. Next, Walters used the phraseology "busing to achieve racial balance." This made it seem as if judges were ordering busing willy-nilly, to suit some liberal vision of social engineering. But in Pontiac, Judge Keith had found that school officials had violated the Constitution. The same went for Judge Roth in Detroit. Desegregation was the *remedy* for that constitutional violation. Busing simply facilitated it.

The newscaster's remarks made McCabe's march seem like a juggernaut. It wasn't. McCabe had predicted that 250,000 supporters would meet her in Washington. She was met by a retinue of elected officials, including Michigan Senator Robert Griffin, Representative William Broomfield of Royal Oak, and Representative (and future president) Gerald Ford of Grand Rapids, all Republicans.[126] But fewer than five hundred people overall welcomed her when she arrived at the Capitol.[127] The march was enough of a dud that the liberal *Detroit Free Press* editorialized that McCabe had overplayed her hand. Arguing that McCabe's march was a "double-barreled fiasco," the paper implored elected officials such as Griffin to reevaluate their position.[128] "As Mrs. McCabe has demonstrated so ably, if not intentionally, the issue simply doesn't rate hysteria. More importantly, it isn't worth the potential price in damage to our Constitution, our nation and our children," the paper urged.

As for the debate itself, McCabe cleverly defended her position using a new rhetorical strategy that would become key to undermining racial justice initiatives in the years to come: colorblindness. Race and drawing attention to race was "the sole reason for busing," she argued. The implication was clear. It was the probusing side that was suspect, race-based, racist. In contrast, she was "colorblind." "This is how I have lived, this is how I have raised my children," she told *The Today Show* viewers. For her part, Stallworth focused on quality education. The question was how to get it. "Because of racism our children are denied the proper funding, the proper facilities, the proper resources," the legislator asserted. "In the city of Detroit, we face a deficit of more than $31 million, and if we do not pass our millage then our schools will close in September . . . In those areas where we have predominantly white residing . . . they are opposing the millage on the basis of the busing."

Walters interrupted Stallworth seeking clarification, "Does everybody know what you mean by millage?" It was a good question. Millage was the formula for determining property tax rates, based upon the assessed value of property within a locality. Higher millage rates—and more valuable property—typically meant more money for the public schools.

Stallworth now had the chance to plead her case on national television: "We have to renew [the millage] plus increase it . . . to make up the deficit and to sustain us." It wasn't an idle appeal. Detroit voters weren't going to the polls just to choose a presidential nominee that day. They were also voting on a package of millage proposals designed to keep the school system afloat. Wallace won; the millage proposals didn't. Mirel attributed both results to antibusing sentiment.[129] The Detroit public school system was on the brink of collapse. Responding to the proposals' defeat, one board member reportedly said: "We have just discovered the death of the school system, and we don't want to recognize it."[130]

Toward the end of the debate, Walters teed up a question about blacks' attitudes on the issue of the day. Speaking to the black legislator in a conversational tone, the newscaster remarked: "I remember when this question was raised when we were in Florida." She paused and then continued: "That there were a great many blacks who were against busing." Acknowledging that "blacks have mixed feelings about busing," Stallworth handled Walters like a pro. Walters's question was premised on the idea that "forced busing" was the issue. Stallworth wasn't buying. So she pivoted, making a familiar connection. The issue was educational equality and how to get it. "But I think most of us have to realize that if we're going to get the benefit of our tax dollars . . . then we will have to force the issue." The legislator continued, "Of course we would like to have the community school concept but what we found since we are segregated and isolated, we never get the kind of attention that's necessary . . . if the situation is integrated . . . then everyone will get the benefit." Stallworth was channeling Verda Bradley, the first named plaintiff in the *Bradley v. Milliken* lawsuit.

16

GOING FOR METRO

In early June 1972, and just a few days before Roth issued his metropolitan ruling in the Detroit case, the United States Court of Appeals for the Fourth Circuit reversed Judge Merhige in the Richmond case. The Fourth Circuit ruling had a "through the looking-glass" quality to it. On the one hand, it accepted the validity of many of the facts upon which Merhige's opinion was based. The appellate court wrote, "It is urged upon us that within the City of Richmond there has been state (also federal) action tending to perpetuate apartheid of the races in ghetto patterns throughout the city, and that there has been state action within the adjoining counties also tending to restrict and control the housing location of black residents. *We think such findings are not clearly erroneous, and accept them.*"[1] In Richmond, there was classic southern-style de jure segregation. In addition, the city, the state, and the federal government had "discriminated against blacks with respect to places and opportunity for residence."[2] The appellate court acknowledged all of this.

On the other hand, the Fourth Circuit overturned Judge Merhige's order. Sure, the schools were de jure segregated—this was Virginia after all; sure, there were racially restrictive covenants; sure, there were discriminatory school construction policies; sure, the counties refused to participate in federally assisted low income housing; sure, there was private residential segregation. But none of that translated into a specific showing that the governmental defendants "had any impact upon movement by blacks out of the city and into the counties."[3] Notwithstanding whatever past discrimination there had been, there was no showing "that there was ever *joint interaction* between any two of the units involved (or by higher state officers) for the purposes of keeping one unit relatively white by confining blacks to another."[4]

It was hard to follow the appellate court's logic unless one viewed racially discriminatory acts in isolation, as individual bad acts unconnected to the larger system of racial discrimination. This was why the Fourth Circuit sought evidence of "joint interaction," of collusion, of overt agreement among responsible officials to discriminate against blacks. Seeing none, the court professed mystification. It wrote: "We think that the root causes of the concentration of blacks in the inner cities of America are simply not known."[5] After reading Judge Merhige's 325-page, meticulously reasoned, trial court opinion below, it was hard to take that statement seriously. It was a fairy tale. But it was now sanctioned by the law.

Irene McCabe was ebullient: "It is our first ray of sunshine," she stated.[6] Michigan attorney general Frank Kelley thought the Fourth Circuit decision was a harbinger of things to come. The ruling fortified his judgment that "upon conclusion of legal proceedings involving Michigan there will be no cross-district busing in this state."[7] But the trial team in the Detroit case was undeterred. Lou Lucas—who served as lead counsel in both the Detroit and Richmond cases—had correctly predicted that the conservative Fourth Circuit would overturn Judge Merhige's consolidation order, which would have opened the door to city-suburban desegregation.[8] He was putting all of his chips on the table when it came to the U.S. Supreme Court. In an article on the Richmond decision for the *Detroit Free Press*, William Grant reported that Lucas predicted "that the U.S. Supreme Court will reverse the Court of Appeals [Richmond] decision."[9] The journalist was starting to count votes. He noted that since 1971, when a unanimous Supreme Court in *Swann* authorized busing as a desegregation technique, President Nixon had added two conservative justices to the high court bench. "This means the majority of the present court has said busing is permitted even if the two new justices do not share that view," Grant wrote.[10]

On June 14, 1972, Nate Jones wrote to Roy Wilkins to tell him that Judge Stephen Roth's desegregation plan had been announced—and that it went way beyond Detroit. "Judge Stephen J. Roth has ordered the State of Michigan and the Detroit School Board to implement a Metropolitan School Plan to be completed by 1973, and to commence its initial stages this fall," Jones reported. He went on: "It involves 900,000 students in the metropolitan area and three counties, and is the largest school case that has ever been decided." In case Wilkins was missing the magnitude of the case, for which Nate Jones's legal team at the NAACP had devoted six attorneys and more than $1 million (in today's dollars) of the organization's money, Jones underscored just what this meant: *This is the most significant development in school litigation since* Brown."

After almost two years of litigation, Jones's enthusiasm—and even a bit of hyperbole—was understandable. Indeed, he overstated the total number of students affected by Judge Roth's ruling, which was closer to eight hundred thousand. But in light of a decision that threatened to totally upend public education in southeastern Michigan, the ferocious reactions for and against Roth's order were understandable. Roth was going to bring *Brown* North. And if the ruling stood, the NAACP would use it like a sword. The organization had placed a huge bet on the Detroit litigation, and it had won.

The Fourth Circuit's ruling in the Richmond case might have caused Roth to think twice. But what it didn't do was prevent him from ordering metropolitan desegregation, staking his claim on history and with it a belief that racial equality—and reconciliation—was still possible. Acknowledging the nation's hard-won progress, he wrote: "The racial history of this country is writ large by constitutional adjudication from Dred Scott v. Sanford to Plessy v. Ferguson to *Brown*."[11] Public education was singularly important. But it could also reify racist beliefs, as the judge recognized: "The Court [in *Brown*] held that "state-imposed" school segregation immeasurably taints the education received by all children in the public schools; perpetuates racial discrimination and a history of public action attaching a badge of inferiority to the black race in a public forum which importantly shapes the minds and hearts of succeeding generations of our young people."[12]

Broadly, Roth's pathbreaking metropolitan ruling did three things: First, it established a metropolitan "desegregation area," consisting of Detroit and roughly fifty suburban school districts nearby. As Roth put it, "In many respects—patterns of economic life, work, play, population, planning, transportation, health services—the tri-county area [Wayne, Oakland, and Macomb Counties] constitutes a rough series of interrelated communities constituting, in the view of the United States Census Bureau, a single standard metropolitan statistical area."[13]

Roth's conclusion that the Detroit metropolitan area was a single region, for educational purposes, was based on the actions of school authorities themselves, who had ignored school district lines when it suited their interests. Roth hadn't forgotten how black children living in the Carver School District, located in the Oakland County suburb of Royal Oak Township, were bused past white schools so they could attend black schools in Detroit.[14] In addition, the city and the suburbs routinely created organizations and pursued regional solutions for intractable problems that crossed jurisdictional boundaries: regional recreational authorities, a tri-county sewage system, and so on.[15] During the metropolitan hearings, Roth observed that local units of government had not "hesitated to join together for the purpose of providing better solutions to problems confronting them."[16]

The board and CCBE's proposed desegregation plans would have included the entire tri-county area.[17] Roth declined to go that far. In all likelihood, he agreed that the highest level of socioeconomic integration was optimal. But Roth was worried about the law. *Brown* and its progeny focused on eliminating racially identifiable schools and reducing travel times for students undergoing desegregation. Even if the available evidence pointed toward the importance of economic integration, the Supreme Court had not recognized socioeconomic diversity as a key component of a school desegregation plan. Roth did not want to get out too far over his skis, injecting novel and appealable issues into what was already a complicated and controversial case. So he struck a cautious, prudential tone: "In terms of what the [Supreme] court views as the primary obligation established by the Constitution—racial discrimination—the court deems the proper approach is to be more conservative: [this] court finds it appropriate to confine the desegregation area to its smallest effective limits."[18] This explained the contours of Roth's metropolitan desegregation area, with approximately fifty suburban school districts and Detroit.[19] Fifty school districts sounded like a lot. But in 1970, the Detroit metro tri-county area—Wayne, Macomb, and Oakland Counties—contained among them more than one hundred and fifty cities and towns.[20] So while including fifty-odd suburban school districts meant the plan was significant, it did not include every suburban school district within the Detroit metropolitan area. The desegregation area was big enough to provide for meaningful desegregation, but not so large as to require overly lengthy bus rides. The area did, however, include some of the toniest locales in southeastern Michigan: Bloomfield Hills, Birmingham, and Grosse Pointe.

Second, Roth created a desegregation panel and charged it with developing a specific metropolitan desegregation plan consistent with the broad outlines established in his order.[21] One question was why an independent panel was needed. Surely he could have placed this obligation on the state. But Michigan was effectively in default. The state had submitted six proposed metropolitan desegregation plans to the court, none of which meaningfully integrated the Detroit school system with the surrounding suburban school systems. Likening Michigan's oppositional behavior throughout the litigation to the state legislature's attempt to overturn Zwerdling's April 7 plan, he wrote: "Put bluntly, State defendants . . . deliberately chose not to assist the court in choosing an appropriate area for effective desegregation of the Detroit public schools."[22] Better to have the panel make independent recommendations consistent with the court's mandate. But there was another reason why this made sense: the state's role in facilitating suburban—and racially exclusionary—school construction.

Roth's order referenced the plaintiffs' containment theory to explain why blacks lacked access to suburban schools. The judge wrote: "The white population of the city declined and in the suburbs grew; the black population in the city grew, and largely, was contained therein by force of public and private racial discrimination at all levels."[23] Good schools were a big part of the suburbs' attraction. After World War II, suburban school systems in southeastern Michigan added thousands of new classrooms, few

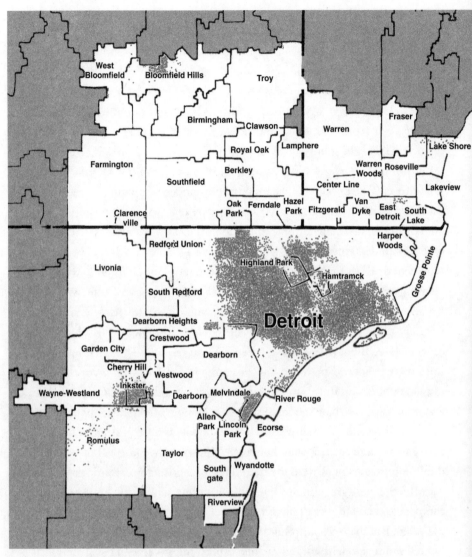

Map of Judge Roth's Metropolitan Detroit Desegregation Area.
Each dot represents one hundred black residents.

of which were available to black children.[24] Roth would not let Michigan forget the role it played in making such "massive school construction" possible. "Unfortunately, the State, despite its awareness of the important impact of school construction and announced policy to control it, acted 'in keeping generally, with the discriminatory practices which advanced or perpetuated racial segregation in these schools.'"[25] Perhaps distrusting the state's ability to undertake the task given its past behavior, Roth charged the panel with the responsibility of considering "future [school] construction throughout the metropolitan area."[26]

Roth noted, however, that he had "taken no proofs with respect to the establishment of the boundaries of the 86 public school districts in the counties of Wayne, Oakland, and Macomb, nor on the issue of whether, with the exclusion of the city of Detroit school district, such school districts have committed acts of de jure segregation."[27] This unsettled the plaintiffs' counsel. Throughout, they had continued to assert that the suburban school districts were merely political subdivisions of the state, and that the state defendants were the only parties against whom they needed to prove their case. Which they did. But after Roth rejected a Detroit-only desegregation plan, the trial team became concerned about what might happen on appeal once Roth ordered metropolitan desegregation. As Dimond described it, this was the plaintiffs' "legal dilemma": the law on the books pointed to the state defendants as the responsible officials. And the plaintiffs didn't want to cede any ground to the suburban school districts' argument that they were in effect mini sovereigns, against whom the plaintiffs had to plead and prove that each had violated the law by engaging in, as Dimond put it, "independent acts of segregation."[28] The plaintiffs tried to resolve their dilemma by providing additional evidence during the metropolitan hearings that the containment was a regional rather than a Detroit-only phenomenon. Dimond wrote that "we hoped that this additional evidence would demonstrate that the 'containment' violation did not end at the boundaries of the Detroit school district."[29] Roth's ruling was consistent with this view. But in expressly confirming that he had "taken no proofs" with respect to the suburbs, Roth's statement implied that perhaps a case against them—directly asserting that the suburbs had violated the Constitution—was warranted. This was why the plaintiffs greeted Roth's "taken no proofs" statement with dismay.

Roth set out general principles for integrating the schools within the desegregation area, which the panel was charged with implementing. But Roth's ruling only set out the parameters for metropolitan desegregation. The judge wrote, "Based on the entire evidence amassed in this case, the court finds that an educationally sound, administratively feasible, constitutionally adequate, practicable and effective plan of desegregation *may be developed* . . . for the desegregation area as set forth."[30] This meant that Roth did not issue a final metropolitan desegregation plan. Instead, he charged the desegregation panel with the job of developing it consistent with the principles he laid out. These included: a requirement that black and white students equally shared the burden of desegregation, that the number of students bused be minimized, that *all* faculty and staff serving schools within the area be desegregated, that "affirmative action" be used to increase the number of minority teachers and administrators, and that school capacity (number of students per class and attending each school) be uniform.[31] The overall goal was to achieve the "greatest degree of actual desegregation [so that] no school, grade or classroom be substantially disproportionate to the overall pupil racial composition."[32] This principle, and the metropolitan order more generally, felt similar to Ribicoff's ambitious integration bill, which had failed to become law. Perhaps Roth would succeed where Congress could not.

Verda Bradley's rationale for joining the *Bradley v. Milliken* litigation was school quality. Roth's order spoke directly to that concern by requiring that all schools in the desegregation area achieve substantial equality with respect to "facilities, extracurricular activities and staff." This, along with the uniformity requirement, meant that the order provided for desegregation *and* equalization of urban and suburban schools. This was a powerful and underappreciated aspect of the metropolitan ruling. Relying on this mandate, Judge Roth later prohibited the Detroit Board of Education from enacting draconian cutbacks because of budget shortfalls. His action preserved more than fifteen hundred faculty positions and ensured that Detroit students would attend school for 180 rather than 117 days during the 1972–73 academic year.[33] "It's the state's obligation to provide education with [in] [the metropolitan] desegregation area. It seems to me it cannot be discharged with the proposed reduction in both the school year and the school staffs," Roth declared at a hearing a few weeks after issuing the metropolitan desegregation order.[34]

The equalization aspect of the metropolitan order also held financial promise for some suburban school districts. As William Grant noted, some of the suburbs included in the large metropolitan desegregation area were experiencing financial difficulty.[35] An order to equalize "facilities, extracurricular activities, and staff" might bring more money and resources into these cash-starved school districts. As Grant put it, compared to Detroit "some suburban school systems are in equally grave condition, and they too may be helped by the busing plan they have fought so hard."[36]

Although the panel had a variety of desegregation techniques at their disposal, the judge pointed approvingly to the "cluster" scheme proposed by the Detroit Board of Education.[37] Under the cluster scheme, the desegregation area was divided into smaller regions or clusters, which included both city and suburban schools. Students would then be assigned to a school within the cluster (disrupting the default neighborhood school rule) and bused to that location, if necessary. The smaller clusters would both reduce the time that any child would spend in transit, and subdivide the larger metropolitan desegregation area into more manageable, "bite-size" units. Roth wanted the panel to develop a plan quickly. His order expected desegregation "to proceed in no event later than the fall of 1973."[38]

Third, and finally, the judge charged the state (and particularly the State Board of Education) with creating the governmental, financial, and administrative structures necessary to facilitate metropolitan desegregation.[39] Instead of formally consolidating the Detroit and suburban school systems, Roth imagined that some sort of regional planning authority— along the lines of the Southeastern Michigan Transportation Authority, or SEMTA—could get the job done.[40] It was up to the state defendants to submit a plan to the court fleshing out the details.

The metropolitan ruling reflected the sum total of what Judge Roth had learned in the almost two years since the NAACP had filed the case. One lawyer familiar with the case stated that the judge had "the most striking change of heart I have ever seen."[41] Reflecting on Roth's actions just before the metropolitan ruling was handed down, a leader of Michigan's Democratic

Party remarked, "Who would have thought Steve would have done this?"[42] A few weeks later, Roth had a private conversation with a reporter. It showed how much the case had changed him: "I hope I get a chance before this case is over to say publicly, from the bench, why I think this has to happen."[43] The judge continued, "We took this country away from the Indians and put them on reservations. We imported the Chinese and made them build the railroads. We got the Irish, the Italians, and the rest and shoved them into the mills. Now I guess we are reserving the ghettos for the Blacks. Everybody seems to have forgotten 1967 but I have not. Black people will not take being locked up in the ghettos without a fight."[44]

The reaction in Detroit to Roth's metropolitan order could be summed up in one word: "busing." On June 15, 1972, the day after he released the order, the front page of the *Detroit Free Press* blared: "Full Integration Set for '73, Roth Orders Busing to Begin in Fall."[45] William Grant's article distilled the multipage order in its very first sentence: "U.S. District Judge Stephen J. Roth Wednesday ordered Detroit and 52 suburban school systems to begin the most massive school busing program in the nation." The article was silent as to why "busing" was needed in the first place, and failed to remind the reader that state and local authorities had violated the Constitution by repeated and intentional acts of racial segregation.

Bradley v. Milliken's national implications were clear immediately. At around 5:00 p.m. on the very same day, President Nixon called Governor Milliken to discuss the case.[46] Nixon had been following the litigation closely. During the call, Nixon gave Milliken some key information. While Broomfield's busing moratorium had just passed, and Nixon intended to sign it, U.S. attorney general Richard Kleindienst had concluded that the law would not prevent Roth from implementing his order. "Preliminary indications are that it would not cover the Detroit situation," Nixon told Milliken.[47] On Thursday, June 29, 1972, *The Detroit News* ran an article titled "Nixon to fight Roth bussing order."[48] In it, the paper reported that President Nixon had pledged to "leave no stone unturned" in fighting against "forced school integration bussing" in Detroit. John Ehrlichman, one of the president's top advisers, was set to meet with Governor Milliken in connection with the case.

Locally, the Detroit branch of the NAACP hailed the metropolitan ruling. Jesse Goodwin, chairman of the branch's education committee, wrote that the decision held "bright promise for all school children in the Metropolitan Area."[49] The branch's official publication, *The NAACP Reporter*, devoted the majority of both its June and July/August issues to analysis of the metropolitan ruling and related articles. An article in *The Detroit News* explored black reaction to Roth's order. William Penn, the NAACP Detroit branch's executive secretary, stated: "I don't favor bussing, but the NAACP is for any means that will desegregate the schools, including bussing."[50] It was interesting to speculate what Penn might have meant by the remark. One possibility was that desegregation still retained popular support in the black community, even as black parents feared—rationally— that their children would shoulder the majority of busing's burdens and dangers. "If the nation plans on keeping the Constitution, then what the NAACP has done is right," Penn added.[51] Mrs. Helen Moore, president of Black Parents for Quality Education, worried that suburban teachers' "stereotyped attitudes" might make it impossible for black children to be educated in suburban schools. Sounding a theme that would come to dominate the desegregation debate, she argued, "Black children should be able to get quality education no matter who they sit next to or where."[52] But she wasn't against desegregation altogether. Instead, Moore proposed "one-way bussing" of white students into Detroit's schools.[53] Harvey Grant, editor of *The Ghetto Speaks* newspaper, thought the emphasis on busing was a red herring. The real issue, he said, was "quality education for black children."[54]

There had always been differences of opinion among blacks about how best to achieve freedom and equality. It would have been strange if there were not. The pitched debate between Albert Cleage and Remus Robinson about the Detroit Public School system was just one example. But the article alluded to another aspect of that dispute: captured black political constituencies. *The Detroit News* paraphrased Penn's concern: he "said they [black folks] should beware of black leaders who might oppose the bussing program because they want to keep certain communities isolated, so they can continue their political control over them."[55] Perhaps, then, each side had a cudgel. The pro-integration forces could accuse the quality education backers of promoting a system that entrenched the power of politically insulated black representatives, who might or might not protect the interests of black children. Conversely, the quality education proponents might indict the integrationists for insufficient attachment to the black community.

To the extent this dichotomy existed it was unfortunate, as there was a good argument that the two groups were really on the same side. After all, quality education was what drew Verda Bradley to the *Bradley v. Milliken* lawsuit in the first instance. For her, desegregation was a means to an end.

In suburban Detroit, antibusing forces sprang into action. In Oak Park, almost two dozen suburban mayors and other officials held a meeting to discuss Roth's ruling.[56] *The Detroit News* reported that the group "passed a resolution opposing cross-district bussing and named a seven-member committee to formulate legal plans."[57] In Warren and Berkley, parent groups moved to organize private schools to provide a segregated educational alternative for their children. The chairman of one such group said: "Now if there is definitely going to be desegregation busing, we will go ahead and organize a private school system."[58] Protesters picketed the federal court building in downtown Detroit.[59] One young boy was pictured holding a sign that read "Judge Roth Child Molester." Upstairs in the judge's chambers, the phone was ringing off the hook. One caller warned menacingly: "You'll get yours."[60]

Dearborn mayor Orville Hubbard predicted that Roth's decision and others like it would lead to an "end to democracy."[61] The judge had been born in Hungary, and Hubbard attacked him for it. "His roots are not deep enough in America. He should be crated up and shipped back," the mayor declared. The front page of the June 15 edition of *The Detroit News* featured a veritable cornucopia of white dissent.[62] Mrs. Miles Brasch of Huntington Woods: "No one wants their children bussed into the inner city."[63] Mrs. John Hambrick of Ferndale: "I don't want my kids taken to Detroit."[64] Mrs. Robert Winters of Troy: "If we have to keep them at home, we will. The people won't stand for it."[65] Troy City Clerk Kenneth Courtney: "My kids won't go there [to Pershing High School in Detroit] even if they have to send my wife to jail."[66] And another Troy city official, Carlos W. Lynch, worried that busing children to Detroit would "stunt the economic growth" of the city of Troy and other suburban areas.[67] He wondered if Roth could be sued directly for the damages.

Taylor, another mostly white suburb of Detroit that had overwhelmingly voted for Wallace in the primary, was a locus of antibusing resistance. On June 19, 1972, *The Detroit News* reported that the city's community leaders, including several elected officials, had formed a "blue ribbon" committee to develop a boycott strategy if Roth's metropolitan ruling was implemented.[68] Taylor mayor Richard J. Trolley was chairman of the committee. "All Taylor is together on this issue," the mayor asserted.[69] Trolley issued a cautionary warning. "This type of action [Roth's metropolitan ruling] and thinking is causing people within the Democratic Party to move further to the right, and it's why I am a Wallace delegate to the Democratic convention."[70]

In late June, *The Detroit News* reported that five Detroit-area Democratic congressmen, citing Roth's order, had written the Democratic platform committee urging it to reject busing for the purposes of achieving "racial balance."[71] The plea fell on deaf ears. In advance of the national convention in Miami Beach, the committee adopted a probusing plank anyway. It characterized busing as a technique for eliminating "legally imposed segregation" and improving "quality of education for all children." The plank was subject to reconsideration at the convention, however. Anticipating that possibility, the article noted, "The busing issue is certain to cause a floor fight at the convention, which opens July 10 in Miami Beach."[72]

That piece was right on the money.[73] The debate in Miami didn't come to blows, but one report had probusing delegates brandishing "clenched fists as they shouted down the Wallace planks."[74] And, as Trolley vowed, he was in the center of the action. Speaking in support of Wallace's proposal to ban busing for the purposes of racial integration, the Taylor mayor poured it on thick. Courts took "innocent children from their homes," he said, whereas racial balance and quality education could never be achieved "on a government bus."[75] (Weren't all public school buses "government" buses?) Trolley's purportedly race-neutral rationale for opposing busing didn't pass the laugh test: "Children cannot be properly educated in strange environments."[76] But he didn't persuade the platform committee. It again characterized busing as a tool to achieve desegregation, one among many. The probusing plank stayed in the Democrats' platform. Wallace predicted his party would lose in the general election.

On July 12, 1972, the convention nominated George McGovern as their standard-bearer.[77] The Democratic nominee famously gave his acceptance speech at 2:45 a.m.[78] Most Americans were asleep. "I'm happy to join you for this benediction of our Friday sunrise service," he quipped.[79]

The possibility of metropolitan desegregation was not received as a death knell in every corner of suburbia, however. The *Detroit Free Press* reported that the Metropolitan Coalition for Peaceful Integration was trying to build some bridges. The group was mobilizing mothers—from both Detroit and its suburbs—to facilitate the desegregation process.[80] The coalition's cochairman, Elwood Hain, emphasized the importance of city-suburban collaboration. "We want to get parents together and plan for the safety of children, to get the women there, on the bus, at the schools, who by their sheer physical presence create an aura of calm," Hain explained.[81] In Livonia, a racially mixed group of thirty Detroiters with school-age children met with fifty suburban parents to discuss desegregation planning. In Grosse Pointe, ninety parents met for the same purpose. The group anticipated the formation of "citizens coalitions," neighborhood teams that would prepare for desegregation and "talk with those parents who feel strongly against busing."[82]

That some suburban whites were open to integration should have been big news, yet few were aware of it. Perhaps one reason why was how the newspapers chose to report the story. The *Detroit Free Press* was the more liberal of the two major daily papers, yet the article about the coalition was buried in the "C" section, in the "for and about women" column. The hard news about the busing pushback, meanwhile, was often right up front.

There was also support from some religious leaders, including within the Catholic church. Just a few days after Roth released the metropolitan ruling, John Cardinal Dearden and eight other Detroit-area religious leaders issued a joint statement urging compliance with the judge's opinion.[83] Dearden's participation was unsurprising. From the time a metropolitan remedy in *Bradley v. Milliken* became a realistic possibility, the head of Detroit's archdiocese had worked to support desegregation. In late 1971, Dearden instructed Detroit Catholic school officials to freeze enrollments at parochial schools so that they would not become a "place of refuge" for whites attempting to avoid court-ordered desegregation.[84] At the time, the city's Catholic schools were experiencing an extraordinary financial crisis and many closed as a result. But Dearden pursued this policy anyway, even when, as one observer noted, "enhanced enrollment might have saved the school in question."[85] In mid-May 1972, he challenged a pastor who had allowed non-Catholic out-of-parish students to attend parochial schools.[86] "The acceptance of so many transfers from Pontiac public schools has raised some questions," the cardinal wrote.[87] The chastised priest retired a short time later.[88]

Lutherans, Episcopalians, Presbyterians, Protestants, Jews, Baptists, and Methodists all signed on to the statement supporting Roth. Where the protesters saw only unmitigated harm, the faith leaders saw a rare opportunity "to make the classrooms of the metropolitan area a living lesson in American pluralism, and this great lesson can go beyond the classroom and renew the spirit of our country." The statement was an appeal to unity. But it also sought to subtly frame public opinion. By referencing "the American goal of good public education," the clergy depicted proponents of Roth's order as supporters of core American values. The ruling's opponents presumably stood for something else entirely.

This was no small thing. Dearborn's Mayor Hubbard had portrayed Roth as an outsider, a stranger to American norms and values. The faith leaders offered a different and competing view of the American creed: pluralistic, expansive, inclusive, integrationist. But one sensed a certain anxiety behind their appeal.

PART III
MILLIKEN V. BRADLEY

17

NOW MORE THAN EVER

J udge Roth had issued a momentous decision. Michigan state attorney general Frank Kelley, however, strongly disagreed with the ruling. He would write later in his autobiography of his concern that court-ordered metropolitan desegregation might derail his prospects for higher office. "What I could instantly see was how unpopular this idea [cross-district busing] was. I also knew, however, that if the courts were to order such a thing, I would legally have to defend and enforce that ruling. Which, politically, would be the kiss of death."[1] Pointing to the fact that Roth had made no finding of intentional segregation against the suburbs, the state attorney general called the decision to include them in the remedy "wrong" and legally unsustainable.[2] Kelley vowed to appeal all the way to the U.S. Supreme Court, if necessary. There, the state attorney general anticipated a receptive audience. Conservative justices would vindicate Michigan's position, he believed. As the *Detroit Free Press* put it, "It was still [Kelley's] opinion that the present Supreme Court, appointed in part by Mr. Nixon, will not uphold cross-district busing orders such as those issued by Roth."[3] Kelley made good on his promise, immediately appealing to the Sixth Circuit Court of Appeals—along with the rest of the defendants—Roth's June 14, 1972, metropolitan ruling.[4]

Roth's metropolitan ruling had set out the broad guidelines for desegregation, but it was up to the desegregation panel to work out the details.

It was hard at work. In late June 1972, the panel ordered several "test runs" between two Detroit high schools and the Bloomfield Hills and West Bloomfield Hills school districts to check school bus trip times and traffic conditions.[5] Acting on the panel's recommendations, in mid-July Roth added the state treasurer as a defendant and ordered her to pay for the acquisition of 295 buses "for the purposes of providing transportation under an interim [desegregation] plan."[6] The extra buses, if purchased, would roll when school opened in just a few short months.

On July 13, 1972, the Sixth Circuit stayed Judge Roth's order requiring the bus purchase.[7] Then, just a few days later, the appellate court clarified its intentions. It continued the stay on the purchases "until entry by the District Judge of a final desegregation order or until certification by the District Judge of an appealable question."[8] What this really meant was that the appellate court didn't want Roth to take any significant steps toward ordering metropolitan desegregation—such as by requiring the expenditure of significant funds to purchase buses—until it had had a chance to weigh in on the major issues in the case. Or, as Dimond explained, the "Sixth Circuit, with the reputation of a defender of segregation in the North and South and one of the most conservative of the courts of appeal, was not about to allow Judge Roth to implement the nation's first substantial cross-district desegregation plan before any appellate review."[9]

Typically, parties cannot appeal to a higher court until a case has concluded. Only then are the questions presented by the case ready for appellate review. But the *Bradley* case was far from over. The desegregation panel had yet to issue its recommendation; Roth had issued no final desegregation order. Notwithstanding these facts, all the parties—including the plaintiffs—agreed that it would be best if the appellate court weighed in as soon as possible. Pursuant to federal practice, all the parties asked Judge Roth to "certify" that several major issues in the case were ready for appellate review, which he did.[10] The plaintiffs' counsel thought there was little choice. Per Dimond: further "delay of appeals would only delay any desegregation and increase the risk that plaintiffs would offend the court of appeals . . . We were resigned: we had to try to convert the Sixth Circuit on appeal as we had Judge Roth at trial."[11]

On July 20, 1972, the Sixth Circuit Court of Appeals agreed to review several major issues in the *Bradley v. Milliken* case, including Judge Roth's initial liability determination and whether any relief for the constitutional violations could traverse Detroit's borders. In doing so, the Sixth Circuit stayed virtually all of Judge Roth's activities in the case. As *The Detroit News* put it, the ruling "effectively block[ed] further progress in [the] busing plans."[12] The stay that prevented Roth from issuing any substantive orders remained in place throughout the remaining litigation, and he never conducted any further substantive proceedings.

For Roth, the *Bradley* case was effectively over. Of the appeal, the judge retained at least some optimism. *The Detroit News* reported Roth's mixed prediction. He believed that "even if he is reversed on his metropolitan bussing order, 'there is a good chance—at least 50–50—that I will be upheld in my finding de jure (intentional) segregation in Detroit.'"[13] The judge had an excellent crystal ball.

———

The Sixth Circuit did allow Roth to engage in "planning proceedings," and the stay did not apply to "studies and planning of the [desegregation] panel."[14] This allowed the panel to release its report, which it did. On July 29, 1972, the panel submitted a fifty-three-page report to Judge Roth, "The Panel's Response to the Court's Ruling on Desegregation Area and Order for Development of Plan of Desegregation."[15] It was worth taking a moment to contemplate perhaps the panel's most breathtaking conclusion: if its recommendations were implemented, they would result in "no 'racially identifiable' schools . . . remain[ing] in the desegregation area." Roth had created a desegregation area spanning much of southeastern Michigan, pulling in *the entire city of Detroit* along with just over fifty suburban school districts. It was astonishing to imagine the idea of almost eight hundred thousand Michigan students attending racially desegregated schools. But this was exactly what the panel had on offer.

In the report, the panel made several important suggestions. First, building on the cluster concept identified in Judge Roth's metropolitan ruling, the panel created a student assignment plan that enhanced desegregation with the most minimal—and equal—transportation of students. The panel wrote: "The pupil assignment plan provides for two-way movement of black and white pupils with the burden of transportation requirements being shared as equally as possible among the children of the Detroit school district and the suburban school district or districts with which they are paired."[16] This recommendation spoke to many black parents' fears, namely that the burden of desegregation—and transportation—would fall primarily on black students. Additionally, the panel didn't ignore many parents' attachments to their neighborhood schools. The panel noted that "in most cases a portion of each student's elementary school experience will be in a school in his home district and a portion in another district in the cluster." The report detailed minimum class sizes, the need for "multi-racial and multi-ethnic" textbook and curricular offerings, and the equalization of school facilities in the desegregation area, and it provided school site selection and construction guidelines, as well as highlighting the need for personnel training to facilitate the desegregation process, and the necessity of including biracial committees of staff members, parents, and students to make desegregation a success.

The panel's report also spoke to another common concern about desegregation. The critique was that the policy was mere window dressing, bringing students of different races to the same school, but not into the same classroom. "Every effort must be expended to avoid creating segregation within schools. Grouping, tracking, and other processes which tend to separate the races must be kept to a minimum," the panel admonished.[17]

In unconstitutionally segregated southern school districts undergoing court-ordered desegregation, black teachers often suffered. Many put their heart and soul into teaching black students under a segregated and unequal system, typically earning much less than similarly situated white teachers. Yet they were often let go when the formerly racially separate school districts were unified.[18] The panel's recommendation blunted this possibility by establishing a minimum baseline for black faculty and staff—no less than 17.5 percent and in many cases 25 percent—in any of the newly desegregated schools.[19] And the panel wasn't interested in achieving these numbers at a discrete point in time, and then moving on. Instead, it recommended "vigorous efforts and affirmative hiring practices to increase the number of black faculty and staff."[20] The affirmative action requirement was no slapdash affair. Section VIII of the panel's report, titled "Affirmative Action Plan," comprised six and a half pages of the fifty-three-page document.[21] As *The Detroit News* explained in a contemporaneous article, the panel's recommendations would mean "an exodus from Detroit schools—where most black teachers are employed—to suburban schools. White suburban teachers would take the black teachers' places in the city."[22]

The panel neither destroyed local school systems nor eliminated local school boards. Instead, it placed the responsibility for administering its recommendations exactly where they needed to be: with the state defendants, who were responsible for educating *all* Michiganders, and who had violated black children's rights under the Fourteenth Amendment of the United States Constitution.[23]

But the panel recommendation that got the most press had to do with money. On July 30, 1972, the *Detroit Free Press* ran a front-page, top-of-the-fold article titled "Panel Wants State Dole of School Funds."[24] The very first sentence of William Grant's article told the paper's readers all they needed to know: "The state would collect all school tax money in Detroit and 52 suburban school systems and hand it out on an 'equitable' basis under the final school integration plan drawn up by the panel appointed by U.S. District Judge Stephen J. Roth."[25] This was consistent with the school finance portion of the report: "The panel recommends that . . . the State defendants be required to . . . provide for the collection and equitable redistribution by the State of all school tax dollars for school districts in the desegregation area."[26] Grant predicted that the "sweeping school finance reform provision" would be "the most controversial section of the report." On this, the reporter was certainly correct.

The phrase "local control" was heard often in connection with the school desegregation controversy. What did "local control" really mean? It certainly meant controlling student assignments, determining which students were assigned (or not assigned) to which schools. But the essence of local control was the ability of local residents to control the direction and distribution of school funds, funds that typically were raised by taxing the assessed value of the homes *within that same local school district*. But now the desegregation panel was suggesting wholesale redistribution. It was recommending that the state of Michigan "take" proceeds raised from local taxation in suburban locales, which often had more valuable homes, and redistribute them equitably to "all school districts in the desegregation area." What this really meant was that white suburbanites would help fund Detroit's majority black public schools. This was how desegregation was a form of resource redistribution. Consistent with the findings of the Coleman Report, the desegregation panel reallocated students with more wealth and income by putting them into classrooms where they tended to raise the overall educational performance of the class. And it redistributed wealth directly by using suburban tax dollars to subsidize black students' education—after all, their parents' homes were typically much less valuable than suburban homes, largely because of racially constrained housing markets.

The state, of course, always had the power to determine how taxes in the state were raised and spent. But this was no longer about choice. The state defendants were adjudicated discriminators. Unless the Sixth Circuit stopped Judge Roth, he likely would turn the panel's recommendations into a federal court-ordered mandate. With these stakes in mind, the state defendants' immediate appeal was no surprise.

———

On Thursday, August 24, 1972, and in the thick of his reelection campaign, Richard Nixon visited the Dwight D. Eisenhower High School in Shelby Township, which was located in Macomb County, about twenty-five miles north of Detroit.[27] The ostensible purpose of his visit was to dedicate the brand-new school, but everyone knew it was really a campaign stop.

The president received a hero's welcome. One picture of the event depicted several thousand white people crammed into the school's gym to hear his address. People appeared to be almost literally hanging from the rafters. The press described the atmosphere inside the gym as "delirious" and "oven-like." Ten thousand more well-wishers were outside. Hundreds fainted from the heat. Carol Wilt of Sterling Heights was ebullient about the president's visit: "To some people it doesn't mean anything, but to me it's the same feeling you get when you go to church."[28]

The night before, Nixon had given a rousing speech accepting the Republican presidential nomination at the party's national convention in Miami Beach, and he had hinted at the idea that desegregation constituted some kind of reverse racism against whites. "Let us commit ourselves to root out every vestige of discrimination in this country of ours. But my fellow Americans, the way to end discrimination against some is not to begin discrimination against others," he told the cheering crowd.[29]

Now, at the high school, the president kept his remarks light, apolitical. He spoke of his youth, reminisced about President Eisenhower, and avoided mentioning busing. But the subject couldn't have been far from anyone's mind. For one thing, several school districts in Macomb County were included in Judge Roth's metropolitan desegregation order.[30] And, just before he took the stage, White House aides released a statement to the press blasting busing. "Busing forced by a court to achieve an arbitrary racial balance is wrong," it declared. "It adds nothing whatever to the children's learning. An hour and half a day on a bus will, if anything, impair the education process whatever a child's race or color."[31]

Nixon was trolling for Wallace voters. The Alabama governor had carried Shelby Township easily in the Democratic primary in May, in part because of his rival McGovern's support for desegregation. "I believe that school busing and redistricting, as ordered by the federal courts, are among the prices we are paying for a century of segregation in our housing patterns," McGovern had written in a letter to *The Washington Post*. "One of the more cynical aspects of our present debate is that President Nixon, seeking to make political capital of this difficult situation, is ignoring history and asking the nation to believe this problem began yesterday."[32] It was hard to backtrack from statements like that. The Republicans had little trouble painting him as "pro-busing."

In 1968, Democrat Hubert Humphrey beat Nixon in Michigan. One scholar observed that the state was "untouchably Democratic late into 1971 due to its high level of unemployment and [public] disapproval" of Nixon's record.[33] But now Nixon's team believed he could carry the state;

the busing issue had changed the calculus. Just a few days after the Republican National Convention in Miami Beach, the Nixon campaign released a television commercial that showed how much of a national issue busing had become.[34] Shot in a cinema verité style, the ad showed what appeared to be an unrehearsed conversation between Nixon and his adviser John Ehrlichman in the Oval Office. "Education's the name of the game," Nixon said. In a deep baritone, an announcer spoke as the camera widened to show the two men talking: "President Nixon believes busing is wrong. And he intends to do something about it." The president continued, underlining his support of the neighborhood school, "But when you take kindergarten kids and put them on a bus for an hour and a half, when they got a school they can walk to five minutes away, now that's wrong." He banged his pen on the desk for emphasis. "It's wrong for the white children." Bang. "It's wrong for the black children." Bang. The camera cut to a close-up of Nixon's hands holding the pen. Referencing the reelection campaign's official slogan, the announcer closed the deal: "There is still much to be done to improve the education of all of our children. This is why we need President Nixon. Now More Than Ever."[35]

As the president spoke, his team was anxiously monitoring events in Cincinnati. It was there that a three-judge "panel" for the Sixth Circuit Court of Appeals was hearing oral arguments in *Bradley v. Milliken*. (Pursuant to federal practice, cases at the intermediate appellate level were typically heard by a panel of three judges.) Frank Kelley personally argued much of the state's case. This was unusual. Typically, a subordinate would have handled the oral argument. But Senator Robert Griffin, the Republican incumbent Kelley hoped to unseat in the fall, had accused the attorney general of insufficient attention to the *Bradley v. Milliken* litigation.[36]

Just a few weeks before the argument, Griffin purchased full-page ads in Detroit metropolitan area newspapers. The ads took the form of an open letter to Kelley. The letter castigated the Democratic attorney general for his "foot-dragging" and "inaction in the Roth case" and for waffling on the busing issue.[37] Several weeks earlier, *The Detroit News* had gotten in on the action. In an editorial, it blasted the state's highest legal officer. "Michigan's legal defense in the bussing controversy rests in the hands of an attorney general who has signed a manifesto in favor of bussing." The paper then posed an obviously rhetorical question: "Who's working for the people?"[38] (Not surprisingly, *The Detroit News* later endorsed Griffin.)[39] The oral argument before the appellate court was an opportunity for Kelley to show that he meant business. Of the contest between the two men, one publication later observed that both candidates "based their campaigns on who could out-antibus the other."[40]

Kelley didn't have the easiest oral argument. According to Dimond, Judge George C. Edwards pounced on "his old friend and political ally."[41] Pointing to the state's long-standing prohibition against segregated education, the attorney general maintained that the state of Michigan bore no responsibility for any segregation in Detroit's schools.[42] According to Kelley, the state's hands were clean. The plaintiffs had failed to demonstrate a "causal connection" between the state's actions and racial segregation in the Detroit public school system.[43] But it was hard to imagine the appellate court overturning Roth's liability determination. As the *Detroit Free Press* reported, the judges "had little doubt that intentional segregation of the Detroit's school system had been proved in Judge Roth's court."[44] The real question was whether the appellate court would uphold the metropolitan desegregation plan.

Which side had the better of the argument was anyone's guess. Dimond was optimistic that the plaintiffs had won over at least two of the three judges.[45] The *Detroit Free Press* was more circumspect: the "appeals judges gave no indication Thursday of which way they were leaning on the integration question."[46] Kelley didn't appear worried. He boldly predicted that the Supreme Court would vindicate the state "regardless of the decision of the appeals court."[47] One thing was clear: no metropolitan plan would be implemented that fall. The school year was fast approaching, and the case was exceedingly complex. The judges would not issue an instant determination. At the end of the three-hour oral argument, the federal appellate court continued its stay of Judge Roth's metropolitan order indefinitely.[48]

The Inter-Faith Centers for Racial Justice took an active role in the *Bradley v. Milliken* litigation, submitting an amicus brief in the appeal.[49] The group spoke for four interfaith centers scattered across suburban Detroit.

It was sponsored by a wide variety of Catholic, Protestant, and Jewish religious denominations, which included more than eighty churches, parishes, and synagogues. It counted more than seven hundred individual members. What the group offered was effectively the dissenting white perspective on metropolitan segregation, making it more difficult for the suburban intervenors to portray themselves as representing the sole or monolithic view of *all* Detroit-area suburban whites. The group told the court that it—along with dozens of other local organizations listed in the brief—stood ready to assist with the implementation of a metropolitan order.

The group was remarkably clear-eyed about the effects of a Detroit-only remedy. Incentivizing Detroit's remaining whites to leave the city would "be worse than the disease as it would give judicial sanction to racial separation along school district lines," the amicus brief said.[50] Such a result would have sweeping ramifications, the group predicted: "A Detroit-only plan, leading as it would to a black school system surrounded by white school systems, would leave the black pupils of Detroit even more vulnerable to discriminatory treatment by a suburban dominated state legislature than they have been in the past."[51] This was a stunning statement. As expansive as the discussion of the harms of segregation was in Judge Roth's court below, it never encompassed the prospective political ramifications of an all-black city surrounded by white suburbs. The implication was clear: if the appellate court overturned Judge Roth's metropolitan order, Detroit would effectively become a black colony within a white state.

═══

Reporting on the Nixon-McGovern race on election day, November 7, 1972, the morning papers said the state was up for grabs.[52] But most national polls clearly showed McGovern losing the election.[53] The only real question was the size of the defeat. The day was a full one for Stephen Roth. After casting his vote (against Nixon) and visiting courtrooms in Detroit, Bay City, and Flint, the judge headed to Henry Ford Hospital.[54] There his wife, Evelyn, was recovering from surgery.[55]

As it turned out, Roth was at the right place at the right time, because he suffered a massive heart attack that evening. The judge was admitted to the hospital's cardiology unit with an acute myocardial infarction at 8:45 p.m.[56] *Bradley v. Milliken* had taken an extraordinary amount of the judge's time; he was now working long hours and driving many miles between courtrooms in three cities to clear up the backlog in his other cases.[57] One newspaper wrote about the attack that week: "Roth's friends speculated he was feeling the strain of intense opposition to his finding of de jure segregation in the Detroit Public Schools, and the subsequent order of cross-district busing between Detroit and 52 suburban districts."[58] Later that day, the result of the presidential election added insult to injury for the judge, with Nixon crushing McGovern.

By late in the week, Roth was out of the woods. The *Detroit Free Press* reported that the judge, "whose Detroit-area school-busing decision had a major influence on voting trends in Tuesday's election . . . is expected to recover."[59]

Roth had indeed apparently had an effect on local election results. Nixon won the highest percentage of the vote in Macomb County of any Republican presidential candidate since 1924.[60] "The busing issue enabled Republicans to split off a major chunk of the white blue-collar vote that Democrats had depended on for a quarter of a century to win elections in Michigan," the *Detroit Free Press* opined.[61] The contest between Attorney General Frank Kelley, a Democrat, and Republican Robert P. Griffin for United States Senate was tight, but Griffin successfully defended his seat. Kelley had known things weren't going his way as he watched the election returns roll in at the Sheraton-Cadillac Hotel in downtown Detroit. At about 10:00 p.m. on the evening of the election, he received a call from his aide Jim Blanchard (who would later become governor of the state). "Frank, it's not good. You are trailing too many places outstate where you shouldn't be. The suburbs are weak because of busing."[62] The segregation ruling helped the incumbent get reelected.[63] Later, the numbers confirmed that Kelley held his own except in areas impacted by Judge Roth's ruling.[64] As he reportedly quipped, "I got hit by a yellow bus on my way to Washington."[65]

But to chalk up Republican electoral success solely to "antibusing sentiment" was too polite. Douglas Fraser, United Auto Workers vice president and chairman of McGovern's campaign in Michigan, put it in broader terms. "If you want to get to the crux of it, under the surface there is a new racism that we haven't seen in a good number of years. Saying it's busing or welfare is oversimplification. And if that's the case, it's much more serious (than the busing issue alone)."[66]

He was right. On election day, Michigan voters declined to adopt an education reform package—championed by Governor Milliken—that would have abolished the property tax based system for financing public education and effectively replaced it with a graduated income tax.[67] (The state's flat tax scheme capped income taxes at 3.9 percent.)[68] Milliken argued that eliminating property taxes would save Michigan property owners more than $1 billion a year.[69] The state would then recoup that money through the new graduated income tax. As *The Detroit News* explained it, "the legislature then could dole out to local school districts [money] on an equal basis for each pupil."[70] In this way, the proposal would have broken the link between local property taxes and school finance, creating the possibility of equitable education funding in urban and suburban districts.[71] Voters also rejected (again) a school millage tax increase for Detroit's schools, which had devastating consequences. As Jeffrey Mirel put it, "The 1972 election reaffirmed the 1968 trend of white Detroiters shifting allegiance towards conservative presidential candidates, with busing as a strong motivating factor. That same trend also brought the Detroit schools to the brink of bankruptcy."[72]

═══

By early December 1972, Judge Roth was at home convalescing. On the eighth of that month, he received an advance copy of the panel's decision in the *Bradley v. Milliken* case. As a courtesy, the circuit judges had provided him with the opinion just before releasing it to the press.[73]

Although the Sixth Circuit had a few qualms with Roth's approach, it affirmed his most important decisions in the case. In an eighty-page opinion authored by Chief Judge Harry Phillips, the Sixth Circuit panel ruled that the Detroit Board of Education and the state engaged in unconstitutional school segregation, that a Detroit-only plan could not achieve desegregation, that local school districts were state instrumentalities over which

Michigan exercised ultimate control, that school district lines were not sacrosanct, and that the remedy for the proven constitutional violation was not limited to the geographic boundaries of the city of Detroit.[74] Roth was "elated" by the ruling, Dimond wrote in a lengthy analysis of the case.[75]

The determination that the suburban school districts were arms of the state was a particularly big win for the plaintiffs. Citing the Michigan Supreme Court, the panel stated flatly: "The school district is a State agency."[76] This wasn't an offhand remark. The panel dedicated an entire section of its opinion—"A. Status of School Districts Under Michigan Law"—to this analysis. Reviewing state law dating back to 1787, the panel explained how education in Michigan was a state rather than a local function. When it came to education in Michigan, it was the state that called the shots and furnished much of the money. The panel noted that Michigan provided "on average 34% of the operating budgets" of the school districts included in Roth's metropolitan order. And in eleven of those districts, that number exceeded 50 percent.[77] This was a key holding. It strongly suggested that there was no need to go through the painstaking process of establishing that each individual suburban school district had committed a constitutional violation before that district could be included in a metropolitan desegregation plan.[78] The plaintiffs had already done that with respect to the state. Notwithstanding the suburbs' protest to the contrary, no additional proof was necessary.

The panel did order that all school districts affected by Roth's desegregation order be officially joined in the case, which made sense.[79] While the suburban school districts lacked independent sovereignty, they could sue and be sued under state law. So the panel ruled that all school districts affected by Roth's metropolitan order were "necessary parties" under federal procedural rules in that complete relief could not be provided to the plaintiffs without them.[80] Some of the suburban school districts were still on the sidelines. Now all would become parties to the lawsuit. But the appellate judges were crystal clear on those districts' subordinate status: they were "arms and instrumentalities of the State of Michigan."[81]

After all was said and done, the question of what remedy was appropriate in the *Bradley v. Milliken* case was actually pretty simple. The state had violated the Constitution by intentionally segregating Detroit's school-children. The suburban school districts lacked independent sovereignty. Michigan had the power to create, dissolve, merge, and reorganize school districts at will, and so therefore the state retained "ultimate control" over public education in Michigan.[82] The panel spoke with moral clarity: "If we hold that school district boundaries are absolute barriers to a Detroit school desegregation plan, we would be opening a way to nullify *Brown v. Board of Education* which overruled *Plessy*."[83] But even as the panel did its best to prevent a *Plessy* "do-over," Detroit's two major papers character-ized the ruling as a "busing" decision—even though no final metropolitan desegregation order specifying busing routes had been issued.[84]

The Sixth Circuit panel recognized just how much evidence regarding residential segregation—both within and outside of Detroit—had come in during the trial. It wrote, the "record contains a substantial volume of testimony concerning local and State action and policies which helped produce residential segregation in Detroit and in the metropolitan area of Detroit."[85] The causes of segregation in southeastern Michigan were in the record for anyone curious enough to investigate it. But in reaching its conclusion, the panel pointedly did not rely "at all upon testimony pertain-ing to segregated housing."[86] Why? Perhaps it was because, as Dimond ac-knowledged, the plaintiffs in their brief to the Sixth Circuit "downplayed, but did not omit, the housing proof that had played such a critical role in the trial court."[87] They did so because they were worried about *Deal*, the recent Sixth Circuit case that held that the public schools in Cincinnati were not unconstitutionally segregated. The plaintiffs' number-one priority on appeal was defending Roth's *liability* determination. The metropolitan *remedy* was a secondary concern.

But this left the plaintiffs in a precarious position vis-à-vis metropolitan relief. If the plaintiffs were successful in sidestepping *Deal* and defending Roth's liability determination, their theory of metropolitan relief would rely primarily on the fact that Michigan—which was responsible for provi-sion of education in the state and could alter school district lines at will—was in the dock. The remedial argument would center on the idea that the state was not only liable for the constitutional violation, but was fully capable of providing metropolitan relief. This approach carried several weaknesses, however, which Dimond admitted. First, the "court would have to conclude that effective desegregation could not be provided within the confines of the Detroit school district," even though the plaintiffs had deemphasized much of the evidence that went beyond the city limits.[88] Second, it left the plaintiffs open to a counterattack, which sounded intuitive and commonsensical: if the violation occurred within the city of Detroit, then the remedy should center there, too.

But even as the Sixth Circuit panel foreswore reliance on the housing evidence, the containment argument hadn't entirely disappeared. First, the appellate court affirmed the symbiotic relationship between school and housing segregation. It wrote that the "segregation of the Detroit public schools, however rooted in private residential segregation, also was validated and augmented by the Detroit Board of Education and Michigan State Board action of pervasive influence through the system."[89] These practices, as the panel observed, might have been "a bit more subtle than the compulsory segregation statutes of the Southern States" but were equally unconstitutional.

Second, the panel chose to leave aside the housing evidence, "except as school construction programs helped cause or maintain such segregation."[90] This seemed a small aside. But it wasn't. School construction was one of the main lynchpins of the state's liability. It was, said the panel, "the clearest example of direct state participation in encouraging the segregated condition of Detroit public schools."[91] This had profound implications. The state's role in school construction—site planning for new schools and approving school building plans—was hardly confined to the city of Detroit. Michigan's actions spanned the southeastern portion of the state. As the panel explicitly recognized, the state "fostered segregation throughout the Detroit Metropolitan area."[92] That was what the containment was all about. Still, the plaintiffs wasted an opportunity to drive home their point about the containment and lay a firmer foundation for metropolitan relief. As Dimond admitted: "We still had not articulated our basic conception of an areawide violation with clarity."[93]

The plaintiffs' lawyers responded to the ruling with jubilation. Louis Lucas: "This is a victory for all of the children in metropolitan Detroit."[94] Alexander Ritchie was particularly pleased. "This is really stunning," he

stated. "The old man (Judge Roth) did it. I didn't think they could disman-
tle that work of art," CCBE's lawyer added.[95]

But their triumph at the Sixth Circuit Court of Appeals did raise a
concern. In the other *Bradley* metropolitan school desegregation case,
Bradley v. Richmond, the plaintiffs lost at the appellate level. In effect,
the Fourth and Sixth Circuits had reached different conclusions about the
propriety of metropolitan desegregation. This created what lawyers called
a "circuit split," a disagreement between two or more federal appellate
courts on an important legal issue. Supreme Court review of lower court
decisions was (and is) largely discretionary. Parties could ask the court to
review a case by filing a petition for a "writ of certiorari," but it granted
few such writs. The presence of a circuit split, however, increased the likelihood of review, because it gave the court an opportunity to clarify the law
throughout the nation by resolving the circuit split.

One of the *Bradley* cases, or both, was likely headed to the Supreme
Court, and everyone knew it. On December 9, 1972, the *Detroit Free
Press* published a piece by William Grant titled "Ruling Means High Court
Can't Avoid Busing Issue." Grant wrote it was now "impossible for the
United States Supreme Court to avoid the explosive political issue of bus-
ing between city and suburbs." The case would likely be "the most import-
ant school integration decision since the Supreme Court in 1954 struck
down the laws . . . which required separate schools for blacks and whites."[96]

18

FAREWELL TO THE WARREN COURT

B ack on Sunday, April 26, 1970, the Detroit branch of the NAACP had hosted its fifteenth annual Freedom Fund Dinner. A seated formal dinner for four thousand that took place at the cavernous Cobo Hall on the banks of the Detroit River, it was a major fundraising event for the organization. *The NAACP Reporter*, the Detroit branch's monthly newsletter, informed its readership that a local rising star would provide the evening's entertainment: "Stevie Wonder For Freedom Dinner—Blind, Black Beyond Soul Singer Booked."[1] The event's keynote speaker was Earl Warren, who had recently stepped down from his post as the chief justice of the United States.[2] During his speech, Warren praised the NAACP for its accomplishments, and took stock of the progress it had made in advancing race relations. But his remarks also sounded a note of caution. Warren believed the country was at an inflection point. He told the attendees: "Our nation has arrived at a crossroad leading in one direction to freedom with equality for all and in the other toward the route of social discrimination and resulting bitterness, disillusionment and discord for our children and their children into the indefinite future."[3] Reading his speech in toto, it was unclear if Warren thought the nation capable of choosing the right path.

The Warren Court era began in late 1953, when Warren was sworn in as chief justice after Fred Vinson's untimely death. It ended sixteen years later in 1969, when the former California governor stepped down from the bench. The Warren Court was committed to equality. Never before had the Supreme Court moved so aggressively—and in so many areas of the law—to defend the rights of the powerless against the will of the powerful. In areas as disparate as the First Amendment, race discrimination, reproductive freedom, illegitimacy, criminal law, criminal procedure, voting rights, and legislative reapportionment, the Warren Court was a fierce protector of individual rights. It empowered those whose voices had long been silent.[4] As the Supreme Court historian Lucas A. Powe Jr. put it, "The Warren Court created the image of the Supreme Court as a revolutionary body, a powerful force for social change."[5]

The Warren Court also protected the poor, at least to the extent that indigency affected a person's ability to defend herself against felony criminal charges, appeal a criminal case, or exercise the "fundamental" right to vote.[6] (A fundamental right is one that is so important that it cannot be deprived unless the government can provide an extremely important justification for the deprivation.) The court even toyed with the idea of constitutionalizing the welfare state.[7] And although it did not do so, as one prominent commentator noted, the court's interventions were "mainly designed to move us towards a condition of economic equality."[8] If the Supreme Court under Warren's leadership had one abiding principle, it was egalitarianism, which for the court meant "equality before the law—equality of races, of citizens, of rich and poor, of prosecutor and defendant."[9]

Running for president in 1968, Nixon campaigned vigorously against Earl Warren's Court. He told anyone who would listen that he would name only "strict constructionists" to the federal bench. The phrase sounded fancy and pretentious; it implied that judges who weren't "strict constructionists" were somehow illegitimate. Journalist Tom Wicker certainly had it right when he wrote that "strict constructionist" suggested a judge who abided "by the Constitution while others—say, those of the type that formed the Warren Court majority—are willing to distort it for their own social and political ends."[10] Beyond that, a clear definition of the term was hard to come by. On one view, "strict construction" was a legitimate and objective mode of judicial interpretation. In the constitutional context, it meant a court's refusal to recognize constitutional rights unless those rights were expressed in the text or clearly implicit in that text. But there was another view, one that suggested that the term served as a highfalutin dog whistle. Or, as legal scholar John Hart Ely deftly put it, strict constructionism has been used "perhaps most notably in recent years by President Nixon, to signal . . . a proclivity to reach constitutional judgments that will please political conservatives."[11]

One person who knew exactly what strict constructionist meant was the influential senior senator from South Carolina: Strom Thurmond. As Nixon was looking to shore up support for his candidacy for the Republican nomination, he and Thurmond had a tête-à-tête in Atlanta in late May 1968. At the meeting, Nixon informed Thurmond that as president he wouldn't attack *Brown v. Board of Education* because it was settled law.[12] But then Nixon reassured him. The candidate was against busing and promised to appoint only "strict constructionists" to the bench.[13] There was some debate as to whether the two men cut a deal at the meeting or whether they simply developed "an understanding—a position of trust," as one scholar described it.[14] Either way, Thurmond must have liked what he heard. Several weeks after the Atlanta meeting, Thurmond announced the South Carolina delegation's support for Nixon's candidacy.[15] (With Nelson Rockefeller and Ronald Reagan in the mix, it was by no means certain that Nixon would be selected as the party's nominee at the Republican National Convention in Miami Beach that August.) Nixon took the nomination on the first ballot.

On May 21, 1969, Nixon stood in the East Room of the White House to announce that he had nominated Warren E. Burger to be the next chief justice of the United States.[16] The president ticked off Burger's biography: night student with a brilliant law school record ("his education is one that he got the hard way"), former assistant attorney general, and thirteen years of experience as a judge on the prestigious United States Circuit Court of Appeals for the District of Columbia. But Nixon was more focused on the role of the chief justice and the importance of law and order, a key campaign theme. He stated, "the Chief Justice is the guardian of the Constitution of the United States. Respect for law in a nation is the most priceless asset a free people can have, and the Chief Justice and his associates are the ultimate custodians and guardians of that priceless asset."[17] The president's statement was perhaps most notable for what it omitted.

The statement was silent on the achievements of the Warren Court and said nothing about racial equality. A scholarly assessment of Burger's tenure on the court was apt. What the nation got in Burger, the scholar observed, was "a conservative chief for conservative times—a man who deferred to executive rather than legislative or judicial power and who decided overwhelmingly against civil liberties claims during a political era dominated by Richard Nixon and Ronald Reagan."[18]

Nixon's next appointment didn't go as smoothly as the previous one. When Associate Justice Abe Fortas resigned on May 14, 1969, Nixon first nominated Clement Haynsworth and then G. Harrold Carswell to fill the vacant seat. The Senate rejected both southerners' nominations. Neither jurist was strong on civil rights, and Carswell was particularly problematic. The jurist was a publicly avowed segregationist. While his nomination was pending, Pulitzer Prize–winning journalist Anthony Lewis reported in *The New York Times* that "Judge Carswell has a record in the racial field that cannot be overlooked," and that the nominee once gave a political speech affirming his "'belief in the principles of white supremacy.'"[19]

After the two failed nominations, the president turned north and nominated Harry Blackmun, a Minnesotan and longtime friend of Warren Burger. The Senate confirmed Blackmun unanimously on May 12, 1970.[20] Because of their lengthy relationship and many similarities—both were St. Paul Republicans who had risen from modest circumstances to the pinnacle of power by virtue of a Nixon nomination—Burger and Blackmun were often referred to as the "Minnesota Twins."[21] (Blackmun intensely disliked the moniker.) Just after Nixon tapped Blackmun for the high court, *The New York Times* observed that the "two men have so much in common by background and judicial philosophy that it seems logical that if the new nominee is confirmed by the Senate, they will often see things the same way on the Supreme Court."[22] For Blackmun's first five years on the court (1970–75), the prediction was accurate. During that period, Blackmun voted with the chief justice almost 90 percent of the time in closely decided cases.[23] But by the time Blackmun retired in 1994, he had forged a separate identity, and the friendship between the two Minnesotans dissolved. Linda Greenhouse wrote that the relationship dissipated for a variety of reasons.[24] But chief among them was emerging ideological disagreement.

Over the course of his twenty-four years on the court, Blackmun's voting habits transformed from reliably conservative to reliably liberal. During the last five years the two served on the court together, Blackmun voted with Burger only about one-third of the time; he voted with William J. Brennan Jr., the liberal lion, more than 70 percent of the time.[25] At his retirement, Blackmun was, according to Greenhouse, "one of the last liberal voices on a transformed Court."[26]

As the *Bradley* case wound its way through the federal courts, the Nixon administration continued to overhaul the judiciary. "Presidents come and go, but the Supreme Court through its decisions goes on forever. Because they will make decisions which will affect your lives and the lives of your children for generations to come."[27] So began President Nixon's announcement on October 21, 1971, that he would nominate William F. Rehnquist and Lewis F. Powell Jr. to fill the vacancies created by two more retiring justices, John M. Harlan and Hugo Black. Early in the address, Nixon acknowledged that many Americans had called for more diversity on the Supreme Court, "A great number of letters have recommended the appointment of a woman since no woman has ever been appointed to the Supreme Court of the United States."[28] Professing agreement with the idea in principle, he blamed the monolithic nature of the court's composition on its small size. "But with only nine seats to fill, obviously every group in the country cannot be represented on the Court."[29] With that, the president immediately pivoted to a discussion of merit and the appropriate qualifications for a Supreme Court justice. The direct move from calls for racial, ethnic, and gender diversity to a recitation of judicial "standards of excellence" suggested that diversity and excellence occupied two completely different worlds, that they did not overlap. The juxtaposition would not have been lost on anyone. The president then advanced the nomination of two white men.

The president ticked off a long list of Powell's major accomplishments. But Nixon omitted a key piece of information about the nominee's southern roots.[30] Powell had more than a passing interest in public education.

He was chair of the Richmond school board when the court handed down the two *Brown* decisions. And he was a member of the Virginia State Board of Education throughout most of the 1960s, serving as its president during the 1968–69 term.[31] Then the president turned to Rehnquist and detailed his impressive CV. Stating that the nominee had been "outstanding in every intellectual endeavor he has undertaken," he noted that Rehnquist had clerked for Justice Robert Jackson.[32] Nixon explained the duties of a Supreme Court law clerk. "In this position he acted as legal assistant to the justice and his duties included legal research of the highest order."[33] Rehnquist was in private practice in Phoenix, Arizona, for more than fifteen years, the president added. After the brief address, Nixon sent his nominees to the Senate for confirmation as justices of the U.S. Supreme Court.

On November 3, 1971, the Senate Judiciary Committee began confirmation proceedings for President Nixon's two Supreme Court nominees. The NAACP and the Leadership Conference on Civil Rights took no position on Powell's nomination. It was a tactical move. Clarence Mitchell, director of the NAACP's Washington Bureau, wrote: "We are concentrating on the Rehnquist nomination because the record on him is clear."[34] But the Congressional Black Caucus (CBC) openly opposed Powell. Michigan representative John Conyers Jr. led the charge for the CBC (an organization that he cofounded in early 1971).[35] The CBC remembered the 1950s very differently than many of Powell's supporters. "While it is true Mr. Powell sat on the school board of the city of Richmond from 1950 to 1961, serving as its chairman during the last eight years of that period, something less than successful integration took place,"[36] Conyers testified.

The reality was that, almost a decade after *Brown*, the Richmond school board continued to use the same racially dual attendance areas and race-based feeder patterns that it had used before *Brown*.[37] Conyers to the Judiciary Committee: "Mr. Powell's 8-year reign as chairman of the Richmond school board created and maintained a patently segregated school system, characterized by grossly overcrowded black public schools, white schools not filled to normal capacity, and the school board's effective perpetuation of a discriminatory feeder or assignment system whereby black children were hopelessly trapped in inadequate, segregated schools."[38] Powell left the board in 1961. In the fall of that year, "only 37 black children out of a total of more than 23,000 were attending previously all-white schools in the city of Richmond."[39]

For his part, Powell leaned heavily into the idea that the board had acted honorably because it declined to close the schools in the face of *Brown*. "We also made another decision that . . . in view of the emotional situation that began to develop, no member of the school board, white or black, would make any public speeches, and we would direct and concentrate our attention on trying to keep the public schools open until the conflict between the federal and state law was resolved," Powell testified.[40] The statement invited the audience to credit the board for refusing to fan the flames of racism during a period of racial tumult. Powell presented himself as a principled public servant who stood above the fray, even as parts of Virginia were descending into lawlessness and chaos. This was consistent with his public brand as a moderate, as someone who could be a neutral arbiter of the law.

There was more to the story, however, though it wouldn't come to light until after the hearings. Just two months before Nixon nominated him to serve on the high court, Powell had written a thirty-four-page memo to his friend Eugene B. Sydnor Jr., the chairman of the U.S. Chamber of Commerce.[41] Exposing the nominee's fiercely ideological side, the memo undercut Powell's reputation for neutrality and moderation. Instead, it suggested that the author was a deeply committed conservative with a very clear point of view. It was, as one historian characterized it, a "businessman's jeremiad."[42] Titled "Attack on the American Free Enterprise System," the memo read like a David and Goliath story except that the American free enterprise system—in effect, unregulated capitalism—was David and the "extremists of the left" were Goliath.[43] The left included labor unions, the ACLU, college professors, intellectuals, and their enablers: "the college campus, the pulpit, the media, the intellectual and literary journals, the arts and sciences and . . . politicians."[44] They, along with the unwitting assistance of an apathetic business community, threatened the very "survival of what we call the free enterprise system."[45] To quash that threat,

Powell recommended a multifaceted, probusiness campaign affecting the media and advertising, colleges and graduate schools, textbooks, scholarly journals, and, of course, politics.

Then there were the courts. Powell characterized the Supreme Court derisively as "activist-minded."[46] He noted that left-leaning organizations such as "civil rights groups" had been more successful in "exploiting judicial action than American business." That had to change. The Chamber of Commerce and other business interests needed to take note quickly. Powell closed the memo with an urgent plea: "Business and the enterprise system are in deep trouble, and the hour is late."[47] Later, veteran court watcher Linda Greenhouse and law professor Michael J. Graetz characterized the memo as a "bizarre hybrid—a product of [Powell's] careful, analytic, lawyer's mind and an angry screed, something that sounds to today's ear more like Rush Limbaugh than Lewis Powell."[48]

Also testifying at Powell's confirmation hearings was Henry L. Marsh III, president of the Old Dominion Bar Association, Virginia's black bar association.[49] Old Dominion vociferously opposed Powell's nomination. (Later, Marsh would become the first black mayor of the city of Richmond). Senator Birch Bayh Jr., an Indiana Democrat, asked Marsh: "Is it not possible that a member of the school board would have been on the horns of a dilemma where the Virginia State law [providing for state-funded assistance for children who did not want to attend integrated public schools] said one thing and *Brown v. Board of Education* said something else?" Bayh continued: "Was [Powell] not also subject to the laws of the State of Virginia?"[50] After some colloquy, Marsh stated: "In our system of laws Mr. Powell must know as an outstanding attorney that under the supremacy clause the laws of the United States prevail. So we think that . . . his obligation was to the highest law and that under our system was the law of the Constitution of the United States." Now Marsh zeroed in for the kill: "We suggest that therein lies the defect of the nomination. Maybe Mr. Powell did what any reasonable man would have done. But any reasonable man would not necessarily be entitled to sit on the Supreme Court."[51]

This, then, was the heart of the matter. No one was entitled to sit on the U.S. Supreme Court. It was a privilege of the highest order. Good grades in law school weren't enough. Perhaps the nation was entitled to expect more than just an intellectually gifted technician. Maybe the successful nominee needed, when tested in the field, to display uncommon courage and character. Perhaps the most important question was whether the nominee did the right thing, notwithstanding the cost. Powell suggested that there was nothing he could have done to change the reality in Richmond, Virginia.[52] Desegregation was unpopular, so the city's schools would likely have stayed segregated until more powerful players, such as the federal courts, got involved. As an observation of likely outcomes, this was probably true. But what the assertion didn't account for was the complexity of how social change occurs. A principled stand by a respected member of a community could sometimes spur waves of change. Conyers told the Judiciary Committee, "I think we have to put the gentleman in the context of the prestige and the influence and the power that he wields in the State of Virginia. He is clearly one of the ten most influential citizens of that State, and I would suggest that his influence does not stop at the Arlington city line by any means."[53]

At best, there were conflicting views of Powell's tenure as a Virginia school official. One view said he was a man of high character, who did the best he could under extremely difficult circumstances. Reflecting on that period, Powell told the Judiciary Committee: "If you will look back on it now, the situation may be hard to understand. But if one lived through those days, as . . . I did, he may have a different perspective."[54] But there was another view that was at least as compelling, and in hindsight perhaps more so. Circling back to Powell's rejection of massive resistance, Marsh indicted the nominee for having had "sense enough to recognize the futility of the massive resistance program and to go for a more sophisticated scheme of evading . . . Brown."[55] He reminded the committee that the Constitution "outlaws the ingenious as well as the obvious scheme." Marsh pressed a far less complimentary view of Powell: that he "had the knowledge to know how to evade the Constitution more effectively, [which] he did in the city of Richmond during the massive resistance era, without having integration."[56] This did "not commend him to the Supreme Court," Marsh argued. Robert A. Pratt, a scholar who wrote extensively about Richmond's post-Brown experience, agreed. "A fair examination of the record, however, clearly shows that Richmond maintained a patently segregated system during Powell's administration," he concluded.[57] Richmond failed to meet even the excessively permissive standard set out in *Brown II*. "In fact, the school board could not even maintain that a reasonable start had been made towards the elimination of racially discriminatory practices," Pratt observed.[58]

Ultimately, however, none of it mattered. On December 6, 1971, Powell was confirmed by the Democratically controlled Senate. The vote was 89–1. There was little question that he benefited from being paired with William Rehnquist, the younger and more ideologically doctrinaire of the two.[59] And indeed Rehnquist's journey toward confirmation would prove to be more problematic than Lewis Powell's.

———

On November 4, Senator Charles "Mac" Mathias Jr., a Republican from Maryland, asked Rehnquist about his views on public accommodations and school desegregation. The nominee acknowledged that his views on the "public accommodations ordinance have changed."[60] He had to. Rehnquist's earlier position would have been singularly difficult to defend. In mid-June 1964, he appeared at a public hearing in Phoenix to speak against a proposed ordinance that would have prohibited racial discrimination in public accommodations. His was a minority view. Of the thirty-three speakers, only three were opposed.[61] "I venture to say that there has never been this sort of assault on the institution [of private property] where you are told, not what you can build on your property, but who can come on your property. This, to me, is a matter for the most serious consideration and, to me, would lead to the conclusion that the ordinance ought to be rejected," he had stated.[62] The city council passed the antidiscrimination ordinance unanimously the very next day.

But Rehnquist wasn't ready to throw in the towel. In a letter to *The Arizona Republic*, he reaffirmed his view. The city council's action was "a mistake," he wrote. "It is, I believe, impossible to justify the sacrifice of even a portion of our historic individual freedom for a purpose such as this," he added.[63] At the very same moment that he was railing against a local public accommodations law, Congress was debating a federal analog that would change the nation. President Johnson signed the historic bill, Title II of the Civil Rights Act of 1964, into law on July 2, 1964. The contemporaneous debate on the similar bill (which had passed the House and survived an epic filibuster in the Senate by the time Rehnquist spoke) should have alerted the witness that he ran the risk of being on the wrong side of history. Rehnquist testified anyway. Shockingly, on this issue he was to the right of conservative Arizona senator Barry Goldwater. Goldwater famously was against Title II because he thought it was unconstitutional. The federal government, he believed, didn't have the power to regulate private property.[64] But he saw no such bar to state and location regulation, and thus supported the Phoenix ordinance.[65]

It was a different story with school desegregation, where Rehnquist made no attempt to walk back his earlier views. In 1967, he had opposed a modest proposal to help desegregate Phoenix's public schools.[66] Gary Orfield, then an assistant professor of politics and public affairs at Princeton University, testified against the nominee. The young professor characterized the proposal as a "voluntary local desegregation effort" that would have made "some relatively minor changes intended to reduce the high level of local segregation" in schools that had been de jure segregated.[67] Orfield testified: "Phoenix had a whole set of schools built and operated as ghetto schools. Even their names—Dunbar, Bethune, and Booker T. Washington—were the classic ghetto school names. The city had a long-established pattern of segregating its black faculty members largely in black schools."[68] The professor asserted that Rehnquist attacked the proposal and "argued that there was nothing wrong with the existence of segregated schools."[69]

Perhaps Orfield exaggerated Rehnquist's position. Indeed, Rehnquist took issue with the professor's testimony in a written response to his claims, calling his description of the proposed desegregation effort "materially inaccurate."[70] But the nominee's response to a series of articles in *The Arizona Republic*, which exposed the extent of racial segregation in Phoenix's schools, corroborated Orfield's testimony.[71] Published between August 27, 1967, and September 1, 1967, the series provided the racial breakdown of numerous schools in the city, explained how the use of the "neighborhood school principle" resulted in "some schools in South Phoenix which are nearly all-Negro or all Mexican-American," advised its readers that the "best way to improve education for Negro and other minority-group children is to permit them to attend integrated schools, rather than rely on 'compensatory programs,'" and asserted that busing would be required in order to achieve integration.

On September 9, 1967, Rehnquist sent a letter to the paper confirming that he'd read—and disagreed with—the entire series ("the combined effect of Harold Cousland's series of articles").[72] He wrote that "the neighborhood school concept" had "served us well for countless years." The difficulty with this assertion was that the series had painstakingly demonstrated how the "neighborhood school concept" necessarily resulted in racially segregated schools. Cousland had written that we "are and must be concerned with achieving an integrated society." But Rehnquist disagreed: "We are no more dedicated to an 'integrated' society than we are to a 'segregated' society." Instead, Rehnquist maintained that the objective was to obtain a "free society," where "each man is accorded a maximum amount of freedom of choice in his individual activities." How blacks were to be accorded freedom of choice when the government mandated that they attend their neighborhood school and it was impossible to move elsewhere was not explained. Or, as Gary Orfield put it in his Senate testimony, "Mr. Rehnquist often talks about freedom. You often wonder whose freedom."[73]

The NAACP's Clarence Mitchell told the Senate Judiciary Committee that he had "grave doubts about whether [Rehnquist] could mete out to the black citizens of America equal justice under law."[74] Notwithstanding opposition from civil rights quarters, however, Rehnquist's nomination was solidly on track. On November 30, 1971, the committee filed its report. It found the nominee "thoroughly qualified" and dismissed concerns about his civil rights record. "The Committee has carefully considered each of these [civil rights] charges against Mr. Rehnquist. On the basis of his testimony, his written public statements and other evidence which has been sent to this Committee, we believe these charges are totally unfounded," the report concluded.[75] The hearings were over. (The Senate Judiciary Committee voted out his nomination twelve to four.) The outcome was a foregone conclusion. Rehnquist was headed to the high court.

But then, just before the largely perfunctory debate on the floor of the

Senate was scheduled to begin, *Newsweek* magazine published a bomb-shell. It released a memo Rehnquist had written while serving as a clerk to Justice Robert H. Jackson. Written in 1952, while the court was considering *Brown*, the memo was signed "WHR" (Rehnquist's initials) and titled "A Random Thought on the Segregation Cases." Whether the thought was in fact "random" would soon become a point of contention because the memo recommended that the court reaffirm rather than overrule the "separate but equal" doctrine of *Plessy v. Ferguson*.

Two days after the Senate became aware of the memo, Rehnquist wrote James O. Eastland, the chairman of the Senate Judiciary Committee, informing him that, "As best I can reconstruct the circumstances after nineteen years, the memorandum was prepared by me at Justice Jackson's request; it was intended as a rough draft of a statement of *his* views at the conference of the justices, rather than as a statement of my views."[76] With his nomination hanging in the balance, Rehnquist could hardly admit warm feelings for *Plessy v. Ferguson*. He affirmed his support of the more recent precedent. The nominee wrote that he fully supported "the legal reasoning and the rightness from the standpoint of fundamental fairness of the *Brown* decision."[77] Senator Bayh called Rehnquist's statement "self-serving," as it undoubtedly was.[78]

Even at the time, the idea that the memo represented Justice Jackson's views strained credulity. Jackson, who had served as both solicitor general and attorney general during the Roosevelt administration, had seen what the evils of race and religious hatred could do firsthand. He famously had taken a leave from the U.S. Supreme Court to serve as the U.S. chief prosecutor at the International Military Tribunal at Nuremberg, which tried members of the Nazi leadership for war crimes and crimes against humanity. Justice Jackson's longtime secretary, Elsie Douglas, was apoplectic. She told *The Washington Post* that Rehnquist had "smeared the reputation of a great justice."[79] "I don't know anyone in the world who was more for equal protection of the laws than Mr. Justice Jackson," she added.[80] A number of Justice Jackson's law clerks were equally outraged.[81] In a letter to *The New York Times*, one of the justice's former clerks wrote: "I consider it ludicrous that Justice Jackson would have asked a law clerk to write a memo expressing his views."[82] In an extensively researched 2017 book examining

Justice Jackson's participation in *Brown*—the justice wrote several draft opinions in the case, none of which were ever published—Supreme Court scholar David O'Brien concluded that "without any doubt, in 1971 and 1986 Rehnquist at the very least misled and misrepresented whose views his memo represented, if not outright lied."[83]

Then there were the words on the page. A close read revealed the memo's true purpose, which was to convince Justice Jackson to reaffirm *Plessy*. The first clue was the young clerk's use of personal pronouns. It was hard to imagine that the memo's last paragraph represented the views of anyone other than the author: "I realize that it is an unpopular and unhumanitarian position, for which I have been excoriated by "liberal" colleagues, but I think Plessy v. Ferguson was right and should be re-affirmed."[84] These were the words of a writer who, notwithstanding the imagined personal sacrifice, was willing to speak truth to power in order to advance an important political objective. The casualness of the memo's title belied the seriousness of the brand of constitutional interpretation it displayed. Rather than a "random thought" on the segregation cases pending before the court, it was instead a wholesale attack on the primacy of the Fourteenth Amendment as a constitutional bulwark against race discrimination.

The young clerk argued that the federal courts were well suited to the role of referee. They could ably resolve disputes among the branches of the federal government and between the federal government and the states. In contrast, the federal courts were "seldom . . . out of hot water when attempting to interpret these individual rights." Why was this? Rehnquist asserted that adjudicating individual rights claims, which often raised strong emotions, invited the court to "read its own sociological views into the Constitution."[85] The problem with this view was that there was no hard-and-fast dichotomy between questions involving "the skeletal relations of the governments to each other" and individual rights. Both kinds of queries often raised "emotionally charged subject matter." Both demanded skillful judging. Many, if not most, judges would have agreed that answering these questions required reference to the constitutional text, its history, the framers' intent, applicable precedent, and constitutional structure. (Although many judges would disagree on how much weight—if any—to give to any particular mode of constitutional interpretation.) But the task was further complicated because deciding some questions of individual rights required mediating *between* competing visions of who and what the Constitution was supposed to protect. To do this successfully required a theory of constitutional interpretation. But no theory of constitutional interpretation was neutral, without political valence.

The mode of constitutional interpretation Rehnquist favored in his memo was deference to majoritarian interests. And the court, being an unelected, largely democratically unaccountable body, should defer to the majority. Otherwise, the will of the people would be thwarted. He put it this way: "Where the legislature was dealing with its own citizens, it was not part of the judicial function to thwart public opinion except in extreme cases."[86] How did the court *know* when a case was extreme enough to warrant intervention? This was a hard question. But by the early 1950s, the court had already supplied an answer.

In a somewhat obscure case decided in 1938, *United States v. Carolene Products*, the court dropped a footnote that had an earthshaking effect on the development of constitutional doctrine.[87] In the *Carolene Products* footnote, the court—agreeing with the young Rehnquist—opined that it should usually defer to the majority in most constitutional cases. But this deferential rule didn't decide every case, nor could it. The footnote indicated that there were times when the court should be suspicious of, rather than deferential to, the majority. Legislation was the product of a presumptively fair process. But what if the process that produced the statute was tainted? Perhaps *Brown* presented a situation where the court should ask a few more questions before taking the states' word on faith that there was a legitimate government rationale for the race-based school statutes. Perhaps the reason why was because the state statutes harmed "discrete and insular minorities," groups that because of systematic voter disenfranchisement, residential segregation, over-criminalization, and other related disabilities couldn't adequately protect their own interests in the political process. Even in a democracy, if the school segregation statutes were tainted goods, there was no reason the court should pay fealty to them. Laws directed at "discrete and insular minorities" were inherently suspect precisely because those groups had been the subject of governmental discrimination, social exclusion, and relative political powerlessness.

Rehnquist thought *Brown* was an easy case. The court should defer to the preferences of the majority in Kansas, Delaware, South Carolina, and Virginia. This "quite clearly is not one of those extreme cases which commands intervention," he wrote.[88] The logic of the *Carolene Products* footnote dictated otherwise. Perhaps the case "quite clearly" didn't require judicial intervention because all blacks were entitled to was what the states deigned to give them. "To the argument made by (Thurgood, not John) Marshall* that a majority may not deprive a minority of its constitutional right, the answer must be made that while this is sound in theory, in the long run it is the majority who will determine what the constitutional rights of the minority are," he argued.[89] The only problem with this assertion was that the Fourteenth Amendment explicitly constrained the states when it came to certain individual rights, such as the right to "equal protection" of the laws. The states no longer enjoyed the "run of the house" when it came to blacks. There was now a baseline below which the states could not fall. The Civil War and the Fourteenth Amendment that came after it changed the Constitution for all time or at least until "the people"—and not the U.S. Supreme Court—amended the document to strike out those provisions.

The NAACP thought the memo—alone—disqualified Rehnquist from serving on the Supreme Court. In a telegram to several senators, Roy Wilkins wrote that the memo, "in his own words, brands Mr. Rehnquist as a segregationist, one who holds a view contrary to the unanimous opinion of the Court in the Brown Case."[90]

In early 1972, Lewis F. Powell Jr. and William H. Rehnquist were sworn in as associate justices of the U.S. Supreme Court. With four appointments, all made in his first term, Nixon had dramatically changed the high court. It was no longer the Warren Court. It was now the Burger Court. Underlining the shift, *The New York Times* observed that "the additions made today gave the tribunal a strongly conservative flavor."[91] Later, after having ascended to the bench, Rehnquist would reflect on his judicial

* John Marshall was the Supreme Court's fourth chief justice.

philosophy: "I can remember arguments we would get into as law clerks in the early '50s, and I don't know that my views have changed much from that time."[92]

———

Warren Burger served as chief justice for nearly a generation, from 1969, when he first took his seat on the court, until 1986, when he retired.

Early assessments of the Burger Court era stressed the court's moderation. The consensus was that the Burger Court, with four justices appointed in quick succession by a "law and order" president who had run against "judicial activism," had under-delivered. The Burger Court was hardly a conservative juggernaut. An entire book published just a few years before the chief justice stepped down, *The Burger Court: The Counter-Revolution That Wasn't*, attested to this view.[93]

Justice Powell agreed. In August 1986, Powell addressed the annual meeting of the American Bar Association. "There has been no conservative counterrevolution by the Burger Court," he told the crowd.[94] One could understand the argument. After all, many liberal Warren Court precedents that had inflamed conservatives, including *Gideon v. Wainright* (guaranteeing a right to counsel for indigent defendants in criminal cases) and *Reynolds v. Sims* (establishing the "one person, one vote" principle), survived. Perhaps the most prominent of the survivors was *Miranda v. Arizona*, which required police officers to inform criminal suspects held for interrogation of their "right to remain silent and to have counsel present during questioning."[95] Against this background, one scholar stated definitively: "No important Warren Court decision was overruled during the Burger tenure. Some of them were narrowed by Burger Court decisions; others were, however, not only fully applied but even expanded."[96]

But not everyone agreed. In 1972, Patrick Buchanan, one of President Nixon's speechwriters and most trusted advisers, told his boss that he had reason to celebrate: you have "recaptured the institution [the Supreme Court] from the Left; [your] four appointments have halted much of its social experimentation."[97] And more recent scholarship has undermined the argument that the Burger Court era was a period during which "nothing much happened."[98] In 2016, Linda Greenhouse and Michael J. Graetz published *The Burger Court and the Rise of the Judicial Right*, which was explicitly intended to refute the early consensus view.[99] The Burger Court wasn't agendaless and nonideological, merely a transitory way station to the later and truly conservative Rehnquist and Roberts Courts. Instead, they argued that the three courts were all on the same team. Sure, major Warren Court–era precedents survived. But the Burger Court undermined their foundations. Many of those cases, Greenhouse and Graetz argued, were "hollowed out" even as the Burger Court erected "daunting barriers to defendants seeking to vindicate their rights in federal court."[100]

Surveying the Burger Court's work across a variety of doctrinal areas, including criminal law and procedure, church and state, commercial speech, campaign finance, labor rights, and government officials' immunity for illegal acts, Greenhouse and Graetz concluded that that court had flipped the defaults that had obtained under Chief Justice Warren. The Warren Court had been committed to equality in many spheres of American life. But under the Burger Court, equality took a backseat to other objectives: federalism and local control, criminal justice efficiency, promoting business interests, and most importantly "rolling back the rights revolution the Warren Court had unleashed."[101] Writing four years later, lawyer and journalist Adam Cohen largely agreed with Greenhouse and Graetz's conclusion. He wrote, the Burger Court "killed off the liberal Warren Court."[102]

19

A TICKING CLOCK

The Sixth Circuit decision that affirmed Roth's metropolitan desegregation ruling was issued by a panel of three federal judges. The defendants could have asked the U.S. Supreme Court to review the panel's decision immediately. But they decided to request a rehearing first. Federal court rules allowed a party to ask that a panel's determination be reviewed "en banc," meaning reconsidered by all the judges on that court if the case involved an exceptionally important issue.[1] Arguing that the panel's decision was "unquestionably unique, unprecedented and . . . erroneous," the defendants sought "en banc" review.[2]

It was a low-probability play. The Sixth Circuit—like most circuits—denied the vast majority of such petitions. But on January 16, 1973, it granted the defendants' request. The move surprised some counsel, Louis Lucas among them.[3] *The New York Times* called the court's action "an extraordinary move."[4] Kelley praised the decision, characterizing review by the entire court as a "victory" for the state.[5] The attorney general might have been referring to the technical effect of the court's action. The court's decision to rehear the case meant that the panel's decision was "vacated," or voided in its entirety. It was as if the prior decision had never been handed down. As one lawyer remarked, "This is a new ballgame."[6]

William Grant openly speculated about the appellate court's rationale for granting "en banc" review. Just one day earlier, the U.S. Supreme Court had elected to wade into the question of metropolitan desegregation by agreeing to review the *Bradley v. Richmond* case—which made front-page news in Detroit.[7] This meant that at least one of the two *Bradley* metropolitan desegregation cases would be reviewed by the highest court in the land. Perhaps the Sixth Circuit had one eye on the appellate court to the south and another on the nine justices in Washington, D.C. This was Grant's take: "It is possible that the Sixth Circuit judges simply wanted a full nine-judge hearing in the Detroit case because the U.S. Fourth Circuit Court of Appeals gave a similar hearing by the full court in the Richmond [Virginia] metropolitan integration case."[8] If both cases were going to go up, best that they each receive full court review.

Oral argument was scheduled for Thursday, February 8, 1973, at 2:00 p.m. Everyone knew the argument had national implications. *The Washington Post* sent a journalist to Cincinnati to cover the proceeding. *The New York Times* also reported on the hearing.

Kelley argued on behalf of the state defendants. The state defendants had, from day one, denied any responsibility for segregation in Detroit's schools. But now Kelley admitted the state's unclean hands. The state legislature should never have overturned Zwerdling's April 7 integration plan, he offered. But the attorney general asserted that he had no "obligation under the circumstances to point out to the Legislature that it was acting in an illegal manner."[9] He put a positive spin on the appellate court's action. The Sixth Circuit's quick invalidation of the state law back in October of 1970, before it went into effect, foreclosed state culpability, Kelley believed.[10] Kelley also admitted for the very first time that every school district in the state—including the suburban school systems—was in effect a state agency. Notwithstanding these admissions, however, the state defendants maintained that the suburban school districts could not be included in a plan intended to remedy segregation in Detroit.[11] They might have been arms of the state, but the suburban school systems had done nothing that would warrant forcing them into an arranged marriage with the Detroit public schools. "The scope of the remedy cannot exceed the scope of the violation," another of the state's lawyers added.[12]

According to Dimond, George Roumell, counsel for the Detroit Board of Education, "stunned the parties and the court" by effectively accepting the liability determination against it. What the board wanted now more than anything was metropolitan desegregation. Roumell: "Although I may not be happy with [the liability] judgment, I do not intend to argue any further on that score. Instead, I want to explain the compelling reasons supporting a metropolitan remedy in this case."[13] If Roth's liability determination was going to stand, best to have the suburban school districts on the hook, too. Dimond provided more color on the eventful argument: Judge Paul C. Weick, who had written the *Deal* decision, "visibly quaked" at Roumell's "impassioned defense of [the] metropolitan ruling."[14] Incredulous, Weick asked, "If that is not effective, can you include the whole state?" "And if that is not sufficient, how about going into Ohio?" the judge quipped. "Detroit doesn't stop at the city line. It is an integrated community economically and socially," was Roumell's reply.[15]

A full transcript of the three-hour oral argument could not be located. But a draft of Nathaniel Jones's weary and exasperated remarks to the court that day has survived. He reminded the court that *Brown v. Board of Education* was the lodestar. "My comments will be limited to the policy concerns which justify our insistence that there be no judicial 'walk away' from the constitutional imperatives so carefully constructed since 1954," he began.[16] The plaintiffs had conducted a lengthy and exhausting trial. They had turned a once-suspicious trial judge into an implacable foe of segregation. They had convinced a federal appellate panel of the rightness of the cause. They won the case the hard way. Yet little had changed on the ground. The Detroit public school system was still in deep financial trouble. In mid-February, it asked the state legislature for authority to impose an additional tax on Detroiters in order to keep the schools open for the full 180-day school year.[17] (The state legislature provided the authorization the following month.)[18] The city's schools were still segregated.

Jones believed that the defendants would do everything in their power to obstruct, to obfuscate, to impede desegregation. "This record clearly shows a series of acts which can be characterized, in their effect, as constantly a changing of the rules in the middle of the game." A bit later he added, minorities "see the ante constantly being upped, the rules forever being changed."[19] The defendants were going to keep on moving the goalposts. The question was whether any court, high or low, would stop them. Now, almost three years after the NAACP filed the complaint in the

Detroit case, the organization's general counsel stood before the entire Sixth Circuit Court of Appeals and asked simply that his clients be treated as what they were: prevailing parties.

Beneath the formality of his argument was a simmering rage. All his life, Jones had played by the rules. So had the vast majority of black people. They had been told to trust the system. "Minorities are counselled to believe in and resort to the law in seeking redress of grievances," Jones told the court. The general counsel pointed to Zwerdling's April 7 integration plan, which the state legislature overturned. Black reaction to that act was measured, tempered. They did "not take matters to the street," he observed. Instead, blacks "went to court." Were they foolish to do so? Were they naive? Now Jones asked the court: "What are people to do for redress, when on a record such as this they are told that a Court can't go beyond the political bounds of Detroit in fashioning a remedy?"[20]

A few weeks before the Sixth Circuit granted the defendants' request for a rehearing, the U.S. Senate Select Committee on Equal Educational Opportunity had published an extraordinary report.[21] The committee had been "created to 'study the effectiveness of existing laws and policies in assuring equality of educational opportunity . . . with regard to segregation on the ground of race . . . whatever the form of such segregation, and to examine the extent to which policies are applied uniformly in all regions of the United States.'"[22] Translation: to what extent has *Brown's* vision of equal educational opportunity been achieved? Chaired by Walter Mondale, the committee had done its homework. The result of almost three years of investigation, the committee's report clocked in at a cool 440 single-spaced pages. It included the testimony of hundreds of witnesses: "students and their parents, teachers, school principals and superintendents, school board members, educational economists, lawyers, psychologists, sociologists, State, local and Federal public officials, representatives of civil rights and other nonprofit organizations."[23] Along with this voluminous testimony, the report was based on committee-commissioned research studies and school visits in more than a dozen states.

The report was extraordinary in its breadth, covering educational disadvantage and child development, the education of language minorities, educational finance, the racial educational achievement gap, rural education, the effects of housing segregation on school segregation, compensatory education, and, of course, school integration. The problem the report identified—public education was failing millions of children "who are from racial and language minority groups, or who are simply poor"[24]—threatened not just those children but, the committee wrote, the vitality of the nation. The lack of equal educational opportunity for all meant substantial economic and human capital losses, more crime, higher welfare costs, and unemployment for those incapable of meeting employers' increasingly rigorous demands for an educated workforce.

The report was extraordinary for its crystal-clear enunciation of the problem's cause: racial discrimination. The committee pointed the guilty finger at the housing-schools nexus. It was racial discrimination that caused residential segregation, and residential segregation was a powerful driver of school segregation. School segregation today, the report charged, particularly in metropolitan areas, was mainly the result of "segregated residential patterns" caused by government policy and the actions of school authorities that intentionally incorporated those policies into the schools' operations for the purpose of segregating the schools.[25] The evidence for this proposition was none other than Judge Roth's findings in *Bradley v. Milliken*: "The pattern of combined governmental official action which produces residential and school isolation in most of our large cities was best described by the Federal District Court in Michigan in *Bradley v. Milliken*."[26]

The situation was dire, the committee believed: "The roots of the extreme social and economic tensions which threaten to divide the Nation, and of much educational deprivation, lie in the extreme racial and economic segregation of our urban areas."[27] For this reason, it advocated that low- and moderate-income families be given the choice to "live near suburban employment and integrated suburban schools." The report also called for the federal government to fund some number of model education parks that would serve "perhaps 12,000 to 20,000 students from kindergarten through high school."[28]

304 | THE CONTAINMENT

The report's clarion call: "It is among our principal conclusions . . . that quality integrated education is one of the most promising educational policies that this Nation and its school systems can pursue if we are to fulfill our commitment to equality of opportunity for our children."[29]

At the same time, it acknowledged—and credited—some blacks' call for community control of their children's schools.[30] Given that, why was the committee so keen on integration? The short answer was the data. The committee largely accepted the findings in the Coleman Report, but it also cited subsequent data suggesting that resource allocation also affected academic achievement.[31] If this was the case, the answer wasn't either-or, it was both-and. The committee called for "focused compensatory efforts" *and* socioeconomic integration. And while it was at it, the committee suggested a more equitable school finance system, too: "The major role in financing education should be shifted away from the local property tax to state funding. In addition, education revenue should be borne in larger part by progressive state income taxes, rather than regressive sales or property taxes."[32] This was going to be a hard sell. Michigan voters had rejected just such a proposal—favored by Governor Milliken—a few weeks before the committee published its report. And just a few months after the committee released its report, the U.S. Supreme Court would go in precisely the opposite direction in a case called *San Antonio Independent School District v. Rodriguez.*[33]

In *Rodriguez*, the court upheld a Texas school financing scheme that relied heavily on local property taxes, which varied—often dramatically—by school district. The Texas scheme was similar to many others around the nation. School taxes were based on a property's assessed value, with local school districts having the ability to determine the specific tax rates applicable within the district. What this meant in practice was that even if poorer districts decided to tax themselves at extraordinarily high levels, they could not raise as much money per pupil as richer districts with much more expensive homes. In an opinion written by Justice Powell, the court acknowledged that the scheme created substantial disparities in school financing between districts. But the court ruled that such disparities didn't violate the equal protection clause. Instead, what really mattered was local control and the inviolability of school district lines.

The committee wasn't pushing integration solely because it was linked to increased academic achievement for minority students. It also believed that integration could foster democracy. In a truly functional multiracial democracy, citizens needed to communicate, debate, and ultimately compromise across racial lines. They needed to resolve disputes without resorting to violence, intimidation, and chicanery. Integration in the schools, particularly when the process was begun in the early grades, powerfully facilitated this process. In a conclusion that jibed with Gordon Allport's insights, the committee wrote: "In a society increasingly divided along racial and social class lines, the social skills that can be learned in a sensitively conducted integrated school may be the most crucial lesson which can be imparted by public education."[34]

The committee's report was astonishing in many ways. But looking back from a distance of more than fifty years, one thing in particular stood out: the issue was completely in flux. On December 31, 1972, when the report was published, the question of whether there would be meaningful metropolitan desegregation—the issue at the core of the *Bradley* case—had yet to be decided. And the committee knew it. It wrote against the background of a ticking clock.

The length and specificity of the report suggested that the committee still believed it was possible to persuade elected officials—and members of the public—to adopt policies that furthered integration rather than double down on racial segregation. It was acutely aware of the Richmond and Detroit metropolitan desegregation decisions and the circuit split that heightened the possibility of Supreme Court review, but it remained skeptical of the courts. Of the two cases, the committee wrote: "The future of these housing and school desegregation decisions and the legal theories on which they rest cannot be predicted with confidence."[35] The committee believed that elected officials were far better suited than the courts to deal with the flinty complexities of "breaking down racial and economic barriers" to facilitate metropolitan desegregation. It wrote: "A court cannot offer subsidies to compensate suburban communities for increased costs, including educational costs of serving low-income families or provide assistance to replace revenues lost through location of tax-free public housing units; a court is ill equipped to require that low-income housing be scatter-site, rather than in huge apartment projects or to implement the metropolitan planning needed to prevent some suburban communities from being swamped by low-income housing while others are untouched."[36]

It was true that in an ideal world, the political branches were better situated than the federal courts to deal with the myriad difficulties of school desegregation. And it was also true that the strongest desegregation gains in the South occurred during the short period when all three branches of the federal government—legislative, executive, and judicial—were on the same page and worked together to ensure that result.[37] And it was also true that the federal courts' primary function was to resolve disputes between the parties, not make wide-ranging policy determinations. In a democracy, it was better for the more politically accountable branches of government to do that. But the federal courts retained a vital law announcement function. They could protect minority rights—as Judge Roth had done—forcing reluctant public officials to deal with a problem they would have preferred to avoid. And, in announcing the law, they could tell the public what the Constitution prohibited and what actions were required of public officials. They were a line in the sand, shifting the defaults against which public officials acted and making it that much easier or that much harder to address the effects of race discrimination. And, because of their institutional prestige, the federal courts had the power to change some minds along the way.

The fifteen-member bipartisan committee was closely divided; it included some of the Senate's leading lights: Daniel K. Inouye of Hawaii, Jacob K. Javits of New York, Edward W. Brooke of Massachusetts, and Mark O. Hatfield of Oregon. Eight members endorsed the final report in full, while seven declined to do so. One of the dissenters hailed from Nebraska; another was from Colorado. The rest were from southern or border states. The seven dissenters filed various statements explaining their positions. Perhaps the key disagreement was over busing and racial balance. A majority of the committee thought those terms were misleading, deflecting from the real issues, which were the well-being of minority and poor children.[38] But Senator Sam Ervin of North Carolina, emphasizing individual freedom, said the majority had it exactly backward. Busing and racial balance were exactly what he was fighting against. It was "as clear as the noonday sun in a cloudless sky."[39]

=====

On May 21, 1973, the U.S. Supreme Court issued a ruling in the Richmond case. A ruling—but not an opinion. In fact, the decision included only one sentence: "The judgment is affirmed by an equally divided Court."[40]

That short statement was loaded with meaning. "The judgment is affirmed" meant that the court was upholding the appellate court's determination to halt Judge Merhige's city-suburban desegregation plan. The phrase "equally divided" raised an eyebrow, as it wasn't possible to divide a nine-member court into two equal parts. In fact, only eight justices had participated in consideration of the Richmond case, with one recusal. "Mr. Justice POWELL," the former chair of the Richmond school board and longtime member of the Virginia State Board of Education, "took no part in the consideration or decision of these cases."[41]

As a technical matter, the four-four split limited its effect. The Fourth Circuit ruling was still controlling law in that circuit, but nowhere else. A court majority was needed to produce a ruling with nationwide effect. As *The Baltimore Sun* explained, "yesterday's decision left open, for all . . . school systems except Richmond's the question of whether the courts may order the merger of city and suburban schools to achieve integration."[42] The tie also had the effect of leaving the circuit split unresolved. Still, the four-four split didn't bode well for the Detroit plaintiffs. The close vote in the Richmond case suggested that the constitutionality of metropolitan desegregation was on a knife's edge.

Richmond was a "per curiam" decision, meaning "by the court." This meant that the justices' votes were not released. By late May 1973, President Nixon had appointed four justices to the U.S. Supreme Court. They joined the Warren Court holdovers—Thurgood Marshall, William O. Douglas, Potter Stewart, William J. Brennan, and Byron White—to form the nine-member court. With Powell recused, it was likely that the remaining Nixon appointees, Burger, Rehnquist, and Blackmun, all voted to affirm the Fourth Circuit. But who provided the fourth vote? *The Brethren*, Bob Woodward and Scott Armstrong's account of the inner workings of the Supreme Court during this period, provided the answer: Justice Potter Stewart.[43]

President Eisenhower had appointed the Cincinnati native and moderate Republican to serve on the court during a congressional recess in 1958. At the relatively tender age of forty-three, Stewart was one of the youngest men ever confirmed to sit on the high court.[44] Assessing his judicial philosophy, commentators often emphasized Stewart's moderation and restraint.[45] They characterized him as "pragmatic," "non-ideological," "a lawyer rather than a philosopher."[46] *The New York Times* offered this helpful appraisal: "For half of his time on the Court Justice Stewart was a conservative, often dissenting member of the Warren Court; for the other half he was at the decisive center of the more conservative Burger Court."[47]

According to Woodward and Armstrong, Stewart voted to overturn the Richmond desegregation plan because no "violation in the suburban district had been proven." Additionally, he was "deeply affected by non-judicial considerations," namely, that the "mainstream of society opposed forced integration of the schools when it meant busing."[48] It was hard to interpret the phrase "mainstream of society" as meaning anything other than "the white majority." The two journalists continued: "Stewart told his clerks that he had ridden the bus on the Charlotte [*Swann*] and Denver [*Keyes*] decisions, [discussed in the next chapter] but that Richmond was different. 'It is where I get off,' he said."

20

MILLIKEN V. BRADLEY

I n early June 1973, the full Sixth Circuit released its decision in *Bradley v. Milliken*. Citing liberally from the panel's earlier ruling, the court affirmed it in virtually all respects.[1] One commentator observed, "The full court reissued the original opinion, with minor changes, on June 12, 1973. Three judges dissented from all or part of the decision."[2] (Judge Weick wrote a particularly bitter dissent, characterizing the suburban school districts as being "invaded.")[3]

Like the panel, the full Sixth Circuit again refused to rely on the area-wide housing evidence: "We have not relied at all upon testimony pertaining to segregated housing."[4] But it, again like the panel, made an exception when it came to "school construction programs [that] helped cause or maintain such segregation." It was an exception that effectively swallowed the rule, as the school construction evidence spanned the Detroit metropolitan area. As Dimond correctly recognized, "State discrimination not only caused segregation *within* the Detroit school district, but also promoted segregation *of* the Detroit school district from its suburban neighbors."[5] Additionally, the circuit's decision reminded the reader of the plethora of metropolitan evidence that Judge Roth *had* heard. It noted that the "record contains a substantial volume of testimony concerning local and State action and policies which helped produce residential segregation in Detroit and in the metropolitan area of Detroit."[6] This testimony plus Judge Roth's fulsome opinion itself would make it difficult for later

readers to credibly argue that the causes of segregation in the Detroit metropolitan area were "unknown and unknowable." There was voluminous
evidence of, as Dimond put it, "the causal interaction between school and
housing segregation and . . . proof of discrimination and housing throughout the metropolitan area" for anyone who cared to see it.[7]

The full appellate court agreed with the panel that any suburban school
district that could be affected by Roth's order had to be "made a party to
this litigation and afforded an opportunity to be heard."[8] The court ordered
Roth to conduct a new hearing with all the affected suburban school districts. William Grant characterized this portion of the appellate court's ruling as a "technicality," which wasn't far off the mark.[9] The suburban school
districts would be permitted to cross-examine witnesses and offer evidence,
but only to a point. They would not be allowed to attack the most important
of Roth's findings, that the defendants had violated the Constitution and
that metropolitan relief was necessary and appropriate. As one commentator put it, the new hearing would focus on "how many school districts
should be included in the plan, which they will be, when bussing will start
and how many students will be involved."[10] The districts would have a say
on the metropolitan plan's design. But, for the moment, its existence was
not in question. (Pursuant to the Sixth Circuit's mandate, Roth later added
to the lawsuit every suburban school district in Wayne, Oakland, and Macomb Counties. Pontiac, still under Judge Keith's desegregation order, was
omitted.)[11] Finally, the full Sixth Circuit chose to distinguish rather than to
overrule *Deal*: "There the District Court made findings of fact that there
had been no unconstitutional conduct on the part of the Cincinnati Board
of Education."[12] The situation was different in Detroit.

Not surprisingly, the Sixth Circuit's ruling was front page news in Detroit. William Grant's article for the *Detroit Free Press* highlighted the
likelihood of high court review: "The unusually strongly worded [Sixth
Circuit] opinion places the issue of city-suburban busing squarely before
the U.S. Supreme Court, which last month deadlocked 4-4 and was unable
to issue any opinion on a similar case from Richmond, Va."[13]

Reacting to the decision, Nate Jones was ebullient. The NAACP "re-
joices" in the opinion, he said.[14] Indeed, the organization had now notched
three wins—four if one counted the Sixth Circuit's early invalidation of

Act 48—in an exceedingly difficult and complex case. It was an extraordinary accomplishment. In mid-July 1973, William Grant offered an astute assessment.[15] *Bradley v. Milliken* was less about busing than about the federal courts' role in society. He linked the Sixth Circuit Court of Appeals to the Warren Court and the "activist role" that court assumed. But by the time Grant wrote this assessment, the Warren Court was already gone. And another, much more conservative court had taken its place.

On June 22, 1973, Nate Jones briefed Roy Wilkins and several others on the status of the Detroit case.[16] Jones's assessment was almost breathless. "With the decision by the Sixth Circuit in the Detroit Case, it is fair to say that it has now ripened into the most significant school case pending in any Court," he wrote.[17] The general counsel assessed the stakes of a case that was poised for review at the highest court in the land. "Without question, it may now be the case in which the U.S. Supreme Court will definitively deal with the question of metropolitan remedy and in other respects, speak to the 'de jure,' 'de facto' issue," he declared.

The road ahead would be hard. "The full resources of the Federal Government, the State of Michigan, and those of the various suburbs will be allied against us," the general counsel warned. But Jones wasn't worried just about the defendants and the feds. Other powerful players also had a dog in the fight. "Joining with them, most certainly, will be the 'troops' of other states anxious to resist the crossing of district boundaries, now that the Court has spoken in Denver." It was the NAACP against the world.

By "Denver" the general counsel meant *Keyes v. School District No. 1, Denver, Colorado*, which the Supreme Court had decided just one day before Jones wrote the memo.[18] In an opinion written by Justice William Brennan, the U.S. Supreme Court—for the very first time—extended *Brown* to a non-southern school district. In Denver, just as in Detroit, there was no law requiring that the schools be racially segregated, but somehow they were anyway. The techniques school officials used to perpetuate segregation were familiar, too: racial gerrymandering of school zones, siting new schools to maximize segregation, the neighborhood school rule.[19] At the core of the case was a technical question: How much evidence did the plaintiffs need to prove that school officials deliberately segregated the schools? Was evidence of intentional segregation in one neighborhood within a school district sufficient to entitle the plaintiffs to an order requiring desegregation of the entire district? Or was the evidentiary burden much higher? Perhaps the plaintiffs needed to make a fresh showing of intentional segregation—of deliberate action on the part of school authorities—with respect to every single school in the district before they were entitled to system-wide desegregation.

In *Keyes*, the court declined to go that far. It ruled that evidence of de jure segregation in a "substantial portion" of the school system created a presumption that the rest of the school system was illegally segregated, too.[20] But why make that assumption? The answer was that de jure segregation had a hydraulic effect. A student could attend only one school. If students of color were trapped in one area or within specific schools because of the deliberate acts of school officials, they were necessarily unavailable to attend other schools. Confining minority students to minority schools didn't just change the complexion of those schools. Those acts also drained minority students from white schools. Race discrimination metastasized, affecting the entire school district. So the court pushed back against a myopic focus on single schools and individual neighborhoods: "It is obvious that a practice of concentrating Negroes in certain schools by structuring attendance zones or designating 'feeder' schools on the basis of race has a reciprocal effect of keeping other nearby schools predominantly white."[21]

The Denver case accepted rather than refuted the idea that there was a strict separation between de jure and de facto segregation. But the court interpreted de jure segregation broadly enough to give the plaintiffs litigating non-southern school desegregation cases a crucial assist. Nate Jones recognized this almost instantly. Per his June 22, 1973, memo: the "Denver rationale buttresses Roth's rulings on Detroit segregation."[22] Vernon E. Jordan Jr., the executive director of the National Urban League, was also hopeful. In an op-ed, he wrote that *Keyes* "opens the way for widespread desegregation of northern schools."[23] Law professor and school desegregation expert Myron Orfield (Gary Orfield's brother) later contextualized their enthusiasm. He argued that the *Keyes* court adopted a generous approach for establishing legal responsibility in northern school segregation cases.[24] The effects of discrimination tended to spread rather than stay localized, so that if "one school was made black by a discriminatory act . . .

another school would be made whiter even though the white students may have been assigned based on neutral geography."

But that wasn't all. The court also assumed that evidence of de jure segregation in a "substantial portion" of a school district—as little as 5 to 10 percent of the student population—was indicative of state-imposed segregation in the rest of the district.[25] School defendants could overcome these presumptions, but the court made them difficult to rebut. In effect, *Keyes* said that where there was smoke, the court would assume there was a fire. And, once the plaintiffs established that school officials had violated the Constitution, they were entitled to the full panoply of desegregation remedies as outlined in *Green* and *Swann*. Justice Brennan remanded the case to the lower court "for further proceedings consistent with this opinion."[26] The four-four split in the Richmond case was a yellow "caution" light for the plaintiffs in the Detroit case. But *Keyes* let the *Bradley v. Milliken* trial team exhale.

Although Justice Powell agreed with the court that the case should be sent back to the lower courts, he disagreed on the reason for the remand. Powell wrote separately to explain his views. The justice noted that segregation was pervasive throughout the United States.[27] Segregated schools were evil, whether in Denver or Atlanta, the justice declared.[28] Housing and school segregation were deeply interrelated, he added.[29] Therefore, he wanted to "formulate constitutional principles of national rather than merely regional application."[30] Referring to *Green* and in particular *Swann*, the justice wrote: "In imposing on metropolitan southern school districts an affirmative duty, entailing largescale transportation of pupils, to eliminate segregation in the schools, the court required these districts to alleviate conditions which in large part did not result from historic, state-imposed de jure segregation."[31] What Powell seemed to be getting at was that it was too late to attribute southern school segregation to the kinds of overt governmental policies—classic de jure segregation—that the court struck down in 1954. Instead, the schools were segregated by other means, ones that were prevalent throughout the country. From Justice Powell's perspective, the de jure / de facto dichotomy, upon which the *Keyes* ruling was based, was just a fancy way of saying "double standard." Why should southern school districts be deemed guilty until proven innocent when segregation—north, east, south, and west—all originated from the same source?

This, then, was the crux of the issue. In the South, there was no requirement that the plaintiffs prove deliberate action on the part of school officials before busing was ordered—*Green* required southern school districts to desegregate whether they had been sued or not. Even if that obligation was often ignored, it hung over southern school officials like the Sword of Damocles. Northern school districts, which were often even more segregated than their southern counterparts, got the benefit of the doubt. There, the plaintiffs had to painstakingly show intent. The Detroit case showed just how much northern litigants had to do to convince a federal court to rule in their favor. In fact, it was the plaintiffs' overarching and justified concern about defending Judge Roth's liability determination—in the shadow of the *Deal* case—that so complicated their litigation position on metropolitan relief. As Powell understood it, the de jure / de facto distinction allowed segregated northern school districts to get off easy, and southern ones to be controlled aggressively even though the causes of segregation were comparable to those in the North. The Virginian preferred a level playing field.

Powell clearly disfavored the de jure / de facto distinction upon which the majority relied. Powell's biographer John Jeffries reported that Brennan apparently offered to drop the distinction if a majority of the justices—and Powell in particular—would support doing so. Jeffries cited a memorandum Brennan wrote to his colleagues suggesting that the two justices actually agreed when it came to de jure and de facto segregation: "Lewis and I seem to share the view that de facto segregation and de jure segregation . . . should receive like constitutional treatment."[32] This statement suggested that a deal was in the offing. But it wasn't to be. As Jeffries explained it, Powell could have agreed to discard the distinction, "but at what price? Would he have had to give up his opposition to busing? That, of course, he was unwilling to do." Brennan's memo put a finer point on the source of their disagreement: "Lewis's approach has the virtue of discouraging an illogical and unworkable distinction, but only at the price of a substantial retreat from our commitment of the past twenty years to eliminate all vestiges of state-imposed segregation in public schools." The issue that divided the two justices *wasn't* how best to establish liability in a non-southern school segregation case. Instead, it was how robust the remedy for school segregation needed to be—specifically, busing. Jeffries: "Brennan had offered to take Powell's views on the de facto-de jure distinction, but not on busing."

Justice Powell's hostility to the de jure / de facto distinction raised a question that his colleague Justice Blackmun would later point out after the *Bradley v. Milliken* case had reached the Supreme Court. In a pre-argument memo summarizing his thoughts on the case, Blackmun was particularly concerned about Justice Powell's role in the court's deliberations.[33] (Prior to oral argument and after having reviewed the case material, the justice's customary practice was to dictate a memo to himself condensing the parties' arguments and providing his preliminary thoughts on the case.)[34]

Predicting that "the eight votes will split as they did in Richmond," Blackmun believed that "Justice Powell's vote [will be] very critical."[35] But it wouldn't be uncomplicated. Blackmun pointed to Powell's opinion in the *Keyes* case. Powell was "in a bit of a box," the justice wrote, "because of his long opinion in the Denver case arguing that the de jure-de facto distinction is not a valid one." Denver "substantially weakens [Powell's] position here if he is at all inclined to reverse," he added.

Presumably Blackmun thought Powell's position in *Keyes* put him on record as accepting the view that all school segregation, south or north, was equally suspect constitutionally and that all school authorities regardless of location had the same obligation to eliminate it.[36] And when it came to eliminating the vestiges of de jure segregation, the court said that desegregation had to be real: "The district judge or school authorities should make every effort to achieve the greatest possible degree of actual desegregation and thus will necessarily be concerned with the elimination of one-race schools," the court wrote in *Swann*.[37] Later in the memo, Blackmun reiterated his concern, writing that the case "will be a terribly difficult case for Justice Powell, and his vote will probably determine the outcome."[38]

As for Justice Blackmun's vote, it was never in play. He believed school district lines were sacrosanct. "I have always been concerned . . . with an approach that would completely ignore long-established and innocently drawn boundary lines," he wrote in his memo.[39] The justice was also concerned about the proverbial barn door: "Once we cross that barrier, we open the way to doing the same thing in all possible types of situations." Blackmun continued, "If Detroit can be desegregated on a metropolitan basis, by getting into surrounding districts, why may not the city of Washington be desegregated by getting into adjacent portions of Maryland and Virginia?" It was a good question.

———

On November 19, 1973, the U.S. Supreme Court granted the defendants' cert. petition requesting that the Supreme Court hear the *Bradley v. Milliken* case.[40] The Detroit case was headed to the nation's highest court. The paper of record took notice, suggesting that *Bradley v. Milliken* was of national, not just regional, interest. *The New York Times* informed its readers of the cert. grant and predicted that the court would hand down a decision by the end of its current term.[41] This meant that the public could expect a decision in late spring or early summer of 1974.

In a long memo a few days earlier, Nate Jones had written to Roy Wilkins with an update on the Detroit case, correctly surmising that the Supreme Court would soon announce the cert. grant. His goal was to put all the facts at Wilkins's fingertips in the (not unlikely) event that he was called on to comment. As in earlier missives, Jones reiterated his belief that *Bradley v. Milliken* was singularly important. "The Detroit case is the most significant school desegregation case pending in any Court in the nation," he declared. "Upon the outcome of this case, hinges the fate of Negro and other [minority] children in numerous Northern communities around the country."[42]

As an advocate with a very particular point of view, the general counsel might have gotten carried away. But he wasn't alone in his thinking. William Grant supported Jones's view of the litigation, writing in the *Detroit Free Press* that a Supreme Court decision in the case "could be the most important high court pronouncement on school integration since 1954."[43] The conservative *Detroit News* agreed that the case had the makings of a landmark. Calling the lawsuit "historic" and comparing it to *Brown*, it wrote that the Detroit litigation was "one of the most significant civil rights cases to come before the [Supreme Court] in more than a decade."[44]

Why was the Detroit case so important? Grant's answer was that Detroit was both a very large school district, and thus important in its own right, and a bellwether. The structure of the Detroit metropolitan area, a majority black city bounded by majority white suburbs with separate school districts, was far from unusual in the early 1970s. It was a metropolitan arrangement that was prevalent from coast to coast. Grant wrote that a Supreme Court decision in the Detroit case would "have sweeping implications not only for Detroit but for most major U.S. cities where predominantly black city schools are surrounded by predominantly white suburban schools."[45] Specifically, he wrote, "many civil rights attorneys" feared that a decision "against metropolitan integration would, in effect, re-establish the 'separate but equal' rule by permitting segregated black city schools and segregated white suburban schools."[46]

Grant was right in seeing the Detroit litigation as a watershed. If the Supreme Court upheld Judge Roth, the ruling had the potential to become the judicial version of Ribicoff's pathbreaking integration bill, knitting together city and suburb from coast to coast. That bill's failure suggested judicial action was the most promising avenue for blacks to have access to the benefits of suburban schools. In fact, the Detroit and Richmond school cases weren't the only lawsuits testing the possibility of metropolitan desegregation, as *The New York Times* reported. In the article on the cert. grant, the paper observed that several cases with the potential to result in "similar city-suburban school desegregation plans are pending in a number of cities, including Atlanta, Buffalo, Hartford, Indianapolis, Louisville and Wilmington, Del."[47] A Supreme Court ruling upholding Roth would likely green-light metropolitan desegregation in the pending cases and create an incentive for other plaintiffs to bring copycat lawsuits.

There was yet another reason why the cert. grant in *Bradley v. Milliken* was so monumental: the trial record. The proofs the plaintiffs put on in Detroit did much more than provide the evidence necessary to convince the trial court judge to assign liability to the defendants. The trial record in *Bradley v. Milliken* was special; it read like a novel. That record didn't just explain how the Detroit public school authorities segregated the schools. Nor did it simply elucidate the housing-schools nexus. Instead, it was a road map, an explainer, a treatise on northern Jim Crow. It was almost unimaginable, after having read the trial transcripts, that one could sustain the belief that racial segregation in the North wasn't the result of racial discrimination, which, in turn, was deeply embodied in governmental policy. The record indicted government at every level for segregating schools, for segregating neighborhoods, and for creating the stark racial divisions *between* city and suburb. This was the northern Jim Crow story, as it had unfolded day after day in Judge Roth's courtroom in downtown Detroit. That story involved multiple actors, levels of government, and time frames. It was complicated and, at times, byzantine. But it was comprehensible. It was knowable.

The record the NAACP lawyers compiled—and Judge Roth and the Sixth Circuit's reaction to it (twice!)—was profoundly threatening to the racial status quo. It encompassed the containment, snakes in the basement, physical segregation barriers that resembled prison walls, redlining, racially restrictive covenants, white neighborhood associations with violent tendencies, segregated public housing, racially separate real estate salespersons associations, and school authorities that hoovered it all up when they insisted on neighborhood schools. The record was vertigo inducing. It was so powerful that it could prompt a shift in one's worldview. This was exactly what happened to Judge Roth, who then acted in accordance with those changed beliefs. For some this was a terrifying prospect. At the core of *Bradley v. Milliken* was the northern Jim Crow story: how it happened, who was responsible, and what it might take to heal an open wound. If more Americans learned that story, if more understood that history, perhaps they might undergo a similar conversion. Perhaps.

<hr>

For just over three years, the official caption of the Detroit case had listed the Bradleys' names first. The Detroit school segregation case was the *Bradley* case. When the case reached the U.S. Supreme Court, that changed. Pursuant to long-standing Supreme Court practice, the party asking the court to review a determination—the petitioner—was listed first.[48] The Detroit case now had a new name that, coincidentally, highlighted the state's role in segregating the city of Detroit: *Milliken v. Bradley*.

21

THE STORY

W e will hear arguments next in . . . Milliken against Bradley," Chief Justice Warren Burger intoned before a packed courtroom. In the audience at the Supreme Court Building in Washington, D.C., that day were various luminaries of the case: Roy Wilkins, several school superintendents, a bevy of officials from Detroit and the state of Michigan, and a group of law students who had camped all night on the building's steps with the hope of scoring seats for the hotly anticipated event.[1] And somewhere in the courtroom sat a former school board president who had a particularly keen interest in the outcome: Abraham Zwerdling. The date was February 27, 1974.

First up were the petitioners. Attorney General Frank Kelley represented the state defendants. William Saxton spoke on behalf of the suburban school districts. The court also heard from Robert Bork, the United States solicitor general, who was backing them. It was clear from the outset that one of the petitioners' main goals was to cast Judge Roth as the villain, a judicial activist hell-bent on mandating social change from the bench. That he began the litigation skeptical of the plaintiffs' claims, if not outrightly hostile to them, was immaterial. Less than five minutes into his presentation, Kelley attacked the judge by suggesting that Roth had become "preoccupied with the majority black character of the Detroit school district."[2] The attorney general was planting a seed. This and other comments—which wrenched several of the judge's statements out of context—suggested that

Roth was insufficiently objective. Here was a judge, the attorney general seemed to be saying, who was less concerned with what the Constitution required than with achieving a racialized, pro-black agenda.

Proceeding further, Roth's ruling had a crucial deficiency, Kelley and Saxton argued. There was no "interdistrict violation." Saxton told the court: "You will search this record in vain to find one whit, one jack of evidentiary material that any suburban school district committed any de jure act of segregation, either by itself, in complicity with the state, or complicity with anyone else. There is no such evidence."[3] But what was an interdistrict violation?

Solicitor General Bork's brief on behalf of the United States in the case had featured a lengthy discussion of the "interdistrict violation-interdistrict remedy" concept. In the brief, Bork argued that metropolitan or "interdistrict" remedies in school desegregation cases were generally disfavored. Only an interdistrict violation could justify such a remedy. If the government created a school district solely for black students, that would amount to an interdistrict violation. Similarly, if students were transferred across school district lines on the basis of race, that would also amount to an interdistrict violation. But as the government's brief emphasized, these were "unusual circumstance[s]."[4] What all this really meant was that a Brown violation alone wasn't enough to justify a metropolitan remedy. What's more, this argument was just that: an argument. No preexisting precedent required this approach. If anything, the weight of the precedent—Brown and the rest—cut the other way.

The interdistrict violation question was the subject of the most arresting interchange of the entire oral argument. It occurred during the solicitor general's presentation. Bork told the court that if the respondents (the Bradley plaintiffs) wanted to include the suburban school systems in the remedy, the case had to be remanded for what was, in effect, a new trial. There, the plaintiffs would be required to demonstrate the presence of an interdistrict violation, one that "directly altered or substantially affected the respective racial compositions of the Detroit school system and the specific suburban school systems."[5] The chief justice interrupted: "Can you tell me, Mr. Solicitor General, when in the course of this litigation, the allegations were made that the outlying districts . . . had engaged in conduct violative of the Constitution."[6] Bork responded immediately: "Mr. Chief Justice, it is my understanding that no such allegation had been made to date."

Burger surely knew that there had been no such showing. It was a rhetorical question. What the jurist really meant was: If such a showing had not already been made, how could the suburbs possibly be on the hook? It appeared that the solicitor general and the chief justice agreed that every single suburban school district was entitled to an extraordinary level of autonomy and respect. Their colloquy suggested that before any outlying district could be included in a metropolitan desegregation plan, there had to be a finding that *it* had violated the Constitution. This was a vision of the suburban school districts as, in effect, little mini-states, even though nothing in Michigan law suggested that they be accorded such protection. Every school district in the state of Michigan was a state agency, as the lower courts had held. But clearly that wasn't enough for the chief justice. In this moment, it was clear to all present that he was inclined to vote against the respondents.

Addressing the matter, Justice Potter Stewart asked: "Mr. Solicitor General, what do you mean exactly by interdistrict violations?" "A violation that results in altering the racial composition of two districts. So that blacks tend to be confined to one and whites confined to another," was Bork's reply. Justice Stewart continued: "Does it require cooperative action on the part of two or more districts?" That was one possibility, said the solicitor general, but joint action wasn't necessarily required. Bork provided additional clarification: the interdistrict violation could occur either by action taken by the state or through "collusion or cooperation between the two districts." Justice William Rehnquist jumped in to make sure he was following him correctly: "Some sort of a shifting of a district line in order to preserve segregation," he clarified.[7] Rehnquist's restatement suggested that the predicate for a city-suburban school desegregation remedy existed only when public officials gerrymandered school district lines to preserve segregation. The solicitor general had used the word "confined," which one might have taken as referring to the fact that blacks were confined to an ever-expanding area within the city and were correspondingly locked out of the suburbs, as the plaintiffs had shown at trial. But that wasn't it. Instead, he, along with Justices Stewart and Rehnquist, was describing the unicorn: the elusive piece of evidence that might hypothetically entitle the plaintiffs to interdistrict relief.

J. "Nick" Harold Flannery, civil rights expert and trusted member of the NAACP trial team, used a large portion of his argument time to explain how the containment actually worked. He noted how Detroit and the state of Michigan operated in unison: "It wasn't the state's role in isolation today and the Detroit Board's role in isolation tomorrow." And he detailed how various actors used a variety of techniques to perpetuate the containment. "All of these factors, especially the segregative school practices, operated in lock step with an areawide metropolitan policy of confining by housing discrimination at the local level, at the governmental levels, both state and federal, and the private level," Flannery said, "confining black families to an identifiable core in Detroit which is, to be sure expanding, but still surrounded by a white ring of reciprocal corresponding schools now separated only by the border—or soon to be separated only by the border, as Judge Roth observed."[8]

Flannery also spoke at length about Michigan's de jure acts of segregation—among them, segregated school site selection, and state aid formulas that disfavored Detroit's school system. And there was Act 48, the state statute that overturned the April 7 high school integration plan. The advocate told the court that Act 48 showed how the state was perfectly capable of micromanaging a school district's affairs "when the objective was the retention of segregation."[9] Then he put it all together: "So it appears to us that a variety of state practices, some implemented at the local level, some by state education officials, have combined with massive housing segregation throughout the Detroit metropolitan area. Each reinforcing the other as noted by this Court in *Swann* and again in *Keyes*."[10] Still, looking back at the transcript, one had the sense that, notwithstanding his erudition, the advocate was failing to connect. Flannery spoke for long stretches without interruption. Were the members of the Supreme Court listening attentively, or had they already made up their minds?

For his part, Nate Jones spoke to the practicalities of interdistrict desegregation. He told the court that Wayne, Oakland, and Macomb Counties—the Tri-County Area—were a single "community of interest" united by the ties that bound them: "economic interests, recreation interests, social concerns and interests, governmental interests of various sorts and a transportation network."[11] He reiterated the containment theme. The NAACP's general counsel stated yet again that the constitutional violations were committed by the state of Michigan and its entity, the Detroit school district. Their actions "led to the containment of 133,000 Black children in 133 core schools surrounded by a ring of white schools," Jones declared. And, just in case any of the justices had forgotten it, he reminded them that Judge Roth had yet to issue an actual desegregation plan. Replying to a question from Justice Brennan, Jones stated: "All that is before the court now is the narrow question of whether or not these boundaries, these geographical boundaries, are impermeable and whether they may be crossed."[12] It was true. When all the technical legal jargon was stripped away, this was what *Milliken v. Bradley* was about: Would the suburban fences come down? Jones took his seat. Would it be enough?

At around 1:40 p.m., Chief Justice Burger said: "Thank you, gentlemen. The case is submitted."[13] The fate of the Detroit case was now in the hands of the U.S. Supreme Court.

On Thursday, April 4, 1974, Judge Roth suffered a second heart attack.[14] Although this attack was milder than his first—doctors predicted he would recover—the press sounded a note of caution about Roth's continued participation in the *Milliken* case. One paper observed that the judge's ability to preside over the Detroit case after the Supreme Court issued its ruling "depends largely on his health."[15]

At the end of the month, Roth underwent a coronary bypass procedure. He was listed in serious but improving condition and was released from St. Joseph Hospital in Flint in early May.[16] It was around this time that Roth reportedly considered retiring from the bench.[17] Then, in mid-July, the judge returned to St. Joseph's, in critical condition after a third—and final—heart attack.[18] Roth died on July 11, 1974. He was 66.[19]

It was hard to imagine that the stress of the Detroit case had nothing to do with the judge's death. John Runyan, one of Roth's law clerks, certainly believed there was a connection. In 2018, Runyan told me, "He gave his life for what he thought was right."[20]

Reverend David E. Molyneaux, a longtime friend, seemed to agree. Speaking on July 15, 1974, to several hundred attendees at Roth's memorial service in Flint, he remarked: "If controversy troubled his days and laid a heavy strain upon him, it also awakened the appreciation of his country for his honest, thoughtful and forthright service to humanity."[21] The federal courts in Detroit, Flint, and Bay City all closed that day, in observance of Roth's memory.[22]

On Wednesday, June 26, 1974, approximately two weeks before Roth's death, the Supreme Court's 1973–74 term came to an end. To the surprise of some observers, the justices issued no decision in the Detroit case. Supreme Court deliberations routinely took months, but cases argued in February typically were decided by the end of the term. *The New York Times* wrote, it "was the last regular decision day of the high court's 1973–74 term, and a decision on the [Detroit] case—probably the single most important controversy of the term—had been expected."[23] The paper speculated that the case might be held over until the following term.[24]

Indeed, earlier in the month, Justice Marshall had written his colleagues seeking just such a delay.[25] "After much work, and even greater deliberation, I have come to the conclusion that it will be impossible for me to complete my dissent . . . before adjournment," he pleaded.[26] But the outcome was already a conclusion. At the justices' conference just after oral argument in the case, five members of the court—Chief Justice Burger and Justices Powell, Rehnquist, Blackmun, and Stewart—voted to reverse Judge Roth. Marshall and Justices White, Douglas, and Brennan were in Roth's corner. It was hard to imagine giving Thurgood Marshall, whose name was practically synonymous with school desegregation, more time to poke holes in the majority opinion. Predictably, his efforts failed. The case remained on the docket for the 1973–74 term.

So why wasn't the Detroit ruling released by the end of the term? One answer was that, by the time the chief justice circulated the first draft of the opinion, there was precious little time before the end of the term for his colleagues to review it.[27] (Because the chief justice voted with the majority, Burger held the power to determine who would write the court's opinion. He assigned it to himself.) Another answer was that even though the regular term ended in late June, the court did not recess for the summer as was its normal practice. The reason why was Watergate. In effect, the court decided to sit for a rare special term in the summer of 1974 in order to decide whether the president of the United States could be forced to provide evidence in a federal criminal case against seven of his aides for attempting to conceal the Watergate scandal.[28] On July 24, 1974, the court issued *United States v. Nixon*, ruling that the answer to that question was yes.[29] It released the *Milliken v. Bradley* decision the very next day.

In the end, the delay made little difference—except perhaps to one man. Having survived the end of the Supreme Court term, Judge Roth had passed away just two weeks before the court finally issued its ruling. He never had a chance to read the decision. John Runyan thought that was a good thing. As he told me, more than four decades after his old boss's death: "I'm glad that Judge Roth didn't live to see what the Supreme Court did to his ruling."[30]

The conservative *Detroit News* and the more liberal *Detroit Free Press* weren't always in agreement. But in late July 1974, the papers reached for the same metaphor. *"Roth Bussing Plan Killed,"* read the front page of *The Detroit News* on July 25.[31] The next morning, the *Detroit Free Press* agreed, on A1 above the fold: *"High Court Kills Cross-District Busing."*[32] The metropolitan desegregation order was dead. But how, exactly, did the high court kill it?

First, Chief Justice Burger adopted the petitioners' story of the case, which was grounded in white innocence. His analysis of Roth's findings of de jure segregation against the defendants—which the court never overturned—was short and clinical. There was no discussion of school segregation's effect on black children. There was no mention of the containment. There was no acknowledgment of how blacks were locked in specific

Detroit neighborhoods and mostly black schools, and then into an ever-expanding urban core that was hermetically sealed off from the suburbs. Instead, Burger portrayed the record as containing little or no evidence entitling the Detroit plaintiffs to metropolitan relief. The chief wrote, with "a single exception [when the Carver School District sent black high schoolers past a closer suburban high school to a more distant Detroit high school with state approval] there has been no showing that either the State or any of the 85 outlying districts engaged in activity that had a cross-district effect." The entire discussion was reduced to a single point: "the District Court's findings of the condition of segregation were limited to Detroit."[33]

Notwithstanding the fact that there were ten full trial days on the issue, the Supreme Court dispensed with the issue of residential segregation in a footnote. In it, the court minimized the extent to which Judge Roth's ruling was informed by the containment: "The District Court briefly alluded to the possibility that the State, along with private persons, had caused, in part, the housing patterns of the Detroit metropolitan area which, in turn, produced the predominantly white and predominantly Negro neighborhoods that characterize Detroit."[34] But the court said it was free to ignore that because the Sixth Circuit Court of Appeals, in affirming Roth, did not rely "at all upon testimony pertaining to segregated housing except as school construction programs helped cause or maintain such segregation."[35] "Accordingly, in its present posture, the case does not present any question concerning state housing violations," the chief justice concluded. Just like that, the housing evidence—crucial to understanding the containment, northern Jim Crow's essential ingredient—was out of the case.

Ignoring the containment was a choice the court made. With the housing evidence shunted to the side, the *Milliken* case was really about two utterly different versions of reality. In one version, white America had little or nothing to do with segregation in Detroit's schools and, by extension, school segregation in other urban areas. In another version of reality, one that echoed the Kerner Commission's findings, white America was responsible for northern Jim Crow. By "ignoring housing, the Supreme Court [in *Milliken*] began to lift from white America responsibility for the ghetto," the former Powell clerk and prominent conservative jurist J. Harvie Wilkinson III observed in his examination of the case.[36]

In the heart of the decision, the court roundly threw out the metropolitan remedy: it chastised the lower courts for rejecting a Detroit-only plan "because of their conclusion that total desegregation of Detroit would not produce the racial balance which they perceived as desirable."[37] It was this section of the opinion that had sparked the most debate among the justices during their deliberations.

In early drafts of his opinion for the majority, Burger argued at great length that the lower courts' main error was their quest to achieve a racially balanced school system in Detroit, a goal that could not be obtained without suburban involvement. In one draft he wrote, "To approve the remedy imposed by the District Court on these facts would make racial balance the constitutional objective and standard; a result not even hinted at in Brown I and Brown II, which held that the operation of dual school systems, not some hypothetical level of racial balance, is the constitutional violation to be remedied."[38] This was consistent with the arguments made by Frank Kelley on behalf of the state petitioners in his brief. Kelley portrayed the lower courts as unfaithful "to the Constitution and the binding precedents of this Court." Instead, their objective was to "use the law as a lever in attaining" their preferred "social goal."[39] And what was that goal? Racial balance. The lower courts' rulings that the defendants "had committed acts resulting in de jure segregation are mere makeweights designed to provide the legal window dressing for the achievement of multi-district racial balance," Kelley asserted in his brief.[40]

Several of the chief's colleagues, however, thought the chief was missing the forest for the trees. Sure, Judge Roth's emphasis on racial balance was incorrect, but that wasn't the real issue in the case. The key question—which the chief underemphasized—was the propriety of suburban involvement in a desegregation remedy where the constitutional violation took place solely within the city. One of Justice Blackmun's clerks framed the concern with the chief's early drafts: the "primary mistake committed below was not the preoccupation with racial balance as a goal, rather it was the legal assumption that district lines are simply artificial creatures of the state that can be disregarded whenever necessary."[41]

Along these lines, on June 3, 1974, Justice Rehnquist wrote a memo to the chief that stated: "As I told you on the telephone, I am with you in this case, and the following suggestions are designed only to make even more clear what I think is the basic thrust of your opinion—that without a cross-district violation, there cannot be a cross-district remedy."[42] Rehnquist was also concerned that the first draft of the *Milliken* opinion left the impression that a metropolitan remedy could be supported in any number of ways, including on a showing that the neighboring school districts were given "a meaningful opportunity . . . to present evidence or be heard on the propriety of a multidistrict remedy or on the question of constitutional violations by those neighboring districts."[43] Rehnquist clearly believed that such a standard was too low. The justice then proposed several editorial changes to "make even clearer" that "without a cross district violation, there cannot be a cross district remedy."

Two days later, Justice Powell wrote a more substantive—and pointed— memo to the chief.[44] Powell told the chief that *Milliken* was a test case meant to resolve two "burning issues of great public concern." First, could two or more school districts be "consolidated" to achieve desegregation? And, if so, could federal courts order "extensive interdistrict" busing to cure the constitutional violation? Powell believed Burger's opinion was inadequate to the task: "The draft opinion . . . deals summarily and not entirely clearly with the first of these issues. It does not mention transportation or busing at all."[45] Focusing on racial balance "misses the core issue," Powell continued.[46] The Virginian zeroed in on the constitutional violation: "The only violation found was by and within the Detroit district, namely, the operation there of a segregated school system."[47] So if the violation was confined to the city of Detroit, the remedy had to be, too.

Drawing on Solicitor General Bork's influential brief, Powell told the chief exactly where he stood. "I would hold expressly that there must be a finding that unlawful segregatory acts of a suburban school district have contributed substantially to the unlawful segregation of the city school district."[48] (In a memo to his boss, one of Justice Blackmun's law clerks later confirmed the importance of Bork's role in *Milliken*: "As I understand it, the conference voted to adopt the position taken by the S.G. in this case.")[49] But what rule of law, what legal doctrine required this new rule? It wasn't Michigan state law under which local school districts were state agencies. And it certainly wasn't the Fourteenth Amendment, which expressly constrained the actions of the states. Instead, Powell pointed to values, traditions. He wrote that "public education in this country has been organized around the concept of local control."[50] "The values of local school board autonomy and responsibility are fundamental," he added.[51]

In his *Keyes* opinion, Powell had written that "we should abandon [the de jure / de facto] distinction, which long since has outlived its time,"[52] but in his memo to the chief, he relied on it to put metropolitan desegregation out of judicial reach. Pointing to his recommendation that the court adopt a clear rule against interdistrict remedies, he wrote: "It is important to bear in mind the difference between states which, for historic and other reasons, practiced school segregation, and on the other hand states (of which Michigan may be one) in which there is no past history of segregated schools."[53]

Powell then pivoted to the Richmond case, comparing the outcome there to the Detroit litigation. Richmond, of course, was a split decision, with Powell recusing himself because of his long history as a school official in Virginia. But even there, in a jurisdiction with a long history of de jure segregation, a plurality of the court paid fealty to school district lines. Powell implied that if four members of the court had refused to allow federal courts to permeate school district lines to implement *Brown* in the South, how could the court even consider allowing federal courts to do so in the North? It appeared that Powell's flirtation with a single national standard was over.

The justice left little doubt about what he thought of the lower courts' work. The Sixth Circuit Court of Appeals had "denigrate[d] school districts as little more than lines on a map," which was "nonsense."[54] He claimed that the "decree approved by the courts below" was "radical."[55] The decree was "just about as absurd as any court decree I have ever read." Racial balance requirements had "no purpose except the neglect of quality education!"

In a private memo, Justice Blackmun had noted his anticipation that the Detroit case would be "terribly difficult" for Justice Powell "because of his long opinion in the Denver case [*Keyes*] arguing that the de jure–de facto distinction is not a valid one." But Powell's memo to the chief gave no sense that the justice was struggling with a difficult decision, that *Milliken* was a close case. Instead, its tone suggested a piece of advocacy intended to push the chief justice as hard as possible to draft an opinion that left no doubt whatsoever that interdistrict remedies were impermissible except in extraordinary circumstances. In his autobiography, Nathaniel Jones made this observation about the majority opinion's birth: "Research of the papers of Supreme Court justices revealed the role of Justice Lewis Powell in virtually taking over the drafting of the majority opinion from Chief Justice Warren Burger, following a memorandum-driven tug-of-war."[56] "It was as though the opinion were based on a different trial," he added.

Chief Justice Burger wrote several drafts of the *Milliken v. Bradley* opinion, seeking to satisfy the concerns of the four justices who had voted to reverse. The racial balance discussion remained a sticking point. One of Justice Blackmun's clerks wrote, "Justice Powell's earlier letter to the Chief has, for the most part gone unheeded. The major and overriding criticism . . . is the preoccupation with racial balance and the continual discussion of how the D.Ct erred in ordering 'racial balance.'"[57] On June 17, Justice Stewart wrote a memo to the chief raising the same concern: "I continue firmly to believe that 'racial balance' is not a question in this case, and that a discussion of that subject in the Court opinion will serve only to distract attention from the real issue."[58]

In mid-July, and with Burger having revised the opinion several times to minimize the racial balance discussion, Justice Rehnquist moved to neutralize the dissenters. In a memo, he wrote, our "dissenting Brothers White and Marshall take pains to demonstrate that state agencies participated in maintaining the dual school system found to exist in Detroit."[59] As Rehnquist characterized the dissenters' view, the suburban school districts' status as state, as opposed to local, units of government suggested that "the District Court should have a relatively free hand to reconstruct school districts outside of Detroit in fashioning relief."[60] Rehnquist *agreed* that the suburban school districts were state agencies. But that was irrelevant. What mattered was where the constitutional violation took place. The justice wrote, the "constitutional right of the Negro respondents residing in Detroit was to attend a unitary school system in that district. Unless the petitioners had drawn the district lines in a discriminatory fashion, or arranged for white students residing in the Detroit district to attend schools in Oakland and Macomb Counties, they were under no constitutional duty to make provision for black students to do so."[61]

The chief inserted Rehnquist's text, and his response to the dissenters, almost verbatim into the final draft he sent to his colleagues for review.[62] That same language appeared at the end of Part II of the official *Milliken v. Bradley* decision. It supported the court's holding—no interdistrict violation, no interdistrict remedy—quite nicely.[63]

Justice Stewart wrote a remarkable concurring opinion in the *Milliken* case. In it, he argued—incorrectly—that "no record has been made in this case showing that the racial composition of the Detroit school population or that residential patterns within Detroit and in the surrounding areas were in any significant measure caused by governmental activity." It was hard to read that assertion without shaking one's head in disbelief. It wiped out hundreds of hours of trial testimony, countless witnesses, the map. But even if this claim were accurate, which it wasn't, if government action didn't explain the racial makeup of Detroit's schools, what did? Here was the justice's answer: no one knew and it was probably impossible to find out. In a footnote, the justice wrote: "It is this essential fact of a predominantly Negro school population in Detroit—*caused by unknown and perhaps unknowable factors*, such as in-migration, birth rates, economic changes, or cumulative acts of private racial fears—that accounts for the 'growing core of Negro schools,' a 'core' that has grown to include virtually the entire city."[64]

As one of our nation's most important national institutions, the Supreme Court's view of the past helps construct Americans' beliefs about what they think actually happened (or didn't happen). Perhaps the best way to think about Justice Stewart's footnote was that it exemplified *Milliken's* "takeaway" narrative; the impression the reader was left with if all they knew about the Detroit case and its causes was what the Supreme Court told them. In that story, people lived where they did because of private choices and individual preferences. Racial separation in schools and housing was natural, unaffected by prejudice, race discrimination, or official government policy. The unspoken rationale behind Judge Roth's order was that suburban whites had benefited from generations of public and private racial discrimination; requiring them to participate in a metropolitan desegregation plan was only fair. But in Justice Stewart's story, the containment never happened. The only problem with Justice Stewart's story was that it had been conclusively refuted during a forty-one-day trial in Judge Roth's courtroom in downtown Detroit.

＝＝＝

Thurgood Marshall, having failed to persuade his colleagues to hold the case until the following term, was equal parts dejected and apoplectic. His dissent was elegiac. "After 20 years of small, often difficult steps . . . the Court today takes a giant step backwards," he wrote.[65] Black children in Detroit would "receive the same separate and unequal education in the future as they have been unconstitutionally afforded in the past," he added. His dissent was a statement of first principles: the overarching importance of education, the equality of opportunity, the promise of American citizenship, the fabric of the nation. As Marshall saw it, all were threatened by the court's ruling.

Marshall wrote: "We deal here with the right of all of our children, whatever their race, to an equal start in life and to an equal opportunity to reach their full potential as citizens."[66] This was Marshall's understanding of *Brown*: it protected nothing less than a right to equal educational opportunity and, through that right, to equal citizenship. *Brown*'s rule applied nationwide. Thus, his next sentence: "Those children [in Detroit] who have been denied that right in the past deserve better than to see fences thrown up to deny them that right in the future."

Fences. During the Jim Crow era, black children were confined to all-black schools. Southern fences typically divided children on the basis of race with respect to individual school assignments. The lesson of *Milliken* was that, absent extraordinary circumstances, children should attend school where they live. But because of residential segregation, black and other minority students were largely concentrated in the urban core or in separate suburban neighborhoods, and within those areas to separate school districts. But fences were fences, whether they were located at the school or the school district level. Either way, they were still fences. In effect, the highest court in the land told the nation that suburban school district lines could be used as fences to exclude blacks. This was what Justice Marshall was pointing out.

Then there were the perverse incentives the majority's ruling created, which doubled down on Michigan's discriminatory acts. Marshall wrote, "By limiting the District Court to a Detroit-only remedy and allowing [white] flight to the suburbs to succeed, the Court today allows the State to profit from its own wrong and to perpetuate for years to come the separation of the races it achieved in the past by purposeful state action."[67] *Milliken* provided whites who wanted to avoid school desegregation with a clear-cut exit strategy. All they had to do was leave the city, further undermining the ability of a "Detroit-only" desegregation plan to succeed. (Marshall thought such moves would be "forthcoming.") And, once whites moved to the suburbs, whatever ties they had to blacks in Detroit, by virtue of living in the same city, were severed. It wasn't exactly a recipe for a functioning multiracial democracy, as Justice Marshall noted: "Our Nation, I fear, will be ill served by the Court's refusal to remedy separate and unequal education, for unless our children begin to learn together, there is little hope that our people will ever learn to live together."[68]

Marshall's defense of Judge Roth was striking. The justice thought the court had done "a great disservice to the district judge."[69] Roth wasn't a liberal ideologue, hell-bent on imposing "his own philosophy of racial balance on the entire Detroit metropolitan area."[70] Instead, he was focused on curing the constitutional violation. Marshall wrote, "The District Court determined that interdistrict relief was necessary and appropriate only because it found that the condition of segregation within the Detroit school system could not be cured with a Detroit-only remedy. It is on this theory that the interdistrict relief must stand or fall." If anything, it was the justices in the majority who were the partisans, the judicial activists. The court's ruling was a "reflection of a perceived public mood" that the Constitution's promise of equal justice should go no further, Marshall charged.[71] *Milliken v. Bradley* was many things. But one thing it wasn't, he said, was "the product of neutral principles of law."

Justices Douglas and White also filed separate dissents. But in the end, there were still five votes to reverse Roth.

A new trial judge would be needed to oversee the implementation of a Detroit-only desegregation plan. The court's directive was clear: "the case is remanded for further proceedings consistent with this opinion," meaning no suburban school districts were to be included in the remedy.[72] At the same time, the lower court was expected to eliminate "the segregation found to exist in Detroit city schools, a remedy which has been delayed since 1970" in a school district that was approximately 75 percent black. On January 6, 1975, United States District Judge Robert E. DeMascio was chosen through random assignment to succeed Judge Roth. He was a Nixon appointee with, as the *Detroit Free Press* put it, "a reputation as a conservative law-and-order judge."[73] The judge's assignment would not be easy. Several years later, the Sixth Circuit would remark that DeMascio's task on remand was "extremely difficult (if not impossible.)"[74]

22

FENCES

Milliken's implications were clear immediately. On the day the decision was announced, Nate Jones issued a blistering press release accusing the court of turning the clock back to the days of *Plessy v. Ferguson*.[1] The decision was unfortunate, "not only for the thousands of black school children trapped in inner city schools, but also for the nation as a whole," the general counsel declared.

Jones zeroed in on the two sides' dueling narratives. The plaintiffs had presented "clear-cut evidence that the State of Michigan was wholly responsible for education in the state." But the court had "side-step[ped] these facts." Instead of focusing on Michigan's culpability for violating the constitutional rights of thousands of black schoolchildren—a determination that was never disturbed on appeal—the court moved the goalposts and "declared that it was not demonstrated that the suburban school districts were found to have been guilty of a constitutional violation." "We feel that this claim was specious and unfounded," Jones wrote.

Not only did the Supreme Court kill Judge Roth's metropolitan desegregation plan, but it made the standard for sustaining an interdistrict plan anywhere in the nation extraordinarily high. The day after the Supreme Court released its decision, *The New York Times* wrote that metropolitan desegregation plans, based on the ruling, could only be seen as justified where "discriminatory acts in one district produced segregation in the other, or where districts lines had been deliberately drawn to separate the races."[2]

Both requirements would be hard for the plaintiffs to meet. Showing that suburban school districts caused segregation in urban areas was difficult given that, as one commentator put it, "suburban school officials, who have as little as possible to do with their central city counterparts, can even less frequently be found responsible for the segregation in the central school system.[3] Showing that school district lines, which were typically drawn by the state, were deliberately racially gerrymandered wouldn't be much easier. This required proving intent, which was difficult. And in the Detroit case there was already a finding of de jure segregation against the state of Michigan. But that wasn't enough. Perhaps not surprisingly, *The New York Times* reported that civil rights attorneys believed that these requirements barred "metropolitan plans for all practical purposes."[4] Columnist William Raspberry agreed: "Busing across school district lines for purposes of racial integration is all but dead following the Supreme Court's ruling . . . in the Detroit case."[5]

———

The Supreme Court had remanded the Detroit case to the lower courts with a clear directive: desegregate Detroit's majority black school system. For DeMascio this meant evaluating the competing desegregation plans submitted by the parties, reviewing various desegregation techniques, transportation routes, bus travel times, the city's changing demography, and budgetary proposals for educational components such as remedial reading programs to ameliorate the effects of segregation, all in an attempt to establish effective desegregation in a school district that was roughly 26 percent white.[6]

On May 22, 1975, anticipating that he would issue a final desegregation plan prior to the start of the 1975–76 school year, DeMascio ordered the state to purchase 150 school buses to be used for integrating the Detroit school district.[7] The state took an immediate appeal to the United States Court of Appeals for the Sixth Circuit, where it received a frosty reception. A month later, the court reluctantly upheld DeMascio's order—"this court has no choice under [*Milliken*] . . . except to affirm"—although it did require the Detroit school board to cover 25 percent of the cost.[8] Joining the court's order was Judge Harry T. Edwards, who wrote a remarkable concurring opinion. Edwards had graduated from the University of Michigan Law School in 1965 with distinction, as the only black student in the entire school at the time.[9] After a stint as a management-side labor lawyer, in 1970 Edwards became Michigan's very first full-time, tenure-track African American professor, and from there had gone on to become a federal judge.[10]

The judge wrote that "conscience compel[led]" him to state his profound disagreement with the *Milliken v. Bradley* decision. Edwards believed that *Milliken's* single most important sentence was this: "The constitutional right of the Negro respondents residing in Detroit is to attend a unitary school system in that district."[11] He interpreted this to mean that an all-black urban school district surrounded by all-white suburban school systems was effectively constitutionally invisible. Such a situation appeared to raise "no problem of federal constitutional significance," the judge wrote. If this was true, "it can come to represent a formula for American apartheid."

This was strong language coming from a sitting federal appellate court judge. But he went further. "I know of no decision by the Supreme Court of the United States since the Dred Scott decision . . . which is so fraught with disaster for this country," he concluded.[12] This was a jaw-dropper. To the extent that commentators criticizing *Milliken* had reached back for doctrinal parallels, they tended to land on *Plessy v. Ferguson. Plessy*, of course, ushered in the era of "separate but equal." A majority black urban school system surrounded by vastly predominantly white suburban schools would seem to fit that bill. But *Dred Scott* was of a different order of magnitude: it famously held that blacks, whether enslaved or free, were not citizens of the United States.[13]

What did Edwards mean by "fraught with disaster for this country?" Perhaps the judge was referring to the distance between the court's ambition in *Dred Scott*, which was to constitutionalize the slavery issue, thereby taking it out of the political realm, and its result, which was to accelerate the onset of civil war. Or maybe his meaning was even simpler: *Milliken v. Bradley*, like *Dred Scott*, was one of the high court's worst decisions, one the court, and the nation, would come to regret.

In late June 1975, *The New York Times* reported that an intracity busing

order in Detroit was imminent.[14] The paper noted concerns on the ground
that such an order "would succeed only in driving even more whites out
of the system and thereby defeat the integration that busing is intended to
achieve." It reported that Coleman Young—who in 1974 became Detroit's
first black mayor—had submitted a brief to Judge DeMascio arguing that
a large-scale intracity busing order would "have the opposite effect of that
desired—schools will be resegregated instead of desegregated."

Others, too, predicted that the decision would accelerate white flight.
James Coleman, the Johns Hopkins sociologist who had authored the influential Coleman Report, believed it would, and that summer he released
a study asserting that in "districts with certain characteristics [such as being about 75 percent black] as in Detroit . . . the impact of full-scale desegregation would be . . . very large, moving the city's schools to nearly
all black in a single year."[15] But some experts disagreed. Responding to
Coleman, social scientist and school desegregation expert Gary Orfield offered a variety of data points that might have led a white family to depart
Detroit at that point in time. These included "the city's income tax, its 1967
riot, the extremely high level of violent crime, the cutbacks in the police
force, the controversial black mayor, the massive housing abandonment in
the city, the recent loss of more than a fifth of the city's job base, its severe
current economic crises, etc."[16] Given this and the lack of national survey
data, Orfield asserted that "it is impossible now to demonstrate that school
integration, in itself, causes substantial white flight."[17]

Perhaps there was some merit to both views. As John Logan, a prominent sociologist, told me in 2021, "Court ordered desegregation was a
modest stimulus to white flight at a national level, not typically reaching
the magnitude that some anticipated."[18] But he was careful to contextu-
alize that conclusion when it came to Detroit. "Detroit was already losing population, and especially white population, on a large scale before
desegregation. That makes it hard to say specifically how big a role desegregation played in the outcome." Still, whatever stimulus desegregation exerted, one way to blunt its effect would have been to break white
families' assumption that there would always be a nearby nonintegrated
safe haven to welcome them. An excellent way to do this was through a
metropolitan desegregation plan. Assessing the social science research on

white flight, law professor Myron Orfield concluded that the relationship between court-ordered desegregation and white flight was commonsensical: "The easier it was for whites to move to nearby all-white districts, the greater the level of flight. In areas where the white suburban school districts were relatively far away or where the suburbs were racially diverse, white flight declined sharply."[19]

After nine weeks of hearings, in mid-August 1975 DeMascio released a lengthy opinion adopting guidelines for a forthcoming remedial order that would desegregate Detroit's schools. Perhaps the most striking element of the opinion was its candor: meaningful desegregation in Detroit wasn't going to happen. It is impossible, the judge wrote, "to avoid having a substantial number of all black or nearly all black schools in a school district that is over 70% black."[20] *Milliken v. Bradley* left him with no choice. Later, the judge expressed his frustration: "If I could have used the suburbs, I could have had children walking to school. For example, Dearborn was 100 percent white. Detroit schools that were very close to the border, 70 to 90 percent black. It would have been so easy to reduce that by having the children walk to the schools."[21] Desegregation and busing weren't synonyms. Even if meaningful desegregation could have been achieved via the "walk in" school, it wasn't going to happen if it meant crossing school district lines. When everything else was stripped away, this was what the *Milliken* decision was all about. School district lines were fences; whites were on one side and blacks were on the other.

DeMascio's desegregation order had two major components. The first was a pupil reassignment plan that, through busing and rezoning, reassigned only about 10 percent of the Detroit school system's students.[22] The judge's plan was limited—it omitted about 80 percent of the system's black students—and did not call for widespread busing. The order excluded all of the schools in three of the Detroit school system's eight regions, those that had the highest concentration of black students. The judge believed that including them in the plan "would be futile" given their homogeneous racial composition—in 1970, they had all been more than 90 percent black.[23] The subject of whether regions 1, 5, and 8 were properly excluded from the student assignment plan was extensively litigated, with the Sixth Circuit Court of Appeals ruling several times that DeMascio had erred by omitting the schools in those regions. The last of these determinations was issued in 1980. There, the appellate court let its exasperation show. Senior Judge Harry Phillips wrote: "From the outset of this litigation . . . Judge DeMascio seems to have assumed that the inner-city regions must be treated in isolation from the rest of the district. Yet it was exactly this unitary treatment of regions 1, 5, and 8 that led us to reverse and remand the last time this case was before us."[24]

But, as an astute commentator later pointed out, the Sixth Circuit's real beef was with the Supreme Court. DeMascio was just saying the quiet part out loud: it was impossible to desegregate those regions because of their racial composition. The commentator wrote that the Sixth Circuit's frustration was one "that no court order or plan could remedy. When the Supreme Court erected a barrier to interdistrict reassignment of white and black students in 1974, it was all but inevitable that the racial composition of the entire Detroit school district would, over time, become the same as the racial mix in regions 1, 5 and 8 in 1970: 94% minority; 6% white . . . 30 years later in 2000, it did."[25] But another commentator was much more critical of DeMascio. Of the judge's student assignment plan, law professor Elwood Hain wrote in a lengthy analysis of the case that DeMascio's "over-riding concern for the interests of whites is apparent in the retention of majority white schools, the small number of pupils bused, and the number of blacks left in overwhelmingly black schools. Blacks bear a vastly disproportionate share of the inconvenience associated with desegregation."[26]

The other component of DeMascio's order recognized that segregation harmed black students. He ruled that the defendants were required to provide certain "educational components" to facilitate the transition to a desegregated school system and to "remedy [the] effects of past segregation."[27] Some of the components were clearly designed to raise Detroit students' academic achievement, such as comprehensive reading instruction. "Minority students lag significantly behind their white counterparts in reading skills, which in turn affects [their] ability . . . to follow written instructions, succeed on aptitude tests, pass entrance examinations for colleges and universities and compete in the world of arts, sciences, occupations and skills," the judge observed.[28] Others were designed to eradicate a racially discriminatory school environment and to facilitate the process of desegregation, including teacher training programs, provisions for student counseling and career guidance, and the elimination of discriminatory testing. "While it is true that the delivery of quality desegregated educational services is the obligation of the school board, nevertheless the court deems it essential to mandate educational components where they are needed to remedy effects of past segregation, to assure a successful desegregative effort and minimize the possibility of resegregation," the judge wrote. DeMascio ordered the state and local defendants to split the costs of the educational components.

The state officials appealed this part of DeMascio's order, and the *Milliken v. Bradley* case returned to the U.S. Supreme Court for a second time in 1977. They argued that the remedy—the educational components—exceeded the scope of the violation which was segregating black students within the city of Detroit.[29] From the officials' perspective, federal judges only had the power to remedy the constitutional violation, no more and no less—and that was segregation on the basis of race. Given that, they asserted that the federal court's desegregation order had to be limited to, as the Supreme Court later characterized their position, "remedying unlawful pupil assignments."[30]

In a decision that came to be known as *Milliken II*, the Supreme Court unanimously rejected the state officials' argument. The lower courts had long included in desegregation orders elements other than student reassignments, such as faculty and staff desegregation requirements, remedial education programs, in-service training for teachers, and curricular offerings designed to compensate for the harms of segregation. Detroit was no different. Consequently, the court ruled that the state officials—effectively the state of Michigan—must pay its fair share of the costs of the educational components.

Chief Justice Burger, again writing for the court in *Milliken II*, noted that segregation isolated black children: "Children who have been thus educationally and culturally set apart from the larger community will inevitably acquire habits of speech, conduct, and attitudes reflecting their cultural isolation. They are likely to acquire speech habits, for example, which vary from the environment in which they must ultimately function."[31] It was an interesting observation. On the one hand, the statement acknowledged that segregation harmed black children. On the other hand, the court's focus on "speech, conduct and attitudes" and none of segregation's other ill effects carried a negative implication. It suggested that there was something wrong with the way black children behaved. With its emphasis on deficiency, the chief justice's statement validated the conclusion that black children were to be avoided. What rational parent would want to send her child to a school where her peers had irregular speech habits and other markers of isolation, deficit, and inadequacy?

Assessing *Milliken II*, Nate Jones highlighted the positive. In his autobiography, he wrote: "*Milliken II* provided needed benefits to all children in the urban district . . . The court did what the political branches in Michigan had refused to do—support the rights of minority children to receive quality education."[32] But in evaluating the success of "*Milliken II* remedies" across the nation almost two decades after the decision was handed down, Gary Orfield was less sanguine.[33] First, district courts implementing such plans did not insist on extensive monitoring or oversight of the results. Because of this there was "no way to tell whether the programs are actually benefiting children."[34] Next, because the funding was not permanent there was no guarantee that any of the quality education programs the funds supported would remain. The temporary nature of *Milliken II* remedies undercut their ability to address long-standing structural inequalities.[35] Finally and relatedly, *Milliken II* remedies—the money—wasn't always spent in ways that directly helped black children. Continued receipt of *Milliken* money wasn't conditioned on increased student achievement or provision of additional educational opportunities.[36] This raised questions about *Milliken II* remedies' true purpose. Was the money a short-term sanction for the defendants' bad acts, or was it intended to develop quality education for black children even under conditions of segregation? Orfield's assessment pointed to the former. He argued that cash-strapped school districts like Detroit often used *Milliken* money for "things the district wanted to do anyway."[37]

At a total cost of $238 million, the Detroit school system received *Milliken II* remedies for twelve years; the case formally closed in 1989.[38] Later, Judge Avern Cohn, one of the judges who presided over the case during its later stages, remarked: "These monies were insignificant considered in light of the school district's budget . . . and were insufficient to serve as an incentive for real change."[39] Gary Orfield agreed. Writing after the end of the 1992–93 school year, he noted that Detroit students scored well below average on statewide educational assessment tests. Detroit students were vastly less likely than other Michiganders to meet the satisfactory standard in every single grade level tested. While acknowledging that achievement gaps between urban and suburban districts occurred for "a variety of complex reasons," Orfield believed that the remedies in Detroit were ineffectual: "Blatant inequities remained after the removal of the *Milliken II* remedies," he concluded.[40] Paul Dimond affirmed the social scientist's view, telling me in 2021 that he considers the *Milliken II* remedies "'guilt money' payment[s] from the State to the Detroit Schools."[41]

After *Milliken II* it was clear that compensatory education programs— even very expensive ones—could be included in desegregation orders. But the ruling didn't change the fact that the children of southeast Michigan would attend racially segregated schools. In fact, by authorizing payments to segregated school systems, *Milliken II* affirmed that separateness was at the core of *Milliken I*.

Looking at the results of *Milliken I* and *Milliken II* as a pair brought an earlier era to mind, that of "separate but equal." During that period, the reality for most black children was that they received a racially separate education that rarely was equal to that of their white counterparts. From a certain perspective, the *Milliken I–Milliken II* combination was an updated twist on an old formula, one the court supposedly discarded in *Brown v. Board of Education*.

Maybe this was an overstatement, a slur on the highest court in the land. Justice William O. Douglas didn't think so. Dissenting in *Milliken I*, he reached a similar conclusion. *Milliken I*, he argued, looked back to a supposedly vanquished era. He wrote: "When we rule against the metropolitan area remedy we take a step that will likely put the problems of the blacks and our society back to the period that antedated the 'separate but equal' regime of Plessy v. Ferguson."[42] Was this hyperbole? After all, *Plessy* authorized the government to *require* racial segregation in all public accommodations—including education—by law. *Plessy* greenlit Jim Crow. *Milliken I*, in contrast, merely limited the scope of the remedy available to prevailing plaintiffs who had proven that the government violated *Brown*.

But that wasn't how Douglas saw it once he added *San Antonio School District v. Rodriguez* to the mix. *Rodriguez*, the justice asserted, stood for the proposition that "the poorer school districts must pay their own way."[43] *Milliken I* meant separate schools; *Rodriguez* meant unequal ones. *Milliken I* and *Rodriquez*, taken together, mean "that there is no violation of the Equal Protection Clause though the schools are segregated by race and though the black schools are not only 'separate' but 'inferior.'"[44] By offering short-term compensation to those inferior schools but no structural remedy, *Milliken II* only strengthened this conclusion.

When the Detroit case began in August 1970, six-year-old Ronald Bradley was just about to start kindergarten at Clinton Elementary. At that time, the school was 97 percent black.[45] By the late summer of 1976—and after the Supreme Court's first ruling in the Detroit case—Bradley, now a rising sixth grader, was still attending Clinton. The school was 99 percent black. Clinton, located in region 5 on Detroit's northwest side, along with 155 other schools that were virtually or all black, was not included in the intracity desegregation plan that DeMascio approved.[46] Bradley and other children like him gained little from the Detroit litigation. In early 1976, the disappointed youngster told a reporter for *The Detroit News*: "I wanted to be bussed."[47] Ronald's mother was also saddened. Even after the first *Milliken* ruling, Verda Bradley still hoped that a metropolitan desegregation plan might be possible. "When the children start going to school together the parents will be willing to live together," she stated.[48]

Frustrated with the lack of educational quality at Clinton, in 1977 Bradley enrolled Ronald in St. Theresa-Visitation Catholic School, located on Detroit's west side. Ultimately, however, the cost of the tuition was too high, and she removed her son from the parochial school after just a year and a half. Ronald then enrolled in Cass Tech High School, but soon dropped out. (He later earned a GED.) By the age of seventeen, he was ready to turn the page on the Detroit school case. The teenager wanted anonymity. "All my life, people have kept asking me what I did to get my name in the paper," Ronald told a reporter for *The Detroit News*.[49] "I've had a lot of explaining to do. I'm just glad for it to be all over."

In 1980, the *Detroit Free Press* ran a postmortem on the NAACP's effort to desegregate Detroit's schools. The article, written by Stephen Franklin and titled "Award for Plaintiffs in Desegregation Suit: Frustration, Anger," wasn't an easy read.[50] In effect, the piece concluded that Detroit's schools were both segregated and poorly resourced, separate and unequal. The named plaintiffs, Franklin wrote, got "far less than most had hoped for." Ray Litt was deeply disappointed. He told the reporter that "the court suit was what I really wanted. We cannot live in a separate society." Jeanne Goings was in her early teens when the lawsuit was filed. At twenty-three, she no longer believed in integration. "Back in those times, busing was considered good," she stated. "Now I don't think it is the case anymore. I don't think integration is the answer. The basic answer lies with the teacher and the school system." Marcus and Grace Burden's children had also been named plaintiffs in the lawsuit. Grace Burden felt she had little to show for it. "I know they poured money into the schools. But if there were any improvements, I don't know of any," she remarked. A resigned Verda Bradley was philosophical. "I'm glad it happened," she offered. "Maybe people should have been doing it a little more, a little earlier. I'm just sorry I didn't get involved much sooner. It could have been better for my kids."

23

THE CONSEQUENCES

J ust after *Milliken I* came down, *The New York Times* reported "gloom among civil rights activists." They were particularly concerned that the decision would undermine a bucket of lawsuits pending throughout the country "that would have forced black inner-city districts to exchange pupils with white suburban ones."[1] They were right to worry. Assessing the post-*Milliken* landscape, Gary Orfield explained that the Detroit case "had been exhausting and very expensive, and its loss was discouraging. Almost immediately the steam went out of plans to press for metropolitan solutions in a number of older cities."[2] Educational policy expert Charles T. Clotfelter agreed: after *Milliken*, interracial contact was achieved "through federal courts using radically modified school assignments within existing school districts."[3] It would have been strange if it were otherwise. *Milliken's* take-home message was that metropolitan desegregation was *presumptively invalid*.

This raised a fundamental and very difficult question: Did the NAACP's litigation strategy, which ultimately failed, actually make things worse? Perhaps the *Milliken* case should never have been brought at all. Or, if the NAACP legal team thought it imperative to bring the lawsuit, perhaps a more limited case was in order. The Bradley plaintiffs could have focused their lawsuit narrowly on Act 48—which gutted the April 7 high school integration plan—challenging it alone. Even the act's chief sponsor, Coleman Young, thought that portion of the law was unconstitutional. But according to Dimond, Lucas thought a broader approach was necessary from the beginning. He wrote that Lucas was wary that "the case against Act 48 might well depend on proof and findings of pre-existing illegal school segregation; [Lucas] also suggested that a broader case could and should be made against the Detroit school board to ensure actual desegregation."[4]

The plaintiffs' key decision was broadening the case by targeting segregation throughout the whole of the Detroit school system, which opened the housing door. The housing evidence came in, initially, for a very specific purpose: to convince the judge that, per Dimond, "the school authorities should not get off scot-free by arguing that they only incorporated residential segregation through an allegedly neutral system of neighborhood pupil assignments."[5] But once they did this, the difficulty of the case increased exponentially. "The Detroit school case had no firm legal precedent," Dimond wrote.[6] In fact, the controlling federal law in Michigan, supplied by *Deal v. Cincinnati Board of Education*, presumed that racially identifiable northern schools raised no constitutional concerns. The plaintiffs had to convince a court *why* that was not so. And proving that *why* required opening the Pandora's box of residential segregation—in a school case. What emerged from that box was a multiheaded Hydra: numerous public and private bad actors, multiple and overlapping time frames, and a geographic scope that exceeded the jurisdictional boundaries of the city of Detroit. *This was the containment.*

The plaintiffs did a brilliant job of explicating the containment. They put northern Jim Crow on trial for all to see. And they won. At the same time, they made a series of strategic decisions that in hindsight they might have made differently *if they had known how it would all turn out*. Dimond candidly admitted that the litigation team, preoccupied with establishing liability, lacked "a clear idea at the outset" of the appropriate remedy.[7] And then, once the case reached the Sixth Circuit, he confessed that the trial team "still [had not] articulated our basic conception of an areawide violation with clarity."[8] Did the plaintiffs err before that court when they "downplayed, but did not omit, the housing proof that had played such a critical role in the trial court"?[9] This decision, in particular, enabled the Sixth Circuit to sidestep the implications of the housing evidence—except as it pertained to school construction—while still affirming Judge Roth's determination that the defendants had violated the Constitution. And this, in turn, facilitated the ability of the Supreme Court to relegate the extraordinarily important issue of residential segregation to a footnote.

But it was important to put this information in context. When the Bradley plaintiffs first filed the federal lawsuit in mid-August 1970, their main objective was establishing a *Brown* violation in the North. This was an issue upon which the Supreme Court had not yet spoken, but one that activists had been pushing for years. The court ultimately provided a plaintiff-friendly answer to that question in the *Keyes* case—*in late June of 1973*. But by then, the Detroit case, with the exception of Supreme Court review, was over.

By the time the Detroit plaintiffs got to the high court, the liability question that had so bedeviled them early on was no longer a serious issue; *Keyes* had resolved it. This put the propriety of metropolitan relief front and center.[10] And it was here that some of the trial team's decisions came back to haunt them. Per Dimond, those decisions included postponing "active consideration of the metropolitan issue in Detroit" on the theory that the Richmond, Virginia, case was a "better vehicle for raising the metropolitan issue," and failing to define with specificity the "exact nature of the violation that would call for an areawide remedy for Detroit only segregation." Way back on September 4, 1970, and before he became an official member of the Detroit trial team, Nick Flannery had advised Nate Jones against a "conventional desegregation suit" in Detroit.[11] Flannery thought the issue of metropolitan desegregation was inescapable in the case. And if that were true, best to face it at the outset. "I recommend that you consider metropolitan relief," he urged.[12] In hindsight, it was clear that the lawyer offered sound advice. After all, as Flannery noted, "the educational and housing discrimination facts support[ed] it and . . . the state has already intruded itself." Then again, it was unclear that facing the metropolitan issue earlier rather than later would have led to a different result. In that same letter, Flannery—ever prescient—correctly predicted that the U.S. Supreme Court would not uphold metropolitan relief.

Even after one acknowledged the trial team's fallibility, their misjudgments didn't provide an adequate explanation for the outcome in *Milliken v. Bradley*. The blame for that lay squarely with the court, not with the counsel. Indeed, nothing precluded the Supreme Court from considering the full significance of the containment. The fact that the Sixth Circuit did not explicitly rely on the housing evidence (except when it came to school construction, which was areawide) didn't tie the high court's hands. Supreme Court rules allowed respondents to advance—and for the court to consider—any argument raised in the lower courts, even if those courts had not relied on it or even rejected it.[13] And this is exactly what Nate Jones and company highlighted *on the very first page* of their brief to the court.

According to the respondents, this was the question before the U.S. Supreme Court: "May the State of Michigan continue the intentional confinement of black children to an expanding core of state-imposed black schools within a line, in a way no less effective than intentionally drawing a line around them, merely because petitioners seek to interpose an existing school district boundary as the latest line of containment?"[14] The respondents argued that Michigan and Detroit, acting through their school authorities, had intentionally segregated black from white children in Detroit schools and had "successfully undertaken to confine black children to a nucleus of black schools surrounded by a reciprocal ring of white schools in Detroit and the suburbs."[15] This, then, was the respondents' theory at the U.S. Supreme Court: *the constitutional violation itself was areawide.* The containment was the basis of Judge Roth's ruling, they argued. "All of the proof about areawide housing segregation, the racial identification of a set of separate schools for blacks, segregative school construction, and the discriminatory process of racial ghettoization was marshaled in the brief to inform this vision," Dimond wrote.[16] "If the Court chose to understand the nature of the violation as a color line of containment, we would prevail," he added.[17]

And, even if the court was unpersuaded by the plaintiffs' relatively new articulation of the nature of the violation, nothing precluded it from ordering a "remand." This would have meant sending the case back to the courts below to further develop the record on the issue of state and local culpability for housing segregation and its relationship to the racial makeup of Detroit's—and suburban—schools. But as J. Harvie Wilkinson III rightly observed, there was absolutely no need to do so.[18] Acknowledging the reality of the containment should have shifted the defaults. Courts with cases like the Detroit lawsuit should have begun with the presumption that state and local defendants were at fault, the judge argued. He wrote: "The ultimate question was why blacks should undergo the delay, effort, and expense of proving past segregative practices, in either schools or housing. Where segregation existed, residentially or educationally, was there not a presumption of prior state complicity which it, not black plaintiffs, was obliged to explain?"

Writing the year after the case was handed down, William Taylor argued that in order for the plaintiffs to establish the predicate for an interdistrict remedy, they needed to "flood the zone" with evidence of the containment.[19] This was hard to accept given the amount of containment evidence introduced in Judge Roth's courtroom. According to Taylor, if future plaintiffs wanted metropolitan relief, they needed to develop "an overwhelming factual record demonstrating continuing racial constraints on minority advancement—a record exceeding normal requirements in even complex equity cases." What would it take to prove that water was wet?

=====

Even as the *Milliken* plaintiffs weighed the reasons for the defeat of the metropolitan remedy in Detroit, that remedy lived on elsewhere, although typically in unique situations. As the U.S. Commission on Civil Rights observed, lower federal courts tended to find interdistrict violations sufficient to justify metropolitan relief where the case rested "on factual circumstances somewhat special to the districts involved."[20] One such case was *Evans v. Buchanan. Evans*, one of the lawsuits pending at the time *Milliken* was decided—which *The New York Times* had noted—concerned school segregation in Wilmington, Delaware.

Delaware responded to the *Brown v. Board of Education* decision by instituting a program of "gradual desegregation."[21] (Delaware, which had required that its schools be segregated by law, was one of the original parties to the *Brown* litigation.) What this really meant was resistance and foot-dragging.[22] In 1968, the state passed the Education Advancement Act.[23] Ostensibly an education modernization measure, the statute allowed the state board of education to reorganize and consolidate contiguous school districts statewide.[24] There was a notable exception, however: the majority black Wilmington school district, which was located in the northeastern portion of predominantly white New Castle County.[25] The effect of the state law was to isolate the city school district, which had the largest black population in the county, and prevent it from merging with any suburban school district.[26] One commentator observed that state law not only perpetuated the prior dual school system, but also encouraged "the process of black ghettoization in Wilmington and whites-only development of the suburbs."[27]

Seeking to bring the state into compliance with *Brown*, in 1971 black plaintiffs reopened the lawsuit that had culminated in the *Brown* decision. This was *Evans v. Buchanan*; Lou Lucas later became chief counsel.[28] At trial, the plaintiffs presented a case that looked much like the one litigated in Detroit. Copious evidence of interrelated housing and school segregation was at the core of each case. But one difference stood out. In Delaware, the plaintiffs could point to a state statute that directly regulated school district lines for the purpose of confining black students to an urban school system, thereby keeping the suburban schools white.[29] If ever there was an example of interdistrict violation, this was it. The Third Circuit Court of Appeals later affirmed the federal trial court's metropolitan remedy.[30]

A case in Louisville, Kentucky, also presented a rare chance for metropolitan desegregation. In late 1974, the Sixth Circuit upheld an interdistrict remedy, reasoning that the factual backgrounds in metropolitan Louisville and metropolitan Detroit were meaningfully different. For one thing, the Louisville city school district *and* the suburban Jefferson County school district had committed acts of de jure school segregation. In Michigan, there was no finding that the outlying suburban school districts themselves had committed de jure segregation. As the Sixth Circuit put it, "as contrasted with the outlying Michigan districts, they [the Louisville and Jefferson County school districts] are guilty of maintaining dual school systems."[31] The appellate court pointed to another "crucial difference" between the two cases: the disregard of school district lines to maintain and perpetuate segregation. In one situation, black high school students were transported out of the Jefferson County school district—which had no black high school—and into the Louisville school district so that they could attend "the black Central High School."[32] And this was not an isolated incident. Instead, school district lines were crossed in "by far the two largest districts located in the geographical boundaries of Jefferson County."[33] Finally, while the *Milliken* case involved more than fifty suburban school districts in addition to the Detroit system, in Louisville only a handful of school districts were affected. This meant a metropolitan order there would raise far fewer administrative difficulties. The Louisville and Jefferson County school districts merged into one metropolitan school system shortly after the court's ruling.[34] What followed was one of the most successful metropolitan desegregation plans in the history of the United States.

The two cases taken together suggested that *Milliken's* standard was more easily satisfied in formerly de jure segregated locales where there was substantial evidence that governmental authorities had crossed school district lines to foment segregation. This meant that obtaining metropolitan desegregation in the North would remain more difficult than in the South. This was true for another reason as well. *Milliken* was premised on the inviolability of school district lines. In the North, because of municipal incorporation rules and other legal regulations, it was easier "for residents to create small suburban municipalities,"[35] as one scholar put it. These smaller suburban localities tended to have their own school districts. *Milliken*, of course, provided them with a highly effective shield against desegregation.

But the situation was different in the South. There, larger units of municipal government such as counties, which had their own dedicated school districts, prevailed.[36] *Milliken* changed nothing when it came to *within district* desegregation. This set up a paradox, which Gary Orfield pithily explained: "Much of the South can be desegregated under the one-district principle, but the largest urban centers of the North cannot."[37] In fact, during the 1970s and 1980s, only fifteen metropolitan-level desegregation plans were implemented in the United States, the vast majority of which were in southern or border states.[38] Of those fifteen, only three came as a result of a court finding that the *Milliken* standard had been satisfied.[39] And of those three cases where courts found *Milliken* violations and ordered city-suburban desegregation, only one was in the North; the other two were in the border states of Delaware and Kentucky.[40] The result was that black children received very different levels of constitutional protection based solely on their address. The Detroit school system was de jure segregated—just like southern school systems. In the South, de jure segregation meant desegregation. But in the North, it didn't. That was *Milliken*.

Of course, *Milliken* could have been worse. It didn't overturn *Brown*. *Brown* was still a fixed star in the constitutional constellation, a source of pride for jurists and Americans of many stripes. *Brown* was a famous case. It stated an important principle, and the children of Detroit would learn about it in school. But what did *Brown* mean to Detroit's children and others like them? What did it mean in practice to the middle schooler who wrote Remus Robinson back in 1970, who wanted "an equal education just like the white students are getting"? That student feared that "as long as we stay separated we are not going to get anywhere in this world." And for her, *Milliken* meant that an integrated school was essentially out of reach. It brought Albert Cleage to mind, validating his belief that whites were at best uninterested in and at worst unremittingly hostile to the interests of black youth.

In the South, meanwhile, where school districts often were coextensive with county lines, *Brown* still had the power to force whites to share their resources. This helped explain the news coming out of Charlotte-Mecklenburg County, which had been the subject of the *Swann* decision. Encompassing North Carolina's largest city, its surrounding suburbs, and more than one hundred elementary, middle, and high schools, the county's school system was truly metropolitan.[41] By 1975, an ambitious desegregation plan was in place. Consistent with the *Swann* ruling, it used a variety of techniques, including geographic zoning, pairing black and white schools, magnets, and busing, to integrate the county's schools. Crucially, the plan bused minority children to the suburbs and white children to the city.[42] Absent extraordinary circumstances, this was impossible in Detroit and other northern cities. But in the South, with no school district lines to cross, the buses rolled. One scholarly assessment noted that the result was both "high levels of racial balance that were achieved in the 1970s and early 1980s, and according to the best available information, improved educational outcomes."[43]

In Charlotte-Mecklenburg County, this court-ordered school desegregation ended up helping to reduce residential segregation in the county, too.[44] This shouldn't have been a surprise. In *Swann* itself, the Supreme Court had recognized the tight, symbiotic relationship between school and housing segregation. If building new schools in suburban areas "farthest from Negro population centers" might "promote residential segregation," then the converse held as well.[45] Myron Orfield put it this way: "In areas with metropolitan-level integration, residential integration increased faster and there was much less evidence of housing discrimination by real estate agents than in areas without such integration. Instead of steering families to certain neighborhoods based on schools, agents were more likely to say that all neighborhoods had good schools."[46]

Given this, perhaps *Milliken* was just a bad ruling that undermined northern desegregation, but one that thankfully did not apply nationwide. But what would happen when the de jure era ended, and the South began to look more like the rest of the nation? What would happen when whites in southern jurisdictions sought some form of separation or succession from larger municipalities?[47] What would happen when federal courts declared southern school districts "unitary," meaning that they had recovered from their history of de jure segregation, and then withdrew judicial oversight? Then what?

Perhaps the best way to think about *Milliken*'s impact was by imagining a counterfactual: How might the world have looked if the court had gone the other way? *Milliken* was an anti–racial integration decision, an anti–metropolitan desegregation decision. Now imagine if the court had been serious about enforcing—rather than negating—*Brown*'s promise. Law professor Robert A. Sedler did exactly that. Having served as lead counsel for the plaintiffs in the Louisville-Jefferson County case, he knew what he was talking about.[48] After *Keyes*, proving that a school district, North or South, had violated the Constitution was no longer a significant stumbling block. And, at the time, blacks were largely concentrated in urban areas, with whites safely ensconced in the suburban realm. This meant that intracity desegregation orders wouldn't produce meaningful desegregation.

Against this background, Sedler argued that "if the Court had accepted the theory of metropolitan desegregation advanced by the [Detroit] plaintiffs . . . metropolitan desegregation would have become the *norm* in many of the Nation's metropolitan areas."[49] But today, just the opposite is true. When it was all said and done, this was what *Milliken* was all about.

———

In early 1976, Derrick Bell, a former civil rights attorney and Harvard Law School's first black tenured law professor, published in *The Yale Law Journal* what would become an enormously influential article, "Serving Two Masters: Integration Ideals and Client Interests in School Desegregation Litigation." Today, "Serving Two Masters" has been cited hundreds if not thousands of times and has appeared on countless college and law school syllabi. In it, Bell argued that the "great crusade to desegregate the public schools has faltered."[50] To blame, he wrote, were rising public antipathy to desegregation, federal courts that had retreated from protecting civil rights plaintiffs, and an "increasing number of social science studies [that] question[ed] the validity of [desegregation's] educational assumptions."

Bell asserted that none of that mattered to civil rights lawyers like Nate Jones, whom he expressly referred to in the article.[51] These lawyers, blinded by an evergreen commitment to implement *Brown*, persisted in a misbegotten effort to achieve "racial balance measures." Again and again, Bell portrayed the "established civil rights organizations" as preoccupied, if not obsessed, with forcing white children into black classrooms. The lawyers' ultimate goal, said Bell, was "racial balance," not improving black schools.[52] What the lawyers were effectively doing, Bell argued, was ignoring their own clients.

The civil rights lawyers and the families whose rights they were defending had different objectives. The lawyers had "convinced themselves that *Brown* stands for desegregation and not education," Bell asserted.[53] The lawyers' quest for desegregation was symbolic rather than instrumental. If achieved, it would signal "the nation's commitment to equal opportunity."[54] In contrast, their clients wanted something real: "education-oriented remedies" and more effective black schools.[55] In short, Bell argued that the civil rights lawyers weren't adequately representing their clients' interests. This raised ethical concerns, undermining the lawyers' "basic professional obligation[s]," and eroding the duty to display "ethical sensitivity and self-restraint."[56] These were serious charges.

Far less well-known than "Serving Two Masters" was Jones's response to it, which also was published in *The Yale Law Journal* a few months later.[57] What played out was an extraordinary debate between the two men, both destined to become civil rights legends. On the question of negative public reaction to desegregation, Jones cited the Constitution. Public opinion didn't determine the scope of constitutional guarantees, Jones argued, and it would be problematic if it did.[58] Jones also asserted that public opinion itself had been manipulated. But Bell ignored "the factors that have created his negative public climate." Jones accused the Harvard professor of capitulation rather than resistance, which must have stung. Bell's "prescription is to switch rather than fight," Jones declared.

"Serving Two Masters" clearly indicted civil rights lawyers, but in doing so Jones believed that Bell was punching sideways rather than up. The problem wasn't the NAACP; it was school board lawyers who used public money to deprive black children of their constitutional rights, white mobs "agitated by antibusing statements," and the president of the United States, who egged them on.[59]

Jones rejected the "desegregation versus educational quality" frame that Bell had adopted. Bell wrote as if the lawyers were breathlessly litigating desegregation cases when they should have been raising federal claims on behalf of their clients for quality education instead. But there was no federal constitutional right to quality education, Jones shot back. Another case, *San Antonio Independent School District v. Rodriguez*, had proved it. What black children did have a right to was outlined in *Brown* and its progeny. And so this was where the NAACP had been active. Jones noted that successful school desegregation cases could in fact produce "educational components" "necessary to repair the effects of past discrimination, ensure a successful desegregation effort, and minimize the possibility of resegregation."[60] The Detroit case's second trip to the Supreme Court confirmed that this was true.

On *Brown*, Jones unleashed a zinger: "The courts until now have evidently understood, as Professor Bell apparently has not, that segregation is itself the deepest educational harm because it is the result of institutional racism and a condition of state-imposed racial caste."[61] Although this was a generous reading of *Brown* and the other school segregation cases (they never explicitly mentioned racial caste), on the effect of segregation, Jones was right on the money. White students, clustered in high-opportunity schools and neighborhoods, were like winners at the poker table. They sat back and raked in the advantages. This was how a caste system was perpetuated. Jones countered Bell's assertion that civil rights lawyers were unconcerned about improving black schools, firing back: "With integrated schools it is much more difficult to subordinate blacks as a group through unequal or inadequate school resources. Blacks have learned that 'green follows White.' With desegregation—and white children being reassigned to previously black schools—also comes new resources."[62] In this, Nate Jones and Verda Bradley were in violent agreement.

This argument had empirical support. Black children benefited *enormously* from school desegregation in the South. Later research confirmed that, compared to black students in still segregated school districts, black children in desegregated school districts had better educational outcomes, completed more years of higher education, and attended more selective colleges.[63] And the benefits didn't stop there; school desegregation improved black students' lives for years to come. As adults, black children who had attended desegregated schools received superior wages and annual earnings, had higher rates of marital stability, had less exposure to the criminal justice system, and were in better health, because they had lower rates of disease and obesity.[64] In fact, the advantages of desegregation even extended to the children of black Americans who attended integrated schools, enhancing intergenerational upward mobility.[65] It was the gift that kept on giving.

What explained this enormous positive impact on black students? The short answer was money. Southern school authorities, faced with the requirement that they integrate not just children but school facilities and services, had to determine how to fund their newly integrated schools. In most cases they "leveled up" school funding so that desegregated schools would get the same or similar resources as the all-white schools had previously received.[66] In this way, desegregation made it more difficult for whites to hoard educational resources.

The resource reallocations benefited black children. Per-pupil spending went up, teacher salaries increased, instructional time rose, and class sizes shrank.[67] But on top of that, desegregation was a "two-fer." As black students benefited, white students experienced none of the drawbacks that segregationists predicted. Instead, racially diverse schools also better prepared white students to function in a multiracial environment, reduced white bias, and lowered intergroup prejudice.[68]

In 2022, several researchers published an extraordinary, first-of-its-kind study assessing court-ordered integration's impacts on minority children.[69] Never before had researchers had access to such a comprehensive data set. Using Census and American Community Survey data, birth dates, Social Security numbers, and other inputs, the researchers observed "both the childhood geographic locations and adult human capital and labor market outcomes for several million individuals who were attending school in the period when major desegregation orders were being rolled out."[70] They found that black students in the South were strongly positively affected by court-ordered desegregation, which "increased high school graduation rates by approximately 15 percentage points, increased employment rates by approximately 10 percentage points, and increased hourly wages by approximately 30%."[71] The researchers were careful to cabin their findings, however. In the South, black students experienced "qualitatively quite large" positive impacts from court ordered desegregation. But in the North, the effects of court-ordered desegregation for black students were "indistinguishable from zero."[72] Why might that have been? The researchers offered several potential explanations, but chief among them was one that spoke directly to Detroit's experience: the "nature and intensity of white resistance to integration orders in the North may well have contributed to these regional differences as well, with the close proximity of racially homogeneous suburban districts and relatively affordable private school alternatives facilitating large scale white flight and mitigating the benefits of desegregation activity."[73]

If the real differentiator for better educational and other life outcomes was money, both Cleage and Bell might have asked, Why bother with desegregation at all? Why not simply invest more resources in schools that served children of color and leave it at that? But labor economist and school inequality expert Rucker Johnson disagreed. In his book *Children of the Dream: Why School Integration Works*, coauthored with Alexander Nazaryan, he observed that "funding increases that flowed from the desegregation plan were far less effective when they were not coupled with actual desegregation efforts."[74] The statement was curious. Was the economist reviving the old canard that black students were internally deficient, that they needed to sit next to white kids to learn? Hardly. But one had to focus on race and poverty simultaneously to understand what he meant.

As sociologist Sean F. Reardon explained, "high-poverty schools provide, on average, lower educational opportunity than low-poverty schools."[75] Children who came to school hungry often had difficulty concentrating. Homeless children, who moved frequently, arrived stressed or missed school entirely. If they fell behind, they often had difficulty catching up. Students were more frequently exposed to environmental hazards in low-income than middle-class areas—hazards like factories, refineries, and Superfund sites—and experienced more health problems and school absences that undermined the educational process. Low-income neighborhoods often had fewer quality preschool options, social services, and extracurriculars. Low-income parents, frequently struggling to hold down one job (or several) with irregular hours, had less time and energy to devote to homework assistance, the PTA, or interacting with teachers—all of which made a difference, because the "squeaky wheel gets the grease." Fewer affluent parents meant fewer of the demands on school authorities that might spur them to provide a better-quality education, and less money to donate to the local school, helping to defray the costs of books, school supplies, and class trips. These were just a few of the reasons why concentrating children in high-poverty schools undermined academic achievement. This litany also helped explain why allocating equal amounts of money to low-income and middle-class schools didn't produce equal outcomes. Poorer schools, tasked with educating children with greater needs, required *more* money than middle- and upper-middle-class schools. Usually they got less.

The mid-1970s were a turning point in public education in the United States. Desegregation's heyday—the period during which, scholars argue, it "was most actively pursued"—was from the mid-1960s to the early 1970s.[76] The violent response to court-ordered integration in Boston demoralized the policy's advocates.[77] But *Milliken I*, decided in 1974, was a hinge, the critical moment that separated two eras.

During that heyday, the nation actively pursued a policy of desegregation, but one largely centered on the South. As journalist and school desegregation expert Nikole Hannah-Jones has written, southern desegregation was an incredible success story. In as early as 1972, "nearly half [of southern black children] were attending predominantly white schools."[78] The number of black children attending desegregated schools actually reached its highest point in 1988. Most of them lived in the South, where federal trial courts continued to enforce desegregation orders. But *Milliken* put the kibosh on northern desegregation. In so doing, it also ushered in a different era, one of reaction and backlash.

In the 1990s, the Supreme Court decided a trio of school desegregation cases that set court-ordered desegregation back still further. The first case was *Board of Education of Oklahoma City Public Schools v. Dowell*, decided in 1991.[79] There, the court expressed its frustration that federal trial courts were still supervising school districts that had violated the Constitution by segregating black students. Desegregation orders were not intended to "operate in perpetuity," the court ruled.[80] Instead, the lower courts should bring desegregation orders to a close expeditiously and return school districts to local control.

In 1992, in *Freeman v. Pitts*, the court ruled that school districts could be released from federal court oversight incrementally, increasing as one commentator put it "the likelihood that school districts will *de facto* resegregate before fully complying with *Brown*."[81] More importantly, the court ruled that once "the racial imbalance due to the *de jure* violation has been remedied, the school district is under no duty to remedy imbalance that is caused by demographic factors."[82] This is the rule that effectively ended court-ordered desegregation in the South. Finally, in *Missouri v. Jenkins*, decided in 1995, the court directed federal trial courts to "sharply limit, if not dispense with" reliance on student achievement levels in determining whether desegregation orders should be lifted.[83]

Since 1990, segregation has increased in every part of the country.[84] Today, most American children attend racially segregated schools. Not only that, the school districts that serve nonwhite children receive far less financial support than those that mainly serve white children.[85] One study found that "for every student enrolled, the average nonwhite school district receives $2,226 less than a white school district."

Assessing the school segregation landscape in late 2020, researchers Gary Orfield and Danielle Jarvie observed that the year 1974 was pivotal for urban desegregation. There "have been no major legal or policy advances" since *Milliken* was decided, they wrote. *Milliken* was where the promise of *Brown* ended.

24

"TRUE INTEGRATION"

Today, the Detroit Public Schools Community District (DPSCD)—
which includes all of the city's public noncharter schools—is vastly
majority minority and overwhelmingly low-income. Eighty-two
percent of the students are African American; about 15 percent are Latino,
Asian Pacific Islander, or multiracial. The white population of the city's
school district hovers around 2 percent.[1] Almost 80 percent of the district's
students are eligible for a free or a reduced-price lunch. This means that
most students in the Detroit Public Schools Community District are either at or near the federally defined poverty level.[2] Social scientists have
a term for this: "racial economic segregation."[3] The term is important for
two reasons. First, scholars caution that it is important not to treat race and
class as independent variables. Instead, it is the combination of the two
that carries the most destructive weight. Second, and relatedly, the presence of high levels of racial economic segregation is highly predictive of
racial achievement gaps. As one scholar put it, "Black/Hispanic students
have test scores lower than their White peers, not because their schools
are populated with students of color, but because they go to schools with
higher poverty rates."[4]

In 2016, students attending some of the lowest performing schools in
Detroit, both DPSCD and charter, sued state school officials in federal
court, alleging that the state of Michigan had deprived them of "access to

the most basic building block of education: literacy."[5] The case was called *Gary B. v. Snyder*. As the *Milliken* plaintiffs had before them, the *Gary B.* plaintiffs noted in their complaint that in Michigan "the ultimate legal obligation for providing education and for protecting legal rights with respect to education rests with the State."[6] This was even more true than in the 1970s, given the state's repeated takeover of the city's schools. By 2016, "the State [had] been the de facto administrator of the school district for most of the past fifteen years."[7]

The complaint, complete with color pictures, read like a gothic horror story: deteriorated and unsanitary physical facilities; a widespread vermin and rodent infestation—cockroaches, bedbugs, maggots, mice, rats; mold; broken windows and doors; lack of heat and air-conditioning; roof and pipe leaks; falling plaster and ceiling tiles; nauseating odors; inoperable water fountains, bathrooms, and fire alarms; sewage backups; lack of (or unsafe) playground equipment. During the 2015–16 school year "*none* of the [DPSCD's] buildings were in compliance with city health and safety codes," the complaint asserted.[8] Classrooms were extremely overcrowded; in some instances there were sixty students in a single class. School supplies were scant. Textbooks were out of date, damaged, or unavailable. Teacher turnover and vacancies were high. Classes often were taught by uncertified teachers, by substitutes, or not staffed at all. In one instance, a high-performing eighth grade student taught two math classes for a month.[9]

Accusing the state of "long-term disinvestment," the complaint reported the impact on Detroit students who were "overwhelmingly African-American and socioeconomically disadvantaged." The statistics were shocking. The "data show that students in [the DPSCD and the city's charter schools] are, on average, 2.3 grade levels below their actual grade level in basic reading proficiency."[10] Detroit students ranked last in the nation when it came to literacy.[11] Detroit was perhaps the single lowest-performing large urban school district in the nation.

"Detroit is bounded by the most economically and racially segregating school district boundary in the country," the plaintiffs noted.[12] *Gary B.* was, in effect, a lawsuit challenging the pernicious effects of "racial economic segregation" at the school *district* level. The focus was completely consistent with recent social science research, which finds that "most racial economic segregation occurs *between districts in the same state*, rather than between states or between schools in the same district."[13] Most school segregation in the United States is between district segregation.[14] And the incidence of such between district segregation is very high, "accounting for 60 to 70% of total segregation in the nation from 1991 to 2020."[15]

A study conducted by the United States Government Accountability Office (GAO) that was published in 2022 found that even though the nation's school population is increasingly racially diverse, our schools are deeply segregated whether they are located in urban, suburban, or rural areas.[16] The GAO found that "more than a third of students (about 18.5 million) attended a predominantly same-race/ethnicity school—where 75 percent or more of the student population is of a single race/ethnicity." The GAO also found that "14 percent of students attended schools where 90 percent or more of the students were of a single race/ethnicity." And the GAO put its finger directly on a main culprit: school district boundary lines, which "can contribute to continued divisions along racial/ethnic lines."[17] The government study also noted the rising problem of school district secession, a process by which "schools sever governance ties from an existing district to form a new district." School district secession, the government report said, "generally results in shifts in racial/ethnic composition and wealth."[18]

Just as Justice Thurgood Marshall had fatefully prophesized, the Detroit school district line—and thousands of others throughout the United States—have operated as fences, separating schoolchildren on the basis of race and class. One attorney representing the plaintiffs in the *Gary B.* case asked: "Would Governor Snyder assign the children of Grosse Pointe or Ann Arbor to the schools of Detroit?"[19] It was a question that answered itself. While it is true that there are more children of color living in Detroit's suburbs than ever before, it remains the case that Detroit's population is overwhelmingly nonwhite, as is its public school population.

RACIAL DEMOGRAPHICS OF DETROIT VS. DETROIT SUBURBS OVER TIME

DECADE	PERCENT OF METRO AREA POPULA- TION IN SUBURBS	DETROIT POPULATION[1]		DETROIT SUBURBS POPULATION[2]	
		White	Non-white	White	Non-white
1920s	24	96	4	98	2
1930s	28	92	8	98	2
1940s	32	91	9	97	3
1950s	39	84	16	97	3
1960s	56	71	29	97	3
1970s	64	56	44	96	4
1980s	70	34	66	94	6
1990s	74	22	78	92	8
2000s	76	12	88	86	16
2010s	82	11	89	80	20
2020s	84	11	89	76	24

1 Population of Detroit pulled from U.S. Census.

2 Population of Detroit suburbs calculated by adding the total populations of Oakland, Macomb, and Wayne Counties, and then subtracting from that the population of Detroit in Wayne County.

In April 2020, a three-judge panel of the Sixth Circuit Court of Appeals ruled that "it may never be that each child born in this country has the same opportunity for success in life, without regard to the circumstances of her birth. But even so, the Constitution cannot permit those circumstances to foreclose *all* opportunity and deny a child literacy without regard to her potential."[20] The decision was historic. It was the first time in history that a federal appellate court had ruled that the federal Constitution protects the "right to a basic minimum education."[21]

The plaintiffs' historic victory was short-lived. Just a few weeks after the panel handed down its decision, a majority of the judges on the Sixth

Circuit Court of Appeals voted to rehear the case "en banc." This had the effect of vacating (nullifying) the panel's decision below.[22] Anticipating that the panel's decision might well be nullified, the parties settled the lawsuit just days before the Sixth Circuit voted to rehear the case.[23] A key aspect of the settlement was Governor Gretchen Whitmer's pledge to propose legislation that, if passed, would supply Detroit's schools with more than $94 million in funding for literacy programs.[24]

Ultimately, it would be more than three years before the state legislature approved that funding as part of Michigan's K–12 2023–24 school aid budget.[25] Alice Thompson of the Detroit NAACP described the legislature's action as "a giant step forward toward righting past wrongs." The "unprecedented funding for students with the greatest needs, particularly those living in concentrated poverty, will be tremendously important to address the wide and unfair opportunity gaps that exist for students who are most underserved, especially Michigan's Black and Latino students," she added."[26] Derek W. Black, a law professor and education law expert, was more circumscribed: "The panel decision in *Gary B* was breathtaking for what it symbolized. It was the first federal appellate court to recognize that the federal constitution can and must protect some baseline of educational opportunity if equal citizenship is to mean anything in America. The fact, however, that plaintiffs had to settle for education remedies far short of what is necessary to guarantee a reasonable chance at equal citizenship—because the current U.S. Supreme Court was highly unlikely to validate a right to literacy much less basic education—is a sad reminder of just how little has changed since *Milliken* and *Rodriguez*."[27]

———

So what can be done now? First, it is important to remember what *Milliken* does and does not do. The court's decision makes it very difficult to *require* metropolitan desegregation, even when the Constitution has clearly been violated. But nothing in that ruling—or in *Parents Involved*, for that matter—*prohibits* school authorities from taking voluntary race-neutral action with an aim to desegregate. For example, school authorities may redraw school boundaries, combine attendance zones, site new schools, and create school choice policies with an eye toward integrating the public schools.[28] Such initiatives are consistent with constitutional requirements as long as they do not employ explicit racial classifications to achieve diversity gains.[29] In fact, in 2020, the U.S. House of Representatives took a giant step forward in assisting school authorities in just this regard.

In September of that year, the House passed the Strength in Diversity Act. Were the act to become law it would represent the first time since 1972 that the federal government has created a program expressly designed to support school integration.[30] Invoking *Brown v. Board of Education*, the Committee on Education and Labor's report on the bill noted the federal government's failure to provide the necessary leadership in this area. "Federal intervention is needed to confront this persistent, pervasive injustice, yet the federal government has continually retreated from its role in promoting school integration," the committee observed. The committee also pointed an accusatory finger at the Supreme Court: "The retreat [from integration] began in *Milliken v. Bradley* (1974) which held that school districts in the suburbs of Detroit were not obligated to participate in intra-district [*sic*] desegregation unless they committed a constitutional violation, effectively ending state-ordered regional desegregation across school district lines."[31] And it noted the strong relationship between desegregation and academic achievement gains for black students. "Simply put, in the two decades the federal government was most active in supporting and advancing school integration, the U.S. was able to cut the achievement gap nearly in half."[32]

Against that background, the landmark bill leveraged one of the federal government's biggest strengths in this area—its ability to use federal funds to incentivize school authorities to create school integration opportunities. The act would direct the Department of Education to award grants to school authorities to "develop or implement plans to improve diversity and reduce or eliminate racial or socioeconomic isolation in publicly funded early childhood education programs, public elementary schools, or public secondary schools."[33] This might not sound earth-shattering, but in some ways it is. The federal money would support *communities*—as they come together to envision, plan, coordinate, study, and implement practices that will result in racial and socioeconomic integration.[34] The House passed the Strength in Diversity Act in 2020, but the bill failed to receive a floor vote in the Senate and did not become law.[35] It should. The Congress should pass and the president should sign this vitally important legislation into law.

The Elementary and Secondary Education Act of 1965 is the largest source of federal money flowing to K–12 education in the states.[36] The purpose of Title I of the act, *Improving the Academic Achievement of the Disadvantaged*, is to "provide all children significant opportunity to receive a fair, equitable, and high-quality education, and to close educational achievement gaps."[37] It is hard to overstate the importance of Title I money. Congress appropriated more than $18 billion in financial year 2023 for Title I funding.[38] This is a very substantial sum, yet as commentators have pointed out, Title I's funding formulas disincentivize poverty deconcentration and racial integration.[39]

The funding formulas are based on several indicia, including the amount of concentrated poverty in a school district and particular school. As a general matter, the greater the number of high-poverty students, the more Title I money schools receive. This creates perverse incentives. As the National Coalition on School Diversity put it, "Title I funding formulas provide incentives for school districts to maintain high poverty levels and no incentive to deconcentrate poverty or foster voluntary transfer or assignment policies with surrounding districts," which enhance integration.[40] As it stands right now, school districts *lose money* when high-poverty students transfer or otherwise leave the district. Similarly, school districts suffer no financial consequences whatsoever if they concentrate all or most of their high-poverty students in particular schools within the district.

To better align school districts' incentives with the goals of integration and poverty deconcentration, Professor Derek Black has proposed a "hold harmless" rule.[41] Under this rule, school districts that engage in interdistrict integration or transfer programs and the like would not be penalized by the loss of Title I funding. Instead, their Title I funding would be held steady for at least three years.[42] And school districts *accepting* such interdistrict transfer students would also be incentivized by receiving additional Title I money for doing so. And while we're at it, let's create an affirmative right to transfer, as the National Coalition on School Diversity has suggested. Per the coalition: any school district receiving Title I money should also "be required to accept transfers, assuming space availability."[43]

Relatedly, as the Century Foundation has proposed, the federal government should both expand Title I funding and earmark a portion of that funding specifically for school integration efforts.[44] This new earmarked money should be used to fund "magnet schools, rezoning to promote diversity, districtwide 'controlled choice' plans that combine choice with civil rights protections, and interdistrict integration efforts such as transfer programs."[45]

Another portion of the Elementary and Secondary Education Act, Title IV, creates the Magnet Schools Assistance Program.[46] This program was expressly designed to desegregate the public schools by providing modest awards to school districts implementing either voluntary or court-ordered desegregation plans.[47] It is, as the Century Foundation researchers put it, "the primary existing vehicle of federal support for school integration."[48] When properly designed and funded, magnet schools hold tremendous potential because they have the capacity to satisfy student and parental preferences while simultaneously providing sought-after educational offerings in a racially diverse setting. The Magnet Schools Assistance Program has consistently been underfunded. In financial year 2023, the federal government appropriated $139 million to fund program, which, as the Learning Policy Institute points out, was "a decline in real dollar terms since 1984 and provides a very modest level of support given that there are thousands of magnet schools in the country."[49] The institute recommends raising the level of federal funding for the program to at least $500 million.

One of the lessons of Detroit's experience is that schools and housing are inextricably linked—as are race and class. This means that increasing racial and class diversity in our neighborhoods has significant "knock on" effects for education. One of the best ways to overcome the pernicious effects of the "neighborhood school rule" is to reduce or eliminate "exclusionary" zoning. Exclusionary zoning means the prohibition on the construction of higher-density housing units, accessory units, duplexes, fourplexes, and other types of multifamily housing in certain residential areas. Excluding higher-density units raises housing costs and helps maintain the racial and economic fences that deny access to a particular neighborhood's schools. As an Atlanta housing official recently explained, "Exclusionary, single-family zoning has its origins in maintaining racial and economic segregation and today is related to persistent segregation, a lack of diversity in housing, restricting access to high opportunity neighborhoods, and making housing less affordable."[50]

Against this background, some cities have either reduced or eliminated single family zoning. In late 2018, Minneapolis became the first major city in the United States to end single family zoning.[51] *Slate* magazine characterized Minneapolis mayor Jacob Frey's rationale for supporting the policy change this way: "Single-family home zoning was devised as a legal way to keep black Americans and other minorities from moving into certain neighborhoods, and it still functions as an effective barrier today. Abolishing restrictive zoning, the mayor said, was part of a general consensus that the city ought to begin to mend the damage wrought in pursuit of segregation." The city's policy initiative, which included eliminating minimum parking requirements for new developments, encouraging apartment development on commercial corridors, establishing building height minimums in high-density zones, and allowing duplex and triplex construction on all residential lots, has been a resounding success. In early 2024, the Pew Charitable Trusts published an article calling Minneapolis's land use reforms a "blueprint for housing affordability."[52] The foundation concluded that the policy substantially expanded the city's housing supply, which, in turn, reduced rent growth. At the same time, the number of blacks in the city increased. The foundation wrote that "census data shows that Minneapolis gained black residents from 2017 to 2022." In mid-2019, Oregon became the first state to eliminate single-family zoning.[53] Since that time, the cities of Seattle, Washington, D.C., and Arlington, Virginia, and several other states—California, Washington, and Montana—have followed suit with laws intended to increase residential density.[54]

But land use reform, as important as that is, isn't enough. We also need to give low-income families a meaningful option to move to higher-opportunity and more racially diverse neighborhoods. Such moves would, in turn, expose children to higher-opportunity schools. The federal "Housing Choice Voucher" program is the nation's largest housing assistance program for low-income individuals.[55] Federal housing choice vouchers provide rental assistance so that individuals meeting certain income requirements can secure housing in the private market. The majority of housing choice voucher recipients are nonwhite.[56] Given that the vouchers are not place-based and can be used in many areas, the program could have a strong desegregative effect—at least theoretically. But that hasn't happened. Instead, researchers have characterized the program as a "lost opportunity to counter longstanding racial segregation and rising residential income segregation."[57] So a perennial question about the program has been why more voucher recipients do not use the assistance to move to higher-opportunity neighborhoods. Focusing on the word "choice," it might be that recipients simply prefer to stay in low-opportunity neighborhoods. This was how one study summarized the "taste" explanation: "Low-income families [might] prefer to stay in low-opportunity areas because these neighborhoods have other valuable amenities, such as shorter commutes, proximity to family and community, or greater racial and ethnic diversity."[58] However, a recent experiment has conclusively refuted this hypothesis.

Recognizing that some neighborhoods expand life chances, a research team that included noted Harvard economist Raj Chetty, together with the Seattle and King County Housing Authorities, designed the "Creating Moves to Opportunity" (CMTO) experiment.[59] Building on previous "moving to opportunity" programs, the CMTO experiment provided one group of recipients of federal housing choice vouchers with several types of augmented resources that typically are unavailable to voucher recipients: enhanced housing counseling, landlord interface, short-term financial assistance for security deposits and application fees, and information about which neighborhoods had the highest opportunities for children. This was the "treatment group." Another group of voucher recipients—the "control group"—were provided with the standard information typically available to participants in the program.

In mid-2023, the researchers released a comprehensive assessment of the experiment's results. In a word, they were astonishing. The researchers found that 53 percent of families in the treatment group moved to high-opportunity neighborhoods, versus 15 percent of families in the control group. Additionally, members of the treatment group were very likely to stay in those high-opportunity areas when their leases were renewed. And treatment group members were much more likely to report being "very satisfied" with their neighborhoods than members of the control group.[60] Based upon this assessment, the researchers concluded that it is "challenges in the housing search process itself," not individual preferences, that explain why many housing choice voucher recipients do not use their assistance to move to higher-opportunity areas.[61] In undermining the "taste" explanation, the CMTO experiment suggests that many voucher recipients do not possess a strong preference to stay in low-opportunity neighborhoods. The researchers' conclusion: "Redesigning affordable housing programs and other policies (e.g., zoning laws and the location of affordable housing developments) to facilitate more moves to opportunity could have substantial impacts on residential segregation by race and socioeconomic status."[62]

Providing the necessary "high intensity, customized [housing] support" to facilitate moves to opportunity is not cost-free. Researchers estimate the cost of providing augmented housing support to total about $2,670 per voucher plus $2,500 to $3,000 per year in additional rental assistance because of the increased rent in high-opportunity neighborhoods.[63] Some commentators have argued, however, that the higher cost of the program might potentially be offset via future taxes. Children raised in higher-opportunity areas are projected to have substantially higher lifetime earnings than those raised in lower-opportunity neighborhoods.[64] In 2020, House and Senate leaders agreed to double the amount of funding previously allocated for a mobility housing voucher demonstration program.[65] In financial year 2023, Congress increased this funding again.[66] This is a step in the right direction, but millions more are needed so that every family wishing to use a housing voucher to move to a higher-opportunity area may do so.

Across the country, school desegregation advocates continue to push for change. In many cases, these efforts have met with success. In late 2019, the Howard County school district, the top-ranked school district in all of Maryland, approved a redistricting proposal aimed at increasing racial and socioeconomic integration.[67] It was the largest such effort in the district's history.[68] According to one report, by the fall of 2020, "over 5,500 students had been welcomed—virtually—into newly integrated schools."[69]

Plaintiffs have brought lawsuits challenging the status quo. Two recent cases stand out. Seeking to capitalize on New Jersey state law that expressly prohibits school segregation, the Latino Action Network, the New Jersey NAACP, and several other groups and individuals filed a landmark school desegregation lawsuit against the State of New Jersey. In *Latino Action Network v. the State of New Jersey*, the plaintiffs argue that the state's public schools, including its charter schools, are extraordinarily segregated. The cause is familiar, as a paragraph of the complaint demonstrates: "Residential segregation translates to public school segregation through the design of school districts that are mainly contiguous with the boundaries of residentially segregated municipalities and enforcement of an attendance statute . . . which, with minor exceptions, mandates that students attend public school in the municipality in which they reside."[70] Nothing less than statewide school desegregation is the lawsuit's aim. In October 2023, a state court judge issued a pretrial order, dismissing some but not all of the plaintiffs' claims.[71] He also ruled—crucially—that "defendants intentionally failed to exercise their constitutional obligations and authorities to remedy segregation," and that the "problems of racially isolated districts persist, and plaintiffs adequately allege that defendants have . . . failed to take sufficient steps to remedy that segregation."[72] This result is promising. As University of Michigan Law School Professor Elise C. Boddie, who served as a consultant to the plaintiffs, noted, the ruling serves as a "good indication the court recognized the importance of these claims."[73] The case is still being actively litigated.

Integration proponents also have reasons to cheer another recent state court decision. In 2015, a group of parents whose children attended public schools in Minneapolis and Saint Paul brought a case alleging that those schools were racially and socioeconomically segregated in violation of "their children's right to an adequate education under the education clause of the Minnesota constitution."[74] In December 2023, the Minnesota State Supreme Court ruled in *Cruz-Guzman v. State of Minnesota* that while racial imbalances alone did not violate the state constitutional provision, the plaintiffs could prevail if they could show that "the racial imbalances are a substantial factor in causing their children to receive an inadequate education."[75]

At first blush, this result might not seem consequential. But it is. Under the state high court's ruling there is no requirement the plaintiffs establish that the segregated conditions in their schools came as a result of de jure segregation in order to prevail. Instead, the court expressly recognized that state liability *could be* established on a showing of de facto segregation. The Minnesota Supreme Court wrote: "De facto segregation in public schools is fueled by a constellation of public and private forces, both historic and modern . . . These forces include racially restrictive covenants, discriminatory housing finance programs, exclusionary zoning policies, wealth disparities, and implicit and explicit bias."[76] So if the plaintiffs can prove the existence of de facto segregation and that it was a substantial factor in causing their children's inadequate education, they can recover, even though the school authorities are not directly responsible for racially restrictive covenants, exclusionary zoning, or any of the other forces that fuel de facto segregation. Myron Orfield explained how the state supreme court ruling in *Cruz-Guzman* could have a significant effect even outside the state. He told me: "Minnesota does not have a segregation clause in its constitution, unlike Connecticut and New Jersey. So plaintiffs throughout the country can use it as precedent."[77] It was important to put Orfield's comment in context. The Minnesota State Supreme Court recognized that its state constitutional provision that requires an adequate (or equal) education necessarily includes an *integrated or non-segregated education*. Because most state constitutions have similar public education provisions, the Minnesota ruling opens the door to bringing similar suits in those states.

Integrated Schools is a group of parents dedicated to building a "true multiracial democracy." It fights separate and unequal schools and is creating pro-integration chapters across the country.[78] The core mission of the Diverse Charter Schools Coalition is to promote integration and "diverse-by-design" public charters.[79] Since 2017, there's been a significant uptick in the number of schools that have taken steps to integrate. And as one report put it, "More than 900 school districts and charter schools across the country [have] integration policies or legal instruments that address segregation."[80]

These organizations and initiatives are consistent with an underappreciated reality: many Americans believe racial diversity in the schools is important—at least in principle. A recent study found that large numbers of survey respondents favored racially and ethnically integrated schools in their communities.[81] Support for integration fluctuated based upon race, political affiliation, and geographic location, of course. But integration's biggest obstacle was the widespread perception that achieving it would come at an unacceptably high price. As the sponsors of the study put it, if "people think—or are led to think—that reducing segregation will come at a (broadly defined) cost to students, they are much less likely to support taking steps to integrate."

The sponsors of the study propose a solution to the "negative framing" around integration that has the added virtue of being true: *all* students benefit from a racially and socioeconomically integrated education. The challenge is the need to continually dispute the perception that integration was a failed social policy. Instead, students in racially and socioeconomically integrated schools and classrooms have stronger academic outcomes and higher test scores, are more likely to enroll in college, have higher earnings and health outcomes as adults, and are less likely to become incarcerated.[82] And integrated schools reduce racial bias and stereotyping as well. Even the longer school commute times many parents assume must necessarily accompany integration can be reframed. As the study's sponsors note, in many cities, racially gerrymandered attendance zones actually make segregation levels *higher* than assigning students to schools closer to their homes. "In other words, undoing these segregative district and school boundaries results in opportunities to integrate schools without significant increases in students' travel times," the sponsors wrote. But reframing integration isn't going to be easy; busing and the assumption that integration failed are stubbornly synonymous in the public mind.

Law professor and civil rights expert john powell has developed the concept of "true integration," which builds upon King's teachings.[83] According to powell, the purpose of true integration isn't assimilation, but rather the complete and utter transformation of the mainstream. Schools with roughly equal racial group representation and a diverse and responsive faculty and administration, that have eliminated ability grouping and tracking, where positive interracial contact among students is encouraged, where classrooms are racially and economically balanced, and with multicultural curricula and programming, are truly integrated. This achievement was—and is—what so many activists are still fighting for.

EPILOGUE

I went back to Detroit in late 2019 trying to make sense of all that I had learned. I had left in 1981. What did I know about the city now? To say that much had happened since then was an extraordinary understatement.

There had been a state takeover of the public schools—twice. The city had suffered the largest municipal bankruptcy in American history. More recently, the city's downtown had seen a billion-dollar development boom. There had been a tidal wave of change since I'd called the city home. My information is stale, I thought to myself; my memories were intermittent. I had forgotten, if I ever knew it, the difference between Gratiot and Grand River. I needed GPS to get around.

I wanted to visit Clinton Elementary School, where Verda Bradley had served as a lunch-hour aide. It was her displeasure with Clinton that convinced her to approach the NAACP. I typed the address into my cell phone and let the GPS take over. Soon, I was at the corner of Chalfonte and Greenlawn. But there was no school there anymore. In 2010, the school shut its doors as part of a wave of school closures in the city.[1] At the time it had a 99 percent black enrollment.[2]

The area where the school once stood is now the DeWitt Clinton public park, complete with playground and swing set. The park's rectangular area was lined with sidewalks, set off by decorative boulders. There was plenty of open space. Modest houses framed the park on all four sides. It was quiet: a few cars in the street, and a pedestrian or two. It was easy to see how Clinton Elementary once served this neighborhood. One could imagine a parent walking her child to school, dropping her off, and waving goodbye. If one were looking for the quintessential example of a neighborhood school, this would have been it.

I sat in my rental car and thought long and hard about the neighborhood school. The phrase used to sound neutral to me. It rolled off my lips without a second thought. No more. As I looked out the car window, I started taking the words apart. *Neighborhood.* A neighborhood isn't just a place where a group of people live. It is a legal and social construction. In my research, I had learned the extent to which where people live was the result of a whole variety of forces and factors—racially restrictive covenants, redlining, urban renewal policies, public housing siting determinations, realtors' discriminatory actions, zoning—that structure their neighborhood choices. *School.* In theory, most schools in the United States are public, open to all. But if "neighborhood" modifies the word "school," the schools are no more public than the neighborhood is. Neighborhood schools typically are reserved for children who live in the community, whose parents can afford to own or rent homes and pay local property taxes, which in effect are a form of tuition. And a school district's reputation—good, bad, or indifferent—was bundled into the rent or the cost of the house. So while a "neighborhood school" is a public school, it is one that excludes far more students than it serves.

Maybe this characterization of the neighborhood school was too negative. Perhaps the forces and factors that helped explain why different people lived in different neighborhoods were less important than the simple fact that they did. Neighborhoods could be a beautiful thing, too. They could foster community and nurture a sense of individual identity. This was particularly true when the members of that community were part of a historically disfavored minority group. Then a neighborhood could be a place of refuge, a font of camaraderie, a respite from outside and often hostile forces. And when people felt they were part of a community, they often acted not just for their own individual benefit, but for the good of the whole. Maybe racial and cultural bonds coupled with a shared sense of common purpose could make up for whatever blacks' neighborhood schools lacked. I thought of this as I headed to 7625 Linwood Street. My destination: the Shrine of the Black Madonna.

I was warmly greeted there by Reverend Gary "Muthamaki" Bennett and Bishop Menelik Kimathi, who walked me through the stately Classical Revival–style building. As I moved into the nave and gazed behind the pulpit, I was struck by the beauty and power of the immense Black Madonna. A spacious side room used for meetings, meals, and other gatherings featured a multipanel exhibition depicting Cleage's life and times, the history of Black Christian Nationalism, and a survey of the fruits of "Fifty Years of Nation Building." It was all there. Youth centers, bookstores, housing, food co-ops, and, of course, education. The scope and sheer audacity of Cleage's ambition was on full display. He wanted black self-determination above all. Nothing less than a complete divorce from white America would do. There was something so attractive about his vision, particularly given its emphasis on black beauty, culture, music, and art. As I stood there, it was as if I could hear Cleage's voice in my head like a drumbeat. We have the ability to fix our own schools. Black schools for black children. All we need are the resources. Given what I had learned about northern Jim Crow, about the suffocating nature of the containment, it made perfect sense.

At the end of my visit to the shrine, famed local historian and former public school teacher Jamon Jordan met me for a personal tour of the city. Over the years, Jordan has exposed thousands of people to Detroit's unique history. One of his specialties is introducing native Detroiters to hidden parts of a town they thought they already knew.[3] I was in the right hands. As we crisscrossed the city, Jordan dropped his considerable knowledge in rapid-fire bursts. He pointed out Underground Railroad stops; the homesite of Fannie Richards, Detroit's first black public school teacher; the Boston-Edison neighborhood that saw the rise of the auto industry; the block where Smokey and Diana once lived.

Our last stop was the Eight Mile segregation wall. The Birwood Street side of the wall—what had been the black side—boasts a gorgeous, multicolor mural depicting moments of uplift and local and historical figures: Rosa Parks and the Montgomery Bus Boycott, neighborhood hero and community activist Alfonso Wells, Sojourner Truth leading enslaved people to freedom.[4] The mural also contains less uplifting images. A member of the Ku Klux Klan in a flowing white robe is pictured there, too. The Mendota side of the wall—what had been the white side—is unremarkable, just a thick gray partition dividing two streets. You wouldn't know what you were looking at unless someone told you. As we drove from one end of the barrier to the other, I was transfixed. The hour was late, and the tour was over. But I knew I would be coming back.

The next day, I drove from my old house in Palmer Woods to the wall. I was there in all of eight minutes. I sat in my car and stared. I could hardly believe it had been there my entire childhood, so close by, and yet I never knew it. I never fully understood the intensity of my parents' desire to build their dream home. But there was something about the segregation wall that clarified things. I now understood something I hadn't before. *This is what they were up against. The containment.*

Maybe the house was a declaration: *Your walls can't stop us. We are living where we want to live.* From this perspective, it's not surprising that even if my parents had known about the wall, they wouldn't have shared the information. They were going to look forward, not back. But whether they knew about it or not, what this barrier represented had defined their lives. Most of the time, northern Jim Crow lacked the outward symbolism— "whites only"—that characterized southern Jim Crow. The wall between Birwood and Mendota was an exception. The wall never displayed a "whites only" sign, but it was a physical personification of racist ideology. Maybe northern blacks had to internalize where the barriers were. Perhaps the wall was what my parents carried inside them every single day. It's what they had to get over. It's what they had to get around.

I turned the motor off. I thought back to the central ideological clash I had encountered again and again in my research, the conflict that led to the *Milliken* litigation: integration versus separatism. Malcolm versus Martin. Cleage versus Robinson. Bell versus Jones. It was a long-running conversation, one that might never end. But the wall provided new insight. All black folk had to find a way to cope with what it represented. The tools of the trade were many. Humor. Style. Art. Music. Fashion. Erudition. Audacious—and never-ending—displays of black excellence. Some chose to go over the wall. Some chose to burrow under it. Some chose to go around it. But it wasn't going to stop us.

Some built movements—religious, political, social. Some organized others. Some led the faithful. Some taught the next generation. Some ran for office. Some labored in the courts. And some tried to shake hands with the whites who would unclench their fists. Of course, there were serious tactical disagreements about the best way to achieve black freedom and equality. It would have been surprising if there hadn't been. There was no single black community. People had different views, different strengths, different weaknesses. But everyone was in the same army.

King's words spilled into my mind. *Soul force.* King, of course, was committed to nonviolence, and at the March on Washington he advocated for that strategy. "Again and again we must rise to the majestic heights of meeting physical force with soul force," he urged. This was his call to black folks, beseeching them to hold their fire even when intentionally provoked.

He mentioned whites, too. "For many of our white brothers, as evidenced by their presence here today, have come to realize that their destiny is tied up with our destiny. And they have come to realize that their freedom is inextricably bound to our freedom," he declared. The minister's words suggested that the two races could only move forward together. What some saw as an anodyne description of brotherly love—"we cannot walk alone"—I heard as a pragmatic call to build a multiracial coalition that would strengthen blacks' hand. Many whites had earned blacks' mistrust. But not all. Some had realized that their destiny was intertwined with blacks' fate. They were part of the soul force, too.

King's words had two implications for me. First, I thought about Judge Roth. Of all of the characters I'd met along the way, he was the one who had shifted the most. What he learned during the Detroit trial changed him. All of that new information spurred him to do the right thing. It was tempting to call him a hero. After all, his efforts to enforce the Fourteenth Amendment probably shortened his life. Yet I hesitated. It wasn't that I didn't appreciate what he had done. I did. It was that I couldn't view his actions in isolation. His transformation was the fruit of the efforts of countless individuals. The lawyers and advocates—including Alexander

Ritchie—responsible for the lengthy trial, the briefs, the expert witnesses, the map. And, before that, the table had been set by the thousands of black activists across the South and North who pressed for desegregation, often at extraordinary cost.

Then there were the actions of community organizers like June Shagaloff; speak-truth-to-power politicians like Coleman Young; pillars of the community like Remus Robinson; lightning-smart radicals like Albert Cleage; parents fighting for their children like Verda Bradley; black judges like Wade McCree, Damon Keith, and Harry Edwards; school board officials like Abraham Zwerdling; politicians like George Romney, Shirley Chisholm, and Abraham Ribicoff; lawyers and advocates (and later judges) like Robert Carter, Constance Baker Motley, Nate Jones, and Thurgood Marshall. The NAACP. "Hero" is a label that tends to emphasize individual acts of bravery while obscuring the rest of the story. So instead of calling him a hero, I would pay Roth a more accurate compliment. He was a member of the soul force.

Second, King's words held a warning. Everyone benefited when the two groups' fates were tied, the minister seemed to be saying. Doing the opposite meant that everyone—the entire nation—would suffer. I looked at the segregation wall just steps from Eight Mile Road, the border between Detroit and its northern suburbs, and I knew King was right. On one side of the road sat some of the most affluent towns in the nation. On the other, one of the most segregated cities in the United States.[5]

The Supreme Court ignored King's advice. *Milliken I* incentivized whites to leave Detroit and other urban places to avoid court-ordered desegregation. John Mogk, a former member of the Detroit school board, once claimed: "Some people were leaving at that time [the 1967 riots] but, really, it was after *Milliken* that you saw mass [white] flight to the suburbs."[6] Later, Pulitzer Prize–winning historian and Detroit native Heather Ann Thompson would argue that the key event that explained white flight during this period was not *Milliken* but the mayoral election of 1973. She argued that the election of Coleman Young as the city's first black mayor was a watershed, signaling that whites no longer enjoyed full political control of the city. Thompson wrote: "The irrevocable *political* loss that whites experienced in the election of 1973—not neighborhood desegregation, perceptions about crime, welfare dependency, or black militancy alone—finally sent them out of the city in droves and led them, enthusiastically into the Republican fold."[7] But this hardly meant *Milliken* didn't matter. Coming down less than seven months after Young was inaugurated, the case amplified the message that white Detroiters would have to share *both* political power and their schools with blacks if they stayed. They left instead. White abandonment eroded the city's tax base. That, combined with the recession that began in 1973, was a disaster for Detroit.

And it wasn't just Detroit that got hurt. In early 1976, Governor William Milliken proposed a regional tax-sharing plan that he said "could well be [Detroit's] salvation."[8] Under the plan, some of the tax proceeds collected from business property in high-growth suburban areas would be shifted to Detroit (and some low-growth suburbs) to help alleviate the effects of its declining tax base.[9] The governor's budget director believed the plan would benefit the entire metropolitan area by building a strong regional economy.[10] The *Detroit Free Press* characterized the budget director's views on the plan this way: it "recognizes the long-range interest of all southeast Michigan governments in a sound economy in which all units are basically interdependent."[11] The plan was dead on arrival. Most suburban lawmakers were vehemently opposed to the proposal.[12] And, in Detroit, it was too little, too late. "What the governor is proposing is a plan for 1979 in which we are going to share. But you have got to be alive to share," said one Detroit official.[13]

The reality was that many whites, having departed for the suburbs, now wanted nothing to do with the city that anchored their regional area. For some, Detroit was effectively a foreign country. In 1990, Macomb County commissioner Richard D. Sabaugh told *The New York Times* that "we view the values of people in Detroit as completely foreign. We just want to live in peace. And we feel that anybody coming from Detroit is going to cause problems."[14] The commissioner's remarkable statement also reflected the county's political transformation. As recently as 1960, it was, according to the political strategist Stanley B. Greenberg, "the most democratic suburb in America, giving John Kennedy 63% of the vote."[15] But by the early 1980s, Macomb County—which would have been significantly impacted had Judge Roth's desegregation order survived—had completed its political conversion. In the 1984 presidential election, Ronald Reagan won the county in a landslide. "Macomb was now the national home of Reagan Democrats and the working material for a new American political alignment," was Greenberg's assessment.[16]

Of course, it is impossible to state with certainty exactly what would have happened to Detroit and its suburbs if *Milliken* had gone the other way. Obviously, there would have been white resistance to desegregation, just as there had been in the South. But, as the journalist Adam Cohen observed, that didn't necessarily mean that integration was doomed to fail.[17] He pointed to several elements of Judge Roth's desegregation order—holding busing to a minimum and 70 to 80 percent white post-desegregation schools and classrooms—that would have "done a great deal to address the white community's concerns about busing." After the initial furor died down, cross-district desegregation might well have succeeded as it did in Louisville, Kentucky.

Louisville was one of the few jurisdictions where plaintiffs were able to satisfy *Milliken*'s high burden for obtaining metropolitan desegregation. Decades later, a comparison between the two metro areas is illuminating. Although Detroit was far larger than Louisville, initially the two regions had strong similarities. In the early 1970s, both were proportionally comparable, with roughly the same number of blacks and whites in their school systems and similar levels of neighborhood and school segregation.[18] Two generations later, the two were very different. Detroit had one of the nation's most segregated school systems, with the city and public school populations in steep decline. Detroit's neighborhoods also became more racially segregated. The city was plagued by slow job growth, a low tax base, and a bond rating that was at or just above junk bond status. Ultimately, the state twice took over Detroit's public schools.[19] In 2013, the city went bankrupt.[20]

Over this same period, Detroit's suburbs did become more racially diverse. But it was a late-breaking development. As University of Michigan sociologist Reynolds Farley put it, "Metropolitan Detroit came to be the epitome of American Apartheid in 1990 when African Americans made up 77% of the city's residents while 93% of the suburban residents were White."[21] Significant numbers of Detroit's black population with the financial wherewithal to do so moved to the suburbs, but only after 1990 as discriminatory barriers receded.[22] Whites had an enormous head start, and they continued to flee as blacks moved into "inner ring" suburbs with closer proximity to Detroit. Integration has not been stable in these newly more racially diverse suburbs. In 2015, Myron Orfield observed: "Newer white suburbs continue to grow at Detroit's sprawling periphery. These predominantly white suburbs have tax bases that are 120 percent of regional average, lower taxes, better services, and all-white schools to attract white flight from the . . . suburbs" that intervened in the Detroit lawsuit.[23]

The Louisville-Jefferson County School District was a very different story. While Detroit's schools were falling further into decline, the combined school district boasted some of the nation's most racially integrated schools, and its school and regional population rose. Louisville enjoyed a high-quality bond rating, its neighborhoods became more racially integrated, and the tax base and job opportunities expanded. Perhaps most importantly, there was no comparison in *black students' academic achievement*. Black students in Louisville performed much better—sometimes two to three times better—on reading, math, and science tests at both the fourth- and eighth-grade levels than black children attending school in Detroit.[24] The metropolitan school desegregation plan also had a synergistic effect on housing, promoting stable residential integration.[25] Louisville was so enamored with metropolitan desegregation that it kept the plan in place even after a federal court said it was no longer legally required to do so. Then, when a small group of disaffected white parents sued to kill the plan, Louisville defended it all the way to the U.S. Supreme Court, where the case was combined with the similar case involving the Seattle schools. This was the case I witnessed being argued before the high court in December 2006. Louisville lost the case—*Parents Involved in Community Schools v. Seattle School District*—just as I feared it would. In his decision, Chief Justice John Roberts famously wrote, "The way to stop discrimination on the basis of race is to stop discriminating on the basis of race."[26]

Of course, it is important not to confuse causation with correlation. The two cities are in different regions of the country. They have different histories and different economies. No one can prove definitively that the sole reason why Louisville and Detroit's fortunes diverged so dramatically was because of the Supreme Court's decision in *Milliken*. But it is enough to observe that, as Myron Orfield put it, "there is no region in the United States that would have chosen Detroit's fate over Louisville's if it had the chance."[27]

In letting white families escape Detroit, *Milliken* mattered. In 2015, Judge Damon Keith explained to me, "If Roth's decision had been upheld by the Supreme Court there would have been no place for the white suburbs to go, and that's why that case was so important . . . The whites were fleeing the cities and Roth's decision" would have mitigated that.[28] The political scientist Joyce Baugh added context on how a metropolitan desegregation plan might have affected resource allocations for Detroit's public schools: "The white folks who had to send their kids to black schools would have been more inclined to push the legislature. I just can't imagine that if their kids had to go to those schools in Detroit, they wouldn't have done everything they possibly could to make sure that those schools had all of the resources that they needed."[29]

═══

I heard King's warning as I thought of integration's effect on whites. There is plenty of data suggesting that integration benefits them in a variety of ways.[30] White students who have attended racially diverse schools routinely report a better understanding of different viewpoints and enhanced cultural competency, which increases the ability to work in diverse settings.[31] Racially diverse schools facilitate cross-racial friendships, which are linked to prejudice and stereotype reduction.[32] Attending a racially diverse school also changes whites' behavior later in life. One researcher wrote that "white graduates of diverse schools often seek out diverse colleges, work environments, and neighborhoods."[33]

And that harmony is critical. Assessing the impact of foreign interference on the 2016 election, Sherrilyn Ifill, then president and director-counsel of the NAACP Legal Defense and Educational Fund, noted the potential for our nation's enemies to "seize upon these divisions because they are real—because racism remains the United States' Achilles' heel."[34] Racism is a national security issue. The United States will be a majority minority country by 2045.[35] Changing white attitudes—and undermining the growing threat of violent white nationalism—is absolutely vital if we ever hope to become a functioning *multiracial* democracy. On January 6, 2021, the nation got a tragic and very violent reminder of how far we are from achieving that goal. Janai Nelson, LDF's current president and director-counsel, agrees: "The threat of racial apartheid in America is more present today than it has been in the 70 years following *Brown v. Board of Education*. Rather than working to build an inclusive multiracial democracy in which everyone has the potential to thrive, the efforts to maintain a white nationalist patriarchy are in overdrive. There is no sustainable democratic future in the latter strategy."[36]

Then there is the overtly racist "great replacement theory," the fear that "white people are being stripped of their power through the demographic rise of communities of color."[37] Media figures have weaponized the theory, with Tucker Carlson championing it more than four hundred times on his popular political talk show between 2016 and 2023.[38] This has hardly been idle chatter. As *The New York Times* has reported, replacement theory has moved from the fringe to the mainstream: "Sanded down and shorn of explicitly anti-Black and antisemitic themes, [it has] become commonplace in the Republican Party—spoken aloud at congressional hearings, echoed in Republican campaign advertisements and embraced by a growing array of right-wing candidates and media personalities."[39] Violent white extremists have heard the call. Mass shooters in Pittsburgh, El Paso, and Buffalo have drawn homicidal inspiration from replacement theory, killing dozens because of their race or religion.[40] Without an education in a diverse, multiracial environment, it is that much easier for opportunists, demagogues, and politicians to achieve their aims by capitalizing on—and amplifying—our differences. Politicians win elections by putting fear into white parents that their young children will somehow be forcibly indoctrinated by the anti-white teachings of "critical race theory."[41] Never mind that critical race theory is an upper-level *law school elective* and isn't part of the secondary school curriculum.[42] Nor does it matter that the course provides a useful corrective to the sanitized version of American history that so many students routinely encounter throughout the educational process.

In 2004, a young U.S. senator from Illinois, Barack Obama, gave the keynote address at the Democratic National Convention. The speech, which instantly catapulted him into the top rank of future presidential contenders, is perhaps most widely remembered for the following statement: "There's not a liberal America and a conservative America—there's the United States of America. There's not a black America and white America and Latino America and Asian America; there's the United States of America." Looking back at that statement after all that has transpired, Obama's remark seems naive if not patently ridiculous. Since that time, the country has become even more polarized into an "us" and "them." Today, we feel less like a nation and more like two warring tribes. It's the Democrats versus the Republicans, the "blue" versus the "red" states. Discussions of disunion, secession, and even civil war are increasingly common. But where Obama's statement had real value was as an evergreen declaration of national identity. It was about a vision of who we *wanted* to be. We may never become that people: an awesome multiracial democracy that provides true opportunities for all—and not just the wealthiest—to succeed. We may never become a nation where a child's zip code—or school district—does not largely determine her opportunity to reach her full potential. But the American experiment is over when we forget that our boats rise together or they don't rise at all. The American experiment is over when we stop trying to become the country President Obama imagined. All of my research, all of my reading, all of the conversations I had over the years led me to a single conclusion: that pursuing the vision first outlined in *Plessy v. Ferguson* and later confirmed in *Milliken v. Bradley* would never take us there. Instead, it was *Brown v. Board of Education* that led the way.

As I drove away from the segregation wall, I was overcome with sadness. 1974 was a long time ago. Maybe there was too much water under the bridge. Perhaps *Milliken* was our last, best chance to desegregate our schools and our neighborhoods. As much as I tried to keep it at bay, I felt the ripples of despair, of resignation, of bitterness, of anger creeping into my psyche. I could feel tears welling in my eyes. Needing to self-soothe, I flipped through my phone furiously looking for a particular tune. The song I was thinking of was released in 1974, the very same week the court decided the *Milliken* case.

I tapped the screen, and the whirling staccato sound of the Hohner

Clavinet washed over me. Next came a beat you could walk on—backward—so devastatingly funky it was almost disorienting. I heard Stevie yelp "ow" and I was instantly transported back to the living room of our house in Palmer Woods. The cover of the album, *Fulfillingness' First Finale*, flashed into my mind. With a milk-chocolate brown, rust, and orange palette, the jacket featured a psychedelic drawing of Stevie, keyboards rising upward, perhaps to heaven, behind him. The album was one of my parents' favorites, and the song "You Haven't Done Nothin'" was one of the record's highlights. I remember the moment as one of happiness and optimism. I can see my father snapping his fingers as my mother executed her patented dance moves across the green shag carpet. By that time, she was enrolled in Marygrove College, finishing the degree she had begun years earlier at Howard University. My father's clients visited the house frequently. He was well respected in the community. They were moving forward, not back.

I don't know that any of us ever really paid that much attention to the song's lyrics. Listening to them now, I can see that Stevie was talking directly to Nixon. He was taking the fight right to the man. "You Haven't Done Nothin'" was a hard-core dance tune with an in-your-face political message. It indicted the president of the United States—who was to resign less than a month later—for hypocrisy. Yet with its infectious beat, Stevie fought back against despair.

There was a moment—right before *Milliken v. Bradley* was decided—when more than one possibility for seriously reducing both school *and* residential segregation was available. In 1974, the U.S. Supreme Court took us down the wrong path. But we can still choose another.

It's not too late.

I thought of King yet again. If he was right, as I believed he was, then the presumption of validity lies with the laws, policies, and decisions that bring us together—the work of the soul force—rather than with those that tear us apart. *Separate is still unequal.* It is the forces promoting racial and economic segregation that must overcome the heavy burden of presumptive invalidity. It should never have been the other way around.

KEY EVENTS TIMELINE

DATE	EVENT
May 17, 1954	*Brown v. Board of Education*—the Supreme Court rules that state-mandated racially separate public schools violate the equal protection clause of the Fourteenth Amendment.
May 31, 1955	*Brown v. Board of Education II*—the Supreme Court rules that the *Brown I* mandate shall be implemented "with all deliberate speed."
1955	Remus Robinson becomes the first African American member of the Detroit Board of Education.
September 12, 1958	*Cooper v. Aaron*—the Supreme Court rules that Arkansas state officials must comply with *Brown v. Board of Education.*
January 24, 1961	*Taylor v. Board of Education of New Rochelle*—a federal trial court rules that the northern city had violated *Brown* by intentionally "perpetuat[ing] and maintain[ing] a segregated school."
1962	Robert Carter and June Shagaloff tour ten cities on the West Coast, surveying the extent of school segregation outside the Deep South; NAACP sponsors or files ten lawsuits challenging northern-style segregation.
January 29, 1963	*Bell v. School City of Gary, Indiana*—a federal trial court rules that the plaintiffs failed to show that the northern city "deliberately or purposely segregated the Gary schools according to race;" "the problem in Gary is not one of segregated schools but rather one of segregated housing."
1964	Citywide boycotts of the public schools in New York and Cleveland; activists seek comprehensive plan to desegregate the schools.

DATE	EVENT
July 1, 1965	A liberal, pro-integration majority—including Remus Robinson and Abraham Zwerdling—take control of the Detroit Board of Education.
January 1966	Martin Luther King Jr. and his family move to Chicago; opening phase of the Chicago Freedom Movement.
August 26, 1966	The Chicago Freedom Movement and the City of Chicago agree to terms embodied in the Summit Agreement. Chicago promises to enforce antidiscrimination law and to urge passage of state fair housing law; no enforcement mechanisms are included in the agreement.
December 6, 1966	*Deal v. Cincinnati Board of Education*—the United States Court of Appeals for the Sixth Circuit—governing the state of Michigan—rules that a neighborhood school policy does not violate *Brown*; burden of integration on black parents rather than school authorities.
March 1967	The U.S. Commission on Civil Rights publishes *Racial Isolation in the Public Schools*; finds that properly designed and executed school desegregation programs stand the best chance of producing significant gains in student achievement.
June 13, 1967	President Lyndon Johnson nominates Thurgood Marshall to become the first African American justice of the U.S. Supreme Court.
June 13, 1967	Clash in Midtown: Reverend Albert Cleage Jr. calls for black control of black schools at a Detroit Board of Education meeting.
July 23, 1967	Detroit police raid a "blind pig" on Twelfth Street and Clairmount, catalyzing civil unrest in Detroit.
March 1, 1968	The Kerner Commission releases comprehensive findings (the Kerner Commission report) on the causes of recent civil disorders throughout the United States, including Detroit, Newark, and Watts.
April 4, 1968	Martin Luther King Jr. is assassinated.
April 6, 1968	*The New York Times* reports that King's assassination has likely changed the political realities on the ground: "Congressional leaders said that Dr. King's murder could assure passage next week of a landmark civil rights bill."
April 11, 1968	President Lyndon B. Johnson signs the Fair Housing Act into law.

DATE	EVENT
May 27, 1968	*Green v. County School Board of New Kent County*—the Supreme Court rules that southern school authorities have an affirmative obligation—even in the absence of litigation—"to convert to a unitary system in which racial discrimination would be eliminated root and branch."
June 1968	Chief Justice Earl Warren announces that he will retire at the end of the 1968–69 Supreme Court term.
November 5, 1968	Richard Nixon is elected president of the United States.
November 1968	Community control advocate Andrew Perdue is elected to the Detroit Board of Education with Cleage's support.
April 14, 1969	Responding to calls for community control, state senator Coleman Young introduces a bill in the Michigan legislature requiring the Detroit school system to reorganize; bill provides significant implementation discretion to the Detroit Board of Education.
May 21, 1969	President Richard Nixon nominates Warren E. Burger to be chief justice of the U.S. Supreme Court.
August 11, 1969	Governor William Milliken signs Young's school reorganization bill into law.
October 29, 1969	*Alexander v. Holmes County Board of Education*—the Supreme Court discards the *Brown II* "all deliberate speed" standard; "the obligation of every school district is to terminate dual school systems at once."
April 7, 1970	Using its discretion under Young's bill, the Detroit Board of Education votes to reorganize the Detroit public school system *and* adopt a modest high school integration plan at a raucous meeting at the School Center Building in Midtown Detroit.
April 14, 1970	President Richard Nixon nominates Harry A. Blackmun to the U.S. Supreme Court.
May 4, 1970	Citizens Committee for Better Education (CCBE) announces a campaign to recall the four members of the Detroit Board of Education who voted in favor of the high school integration plan.
June 14, 1970	Remus Robinson dies.
July 7, 1970	Governor Milliken signs Public Act 48, "Young's compromise," into law; statute invalidates the high school integration plan, reorganizes the Detroit public school system by creating new educational regions, and shortens the terms of three board members who had voted in favor of the high school integration plan.

DATE	EVENT
August 4, 1970	Detroiters recall board president Abraham Zwerdling, and three other board members, all of whom had voted in favor of the high school integration plan.
August 18, 1970	Lou Lucas files the *Bradley v. Milliken* complaint in federal district court; the case is randomly assigned to federal district court judge Stephen J. Roth.
September 3, 1970	Judge Roth denies the plaintiffs' request to restore the high school integration plan the board had adopted on April 7.
October 13, 1970	The United States Court of Appeals for Sixth Circuit rules that Public Act 48, which invalidated the high school integration plan, is unconstitutional; remands the case to Judge Roth to determine whether Detroit had been operating a "separate and unequal" school system.
March 22, 1971	Judge Roth allows CCBE to intervene as a defendant.
April 6, 1971	The *Bradley v. Milliken* trial begins.
April 19, 1971	The United States Senate begins debate on Senator Abraham Ribicoff's proposal to tie state and local education authorities' receipt of billions of dollars of federal education money to a requirement that they integrate their schools; bill dies on the Senate floor.
April 20, 1971	*Swann v. Charlotte-Mecklenburg Board of Education*—the Supreme Court rules that federal courts have broad remedial authority in school desegregation cases, including the ability to order busing. "The district judge or school authorities should make every effort to achieve the greatest possible degree of actual desegregation and will thus necessarily be concerned with the elimination of one-race schools."
May 28, 1971	*Davis v. School District of the City of Pontiac*—the United States Court of Appeals for the Sixth Circuit upholds trial court judge Damon Keith's ruling that the Pontiac school system (roughly twenty-five miles from Detroit) is unconstitutionally segregated.
Mid-July, 1971	CCBE asks Judge Roth to add more than eighty suburban school districts to the *Bradley v. Milliken* lawsuit. Roth takes CCBE's motion under advisement.
August 30, 1971	Fifty-seven school buses are bombed in Pontiac before Judge Keith's integration order goes into effect.
September 27, 1971	Judge Roth rules in the *Bradley v. Milliken* case that the Detroit Board of Education and the State of Michigan have intentionally segregated Detroit's schools in violation of the Constitution.

DATE	EVENT
October 21, 1971	President Nixon nominates William F. Rehnquist and Lewis F. Powell Jr. to the U.S. Supreme Court.
March 15, 1972	Irene McCabe begins Pontiac-to-Washington antibusing protest march.
March 15, 1972	Judge Roth allows forty-three suburban school systems located in the Detroit metropolitan area to intervene in the *Bradley v. Milliken* lawsuit. Roth continues to defer ruling on CCBE's earlier motion to add more than eighty suburban school districts to "await further developments in this proceeding."
March 28, 1972	Judge Roth rules that a Detroit-only desegregation plan cannot remedy the constitutional violation because it would not achieve "the greatest possible degree of actual school desegregation." Additionally, a Detroit-only plan would "change a school system which is now Black and White to one that would be perceived as Black, thereby increasing the flight of Whites from the city." On the same day, Roth also begins hearings on the proposed metropolitan plans.
May 16, 1972	George Wallace wins Michigan's Democratic presidential primary.
June 14, 1972	Judge Roth rules that only a metropolitan desegregation plan can remedy the constitutional violation; establishes a large city-suburban metropolitan desegregation area affecting approximately 800,000 students; and creates desegregation panel to implement his order.
July 20, 1972	The United States Court of Appeals for the Sixth Circuit agrees to review Judge Roth's metropolitan desegregation ruling, effectively ending Roth's management of the case.
November 7, 1972	Richard Nixon is reelected president of the United States; Nixon carries Michigan, performing particularly well in areas that stand to be affected by Roth's metropolitan desegregation order.
November 7, 1972	Judge Roth has first heart attack.
December 8, 1972	A three-judge panel of the United States Court of Appeals for the Sixth Circuit affirms Judge Roth's metropolitan desegregation order.
December 31, 1972	The Senate Select Committee on Equal Educational Opportunity publishes report noting that "the pattern of combined governmental official action which produces residential and school isolation in most of our large cities was best described by the federal district court in Michigan in *Bradley v. Milliken*."

DATE	EVENT
March 21, 1973	*San Antonio School District v. Rodriguez*—the Supreme Court rules that education is not a "fundamental" right, school finance systems that produce substantial interdistrict funding disparities do not violate U.S. Constitution.
May 21, 1973	*School Board of the City of Richmond v. State Board of Education of Virginia*—an evenly divided Supreme Court issues a "per curiam" decision affirming lower court judgment that had halted Judge Merhige's city-suburban desegregation plan.
June 12, 1973	The full United States Court of Appeals for the Sixth Circuit affirms the three-judge panel decision, again upholding Judge Roth's metropolitan desegregation order.
June 21, 1973	*Keyes v. School District No. 1, Denver, Colorado*—the Supreme Court extends *Brown* to a non-southern school district for the very first time.
November 19, 1973	The Supreme Court agrees to hear *Milliken v. Bradley*.
February 27, 1974	*Milliken v. Bradley* oral argument.
April 4, 1974	Judge Roth suffers second heart attack.
July 11, 1974	Judge Roth dies at age sixty-six.
July 25, 1974	*Milliken v. Bradley*—the Supreme Court strikes down Judge Roth's metropolitan desegregation order; remands case so that Detroit's majority-black schools can be "desegregated" without including the suburban school districts.
August 8, 1974	President Nixon resigns from office.
August 15, 1975	Federal District court judge Robert DeMascio, now presiding over the *Milliken* case, orders a limited student reassignment plan and requires defendants to fund "educational components" to address the harms associated with segregated schools; state officials object to the funding requirement and appeal.
November 15, 1976	*Milliken v. Bradley II*—the Supreme Court grants certiorari; the Supreme Court will again review the *Milliken* case.
March 22, 1977	*Milliken v. Bradley II* oral argument.
June 27, 1977	*Milliken v. Bradley II*—rejecting state officials' argument, the Supreme Court rules that the state can be made to pay its fair share of the costs of the educational components.

NOTES

PROLOGUE

1. Gwenn Bashara Samuel, *The First Hundred Years Are the Hardest: A Centennial History of the Detroit College of Law* (Detroit: Detroit College of Law, 1993), 39.
2. Ernest Gellhorn, "The Law Schools and the Negro," *Duke Law Journal* 1968, no. 6 (December 1968): 1069, 1077.
3. Leigh Ann Mort and Milton Moskowitz, "The Best Law Schools for Blacks," *The Journal of Blacks in Higher Education* 4 (1994): 57, 57.
4. Parents Involved in Community Schools v. Seattle School District No. 1, 551 U.S. at 701 (2007).
5. *Parents Involved*, 551 U.S. at 747.
6. Transcript of Oral Argument at 4, Parents Involved in Community Schools v. Seattle School District No. 1, 551 U.S. at 701 (2007) (No. 05–908).
7. Transcript of Oral Argument at 5, *Parents Involved*, 551 U.S. at 701 (2007).
8. Transcript of Oral Argument at 5, *Parents Involved*, 551 U.S. at 701 (2007).
9. Transcript of Oral Argument at 6, *Parents Involved*, 551 U.S. at 701 (2007).
10. Transcript of Oral Argument at 37, *Parents Involved*, 551 U.S. at 701 (2007).
11. Transcript of Oral Argument at 37, *Parents Involved*, 551 U.S. at 701 (2007).
12. Transcript of Oral Argument at 37, *Parents Involved*, 551 U.S. at 701 (2007).
13. Bradley v. Milliken, Ruling on Propriety of Considering a Metropolitan Remedy to Accomplish Desegregation of the Public Schools of the City of Detroit, Mar. 24, 1972 at 4–5, Box 2, Bradley v. Milliken Case Files, Bentley Historical Library, University of Michigan; Bradley v. Milliken, 345 F. Supp. 914, 939 (E.D. Mich. 1972), *aff'd in part, vacated in part*, 484 F.2d 215 (6th Cir. 1973), *rev'd*, 418 U.S. at 717, 94 S. Ct. 3112, 41 L. Ed. 2d 1069 (1974).
14. Reynolds Farley et al., "'Chocolate City, Vanilla Suburbs': Will the Trend Toward Racially Separate Communities Continue?," *Social Science Research* 7, no. 4 (December 1978): 319–44.
15. Parliament, "Chocolate City," *Genius*, accessed Apr. 22, 2024, https://genius.com/Parliament -chocolate-city-lyrics.
16. Joe T. Darden, "Residential Segregation of Blacks in Metropolitan Areas of Michigan, 1960–1990," in *The State of Black Michigan, 1967–2007*, ed. Joe T. Darden, Curtis Stokes, and Richard Walter Thomas (East Lansing: Michigan State University Press, 2007), 132.

17. "200 Protest in Warren: Negro Home Cleared," *Detroit Free Press*, June 14, 1967.
18. "200 Protest in Warren."
19. David Riddle, "HUD and the Open Housing Controversy of 1970 in Warren, Michigan," *The Michigan Historical Review* 24, no. 2 (1998): 1, n. 2.
20. Richard Rothstein, *The Color of Law: A Forgotten History of How Our Government Segregated America* (New York: Liveright, 2017), 146–67.
21. Ta-Nehisi Coates, "The Other Detroit: The City's Grandest Enclave Clings to the Dream," *The Atlantic*, Apr. 2011, https://www.theatlantic.com/magazine/archive/2011/04/the-other-detroit/308403/ (noting that in 1967, there were only nine black families living in the neighborhood, which had more than three hundred homes).
22. Kevin Boyle, "The Fire Last Time: 40 Years Later, the Urban Crisis Still Smolders," *Washington Post*, July 29, 2007.
23. Warranty Deed, Palmer Woods lot 48, given pursuant to a land contract executed between Phyllis B. Korten and Priscilla B. Burck to David E. Curtis and subsequently assigned to Bernard Adams Jr. and Frederica D. Adams on Oct. 5, 1967.
24. M. Ruff, "The Origins of the Roeper School," The Roeper School, fall 2016, https://www.roeperschoolhistory.org/history/origins/.
25. Kerner Commission, *Report of the National Advisory Commission on Civil Disorders*, 1968, v.
26. Gary Blonston, "Detroit School Chief Backs Integration Plan," *Detroit Free Press*, Feb. 21, 1967.
27. Blonston, "Detroit School Chief Backs Integration Plan."
28. Philip Meyer, "Segregation in Detroit Area Intensifying, Study Shows," *Detroit Free Press*, Sept. 10, 1967.
29. Meyer, "Segregation in Detroit Area Intensifying."
30. Meyer, "Segregation in Detroit Area Intensifying."
31. "The Roeper School, History," The Roeper School, accessed Dec. 3, 2023, https://www.roeperschoolhistory.org/history/.
32. "Decennial Census Historical Facts," United States Census Bureau, https://www.census.gov/programs-surveys/decennial-census/decade/decennial-facts.1950.html.
33. "Decennial Census Historical Facts," United States Census Bureau.
34. Brown v. Board of Education of Topeka, Kansas, 349 U.S. at 294 (1955).
35. *Parents Involved*, 551 U.S. at 876 (Breyer, J., dissenting).
36. *Parents Involved*, 551 U.S. at 878 (Breyer, J., dissenting).

1. CLASH IN MIDTOWN

1. Audiotape, "Johnson offers Marshall SG post," Miller Center of the University of Virginia (July 7, 1965).
2. President Lyndon Baines Johnson, 36th President of the United States, Remarks to the Press Announcing the Nomination of Thurgood Marshall as Associate Justice of the Supreme Court (June 13, 1967), available at https://www.presidency.ucsb.edu/documents/remarks-the-press-announcing-the-nomination-thurgood-marshall-associate-justice-the.
3. "About DPL," Detroit Public Library, accessed Apr. 18, 2024, https://detroitpubliclibrary.org/about; "Cass Gilbert-Designed Works," Cass Gilbert Society, accessed Apr. 18, 2024, https://cassgilbertsociety.org/works/.
4. Linda Bank Downs, *Diego Rivera: The Detroit Industry Murals*, (London, UK: Scala, 2006), 35.
5. Jeffrey Mirel, *The Rise and Fall of an Urban School System: Detroit, 1907–1981* (Ann Arbor: University of Michigan Press, 2000), 250–58.
6. Brown v. Board of Education of Topeka, Kansas, 347 U.S. at 483, 494 (1954).

7. Inner City Parents Council, "Inner City Parents' Program for Quality Education in Detroit Inner City Schools," at 40 (June 13, 1967).
8. Inner City Parents Council, "Program," 41.
9. Inner City Parents Council, "Program," 40–41
10. Inner City Parents Council, "Program," 41.
11. Regular Meeting Proceedings of the Board of Education of the City of Detroit (June 13, 1967), at 614.
12. Albert Cleage, "Special Series on our Leaders; 'The Strange Role of Dr. Remus Robinson on the School Board,'" *Illustrated News*, Apr. 2, 1962, 6.
13. Hiley H. Ward, *Prophet of the Black Nation* (Philadelphia: Pilgrim Press, 1969), 72; Roberta Mackey, "Outbursts Mar School Meeting," *Detroit Free Press*, June 14, 1967, A5.
14. Ward, *Prophet of the Black Nation*, 72.
15. Ward, *Prophet of the Black Nation*, 72.
16. Ward, *Prophet of the Black Nation*, 72–73.
17. Ward, *Prophet of the Black Nation*, 73.
18. Ward, *Prophet of the Black Nation*, 73; see also Mackey, "Outbursts," A5.
19. Mackey, "Outbursts," A5.
20. Mackey, "Outbursts," A5.
21. Sidney Fine, *Violence in the Model City: The Cavanagh Administration, Race Relations, and the Detroit Riot of 1967* (East Lansing: Michigan State University Press, 2012), 45.
22. Malcolm X, "Message to the Grass Roots," Nov. 10, 1963, available at https://www.youtube.com/watch?v=mEG6WiPShY4.
23. Albert Cleage and George Breitman, *Myths About Malcolm X; Two Views* (New York: Pathfinder Press, 1971), 3.
24. Cleage and Breitman, *Myths About Malcolm X*, 10.
25. Cleage and Breitman, *Myths About Malcolm X*, 11.
26. "1916: The Detroit Urban League Formed," Charles H. Wright Museum of African American History, www.motorcities.org/images/making_tracks/1916-The-Detroit-Urban-League.pdf.
27. Fine, *Violence in the Model City*, 31.
28. Fine, *Violence in the Model City*, 31.
29. Mackey, "Outbursts," A5; Regular Meeting Proceedings of the Board of Education of the City of Detroit (June 13, 1967), at 616.
30. Mackey, "Outbursts," A5; Regular Meeting Proceedings of the Board of Education of the City of Detroit (June 13, 1967), at 617.
31. For a definition of the term "race man," see W. E. B. Du Bois, "The Conservation of Races, Mar. 5, 1897 ("For the development of Negro genius, of Negro literature and art, of Negro spirit, only Negroes bound and welded together, Negroes inspired by one vast ideal, can work out in its fullness the great message we have for humanity").
32. Ward, *Prophet of the Black Nation*, 34 ("For all outward appearance, the *enfant terrible* of the black nationalist clergy is a 'white' man").
33. Ward, *Prophet of the Black Nation*, 53.
34. Ward, *Prophet of the Black Nation*, 53.
35. Kristin Cleage, "St Mark's United Presbyterian Church 1951 & 1953," *Finding Eliza*, Sept. 11, 2016, https://findingeliza.com/archives/22655; Angela D. Dillard, *Faith in the City: Preaching Radical Social Change in Detroit* (Ann Arbor: University of Michigan Press, 2007), 244.
36. Dillard, *Faith in the City*, 250.
37. Dillard, *Faith in the City*, 250.
38. Dillard, *Faith in the City*, 250–51; Ward, *Prophet of the Black Nation*, 9.
39. Dillard, *Faith in the City*, 251.
40. Ward, *Prophet of the Black Nation*, 7.

41. Ward, *Prophet of the Black Nation*, 7–8.
42. Ward, *Prophet of the Black Nation*, 9.
43. Rosetta E. Ross, "Black Theology and the History of U.S. Black Religions: Post Civil Rights Approaches to the Study of African American Religions," *Religion Compass* 6, no. 4 (Apr. 2012): 249–61, 253.
44. Craig R. Prentiss, "Coloring Jesus: Racial Calculus and the Search for Identity in Twentieth-Century America," *Nova Religio* 11, no. 3 (Feb. 1, 2008): 64–82, 73–76.
45. Albert B. Cleage Jr., *Black Christian Nationalism: New Directions for the Black Church* (Detroit: William Morrow and Company, 1972), xii.
46. Cleage and Breitman, *Myths About Malcolm X*, 11.
47. Stokely Carmichael and Charles V. Hamilton, *Black Power: The Politics of Liberation in America* (New York, NY: Random House, 1967), 44.
48. Cleage and Breitman, *Myths About Malcolm X*, 11.
49. Martavyrene L. Tootle, "The Political Philosophy Incorporated within Black Theology: A Case Study of the Shrine of the Black Madonna," (MA thesis, Atlanta University, 1988), 24.
50. Tootle, "The Political Philosophy," 54–57.
51. Fine, *Violence in the Model City*, 25, 372; Albert B. Cleage Jr., *The Black Messiah*, 229–31 (1968).
52. Kwame Ture and Charles V. Hamilton, *Black Power: The Politics of Liberation in America* (New York: Vintage, 1992), 167.
53. Ernest C. Smith, "Support the Freedom Now Party: Vote Black, Why An All Black Party?," *Illustrated News*, undated.
54. Fine, *Violence in the Model City*, 28; Margalit Fox, "William Worthy, a Reporter Drawn to Forbidden Datelines, Dies at 92," *New York Times*, May 17, 2014; Harold Cruse and Jerry Gafio Watts, *Harold Cruse's the Crisis of the Negro Intellectual Reconsidered* (New York: Routledge, 2004), 27.
55. Cruse and Watts, *Harold Cruse's the Crisis of the Negro Intellectual Reconsidered*, 28.
56. "New Freedom Now Party Blanked but Not Broken," *Detroit Free Press*, Nov. 5, 1964.
57. Mirel, *The Rise and Fall of an Urban School System*, 250–58.
58. Mirel, *The Rise and Fall of an Urban School System*, 376, n.54.
59. Stan Latreille, "Chief School Critic Trampled; Robinson Leads Board Race," *Detroit News*, Aug. 3, 1966.
60. James Harris Jr., "Decentralization and Recentralization of the Detroit Public Schools: A Study of the Transition of the School System 1969–1983" (PhD dissertation, University of Michigan, 1985), 83.
61. Fine, *Violence in the Model City*, 160.
62. The Detroit Historical Society, Encyclopedia of Detroit, "Uprising of 1967" (calling the Detroit riot "the largest civil disturbance of twentieth century America"), https://detroithistorical.org/learn/encyclopedia-of-detroit/uprising-1967.
63. The Detroit Historical Society, "Uprising of 1967."
64. Fine, *Violence in the Model City*, 293–95.
65. Fine, *Violence in the Model City*, 291.
66. Kerner Commission, *Report*, 70.
67. Associated Press, "President Proclaims Sunday as Day of Prayer for Racial Peace," *Longview Daily News*, July 28, 1967, 1.
68. Associated Press, "President Proclaims Sunday as Day of Prayer for Racial Peace."
69. Peter Charles Hoffer, *Seven Fires: The Urban Infernos That Reshaped America* (New York: PublicAffairs, 2006), 239.
70. Elliot D. Luby and James Hedegard, "A Study of Civil Disorder in Detroit," *William and Mary Law Review* 10, no. 3 (Mar. 1969): 629.

71. Albert Cleage Jr., "The Morning After - July 23, 1967 Rev. Albert B. Cleage, Jr.," YouTube, uploaded by Ribbron JW, https://www.youtube.com/watch?v=2NY-WLy-up4.
72. Albert Cleage Jr., "67-7-30, JAA, 'The Grapes of Wrath,'" *Finding Eliza*, uploaded by Kristin Cleage, https://findingeliza.com/archives/18598.
73. Fine, *Violence in the Model City*, 293.
74. Hoffer, *Seven Fires*, 233–35.
75. Fine, *Violence in the Model City*, 293.
76. Fine, *Violence in the Model City*, 303–305.
77. Heather Ann Thompson, *Whose Detroit? Politics, Labor, and Race in a Modern American City* (Ithaca, NY: Cornell University Press, 2017), ix.
78. Thompson, *Whose Detroit?*, ix.
79. Kerner Commission, *Report*, 91.
80. Letter from Thurgood Marshall to Roger Baldwin (June 9, 1944), in Michael G. Long, *Marshalling Justice: The Early Civil Rights Letters of Thurgood Marshall* (New York: Amistad, 2010), 136.
81. John Steckroth, "Gov. Romney Addresses the State After Detroit Riots Are Contained," WDIV Click on Detroit, July 23, 2017, https://www.clickondetroit.com/features/gov-romney-addresses-the-state-after-detroit-riots-are-contained.
82. Steckroth, "Gov. Romney Addresses the State After Detroit Riots Are Contained."
83. Steckroth, "Gov. Romney Addresses the State After Detroit Riots Are Contained."
84. Steckroth, "Gov. Romney Addresses the State After Detroit Riots Are Contained."
85. Steckroth, "Gov. Romney Addresses the State After Detroit Riots Are Contained."
86. Steckroth, "Gov. Romney Addresses the State After Detroit Riots Are Contained."
87. Coleman Young and Lonnie Wheeler, *Hard Stuff: The Autobiography of Coleman Young* (New York: Viking, 1994), 179; Fine, *Violence in the Model City*, 434.
88. Young and Wheeler, *Hard Stuff*, 179–80; See, e.g., Leah Platt Boustan, "Black Migration and White Flight: Essays on the Northern Housing and Labor Markets, 1940–1970" (PhD dissertation, Harvard University, 2006).
89. Young and Wheeler, *Hard Stuff*, 179–80.

2. SYMPATHY, KNOWLEDGE, AND THE TRUTH

1. Mirel, *The Rise and Fall of an Urban School System*, 226.
2. Mirel, *The Rise and Fall of an Urban School System*, 194–96.
3. Mirel, *The Rise and Fall of an Urban School System*, 217–18.
4. Mirel, *The Rise and Fall of an Urban School System*, 225–26.
5. Mirel, *The Rise and Fall of an Urban School System*, 227.
6. Mirel, *The Rise and Fall of an Urban School System*, 252–55.
7. Mirel, *The Rise and Fall of an Urban School System*, 275.
8. Sherrill School Parents Committee v. Detroit Board of Education, No. 22092 (E.D. Mich., filed Jan. 22, 1962); "Suit Charges Segregation in Detroit Schools," *Detroit Free Press*, Jan. 23, 1962.
9. Complaint at 1, *Sherrill*, No. 22092 (E.D. Mich., 1962).
10. Complaint at 3, *Sherrill*, No. 22092 (E.D. Mich., 1962).
11. Mirel, *The Rise and Fall of an Urban School System*, 264; Dillard, *Faith in the City*, 259.
12. Dillard, *Faith in the City*, 257–58.
13. "Detroit NAACP 'Not Ducking' Sherrill Issue," *Michigan Chronicle*, Mar. 10, 1962. In response to a question about the Detroit branch's purported reluctance to join the Sherrill lawsuit, the chairman of the Legal Redress Committee, H. Franklin Brown, reportedly stated: the "Detroit NAACP is not ducking the Sherrill School issue and will never duck an issue." Mirel, *The Rise and Fall of an Urban School System*, 263.

14. Dillard, *Faith in the City*, 257.
15. Albert B. Cleage Jr., "NAACP Must Support the Court Fight! NAACP Action Threatens Important Sherrill School Suit," *Illustrated News*, Feb. 26, 1962.
16. Fine, *Violence in the Model City*, 47.
17. Detroit NAACP, "Detroit and NAACP Is Forming School Integration Body," Press Release, Feb. 22, 1962, NAACP Records, Manuscript Division, Library of Congress, Washington, D.C.
18. William R. Grant, "Community Control vs. School Integration—The Case of Detroit," *The Public Interest* 24 (Summer 1971): 66–67.
19. Dillard, *Faith in the City*, 257.
20. Dillard, *Faith in the City*, 257.
21. "Race Bias in Schools Denied," *Detroit Free Press*, Aug. 15, 1962, A3.
22. "Race Bias in Schools Denied."
23. "Meet the Committee, They Worked for Two Years," *Detroit Free Press*, Mar. 11, 1962, at B1.
24. Mike Wowk, "Nathan J. Kaufman, 81, Judge for Nearly Three Decades, Fought For Youths, Unions," *Detroit News*, Jan. 1. 1990.
25. "Segregated Schools 'a Fact'—Kaufman," *Detroit News*, Mar. 11, 1962, A1.
26. Mirel, *The Rise and Fall of an Urban School System*, 264.
27. Mirel, *The Rise and Fall of an Urban School System*, 298.
28. Mirel, *The Rise and Fall of an Urban School System*, 307.
29. Mirel, *The Rise and Fall of an Urban School System*, 228.
30. Mirel, *The Rise and Fall of an Urban School System*, 274.
31. Mirel, *The Rise and Fall of an Urban School System*, 298.
32. David Arsen, Tanner Delpier, and Jesse Nagel, "Michigan School Finance at the Crossroads: A Quarter Century of State Control," Michigan State University, Education Policy Report (2019), 13, available at https://education.msu.edu/ed-policy-phd/pdf/Michigan-School-Finance-at-the-Crossroads-A-Quarter-Center-of-State-Control.pdf.
33. Kerner Commission, *Report*, 341 (finding that "there are more than 295,000 students in the Detroit public schools, of whom 43 percent are white and 56 percent Negro. Nearly 60 percent (about 175,000) are educationally disadvantaged within the definition of Title I").
34. Education Committee of the Detroit Branch of the NAACP, *A Report on Counseling and Guidance to the Board of Education of the City of Detroit*, Dec. 1965, NAACP Detroit Branch Records, Box 63, Folder 1, Walter P. Reuther Library, Archives of Labor History and Urban Affairs, Wayne State University.
35. Northern High School, available at https://historicdetroit.org/buildings/northern-high-school; Mirel, *The Rise and Fall of an Urban School System*, 300.
36. Roberta Mackey, "2,300 Picket at Northern; Brownell Grants Demands," *Detroit Free Press*, Apr. 8, 1966.
37. Mackey, "2,300 Picket at Northern."
38. Susan Holmes, "Concern Is Voiced on School Protest," *Detroit Free Press*, Apr. 9, 1966.
39. Joseph Strickland, "Brownell Pledges Improvement After Northern Picketing," *Detroit News*, Apr. 8, 1966.
40. Strickland, "Brownell Pledges Improvement After Northern Picketing."
41. Susan Holmes, "In Northern Walk Out, Ringleaders Explain Revolt," *Detroit Free Press*, Apr. 20, 1966.
42. Holmes, "In Northern Walk Out."
43. Holmes, "In Northern Walk Out."
44. Holmes, "In Northern Walk Out."
45. William Serrin, "Pupils End Student Boycott; Principal's Status Is Unclear," *Detroit Free Press*, Apr. 27, 1966.
46. Mirel, *The Rise and Fall of an Urban School System*, 305.
47. "Eight Students Arrested in Protest," *Detroit Free Press*, Apr. 28, 1966.

48. "Protests Bring Aid to School," *Detroit Free Press*, Oct. 4, 1966.

49. Open Letter from the Ad Hoc Executive Committee to the Detroit Board of Education and the Public (June 2, 1966).

50. Jim Treloar, "An Inside View: What the Schools and Students Need," *Detroit Free Press*, Sept. 28, 1966, at A1.

51. Mirel, *The Rise and Fall of an Urban School System*, 298–99.

52. Grant, "Community Control vs. School Integration," 65.

53. Roberta Mackey, "City Schools Rapped, 'Equality Lag' Hit by Teacher Unit," *Detroit Free Press*, Apr. 5, 1967.

54. Mackey, "City Schools Rapped."

55. Roberta Mackey, "Schools Ask $225.5 Million," *Detroit Free Press*, Apr. 12, 1967, A10.

56. *How School Funding Works in Michigan*, A Mackinac Center Report 14 (2017), available at https://files.eric.ed.gov/fulltext/ED594032.pdf; Arsen, Delpier, and Nagel, "Michigan School Finance at the Crossroads," 13; Daphne Kenyon, Bethany Paquin, and Semida Munteanu, *Public Schools and the Property Tax: A Comparison of Education Funding Models in Three U.S. States*, Lincoln Institute of Land Policy (2022), available at https://www.lincolninst.edu/publications/articles/2022-04-public-schools-property-tax-comparison-education-models.

57. "Detroit Urges US Senators to Boost Funds for Schools," *Detroit Free Press*, Aug. 10, 1967, C15.

58. "Detroit Urges US Senators to Boost Funds for Schools."

59. "Detroit Urges US Senators to Boost Funds for Schools."

60. "Detroit Urges US Senators to Boost Funds for Schools."

61. Congressional Research Service, *The Elementary and Secondary Education Act (ESEA), as Amended by the Every Student Succeeds Act (ESSA): A Primer*, Apr. 20, 2022, available at https://crsreports.congress.gov/product/pdf/R/R45977.

62. "Detroit Urges US Senators to Boost Funds for Schools."

63. Roberta Mackey, "Schools Closed for Indefinite Time, Talks Remain Bogged Down," *Detroit Free Press*, Sept. 7, 1967.

64. William Pannill and Mary Ann Weston, "School Starts Today, Contract OKd by Teachers," *Detroit Free Press*, Sept. 19, 1967.

65. Pannill and Weston, "School Starts Today."

66. "Nearly 6000 Pupils Missing, Schools Face Loss of 1.7 Million," *Detroit Free Press*, Sept. 30, 1967.

67. "Nearly 6000 Pupils Missing, Schools Face Loss of 1.7 Million."

68. Mirel, *The Rise and Fall of an Urban School System*, 312–13.

69. Mirel, *The Rise and Fall of an Urban School System*, 309.

70. William Grant, "Who Will Control Detroit's Schools?," *Detroit Free Press*, Nov. 17, 1968.

71. W. E. B. Du Bois, "Does the Negro Need Separate Schools?," *The Journal of Negro Education* 4, no. 3 (July 1935): 335.

72. Jerald E. Podair, *The Strike That Changed New York: Blacks, Whites, and the Ocean Hill-Brownsville Crisis* (New Haven, CT: Yale University Press, 2002), 82.

73. Podair, *The Strike That Changed New York*, 43–44.

74. Wendell E. Pritchett, *Brownsville, Brooklyn: Blacks, Jews and the Changing Face of the Ghetto* (Chicago: University of Chicago Press, 2003), 231–35.

75. Pritchett, *Brownsville, Brooklyn*, 236.

76. Edward B. Fiske, "Community Run Schools Leave Hope Unfulfilled," *New York Times*, June 24, 1980.

77. Marcia Chambers, "Politics and Patronage Dominate Community-Run School Districts," *New York Times*, June 26, 1980.

78. Richard Severo, "Kenneth Clark, Who Fought Segregation, Dies," *New York Times*, May 2, 2005.

79. Fiske, "Community Run."

80. Albert Cleage, "Message to the Nation, What Do We Owe Our Children?," *Michigan Chronicle*, Nov. 4, 1967.

81. Cleage, "Message to the Nation."

82. Cleage, "Message to the Nation" ("the Inner City Organizing Committee has reported [that the situation in the inner city schools is critical] regularly since last June 13 when the Parents Council of the Inner City Organizing Committee submitted a comprehensive report and specific recommendations for improving inner city schools").

83. Sidney J. Berkowitz, "An Analysis of the Relationship between the Detroit Community Control of Schools Movement and the 1971 Decentralization of Detroit Public Schools" (PhD dissertation, Wayne State University, 1973), 92–93.

84. Berkowitz, "An Analysis," 102.

85. Grace Boggs, *Living for Change: An Autobiography* (Minneapolis: University of Minnesota Press, 2016), 139.

86. "Parents Boycott at Post," *Michigan Chronicle*, Mar. 23, 1968, A1; C. C. Douglass, "Rev. Cleage Blasted by Ousted School Principal," *Michigan Chronicle*, Sept. 14, 1968, A1.

87. Joe Rossiter, "Andrew Perdue: Lawyer Fought Bias, Raised 2 Girls," *Detroit Free Press*, May 10, 2006.

88. Grant, "Community Control vs. School Integration," 68; Albert Cleage, "Andrew Perdue Fights for Community Control," *Michigan Chronicle*, May 24, 1969.

89. William Grant, "Officials Won't Rename School," *Detroit Free Press*, Mar 26, 1969.

90. William Grant, "Board Favors Citizen Councils for Public Schools," *Detroit Free Press*, Apr. 24, 1969.

91. William Grant, "Schools Seek Shift in Control," *Detroit Free Press*, May 14, 1969.

92. Cleage, "Andrew Perdue Fights for Community Control," 1969.

93. Joel D. Aberbach and Jack L. Walker, "Citizen Desires, Policy Outcomes, and Community Control," *Urban Affairs Review* 8, no. 1 (Sept. 1972): 62, https://doi.org/10.1177/107808747200800107; see also Thomas J. Sugrue, *Sweet Land of Liberty: The Forgotten Struggle for Civil Rights in the North* (New York: Random House, 2008), 477.

94. Aberbach and Walker, "Citizen Desires," 57, 62 ("In the 1967 survey, 855 respondents were interviewed [394 whites and 461 blacks]. Approximately 62 percent of the respondents in 1967 were chosen in a sample of the households in the entire city; the rest represent a supplementary sample of the zone within the city in which Detroit's 1967 civil disorders took place").

95. Commission on Civil Rights, *Racial Isolation in the Public Schools* (Mar. 1967).

96. Commission on Civil Rights, *Racial Isolation in the Public Schools* (Mar. 1967), 5.

97. Commission on Civil Rights, *Racial Isolation in the Public Schools* (Mar. 1967), 6.

98. Commission on Civil Rights, *Racial Isolation in the Public Schools* (Mar. 1967), 6, n. 23.

99. Commission on Civil Rights, *Racial Isolation in the Public Schools* (Mar. 1967), 14.

100. Commission on Civil Rights, *Racial Isolation in the Public Schools* (Mar. 1967), 114.

101. Commission on Civil Rights, *Racial Isolation in the Public Schools* (Mar. 1967), 127.

102. Commission on Civil Rights, *Racial Isolation in the Public Schools* (Mar. 1967), 100, 105, 110, 114, 154.

103. Commission on Civil Rights, *Racial Isolation in the Public Schools* (Mar. 1967), 193.

104. George R. LaNoue and Bruce L. R. Smith, *The Politics of School Decentralization* (Lexington, MA: Lexington Books, 1973), 121.

105. June Shagaloff, *Children Apart: Crisis and Conflict in Equality of Educational Opportunity in Large Cities in America: The Relationship between Decentralization and Racial Integration*, Report of the Proceedings of a Special Training Institute on Problems of School Desegregation (June 1968), 41, available at https://files.eric.ed.gov/fulltext/ED030691.pdf.

106. LaNoue and Smith, *The Politics of School Decentralization*, 122.

107. Hiley H. Ward, "Blacks Join Move to Recall Board," *Detroit Free Press*, May 9, 1970.
108. Mirel, *The Rise and Fall of an Urban School System*, 309.

3. SLAY THE DRAGON

1. Commission on Civil Rights, *Racial Isolation in the Public Schools* (Mar. 1967), iv.
2. Commission on Civil Rights, *Racial Isolation in the Public Schools* (Mar. 1967), iv.
3. Commission on Civil Rights, *Racial Isolation in the Public Schools* (Mar. 1967), iv.
4. Memo from Robert L. Carter to Roy Wilkins, dated June 26, 1959, Desegregation Schools De Facto Segregation 1956–65, General Office File, NAACP Records, Manuscript Division, Library of Congress, Washington, D.C.
5. Robert L. Carter, *A Matter of Law: A Memoir of Struggle and the Cause of Civil Rights* (New York: The New Press, 2005), 29, 35, 141.
6. Carter, *A Matter of Law*, 184.
7. "NAACP: A Century in the Fight for Freedom; The Great Depression," Library of Congress, accessed Mar. 8, 2024, https://www.loc.gov/exhibits/naacp/the-great-depression.html; Thurgood Marshall to Arthur B. Spingarn and Walter White, memorandum, July 27, 1939, 087.00.00, NAACP Records, Manuscript Division, Library of Congress, Washington D.C.; NAACP Legal Defense Fund: History, https://www.naacpldf.org/about-us/history/. Federal tax laws prohibited donors from receiving a tax deduction for making contribution to organizations—such as the NAACP proper—that engaged in lobbying efforts. Consequently, two separate organizations were created so that donors could support the NAACP's legal work and still receive a tax deduction. But the relationship between the two organizations would remain close. As constitutional law scholar Mark Tushnet explained it, "To assure donors that the legal work would be coordinated with the NAACP's overall program, the boards of the two groups overlapped: [Thurgood] Marshall served as Director-Counsel of the Inc Fund and as Special Counsel to the NAACP." Mark Tushnet, *Making Civil Rights Law: Thurgood Marshall and the Supreme Court, 1936–1961* (New York: Oxford University Press, 1994), 27.
8. Carter, *A Matter of Law*, 88–90.
9. Justin Driver, "The Lawyers' Revolution," *New Republic*, Mar. 13, 2006, 38.
10. Gilbert Jonas, *Freedom's Sword: The NAACP and the Struggle Against Racism in America, 1909–1969* (New York: Routledge, 2005), 73–74, 77. After almost two decades of sharing board members, staff, and budgets, the LDF and the NAACP formally agreed to sever direct connections in 1957 under intense pressure from hostile southern attorneys general and congressmen who had pressed the treasury department to revoke the LDF's tax-exempt status due to its "close association" with the NAACP. It was part of a larger campaign against the organization. As Robert Carter explained it, "In what was to become a widespread backlash against *Brown*, segregationists who had heretofore dismissed the NAACP as weak and powerless not only began to target our legal work, but threatened to destroy the NAACP itself and to bar it from functioning at the local, state, and national levels." Carter, *A Matter of Law*, 135. Tension developed between the NAACP and the LDF after this split, when the organizations found themselves in competition with one another. The NAACP claimed that the LDF confused donors by continuing to use the "NAACP" initials in its title, and that the media had mistakenly given the LDF credit for the NAACP's achievements. This hostility culminated in the NAACP filing an unsuccessful lawsuit to enjoin the LDF from using the NAACP initials. This competition was exacerbated by the relationship between Carter and Marshall. Carter did not become the NAACP general counsel willingly. In his autobiography he wrote, "Without prior discussion I was summarily removed from the LDF, where I was Thurgood's chief deputy, and named general counsel of the NAACP, with Thurgood's assurance that nothing would change." Carter, *A Matter of Law*, 136. The two men's relationship never

recovered. But, as a close observer of the NAACP later observed, Carter soon "came to the conclusion that there was life after serving as Thurgood Marshall's deputy." Jonas, *Freedom's Sword*, 78.

11. Carter, *A Matter of Law*, 169–70.

12. Memo from Robert L. Carter to Roy Wilkins, dated June 26, 1959, Desegregation Schools De Facto Segregation 1956–65, General Office File, NAACP Records, Manuscript Division, Library of Congress, Washington, D.C.

13. Memo from Robert L. Carter to Roy Wilkins, dated June 26, 1959, Desegregation Schools De Facto Segregation 1956–65, General Office File, NAACP Records, Manuscript Division, Library of Congress, Washington, D.C.

14. Memo from Robert L. Carter to Roy Wilkins, dated June 26, 1959, Desegregation Schools De Facto Segregation 1956–65, General Office File, NAACP Records, Manuscript Division, Library of Congress, Washington, D.C.

15. Report of Robert L. Carter, General Counsel, to Annual Meeting, NAACP, Jan. 5, 1959, at 1, Reports of the General Counsel Annual 1957–65, General Administrative File, NAACP Department, 1956–65, Manuscript Division, Library of Congress, Washington, D.C.

16. Mayor of Baltimore v. Dawson, 350 U.S. at 877 (1955); Gayle v. Browder, 352 U.S. at 903 (1956); Holmes v. Atlanta, 350 U.S. at 879 (1955).

17. Cooper v. Aaron, 358 U.S. at 1, 4 (1958).

18. Cooper v. Aaron, 358 U.S. at 16.

19. Carter, *A Matter of Law*, 169–70.

20. Memo from Roy Wilkins to Robert L. Carter, dated July 8, 1959, Desegregation Schools De Facto Segregation 1956–65, General Office File, NAACP Records, Manuscript Division, Library of Congress, Washington, D.C.

21. Memo from Roy Wilkins to Robert L. Carter, dated July 8, 1959, Desegregation Schools De Facto Segregation 1956–65, General Office File, NAACP Records, Manuscript Division, Library of Congress, Washington, D.C.

22. Green v. County School Board of New Kent County, 391 U.S. at 430 (1968); J. Harvie Wilkinson III, *From Brown to Bakke: The Supreme Court and School Integration: 1945–1978* (Oxford: Oxford University Press, 1981), 79.

23. Keyes v. School District No. 1, Denver, 413 U.S. at 189 (1973).

24. Memo from Roy Wilkins to Robert L. Carter, dated July 8, 1959, Desegregation Schools De Facto Segregation 1956–65, General Office File, NAACP Records, Manuscript Division, Library of Congress, Washington, D.C.

25. Memo from Carter to Wilkins, dated June 26, 1959, Desegregation Schools De Facto Segregation 1956–65, General Office File, NAACP Records, Manuscript Division, Library of Congress, Washington, D.C.

26. Sugrue, *Sweet Land of Liberty*, 459.

27. NAACP Legal Defense and Educational Fund, "Conversation with June Shagaloff," LDF Thurgood Marshall Institute, recorded July 15, 2014, available at https://tminstituteldf.org/archives/ldf-legends/june-shagaloff/.

28. "Conversation with June Shagaloff," July 15, 2014.

29. Tomiko Brown-Nagin, *Civil Rights Queen: Constance Baker Motley and the Struggle for Equality*, (New York: Vintage Books, 2023), 5–7; Gary L. Ford Jr., *Constance Baker Motley: One Woman's Fight for Civil Rights and Equal Justice under Law* (Tuscaloosa: University of Alabama Press, 2017), 1–7; Douglas Martin, "Constance Baker Motley, Civil Rights Trailblazer, Dies at 84," *New York Times*. Sept. 5, 2005; "Conversation with June Shagaloff," July 15, 2014.

30. "Conversation with June Shagaloff," July 15, 2014.

31. "Conversation with June Shagaloff," July 15, 2014.

32. *Black's Law Dictionary* (5th ed., 1979), 375.

33. "Conversation with June Shagaloff," July 15, 2014.
34. "Conversation with June Shagaloff," July 15, 2014.
35. Jonas, *Freedom's Sword*, 80.
36. Juan Williams, *Thurgood Marshall: American Revolutionary* (New York: Times Books, 1998), 206.
37. "Conversation with June Shagaloff," July 15, 2014.
38. "Conversation with June Shagaloff," July 15, 2014.
39. Jonas, *Freedom's Sword*, 81.
40. Clay Risen, "June Shagaloff Alexander, School Desegregation Leader, Dies at 93," *New York Times*, Apr. 6, 2022.
41. Risen, "June Shagaloff Alexander."
42. "Conversation with June Shagaloff," July 15, 2014.
43. "Conversation with June Shagaloff," July 15, 2014.
44. David Leeming, *James Baldwin: A Biography* (London: Penguin Books, 1994), 216.
45. Leeming, *James Baldwin*, 515.
46. Herb Boyd, *Baldwin's Harlem: A Biography of James Baldwin* (New York: Atria Books, 2008), 76.
47. Michelle Adams interview with June Shagaloff, July 10, 2018 (on file with author).
48. Jonas, *Freedom's Sword*, 81.
49. Jonas, *Freedom's Sword*, 81–82.
50. Jonas, *Freedom's Sword*, 82.
51. Memo from June Shagaloff to Robert Carter, *NAACP Program on De Facto Segregated Public Schools*, Aug. 28, 1959, at 1, Desegregation Schools De Facto Segregation 1956–65, General Office File, NAACP Records, Manuscript Division, Library of Congress, Washington, D.C.
52. Memo from Shagaloff to Carter, *NAACP Program on De Facto Segregated Public Schools*, Aug. 28, 1959, 1–4, Desegregation Schools De Facto Segregation 1956–65, General Office File, NAACP Records, Manuscript Division, Library of Congress, Washington, D.C.
53. Sugrue, *Sweet Land of Liberty*, 188.
54. Sugrue, *Sweet Land of Liberty*, 188.
55. Sugrue, *Sweet Land of Liberty*, 188.
56. Taylor v. Board of Education of New Rochelle, 191 F. Supp. 181 (SDNY, 1961), *aff'd* 294 F.2d 36 (2nd Cir. 1961), *cert. denied*, 368 U.S. at 94.
57. *Taylor*, 191 F. Supp. at 185.
58. Joan Cook, "Paul B. Zuber Is Dead at Age 60; Fought Segregated School Systems," *New York Times*, Mar. 10, 1987.
59. Memo from Robert L. Carter to Wilkins, Morsell, Current, Black, Wright, and Farmer, dated Oct. 14, 1960, at 3, NAACP Records, Manuscript Division, Library of Congress, Washington, D.C.
60. Memo from Carter to Wilkins, Morsell, Current, Black, Wright, and Farmer, dated Oct. 14, 1960, at 3, NAACP Records, Manuscript Division, Library of Congress, Washington, D.C.
61. *Taylor*, 191 F. Supp. at 192.
62. *Taylor*, 191 F. Supp. at 194.
63. U.S. Commission on Civil Rights, Book 2: Education 103 (Washington, D.C., 1961), available at https://www.crmvet.org/docs/ccr_edu_us_6100.pdf.
64. *Taylor*, 191 F. Supp. at 197–98.
65. Jonas, *Freedom's Sword*, 84–85.
66. U.S. Commission on Civil Rights, Book 2: Education at 173.
67. James Feron, "New Rochelle Recalls Landmark Bias Ruling," *New York Times*, June 1, 1986.
68. Memo from Robert L. Carter to Wilkins, Morsell, Current, Black, Wright, and Farmer,

dated Oct. 14, 1960, at 1, NAACP Records, Manuscript Division, Library of Congress, Washington, D.C.

69. Memo from Robert L. Carter to Wilkins, Morsell, Current, Black, Wright, and Farmer, dated Oct. 14, 1960, at 2, NAACP Records, Manuscript Division, Library of Congress, Washington, D.C.

70. Letter from A. Leon Higginbotham Jr. to Roy Wilkins and Dr. John Morsell, dated July 3, 1961 (stipulation attached), NAACP Records, Manuscript Division, Library of Congress, Washington, D.C.

71. 1961 NAACP Convention Schedule, Sheraton Hotel, Philadelphia, Pennsylvania, NAACP Records, Manuscript Division, Library of Congress, Washington, D.C.

72. Address by Thurgood Marshall, Director Counsel, NAACP Legal Defense and Educational Fund, Inc., at NAACP 52nd Annual Convention Freedom Fund Report Dinner, Sheraton Hotel, Philadelphia, PA, July 13, 1961, 7:00 p.m., at 1, NAACP Records, Manuscript Division, Library of Congress, Washington, D.C.

73. Marshall Address at NAACP 52nd Annual Convention Freedom Fund Report Dinner, July 13, 1961, at 1, NAACP Records, Manuscript Division, Library of Congress, Washington, D.C.

74. Marshall Address, NAACP 52nd Annual Convention Freedom Fund Report Dinner, July 13, 1961, at 1, NAACP Records, Manuscript Division, Library of Congress, Washington, D.C.

75. NAACP 52nd Annual Convention Resolutions, "12. Segregated Education in Communities Outside of the Deep South," July 15, 1961, at 11, NAACP Records, Manuscript Division, Library of Congress, Washington, D.C.

76. Lewis E. Lomax, *The Negro Revolt* (New York: Harper, 1962), 105; Elliott Rudwick and August Meier, "Integration vs. Separatism: The NAACP and CORE Face Challenge from Within," in *Along the Color Line: Explorations in the Black Experience*, eds. August Meier and Elliott Rudwick (Urbana: University of Illinois Press, 1976), 258.

77. James N. Gregory, "The Second Great Migration: A Historical Overview," in *African-American Urban History Since World War II*, eds. Joe W. Trotter Jr. and Kenneth L. Kusmer (Chicago: University of Chicago Press, 2009), 20–21; Jonas, *Freedom's Sword*, 84.

78. Jonas, *Freedom's Sword*, 84.

79. Jonas, *Freedom's Sword*, 84.

80. June Shagaloff memo, "NAACP Public School Desegregation Front in the North and West: Deliberate and De Facto Segregation, Deliberate Practices Affecting Educational Standards, and/or Faculty Integration," Mar. 25, 1962, at 1, Desegregation Schools De Facto Segregation 1956–65, General Office File, NAACP Records, Manuscript Division, Library of Congress, Washington, D.C; Carter, *A Matter of Law*, 170; Jonas, *Freedom's Sword*, 86.

81. "Survey by NAACP Reveals Western School Jim Crow," Press Release, Apr. 20, 1962, Desegregation Schools De Facto Segregation 1956–65, General Office File, NAACP Records, Manuscript Division, Library of Congress, Washington, D.C.

82. June Shagaloff, "A Review of Public School Desegregation in the North and West," *Journal of Education and Soiology* 36, no. 6 (Feb. 1963): 292.

83. Sugrue, *Sweet Land of Liberty*, 459; Jonas, *Freedom's Sword*, 86; Carter, *A Matter of Law*, 170–73.

84. Jonas, *Freedom's Sword*, 96.

85. Jeanne Theoharis, *A More Beautiful and Terrible History: The Uses and Misuses of Civil Rights History* (Boston: Beacon Press, 2018), 40–45.

86. Theoharis, *A More Beautiful and Terrible History*, 45.

87. Jeanne Theoharis, "Hidden in Plain Sight: The Civil Rights Movement Outside the South," in *The Myth of Southern Exceptionalism*, eds. Matthew D. Lassiter and Joseph Crespino (New York: Oxford University Press, 2009), 64–65.

88. Patrick O'Donnell, *The 1964 Cleveland Schools' Boycott to Protest Segregation, Cleveland*

.com, last modified Feb. 24, 2013, https://www.cleveland.com/metro/index.ssf/2013/02/the _1964_cleveland_schools_boy.html.

89. Brooke Clark, "The Seattle School Boycott of 1966," *Seattle Civil Rights and Labor History Project*, http://depts.washington.edu/civilr/school_boycott.htm (last visited Aug. 25, 2018).

90. *Parents Involved*, 551 U.S. at 701, 808 (2007) (Breyer, J., dissenting).

91. *Parents Involved*, 551 U.S. at 807.

92. *Parents Involved*, 551 U.S. at 720.

93. Theoharis, *A More Beautiful and Terrible History*, 56.

94. Theoharis, *A More Beautiful and Terrible History*, 58.

95. Sugrue, *Sweet Land of Liberty*, 416.

96. Matthew Delmont, "Bernie Sanders and the Unsung Struggle for Civil Rights in the North," *The Atlantic* (Apr. 27, 2016), https://www.theatlantic.com/politics/archive/2016/04/bernie -sanders-and-a-civil-rights-turning-point/479739.

97. Sugrue, *Sweet Land of Liberty*, 416.

98. Sugrue, *Sweet Land of Liberty*, 416.

99. Shagaloff memo, "NAACP Public School Desegregation Front," Mar. 25, 1962, at 1, Desegregation Schools De Facto Segregation 1956–65, General Office File, NAACP Records, Manuscript Division, Library of Congress, Washington, D.C.

100. Cleage Jr., "NAACP Must Support the Court Fight!," 3.

101. "NAACP Intensifies Campaign to End Segregated Schools," Press Release, May 24, 1963, Desegregation Schools De Facto Segregation 1956–65, General Office File, NAACP Records, Manuscript Division, Library of Congress, Washington, D.C.

102. Bell v. School City of Gary, Indiana, 213 F. Supp. 819 (1963).

103. *Bell*, 213 F. Supp. at 823.

104. *Bell*, 213 F. Supp. at 822.

105. *Bell*, 213 F. Supp. at 823.

106. *Bell*, 213 F. Supp. at 829.

107. *Bell*, 213 F. Supp. at 828.

108. *Bell*, 213 F. Supp. at 828.

109. *Bell*, 213 F. Supp. at 822.

110. *Bell*, 213 F. Supp. at 822.

111. *Bell*, 213 F. Supp. at 822.

112. *Bell*, 213 F. Supp. at 822.

113. *Bell*, 213 F. Supp. at 827.

114. *Bell*, 213 F. Supp. at 827.

115. *Bell*, 213 F. Supp. at 827.

116. Sugrue, *Sweet Land of Liberty*, 461.

117. Sugrue, *Sweet Land of Liberty*, 467.

118. Sugrue, *Sweet Land of Liberty*, 463.

119. Statement by Robert L. Carter General Counsel, National Association for the Advancement of Colored People on June 20, 1965, at Workshop of Desegregation Advisory Project, Wayne County, Mich., NAACP Records, Manuscript Division, Library of Congress, Washington, D.C.

120. Statement by Robert L. Carter at 6–7, NAACP Records, Manuscript Division, Library of Congress, Washington, D.C.

121. Statement by Robert L. Carter at 6, NAACP Records, Manuscript Division, Library of Congress, Washington, D.C.

122. Statement by Robert L. Carter at 6–7, NAACP Records, Manuscript Division, Library of Congress, Washington, D.C.

123. Statement by Robert L. Carter at 18, NAACP Records, Manuscript Division, Library of Congress, Washington, D.C.

124. Carter, *A Matter of Law*, 194.
125. Carter, *A Matter of Law*, 194.

4. THE HOUSING-SCHOOLS NEXUS

1. House Bill No. 3801, Journal of the House of Representatives of the State of Michigan 1968, Feb. 21, 1968; "Who Is Del Rio?," *The Blog of James Del Rio*, https://jamesdelrio.wordpress.com/accomplishment/.
2. Harris Jr., "Decentralization and Recentralization of the Detroit Public Schools," 88.
3. "Del Rio Accused Of 'Using' King," *Detroit Free Press*, Apr. 7, 1965.
4. AP, "Sunday Liquor Sale Passed by House," *Escanaba Daily Press*, Apr. 11, 1968, 2.
5. Grant, "Who Will Control Detroit's Schools?," 12A; Conversation between John Ludwig and Jack Faxon (Mar. 31, 2016).
6. Jim Nichols, "House Passes Bill for Vote on Sunday Liquor Sales," *Ironwood Daily Globe*, Apr. 11, 1968, at 15.
7. Frank Angelo, "Freedom March: A Giant Political, Economic Force," *Detroit Free Press*, June 25, 1963.
8. Tom Shawver, "Civil Rights Crusaders to Bare Plan of Action as Sequel to 'Freedom Walk,'" *Detroit Free Press*, June 28, 1963.
9. UPI, "New Powell Protest Asked," *Holland Evening Sentinel*, Mar. 6, 1967, 2.
10. "70 Negro Leaders Hear Plea, Support Urged for Ward Plan," *Detroit Free Press*, May 23, 1963.
11. Robert Pearson, "Negroes Due, Suburbs Told," *Detroit Free Press*, Aug. 15, 1963.
12. Pearson, "Negroes Due, Suburbs Told."
13. Pearson, "Negroes Due, Suburbs Told."
14. "Negroes Told: Speed Move to Suburbs," *Detroit Free Press*, Aug. 30, 1963.
15. William Grant, "19 Separate Districts? School Division Eyed," *Detroit Free Press*, Nov. 30, 1968.
16. Allyson Hobbs, "The Lorraine Motel and Martin Luther King," *New Yorker*, Jan. 16, 2016; Joseph Rosenbloom, *Redemption: Martin Luther King Jr.'s Last 31 Hours* (Boston: Beacon Press, 2018), 155.
17. Hobbs, "The Lorraine Motel and Martin Luther King."
18. Earl Caldwell, "Martin Luther King Is Slain in Memphis; A White Is Suspected; Johnson Urges Calm," *New York Times*, Apr. 5, 1968.
19. CBS Evening News with Walter Cronkite, Martin Luther King Jr. Assassination, Apr. 4, 1968, C-SPAN, available at https://www.c-span.org/video/?443016-1/martin-luther-king-jr-death-announcement.
20. Insider Staff, "The Lone Journalist on the Scene When King Was Shot and the Newsroom He Rallied," *New York Times*, Apr. 3, 2018.
21. Insider Staff, "The Lone Journalist on the Scene."
22. Insider Staff, "The Lone Journalist on the Scene."
23. James R. Ralph Jr., *Northern Protest: Martin Luther King, Jr., Chicago, and the Civil Rights Movement* (Cambridge, MA: Harvard University Press, 1993), 42.
24. Ralph Jr., *Northern Protest*, 31–32; Taylor Branch, *At Canaan's Edge: America in the King Years 1965–68* (New York: Simon & Schuster, 2006), 319; David J. Garrow, *Bearing the Cross: Martin Luther King, Jr., and the Southern Christian Leadership Conference* (1988), at 452–53.
25. Branch, *At Canaan's Edge*, 319; Ralph Jr., *Northern Protest*, 32.
26. Garrow, *Bearing the Cross*, 452.
27. Ralph Jr., *Northern Protest*, 31 (citing speech by Martin Luther King, MLK library, May 31, 1964).
28. Michael K. Honey, *To the Promised Land: Martin Luther King and the Fight for Economic*

Justice (New York: W. W. Norton, 2018), 105; Ralph Jr., *Northern Protest*, 55; Garrow, *Bearing the Cross*, 456–59.

29. Leonard R. Rubinowitz and Kathryn Shelton, "Non-Violent Direct Action and the Legislative Process," *Indiana Law Review* 41, no. 3 (2008): 667; Ralph Jr., *Northern Protest*, 43.
30. Rubinowitz and Shelton, "Non-Violent Direct Action and the Legislative Process," 668–70; Ralph Jr., *Northern Protest*, 39–44.
31. Rubinowitz and Shelton, "Non-Violent Direct Action and the Legislative Process," 671.
32. Garrow, *Bearing the Cross*, 456.
33. Garrow, *Bearing the Cross*, 443, 452, 455–57.
34. Ralph Jr., *Northern Protest*, 88–89.
35. Garrow, *Bearing the Cross*, 468.
36. Branch, *At Canaan's Edge*, 408.
37. Rubinowitz and Shelton, "Non-Violent Direct Action and the Legislative Process," 671.
38. Ralph Jr., *Northern Protest*, 98.
39. Jerrold M. Packard, *American Nightmare: The History of Jim Crow* (New York: St. Martin's Griffin, 2003), 163.
40. Rubinowitz and Shelton, "Non-Violent Direct Action and the Legislative Process," 674.
41. Report of the United States Commission on Civil Rights 1959 at 365.
42. Ralph Jr., *Northern Protest*, 101.
43. Ralph Jr., *Northern Protest*, 102.
44. Ralph Jr., *Northern Protest*, 103–104.
45. Henry Hampton and Steve Fayer, *Voices of Freedom: An Oral History of the Civil Rights Movement from the 1950s to the 1980s* (New York: Bantam Books, 1991), 308.
46. Ralph Jr., *Northern Protest*, 123; "Dr. King Is Felled by Rock," *Chicago Tribune*, Aug. 6, 1966.
47. "Dr. King Is Felled by Rock," *Chicago Tribune*, Aug. 6, 1966; Gene Roberts, "Rock Hits Dr. King as Whites Attack March in Chicago: Felled Rights Leader Rises and Continues to Protest as Crowd of 4,000 Riots," *New York Times*, Aug. 6, 1966; Richard Goldstein, "King in Chicago: Has White Power Killed Love Power?," *The Village Voice*, August 11, 1966; Jonathan Eig, *King: A Life* (New York: Farrar, Straus and Giroux, 2023), 502.
48. Ralph Jr., *Northern Protest*, 123.
49. Ralph Jr., *Northern Protest*, 124.
50. Ralph Jr., *Northern Protest*, 123.
51. Branch, *At Canaan's Edge*, 523.
52. *Meet the Press* (television broadcast Aug. 21, 1966), available at Alexander Street; *Meet the Press*, transcript, https://www.crmvet.org/info/660821_mtp_ckmmwy.pdf.
53. *Meet the Press* (television broadcast Aug. 21, 1966), available at Alexander Street; *Meet the Press*, transcript, https://www.crmvet.org/info/660821_mtp_ckmmwy.pdf.
54. *Meet the Press* (television broadcast Aug. 21, 1966), available at Alexander Street; *Meet the Press*, transcript, https://www.crmvet.org/info/660821_mtp_ckmmwy.pdf.
55. Garrow, *Bearing the Cross*, 501.
56. "Summit Agreement," *Chicago Freedom Movement: Fulfilling the Dream*, accessed Apr. 5, 2024, https://sites.middlebury.edu/chicagofreedommovement/summit-agreement/.
57. Leonard S. Rubinowitz, "The Chicago Freedom Movement and the Federal Fair Housing Act" in *The Chicago Freedom Movement: Martin Luther King Jr. and Civil Rights Activism in the North*, ed. Mary Lou Finley, Bernard LaFayette Jr., James R. Ralph Jr., and Pam Smith (Lexington, KY: University Press of Kentucky, 2015), 117; "Summit Agreement," *Chicago Freedom*.
58. Garrow, *Bearing the Cross*, 501–25; Rubinowitz, "The Chicago Freedom Movement," 117.
59. Kevin Boyle, *The Shattering: America in the 1960s* (New York: W. W. Norton, 2021), 219.
60. Garrow, *Bearing the Cross*, 524.
61. Boyle, *The Shattering*, 220 ("After six months of organizing and a month of marches, after the bricks and bottles and howling mobs, the movement had come away with a set of paper

promises." King left behind "a color line he hadn't been able to break, a system of segregation and domination he couldn't destroy, a city he couldn't transform, and festering wounds
he had failed to salve"). Some recent assessments of the Chicago Freedom Movement have
been more sympathetic, however. See Jonathan Eig, *King: A Life*, 505 (the Summit Agreement "would make those things possible [eradication of housing discrimination], but only
with commitment from the city, private businesses, and the federal government."); James
R. Ralph, "Interpreting The Chicago Freedom Movement: The Last Fifty Years" in *The
Chicago Freedom Movement: Martin Luther King Jr. and Civil Rights Activism in the North*,
eds. Mary Lou Finley, Bernard LaFayette Jr., James R. Ralph Jr., and Pam Smith (Lexington,
KY: University Press of Kentucky, 2015), 92 (discussing an emerging "interpretation of the
Chicago Freedom Movement—that it is significant precisely because it revealed how thor-
oughly embedded racism was in the entire country.")

62. Eig, *King: A Life*, 505.
63. Eig, *King: A Life*, 505.
64. Ralph, *Northern Protest*, 192–93.
65. Rubinowitz, "The Chicago Freedom Movement," 122–23.
66. Kerner Commission, *Report*.
67. Kerner Commission, *Report*, at 1.
68. Robert G. Schwemm, *Housing Discrimination: Law and Litigation* (Eagan, MN: Thomson Reuters, 2013), 5:2, 5–5.
69. Kerner Commission, *Report*, at 237.
70. Kerner Commission, *Report*, at 259.
71. Kerner Commission, *Report*, at 263.
72. Charles M. Lamb, *Housing Segregation in Suburban America Since 1960* (Cambridge: Cambridge University Press, 2005), 41–42; Schwemm, *Housing Discrimination*, 5:4, 5–6.
73. Christopher Bonastia, *Knocking on the Door: The Federal Government's Attempt to Deseg- regate the Suburbs* (Princeton, NJ: Princeton University Press, 2008), 86–87.
74. Branch, *At Canaan's Edge*, 766.
75. Lorraine Boissoneault, "Martin Luther King Jr.'s Assassination Sparked Uprisings in Cit- ies Across America," *Smithsonian Magazine*, Apr. 4, 2018, https://www.smithsonianmag .com/history/martin-luther-king-jrs-assassination-sparked-uprisings-cities-across-america -180968665/.
76. Ben A. Franklin, "Many Fires Set: White House Guarded by G.I.'s—14 Dead in U.S. Out- breaks," *New York Times*, Apr. 6, 1968.
77. "The Four Days in 1968 That Reshaped D.C.," *Washington Post*, Mar. 27, 2018.
78. Letter from Lyndon B. Johnson to the Speaker of the House Urging Enactment of the Fair Housing Bill, Apr. 5, 1968, https://www.presidency.ucsb.edu/documents/letter-the-speaker -the-house-urging-enactment-the-fair-housing-bill.
79. Letter from Lyndon B. Johnson, Apr. 5, 1968.
80. Letter from Lyndon B. Johnson, Apr. 5, 1968.
81. Lyndon B. Johnson, Special Message to the Congress Proposing Further Legislation to Strengthen Civil Rights, Apr. 28, 1966, https://www.presidency.ucsb.edu/documents/special -message-the-congress-proposing-further-legislation-strengthen-civil-rights.
82. Lyndon B. Johnson, Special Message to the Congress, Apr. 28, 1966.
83. Lyndon B. Johnson, Special Message to the Congress, Apr. 28, 1966.
84. Max Frankel, "President Grave: Sets Day of Mourning for Dr. King—Meets Rights Lead- ers," *New York Times*, Apr. 6, 1968.
85. DeNeen L. Brown, "The Fair Housing Act Was Languishing in Congress. Then Martin Luther King Jr. Was Killed," *Washington Post*, Apr. 11, 2018.
86. Bonastia, *Knocking on the Door*, 87.
87. Douglas S. Massey, "The Legacy of the 1968 Fair Housing Act," *Sociological Forum*, 30, no. S1 (June 2015): 575.

88. Rubinowitz and Shelton, "Non-Violent Direct Action and the Legislative Process," 712.

89. Rubinowitz and Shelton, "Non-Violent Direct Action and the Legislative Process," 712.

90. "Education Committee Refers House Bill 3801 to the Committee of the Whole," Mar. 19, 1968, *Journal of the House* 47, 898–99; Stephen J. Pollak, "1968 And the Beginnings of Federal Enforcement of Fair Housing," Civil Rights Division, U.S. Department of Justice, Feb. 1, 2000, https://www.justice.gov/crt/1968-and-beginnings-federal-enforcement-fair-housing1.

91. "Legislator Details—Jackie Vaughn III," Michigan Legislative Biography, accessed Feb. 8, 2024, https://mdoe.state.mi.us/legislators/Legislator/LegislatorDetail/4501.

92. Rep. Vaughn, "Statement on the Floor of the Michigan House of Representatives," Apr. 10, 1968, *Journal of the House* 63, 1572.

93. "Legislator Details—Daisy L. Elliott," Michigan Legislative Biography, accessed Feb. 8, 2024, https://mdoe.state.mi.us/legislators/Legislator/LegislatorDetail/2992.

94. Rep. Elliot, "Statement on the Floor of the Michigan House of Representatives," Apr. 10, 1968, *Journal of the House* 63, 1571.

95. Rep. Vaughn, "Statement on the Floor of the Michigan House of Representatives," Apr. 10, 1968, *Journal of the House* 63, 1572.

96. Rep. Vaughn, "Statement on the Floor of the Michigan House of Representatives," Apr. 10, 1968, *Journal of the House* 63, 1572.

97. Rep. Elliot, "Statement on the Floor of the Michigan House of Representatives," Apr. 10, 1968, *Journal of the House* 63, 1570–71. A coauthor of landmark state civil rights legislation, Elliott was recognized after her death in 2015 by the Michigan Civil Rights Commission as "one of the greatest civil rights leaders this state has ever produced." Michigan Civil Rights Commission, "Statement on the Life and Contributions of Daisy Elliott," Jan. 25, 2016, available at https://www.michigan.gov/-/media/Project/Websites/mdcr/mcrc/statements/2016/daisy-elliott.pdf?rev=d55ed2bd482d4628807122600bcac045.

98. "Legislator Details—David S. Holmes Jr.," Michigan Legislative Biography, accessed Feb. 9, 2024, https://mdoe.state.mi.us/legislators/Legislator/LegislatorDetail/4468.

99. Rep. Holmes, "Statement on the Floor of the Michigan House of Representatives," Apr. 10, 1968, *Journal of the House* 63, 1571.

100. Rep. Holmes, "Statement on the Floor of the Michigan House of Representatives," 1571.

101. "Legislator Details—Rosetta A. Ferguson," Michigan Legislative Biography, accessed Feb. 9, 2024, https://mdoe.state.mi.us/legislators/legislator/LegislatorDetail/2994.

102. Rep. Ferguson, "Statement on the Floor of the Michigan House of Representatives," Apr. 10, 1968, *Journal of the House* 63, 1572.

103. LaNoue and Smith, *The Politics of School Decentralization*, 120.

104. Berkowitz, "An Analysis," 124.

105. William Serrin, "Detroit Schools Sharply Criticized," *Detroit Free Press*, Mar. 25, 1969.

106. Serrin, "Detroit Schools Sharply Criticized."

107. Grant, "Community Control vs. School Integration," 68.

108. Reginald Stuart, "The New Black Power of Coleman Young," *New York Times*, Dec. 16, 1979.

109. Martin Halpern, "'I'm Fighting for Freedom': Coleman Young, HUAC, and the Detroit African American Community," *Journal of American Ethnic History* 17, no. 1 (Fall 1997): 24.

110. Young and Wheeler, *Hard Stuff*, 99–105.

111. Young and Wheeler, *Hard Stuff*, 113–14.

112. Stuart, "The New Black Power of Coleman Young"; Young and Wheeler, *Hard Stuff*, 135–42.

113. Young and Wheeler, *Hard Stuff*, 119–32.

114. Kevin Kearney, "The Radical Background of Michigan's New Democratic National Committeeman," *Human Events*, Oct. 5, 1968.

115. *Communism in the Detroit Area—Part 1: Hearing Before the H. Comm. on Un-American Activities*, 82nd Sess. (Mich. 1952), at 2879.

116. Young and Wheeler, *Hard Stuff*, 121.

117. Young and Wheeler, *Hard Stuff*, 155.
118. Young and Wheeler, *Hard Stuff*, 155–56.
119. Young and Wheeler, *Hard Stuff*, 155.
120. Young and Wheeler, *Hard Stuff*, 164.
121. Wilbur C. Rich, *Coleman Young in Detroit Politics: From Social Activist to Power Broker* (Detroit, MI: Wayne State University Press, 1989), 88.
122. Mirel, *The Rise and Fall of an Urban School System*, 335–36.
123. "Decentralization and Sen. Coleman Young," *Michigan Chronicle*, June 26, 1971.
124. Roger Lane, "Regional School Bill Signed," *Detroit Free Press*, Aug. 12, 1969.
125. William Grant, "Senators Bill Prod City for School Reforms," *Detroit Free Press*, June 12, 1969.
126. William Grant, "Political Battles Loom Over School Breakup," *Detroit Free Press*, Feb. 16, 1970.
127. Mirel, *The Rise and Fall of an Urban School System*, 336–337.
128. Harris Jr., "Decentralization and Recentralization of the Detroit Public Schools," 94.
129. William Grant, "Detroit vs. Suburban Schools: Parents Dilemma," *Detroit Free Press*, Apr. 13, 1969.
130. Grant, "Detroit vs. Suburban Schools."

5. SOUL FORCE

1. Statement by A. L. Zwerdling, *Legislation for Decentralization*, Detroit Board of Education, Regular Meeting Minutes, Aug. 12, 1969, at 57, Accession 447, Box 4, Folder 4–56, Remus Robinson Collection, Walter P. Reuther Library, Wayne State University.
2. Statement by A. L. Zwerdling, *Legislation for Decentralization*, Detroit Board of Education, Regular Meeting Minutes, Aug. 12, 1969, at 57, Box 4, Folder 4–56, Remus Robinson Collection, Walter P. Reuther Library, Wayne State University.
3. Statement by A. L. Zwerdling to Administrators and Supervisors of the Detroit Public Schools on Sept. 5, 1969, *Detroit Schools* (Oct. 28, 1969), at 27, Box 7, Folder 7–6, Detroit Public Schools Community Relations Division, Walter P. Reuther Library, Wayne State University.
4. Statement by A. L. Zwerdling to Administrators and Supervisors of the Detroit Public Schools on Sept. 5, 1969, *Detroit Schools* (Oct. 28, 1969), at 27–28, Detroit Public Schools Community Relations Division, Walter P. Reuther Library, Wayne State University.
5. Statement by A. L. Zwerdling to Administrators and Supervisors of the Detroit Public Schools, *Detroit Schools* (Oct. 28, 1969), at 27, Detroit Public Schools Community Relations Division, Walter P. Reuther Library, Wayne State University.
6. William Grant, "Zwerdling Stands Firm on Integration," *Detroit Free Press*, Apr. 13, 1970.
7. Grant, "Zwerdling Stands Firm on Integration," 3A.
8. Ansley T. Erickson, "Desegregation's Architects: Education Parks and the Spatial Ideology of Schooling," *History of Education Quarterly* 56, no. 4 (November 2016): 563.
9. Erickson, "Desegregation's Architects," 563.
10. James E. Mauch, "The Education Park," *The American School Board Journal* (Mar. 1965): 10.
11. John H. Fischer, "The School Park," in *Education Parks: Appraisals of Plans to Improve Educational Quality and Desegregate the Schools*, US Commission on Civil Rights, Clearinghouse Publication Number 9 (Oct. 1967), 1.
12. "The City Is a Teacher," speech of May 13, 1966, reprinted in *Congressional Record*, June 8, 1966, 12656–57.
13. "The City Is a Teacher," 12656–57.
14. "The City Is a Teacher," 12656–57.
15. Elementary and Secondary Education Amendments Act of 1966, Report of the Committee

of Education and Labor, House of Representatives to accompany H. R. 13161, Aug. 5, 1966, at 24.

16. Max Wolff, "Educational Park Development in the United States 1967, a Survey of Current Development Plans," Center for Urban Education (1967).

17. Gary Orfield, *Must We Bus? Segregated Schools and National Policy* (Washington, D.C.: Brooking Institution, 1978), 282–83.

18. Statement by Congressman Paul A. Fino, Republican of New York, *Congressional Record*, Sept. 15, 1966, 22755.

19. Fino, *Congressional Record*, 22755.

20. Rowland Evans and Robert Novak, "Inside Report: Education Bombshell," *Washington Post*, Sept. 1966, A23.

21. Evans and Novak, "Inside Report."

22. Erickson, "Desegregation's Architects," 565.

23. Ward, *Prophet of the Black Nation*, 73.

24. Lyndon B. Johnson, Remarks at the University of Michigan, May 22, 1964, https://www .presidency.ucsb.edu/documents/remarks-the-university-michigan.

25. Howard Schuman, *Racial Attitudes in America: Trends and Interpretations* (Cambridge, MA: Harvard University Press, 1997), 10.

26. "Editorial: Defeat at Detroit," *The Nation*, July 3, 1943, 4.

27. Gunnar Myrdal, *An American Dilemma* (New York: New Press, 1944), 13.

28. Ralph Ellison, *An American Dilemma: A Review* (1944).

29. David Carroll Cochran, *The Color of Freedom: Race and Contemporary American Liberalism* (Albany, NY: State University of New York Press, 1999), 27.

30. Brown v. Board of Education, 347 U.S. at 483, 495 (1954).

31. Martin Luther King Jr.'s "I Have a Dream" speech, Aug. 28, 1963, https://www.npr.org/2010 /01/18/122701268/i-have-a-dream-speech-in-its-entirety.

32. Martin Luther King Jr.'s "I Have a Dream" speech.

33. Garrow, *Bearing the Cross*, 43.

34. Garrow, *Bearing the Cross*, 43; Eig, *King: A Life*, 208–13.

35. M. K. Gandhi, *Non-violent Resistance* (New York: Schocken Books, 1961), 7.

36. Gandhi, *Non-violent Resistance*, 6.

37. Gandhi, *Non-violent Resistance*, 6.

38. Gandhi, *Non-violent Resistance*, iii (editor's note).

39. Martin Luther King Jr.'s "I Have a Dream" speech.

40. Martin Luther King Jr.'s "I Have a Dream" speech.

41. David Levering Lewis, *King: A Biography* (Urbana: University of Illinois Press, 2013), 101; Eric J. Sundquist, *King's Dream* (New Haven, CT: Yale University Press, 2009), 116–17.

42. Martin Luther King Jr., *A Testament of Hope: The Essential Writings and Speeches of Martin Luther King Jr.* (San Francisco: Harper & Row, 1986), 117.

43. King Jr., *A Testament of Hope*, 119.

44. King Jr., *A Testament of Hope*, 118.

45. Malcolm X, "The Black Revolution," Speech at the Abyssinian Baptist Church (June 1963).

46. King Jr., *A Testament of Hope*, 121.

47. King Jr., *A Testament of Hope*, 124.

48. King Jr., *A Testament of Hope*, 124.

49. James Baldwin, "Malcolm and Martin," *Esquire*, Apr. 1972, 94, 201.

50. Peniel E. Joseph, *The Sword and the Shield: The Revolutionary Lives of Malcolm X and Martin Luther King Jr.* (New York: Basic Books, 2020), 17–19.

51. Eig, *King: A Life*, 544–45.

52. A Position Statement of the Michigan Civil Rights Commission on the Implementation of

Public Act 244 in the Detroit Public Schools (Nov. 4, 1969), Box 14, Folder 14–1, Public Act 244 (635), 1970, Coleman A. Young Collection Part I, Walter P. Reuther Library, Wayne State University.

53. Position Statement of the Michigan Civil Rights Commission on the Implementation of Public Act 244 in the Detroit Public Schools (Nov. 4, 1969), Box 14, Folder 14–1, Public Act 244 (635), 1970, Coleman A. Young Collection Part I, Walter P. Reuther Library, Wayne State University.

54. William L. Taylor, *The Passion of My Times* (New York: Carroll and Graf Publishers, 2004), 121.

55. Taylor, *Passion*, 121.

56. Taylor, *Passion*, 11–15.

57. Brown v. Board of Education, 347 U.S. at 490 n. 5.

58. Civil Rights Cases, 109 U.S. at 3, 25 (1883).

59. *Keyes*, 413 U.S. at 189, 202–203 (1973).

60. Korematsu v. United States, 323 U.S. at 214, 216 (1944).

61. *Korematsu*, 323 U.S. at 217–18.

62. Plessy v. Ferguson, 163 U.S. 537, 540 (1896).

63. Plessy v. Ferguson, 163 U.S. at 560.

64. Brown v. Board of Education, 347 U.S. at 495.

65. Plessy v. Ferguson, 163 U.S. at 559 (1896) (J. Harlan dissenting).

66. Plessy v. Ferguson, 163 U.S. at 559 (J. Harlan dissenting).

67. Brown v. Board of Education, 347 U.S. at 494.

68. Brown v. Board of Education, 349 U.S. at 294.

69. Brown v. Board of Education, 349 U.S. at 301.

70. Green v. County School Board of New Kent County, 391 U.S. at 430, 441 (1968).

71. *Green*, 391 U.S. at 430 (1968).

72. Alexander v. Holmes County Board of Education, 396 U.S. at 20, 20 (1969).

73. *Alexander*, 396 U.S. at 20.

74. Swann v. Charlotte Mecklenburg Board of Education, 402 U.S. at 1 (1971).

75. See Michigan Act of 1842, 1842 Mich. Pub. Acts 112 ("the city of Detroit shall be considered as one school district, and hereafter all schools organized therein . . . shall . . . be public and free to all children residing within the limits thereof"); see also People ex rel. Workman v. Detroit Board of Education, 18 Mich. 400, 409–10 (1869) ("It cannot be seriously urged that with this provision in force, the school board of any district which is subject to it may . . . exclude any resident of the district from any of its schools, because of race or color . . . It is too plain for argument that an equal right to all the schools, irrespective of all such distinctions, was meant to be established").

76. Memorandum from William L. Taylor to A. L. Zwerdling Re: Obligations of the Detroit Board of Education Under the U.S. Constitution in Establishing Regional School Districts Pursuant to Public Act No. 244, at 4 (Dec. 2, 1969), Box 3, School Desegregation and Decentralization, Remus Robinson Collection, Walter P. Reuther Library, Archives of Labor and Urban Affairs, Wayne State University.

77. Green v. County School Board of New Kent County, 391 U.S. at 430 (1968).

78. Taylor Memo to Zwerdling Re: Obligations, at 5, Remus Robinson Collection, Walter P. Reuther Library, Archives of Labor and Urban Affairs, Wayne State University.

79. See, e.g., Hobson v. Hansen, 269 F. Supp. 401 (D.D.C. 1967).

80. See, e.g., Bell v. City of Gary, 324 F.2d 209 (7th Cir. 1963).

81. Deal v. Cincinnati Board of Education, 369 F.2d 55, 61 (6th Cir. 1966).

82. *Deal*, 369 F.2d at 58–61.

83. *Deal*, 369 F.2d at 60.

84. *Deal*, 369 F.2d at 60.

85. Taylor Memo to Zwerdling Re: Obligations, at 14, Remus Robinson Collection, Walter P. Reuther Library, Archives of Labor and Urban Affairs, Wayne State University.

86. Taylor Memo to Zwerdling Re: Obligations, at 14, Remus Robinson Collection, Walter P. Reuther Library, Archives of Labor and Urban Affairs, Wayne State University.

87. Taylor Memo to Zwerdling Re: Obligations, at 13, Remus Robinson Collection, Walter P. Reuther Library, Archives of Labor and Urban Affairs, Wayne State University.

88. Taylor Memo to Zwerdling Re: Obligations, at 19, Remus Robinson Collection, Walter P. Reuther Library, Archives of Labor and Urban Affairs, Wayne State University.

89. Taylor Memo to Zwerdling Re: Obligations, at 19, Remus Robinson Collection, Walter P. Reuther Library, Archives of Labor and Urban Affairs, Wayne State University.

6. DEMOCRACY'S FINEST HOUR

1. William Grant, "Pupil Integration Plan OKd, Schools Get Race Balance," *Detroit Free Press*, Apr. 8, 1970, A1.

2. Grant, "Pupil Integration Plan OKd," A1.

3. Harry Salsinger, "New Formula to Integrate High Schools," *Detroit News*, Apr. 5, 1970.

4. William Grant, "City to Shuffle School Areas in Broad Integration Plan: Board to Vote Tuesday," *Detroit Free Press*, Apr. 5, 1970.

5. William Grant, "The Detroit School Case: An Historical Overview," *Wayne State Law Review* 21, no. 2 (1975): 857.

6. William Grant, "School Board Fears Bias in Decentralizing," *Detroit Free Press*, Jan. 18, 1970, A4.

7. Abraham Zwerdling statement, Detroit Board of Education, Regular Meeting, Apr. 7, 1970, Accession 449, Box 14, Folder 14–2, Public Act 244 (635), 1970, Coleman A. Young Collection Part I, Walter P. Reuther Library, Wayne State University.

8. Grant, "Community Control vs. School Integration," 70.

9. Grant, "Community Control vs. School Integration," 68–70.

10. Andrew W. Perdue, Views on Decentralization as it Pertains to the Implementation of Public Law 244 (Mar. 16, 1970), at 5, 10–12, Accession 449, Box 14, Folder 14–2, Public Act 244 (635), 1970, Coleman A. Young Collection Part I, Walter P. Reuther Library, Wayne State University (citing statement released by the Metropolitan Detroit Society of Black Educational Administrators on the Establishment of Regional Districts for the city of Detroit school district, submitted to the Detroit Board of Education).

11. Perdue, Views on Decentralization, Mar. 16, 1970, at 11, Coleman A. Young Collection Part I, Walter P. Reuther Library, Wayne State University.

12. Perdue, Views on Decentralization, Mar. 16, 1970, at 16–17, Coleman A. Young Collection Part I, Walter P. Reuther Library, Wayne State University.

13. Perdue, Views on Decentralization, Mar. 16, 1970, at 19, Coleman A. Young Collection Part I, Walter P. Reuther Library, Wayne State University.

14. Perdue, Views on Decentralization, Mar. 16, 1970, at 19, Coleman A. Young Collection Part I, Walter P. Reuther Library, Wayne State University.

15. Grant, "Community Control vs. School Integration," 71.

16. Grant, "Community Control vs. School Integration," 71.

17. Grant, "The Detroit School Case," 855–56; Mirel, *The Rise and Fall of an Urban School System*, 340.

18. Grant, "Community Control vs. School Integration," 71.

19. Mirel, *The Rise and Fall of an Urban School System*, 340.

20. Mirel, *The Rise and Fall of an Urban School System*, 340.

21. LaNoue and Smith, *The Politics of School Decentralization*, 127.

22. Grant, "Community Control vs. School Integration," 73.

23. Grant, "Community Control vs. School Integration," 70–71.

24. Elwood Hain, "Sealing Off the City: School Desegregation in Detroit," in *Limits of Justice: The Courts' Role in School Desegregation*, eds. Howard I. Kalodner and James J. Fishman

(Cambridge, MA: Ballinger, 1978), 233–34; William Grant, "Rise and Fall of Patrick Mc-Donald," *Detroit Free Press*, July 3, 1971, 1A, 5A.

25. Mirel, *The Rise and Fall of an Urban School System*, 340.

26. Harry Salsinger, "Parents' Protest Over Integration Shuts 2 Schools," *Detroit News*, Apr. 6, 1970.

27. Salsinger, "Parents' Protest."

28. Telephone Calls Received Apr. 6, 1970, Re: Boundary Plans, Box 2, Folder 2–24, Decentralization; corres., 1970 Apr., Remus Robinson Collection, Walter P. Reuther Library, Archives of Labor and Urban Affairs, Wayne State University.

29. Telephone Calls Received Apr. 6, 1970, Re: Boundary Plans, Remus Robinson Collection, Wayne State University.

30. Telephone Calls Received Apr. 6, 1970, Re: Boundary Plans, Remus Robinson Collection, Wayne State University.

31. Telephone Calls Received Apr. 6, 1970, Re: Boundary Plans, Remus Robinson Collection, Wayne State University.

32. Telegram from J. E. Cappy to Remus Robinson, Apr. 6, 1970, Box 2, Folder 35, Decentralization-integration; corres. from citizens, 1970, Remus Robinson Papers, Walter P. Reuther Library, Archives of Labor and Urban Affairs, Wayne State University.

33. Edward Shanahan and William Schmidt, "750 Whites Rap School Changes," *Detroit Free Press*, Apr. 8, 1970.

34. Shanahan and Schmidt, "750 Whites Rap School Changes"; Stephen Cain and W. Howard Erickson, "Protests Get Hotter over School Switching," *Detroit News*, Apr. 8, 1970.

35. Shanahan and Schmidt, "750 Whites Rap School Changes"; Grant, "Community Control vs. School Integration," 72.

36. Shanahan and Schmidt, "750 Whites Rap School Changes."

37. Cain and Erickson, "Protests Get Hotter."

38. Shanahan and Schmidt, "750 Whites Rap School Changes."

39. Cain and Erickson, "Protests Get Hotter."

40. Cain and Erickson, "Protests Get Hotter."

41. Hain, "Sealing Off the City," 234.

42. Shanahan and Schmidt, "750 Whites Rap School Changes."

43. Detroit Board of Education, Regular Meeting, Apr. 7, 1970, Official Transcript, at 499, Remus Robinson Papers, Walter P. Reuther Library, Archives of Labor and Urban Affairs, Wayne State University.

44. Detroit Board of Education, Regular Meeting, Apr, 7, 1970, Official Transcript, at 499, Remus Robinson Papers, Walter P. Reuther Library, Archives of Labor and Urban Affairs, Wayne State University.

45. Detroit Board of Education, Regular Meeting, Apr. 7, 1970, Official Transcript, at 501, Remus Robinson Papers, Walter P. Reuther Library, Archives of Labor and Urban Affairs, Wayne State University.

46. Detroit Board of Education, Regular Meeting, Apr. 7, 1970, Official Transcript, at 501, Remus Robinson Papers, Walter P. Reuther Library, Archives of Labor and Urban Affairs, Wayne State University.

47. Detroit Board of Education, Regular Meeting, Apr. 7, 1970, Official Transcript, at 522, Remus Robinson Papers, Walter P. Reuther Library, Archives of Labor and Urban Affairs, Wayne State University.

48. Detroit Board of Education, Regular Meeting, Apr. 7, 1970, Official Transcript, at 523, Remus Robinson Papers, Walter P. Reuther Library, Archives of Labor and Urban Affairs, Wayne State University.

49. Detroit Board of Education, Regular Meeting, Apr. 7, 1970, Official Transcript, at 523, Remus Robinson Papers, Walter P. Reuther Library, Archives of Labor and Urban Affairs, Wayne State University.

50. Detroit Board of Education, Regular Meeting, Apr. 7, 1970, Official Transcript, at 533, Remus Robinson Papers, Walter P. Reuther Library, Archives of Labor and Urban Affairs, Wayne State University.

51. Detroit Board of Education, Regular Meeting, Apr. 7, 1970, Official Transcript, at 532, Remus Robinson Papers, Walter P. Reuther Library, Archives of Labor and Urban Affairs, Wayne State University.

52. Detroit Board of Education, Regular Meeting, Apr. 7, 1970, Official Transcript, at 532, Remus Robinson Papers, Walter P. Reuther Library, Archives of Labor and Urban Affairs, Wayne State University.

53. Mirel, *The Rise and Fall of an Urban School System*, 339.

54. Grant, "Community Control vs. School Integration," 70 ("Zwerdling delayed the vote for weeks in the hope that Robinson would be well enough to appear and vote").

55. Mirel, *The Rise and Fall of an Urban School System*, 340.

56. L. J. Zacharias Statement, Detroit Board of Education, Regular Meeting, Apr. 7, 1970, Official Transcript, at 517, Remus Robinson Papers, Walter P. Reuther Library, Archives of Labor and Urban Affairs, Wayne State University.

57. Harold Ryan Statement, Detroit Board of Education, Regular Meeting, Apr. 7, 1970, Official Transcript, at 531, Remus Robinson Papers, Walter P. Reuther Library, Archives of Labor and Urban Affairs, Wayne State University.

58. Harold Ryan Statement, Detroit Board of Education, Regular Meeting, Apr. 7, 1970, Official Transcript, at 531, Remus Robinson Papers, Walter P. Reuther Library, Archives of Labor and Urban Affairs, Wayne State University.

59. Wayne State University, "Detroit Area Ethnic Groups 1971," Detroit Historical Society: Digital Collections, http://detroithistorical.pastperfectonline.com/archive/197E1D3C-449A-454C-85ED-765155362100 (accessed Nov. 2, 2022).

60. "Median Home Value vs. Race by Census Tract in 1970," created by Myles Zhang on Social Explorer with data from the 1970 U.S. Census, socialexplorer.com/a2feddfc92/view (accessed Nov. 2, 2022).

61. Mirel, *The Rise and Fall of an Urban School System*, 219.

62. "Median Home Value vs. Race by Census Tract in 1970"; Mirel, *The Rise and Fall of an Urban School System*, 219.

63. "Median Home Value vs. Race by Census Tract in 1970."

64. "Black vs. White Poverty Rate by Census Tract in 1970," created by Myles Zhang on Social Explorer with data from the 1970 U.S. Census, socialexplorer.com/a92c408447/view (accessed Nov. 2, 2022).

65. "Median Home Value vs. Race by Census Tract in 1970."

66. Aberbach and Walker, "Citizen Desires," 61.

67. Aberbach and Walker, "Citizen Desires," 61.

68. Telephone Calls Received Apr. 6, 1970, Re: Boundary Plans, Remus Robinson Collection, Box 2, Folder 2–24, Decentralization; corres., 1970 Apr., Remus Robinson Collection, Walter P. Reuther Library, Archives of Labor and Urban Affairs, Wayne State University.

69. Aberbach and Walker, "Citizen Desires," 61.

70. Detroit Board of Education, Regular Meeting, Apr. 7, 1970, Official Transcript, at 533, Remus Robinson Papers, Walter P. Reuther Library, Archives of Labor and Urban Affairs, Wayne State University.

71. Reynolds Farley, Suzanne Bianchi, and Diane Colasanto, "Barriers to the Racial Integration of Neighborhoods: The Detroit Case," *Annals of the American Academy* 441 (1979): 97; David R. Harris, "'Property Values Drop When Blacks Move In, Because . . .'; Racial and Socioeconomic Determinants of Neighborhood Desirability," *American Sociological Review* 64, no. 3 (June 1999): 476.

72. In a pathbreaking article published in 2000 and titled "The Integration Game," scholars

Abraham Bell and Gideon Parchomovsky provided a game-theoretic account demonstrating the complexity of this process. They concluded:

> First, black entry into predominantly white neighborhoods sets in motion a process that may lead to resegregation or to integration. The process may be mapped in three game-theoretic models—the resegregation game, the assurance game, and the weak integration game. Second, the particular game form that the process will take depends on white homeowners' integration preferences and their relative intensity, as well as changes in property values. Third, perceived declines in property values of sufficient magnitude drive white homeowners away from weak integration models, and accelerate the movement toward resegregation of racially changing neighborhoods. Fourth, and finally, perceptions (even inaccurate ones) are crucial in determining how white homeowners will respond to racial change. The likelihood that a white homeowner will abandon a racially changing neighborhood is dramatically enhanced by a perception that property values will decline or that one's white neighbors will leave the neighborhood. (Abraham Bell and Gideon Parchomovsky, "The Integration Game," *Columbia Law Review* 100, no. 8 [December 2000]: 1965–2029.)

73. Farley, Bianchi, and Colasanto, "Barriers to the Racial Integration of Neighborhoods," 107.
74. Francis Kornegay Statement, Detroit Board of Education, Regular Meeting, Apr. 7, 1970, Official Transcript, at 521, Remus Robinson Papers, Walter P. Reuther Library, Archives of Labor and Urban Affairs, Wayne State University.
75. Francis Kornegay Statement, Detroit Board of Education, Regular Meeting, Apr. 7, 1970, Official Transcript, at 522, Remus Robinson Papers, Walter P. Reuther Library, Archives of Labor and Urban Affairs, Wayne State University.
76. Francis Kornegay Statement, Detroit Board of Education, Regular Meeting, Apr. 7, 1970, Official Transcript, at 522, Remus Robinson Papers, Walter P. Reuther Library, Archives of Labor and Urban Affairs, Wayne State University.
77. Francis Kornegay Statement, Detroit Board of Education, Regular Meeting, Apr. 7, 1970, Official Transcript, at 522, Remus Robinson Papers, Walter P. Reuther Library, Archives of Labor and Urban Affairs, Wayne State University.
78. Detroit Board of Education, Regular Meeting, Apr. 7, 1970, Official Transcript, at 548–49, Remus Robinson Papers, Walter P. Reuther Library, Archives of Labor and Urban Affairs, Wayne State University.
79. Grant, "Pupil Integration Plan OKd."
80. Grant, "Pupil Integration Plan OKd."
81. Mirel, *The Rise and Fall of an Urban School System*, 342.
82. Telephone Calls Received Apr. 6, 1970, Re: Boundary Plans, Box 2, Folder 2–24, Remus Robinson Collection, Walter P. Reuther Library, Archives of Labor and Urban Affairs, Wayne State University.
83. Richard Nixon, "Statement About Desegregation of Elementary and Secondary Schools," The American Presidency Project, Mar. 24, 1970, available at https://www.presidency.ucsb.edu/node/241065.
84. William Safire, *Before the Fall: An Inside View of the Pre-Watergate White House* (New York: Doubleday, 1975), 238.
85. The Gallup Poll Public Opinion 1935–1971, at 2240 (Interview dates Feb. 27–Mar. 2, 1970).
86. The Harris Survey, Yearbook on Public Opinion (1970), at 228.
87. The Harris Survey, at 228; Kevin J. McMahon, *Nixon's Court: His Challenge to Judicial Liberalism and its Political Consequences* (Chicago: The University of Chicago Press, 2011), 99.
88. The Harris Survey, at 228.

89. The Harris Survey, at 227; see also McMahon, *Nixon's Court*, 99.
90. The Harris Survey, at 229.
91. McMahon, *Nixon's Court*, 90–91; Hugh Davis Graham, *Civil Rights and the Presidency: Race and Gender in American Politics, 1960–1972* (New York: Oxford University Press, 1992), 139.
92. McMahon, *Nixon's Court*, 100.
93. Safire, *Before the Fall*, 237.
94. Nixon, "Statement About Desegregation," Mar. 24, 1970.
95. Nixon, "Statement About Desegregation," Mar. 24, 1970 [emphasis added].
96. Nixon, "Statement About Desegregation," Mar. 24, 1970.
97. John Pierson, "Nixon Declares U.S. Won't Demand End of De Facto School Segregation," *Wall Street Journal*, Mar. 25, 1970.
98. Pierson, "Nixon Declares U.S. Won't Demand End of De Facto School Segregation."
99. Nixon, "Statement About Desegregation Schools," Mar. 24, 1970.
100. Pierson, "Nixon Declares U.S. Won't Demand End of De Facto School Segregation."
101. Carl T. Rowan, "The $1.5 Billion Misunderstanding," *Chicago Sun-Times*, Apr. 1, 1970.

7. MONEY IS POWER AND IT WORKS

1. Barbara Doerr, "Tears, Cheers and Jeers, Shift Stirs Redford Pupils," *Detroit News*, Apr. 8, 1970.
2. Doerr, "Tears, Cheers and Jeers."
3. Doerr, "Tears, Cheers and Jeers."
4. Doerr, "Tears, Cheers and Jeers."
5. "Police Block Student Clash," *Detroit Free Press*, Apr. 9, 1970, 8A.
6. W. Howard Erickson, "Talks Urged on School Unrest," *Detroit News*, Apr. 9, 1970.
7. While Detroit's two major papers had different accounts of the total number of students involved in the incident, they both agreed that the police arrested fourteen students.
8. "Murphy Urges Calm at Schools," *Detroit Free Press*, Apr. 10, 1970.
9. Jerome F. Hansen, "Walkouts, Protests Flare at 11 Schools," *Detroit News*, Apr. 10, 1970.
10. "Murphy Urges Calm at Schools."
11. Gary Blonston, "Junior Highs Boycotted, Blacks Protest School Plan," *Detroit Free Press*, Apr. 11, 1970.
12. Blonston, "Junior Highs Boycotted."
13. Blonston, "Junior Highs Boycotted."
14. Blonston, "Junior Highs Boycotted."
15. Blonston, "Junior Highs Boycotted."
16. Blonston, "Junior Highs Boycotted," 3A.
17. Blonston, "Junior Highs Boycotted," 5A.
18. Blonston, "Junior Highs Boycotted," 1A, 5A.
19. Blonston, "Junior Highs Boycotted," 1A, 5A.
20. "Citizens Ask Aid for School," *Detroit Free Press*, Mar. 25, 1970, at 7B.
21. Tom DeLisle, "Served Up Western Style," *Detroit Free Press*, June 13, 1970.
22. "Citizens Ask Aid for School," 7B.
23. "Citizens Ask Aid for School," 7B.
24. "Citizens Ask Aid for School," 7B.
25. Letter from the Western High School Student Body to the Detroit Board of Education, Apr. 14, 1970, Box 2, Folder 2–23, Decentralization, 1970 Apr., Remus Robinson Papers, Walter P. Reuther Library, Wayne State University.
26. Letter from the Western High School Student Body to the Detroit Board of Education, Apr. 14, 1970, Remus Robinson Papers, Walter P. Reuther Library, Wayne State University.

27. Chris Singer, "Program Approved, Western Students Win Their Case," *Detroit Free Press*, May 27, 1970, 14A.
28. William Grant, "Board Takes to TV to Calm Fears on School Integration," *Detroit Free Press*, Apr. 10, 1970, 3A.
29. Grant, "Board Takes to TV," 3A.
30. William Grant, "Board's Plan: 'Finest Hour' or Mistake?," *Detroit Free Press*, Apr. 9, 1970, 3A.
31. Associated Press, "Detroit School Plan Brings on Some Opposition," *Lansing State Journal*, Apr. 9, 1970.
32. Allen Phillips, "House Votes to Kill Detroit School Shifts," *Detroit News*, Apr. 10, 1970.
33. Phillips, "House Votes to Kill Detroit School Shifts."
34. Phillips, "House Votes to Kill Detroit School Shifts."
35. Associated Press, "House, Senate Vote Decentralizing Halt," *Lansing State Journal*, Apr. 10, 1970.
36. Grant, "Community Control vs. School Integration," 65.
37. Telegram from Roy Wilkins to all NAACP Branches in Michigan, Apr. 10, 1970, NAACP Records, Manuscript Division, Library of Congress, Washington, D.C.
38. Telegram from Roy Wilkins to all NAACP Branches in Michigan, Apr. 10, 1970, NAACP Records, Manuscript Division, Library of Congress, Washington, D.C.
39. Telegram from Roy Wilkins to all NAACP Branches in Michigan, Apr. 10, 1970, NAACP Records, Manuscript Division, Library of Congress, Washington, D.C.
40. Telegram from Roy Wilkins to all NAACP Branches in Michigan, Apr. 10, 1970, NAACP Records, Manuscript Division, Library of Congress, Washington, D.C.
41. Telegram from Roy Wilkins to all NAACP Branches in Michigan, Apr. 10, 1970, NAACP Records, Manuscript Division, Library of Congress, Washington, D.C.
42. Telegram from Roy Wilkins to Norman Drachler, Apr. 13, 1970, NAACP Records, Manuscript Division, Library of Congress, Washington, D.C.
43. Telegram from Roy Wilkins to Norman Drachler, Apr. 13, 1970, NAACP Records, Manuscript Division, Library of Congress, Washington, D.C.
44. Telegram from Roy Wilkins to Norman Drachler, Apr. 13, 1970, NAACP Records, Manuscript Division, Library of Congress, Washington, D.C.
45. Telegram from Roy Wilkins to Norman Drachler, Apr. 13, 1970, NAACP Records, Manuscript Division, Library of Congress, Washington, D.C.
46. Yvonne Ryan, *Roy Wilkins: The Quiet Revolutionary and the NAACP* (Lexington, KY: University Press of Kentucky, 2013), 5–25.
47. Roy Wilkins and Tom Mathews, *Standing Fast: The Autobiography of Roy Wilkins* (New York: Viking Press, 1982), 318.
48. Ryan, *Roy Wilkins*, 199.
49. Wilkins and Mathews, *Standing Fast*, 217.
50. Albin Krebs, "Roy Wilkins, 50-year Veteran of Civil Rights Fights Is Dead," *New York Times*, Sept. 9, 1981, A1.
51. Krebs, "Roy Wilkins," A1.
52. Wilkins and Mathews, *Standing Fast*, 119.
53. Krebs, "Roy Wilkins," A1.
54. Krebs, "Roy Wilkins," A1.
55. Wilkins and Mathews, *Standing Fast*, 127.
56. Associated Press, "House, Senate Vote Decentralizing Halt."
57. Roger Lane, "Senate Votes to Repeal School Plan," *Detroit Free Press*, Apr. 11, 1970.
58. Transcript of news conference, Apr. 8, 1970, at 1 (on file with author).
59. Roger Lane, "City School Decentralization Threatened by Legislature," *Detroit Free Press*, Apr. 9, 1970.

60. Transcript of news conference, Apr. 8, 1970, at 2.
61. William Grant, "Parents Kickoff Campaign to Recall Four on School Board," *Detroit Free Press*, May 5, 1970.
62. "4 on School Board Are Target of Recall," *Detroit News*, May 1, 1970.
63. Grant, "Parents Kickoff Campaign."
64. William Grant, "Petitions Aimed at Integration Backers, School Board Recall Advances," *Detroit Free Press*, June 16, 1970.
65. William Grant, "School Recall Drive Hits the 700,000 Mark," *Detroit Free Press*, May 22, 1970.
66. Lane, "Senate Votes to Repeal School Plan," 5A.
67. Memorandum from June Shagaloff to Roy Wilkins and John A. Morsell, May 5, 1970, at 1, Box V:1041, Folder 1, NAACP Legal Department, Case Files, Michigan, Bradley v. Milliken, General Case Material, 1970 May–Aug., NAAPC Records, Manuscript Division, Library of Congress, Washington, D.C.
68. Mirel, *The Rise and Fall of an Urban School System*, 341.
69. Memorandum from June Shagaloff to Roy Wilkins and John A. Morsell, May 5, 1970, at 1, Box V:1041, Folder 1, NAACP Legal Department, Case Files, Michigan, Bradley v. Milliken, General Case Material, 1970 May–Aug., NAACP Records, Manuscript Division, Library of Congress, Washington, D.C.
70. Board of Directors of the Metropolitan Detroit Council of Churches, Statement and Resolution on Detroit school decentralization voted Apr. 9, 1970, Box 14, Folder 14–2, Public Act 244 (635), 1970, Walter P. Reuther Library, Archives of Labor and Urban Affairs, Wayne State University.
71. Board of Directors of the Metropolitan Detroit Council of Churches, Statement and Resolution on Detroit school decentralization voted Apr. 9, 1970, Walter P. Reuther Library, Archives of Labor and Urban Affairs, Wayne State University.
72. Memorandum from June Shagaloff to Roy Wilkins and John A. Morsell, May 5, 1970, at 1, NAACP Legal Department, NAACP Records, Manuscript Division, Library of Congress, Washington, D.C.
73. "As We See It, Detroiters Must Overcome School Board Ineptitude," *Detroit Free Press*, Apr. 9, 1970, 6A.
74. Editorial, "Quality Schools Still in Doubt," *Detroit News*, Apr. 9, 1970.
75. Editorial, "Quality Schools."
76. Editorial, "Quality Schools."
77. "Detroit School Board Has Shown the Way," *Michigan Chronicle*, Apr. 18, 1970.
78. "Detroit School Board Has Shown the Way."
79. "Detroit School Board Has Shown the Way."
80. Memorandum from June Shagaloff to Roy Wilkins and John A. Morsell, May 5, 1970, at 1, NAACP Legal Department, NAACP Records, Manuscript Division, Library of Congress, Washington, D.C.
81. "Split Community Reaction to Student Bussing Edict," *Michigan Chronicle*, Apr. 18, 1970.
82. Ward, "Blacks Join Move to Recall Board," 14B.
83. Ward, "Blacks Join Move to Recall Board," 14B.
84. Ward, "Blacks Join Move to Recall Board," 14B.
85. "Detroit Recall Campaign Success Is First in the U.S.," *Redford Record*, July 1, 1970.
86. Grant, "Community Control vs. School Integration," 74.
87. Tom Nugent, "Dr. Robinson Dies at 64; School Integration Backer," *Detroit Free Press*, June 15, 1970, A1.
88. Nugent, "Dr. Robinson Dies at 64," A1.
89. Letter from Linda G. Johnson to Remus Robinson, dated Apr. 23, 1970, Box 2, Folder 2–28, Remus Robinson Collection, Walter P. Reuther Library, Archives of Labor and Urban Affairs, Wayne State University.

8. RIGHT THING TO LOSE

1. Grant, "The Detroit School Case," 857.
2. Clark Hoyt, "Milliken Pledges Best for Michigan," *Detroit Free Press*, Jan. 23, 1969, 1A.
3. "1970 Gubernatorial General Election Results - Michigan," *Dave Leip's Atlas of U.S. Elections*, https://uselectionatlas.org/RESULTS/state.php?fips=26&year=1970&f=0&off=5&elect=0.
4. Lane, "Senate Votes to Repeal School Plan."
5. Grant, "The Detroit School Case," 857.
6. Grant, "Community Control vs. School Integration," 73; Lane, "Senate Votes to Repeal School Plan."
7. Hain, "Sealing Off the City," 234; Grant, "Community Control vs. School Integration," 73.
8. "'Act 244 Repeal, Attempt Work of Bigots' . . . Young," *Michigan Chronicle*, May 2, 1970.
9. Lane, "Senate Votes to Repeal School Plan."
10. Lane, "Senate Votes to Repeal School Plan."
11. "'Act 244 Repeal, Attempt Work of Bigots' . . . Young."
12. "'Act 244 Repeal, Attempt Work of Bigots' . . . Young."
13. "'Act 244 Repeal, Attempt Work of Bigots' . . . Young."
14. Grant, "The Detroit School Case," 857.
15. Harry Salsinger, "School Compromise Heads for Senate," *Detroit News*, May 28, 1970.
16. William Grant, "Maneuvering That Broke the School Plan Deadlock," *Detroit Free Press*, July 5, 1970.
17. Grant, "Community Control vs. School Integration," 74.
18. Jerry M. Flint, "Integration Plan Fought in Detroit," *New York Times*, June 13, 1970.
19. Allen Phillips, "Milliken Signs Detroit School Bill," *Detroit News*, July 8, 1970; 1970 Mich. Pub. Act 48, Sec. 12.
20. Grant, "Community Control vs. School Integration," 73.
21. "May 5, 1970 Testimony: Public Law # 244," *NAACP Reporter*, May 1970, 3, NAACP Records, Manuscript Division, Library of Congress, Washington D.C.
22. Grant, "Maneuvering That Broke the School Plan Deadlock."
23. Grant, "Community Control vs. School Integration," 73–74; Phillips, "Milliken Signs Detroit School Bill."
24. 1970 Mich. Pub. Act 48, Sec. 12.
25. Phillips, "Milliken Signs Detroit School Bill"; Grant, "Community Control vs. School Integration," 74.
26. Harry Salsinger, "Legislature 'Saves' Board," *Detroit News*, May 30, 1970.
27. Harry Salsinger, "School Compromise"; William Grant, "School Compromise Near in Legislature," *Detroit Free Press*, May 28, 1970; Harry Salsinger, "Senate Approves School Compromise," *Detroit News*, May 29, 1970.
28. Grant, "School Compromise Near in Legislature."
29. "NAACP National Convention Supports Detroit Board of Education Plan," *NAACP Reporter*, July 1970, 3, NAACP Records, Manuscript Division, Library of Congress, Washington D.C.
30. "NAACP National Convention Supports Detroit Board of Education Plan," *NAACP Reporter*, July 1970, 3, NAACP Records, Manuscript Division, Library of Congress, Washington D.C.
31. 1970 Mich. Pub. Act 48.
32. William Grant, "Stormy Meeting May Bring Changes to Decentralization Bill," *Detroit Free Press*, June 3, 1970.
33. Grant, "Community Control vs. School Integration," 74.
34. William Grant, "Recall Vote Outs 4 from School Board," *Detroit Free Press*, Aug. 6, 1970, A1.
35. William Grant, "School Recall Bid Splits Voters Along Racial Lines," *Detroit Free Press*, Aug. 5, 1970, 9A.
36. Grant, "Community Control vs. School Integration," 75.

37. Aberbach and Walker, "Citizen Desires," 63.
38. Aberbach and Walker, "Citizen Desires," 63.
39. Aberbach and Walker, "Citizen Desires," 69.
40. William Grant, "Drachler Won't Quit Despite Recall: Calls Vote Policy Rejection," *Detroit Free Press*, Aug. 7, 1970, 3A.
41. Grant, "Community Control vs. School Integration," 75.
42. William Grant, "School Regions Divided Evenly Between the Races," *Detroit Free Press*, Aug. 5, 1970, 3A.
43. Grant, "Community Control vs. School Integration," 75.
44. Grant, "School Regions Divided Evenly," 3A.
45. "Milliken Panel's Regional School Plan Denounced," *Michigan Chronicle*, Aug. 22, 1970, A12.
46. Mirel, *The Rise and Fall of an Urban School System*, 343; *Key Facts On Eight Region Plan*, adopted Aug. 4, 1970, by Detroit Boundary Line Commission (on file with author).
47. Berkowitz, "An Analysis," 149.
48. LaNoue and Smith, *The Politics of School Decentralization*, 121.
49. William Grant, "Drachler May Quit School Post," *Detroit Free Press*, Nov. 16, 1970; Grant, "Community Control vs. Integration," 76.
50. Grant, "Community Control vs. Integration," 76–77; LaNoue and Smith, *The Politics of School Decentralization*, 144 ("Almost immediately, the central board replaced James Hathaway and chose Patrick McDonald as its President. The selection of McDonald, the representative of the white neighborhoods who had been censured by the old liberal board, was the first clear indication of the consequence of the election").
51. Berkowitz, "An Analysis," 151.
52. William Grant, "Election Cuts Black School Board Seats," *Detroit Free Press*, Nov. 7, 1970, 12A.
53. Grant, "Election Cuts Black School Board Seats," 12A.
54. Grant, "Community Control vs. Integration," 77.
55. Grant, "Drachler May Quit."
56. Georgea Kovanis, "School Board President Stuck to His Ideals," *Detroit Free Press*, May 18, 1987, 13F.

9. UP FOR GRABS

1. William Grant, "Lawyer's Hard Work and Ego Win Integration Cases," *Detroit Free Press*, June 18, 1972.
2. Paul R. Dimond, *Beyond Busing: Reflections on Urban Segregation, the Courts, and Equal Opportunity* (Ann Arbor: University of Michigan Press, 2009), 26; Wolfgang Saxon, "Louis R. Lucas, 70, Lawyer in School Desegregation Era, Dies," *New York Times*, June 24, 2005.
3. Order, Feb. 16, 1971, quoted in Bradley v. Milliken, 338 F. Supp. 582, 584 (E.D. Mich. 1971).
4. Bradley v. Milliken Complaint, Aug. 1970, at Paragraph IV, Box 1, Bradley v. Milliken Case Files, Bentley Historical Library, University of Michigan.
5. William Grant, "Boy Plays Key Role in Busing Fight, But Football's His Interest," *Detroit Free Press*, June 18, 1972; Stephen Franklin, "Award for Plaintiffs in Desegregation Suit: Frustration, Anger," *Detroit Free Press*, Dec. 3, 1980.
6. Denton Watson, "The Detroit School Challenge," *The Crisis*, June–July 1974, 188; Howard Warren, "Boy in Busing Suit Gets Historic Role," *Detroit News*, July 25, 1974.
7. "Plaintiff in Suit 'Shocked,'" *Benton Harbor News-Palladium*, July 26, 1974.
8. "Plaintiff in Suit 'Shocked.'"
9. Watson, "The Detroit School Challenge," 189.
10. Warren, "Boy in Busing Suit Gets Historic Role."
11. Warren, "Boy in Busing Suit Gets Historic Role."

12. Christine MacDonald and Brad Heath, "Family Named in Case Proud of Equality Fight," *Detroit News*, May 16, 2004.
13. Watson, "The Detroit School Challenge," 188.
14. Watson, "The Detroit School Challenge," 188.
15. MacDonald and Heath, "Family Named in Case Proud of Equality Fight."
16. Grant, "Boy Plays Key Role in Busing Fight."
17. Grant, "Boy Plays Key Role in Busing Fight."
18. Grant, "Boy Plays Key Role in Busing Fight."
19. Cleage Jr., *Black Christian Nationalism*, xxvvii.
20. Philip A. Hart, "School Desegregation: A Northern View," *Congressional Record* 117, Nov. 8, 1971.
21. MacDonald and Heath, "Family Named in Case Proud of Equality Fight."
22. Grant, "Boy Plays Key Role in Busing Fight."
23. Franklin, "Award for Plaintiffs in Desegregation Suit: Frustration, Anger."
24. Ron Russell, "Integration of Schools a 'Dead Issue'?," *Detroit News and Free Press*, May 1, 1994.
25. Grant, "Boy Plays Key Role in Busing Fight."
26. Grant, "Boy Plays Key Role in Busing Fight."
27. Hain, "Sealing Off the City," 236.
28. Dimond, *Beyond Busing*, 29.
29. Dimond, *Beyond Busing*, 29.
30. Hain, "Sealing Off the City," 237.
31. Dimond, *Beyond Busing*, 29.
32. Letter from Nathaniel R. Jones to Thomas Turner, Aug. 24, 1970, Box V:1041, Folder 1, NAACP Records, Manuscript Division, Library of Congress, Washington, D.C.
33. Memo from Nathaniel R. Jones, Roy Wilkins, John A. Morsell, and June Shagaloff dated Aug. 27, 1970, at 2, NAACP Records, Manuscript Division, Library of Congress, Washington, D.C.
34. Memo from Nathaniel R. Jones, Roy Wilkins, John A. Morsell, and June Shagaloff dated Aug. 27, 1970, at 2, NAACP Records, Manuscript Division, Library of Congress, Washington, D.C.
35. Nathaniel R. Jones, *Answering the Call: An Autobiography of the Modern Struggle to End Racial Discrimination in America* (New York: The New Press, 2016), 9–11.
36. Jones, *Answering the Call*, 19.
37. Jones, *Answering the Call*, 18.
38. Jones, *Answering the Call*, 22.
39. Jones, *Answering the Call*, 33.
40. Jones, *Answering the Call*, 33.
41. Jones, *Answering the Call*, 33–58.
42. Jones, *Answering the Call*, 82–84.
43. Jones, *Answering the Call*, 84–85.
44. Jones, *Answering the Call*, 95.
45. Jones, *Answering the Call*, 98.
46. Bradley v. Milliken Complaint, Aug. 1970, at paragraph XIV, Milliken Case Files, Bentley Historical Library, University of Michigan.
47. Nixon, "Statement About Desegregation," Mar. 24, 1970.
48. Bradley v. Milliken Complaint, Aug. 1970, at paragraph XV, Milliken Case Files, Bentley Historical Library, University of Michigan.
49. Bradley v. Milliken Complaint, Aug. 1970, at paragraph XVI, Milliken Case Files, Bentley Historical Library, University of Michigan.
50. Bradley v. Milliken Complaint, Aug. 1970, at paragraph XX, Milliken Case Files, Bentley Historical Library, University of Michigan.
51. Bradley v. Milliken Complaint, Aug. 1970, at paragraph XXIII, 1(a), 1(b), Milliken Case Files, Bentley Historical Library, University of Michigan.

52. Bradley v. Milliken Complaint, Aug. 1970, at paragraph XXIII, 2(f), Bradley v. Milliken Case Files, Bentley Historical Library, University of Michigan.

53. Green v. County School Board of New Kent County, 391 U.S. 430, 438 (1968).

54. Bradley v. Milliken Complaint, Aug. 1970, at paragraph XXIII, 2(g), Milliken Case Files, Bentley Historical Library, University of Michigan.

55. Bradley v. Milliken Complaint, Aug. 1970, at paragraph V, VI, Milliken Case Files, Bentley Historical Library, University of Michigan.

56. City of Monterey v. Del Monte Dunes, 526 U.S. at 687, 719 (1999) (emphasizing it is settled law that the Seventh Amendment does not apply to suits seeking only injunctive relief).

57. Email from Paul Dimond to Michelle Adams, dated Jan. 21, 2019 (on file with author).

58. Michelle Adams interview of John Mogk, Oct. 3, 2018 (on file with the author).

59. Michelle Adams interview of John Mogk, Oct. 3, 2018 (on file with the author).

60. Dimond, *Beyond Busing*, 64.

61. Hunter v. Pittsburgh, 207 U.S. at 161, 178 (1907).

62. Osborne M. Reynolds Jr., *Local Government Law* (5th ed., 2019), 31.

63. Hunter v. Pittsburgh, 207 U.S. at 161, 178–79 (1907).

64. In the South, plaintiffs challenging school segregation typically sued southern school *districts*, not the southern states themselves. *Brown v. Board of Education* itself demonstrated that the defendant was the Topeka Board of Education, not the state of Kansas. As longtime LDF attorney Norman J. Chachkin explained in late 1971, "Desegregation suits had classically proceeded against individual school districts as bodies corporate under state law, and relief was generally assumed to be limited to the entity sued." Norman J. Chachkin, "Metropolitan School Desegregation: Evolving Law," *Equity and Excellence in Education* 10, no. 2 (Mar./Apr. 1972): 16. This approach made sense, as it was the southern school districts themselves that actively enforced and maintained the dual school policy; they were the entities against whom relief would run, if any. But this didn't change the fundamental reality: school districts did not enjoy an independent, inviolable sovereignty separate from the state in which they were located.

65. Dimond, *Beyond Busing*, 30.

66. Brown v. Board of Education, 349 U.S. at 294, 300–301 (1955).

67. Dimond, *Beyond Busing*, 63–64.

68. Editorial, "Law Holds for Detroit as Well as for Dixie," *Detroit Free Press*, Aug. 21, 1970.

69. Editorial, "Law Holds for Detroit."

70. Letter from J. "Nick" Harold Flannery to Nathaniel R. Jones, dated Sept. 4, 1970, NAACP Records, Manuscript Division, Library of Congress, Washington D.C.

71. Letter from Flannery to Jones dated Sept. 4, 1970, NAACP Records, Manuscript Division, Library of Congress, Washington D.C.

72. Letter from Flannery to Jones dated Sept. 4, 1970, NAACP Records, Manuscript Division, Library of Congress, Washington D.C.

73. Lewis M. Steel, *The Butler's Child: An Autobiography* (New York: Thomas Dunne Books, 2016), 146.

74. Louis D. Beer, "The Nature of the Violation and the Scope of the Remedy: An Analysis of *Milliken v. Bradley* in Terms of the Evolution of the Theory of the Violation," *Wayne Law Review* 21 (1975): 903, 904.

75. Bradley v. Milliken, 402 F. Supp. 1096, 1107 (E.D. Mich. 1975).

76. William Serrin, "The Most Hated Man in Michigan," *Saturday Review*, Aug. 26, 1972, 14.

77. William Grant, "Judge Ready in School Case," *Detroit Free Press*, Nov. 23, 1970.

78. Grant, "Judge Ready in School Case."

79. Carrie Sharlow, "Michigan Lawyers in History," *Michigan Bar Journal* (October 2012): 44.

80. "Judge Roth Had to Grow Up to Find Out What Word Segregation Meant," *Sheboygan Press*, June 26, 1972, 31; Nancy Abner, "Judge Roth—No Stranger to Controversy," *Detroit News*, June 18, 1972.

81. Jerry M. Flint, "Judge in Busing Case Stephen John Roth," *New York Times*, June 16, 1972.
82. Walter G. Krapohl, "Stephen J. Roth," *Michigan State Bar Journal* 28 (1949): 23.
83. William Grant, "Judge Ready in School Case," *Detroit Free Press*, Nov. 23, 1970.
84. Krapohl, "Stephen J. Roth."
85. William Grant, "Roth's Views Did Dramatic Turnabout," *Detroit Free Press*, June 18, 1972.
86. Serrin, "The Most Hated Man in Michigan," 14.

10. TAKING ON NORTHERN JIM CROW

1. Dimond, *Beyond Busing*, 32.
2. Jones, *Answering the Call*, 157.
3. Grant, "Roth's Views Did Dramatic Turnabout," 4A.
4. Grant, "The Detroit School Case," 859.
5. Bradley v. Board of Education of the City of Detroit, Rulings on: Application for Preliminary Injunction; Motion to Intervene; Motion to Dismiss as to Defendants Milliken and Kelley, September 3, 1970, Box 10, Bradley v. Milliken Case Files, Bentley Historical Library, University of Michigan.
6. Bradley Rulings on: Application for Preliminary Injunction; Motion to Intervene; Motion to Dismiss as to Defendants Milliken and Kelley, September 3, 1970, Bradley v. Milliken Case Files, Bentley Historical Library, University of Michigan.
7. Bradley Rulings on: Application for Preliminary Injunction; Motion to Intervene; Motion to Dismiss as to Defendants Milliken and Kelley, September 3, 1970, Bradley v. Milliken Case Files, Bentley Historical Library, University of Michigan.
8. Statement of Nathaniel R. Jones, General Counsel NAACP, dated Sept. 3, 1970, Box V:1040, Folder 3, Legal Department, Case Files, Michigan, Bradley v. Milliken General Case Material, 1970 Oct., NAACP Records, Manuscript Division, Library of Congress, Washington, D.C.
9. Statement of Nathaniel R. Jones, dated Sept. 3, 1970, NAACP Records, Manuscript Division, Library of Congress, Washington, D.C.
10. Bradley v. Milliken, No. 20794, Oct. 13, 1970, at 10.
11. Dimond, *Beyond Busing*, 33-34.
12. Dimond, *Beyond Busing*, 33-34.
13. Bradley v. Milliken, No. 20794, Oct. 13, 1970, at 12-13.
14. Bradley v. Milliken, No. 20794, Oct. 13, 1970, at 13.
15. Bradley v. Milliken, No. 20794, Oct. 13, 1970, at 13.
16. Bradley v. Milliken, No. 20794, Oct. 13, 1970, at 13.
17. Bradley v. Milliken, No. 20794, Oct. 13, 1970, at 14.
18. David Cooper, "City School Integration Bid Upheld: State Action Is Overruled," *Detroit Free Press*, Oct. 15, 1970.
19. Bradley v. Milliken, No. 20794, Oct. 13, 1970, at 14.
20. Tom Turner, "NAACP Tells Board of Education 'Carry Out Your Plan,'" Press Release, Oct. 15, 1970, NAACP Records, Manuscript Division, Library of Congress, Washington, D.C.
21. Cooper, "City School Integration Bid Upheld."
22. Statement of Nathaniel R. Jones, Esq. General Counsel—NAACP, Oct. 15, 1970, Box V:1040, Folder 3, Legal Department, Case Files, Michigan, Bradley v. Milliken General Case Material, 1970 Oct., NAACP Records, Manuscript Division, Library of Congress, Washington, D.C.
23. Bradley v. Milliken, No. 35257, Ruling of the Court on Motion to Implement Apr. 7, 1970 Plan, by Honorable Stephen J. Roth, United States District Judge, at Detroit, Michigan, on Wednesday, Nov. 4, 1970.
24. William Grant, "600 Angry Parents Protest Order to Integrate Schools," *Detroit Free Press*, Nov. 15, 1970.
25. Harry Salsinger, "Citizens Tell Opposition to Integration," *Detroit News*, Nov. 15, 1970.

26. Grant, "600 Angry Parents Protest."
27. Grant, "600 Angry Parents Protest"; Salsinger, "Citizens Tell Opposition."
28. Grant, "600 Angry Parents Protest."
29. Salsinger, "Citizens Tell Opposition."
30. Harry Salsinger, "School Board Offers District Plan Package," *Detroit News*, Nov. 17, 1970.
31. Harold Hines, "Drawn to Success: How Do Integrated Magnet Schools Work?," Reimagining Integration, published Feb. 2017, https://rides.gse.harvard.edu/files/gse-rides/files/rides _-_drawn_to_success_how_do_integrated_magnet_schools_work.pdf.
32. Alex Sergienko, "In the Beginning: How a Small City in the Pacific Northwest Invented Magnet Schools," *Education Next* (Spring 2005): 47.
33. Green v. New Kent County, 391 U.S. at 430, 440 (1968).
34. Bradley v. Milliken, Ruling on School Plans Submitted, Dec. 3, 1970, at 2–3, Box V:1041, Folder 5, Legal Department, Case Files, Michigan, Bradley v. Milliken General Case Material, 1970 Dec., NAACP Records, Manuscript Division, Library of Congress, Washington, D.C.
35. Bradley v. Milliken, Ruling on School Plans Submitted, Dec. 3, 1970, at 5, Bradley v. Milliken General Case Material, NAACP Records, Manuscript Division, Library of Congress, Washington, D.C.
36. Bradley v. Milliken, Ruling on School Plans Submitted, Dec. 3, 1970, at 6, Bradley v. Milliken General Case Material, NAACP Records, Manuscript Division, Library of Congress, Washington, D.C.
37. Bradley v. Milliken, Ruling on School Plans Submitted, Dec. 3, 1970, at 8, Bradley v. Milliken General Case Material, NAACP Records, Manuscript Division, Library of Congress, Washington, D.C.
38. Bradley v. Milliken, Ruling on Motion for Continuance, Dec. 3, 1970, at 2, Bradley v. Milliken General Case Material, NAACP Records, Manuscript Division, Library of Congress, Washington, D.C.
39. William Grant, "Voluntary Integration Plan Approved," *Detroit Free Press*, Dec. 4, 1970, 8-A.
40. William Grant, "Black Philosophy Professor Joins City School Board," *Detroit Free Press*, July 2, 1970, 8-C.
41. Grant, "Voluntary Integration Plan Approved," 1-A.
42. John McClendon, "Dr. Cornelius Golightly (1917–1976): The Life of an Academic and a Public Intellectual," BlackPast, published Mar. 25, 2014, accessed May 5, 2024, available at https://www.blackpast.org/african-american-history/dr-cornelius-golightly-1917-1976 -life-academic-and-public-intellectual/.
43. Dimond, *Beyond Busing*, 36.
44. Dimond, *Beyond Busing*, 36.
45. Motion to Intervene as Defendant in a Class Action on the Basis of Common Question in Law and Fact, Aug. 25, 1970, Box 3, Bradley v. Milliken Case Files, Bentley Historical Library, University of Michigan.
46. Motion to Intervene, 3, Bradley v. Milliken Case Files, Bentley Historical Library, University of Michigan.
47. Motion to Intervene, transcript, Aug. 27, 1970, at 14, Box 4, Bradley v. Milliken Case Files, Bentley Historical Library, University of Michigan.
48. Motion to Intervene, 2, Bradley v. Milliken Case Files, Bentley Historical Library, University of Michigan.
49. Motion to Intervene, transcript, Aug. 27, 1970, at 14, Bradley v. Milliken Case Files, Bentley Historical Library, University of Michigan.
50. Rulings On: Application for Preliminary Injunction: Motion to Intervene; Motion to Dismiss as to Defendants Milliken and Kelley, Sept. 3, 1970, Box 10, Bradley v. Milliken Case Files, Bentley Historical Library, University of Michigan.

51. Motion to Intervene, transcript, Aug. 27, 1970, at 24, Box V:1041, Folder 2, Legal Department, Case Files, Michigan, Bradley v. Milliken General Case Material, 1970 Sept., NAACP Records, Manuscript Division, Library of Congress, Washington, D.C.
52. Petition for Rehearing on Motion to Intervene as a Defendant in a Class Action, Mar. 11, 1971, at 6, Box V:1041, Folder 8, Legal Department, Case Files, Michigan, Bradley v. Milliken General Case Material, 1971 Jan.–June, NAACP Records, Manuscript Division, Library of Congress, Washington, D.C.
53. Bradley v. Milliken, Trial Transcript, Apr. 6, 1971, at 10, Box 5, Book 1, Bradley v. Milliken Case Files, Bentley Historical Library, University of Michigan.
54. Bradley v. Milliken, No. 20794 (6th Cir. Oct. 13, 1970), at 14.
55. Bradley v. Milliken, Trial Transcript, Apr. 6, 1971, at 10, Bradley v. Milliken Case Files, Bentley Historical Library, University of Michigan.
56. Bradley v. Milliken, Trial Transcript, Apr. 6, 1971, at 10, Bradley v. Milliken Case Files, Bentley Historical Library, University of Michigan.
57. Bradley v. Milliken, Trial Transcript, Apr. 6, 1971, at 12, Bradley v. Milliken Case Files, Bentley Historical Library, University of Michigan.
58. Bradley v. Milliken, Trial Transcript, Apr. 6, 1971, at 11, Bradley v. Milliken Case Files, Bentley Historical Library, University of Michigan.
59. Bradley v. Milliken, Trial Transcript, Apr. 6, 1971, at 12, Bradley v. Milliken Case Files, Bentley Historical Library, University of Michigan.
60. Deal v. Cincinnati Board of Education, 369 F.2d 55, 60 (6th Cir. 1966).
61. Bradley v. Milliken, Trial Transcript, Apr. 13, 1971, at 460–61, Box 5, Book 4, Bradley v. Milliken Case Files, Bentley Historical Library, University of Michigan.
62. Deal v. Cincinnati Board of Education, 369 F.2d 55, 60 (6th Cir. 1966).
63. Dimond, *Beyond Busing*, 39.
64. Dimond, *Beyond Busing*, 39.
65. *The Kerner Report: The National Advisory Commission on Civil Disorders*, with contributions by Julian E. Zelizer (2016), 441.
66. Abraham A. Ribicoff, "The Future of School Integration in the United States," *Journal of Law and Education* 1 (1972): 17.
67. Tom Wicker, "Mr. Ribicoff Comes Through," *New York Times*, Mar. 21, 1971.
68. Ribicoff, "The Future of School Integration," 19.
69. Ribicoff, "The Future of School Integration," 20.
70. Wicker, "Mr. Ribicoff Comes Through," 65.
71. William Raspberry, "Ribicoff's Bills May Not Hit Mark," *Washington Post*, Mar. 18, 1971.
72. Raspberry, "Ribicoff's Bills May Not Hit Mark."
73. Abraham Ribicoff, *America Can Make It!* (New York: Atheneum, 1972), 42.
74. Ribicoff, "The Future of School Integration," 19.
75. Ribicoff, "The Future of School Integration," 19.
76. Congressional Record—Senate, Apr. 19, 1971, at 10746.
77. Congressional Record—Senate, Apr. 19, 1971, at 10745.
78. Congressional Record—Senate, Apr. 19, 1971, at 10765.
79. Congressional Record—Senate, Apr. 19, 1971, at 10745.
80. Congressional Record—Senate, Apr. 19, 1971, at 10746.
81. Congressional Record—Senate, Apr. 19, 1971, at 10757–59.
82. Ribicoff, "The Future of School Integration," 18.
83. Ribicoff, "The Future of School Integration," 18–19.
84. Ribicoff, "The Future of School Integration," 19.
85. Bureau of the Census, U.S. Dep't of Com., 1970 Census of Population and Housing: Census Tracts, PHC(1)-58, Detroit, Mich. SMSA App-2 (1973).
86. Ribicoff, "The Future of School Integration," 19.

87. Ribicoff, "The Future of School Integration," 19.
88. Jason Sokol, *All Eyes Are Upon Us: Race and Politics from Boston to Brooklyn, the Conflicted Soul of the Northeast* (Amherst: University of Massachusetts Press, 2014), 153.
89. Congressional Record—Senate, Apr. 19, 1971, at 10749–50.
90. Congressional Record—Senate, Apr. 20, 1971, at 10949.
91. Congressional Record—Senate, Apr. 20, 1971, at 10949.

11. ANOTHER BRICK IN THE WALL

1. Bradley v. Milliken, Trial Transcript, Apr. 6, 1971, at 139, Bradley v. Milliken Case Files, Bentley Historical Library, University of Michigan.
2. *Cambridge Dictionary*, s.v. "containment (*n.*)," accessed Apr. 19, 2024, https://dictionary .cambridge.org/us/dictionary/english/containment.
3. Bradley v. Milliken, Trial Transcript, Apr. 27, 1971, at 919, Box 5, Book 8, Bradley v. Milliken Case Files, Bentley Historical Library, University of Michigan.
4. Bradley v. Milliken, Trial Transcript, Apr. 14, 1971, at 569, Box 5, Book 5, Bradley v. Milliken Case Files, Bentley Historical Library, University of Michigan.
5. Bradley v. Milliken, Trial Transcript, Apr. 16, 1971, at 736, Box 5, Book 7, Bradley v. Milliken Case Files, Bentley Historical Library, University of Michigan.
6. Bradley v. Milliken, Trial Transcript, Apr. 7, 1971, at 295, Box 5, Book 2, Bradley v. Milliken Case Files, Bentley Historical Library, University of Michigan.
7. *Merriam-Webster*, s.v. "cat and mouse (*n.*)," https://www.merriam-webster.com/dictionary /cat%20and%20mouse.
8. Dimond, *Beyond Busing*, 39.
9. Dimond, *Beyond Busing*, 39.
10. Thomas A. Mauet, *Fundamentals of Trial Techniques* (Boston: Little, Brown and Co., 1988).
11. Dimond, *Beyond Busing*, 41–42.
12. The original 10 x 20 ft. map with census data overlays could not be located. The maps in this chapter showing the black population of Detroit from 1940 to 1970 were recreated by Myles Zhang, a Ph.D. candidate in the architecture program at the University of Michigan.
13. Grant, "Roth's Views Did Dramatic Turnabout," 4A.
14. Email from Paul Dimond to Michelle Adams, dated Dec. 14, 2022 (on file with author).
15. William Grant, "Suit Unraveled Long History of Race Segregation in City," *Detroit Free Press*, Oct. 11, 1971.
16. Grant, "The Detroit School Case," 862.
17. Grant, "The Detroit School Case," 862.
18. Bradley v. Milliken, Trial Transcript, Apr. 6, 1971, at 131, Bradley v. Milliken Case Files, Bentley Historical Library, University of Michigan.
19. Bradley v. Milliken, Trial Transcript, Apr. 6, 1971, at 145, Bradley v. Milliken Case Files, Bentley Historical Library, University of Michigan.
20. Bradley v. Milliken, Trial Transcript, Apr. 6, 1971, at 145–46, Bradley v. Milliken Case Files, Bentley Historical Library, University of Michigan.
21. Bradley v. Milliken, Trial Transcript, Apr. 6, 1971, at 146, Bradley v. Milliken Case Files, Bentley Historical Library, University of Michigan.
22. Thomas J. Sugrue, *The Origins of the Urban Crisis: Race and Inequality in Postwar Detroit* (Princeton, NJ: Princeton University Press, 2014), 33.
23. Bradley v. Milliken, Trial Transcript, Apr. 8, 1971, at 347, Box 5, Book 3, Bradley v. Milliken Case Files, Bentley Historical Library, University of Michigan.
24. Bradley v. Milliken, Trial Transcript, Apr. 6, 1971, at 146, Bradley v. Milliken Case Files, Bentley Historical Library, University of Michigan.
25. Shelley v. Kraemer, 334 U.S. at 1, 8 (1948).

26. Shelley v. Kraemer, 334 U.S. at 1, 8 (1948).
27. Clement E. Vose, *Caucasians Only: The Supreme Court, the NAACP, and the Restrictive Covenant Cases* (Berkeley: University of California Press, 1959), 122–50.
28. Robert Clifton Weaver, *The Negro Ghetto* (New York: Russell and Russell, 1967).
29. Weaver, *The Negro Ghetto*, 16.
30. Schwemm, *Housing Discrimination*, 3:4.
31. Bradley v. Milliken, Trial Transcript, Apr. 6, 1971, at 153, Bradley v. Milliken Case Files, Bentley Historical Library, University of Michigan.
32. Bradley v. Milliken, Trial Transcript, Apr. 7, 1971, at 186, Bradley v. Milliken Case Files, Bentley Historical Library, University of Michigan.
33. See U.S. Census Bureau, "Booming Cities Decade-to-Decade, 1830–2010" (Oct. 4, 2012), https://www.census.gov/dataviz/visualizations/017/508.php (listing Hamtramck and Highland Park as growing more than ten times larger in population between 1910 and 1920).
34. Bradley v. Milliken, Trial Transcript, Apr. 7, 1971, at 193–94, Bradley v. Milliken Case Files, Bentley Historical Library, University of Michigan.
35. Bradley v. Milliken, Trial Transcript, Apr. 7, 1971, at 187, Bradley v. Milliken Case Files, Bentley Historical Library, University of Michigan.
36. Grant, "Suit Unraveled Long History of Race Segregation in City."
37. Bradley v. Milliken, Trial Transcript, Apr. 7, 1971, at 187, Bradley v. Milliken Case Files, Bentley Historical Library, University of Michigan.
38. Bradley v. Milliken, Trial Transcript, Apr. 13, 1971, Box 5, Book 4, Bradley v. Milliken Case Files, Bentley Historical Library, University of Michigan.
39. James H. Carr and Katrin B. Anacker, "The Complex History of the Federal Housing Administration: Building Wealth, Promoting Segregation, and Rescuing the U.S. Housing Market and the Economy," *Banking & Financial Services Policy Report* 34 (Aug. 2015): 10.
40. Carr and Anacker, "The Complex History," 11.
41. Carr and Anacker, "The Complex History," 11.
42. Carr and Anacker, "The Complex History," 11.
43. Bradley v. Milliken, Trial Transcript, Apr. 13, 1971, Bradley v. Milliken Case Files, Bentley Historical Library, University of Michigan.
44. Bradley v. Milliken, Trial Transcript, Apr. 13, 1971, at 452, Bradley v. Milliken Case Files, Bentley Historical Library, University of Michigan.
45. Bradley v. Milliken, Trial Transcript, Apr. 13, 1971, at 495–96, Bradley v. Milliken Case Files, Bentley Historical Library, University of Michigan.
46. Bradley v. Milliken, Trial Transcript, Apr. 13, 1971, at 446, Bradley v. Milliken Case Files, Bentley Historical Library, University of Michigan.
47. Bradley v. Milliken, Trial Transcript, Apr. 13, 1971, at 445, Bradley v. Milliken Case Files, Bentley Historical Library, University of Michigan.
48. Dimond, *Beyond Busing*, 48.
49. Dimond, *Beyond Busing*, 48.
50. See "Arsenal of Democracy," Detroit Historical Society, https://detroithistorical.org/learn/encyclopedia-of-detroit/arsenal-democracy ("It is generally agreed that no American city contributed more to the Allied powers during WWII than Detroit. Appropriately, then, Detroit grew to become known as 'The Arsenal of Democracy' after a fireside chat conducted by President Franklin D. Roosevelt").
51. Victor G. Reuther, "500 Planes a Day," in *Detroit Perspectives: Crossroads and Turning Points*, ed. Wilma Wood Hendrickson (Detroit: Wayne State University Press, 1991), 41.
52. Bradley v. Milliken, Trial Transcript, Apr. 6, 1971, at 146–47, Bradley v. Milliken Case Files, Bentley Historical Library, University of Michigan.
53. Bradley v. Milliken, Trial Transcript, Apr. 6, 1971, at 149, Bradley v. Milliken Case Files, Bentley Historical Library, University of Michigan.

54. Sugrue, *The Origins of the Urban Crisis*, 72.
55. Sugrue, *The Origins of the Urban Crisis*, 73.
56. Bradley v. Milliken, Trial Transcript, Apr. 7, 1971, at 225, Bradley v. Milliken Case Files, Bentley Historical Library, University of Michigan; Richard Walter Thomas, *Life for Us Is What We Make It: Building Black Community in Detroit, 1915–1945* (Bloomington: Indiana University Press, 1992), 143.
57. Bradley v. Milliken, Trial Transcript, Apr. 7, 1971, at 225–26, Bradley v. Milliken Case Files, Bentley Historical Library, University of Michigan.
58. Sugrue, *The Origins of the Urban Crisis*, 73.
59. Bradley v. Milliken, Trial Transcript, Apr. 14, 1971, at 539, Bradley v. Milliken Case Files, Bentley Historical Library, University of Michigan.
60. Joe T. Darden, et al., *Detroit: Race and Uneven Development* (Philadelphia: Temple University Press, 1987), 115.
61. Darden, *Detroit*, 114.
62. Thomas, *Life for Us*, 144–45.
63. Sugrue, *The Origins of the Urban Crisis*, 73.
64. Charles K. Hyde, "The Arsenal of Democracy-for-Some," in *Detroit 1967: Origins, Impacts, Legacies* (Detroit: Wayne State University Press, 2017), 52; Darden, *Detroit*, 118; Sugrue, *The Origins of the Urban Crisis*, 74.
65. Heather Ann Thompson, "The Racial History of Criminal Justice in America," *Du Bois Review: Social Science Research on Race* 16, no. 1 (2019): 225.
66. Rothstein, *The Color of Law*, 27.
67. Thomas, *Life for Us*, 148.
68. Sugrue, *The Origins of the Urban Crisis*, 75.
69. Bradley v. Milliken, Trial Transcript, Apr. 6, 1971, at 170, Bradley v. Milliken Case Files, Bentley Historical Library, University of Michigan.
70. Bradley v. Milliken, Trial Transcript, Apr. 14, 1971, at 531, Bradley v. Milliken Case Files, Bentley Historical Library, University of Michigan.
71. Douglas S. Massey and Nancy A. Denton, *American Apartheid: Segregation and the Making of the Underclass* (Cambridge, MA: Harvard University Press, 2003), 56.
72. Susan J. Popkin, "Public Housing and the Legacy of Segregation," Urban Institute, Aug. 19, 2013, https://www.urban.org/urban-wire/public-housing-and-legacy-segregation.
73. Bradley v. Milliken, Trial Transcript, Apr. 15, 1971, at 706, Box 5, Book 6, Bradley v. Milliken Case Files, Bentley Historical Library, University of Michigan.
74. Bradley v. Milliken, Trial Transcript, Apr. 15, 1971, at 706, Bradley v. Milliken Case Files, Bentley Historical Library, University of Michigan.
75. Bradley v. Milliken, Trial Transcript, Apr. 16, 1971, at 731, Bradley v. Milliken Case Files, Bentley Historical Library, University of Michigan.
76. Bradley v. Milliken, Trial Transcript, Apr. 13, 1971, at 464, Bradley v. Milliken Case Files, Bentley Historical Library, University of Michigan.
77. Bradley v. Milliken, Trial Transcript, Apr. 13, 1971, at 464, Bradley v. Milliken Case Files, Bentley Historical Library, University of Michigan.
78. Bradley v. Milliken, Trial Transcript, Apr. 6, 1971, at 147, Bradley v. Milliken Case Files, Bentley Historical Library, University of Michigan.
79. Bradley v. Milliken, Trial Transcript, Apr. 6, 1971, at 147, Bradley v. Milliken Case Files, Bentley Historical Library, University of Michigan.
80. Bradley v. Milliken, Trial Transcript, Apr. 6, 1971, at 148, Bradley v. Milliken Case Files, Bentley Historical Library, University of Michigan.
81. Bradley v. Milliken, Trial Transcript, Apr. 6, 1971, at 163, Bradley v. Milliken Case Files, Bentley Historical Library, University of Michigan.
82. Gerald C. Van Dusen, *Detroit's Birwood Wall: Hatred & Healing in the West Eight Mile Community* (Charleston, SC: The History Press, 2019).

83. Sugrue, *The Origins of the Urban Crisis*, 65.
84. Adkins v. Morgan Stanley (SDNY), Expert Report of Thomas J. Sugrue in Support of Class Certification at 19, filed June 27, 2014.
85. Van Dusen, *Detroit's Birwood Wall*, 39.
86. Sugrue, *The Origins of the Urban Crisis*, 38.
87. N. D. B. Connolly et al., "Mapping Inequality: 'Big Data' Meets Social History in the Story of Redlining," essay, in *The Routledge Companion to Spatial History*, eds. Ian Gregory, Don DeBats, and Don Lafreniere (London: Routledge, 2020), 511.
88. Sugrue, *The Origins of the Urban Crisis*, 64.
89. Sugrue, *The Origins of the Urban Crisis*, 64.
90. Sugrue, *The Origins of the Urban Crisis*, 64.
91. Sugrue, *The Origins of the Urban Crisis*, 66–70.
92. Van Dusen, *Detroit's Birwood Wall*, 57.
93. Sugrue, *The Origins of the Urban Crisis*, 71.
94. Sugrue, *The Origins of the Urban Crisis*, 71–72.
95. Sugrue, *The Origins of the Urban Crisis*, 71–72.
96. Bradley v. Milliken, Trial Transcript, Apr. 8, 1971, at 347–50, Bradley v. Milliken Case Files, Bentley Historical Library, University of Michigan.
97. Bradley v. Milliken, Trial Transcript, Apr. 8, 1971, at 363, Bradley v. Milliken Case Files, Bentley Historical Library, University of Michigan.
98. Dimond, *Beyond Busing*, 47.
99. Dimond, *Beyond Busing*, 47.
100. Bradley v. Milliken, Trial Transcript, Apr. 14, 1971, at 592, Bradley v. Milliken Case Files, Bentley Historical Library, University of Michigan.
101. Bradley v. Milliken, Trial Transcript, Apr. 14, 1971, at 592, Bradley v. Milliken Case Files, Bentley Historical Library, University of Michigan.
102. Later, scholars would analogize the exclusionary actions of white groups like homeowners associations to those of anticompetitive cartels. One observed, "Racial cartels generated profit in the same way that market cartels do—by restricting supply and manipulating price." The scholar continued, "In housing markets, a segmented market provided Whites with higher property values." Daria Roithmayr, "Racial Cartels," *Michigan Journal of Race and Law* 16 (2010): 48. See also Darrell A. H. Miller, "Racial Cartels and the Thirteenth Amendment Enforcement Power," *Kentucky Law Journal* 100 (2011–2012): 23.
103. Bradley v. Milliken, Trial Transcript, Apr. 14, 1971, at 596, Bradley v. Milliken Case Files, Bentley Historical Library, University of Michigan.
104. Bradley v. Milliken, Trial Transcript, Apr. 14, 1971, at 598, Bradley v. Milliken Case Files, Bentley Historical Library, University of Michigan.
105. Bradley v. Milliken, Trial Transcript, Apr. 14, 1971, at 596, Bradley v. Milliken Case Files, Bentley Historical Library, University of Michigan.
106. Bradley v. Milliken, Trial Transcript, Apr. 15, 1971, at 647, Bradley v. Milliken Case Files, Bentley Historical Library, University of Michigan.
107. Bradley v. Milliken, Trial Transcript, Apr. 14, 1971, at 525, Bradley v. Milliken Case Files, Bentley Historical Library, University of Michigan. The National Association of Real Estate Boards (NAREB) was founded in 1908. The Detroit Real Estate Board was one of its founding members. In 1972, right after the *Bradley v. Milliken* trial, NAREB changed its name to the National Association of REALTORS® (NAR). NAREB/NAR has owned the registered trademarks REALTORS® and REALTOR® since the late 1940s. "History," National Association of REALTORS®, accessed July 16, 2024, https://www.nar.realtor/about-nar/history. NAREB/NAR formally excluded black members until 1961. Even after that time, however, many local boards—including Detroit's—continued to prevent black real estate professionals from joining their organizations. "From One Voice to Many: Despite Setbacks and

Opposition, How a Growing Chorus Paved the Way to Fair Housing," *Fair Housing Makes U.S. Stronger*, National Association of REALTORS®, Mar. 9, 2018, accessed July 16, 2024, https://www.nar.realtor/sites/default/files/documents/March-2018-Fair-Housing-3-9-2018 .pdf. Tellingly, NAREB/NAR lobbied against the 1968 Fair Housing Act. "Selling Houses While Black," *NAREB REALTIST*, National Association of Real Estate Brokers, accessed July 16, 2024, https://www.nareb.com/press/selling-houses-while-black/#:~:text=Though%20 the%20National%20Association%20of,law%20to%20end%20housing%20discrimination. In 2020, NAR apologized for its past complicity in racist housing practices. Collette Coleman, "Selling Houses While Black," *New York Times*, Jan. 12, 2023. To avoid overstating the role of trademarking in the creation of two racially separate real estate associations, I make note of the trademark here and go on without it.

108. Bradley v. Milliken, Trial Transcript, Apr. 14, 1971, at 525, Bradley v. Milliken Case Files, Bentley Historical Library, University of Michigan.
109. McKibben v. Michigan Corp. and Sec. Comm'n, 119 N.W. 2d 557, 558 (Mich. 1963).
110. McKibben v. Michigan Corp. and Sec. Comm'n, 119 N.W. 2d, 557, 563–65 (Mich. 1963).
111. Dimond, *Beyond Busing*, 46.
112. Bradley v. Milliken, Trial Transcript, Apr. 14, 1971, at 594, Bradley v. Milliken Case Files, Bentley Historical Library, University of Michigan.
113. Bradley v. Milliken, Trial Transcript, Apr. 14, 1971, at 594–95, Bradley v. Milliken Case Files, Bentley Historical Library, University of Michigan.
114. Bradley v. Milliken, Trial Transcript, Apr. 14, 1971, at 607, Bradley v. Milliken Case Files, Bentley Historical Library, University of Michigan.
115. Bradley v. Milliken, Trial Transcript, Apr. 14, 1971, at 607, Bradley v. Milliken Case Files, Bentley Historical Library, University of Michigan.
116. Bradley v. Milliken, Trial Transcript, Apr. 16, 1971, at 728, Bradley v. Milliken Case Files, Bentley Historical Library, University of Michigan.
117. Bradley v. Milliken, Trial Transcript, Apr. 16, 1971, at 737, Bradley v. Milliken Case Files, Bentley Historical Library, University of Michigan.
118. Bradley v. Milliken, Trial Transcript, Apr. 16, 1971, 751–53, Bradley v. Milliken Case Files, Bentley Historical Library, University of Michigan.
119. Bradley v. Milliken, Trial Transcript, Apr. 15, 1971, at 709, Bradley v. Milliken Case Files, Bentley Historical Library, University of Michigan.
120. Bradley v. Milliken, Trial Transcript, Apr. 15, 1971, at 710, Bradley v. Milliken Case Files, Bentley Historical Library, University of Michigan.
121. William Grant, "City Group Begins New Fight Against School Integration," *Detroit Free Press*, Apr. 25, 1971.
122. Grant, "City Group Begins New Fight."
123. William Grant, "Detroiter Switched His Stand: Lawyer Key Figure in Busing Plan," *Detroit Free Press*, June 15, 1972.
124. Grant, "Detroiter Switched His Stand."
125. Grant, "Detroiter Switched His Stand."
126. Bradley v. Milliken, Trial Transcript, Apr. 13, 1971, at 507, Bradley v. Milliken Case Files, Bentley Historical Library, University of Michigan.
127. Bradley v. Milliken, Trial Transcript, Apr. 13, 1971, at 508, Bradley v. Milliken Case Files, Bentley Historical Library, University of Michigan.
128. Bradley v. Milliken, Trial Transcript, Apr. 13, 1971, at 509, Bradley v. Milliken Case Files, Bentley Historical Library, University of Michigan.
129. Bradley v. Milliken, Trial Transcript, Apr. 13, 1971, at 509, Bradley v. Milliken Case Files, Bentley Historical Library, University of Michigan.
130. Bradley v. Milliken, Trial Transcript, Apr. 13, 1971, at 510, Bradley v. Milliken Case Files, Bentley Historical Library, University of Michigan.

131. Bradley v. Milliken, Trial Transcript, Apr. 13, 1971, at 510, Bradley v. Milliken Case Files, Bentley Historical Library, University of Michigan.

132. Bradley v. Milliken, Trial Transcript, Apr. 13, 1971, at 510, Bradley v. Milliken Case Files, Bentley Historical Library, University of Michigan.

133. Bradley v. Milliken, Trial Transcript, Apr. 13, 1971, at 510, Bradley v. Milliken Case Files, Bentley Historical Library, University of Michigan.

134. Bradley v. Milliken, Trial Transcript, Apr. 13, 1971, at 511, Bradley v. Milliken Case Files, Bentley Historical Library, University of Michigan.

135. Bradley v. Milliken, Trial Transcript, Apr. 13, 1971, at 512, Bradley v. Milliken Case Files, Bentley Historical Library, University of Michigan.

136. Bradley v. Milliken, Trial Transcript, Apr. 13, 1971, at 512, Bradley v. Milliken Case Files, Bentley Historical Library, University of Michigan.

137. Bradley v. Milliken, Trial Transcript, Apr. 13, 1971, at 517, Bradley v. Milliken Case Files, Bentley Historical Library, University of Michigan.

138. Bradley v. Milliken, Trial Transcript, Apr. 13, 1971, at 517, Bradley v. Milliken Case Files, Bentley Historical Library, University of Michigan.

139. Dimond, *Beyond Busing*, 50.

140. William Grant, "School Ruling Studied, Tighter Integration Seen," *Detroit Free Press*, Apr. 22, 1971.

141. Dimond, *Beyond Busing*, 55.

142. Grant, "The Detroit School Case," 863.

12. GARBAGE IN, GARBAGE OUT

1. Charlotte-Mecklenburg Schools homepage, http://www.cms.k12.nc.us/mediaroom/aboutus/Pages/History.aspx.

2. Swann v. Charlotte-Mecklenburg Board of Education, 311 F. Supp. 265, 268–71 (W.D.N.C.), *aff'd in part, modified in part*, 318 F. Supp 786, 801–804 (W.D.N.C. 1970).

3. *Swann*, 318 F. Supp. 786, 789.

4. *Swann*, 318 F. Supp. 786, 789.

5. *Swann*, 318 F. Supp. 786, 789.

6. Michael J. Graetz and Linda Greenhouse, *The Burger Court and the Rise of the Judicial Right* (New York: Simon & Schuster Paperbacks, 2017), 86.

7. Brief for the Commonwealth of Virginia at 6–7, *Swann*, 402 U.S. 1, 23 (1971).

8. *Swann*, 402 U.S. at 1, 23 (1971).

9. *Swann*, 402 U.S. at 1, 20–21 (1971).

10. *NAACP Reporter*, Apr. 1971, NAACP Records, Manuscript Division, Library of Congress, Washington D.C.

11. Grant, "School Ruling Studied."

12. John Ehrlichman, *Witness to Power: The Nixon Years* (New York: Simon & Schuster, 1982), 112; Fred Barbash, "Ehrlichman Tells of Nixon, Burger Talks," *Washington Post*, Dec. 10, 1981. We know the meeting occurred because of Ehrlichman's copious notes and because White House logs confirmed it. Audiotape: Conversation between Richard Nixon, Harry Dent, John Mitchell, and others, Oval Office of the White House, Washington, D.C., at 24:19–24:38, Apr. 21, 1971, Nat'l Archives Nixon White House Tape Conversation 484–82 (Nixon commenting to Dent that "Mitchell and Burger and I had breakfast about three months ago and I lit into Burger. I said, 'Now look here, I'll be honest with you, if you insist on busing . . .' So I was sorta disappointed."), available at http://www.easynixon.org/tapes/484-002; *accord* Hon. David S. Tatel, "Judicial Methodology, Southern School Desegregation, and the Rule of Law," *New York University Law Review* 79 (2004): 1100.

13. Barbash, "Ehrlichman Tells," 12.

14. Ehrlichman, *Witness to Power*, 112.
15. Evan Vassar, "Nixon, the Supreme Court, and Busing," Richard Nixon Foundation, Apr. 8, 2022, https://www.nixonfoundation.org/2015/04/nixon-the-supreme-court-and-busing/.
16. Vassar, "Nixon, the Supreme Court, and Busing."
17. Vassar, "Nixon, the Supreme Court, and Busing."
18. Vassar, "Nixon, the Supreme Court, and Busing."
19. Vassar, "Nixon, the Supreme Court, and Busing."
20. Ms. Shagaloff had married Michael Alexander in 1970. Risen, "June Shagaloff Alexander."
21. 1971 Annual Convention, Minneapolis, Minnesota, Excerpt of Address of June Alexander NAACP National Education Director in *NAACP Reporter*, Aug. 1971, NAACP Records, Manuscript Division, Library of Congress, Washington, D.C.
22. Excerpt of Address of June Alexander in *NAACP Reporter*, Aug. 1971, NAACP Records, Manuscript Division, Library of Congress, Washington, D.C.
23. Grant, "Detroiter Switched His Stand."
24. Bradley v. Milliken, Trial Transcript, Apr. 29, 1971, Box 5, Book 10, Bradley v. Milliken Case Files, Bentley Historical Library, University of Michigan.
25. Grant, "Detroiter Switched His Stand."
26. Bradley v. Milliken, Trial Transcript, Apr. 29, 1971, at 1131–32, Bradley v. Milliken Case Files, Bentley Historical Library, University of Michigan.
27. Bradley v. Milliken, Trial Transcript, Apr. 29, 1971, at 1132, Bradley v. Milliken Case Files, Bentley Historical Library, University of Michigan.
28. Bradley v. Milliken, Trial Transcript, Apr. 29, 1971, at 1132, Bradley v. Milliken Case Files, Bentley Historical Library, University of Michigan.
29. Bradley v. Milliken, Trial Transcript, Apr. 29, 1971, at 1132, Bradley v. Milliken Case Files, Bentley Historical Library, University of Michigan.
30. Bradley v. Milliken, Trial Transcript, Apr. 29, 1971, at 1132–33, Bradley v. Milliken Case Files, Bentley Historical Library, University of Michigan.
31. Grant, "Detroiter Switched His Stand."
32. Grant, "Detroiter Switched His Stand."
33. Grant, "Detroiter Switched His Stand."
34. Grant, "Detroiter Switched His Stand."
35. Grant, "Detroiter Switched His Stand."
36. Hain, "Sealing Off the City," 245–46.
37. Bradley v. Milliken, Trial Transcript, Apr. 27, 1971, at 861, Bradley v. Milliken Case Files, Bentley Historical Library, University of Michigan.
38. Bradley v. Milliken, Trial Transcript, Apr. 27, 1971, at 857, Bradley v. Milliken Case Files, Bentley Historical Library, University of Michigan.
39. Robert Lee Green, *At the Crossroads of Fear and Freedom: The Fight for Social and Educational Justice* (East Lansing: Michigan State University Press, 2016).
40. Green, *At the Crossroads of Fear and Freedom*, 10.
41. Green, *At the Crossroads of Fear and Freedom*, 10–11.
42. Green, *At the Crossroads of Fear and Freedom*, 14.
43. Green, *At the Crossroads of Fear and Freedom*, 64.
44. In late August 2020, the Grenada City Council, by a slim 4–3 majority, voted to move the Davis monument to a different location. "Grenada City Council Votes to Remove Confederate Statue," *Delta News*, Aug. 27, 2020, https://www.deltanews.tv/news/grenada-city-council-votes-to-remove-confederate-statue/article_a91e4a28-e841-11ea-ac65-f7db904d69f7.html.
45. Dimond, *Beyond Busing*, 59–60.
46. Bradley v. Milliken, Plaintiffs' Conclusions of Law, July 27, 1971, at 1, Box 1, Bradley v. Milliken Case Files, Bentley Historical Library, University of Michigan.

47. Bradley v. Milliken, Plaintiffs' Conclusions of Law, July 27, 1971, at 3, Box 1, Bradley v. Milliken Case Files, Bentley Historical Library, University of Michigan.
48. Bradley v. Milliken, Plaintiffs' Conclusions of Law, July 27, 1971, at 1, Box 1, Bradley v. Milliken Case Files, Bentley Historical Library, University of Michigan.
49. Brown v. Board of Education, 347 U.S. at 483, 494 (1954).
50. Bradley v. Milliken, Trial Transcript, Apr. 27, 1971, at 862, Bradley v. Milliken Case Files, Bentley Historical Library, University of Michigan.
51. Bradley v. Milliken, Trial Transcript, Apr. 28, 1971, at 1050, Box 5, Book 9, Bradley v. Milliken Case Files, Bentley Historical Library, University of Michigan.
52. Bradley v. Milliken, Trial Transcript, Apr. 27, 1971, at 895, Bradley v. Milliken Case Files, Bentley Historical Library, University of Michigan.
53. Bradley v. Milliken, Trial Transcript, Apr. 27, 1971, at 877, Bradley v. Milliken Case Files, Bentley Historical Library, University of Michigan.
54. Bradley v. Milliken, Trial Transcript, Apr. 27, 1971, at 880, Bradley v. Milliken Case Files, Bentley Historical Library, University of Michigan.
55. Bradley v. Milliken, Trial Transcript, Apr. 27, 1971, at 836–37, Bradley v. Milliken Case Files, Bentley Historical Library, University of Michigan.
56. Bradley v. Milliken, Trial Transcript, Apr. 27, 1971, at 913, Bradley v. Milliken Case Files, Bentley Historical Library, University of Michigan.
57. Elizabeth Evitts Dickinson, "Coleman Report Set the Standard for the Study of Public Education," *Johns Hopkins Magazine*, Dec. 2, 2016, https://hub.jhu.edu/magazine/2016/winter/coleman-report-public-education/.
58. Dickinson, "Coleman Report."
59. Dickinson, "Coleman Report."
60. James S. Coleman, "Equality of Educational Opportunity," U.S. Department of Health, Education, and Welfare (1966), 9.
61. Coleman, "Equality of Educational Opportunity," 9–10.
62. Coleman, "Equality of Educational Opportunity," 9.
63. Coleman, "Equality of Educational Opportunity," 22.
64. Coleman, "Equality of Educational Opportunity," 325. While later social scientists raised some important methodological concerns about the study, all of Coleman's central conclusions—including that "family background, peers, and students' own academic self-concept explain much more of the variability in test scores" than schools—have been repeatedly reaffirmed. Heather C. Hill, "The Coleman Report, 50 Years On: What Do We Know About the Role of Schools and Academic Inequality?," *The Annals of the American Academy of Political and Social Science* 674 (November 2017): 11, https://doi.org/10.1177/0002716217727510.
65. John Herbers, "Negro Education Is Found Inferior, U.S. Public Schools Survey Confirms Racial Disparity," *New York Times*, July 2, 1966.
66. Congressional Record—Senate, Apr. 19, 1971, at 10751.
67. Coleman, "Equality of Educational Opportunity," 307.
68. Congressional Record—Senate, Apr. 19, 1971, at 10750.
69. Sean F. Reardon et al., "Is Separate Still Unequal? New Evidence on School Segregation and Racial Academic Achievement Gaps," *Stanford Center for Education Policy Analysis*, CEPA Working Paper No. 19-06, 2022, https://cepa.stanford.edu/sites/default/files/wp19-06-v082022.pdf.
70. Gary Orfield and Chungmei Lee, "Brown at 50: King's Dream or Plessy's Nightmare?," The Civil Rights Project at UCLA, 2004, http://civilrightsproject.ucla.edu/research/k-12-education/integration-and-diversity/brown-at-50-king2019s-dream-or-plessy2019s-nightmare/?searchterm.
71. Orfield and Lee, "Brown at 50."
72. Reardon et al., "Is Separate Still Unequal?," 42.

73. Reardon et al., "Is Separate Still Unequal?," 43.
74. Coleman, "Equality of Educational Opportunity," 22.
75. Bruce D. Baker, *Does Money Matter in Education?*, Albert Shanker Institute, available at https://www.shankerinstitute.org/resource/does-money-matter-education-second-edition.
76. Bradley v. Milliken, Trial Transcript, Apr. 28, 1971, at 965, Bradley v. Milliken Case Files, Bentley Historical Library, University of Michigan.
77. Brown v. Board of Education, 347 U.S. at 483, 493 (1954).
78. Bradley v. Milliken, Trial Transcript, Apr. 28, 1971, at 966, Bradley v. Milliken Case Files, Bentley Historical Library, University of Michigan.
79. Bradley v. Milliken, Trial Transcript, Apr. 28, 1971, at 966, Bradley v. Milliken Case Files, Bentley Historical Library, University of Michigan.
80. Gordon W. Allport, Kenneth Clark, and Thomas F. Pettigrew, *The Nature of Prejudice* (New York: Basic Books, 2015).
81. Allport et al., *The Nature of Prejudice*, 272.
82. Thomas F. Pettigrew and Linda R. Tropp, "A Meta-Analytic Test of Intergroup Contact Theory," *Journal of Personality and Social Psychology* 90, no. 5 (2006): 766, https://doi.org/10.1037/0022-3514.90.5.751.
83. Allport et al., *The Nature of Prejudice*, 272.
84. Allport et al., *The Nature of Prejudice*, 281.
85. Allport et al., *The Nature of Prejudice*, 276.
86. Allport et al., *The Nature of Prejudice*, 276.
87. Allport et al., *The Nature of Prejudice*, 470.
88. Pettigrew and Tropp, "A Meta-Analytic Test of Intergroup Contact Theory," 766.
89. Mauet, *Fundamentals of Trial Techniques*, 119.
90. Bradley v. Milliken, Trial Transcript, Apr. 27, 1971, at 913–14, Bradley v. Milliken Case Files, Bentley Historical Library, University of Michigan.
91. Bradley v. Milliken, Trial Transcript, Apr. 27, 1971, at 914, Bradley v. Milliken Case Files, Bentley Historical Library, University of Michigan.
92. Grutter v. Bollinger, 539 U.S. at 306 (2003); Fisher v. University of Texas, 570 U.S. at 297 (2013).
93. Bradley v. Milliken, Trial Transcript, Apr. 27, 1971, at 922, Bradley v. Milliken Case Files, Bentley Historical Library, University of Michigan.
94. Bradley v. Milliken, Trial Transcript, Apr. 28, 1971, at 951, Bradley v. Milliken Case Files, Bentley Historical Library, University of Michigan.
95. Bradley v. Milliken, Trial Transcript, Apr. 28, 1971, at 951, Bradley v. Milliken Case Files, Bentley Historical Library, University of Michigan.
96. Bradley v. Milliken, Trial Transcript, Apr. 28, 1971, at 952, Bradley v. Milliken Case Files, Bentley Historical Library, University of Michigan.

13. TEN BUSES

1. Bradley v. Milliken, Trial Transcript, June 8, 1971, at 2897, Box 6, Book 27, Bradley v. Milliken Case Files, Bentley Historical Library, University of Michigan.
2. Bradley v. Milliken, Trial Transcript, Apr. 29, 1971, at 1136–37, Bradley v. Milliken Case Files, Bentley Historical Library, University of Michigan.
3. Bradley v. Milliken, Trial Transcript, Apr. 29, 1971, at 1157, Bradley v. Milliken Case Files, Bentley Historical Library, University of Michigan.
4. Bradley v. Milliken, Trial Transcript, Apr. 29, 1971, at 1156, Bradley v. Milliken Case Files, Bentley Historical Library, University of Michigan.
5. Bradley v. Milliken, Trial Transcript, Apr. 29, 1971, at 1158–59, Bradley v. Milliken Case Files, Bentley Historical Library, University of Michigan.
6. Bradley v. Milliken, Trial Transcript, Apr. 30, 1971, at 1185, Box 5, Book 11, Bradley v. Milliken Case Files, Bentley Historical Library, University of Michigan.

7. Bradley v. Milliken, Trial Transcript, May 5, 1971, at 1396, Box 5, Book 13, Bradley v. Milliken Case Files, Bentley Historical Library, University of Michigan.
8. Bradley v. Milliken, Trial Transcript, May 5, 1971, at 1482–83, Bradley v. Milliken Case Files, Bentley Historical Library, University of Michigan.
9. Bradley v. Milliken, Trial Transcript, June 24, 1971, at 4003, Box 7, Book 36, Bradley v. Milliken Case Files, Bentley Historical Library, University of Michigan.
10. Bradley v. Milliken, Trial Transcript, June 25, 1971, at 4141–43, Box 7, Book 36, Bradley v. Milliken Case Files, Bentley Historical Library, University of Michigan.
11. Bradley v. Milliken, Trial Transcript, June 25, 1971, at 4142–43, Bradley v. Milliken Case Files, Bentley Historical Library, University of Michigan.
12. Bradley v. Milliken, Trial Transcript, May 14, 1971, at 2067, Box 6, Book 19, Bradley v. Milliken Case Files, Bentley Historical Library, University of Michigan.
13. Bradley v. Milliken, Trial Transcript, June 16, 1971, at 3309–10, Box 6, Book 31, Bradley v. Milliken Case Files, Bentley Historical Library, University of Michigan.
14. Dimond, *Beyond Busing*, 67–68.
15. Bradley v. Milliken, Trial Transcript, July 22, 1971, at 4634, Box 6, Book 34, Bradley v. Milliken Case Files, Bentley Historical Library, University of Michigan.
16. Detroit Board of Education Meeting Minutes, July 1, 1969, at 4, Box 4, Folder 4–56, Remus Robinson Collection, Walter P. Reuther Library, Wayne State University.
17. Detroit Board of Education Meeting Minutes, July 1, 1969, at 5, Remus Robinson Collection, Walter P. Reuther Library, Wayne State University.
18. Detroit Board of Education Meeting Minutes, July 1, 1969, at 5, Remus Robinson Collection, Walter P. Reuther Library, Wayne State University.
19. Bradley v. Milliken, Trial Transcript, July 22, 1971, at 4635, Bradley v. Milliken Case Files, Bentley Historical Library, University of Michigan.
20. Bradley v. Milliken, Trial Transcript, July 22, 1971, at 4634–35, Bradley v. Milliken Case Files, Bentley Historical Library, University of Michigan.
21. Detroit Board of Education Meeting Minutes, July 1, 1969, at 6, Remus Robinson Collection, Walter P. Reuther Library, Wayne State University.
22. Dimond, *Beyond Busing*, 65.
23. Bradley v. Milliken, Trial Transcript, June 2, 1971, at 2706, Box 6, Book 24, Bradley v. Milliken Case Files, Bentley Historical Library, University of Michigan.
24. Bradley v. Milliken, Motion to Join Additional Parties Defendant, July 12, 1971, Bradley v. Milliken, Trial Transcript, July 26, 1971, at 4682, Box 7, Book 42, Bradley v. Milliken Case Files, Bentley Historical Library, University of Michigan.
25. "Rule 21. Misjoinder and Nonjoinder of Parties," Legal Information Institute, https://www.law.cornell.edu/rules/frcp/rule_21.
26. "Rule 19. Required Joinder of Parties," Legal Information Institute, https://www.law.cornell.edu/rules/frcp/rule_19.
27. Motion to Join Additional Parties Defendant, July 12, 1971, at 2, Bradley v. Milliken Case Files, Bentley Historical Library, University of Michigan.
28. Bradley v. Milliken, Trial Transcript, July 26, 1971, at 4684, Bradley v. Milliken Case Files, Bentley Historical Library, University of Michigan.
29. Bradley v. Milliken, Trial Transcript, July 26, 1971, at 4685, Bradley v. Milliken Case Files, Bentley Historical Library, University of Michigan.
30. Motion to Join Additional Parties Defendant, July 12, 1971, at 2, Bradley v. Milliken Case Files, Bentley Historical Library, University of Michigan.
31. Bradley v. Milliken, Trial Transcript, July 26, 1971, at 4682–83, Bradley v. Milliken Case Files, Bentley Historical Library, University of Michigan.
32. Bradley v. Milliken, Trial Transcript, July 26, 1971, at 4683, Bradley v. Milliken Case Files, Bentley Historical Library, University of Michigan.

33. Bradley v. Milliken, Trial Transcript, July 26, 1971, at 4683, Bradley v. Milliken Case Files, Bentley Historical Library, University of Michigan.
34. Bradley v. Milliken, Trial Transcript, Apr. 8, 1971, at 385–89, Bradley v. Milliken Case Files, Bentley Historical Library, University of Michigan.
35. Bradley v. Milliken, Trial Transcript, Apr. 14, 1971, at 601–602, Bradley v. Milliken Case Files, Bentley Historical Library, University of Michigan.
36. Bradley v. Milliken, Trial Transcript, Apr. 15, 1971, at 708–709, Bradley v. Milliken Case Files, Bentley Historical Library, University of Michigan.
37. Bradley v. Milliken, Trial Transcript, Apr. 16, 1971, at 728, Bradley v. Milliken Case Files, Bentley Historical Library, University of Michigan.
38. Bradley v. Milliken, Trial Transcript, Apr. 16, 1971, at 733, Bradley v. Milliken Case Files, Bentley Historical Library, University of Michigan.
39. Bradley v. Milliken, Trial Transcript, July 26, 1971, at 4690, Bradley v. Milliken Case Files, Bentley Historical Library, University of Michigan.
40. Bradley v. Milliken, Trial Transcript, July 26, 1971, at 4691, Bradley v. Milliken Case Files, Bentley Historical Library, University of Michigan.
41. Bradley v. Milliken, Trial Transcript, July 26, 1971, at 4705, Bradley v. Milliken Case Files, Bentley Historical Library, University of Michigan.
42. Dimond, *Beyond Busing*, 67.
43. Letter to Nate Jones from Paul Dimond, July 30, 1971, Box V:1042, Folder 2, NAACP Records, Manuscript Division, Library of Congress, Washington, D.C.
44. U.S. Census Bureau, 1970 Census of Population: Characteristics of the Population: Michigan [41] (1970).
45. "The Pontiac Story of Progress & Promise," YouTube, May 13, 2013, https://www.you tube.com/watch?v=B3HTPrs05Ks%3B++https%3A%2F%2Fwww.deadlinedetroit .com%2Farticles%2F11283%2Fvideo_star_of_1960_film_promoting_city_of_pontiac _comes_forward.
46. "The Pontiac Story of Progress & Promise."
47. "The Pontiac Story of Progress & Promise."
48. Davis v. School District, 309 F. Supp. 734, 736 (E.D. Mich. 1970).
49. Davis v. School District, 443 F.2d 573 (6th Cir. 1971).
50. Davis v. School District, 309 F. Supp. 734, 744–45 (E.D. Mich. 1970).
51. Trevor W. Coleman, Peter J. Hammer, and Mitch Albom, *Crusader for Justice: Federal Judge Damon J. Keith* (Detroit, MI: Wayne State University Press, 2014); "The Damon J. Keith Law Collection of African American Legal History, Wayne State University Law School," https:// web.archive.org/web/20100708235606/http://keithcollection.wayne.edu/fighters/keith.htm; U.S. 6th Circuit Judge Damon J. Keith 1922–2019, https://www.mied.uscourts.gov/PDFFIles /Damon_Keith_obituary.pdf.
52. Branden Hunter, "Justice Served: Detroit Says Farewell to Judge Damon J. Keith," *Michigan Chronicle*, May 14, 2019, https://michiganchronicle.com/justice-served-detroit-says -farewell-to-judge-damon-j-keith/.
53. Davis v. School District, 309 F. Supp. 734, 745 (E.D. Mich. 1970).
54. Remus Robinson, telegram to Judge Damon Keith, Feb. 18, 1970, Box 15, Folder 1, Damon J. Keith Collection, Walter P. Reuther Library, Archives of Labor History and Urban Affairs, Wayne State University.
55. Unsigned telegram to Judge Damon Keith, Sept. 30, 1971, Damon J. Keith Collection, Walter P. Reuther Library, Archives of Labor History and Urban Affairs, Wayne State University.
56. Steven J. Jager, "Wade Hampton McCree Jr. (1920–1987)," BlackPast, July 23, 2019, https:// www.blackpast.org/african-american-history/mccree-jr-wade-hampton-1920-1987.
57. Lawrence J. McAndrews, *The Era of Education: The Presidents and the Schools, 1965–2001* (Urbana: University of Illinois Press, 2008), 167.

58. Eric Pace, "Wade H. McCree Jr. Dies at 67; Was Judge and Solicitor General," *New York Times*, Sept. 1, 1987.

59. Davis v. School District, 443 F.2d 573, 575 (6th Cir. 1971).

60. Davis v. School District, 443 F.2d 573, 576 (6th Cir. 1971).

61. Davis v. School District, 309 F. Supp. 734, 741 (E.D. Mich. 1970).

62. Bradley v. Milliken, Plaintiffs' Conclusions of Law, Aug. 5, 1971, at 2.

63. Coleman et al., *Crusader for Justice*, 118.

64. Coleman et al., *Crusader for Justice*, 120.

65. Coleman et al., *Crusader for Justice*, 88.

66. John Oppedahl, "NAACP Unit May Ask GIs for Pontiac," *Detroit Free Press*, Sept. 1, 1971.

67. William K. Stevens, "5 Ex-Klansman Convicted in School Bus Bomb Plot," *New York Times*, May 22, 1973.

68. Jeffrey Hadden, "Pontiac Firemen Spied," *Detroit News*, Oct. 5, 1971.

69. Hadden, "Pontiac Firemen Spied."

70. Maryanne Conheim, "Campaign Hits Busing in Pontiac," *Detroit Free Press*, Aug. 14, 1971.

71. "Nine Students Hurt in Pontiac Clash," *New York Times*, Sept. 9, 1971.

72. Gene Goltz, "Pontiac Parents and Kids Rally to Protest Busing: Peaceful Meeting Draws 500," *Detroit Free Press*, Aug. 15, 1971.

73. Goltz, "Pontiac Parents and Kids Rally to Protest Busing."

74. Goltz, "Pontiac Parents and Kids Rally to Protest Busing."

75. Goltz, "Pontiac Parents and Kids Rally to Protest Busing."

76. Conheim, "Campaign Hits Busing in Pontiac."

77. Conheim, "Campaign Hits Busing in Pontiac."

78. "Pontiac Legislator Urges Busing Boycott," *Detroit Free Press*, Aug. 29, 1971.

79. Jim Neubacher, "School Unrest Led Mother to Push Attack on Busing," *Detroit Free Press*, Aug. 29, 1971.

80. Neubacher, "School Unrest Led Mother."

81. Neubacher, "School Unrest Led Mother."

82. Maureen McDonald, "The Battle of Pontiac: Integration Wins, After All," *Ann Arbor Sun*, Jan. 22, 1976.

83. McDonald, "The Battle of Pontiac."

84. Neubacher, "School Unrest Led Mother."

85. Neubacher, "School Unrest Led Mother."

86. Neubacher, "School Unrest Led Mother."

87. Neubacher, "School Unrest Led Mother."

88. "Judge Dismisses Attempt in Michigan to Bar Busing," *New York Times*, Sept. 2, 1971.

89. "Judge Dismisses Attempt."

90. Michelle Adams interview with Judge Damon Keith, Nov. 21, 2015 (on file with author).

91. Having identified myself as a Detroit native and daughter of local lawyer Bernard Adams Jr., the judge confided that he knew my father well. It was a fact of which I was not aware. As I struggled to assimilate this new knowledge, the judge paid me a compliment I will never forget: "I'm proud of you. The fruit doesn't fall far from the tree."

92. William Grant, "KKK After You, FBI Tells Judge, Threat Linked to Busing Ruling," *Detroit Free Press*, Sept. 23, 1971.

93. "Anti-Busing Protest—Pontiac with Irene McCabe-9-6-71-ABC," Critical Commons, http://www.criticalcommons.org/Members/mattdelmont/clips/anti-busing-protest-pontiac-with-irene-mccabe-9-6.

94. Matthew F. Delmont, *Why Busing Failed: Race, Media, and the National Resistance to School Desegregation* (Oakland: University of California Press, 2016), 144.

95. Delmont, *Why Busing Failed*, 147.

96. Delmont, *Why Busing Failed*, 149.

97. Gene Roberts and Hank Klibanoff, *The Race Beat: The Press, the Civil Rights Struggle, and the Awakening of a Nation* (New York: Vintage, 2007), 407.

98. Delmont, *Why Busing Failed*, 150.

99. Coleman et al., *Crusader for Justice*, 118.

100. Coleman et al., *Crusader for Justice*, 118.

101. Maryanne Conheim and John Oppedahl, "School Buses Built in Pontiac Turn into Symbols of Fear," *Detroit Free Press*, Sept. 7, 1971.

102. John Oppedahl, "Busing Makes Quiet Debut: Pontiac Schools Half Empty," *Detroit Free Press*, Sept. 8, 1971.

103. "Irene McCabe and Her Battle Against Busing," *Detroit News*, May 3, 1997.

104. William Serrin, "They Don't Burn Buses Anymore in Pontiac," *Saturday Review*, June 24, 1972.

105. Oppedahl, "Busing Makes Quiet Debut."

106. Serrin, "They Don't Burn Buses Anymore."

107. "Irene McCabe and Her Battle Against Busing."

108. John Oppedahl and George Cantor, "Judge Considering Marshals to Enforce Pontiac Busing: Enrollment Rises Near Normal," *Detroit Free Press*, Sept. 11, 1971.

109. Jerry M. Flint, "Antibusing Pickets Close Two Car Plants," *New York Times*, Sept. 15, 1971.

110. Flint, "Antibusing Pickets Close Two Car Plants."

111. "CBS Report on End of NAG McCabe Anti-Busing Protest," *CBS Evening News*, Sept. 23, 1971, available at http://www.criticalcommons.org/Members/mattdelmont/clips/cbs-report -on-end-of-nag-mccabe-anti-busing/view.

112. "CBS Report on End of NAG McCabe Anti-Busing Protest."

113. Delmont, *Why Busing Failed*, 166.

114. Delmont, *Why Busing Failed*, 212.

14. ACCIDENT OF GEOGRAPHY

1. Dimond, *Beyond Busing*, 68.

2. Bradley v. Milliken, 338 F. Supp. 582, 585 (1971).

3. Bradley v. Milliken, 338 F. Supp. 582, 585 (1971).

4. Bradley v. Milliken, 338 F. Supp. 582, 586 (1971).

5. Bradley v. Milliken, 338 F. Supp. 582, 586 (1971).

6. Bradley v. Milliken, 338 F. Supp. 582, 586–87 (1971).

7. Bradley v. Milliken, 338 F. Supp. 582, 587 (1971).

8. Bradley v. Milliken, 338 F. Supp. 582, 587 (1971).

9. Bradley v. Milliken, 338 F. Supp. 582, 587 (1971).

10. Bradley v. Milliken, 338 F. Supp. 582, 593 (1971).

11. Bradley v. Milliken, 338 F. Supp. 582, 587 (1971).

12. Bradley v. Milliken, 338 F. Supp. 582, 592 (1971).

13. Bradley v. Milliken, 338 F. Supp. 582, 587 (1971).

14. Bradley v. Milliken, 338 F. Supp. 582, 587 (1971).

15. Bradley v. Milliken, 338 F. Supp. 582, 588 (1971).

16. Bradley v. Milliken, 338 F. Supp. 582, 588 (1971).

17. Bradley v. Milliken, 338 F. Supp. 582, 589 (1971).

18. Bradley v. Milliken, 338 F. Supp. 582, 591 (1971).

19. Bradley v. Milliken, 338 F. Supp. 582, 593 (1971).

20. Bradley v. Milliken, 338 F. Supp. 582, 593 (1971).

21. Bradley v. Milliken, 338 F. Supp. 582, 589 (1971).

22. Bradley v. Milliken, 338 F. Supp. 582, 593 (1971).

23. Bradley v. Milliken, 338 F. Supp. 582, 593 (1971).

24. Bradley v. Milliken, 338 F. Supp. 582, 589 (1971).
25. Bradley v. Milliken, 338 F. Supp. 582, 589 (1971).
26. Bradley v. Milliken, 338 F. Supp. 582, 593 (1971).
27. Bradley v. Milliken, 338 F. Supp. 582, 593 (1971).
28. Bradley v. Milliken, Trial Transcript, May 7, 1971, at 1696, Box 5, Book 15, Bradley v. Milliken Case Files, Bentley Historical Library, University of Michigan.
29. Bradley v. Milliken, Trial Transcript, May 7, 1971, at 1696–97, Bradley v. Milliken Case Files, Bentley Historical Library, University of Michigan.
30. Bradley v. Milliken, 338 F. Supp. 582, 589 (1971).
31. Bradley v. Milliken, 338 F. Supp. 582, 589 (1971).
32. Arguing that the state had little or no power over the Detroit Board of Education, and that any decisions that led to segregation were the city's and not the state's, counsel for the state defendants had moved to dismiss the case against them in early June. Bradley v. Milliken, Trial Transcript, June 2, 1971, at 2678. Roth unceremoniously denied that motion several weeks later. Bradley v. Milliken, Order, June 25, 1971. Much to their chagrin, the state-level defendants remained in the case. And in his "Ruling on Issue of Segregation, Sept. 27, 1971," Roth found them liable for violating the Constitution.
33. Bradley v. Milliken, 338 F. Supp. 582, 592 (1971).
34. Dimond, *Beyond Busing*, 72.
35. Bradley v. Milliken, Proceedings dated Oct. 4, 1971, at 4, Box 7, Bradley v. Milliken Case Files, Bentley Historical Library, University of Michigan.
36. Bradley v. Milliken, Proceedings dated Oct. 4, 1971, at 10, Bradley v. Milliken Case Files, Bentley Historical Library, University of Michigan.
37. Bradley v. Milliken, Proceedings dated Oct. 4, 1971, at 4, Bradley v. Milliken Case Files, Bentley Historical Library, University of Michigan.
38. Bradley v. Milliken, Proceedings dated Oct. 4, 1971, at 9, Bradley v. Milliken Case Files, Bentley Historical Library, University of Michigan.
39. Bradley v. Milliken, Proceedings dated Oct. 4, 1971, at 15–18; 26, Bradley v. Milliken Case Files, Bentley Historical Library, University of Michigan.
40. Bradley v. Milliken, Proceedings dated Oct. 4, 1971, at 28, Bradley v. Milliken Case Files, Bentley Historical Library, University of Michigan.
41. Bradley v. Milliken, Proceedings dated Oct. 4, 1971, at 28, Bradley v. Milliken Case Files, Bentley Historical Library, University of Michigan.
42. Bradley v. Milliken, Proceedings dated Oct. 4, 1971, at 28–29, Bradley v. Milliken Case Files, Bentley Historical Library, University of Michigan.
43. Dimond, *Beyond Busing*, 77.
44. Bradley v. Milliken, Proceedings dated Oct. 4, 1971, at 28, Bradley v. Milliken Case Files, Bentley Historical Library, University of Michigan.
45. Statement of Nathaniel R. Jones, General Counsel, NAACP at Press Conference Today, Sept. 27, 1971, 1:00 p.m., Detroit, MI, Re: Judge Stephen Roth's Decision in Bradley v. Milliken, Box V:1042, Folder 2, NAACP Records, Manuscript Division, Library of Congress, Washington, D.C.
46. Statement of Nathaniel R. Jones, Re: Judge Stephen Roth's Decision in Bradley v. Milliken, NAACP Records, Manuscript Division, Library of Congress, Washington, D.C.
47. Statement of Nathaniel R. Jones, Re: Judge Stephen Roth's Decision in Bradley v. Milliken, NAACP Records, Manuscript Division, Library of Congress, Washington, D.C.
48. Statement of Nathaniel R. Jones, Re: Judge Stephen Roth's Decision in Bradley v. Milliken, NAACP Records, Manuscript Division, Library of Congress, Washington, D.C.
49. Statement of Nathaniel R. Jones, Re: Judge Stephen Roth's Decision in Bradley v. Milliken, NAACP Records, Manuscript Division, Library of Congress, Washington, D.C.
50. Statement of Nathaniel R. Jones, Re: Judge Stephen Roth's Decision in Bradley v. Milliken, NAACP Records, Manuscript Division, Library of Congress, Washington, D.C.

51. Robert Wisler, "Livonia Schools Fight Bus Rumors," *Detroit News*, Oct. 1, 1971.
52. Ted Goczkowski, "500 in Taylor Meet in Furor over Bussing," *Detroit News*, Sept. 30, 1971.
53. Donald P. O'Connor, "Anger Is the Reaction in Suburban Areas," *Detroit News*, Oct. 5, 1971.
54. O'Connor, "Anger Is the Reaction in Suburban Areas."
55. O'Connor, "Anger Is the Reaction in Suburban Areas."
56. Michael Wendland, "NAG Offers to Help Detroit's Bussing Foes," *Detroit News*, Oct. 5, 1971.
57. "Bus Ruling Jars Detroit Suburbs," *New York Times*, Oct. 3, 1971.
58. Wendland, "NAG Offers to Help."
59. Mike Maza, "Months Needed to Decide School Segregation Issue," *Detroit News*, Sept. 28, 1971.
60. Remer Tyson and William Serrin, "State Leaders Surveyed: Busing Issue Has Politicians Jittery," *Detroit Free Press*, Oct. 3, 1971.
61. Tyson and Serrin, "State Leaders Surveyed."
62. Letter from Julian Abele Cook Jr., President of the Michigan State Civil Rights Commission, to Dr. Edwin L. Novak, President State Board of Education, Oct. 21, 1971, at 1, Box V:1042, Folder 3, NAACP Records, Manuscript Division, Library of Congress, Washington, D.C.
63. *Busing Is Backed by Rabbis*, undated, 1582, Box 15, Folder 15–2, Damon Keith Collection, Walter P. Reuther Library, Archives of Labor and Urban Affairs, Wayne State University.
64. Robert Marshall, "In Defense of Busing," Birmingham Unitarian Church, sermon delivered Oct. 3, 1971.
65. Marshall, "In Defense of Busing."
66. Marshall, "In Defense of Busing."
67. Marshall, "In Defense of Busing."
68. Hain, "Sealing Off the City," 251.
69. Robert L. Pisor, "Temporary Measure: Top State Democrats Say Busing Is Needed," *Detroit News*, Oct. 3, 1971.
70. Pisor, "Temporary Measure."
71. Pisor, "Temporary Measure"; Remer Tyson, "State Party Debate: Dems Favor School Busing," *Detroit Free Press*, Oct. 3, 1971; Frank J. Kelley and Jack Lessenberry, *The People's Lawyer: The Life and Times of Frank J. Kelley: The Nation's Longest-Serving Attorney General* (Detroit: Painted Turtle, 2015), 127.
72. Laura Berman, Beth LeBlanc, and Craig Mauger, "Frank Kelley, Michigan's 'Eternal General,' Dies at 96," *Detroit News*, Mar. 6, 2021.
73. Patrick E. Shipstead, *New Perspectives on American Politics: A Report from Michigan on the Busing Issue* (Princeton, NJ: Woodrow Wilson School of Public and International Affairs, Princeton University, 1973), 17.
74. Richard A. Ryan, "Griffin Asks Amendment to Bar Busing," *Detroit News*, Oct. 7, 1971.
75. Ryan, "Griffin Asks Amendment to Bar Busing."
76. Ryan, "Griffin Asks Amendment to Bar Busing."
77. Ryan, "Griffin Asks Amendment to Bar Busing."
78. "Hart Renews His Support for Busing," *Detroit Free Press*, Oct. 17, 1971.
79. David Riddle, "Race and Reaction in Warren, Michigan, 1971 to 1974: 'Bradley v. Milliken' and the Cross-District Busing Controversy," *Michigan Historical Review* 26, no. 2 (2000): 38, https://doi.org/10.2307/20173858.
80. "FBI Puts Guard on Judge Roth," *Detroit News*, Oct. 18, 1971.
81. Governor Milliken Speech Aired on TV, Nov. 3, 1971.
82. Harry Salsinger, "School Board Attorney Resigns," *Detroit News*, Nov. 10, 1971.
83. Governor Milliken Speech Aired on TV, Nov. 3, 1971.
84. Governor Milliken Speech Aired on TV, Nov. 3, 1971.
85. Bradley v. Milliken, Order, Feb. 23, 1972, Box 10, Bradley v. Milliken Case Files, Bentley Historical Library, University of Michigan; Dimond, *Beyond Busing*, 77.
86. Congressional Record—House, Nov. 4, 1971, at 39302.

87. Congressional Record—House, Nov. 4, 1971, at 39303.
88. Winston-Salem / Forsyth County Board of Education v. Scott, 404 U.S. at 1221 (1971).
89. Winston-Salem / Forsyth County Board of Education v. Scott, 404 U.S. at 1221, 1228 (1971).
90. Fred P. Graham, "Burger Cautions Lower Tribunals on Busing Orders," *New York Times*, Sept. 1, 1971.
91. Congressional Record—House, Nov. 4, 1971, at 39305.
92. Brown v. Board of Education II, 396 U.S. at 19 (1969).
93. James Barron, "Shirley Chisholm, 'Unbossed' Pioneer in Congress, Is Dead at 80," *New York Times*, Jan. 3, 2005.
94. Congressional Record—House, Nov. 4, 1971, at 39310.
95. Congressional Record—House, Nov. 4, 1971, at 39310.
96. Congressional Record—House, Nov. 4, 1971, at 39310.
97. Congressional Record—House, Nov. 4, 1971, at 39310.
98. "1972 Education Act: $21-Billion in Aid, Busing Curbs," *CQ Almanac*, 1972.
99. "Governor's Statement Racist Motivated," *NAACP Reporter*, Oct. 1971, NAACP Records, Manuscript Division, Library of Congress, Washington, D.C.
100. "Governor's Statement Racist Motivated."
101. "Governor's Statement Racist Motivated."
102. Governor Milliken Speech Aired on TV, Nov. 3, 1971.
103. "Governor's Statement Racist Motivated."
104. "Cross-District Busing Is Issue: Milliken to Appeal Segregation Ruling, Blacks Protest Decision, Governor Bids to Cool Crisis," *Detroit Free Press*, Nov. 4, 1971.
105. "Cross-District Busing Is Issue."
106. Memo from Nathaniel R. Jones to Executive Staff regarding the Detroit School Decision, Nov. 8, 1971, Box V:1042, Folder 3, NAACP Records, Manuscript Division, Library of Congress, Washington, D.C.
107. Memo from Nathaniel R. Jones to Executive Staff, NAACP Records, Manuscript Division, Library of Congress, Washington, D.C.
108. Memo from Nathaniel R. Jones to Executive Staff, NAACP Records, Manuscript Division, Library of Congress, Washington, D.C.
109. Letter from Roy Wilkins to Judge Stephen M. Roth, Dec. 22, 1971, Box V:1042, Folder 4, NAACP Records, Manuscript Division, Library of Congress, Washington, D.C.
110. Letter from Roy Wilkins to Judge Stephen M. Roth, NAACP Records, Manuscript Division, Library of Congress, Washington, D.C.
111. Letter from Judge Stephen M. Roth to Roy Wilkins to Dec. 29, 1971, Box V:1042, Folder 4, NAACP Records, Manuscript Division, Library of Congress, Washington, D.C.
112. Letter from Judge Stephen M. Roth to Roy Wilkins, NAACP Records, Manuscript Division, Library of Congress, Washington, D.C.
113. Deal v. Cincinnati Board of Education, 369 F.2d 55, 60 (6th Cir. 1966).

15. SOMETHING WE COMFORTABLY TELL OURSELVES

1. Toni Jones and Julie Morris, "Blacks Skeptical of School Busing," *Detroit Free Press*, Oct. 10, 1071.
2. Jones and Morris, "Blacks Skeptical of School Busing."
3. Market Opinion Research, "Quality of Education Study in the Black Community of the City of Detroit for New Detroit, Inc." (December 1971), 4.
4. Market Opinion Research, "Quality of Education Study," 11, 14.
5. "Busing Debates Rage On—Out of Court," *Detroit Free Press*, July 23, 1972.
6. "Busing Debates Rage On."
7. "Busing Debates Rage On."

8. "Busing Debates Rage On."

9. "Busing Debates Rage On."

10. "Busing Backers Get Together," *Detroit Free Press*, Oct. 14, 1971.

11. "Busing Backers Get Together."

12. "Busing Backers Get Together."

13. Citizens for Suburban Responsibility, Political Advertisement, "Bring Us Together," *Detroit Free Press*, Oct. 31, 1971, C-17.

14. Citizens for Suburban Responsibility, Political Advertisement.

15. Citizens for Suburban Responsibility, Political Advertisement.

16. Frank Angelo, "Minister Responds to Burning Issues, Busing Leads List," *Detroit Free Press*, Apr. 24, 1972.

17. Michael F. Wendland, "Pro Bussing: Other Side Has Voice, Too," *Detroit News*, Apr. 14, 1972.

18. Wendland, "Pro Bussing."

19. "New Group Gives Backing to Busing," *Detroit Free Press*, Mar. 24, 1972.

20. Frank Angelo, "She Wants Smiles, Not Growls: Mother's Goal Is Peaceful Busing," *Detroit Free Press*, Apr. 17, 1972; "Hart Hits Nixon Stand on Busing," *Detroit Free Press*, May 21, 1972; Hain, "Sealing Off the City," 263–64.

21. Angelo, "She Wants Smiles, Not Growls."

22. Angelo, "She Wants Smiles, Not Growls."

23. Angelo, "She Wants Smiles, Not Growls."

24. "Six Western Wayne County Cities Form Groups, Parents Work for Peaceful Integration," *Detroit News*, Sept. 4, 1972.

25. "Six Western Wayne County Cities Form Groups."

26. "Six Western Wayne County Cities Form Groups."

27. "Transcript of Nixon's Statement on School Busing," *New York Times*, Mar. 17, 1972.

28. "Transcript of Nixon's Statement."

29. Richard A. Ryan, "The School Bus: Symbol of Our Changing Times," *Detroit News*, Mar. 17, 1972.

30. Robert Pratt, "Simple Justice Denied: The Supreme Court's Retreat from School Desegregation in Richmond, Virginia," *Rutgers Law Journal* 24 (1993): 710.

31. Robert A. Pratt, "A Promise Unfulfilled: School Desegregation in Richmond, Virginia, 1956–1986," *Virginia Magazine of History and Biography* 99 (1991): 435.

32. Pratt, "A Promise Unfulfilled," 435–40.

33. Pratt, "A Promise Unfulfilled," 439.

34. Robert A. Pratt, *The Color of Their Skin: Education and Race in Richmond, Virginia, 1954–89* (Charlottesville: University Press of Virginia, 1993).

35. Bradley v. School Board of City of Richmond, 338 F. Supp. 67, 84 (1972).

36. Pratt, "A Promise Unfulfilled," 445.

37. "Transcript of Nixon's Statement."

38. "Transcript of Nixon's Statement."

39. "Transcript of Nixon's Statement."

40. Education Amendments Act of 1972, Sec. 803.

41. Drummond v. Acree, 409 U.S. at 1228, 1229 (1972) ("the statute requires that the effectiveness of a district court order be postponed pending appeal only if the order requires the 'transfer or transportation' of students 'for the purposes of achieving a balance among students with respect to race.' It does not purport to block all desegregation orders which require the transportation of students").

42. "Transcript of Nixon's Statement."

43. Arnold R. Issaacs, "Nixon's Anti-Busing Proposals Are Forwarded to Congress," *Baltimore Sun*, Mar. 18, 1972; Michael B. Wise, "School Desegregation: The Court, the Congress and the President," *School Review* 82 (1974) 173.

44. "Transcript of Nixon's Statement."
45. Maryanne Conheim, "Irene's Long Walk Starts with a Dance," *Detroit Free Press*, Mar. 16, 1972.
46. Conheim, "Irene's Long Walk."
47. Maryanne Conheim, "Anti-Busing Mom Taking 585-Mile Walk to Capital," *Detroit Free Press*, Mar. 15, 1972.
48. "Michigan Housewife Raps Nixon on Busing 'Copout' . . . Walks On," *Pittsburgh Press*, Mar. 17, 1972.
49. "Michigan Housewife Raps Nixon."
50. Tom Wicker, "The New Jim Crow," *New York Times*, Mar. 23, 1972.
51. Wicker, "The New Jim Crow."
52. Marjorie Hunter, "Nixon's Plan Splits Rivals; Ervin Leads Busing Attack," *New York Times*, Mar. 18, 1972.
53. "Mr. Nixon Urges Us Forward to the Past," *Louisville Courier Journal*, Mar. 19, 1972.
54. "Mr. Nixon Urges Us Forward to the Past."
55. "Excerpts of Nathaniel Jones' Address," *NAACP Reporter*, Apr., 1972, at 3, NAACP Records, Manuscript Division, Library of Congress, Washington, D.C.
56. "Excerpts of Nathaniel Jones' Address," at 4, NAACP Records, Manuscript Division, Library of Congress, Washington, D.C.
57. Bradley v. Milliken, Ruling and Order on Petitions for Intervention, Mar. 15, 1972, Box 10, Bradley v. Milliken Case Files, Bentley Historical Library, University of Michigan; William Grant, "Suburbs Added to City School Integration Suit," *Detroit Free Press*, Mar. 16, 1972. Later, the Bloomfield Hills school district would make exactly that argument. "Since this school district was not one of the initial parties in the suit and we were not one of the suburban school districts that intervened in it, we believe Judge Roth's court does not have jurisdiction over us," the tony enclave asserted. Joel Smith, "Bloomfield Hills files plea against Roth bussing order," *Detroit News*, June 28, 1972; Bradley v. Milliken, Petition for Writ of Mandamus and/or Prohibition, June 26, 1972, Box 8, Bradley v. Milliken Case Files, Bentley Historical Library, University of Michigan.
58. Dimond, *Beyond Busing*, 77.
59. Harry Salsinger, "3,000 School Buses May Be Needed, Roth Told," *Detroit News*, Mar. 16, 1972.
60. Mike Maza, "Detroit's Board Likely to Submit Own School Plan," *Detroit News*, Feb. 27, 1972.
61. Salsinger, "3,000 School Buses May Be Needed."
62. Bradley v. Milliken, Recommendations of Defendant Board of Education for the City of Detroit and Other Defendants for "Conditions of Intervention," Mar. 14, 1972.
63. Bradley v. Milliken, Plaintiffs' Recommendations for Conditions to Be Placed on Interventions, Mar. 14, 1972, at 3, Box 3, Bradley v. Milliken Case Files, Bentley Historical Library, University of Michigan.
64. Bradley v. Milliken, Ruling and Order on Petitions for Intervention, Mar. 15, 1972, at 3–4, Box 10, Bradley v. Milliken Case Files, Bentley Historical Library, University of Michigan.
65. Salsinger, "3,000 School Buses May Be Needed."
66. Bradley v. Milliken, Ruling on Propriety of Considering a Metropolitan Remedy to Accomplish Desegregation of the Public Schools of the City of Detroit, Mar. 24, 1972, at 1, Box 10, Bradley v. Milliken Case Files, Bentley Historical Library, University of Michigan.
67. Findings and Conclusions on Detroit-Only Plans of Desegregation, Mar. 28, 1972, at 4, Bradley v. Milliken Case Files, Bentley Historical Library, University of Michigan; William Grant, "Subdivisions Aren't Sovereign: Roth Case Based on Legal Precedents," *Detroit Free Press*, May 5, 1972.
68. Findings and Conclusions on Detroit-Only Plans of Desegregation, Mar. 28, 1972, at 4, Bradley v. Milliken Case Files, Bentley Historical Library, University of Michigan.

69. Findings and Conclusions on Detroit-Only Plans of Desegregation, Mar. 28, 1972, at 5, Bradley v. Milliken Case Files, Bentley Historical Library, University of Michigan.
70. William Grant, "Roth Orders City-Suburb Integration, Detroit-Only Plans Rejected," *Detroit Free Press*, Mar. 29, 1972.
71. Grant, "Detroiter Switched His Stand."
72. Grant, "Detroiter Switched His Stand."
73. William L. Taylor, "Metropolitan School Integration and the Black Educational Crisis," a background paper for the National Policy Conference on Education for Blacks, Washington, D.C., Mar. 29–Apr. 1, 1972, at 1.
74. Taylor, "Metropolitan School Integration," 6.
75. Taylor, "Metropolitan School Integration," 1.
76. Grant, "Subdivisions Aren't Sovereign."
77. Grant, "Subdivisions Aren't Sovereign."
78. Grant, "Subdivisions Aren't Sovereign."
79. Allen v. County Board of Prince Edward County, 207 F. Supp. 349, 354 (E.D. Vir. 1962).
80. Reynolds v. Sims, 377 U.S. at 533, 575 (1974).
81. Brown v. Board of Education, 349 U.S. at 294, 300 (1955).
82. Grant, "Subdivisions Aren't Sovereign."
83. Letter from George T. Roumell Jr. to Honorable Stephen J. Roth, Mar. 1, 1972, Box V:1042, Folder 2, NAACP Records, Manuscript Division, Library of Congress, Washington, D.C.
84. William Grant, "Conservatives Challenged in School Board Race," *Detroit Free Press*, Oct. 29, 1972.
85. Bradley v. Milliken, Objections of Board of Education for the City of Detroit and other Defendants to the Metropolitan Plan Submitted by the State of Michigan and by Way of an Alternative, A Submission Herein by Said Board of a Metropolitan Detroit Area Integration Plan, Mar. 4, 1972, at 19, Box 1, Bradley v. Milliken Case Files, Bentley Historical Library, University of Michigan.
86. Objections of Board of Education for the City of Detroit, at 8, Bradley v. Milliken Case Files, Bentley Historical Library, University of Michigan.
87. Objections of Board of Education for the City of Detroit, at 8, Bradley v. Milliken Case Files, Bentley Historical Library, University of Michigan.
88. Objections of Board of Education for the City of Detroit, at 19, Bradley v. Milliken Case Files, Bentley Historical Library, University of Michigan.
89. Bradley v. Milliken, Proceedings Transcript, Mar. 30, 1972, at 379–95, Box 7, Book IIII, Bradley v. Milliken Case Files, Bentley Historical Library, University of Michigan.
90. Bradley v. Milliken, Proceedings Transcript, Mar. 30, 1972, at 388, Bradley v. Milliken Case Files, Bentley Historical Library, University of Michigan.
91. "The Designation [sic] and Integration of Public Schools in Metropolitan Detroit: A Proposal for Employing Educational Boroughs in Designationg [sic] Schools," Jan. 25, 1972, Box 2, Bradley v. Milliken Case Files, Bentley Historical Library, University of Michigan.
92. Bradley v. Milliken, Proceedings re: Metropolitan Plans, Mar. 28, 1972, at 14, Box 7, Book I, Bradley v. Milliken Case Files, Bentley Historical Library, University of Michigan.
93. Bradley v. Milliken, Proceedings re: Metropolitan Plans, Mar. 28, 1972, at 29, Bradley v. Milliken Case Files, Bentley Historical Library, University of Michigan.
94. Bradley v. Milliken, Brief of State Defendants on the Legal Propriety or Impropriety of Consideration by this Court of a Metropolitan Plan, Mar. 21, 1972, at 2.
95. Dimond, *Beyond Busing*, 81.
96. Bradley v. Milliken, Proceedings on Metropolitan Plans, Apr. 7, 1972, at 974–75, Box 8, Book VII, Bradley v. Milliken Case Files, Bentley Historical Library, University of Michigan.

97. Bradley v. Milliken, Proceedings on Metropolitan Plans, Apr. 7, 1972, at 974, Bradley v. Milliken Case Files, Bentley Historical Library, University of Michigan.

98. Bradley v. Milliken, Proceedings on Metropolitan Plans, Apr. 7, 1972, at 975, Bradley v. Milliken Case Files, Bentley Historical Library, University of Michigan.

99. Bradley v. Milliken, Proceedings on Metropolitan Plans, Apr. 7, 1972, at 977, Bradley v. Milliken Case Files, Bentley Historical Library, University of Michigan.

100. *Parents Involved*, 551 U.S. at 701, 748 (2007).

101. Bradley v. Milliken, Proceedings on Metropolitan Plans, Apr. 7, 1972, at 991, Bradley v. Milliken Case Files, Bentley Historical Library, University of Michigan.

102. Bradley v. Milliken, Proceedings on Metropolitan Plans, Apr. 7, 1972, at 994, Bradley v. Milliken Case Files, Bentley Historical Library, University of Michigan.

103. William Grant, "Suburbs Pushing Integration Edict for Detroit Only," *Detroit Free Press*, July 24, 1972.

104. Letter from J. "Nick" Harold Flannery to Nathaniel R. Jones, dated Sept. 4, 1970, Box V:1042, Folder 2, NAACP Records, Manuscript Division, Library of Congress, Washington, D.C.

105. Dimond, *Beyond Busing*, 81.

106. Dimond, *Beyond Busing*, 81.

107. Bradley v. Milliken, *Proceedings on Metropolitan Plans*, Apr. 14, 1972, at 1603.

108. Remer Tyson and Billy Bowles, "Governor Draws 10,000: Wallace and Rival Vie in City," *Detroit Free Press*, Apr. 16, 1972.

109. Tyson and Bowles, "Governor Draws 10,000."

110. The Michigan State Fair, available at https://www.loststory.net/history/michigan-state-fair#:~:text=Even%20counting%20the%20successful%201849,of%20the%20state%2C%20Ephradatus%20Ransom; "Detroit State Fair Grounds," Hood Design Studio, http://www.hooddesignstudio.com/detroitfairgrounds.

111. Dickinson, "Coleman Report."

112. Tyson and Bowles, "Governor Draws 10,000."

113. Tyson and Bowles, "Governor Draws 10,000."

114. "A History of Busing in Metro Detroit," *Detroit News*, July 21, 2019, https://www.detroitnews.com/picture-gallery/news/local/oakland-county/2019/07/22/history-busing-segregation-metro-detroit/1791862001/.

115. Tyson and Bowles, "Governor Draws 10,000."

116. Tyson and Bowles, "Governor Draws 10,000."

117. Tyson and Bowles, "Governor Draws 10,000."

118. David Cooper, "State Primary Pivots on Wallace Vote," *Detroit Free Press*, May 14, 1972.

119. William Greider, "Wallace Is Shot, Legs Paralyzed: Suspect Seized at Laurel Rally," *Washington Post*, May 16, 1972.

120. Richard Pearson, "Former Alabama Governor George C. Wallace Dies," *Washington Post*, Sept. 14, 1998.

121. Larry Kurtz, "Wallace Rides Record Vote Tide," *Times Herald* (Port Huron, Michigan), May 17, 1972.

122. Kurtz, "Wallace Rides Record Vote Tide."

123. "Desegregation Busing Debate (1972) | Alma G. Stallworth vs. Irene McCabe," YouTube, Nov. 22, 2016, https://www.youtube.com/watch?v=o20v-NdTvAU.

124. "Barbara Walters Official Biography," ABC News, https://abcnews.go.com/ABCNews/barbara-walters-official-biography/story?id=48450664.

125. "Desegregation Busing Debate (1972) | Alma G. Stallworth vs. Irene McCabe."

126. Maryanne Conheim, "Irene Is Greeted at Capitol," *Detroit Free Press*, Apr. 28, 1972.

127. Conheim, "Irene Is Greeted at Capitol."

128. "As We See It: Anti-Busing Hysteria Fades with a Whimper," *Detroit Free Press*, May 2, 1972.

129. Mirel, *The Rise and Fall of an Urban School System*, 350.
130. Mirel, *The Rise and Fall of an Urban School System*, 351.

16. GOING FOR METRO

1. Bradley v. School Board, 462 F.2d 1058, 1065 (4th Cir. 1972).
2. Bradley v. School Board, 462 F.2d 1058, 1065 (4th Cir. 1972).
3. Bradley v. School Board, 462 F.2d 1058, 1066 (4th Cir. 1972).
4. Bradley v. School Board, 462 F.2d 1058, 1065 (4th Cir. 1972).
5. Bradley v. School Board, 462 F.2d 1058, 1066 (4th Cir. 1972).
6. "Court Overturns Busing Order: No Bias Found In Virginia Case," *Detroit Free Press*, June 7, 1972.
7. "Court Overturns Busing Order."
8. William Grant, "NAACP Expected Richmond Bus Ban," *Detroit Free Press*, June 7, 1972.
9. Grant, "NAACP Expected Richmond Bus Ban."
10. Grant, "NAACP Expected Richmond Bus Ban."
11. Bradley v. Milliken, 345 F. Supp. 914, 921 (E.D. Mich. 1972).
12. Bradley v. Milliken, 345 F. Supp. 914, 921 (E.D. Mich. 1972).
13. Bradley v. Milliken, 345 F. Supp. 914, 935 (E.D. Mich. 1972).
14. Bradley v. Milliken, 345 F. Supp. 914, 925 (E.D. Mich. 1972).
15. Bradley v. Milliken, Proceedings re: Metropolitan Plans, Apr. 13, 1972, at 1486–87, Box 8, Book X, Bradley v. Milliken Case Files, Bentley Historical Library, University of Michigan.
16. Bradley v. Milliken, Proceedings re: Metropolitan Plans, Apr. 13, 1972, at 1486, Bradley v. Milliken Case Files, Bentley Historical Library, University of Michigan.
17. Bradley v. Milliken, 345 F. Supp. 914, 924–925 (E.D. Mich. 1972).
18. Bradley v. Milliken, 345 F. Supp. 914, 927 (E.D. Mich. 1972).
19. Judge Roth's order also included the school districts of two small cities located entirely within the jurisdictional boundaries of the city of Detroit: Highland Park and Hamtramck. The vast majority of the school districts in Judge Roth's order, however, were located in Detroit's suburbs.
20. U.S. Census Bureau, 1970 Census of Population: Characteristics of the Population: Michigan [21–34] (1973), https://www2.census.gov/prod2/decennial/documents/1970a_mi-01.pdf.
21. Bradley v. Milliken, 345 F. Supp. 914, 917–918 (E.D. Mich. 1972).
22. Bradley v. Milliken, 345 F. Supp. 914, 924 (E.D. Mich. 1972).
23. Bradley v. Milliken, 345 F. Supp. 914, 932 (E.D. Mich. 1972).
24. Bradley v. Milliken, 345 F. Supp. 914, 933 (E.D. Mich. 1972).
25. Bradley v. Milliken, 345 F. Supp. 914, 933 (E.D. Mich. 1972).
26. Bradley v. Milliken, 345 F. Supp. 914, 933 (E.D. Mich. 1972).
27. Bradley v. Milliken, 345 F. Supp. 914, 920 (1972).
28. Dimond, *Beyond Busing*, 78.
29. Dimond, *Beyond Busing*, 81.
30. Bradley v. Milliken, 345 F. Supp. 914, 937 (E.D. Mich. 1972).
31. Bradley v. Milliken, 345 F. Supp. 914, 918–919 (E.D. Mich. 1972).
32. Bradley v. Milliken, 345 F. Supp. 914, 918 (E.D. Mich. 1972).
33. Bradley v. Milliken, Preliminary Injunction, July 7, 1972, Box 10, Bradley v. Milliken Case Files, Bentley Historical Library, University of Michigan; William Grant, "Roth to Prohibit City Teacher Cuts," *Detroit Free Press*, June 30, 1972.
34. Bradley v. Milliken, Hearing on Motion to Expand Panel, Temporary Injunction, Stay of Proceedings, June 29, 1972, at 1829, Box 8, Bradley v. Milliken Case Files, Bentley Historical Library, University of Michigan.

35. William Grant, "Suburban Schools Could Reap Financial Help from Busing," *Detroit Free Press*, Aug. 7, 1972.
36. Grant, "Suburban Schools Could Reap Financial Help from Busing."
37. Bradley v. Milliken, 345 F. Supp. 914, 928–929 (E.D. Mich. 1972).
38. Bradley v. Milliken, 345 F. Supp. 914, 917 (E.D. Mich. 1972).
39. Bradley v. Milliken, 345 F. Supp. 914, 935 (E.D. Mich. 1972).
40. Bradley v. Milliken, 345 F. Supp. 914, 935 (E.D. Mich. 1972).
41. Grant, "Roth's Views Did Dramatic Turnabout," 4A.
42. Flint, "Judge in Busing Case Stephen John Roth."
43. Grant, "The Detroit School Case," 866.
44. Grant, "The Detroit School Case," 866.
45. William Grant, "Full Integration Set For '73, Roth Orders Busing to Begin in Fall, *Detroit Free Press*," June 15, 1972. *The Detroit News*'s reaction was similar. Its front-page headline read: "Roth Orders Tricounty Bussing, Picks Panel to Draft Changes." Harry Salsinger, "Roth Orders Tricounty Bussing, Picks Panel to Draft Changes." *Detroit News*, June 14, 1972.
46. David Cooper, "Nixon Says Anti-Busing Bill Will Not Affect Detroit Case," *Detroit Free Press*, June 16, 1972.
47. Al Sander, "In Talk with Milliken: Stronger Bus Bill Urged by Nixon," *Detroit News*, June 16, 1972.
48. Gary F. Schuster, "Nixon to Fight Roth Busing Order," *Detroit News*, June 29, 1972.
49. Jesse F. Goodwin, "Highlights of Judge Roth's Desegregation Order," *NAACP Reporter*, June 1972, NAACP Records, Manuscript Division, Library of Congress, Washington D.C.
50. Gloria Sneed, "Be Calm on Bussing, NAACP Leader Urges," *Detroit News*, June 16, 1972.
51. Sneed, "Be Calm on Bussing."
52. Sneed, "Be Calm on Bussing."
53. Sneed, "Be Calm on Bussing."
54. Sneed, "Be Calm on Bussing."
55. Sneed, "Be Calm on Bussing."
56. Robert S. Wisler, "23 Oppose Roth Order; Suburban Officials Seek Bussing Role," *Detroit News*, June 30, 1972.
57. Wisler, "23 Oppose Roth Order."
58. "Busing Foes Map Plans to Resist Order," *Detroit Free Press*, June 16, 1972.
59. "Youthful Protest," *Detroit Free Press*, June 17, 1972.
60. Flint, "Judge in Busing Case Stephen John Roth."
61. Robert Ankeny, "Irate Hubbard Tees Off on Roth," *Detroit News*, June 15, 1972.
62. Donald P. O'Connor, "Roth Order Outrages Some Suburban Parents, 'The People Won't Stand for Bussing,'" *Detroit News*, June 15, 1972.
63. O'Connor, "Roth Order Outrages Some Suburban Parents."
64. O'Connor, "Roth Order Outrages Some Suburban Parents."
65. O'Connor, "Roth Order Outrages Some Suburban Parents."
66. O'Connor, "Roth Order Outrages Some Suburban Parents."
67. Douglas Ilka, "Troy Official Wants to Sue Roth; Says Growth Is Periled," *Detroit News*, June 27, 1972.
68. "Bus Boycott Committee to Stage Rally in Taylor," *Detroit News*, June 19, 1972.
69. "Bus Boycott Committee to Stage Rally in Taylor."
70. "Bus Boycott Committee to Stage Rally in Taylor."
71. Beverly Craig, "State Group Asks Dems to Oppose Bussing," *Detroit News*, June 28, 1972.
72. Craig, "State Group Asks Dems to Oppose Bussing."
73. UPI and AP, "Wallace Loses Platform Bid," *Detroit Free Press*, July 12, 1972.
74. UPI and AP, "Wallace Loses Platform Bid."
75. UPI and AP, "Wallace Loses Platform Bid."
76. UPI and AP, "Wallace Loses Platform Bid."

77. William Montalbano, "It's McGovern on 1st," *Detroit Free Press*, July 13, 1972.
78. Rick Perlstein, *Nixonland: The Rise of a President and the Fracturing of America* (New York: Scribner, 2009).
79. "McGovern's 1972 Democratic Convention Acceptance Speech," YouTube, May 15, 2011, https://www.youtube.com/watch?v=orx63ix1y-o.
80. Helen May, "Safe, 'Mom Power' Mobilized to Seek Safe, Harmonious School Busing," *Detroit Free Press*, July 14, 1972.
81. May, "Safe, 'Mom Power' Mobilized."
82. May, "Safe, 'Mom Power' Mobilized."
83. Billy Bowles, "Churches Back Busing Order," *Detroit Free Press*, June 17, 1972.
84. "Parochials Freeze Enrollments, Refuge Role Declined," *Lansing State Journal*, Nov. 5, 1971.
85. Leslie Woodcock Tentler,"Through the Prism of Race: The Archdiocese of Detroit," in *Catholics in the Vatican II Era Local Histories of a Global Event*, eds. Kathleen Sprows Cummings, Timothy Matovina, and Robert A. Orsi (New York: Cambridge University Press, 2018).
86. William Mitchell, "700 Rally to Support of Waterford Pastor," *Detroit Free Press*, May 16, 1972.
87. Mitchell, "700 Rally to Support of Waterford Pastor."
88. Mitchell, "700 Rally to Support of Waterford Pastor."

17. NOW MORE THAN EVER

1. Kelley and Lessenberry, *The People's Lawyer*, 122.
2. Cooper, "Nixon Says Anti-Busing Bill Will Not Affect Detroit Case."
3. Cooper, "Nixon Says Anti-Busing Bill Will Not Affect Detroit Case."
4. Hain, "Sealing Off the City," 267.
5. Harry Salsinger, "Bloomfield to Mumford by Bus," *Detroit News*, June 28, 1972.
6. Order Adding Defendant Allison Green, July 11, 1972, Bradley v. Milliken Case Files, Bentley Historical Library, University of Michigan; Order for Acquisition of Transportation, July 11, 1972, Box 10, Bradley v. Milliken Case Files, Bentley Historical Library, University of Michigan.
7. William Grant, "Appeal Delays Roth's Busing Order," *Detroit Free Press*, July 14, 1972.
8. Dimond, *Beyond Busing*, 86.
9. Dimond, *Beyond Busing*, 86.
10. Paul Dimond provided a helpful description of the certification process: "'Certification' is the procedure whereby district courts can state important questions of law for appellate review before entry of appelable orders, in order to advance the final resolution of cases in the appellative courts and to avoid unnecessary proceedings in the trial courts." Dimond, *Beyond Busing*, 86.
11. Dimond, *Beyond Busing*, 87.
12. Jeffrey Hadden and Harry Salsinger, "Court Halts Roth Bussing Orders until Hearing on Aug. 24," *Detroit News*, July 20, 1972.
13. Harry Salsinger, "State to Appeal Roth Order on Bus Funds," *Detroit News*, July 11, 1972.
14. Bradley v. Milliken, 484 F.2d 215, 218 (6th Cir. 1973).
15. Panel's Response to the Court's Ruling on Desegregation Area and Order for Development of Plan of Desegregation, July 29, 1972, Box 2, Bradley v. Milliken Case Files, Bentley Historical Library, University of Michigan.
16. Panel's Response to Ruling on Desegregation, July 29, 1972, at 3, Bradley v. Milliken Case Files, Bentley Historical Library, University of Michigan.
17. Panel's Response to Ruling on Desegregation, July 29, 1972, at 50, Bradley v. Milliken Case Files, Bentley Historical Library, University of Michigan.
18. Madeline Will, "65 Years After 'Brown v. Board' Where Are All the Black Educators?," *Education Week*, May 14, 2019, https://www.edweek.org/policy-politics/65-years-after-brown-v-board-where-are-all-the-black-educators/2019/05; James E. Lyons and Joanne Chesley,

"Fifty Years After Brown: The Benefits and Tradeoffs for African American Educators and Students," *The Journal of Negro Education* 73, no. 3 (2004); Adam Fairclough, "The Costs of Brown: Black Teachers and School Integration," *The Journal of American History* 91, no. 1 (June 2004).

19. Panel's Response to Ruling on Desegregation, July 29, 1972, at 26, Bradley v. Milliken Case Files, Bentley Historical Library, University of Michigan.

20. Panel's Response to Ruling on Desegregation, July 29, 1972, at 26, Bradley v. Milliken Case Files, Bentley Historical Library, University of Michigan.

21. Panel's Response to Ruling on Desegregation July 29, 1972, at 31–37, Bradley v. Milliken Case Files, Bentley Historical Library, University of Michigan.

22. Harry Salsinger, "Panel Asks More Black Teachers in Suburbs," *Detroit News*, July 20, 1972.

23. Panel's Response to Ruling on Desegregation, July 29, 1972, at 41–43, Bradley v. Milliken Case Files, Bentley Historical Library, University of Michigan.

24. William Grant, "Panel Wants State Dole of School Funds," *Detroit Free Press*, July 30, 1972.

25. Grant, "Panel Wants State Dole of School Funds," 1A.

26. Panel's Response to Ruling on Desegregation, July 29, 1972, at 38, Bradley v. Milliken Case Files, Bentley Historical Library, University of Michigan.

27. Gary Blonston et al., "13,000 Welcome President; Nixon Blasts Busing in Macomb Visit, He Dedicates New School," *Detroit Free Press*, Aug. 25, 1972.

28. Gary Blonston et al., "Delirious Crowd Greets President in Macomb County," *Detroit Free Press*, Aug. 25, 1972, 5-A.

29. Richard Nixon, "Remarks on Accepting the Nomination of the Republican National Convention" (Miami, FL, Aug. 23, 1972), YouTube, https://www.youtube.com/watch?v=gYxkde0itOE.

30. Hal Bush, "Throngs Greet Nixon at School Ceremony," *Times Herald* (Port Huron), Aug. 25, 1972.

31. Blonston et al., "13,000 Welcome President."

32. George McGovern, "Letters to the Editor: McGovern Stand on Busing," *Washington Post*, Jan. 31, 1972.

33. Shipstead, *New Perspectives on American Politics*, 1.

34. Museum of the Moving Image, "The Living Room Candidate, Presidential Campaign Commercials 1952–2016, 1972 Nixon v. McGovern," available at http://www.livingroomcandidate.org/commercials/1972/busing; Richard Nixon Presidential Library and Museum, Committee for the Re-Election of the President 2-Inch Quad Collection at 44, Busing—NBC (8/29/72).

35. Tom Porter, "The Winning Slogan from Every US Presidential Campaign Since 1948," *Business Insider*, May 15, 2018, https://www.businessinsider.com/every-winning-slogan-from-us-presidential-campaigns-1948-2016-2019-5.

36. UPI, "In Busing Case, Kelley to Present State's Views," *Times Herald* (Port Huron), Aug. 23, 1972.

37. Robert Grifin, "What Is Your Position on Busing? An Open Letter from U.S. Senator Robert P. Griffin to Attorney General Frank Kelley," *Detroit News*, July 31, 1972.

38. Editorial, "On Bussing Issue: Milliken's Off Base," *Detroit News*, June 30, 1972.

39. Editorial, "In the Senate Race: An Easy Decision: A Vote for Griffin," *Detroit News*, Nov. 6, 1972.

40. UPI, "Griffin, Kelley Exchange Barbs," *South Bend Tribune*, Aug. 28, 1972.

41. Dimond, *Beyond Busing*, 88.

42. Al Sander and Jeffrey Hadden, "Court Continues Stay of Roth Busing Order," *Detroit News*, Aug. 24, 1972.

43. Sander and Hadden, "Court Continues Stay of Roth Busing Order."

44. William Grant, "Bus Ruling Still Far in Future," *Detroit Free Press*, Aug. 25, 1972, 12-A.

45. Dimond, *Beyond Busing*, 89.

46. Grant, "Bus Ruling Still Far in Future."
47. UPI, "Ruling Figured Weeks in Future, Busing Out for The Near Term," *Times Herald* (Port Huron), Aug. 25, 1972.
48. Grant, "Bus Ruling Still Far in Future."
49. Amicus Brief for the Inter-Faith Centers for Racial Justice, Inc., Bradley v. Milliken, 484 F.2d 215, Aug.13, 1972.
50. Inter-Faith Centers for Racial Justice Brief at 5, Bradley v. Milliken, 484 F.2d 215.
51. Inter-Faith Centers for Racial Justice Brief at 5, Bradley v. Milliken, 484 F.2d 215.
52. Billy Bowles and Remer Tyson, "Showdown Comes Today 3.5 Million to Vote in State," *Detroit Free Press*, Nov. 7, 1972.
53. Bowles and Tyson, "Showdown Comes."
54. Dimond, *Beyond Busing*, 89.
55. UPI, "Ordered Detroit Busing Judge Roth Stricken," *State Journal* (Lansing), Nov. 8, 1972.
56. Louis Heldman, "Roth's Condition Remains Serious; Recovery Likely," *Detroit Free Press*, Nov. 9, 1972.
57. AP, "Federal Judge Stephen Roth 'Excused' from Detroit Cases," *State Journal* (Lansing), Oct. 11, 1971.
58. UPI, "Ordered Detroit Busing Judge Roth Stricken."
59. Heldman, "Roth's Condition Remains Serious."
60. Remer Tyson, "Griffin Won on Busing Issue; Can GOP Hold onto Voters?," *Detroit Free Press*, Nov. 9, 1972.
61. Tyson, "Griffin Won on Busing Issue."
62. Kelley and Lessenberry, *The People's Lawyer*, 125.
63. Tyson, "Griffin Won on Busing Issue."
64. Shipstead, *New Perspectives on American Politics*, 27.
65. David Riddle, "Race and Reaction in Warren, Michigan," 1, 42.
66. Tyson, "Griffin Won on Busing Issue."
67. William Grant, "School Tax Revision Rejected," *Detroit Free Press*, Nov. 8, 1972.
68. Robert A. Popa, "Twin Defeat for State Tax Plans," *Detroit News*, Nov. 8, 1972.
69. Popa, "Twin Defeat for State Tax Plans."
70. Popa, "Twin Defeat for State Tax Plans."
71. Grant, "School Tax Revision Rejected."
72. Mirel, *The Rise and Fall of an Urban School System*, 351.
73. Dimond, *Beyond Busing*, 90.
74. Bradley v. Milliken, 484 F.2d 215 (6th Cir. 1973), *rev'd*, 418 U.S. at 717 (1974).
75. Dimond, *Beyond Busing*, 90.
76. Bradley v. Milliken, 484 F.2d at 247.
77. Bradley v. Milliken, 484 F.2d at 248.
78. William Grant, "Court Upholds Busing But New Delay Is Seen," *Detroit Free Press*, Dec. 9, 1972.
79. Bradley v. Milliken, 484 F.2d at 252.
80. Bradley v. Milliken, 484 F.2d at 252.
81. Bradley v. Milliken, 484 F.2d at 252.
82. Bradley v. Milliken, 484 F.2d at 248.
83. Bradley v. Milliken, 484 F.2d at 249.
84. Grant, "Court Upholds Busing But New Delay Is Seen."
85. Bradley v. Milliken, 484 F.2d at 242.
86. Bradley v. Milliken, 484 F.2d at 242.
87. Dimond, *Beyond Busing*, 87.
88. Dimond, *Beyond Busing*, 87.
89. Bradley v. Milliken, 484 F.2d at 242.

90. Bradley v. Milliken, 484 F.2d at 242.
91. Bradley v. Milliken, 484 F.2d at 241.
92. Bradley v. Milliken, 484 F.2d at 241.
93. Dimond, *Beyond Busing*, 89.
94. Grant, "Court Upholds Busing But New Delay Is Seen."
95. Grant, "Court Upholds Busing But New Delay Is Seen."
96. William Grant, "Ruling Means High Court Can't Avoid Busing Issue," *Detroit Free Press*, Dec. 9, 1972.

18. FAREWELL TO THE WARREN COURT

1. "Stevie Wonder for Freedom Dinner," *NAACP Reporter*, Apr. 1970, 1, NAACP Records, Manuscript Division, Library of Congress, Washington D.C.
2. "Excerpts of 1970 Freedom Dinner Address," *NAACP Reporter*, June 1970, 3, NAACP Records, Manuscript Division, Library of Congress, Washington D.C.
3. "Excerpts of 1970 Freedom Dinner Address," *NAACP Reporter*, June 1970, 3–4, NAACP Records, Manuscript Division, Library of Congress, Washington D.C.
4. Kermit L. Hall, "The Warren Court in Historical Perspective," in *The Warren Court: A Retrospective*, ed. Bernard Schwartz (New York: Oxford University Press, 1996), 302.
5. Lucas A. Powe Jr., *The Warren Court and American Politics* (Cambridge, MA: Belknap Press, 2000), 1.
6. Gideon v. Wainwright, 372 U.S. at 335 (1963); Douglas v. California, 372 U.S. at 353 (1963); Griffin v. Illinois, 351 U.S. at 12 (1956); Harper v. Virginia Board of Elections, 383 U.S. at 663 (1966).
7. Powe, *The Warren Court and American Politics*, 446.
8. Frank I. Michelman, "Foreword: On Protecting the Poor Through the Fourteenth Amendment," *Harvard Law Review* no. 1 (1969): 7, 9.
9. Bernard Schwartz, "The Warren Court in Action," in *The Burger Court: Counterrevolution or Confirmation?*, ed. Bernard Schwartz (New York: Oxford University Press, 1998), 268.
10. Tom Wicker, "In the Nation: What's a Strict Constructionist?," *New York Times*, Apr. 16, 1970.
11. John Hart Ely, *Democracy and Distrust: A Theory of Judicial Review* (Cambridge, MA: Harvard University Press, 1980), 1.
12. Perlstein, 284; Dennis D. Wainstock, *Election Year 1968: The Turning Point* (Enigma Books, 2012), 98.
13. Perlstein, *Nixonland*, 284; Nadine Cohodas, *Strom Thurmond and the Politics of Southern Change* (New York: Simon & Schuster, 1993), 397.
14. Perlstein, *Nixonland*, 285; Joseph Crespino, *Strom Thurmond's America: A History* (New York: Hill and Wang, 2013), 211.
15. Perlstein, *Nixonland*, 285.
16. Richard Nixon, "Remarks Announcing the Nomination of Judge Warren Earl Burger to Be Chief Justice of the United States" (speech, Washington, D.C., May 21, 1969).
17. Nixon, "Announcing the Nomination of Warren Earl Burger to Be Chief Justice."
18. Charles M. Lamb, "Chief Justice Warren E. Burger: A Conservative Chief for Conservative Times," in *The Burger Court: Political and Judicial Profiles*, eds. Charles M. Lamb and Stephen C. Halpern (Urbana: University of Illinois Press, 1991), 132.
19. Anthony Lewis, "The Significance of Judge Carswell," *New York Times*, May 7, 1970.
20. Linda Greenhouse, *Becoming Justice Blackmun: Harry Blackmun's Supreme Court Journey* (New York: Times Books, 2006), 51.
21. Linda Greenhouse, "The Blackmun Papers," *New York Times*, Mar. 4, 2004.
22. Fred P. Graham, "Burger and Blackmun: Opinions Similar," *New York Times*, Apr. 15, 1970.

23. Greenhouse, *Becoming Justice Blackmun*, 186.
24. Greenhouse, *Becoming Justice Blackmun*, 186.
25. Greenhouse, *Becoming Justice Blackmun*, 186.
26. Linda Greenhouse, "Justice Blackmun, Author of Abortion Right, Dies," *New York Times*, Mar. 5, 1999.
27. Richard Nixon, "President Nixon's Address to the Nation Announcing His Intention to Nominate Lewis F. Powell, Jr., and William H. Rehnquist to Be Associate Justices of the United States Supreme Court" (speech, Washington, D.C., Oct. 21, 1971), American Presidency Project, https://www.presidency.ucsb.edu/documents/address-the-nation-announcing -intention-nominate-lewis-f-powell-jr-and-william-h-rehnquist.
28. Nixon, "Announcing His Intention to Nominate Powell and Rehnquist," 1.
29. Nixon, "Announcing his Intention to Nominate Powell and Rehnquist," 2.
30. Nixon, "Announcing his Intention to Nominate Powell and Rehnquist," 3.
31. Linda Greenhouse, "Lewis Powell, Crucial Centrist Justice, Dies at 90," *New York Times*, Aug. 26, 1998.
32. Nixon, "Announcing his Intention to Nominate Powell and Rehnquist," 4.
33. Nixon, "Announcing his Intention to Nominate Powell and Rehnquist," 4.
34. Press Release, NAACP Opposes Rehnquist for Supreme Court Judge, Nov. 6, 1971.
35. "Congressional Black Caucus, History," https://cbc.house.gov/history/.
36. Hearings Before the Committee on the Judiciary United States Senate, 92nd Congress, First Session on Nominations of William H. Rehnquist of Arizona, and Lewis F. Powell, Jr., of Virginia, to be Associate Justices of the Supreme Court of the United States, November 3, 4, 8, 9, and 10, 1971 (originally printed for use by the committee, https://www.govinfo.gov /content/pkg/gpo-chrg-rehnquist-powell/pdf/gpo-chrg-rehnquist-powell.pdf).
37. Bradley v. School Board of City of Richmond, Va. 317 F. 2d 429, 437 (1963).
38. *Nomination Hearings of Rehnquist and Powell*, 92nd Cong. 363 (statement of Hon. John Conyers Jr., a Representative in Congress from the State of Michigan).
39. *Nomination Hearings of Rehnquist and Powell*, 92nd Cong. 371 (statement of Hon. John Conyers Jr., a Representative in Congress from the State of Michigan).
40. *Nomination Hearings of Rehnquist and Powell*, 92nd Cong. 278 (testimony of Lewis F. Powell Jr., Nominee to Be Associate Justice of the Supreme Court of the United States).
41. Lewis F. Powell Jr., "Attack on the American Free Enterprise System," confidential memorandum to Eugene B. Sydnor Jr., Chairman of the U.S. Chamber of Commerce, Aug. 23, 1971, https:// scholarlycommons.law.wlu.edu/cgi/viewcontent.cgi?article=1000&context=powellmemo.
42. Lawrence B. Glickman, *Free Enterprise* (New Haven, CT: Yale University Press, 2019), 31.
43. Powell, "Attack on the American Free Enterprise System," 2.
44. Powell, "Attack on the American Free Enterprise System," 2–3.
45. Powell, "Attack on the American Free Enterprise System," 10.
46. Powell, "Attack on the American Free Enterprise System," 26.
47. Powell, "Attack on the American Free Enterprise System," 34.
48. Graetz and Greenhouse, *The Burger Court and the Rise of the Judicial Right*, 237–38.
49. *Nomination Hearings of Rehnquist and Powell*, 92nd Cong. 389 (statement of the Old Dominion Bar Association of Virginia by William A. Smith, President).
50. *Nomination Hearings of Rehnquist and Powell*, 92nd Cong. 392 (statement of the Old Dominion Bar Association of Virginia by William A. Smith, President).
51. *Nomination Hearings of Rehnquist and Powell*, 92nd Cong. 393 (statement of the Old Dominion Bar Association of Virginia by William A. Smith, President).
52. John C. Jeffries, *Justice Lewis F. Powell, Jr.* (New York: C. Scribner's Sons, 1994), 142.
53. *Nomination Hearings of Rehnquist and Powell*, 92nd Cong. 394 (Conyers interjection into statement of the Old Dominion Bar Association of Virginia by William A. Smith, President).

54. *Nomination Hearings of Rehnquist and Powell*, 92nd Cong. 278 (testimony of Lewis F. Powell Jr., nominee to Be Associate Justice of the Supreme Court of the United States).

55. *Nomination Hearings of Rehnquist and Powell*, 92nd Cong. 393 (testimony of Henry L. Marsh, III, spokesperson of Old Dominion Bar Association of Virginia).

56. *Nomination Hearings of Rehnquist and Powell*, 92nd Cong. 393 (statement of Henry L. Marsh, III, chairman of Judicial Appointments Committee).

57. Pratt, "A Promise Unfulfilled," 425.

58. Pratt, "A Promise Unfulfilled," 425.

59. Jeffries, *Justice Lewis F. Powell, Jr.*, 229.

60. *Nomination Hearings of Rehnquist and Powell*, 92nd Cong. 156 (testimony of William H. Rehnquist, Nominee to Be Associate Justice of the Supreme Court of the United States).

61. John A. Jenkins, *The Partisan: The Life of William Rehnquist* (New York: PublicAffairs, 2012), 69.

62. *Nomination Hearings of Rehnquist and Powell*, 92nd Cong. 305 (comments of William Rehnquist, made June 15, 1964, at the Public Hearing on the Public Accommodations Ordinance Proposed for the City of Phoenix introduced into the record during the statement of Joseph L. Rauh Jr., counsel, Leadership Conference on Civil Rights).

63. Individual Views of Messrs. Bayh, Hart, Kennedy, and Tunney, on Nomination of William Rehnquist to Be an Associate Justice of the Supreme Court, 92nd Cong., 1st sess., *Congressional Record* 117, pt. 34: 44638.

64. Ken Rudin, "Flashback Friday: This Day in 1964, Goldwater Says No to Civil Rights Bill," NPR, June 18, 2010, https://www.npr.org/sections/politicaljunkie/2010/06/17/127915281 /flashback-friday-this-day-in-1964-goldwater-says-no-to-civil-rights-bill.

65. "Goldwater's City in Rights Battle: Senator Endorses Phoenix Accommodations Bill," *New York Times*, June 7, 1964.

66. *Nomination Hearings of Rehnquist and Powell*, 92nd Cong. 446 (testimony of Gary Orfield, Assistant Professor of Politics and Public Affairs, Princeton University).

67. *Nomination Hearings of Rehnquist and Powell*, 92nd Cong. 446 (testimony of Gary Orfield, Assistant Professor of Politics and Public Affairs, Princeton University).

68. *Nomination Hearings of Rehnquist and Powell*, 92nd Cong. 446 (testimony of Gary Orfield, Assistant Professor of Politics and Public Affairs, Princeton University).

69. *Nomination Hearings of Rehnquist and Powell*, 92nd Cong. 447 (testimony of Gary Orfield, Assistant Professor of Politics and Public Affairs, Princeton University).

70. *Nomination Hearings of Rehnquist and Powell*, 92nd Cong. 487 (additional questions addressed to William Rehnquist by Senator Birch Bayh, Senator Philip A. Hart, and Senator Edward M. Kennedy).

71. Harold R. Cousland, "Our Schools 'Segregate' Both Negroes and Latins," *Arizona Republic*, Aug. 27, 1967; Harold R. Cousland, "Segregation Self-Perpetuating," *Arizona Republic*, Aug. 28, 1967; Harold R. Cousland, "Minorities Better Off in Integrated Schools," *Arizona Republic*, Aug. 29, 1967; Harold R. Cousland, "Compensatory Education Preferred in Phoenix," *Arizona Rep*, Aug. 30, 1967; Harold R. Cousland, "Integration Needs Busing," *Arizona Republic*, Aug. 31, 1967; Harold R. Cousland, "Limited Compensatory Education Plan Used Here," *Arizona Republic*, Sept. 1, 1967.

72. William H. Rehnquist, "'De Facto' Schools Seen Serving Well, Letter to the Editor," *Arizona Republic*, Sept. 9, 1967.

73. *Nomination Hearings of Rehnquist and Powell*, 92nd Cong. 451 (testimony of Gary Orfield, Assistant Professor of Politics and Public Affairs, Princeton University).

74. *Nomination Hearings of Rehnquist and Powell*, 92nd Cong. 291 (testimony of Clarence Mitchell, Director, Washington Bureaus, NAACP).

75. Committee on the Judiciary United States Senate, 92nd Congress, Nomination of William H. Rehnquist, Committee on the Judiciary, Report at 5, Nov. 23, 1971.

76. C. Evan Stewart, "Did William Rehnquist Lie to Become a Justice, and Then Chief Justice?," *Federal Bar Counsel Quarterly* 15 (Mar. 2018).

77. Fred P. Graham, "Rehnquist Says '52 Memo Outlined Jackson's Views," *New York Times*, Dec. 9, 1971.

78. Graham, "Rehnquist Says '52 Memo Outlined Jackson's Views."

79. John P. MacKenzie, "Controversy Deepens over Rehnquist Memo," *Washington Post*, Dec. 10, 1971, 81.

80. Justice Jackson attended the May 17, 1954, announcement of *Brown* at great personal sacrifice. Against doctor's orders, he returned to the Supreme Court from the hospital where he was recovering from a heart attack. The justice insisted on a united bench to invalidate racial segregation in schools and overturn *Plessy v. Ferguson*. Five months later, Justice Jackson died of another heart attack. Daniel B. Moskowitz, "The Supreme Court Decision That Changed America: Brown v. Board of Education," *History.net*, last modified Mar. 16, 2021, https://www.historynet.com/brown-v-board-of-education/; Special to *The New York Times*, "Justice Jackson Dead at 62 Of Heart Attack in Capital," *New York Times*, Oct. 10, 1954.

81. Brad Snyder and John Q. Barrett, "Rehnquist's Missing Letter: A Former Law Clerk's 1955 Thoughts on Justice Jackson and Brown," *Boston College Law Review* 53, no. 9 (2012): 631, 634.

82. Murray Gartner, "Letter to the Editor, We're All Equal under Law; Whose Memo?," *New York Times*, Jan. 14, 1999, A20.

83. David M. O'Brien, *Justice Robert H. Jackson's Unpublished Opinion in* Brown v. Board: *Conflict, Compromise, and Constitutional Interpretation* (Lawrence: University Press of Kansas, 2017), 77.

84. William H. Rehnquist to Justice Robert H. Jackson, 1952, "A Random Thought on the Segregation Cases," available at https://www.govinfo.gov/content/pkg/gpo-chrg-rehnquist/pdf/gpo-chrg-rehnquist-4-16-6.pdf.

85. Rehnquist to Justice Jackson, "A Random Thought on the Segregation Cases," 1.

86. Rehnquist to Justice Jackson, "A Random Thought on the Segregation Cases," 2.

87. United States v. Carolene Products, 304 U.S. at 144, fn 4. (1938).

88. Rehnquist to Justice Jackson, "A Random Thought on the Segregation Cases," 2.

89. Rehnquist to Justice Jackson, "A Random Thought on the Segregation Cases," 2.

90. Roy Wilkins telegram to Hon. Senators William Proxmire, Thomas J. McIntyre, Charles H. Percy, Robert Taft Jr., Bob Packwood, Hugh Scott, Claiborne Pell, Charles Mathias Jr., Thomas F. Eagleton, William B. Saxbe, Mark O. Hatfield, Richard S. Schweiker, and John O. Pastore, Dec. 9, 1971.

91. Fred P. Graham, "Powell and Rehnquist Take Seats on the Supreme Court," *New York Times*, Jan. 8, 1972.

92. Jenkins, *The Partisan*, xxi.

93. Vincent Blasi, *The Burger Court: The Counter-Revolution That Wasn't* (New Haven, CT: Yale University Press, 1983).

94. Graetz and Greenhouse, *The Burger Court and the Rise of the Judicial Right*, 339.

95. Victor Li, "50-Year Story of the Miranda Warning Has the Twists of a Cop Show," *ABA Journal*, Aug. 1, 2016, https://www.abajournal.com/magazine/article/miranda_warning_history.

96. Schwartz, "The Warren Court in Action," 263.

97. Steven Michael Teles, *The Rise of the Conservative Legal Movement: The Battle for Control of the Law* (Princeton, NJ: Princeton University Press, 2008), 1.

98. Graetz and Greenhouse, *The Burger Court and the Rise of the Judicial Right*, 7.

99. Graetz and Greenhouse, *The Burger Court and the Rise of the Judicial Right*, 1.

100. Graetz and Greenhouse, *The Burger Court and the Rise of the Judicial Right*, 8.

101. Graetz and Greenhouse, *The Burger Court and the Rise of the Judicial Right*, 341.

102. Adam Cohen, *Supreme Inequality: The Supreme Court's Fifty-Year Battle for a More Unjust America* (New York: Penguin, 2020), xviii.

19. A TICKING CLOCK

1. Rule 35, Federal Rules of Appellate Procedure.
2. Petition for Rehearing and Suggestion of Appropriateness of Rehearing En Banc at 14, Bradley v. Milliken, 484 F.2d 215 (2:70-cv-35257), Dec. 12, 1972.
3. William Grant, "Integration Order Delayed: Appeals Court to Review Busing Case," *Detroit Free Press*, Jan. 17, 1973.
4. William K. Stevens, "U.S. Courts Near Busing Decision," *New York Times*, Feb. 11, 1973.
5. Grant, "Integration Order Delayed."
6. Harry Salsinger, "Rehearing Raises Hopes of Anti-Busing Forces," *Detroit News*, Jan. 17, 1973.
7. AP and UPI, "High Court to Eye Metro School Plan," *Detroit Free Press*, Jan. 16, 1972.
8. Grant, "Integration Order Delayed."
9. William Grant, "Kelley Concedes State Aided Segregation in City Schools," *Detroit Free Press*, Feb. 9, 1973.
10. John P. MacKenzie, "Judges Weigh Detroit School Busing Case," *Washington Post*, Feb. 9, 1973.
11. Grant, "Kelley Concedes State Aided Segregation in City Schools."
12. Jeffery Hadden, "No Hint on How Court Will Rule on Busing," *Detroit News*, Feb. 9, 1973.
13. Dimond, *Beyond Busing*, 91.
14. Dimond, *Beyond Busing*, 91.
15. Hadden, "No Hint on How Court Will Rule on Busing."
16. Draft of Oral Argument of Nathaniel R. Jones, Feb. 8, 1973, at 1, NAACP Records, Manuscript Division, Library of Congress, Washington D.C.
17. William Grant, "School Board Asks for Tax Hike," *Detroit Free Press*, Feb. 14, 1973.
18. David Cooper, "Legislature OKs Detroit School Tax," *Detroit Free Press*, Mar. 9, 1973.
19. Draft of Oral Argument of Nathaniel R. Jones, Feb. 8, 1973, at 1, NAACP Records, Manuscript Division, Library of Congress, Washington D.C.
20. Draft of Oral Argument of Nathaniel R. Jones, Feb. 8, 1973, at 2, NAACP Records, Manuscript Division, Library of Congress, Washington D.C.
21. U.S. Senate, Select Committee on Equal Educational Opportunity, *Toward Equal Educational Opportunity: The Report of the Select Committee on Equal Educational Opportunity*, 92nd Cong. 2d sess., 1972, S. Rep. No. 92–000.
22. U.S. Senate, Select Committee on Equal Educational Opportunity, *Toward Equal Educational Opportunity*, 92nd Cong. 2d sess., 1972, S. Rep. No. 92–000, 1.
23. U.S. Senate, Select Committee on Equal Educational Opportunity, *Toward Equal Educational Opportunity*, 92nd Cong. 2d sess., 1972, S. Rep. No. 92–000, vii.
24. U.S. Senate, Select Committee on Equal Educational Opportunity, *Toward Equal Educational Opportunity*, 92nd Cong. 2d sess., 1972, S. Rep. No. 92–000, vii.
25. U.S. Senate, Select Committee on Equal Educational Opportunity, *Toward Equal Educational Opportunity*, 92nd Cong. 2d sess., 1972, S. Rep. No. 92–000, 119–25.
26. U.S. Senate, Select Committee on Equal Educational Opportunity, *Toward Equal Educational Opportunity*, 92nd Cong. 2d sess., 1972, S. Rep. No. 92–000, 124–25.
27. U.S. Senate, Select Committee on Equal Educational Opportunity, *Toward Equal Educational Opportunity*, 92nd Cong. 2d sess., 1972, S. Rep. No. 92–000, 249.
28. U.S. Senate, Select Committee on Equal Educational Opportunity, *Toward Equal Educational Opportunity*, 92nd Cong. 2d sess., 1972, S. Rep. No. 92–000, 44.
29. U.S. Senate, Select Committee on Equal Educational Opportunity, *Toward Equal Educational Opportunity*, 92nd Cong. 2d sess., 1972, S. Rep. No. 92–000, 3.
30. U.S. Senate, Select Committee on Equal Educational Opportunity, *Toward Equal Educational Opportunity*, 92nd Cong. 2d sess., 1972, S. Rep. No. 92–000, 13–14.
31. U.S. Senate, Select Committee on Equal Educational Opportunity, *Toward Equal Educational Opportunity*, 92nd Cong. 2d sess., 1972, S. Rep. No. 92–000, 168.

32. U.S. Senate, Select Committee on Equal Educational Opportunity, *Toward Equal Educational Opportunity*, 92nd Cong. 2d sess., 1972, S. Rep. No. 92–000, 337.

33. San Antonio v. Rodriguez, 411 U.S. at 1 (1973).

34. U.S. Senate, Select Committee on Equal Educational Opportunity, *Toward Equal Educational Opportunity*, 92nd Cong. 2d sess., 1972, S. Rep. No. 92–000, 231.

35. U.S. Senate, Select Committee on Equal Educational Opportunity, *Toward Equal Educational Opportunity*, 92nd Cong. 2d sess., 1972, S. Rep. No. 92–000, 252.

36. U.S. Senate, Select Committee on Equal Educational Opportunity, *Toward Equal Educational Opportunity*, 92nd Cong. 2d sess., 1972, S. Rep. No. 92–000, 252.

37. Gary Orfield, "School Desegregation 50 Years After Brown: Misconceptions, Lessons Learned, and Hopes for the Future," *Center for the Study of Ethics and Society* XVI, no. 1 (2005): 4–5.

38. U.S. Senate, Select Committee on Equal Educational Opportunity, *Toward Equal Educational Opportunity*, 92nd Cong. 2d sess., 1972, S. Rep. No. 92–000, 21.

39. Jack Rosenthal, "Senate Unit Asks Integration Aid," *New York Times*, Jan. 14, 1973.

40. School Board of the City of Richmond v. State Board of Education of Virginia, 412 U.S. at 92 (1973).

41. *School Board of the City of Richmond*, 412 U.S. at 92 (1973).

42. Dean Mills, "School Districts Upheld; Court's Tie Vote Voids Merger of Va. Systems," *Baltimore Sun*, May 22, 1973.

43. Bob Woodward and Scott Armstrong, *The Brethren: Inside the Supreme Court* (Simon & Schuster, 1979), 317.

44. John P. MacKenzie, "Potter Stewart Is Dead at 70; Was on High Court 23 Years," *New York Times*, Dec. 8, 1985.

45. Vincent L. Broderick, "Justice Potter Stewart," *North Carolina Central Law Review* 12 (1981): 297, 301.

46. MacKenzie, "Potter Stewart Is Dead at 70"; Al Kamen, "Retired High Court Justice Potter Stewart Dies at 70," *Washington Post*, Dec. 8, 1985; "Justice Stewart (Retired), The Talk of the Town," *New Yorker*, Oct. 19, 1981, 36.

47. MacKenzie, "Potter Stewart Is Dead at 70."

48. Woodward and Armstrong, *The Brethren: Inside the Supreme Court*, 323.

20. *MILLIKEN V. BRADLEY*

1. Bradley v. Milliken, 484 F.2d 215 (6th Cir. 1973).

2. Hain, "Sealing Off the City," 268.

3. Bradley v. Milliken, 484 F.2d at 267.

4. Bradley v. Milliken, 484 F.2d at 242.

5. Dimond, *Beyond Busing*, 94.

6. Bradley v. Milliken, 484 F.2d at 242.

7. Dimond, *Beyond Busing*, 94.

8. Bradley v. Milliken, 484 F.2d at 252.

9. William Grant, "Roth Plan Is Upheld; High Court Test Next," *Detroit Free Press*, June 13, 1973.

10. Harry Salsinger, "2-year Delay Likely for Any Metro Bussing," *Detroit News*, June 13, 1973.

11. William Grant, "Roth Orders 41 Districts Added to Metro Busing Case," *Detroit Free Press*, Sept. 11, 1973.

12. Bradley v. Milliken, 484 F.2d at 258.

13. Grant, "Roth Plan Is Upheld; High Court Test Next."

14. Statement of Nathaniel R. Jones, June 12, 1973, NAACP Records, Manuscript Division, Library of Congress, Washington, D.C.

15. William Grant, "Busing Case Tests Court Role in Society," *Detroit Free Press*, July 14, 1973.

16. Nathaniel Jones to Roy Wilkins, John A. Morsell, and Richard McClain, June 22, 1973, Memo re: The Detroit Case, NAACP Records, Manuscript Division, Library of Congress, Washington, D.C.
17. Jones to Wilkins, et. al., June 22, 1973, Memo re: The Detroit Case, at 1, NAACP Records, Manuscript Division, Library of Congress, Washington, D.C.
18. *Keyes*, 413 U.S. at 189 (1973).
19. *Keyes*, 413 U.S. at 191.
20. *Keyes*, 413 U.S. at 201.
21. *Keyes*, 413 U.S. at 201.
22. Jones to Wilkins, et. al., June 22, 1973, Memo re: The Detroit Case, at 1, NAACP Records, Manuscript Division, Library of Congress, Washington D.C.
23. Vernon E. Jordan Jr., "The North's Turn to Integrate," *Louisville Defender*, July 12, 1973.
24. Myron Orfield, "Milliken, Meredith, and Metropolitan Segregation," *UCLA Law Review* 62 (2015): 364, 389.
25. Orfield, "Milliken, Meredith, and Metropolitan Segregation," 389.
26. *Keyes*, 413 U.S. at 214.
27. *Keyes*, 413 U.S. at 218.
28. *Keyes*, 413 U.S. at 219.
29. *Keyes*, 413 U.S. at 222–23.
30. *Keyes*, 413 U.S. at 219.
31. *Keyes*, 413 U.S. at 222.
32. Jeffries, *Justice Lewis F. Powell, Jr.*, 303.
33. Memo for Milliken v. Bradley, Feb. 25, 1974, Harry A. Blackmun Papers, Box 187, Manuscript Division, Library of Congress, Washington, D.C.
34. Greenhouse, *Becoming Justice Blackmun*, 31.
35. Memo for Milliken v. Bradley at 4, Harry A. Blackmun Papers, Manuscript Division, Library of Congress, Washington, D.C.
36. *Keyes*, 413 U.S. at 223–24.
37. *Swann*, 402 U.S. at 1, 26 (1971).
38. Memo for Milliken v. Bradley, at 6, Harry A. Blackmun Papers, Manuscript Division, Library of Congress, Washington, D.C.
39. Memo for Milliken v. Bradley, at 5, Harry A. Blackmun Papers, Manuscript Division, Library of Congress, Washington, D.C.
40. Milliken v. Bradley, 414 U.S. at 1038 (1973). The Detroit Board of Education did not seek Supreme Court review. It its brief, it explained why:

   Although the Detroit Board of Education maintains that, as a local state agency, it had taken no actions which resulted in the current condition of segregation forming the basis of the original complaint, but instead had taken positive steps to promote integration in its schools, it has not appealed the lower court findings for the following reasons: (1) the consistent findings of violations in the Courts below; (2) this Honorable Court's recent decision in Keyes: and (3) a recognition by the Detroit Board that it is a mere instrumentality of the State under Michigan law and therefore, regardless of whether violations were found to have been committed either by state officers at the state level alone, or by state officers at the local level, the result would be the same. It is incumbent upon the State of Michigan ultimately to remedy the violations. (Milliken v. Bradley, Brief for Respondents Board of Education for the School District of the City of Detroit, WL 185664 at 8–9.)

41. Warren Weaver Jr., "Justices Will Weigh Detroit School Plan," *New York Times*, Nov. 20, 1973.
42. Nathaniel R. Jones to Roy Wilkins, Memo re: The Detroit Case, Nov. 15, 1973, at 1, NAACP Records, Manuscript Division, Library of Congress, Washington, D.C.

43. William Grant, "Supreme Court to Hear Area School Busing Case," *Detroit Free Press*, Nov. 20, 1973.
44. Richard A. Ryan, "Supreme Court Begins Hearings Tomorrow: The Historic Detroit School Bussing Case," *Detroit News*, Feb. 26, 1974.
45. Grant, "Supreme Court to Hear Area School Busing Case."
46. Grant, "Supreme Court to Hear Area School Busing Case."
47. Weaver Jr., "Justices Will Weigh Detroit School Plan."
48. "GW Law Library: Library Guides: Supreme Court of the United States: Interpreting Citations," https://law.gwu.libguides.com/scotus/tips.

21. THE STORY

1. William Grant, "Busing Case Quietly Put in Court's Hands," *Detroit Free Press*, Feb. 28, 1974.
2. Transcript of Oral Argument, Milliken v. Bradley, 418 U.S. at 717 (1974) available at https://www.oyez.org/cases/1973/73-434.
3. Transcript of Oral Argument at 20, Milliken v. Bradley, 418 U.S. at 717 (1974).
4. Memorandum for the United States as Amicus Curiae at 13, Milliken v. Bradley, 418 U.S. at 717 (1974).
5. Transcript of Oral Argument at 34–35, Milliken v. Bradley, 418 U.S. at 717 (1974).
6. Transcript of Oral Argument at 35, Milliken v. Bradley, 418 U.S. at 717 (1974).
7. Transcript of Oral Argument at 26-27, Milliken v. Bradley, 418 U.S. at 717 (1974).
8. Transcript of Oral Argument at 50, Milliken v. Bradley, 418 U.S. at 717 (1974).
9. Transcript of Oral Argument at 51, Milliken v. Bradley, 418 U.S. at 717 (1974).
10. Transcript of Oral Argument at 51, Milliken v. Bradley, 418 U.S. at 717 (1974).
11. Transcript of Oral Argument at 65, Milliken v. Bradley, 418 U.S. at 717 (1974).
12. Transcript of Oral Argument at 70, Milliken v. Bradley, 418 U.S. at 717 (1974).
13. Transcript of Oral Argument at 82, Milliken v. Bradley, 418 U.S. at 717 (1974).
14. William Grant, "Judge Roth OK After 2nd Heart Attack," *Detroit Free Press*, Apr. 5, 1974; Fred Manardo, "Judge Roth Suffers 2nd Heart Attack," *Detroit News*, Apr. 4, 1974.
15. Grant, "Judge Roth OK After 2nd Heart Attack."
16. AP, "Judge Roth 'Improving,'" *Detroit News*, Apr. 29, 1974; "Roth Is Released from Hospital," *Detroit News*, May 10, 1974.
17. "Roth to Retire?," *Detroit News*, June 25, 1974.
18. "3rd Seizure Hospitalizes Judge Roth," *Detroit News*, July 11, 1974.
19. "3rd Heart Attack Fatal to Roth," *Detroit News*, July 12, 1974.
20. Email between Michelle Adams and John Runyan, May 24, 2018 (on file with the author).
21. Clark Hallas, "Roth Eulogized: 'Never Lost the Common Touch,'" *Detroit News*, July 16, 1974.
22. "Roth Rites Shut Area U.S. Courts," *Detroit News*, July 13, 1974.
23. "Supreme Court Delays Ruling on Critical Detroit School Integration Case," *New York Times*, June 27, 1974.
24. "Supreme Court Delays Ruling on Critical Detroit School Integration Case."
25. Justice Thurgood Marshall, Memo to the Conference, dated June 13, 1974, at 3, U.S. Supreme Court Materials, Manuscript Division, Library of Congress, Washington, D.C.
26. Justice Marshall Memo, dated June 13, 1974, at 1, U.S. Supreme Court Materials, Manuscript Division, Library of Congress, Washington, D.C.
27. Milliken v. Bradley First Draft, dated May 31, 1974, U.S. Supreme Court Materials, Manuscript Division, Library of Congress, Washington, D.C.
28. Anthony Ripley, "Federal Grand Jury Indicts 7 Nixon Aides on Charges of Conspiracy on Watergate; Haldeman, Ehrlichman, Mitchell on List," *New York Times*, Mar. 3, 1974.
29. United States v. Nixon, 418 U.S. at 683 (1974).

30. Email between Michelle Adams and John Runyan, May 24, 2018 (on file with the author).

31. Richard A. Ryan, "Roth Bussing Plan Killed," *Detroit News*, July 25, 1974.

32. William Grant, "High Court Kills Cross-District Busing," *Detroit Free Press*, July 26, 1974.

33. Milliken v. Bradley, 418 U.S. at 717, 739 (1974).

34. Milliken v. Bradley, 418 U.S. at 728, n. 7.

35. Milliken v. Bradley, 418 U.S. at 728, n. 7.

36. Wilkinson, *From Brown to Bakke*, 224.

37. Milliken v. Bradley, 418 U.S. at 740.

38. Milliken v. Bradley First Draft, dated May 31, 1974, at 24, U.S. Supreme Court Materials, Manuscript Division, Library of Congress, Washington, D.C.

39. Brief for Petitioners, at 24, Milliken v. Bradley, 418 U.S. 717 (1974).

40. Brief for Petitioners, at 25, Milliken v. Bradley, 418 U.S. at 717 (1974).

41. Memo from Robert Richter to Justice Blackmun re: Circulation by the Chief Justice (2nd draft) dated June 12, 1974, at 2–3, Harry A. Blackmun Papers, Box 187, Manuscript Division, Library of Congress, Washington, D.C.

42. Letter from William H. Rehnquist to Chief Justice Burger, dated June 3, 1974, U.S. Supreme Court Materials, Manuscript Division, Library of Congress, Washington, D.C.

43. Letter from Rehnquist to Burger, dated June 3, 1974, U.S. Supreme Court Materials, Manuscript Division, Library of Congress, Washington, D.C.

44. Memo to the Chief Justice from Justice Powell, dated June 5, 1974, Harry A. Blackmun Papers, Box 187, Manuscript Division, Library of Congress, Washington, D.C.

45. Memo to the Chief Justice, dated June 5, 1974, at 2, Harry A. Blackmun Papers, Manuscript Division, Library of Congress, Washington, D.C.

46. Memo to the Chief Justice, dated June 5, 1974, at 3, Harry A. Blackmun Papers, Manuscript Division, Library of Congress, Washington, D.C.

47. Memo to the Chief Justice, dated June 5, 1974, at 4, Harry A. Blackmun Papers, Manuscript Division, Library of Congress, Washington, D.C.

48. Memo to the Chief Justice, dated June 5, 1974, at 7, Harry A. Blackmun Papers, Manuscript Division, Library of Congress, Washington, D.C.

49. Memo from Richter to Justice Blackmun, dated June 12, 1974, at 5, Harry A. Blackmun Papers, Box 187, Manuscript Division, Library of Congress, Washington, D.C.

50. Memo to the Chief Justice, dated June 5, 1974, at 8, Harry A. Blackmun Papers, Manuscript Division, Library of Congress, Washington, D.C.

51. Memo to the Chief Justice dated June 5, 1974, at 8–9, Harry A. Blackmun Papers, Manuscript Division, Library of Congress, Washington, D.C.

52. Keyes, 413 U.S. 189, 219–220 (Powell, J., concurring in part).

53. Memo to the Chief Justice, dated June 5, 1974, at 5, Harry A. Blackmun Papers, Manuscript Division, Library of Congress, Washington, D.C.

54. Memo to the Chief Justice, dated June 5, 1974, at 9, Harry A. Blackmun Papers, Manuscript Division, Library of Congress, Washington, D.C.

55. Memo to the Chief Justice, dated June 5, 1974, at 11, Harry A. Blackmun Papers, Manuscript Division, Library of Congress, Washington, D.C.

56. Jones, *Answering the Call*, 161.

57. Memo from Richter to Justice Blackmun, dated June 12, 1974, at 1, Harry A. Blackmun Papers, Manuscript Division, Library of Congress, Washington, D.C.

58. Memo to the Chief Justice from Justice Stewart, dated June 17, 1974, at 1, U.S. Supreme Court Materials, Manuscript Division, Library of Congress, Washington, D.C.

59. Memo to the Chief Justice from Justice William H. Rehnquist, dated July 18, 1974, at 1, U.S. Supreme Court Materials, Manuscript Division, Library of Congress, Washington, D.C.

60. Memo to the Chief Justice from Justice Rehnquist, dated July 18, 1974, at 1, U.S. Supreme Court Materials, Manuscript Division, Library of Congress, Washington, D.C.

61. Memo to the Chief Justice from Justice Rehnquist, dated July 18, 1974, at 2, U.S. Supreme Court Materials, Manuscript Division, Library of Congress, Washington, D.C.
62. Milliken v. Bradley Fourth Draft, dated July 22, 1974, at 24, U.S. Supreme Court Materials, Manuscript Division, Library of Congress, Washington, D.C.
63. Milliken v. Bradley, 418 U.S. at 745.
64. Milliken v. Bradley, 418 U.S. at 756, n. 2.
65. Milliken v. Bradley, 418 U.S. at 782.
66. Milliken v. Bradley, 418 U.S. at 783.
67. Milliken v. Bradley, 418 U.S. at 806.
68. Milliken v. Bradley, 418 U.S. at 783.
69. Milliken v. Bradley, 418 U.S. at 789.
70. Milliken v. Bradley, 418 U.S. at 790.
71. Milliken v. Bradley, 418 U.S. at 814.
72. Milliken v. Bradley, 418 U.S. at 753.
73. William Grant, "DeMascio to Rule on Busing," *Detroit Free Press*, Jan. 7, 1975.
74. Bradley v. Milliken, 540 F.2d 229, 236 (6th Cir. 1976).

22. FENCES

1. Nathaniel Jones, "Supreme Court Detroit Ruling 'Unfortunate,' NAACP Declares," Press Release, July 25, 1974.
2. Warren Weaver Jr., "Decision by 5 to 4," *New York Times*, July 26, 1974.
3. Martin E. Sloane, "Milliken v. Bradley and Residential Segregation," Commission on Civil Rights, *Milliken v. Bradley: The Implications for Metropolitan Desegregation*, Oct. 22, 1974, 5, https://files.eric.ed.gov/fulltext/ED117258.pdf.
4. Weaver Jr., "Decision by 5 to 4."
5. William Raspberry, "Busing and the Court: A 'Giant Step Backward'?," *Washington Post*, July 29, 1974.
6. Bradley v. Milliken, 402 Supp. 1096, 1102, 1138–1140 (E.D. MI 1975).
7. William Grant, "State Told to Give City 150 Buses: School Plan Faces Appeal," *Detroit Free Press*, May 22, 1975.
8. Bradley v. Milliken, 519 F.2d 679, 679 (6th Cir. 1975).
9. Harry T. Edwards, "The Journey from Brown v. Board of Education to Grutter v. Bollinger: From Racial Assimilation to Diversity," *Michigan Law Review* 102, no. 5 (2004): 944, 946.
10. Harry T. Edwards, "Personal Reflections on 30 Years of Legal Education for Minority Students," *University of Michigan Law Quad Notes* 37, no. 2 (Summer 1994): 39, https://repository.law.umich.edu/cgi/viewcontent.cgi?article=1445&context=lqnotes.
11. Bradley v. Milliken, 519 F.2d at 680.
12. Bradley v. Milliken, 519 F.2d at 680–81.
13. Dred Scott v. Sandford, 60 U.S. at 393, 404–405 (1857).
14. William K. Stevens, "Detroit Is Facing Wide Busing Plan," *New York Times*, June 29, 1975.
15. James S. Coleman, Sara D. Kelly, and John A. Moore, "Trends in School Segregation, 1968–73," *The Urban Institute* (Aug. 1975), 98.
16. Gary Orfield, "National Data and Methods of Analysis," *Symposium on School Desegregation and White Flight*, Catholic University of America (Aug. 1975), 50–51.
17. Orfield, "National Data and Methods of Analysis," 44–45.
18. Email message from John Logan to Michelle Adams, Jan. 8, 2021 (on file with the author).
19. Orfield, "Milliken, Meredith, and Metropolitan Segregation," 364, 437.
20. Bradley v. Milliken, 402 F. Supp. at 1102.
21. Samuel C. Damren, *"Milliken v. Bradley I* On Remand: The Impossible Assignment," His-

torical Society for the United States District Court for the Eastern District of Michigan, *Court Legacy* XVI, no. 1 (Feb. 2009): 3, https://federalcourthistoricaledmi.org/wp-content/uploads/2021/11/Court.Legacy.2009.02.pdf.

22. Bradley v. Milliken, 540 F.2d at 236–37.
23. Bradley v. Milliken, 402 F. Supp. at 1129.
24. Bradley v. Milliken, 620 F.2d 1143, 1151 (6th Cir. 1980).
25. Damren, "*Milliken v. Bradley I* On Remand," 9.
26. Elwood Hain, "School Desegregation in Detroit: Domestic Tranquility and Judicial Futility," *Wayne Law Review* 23 (1976): 65, 142.
27. Bradley v. Milliken, 402 F. Supp. at 1118.
28. Bradley v. Milliken, 402 F. Supp. at 1138.
29. Milliken v. Bradley, 433 U.S. at 267, 281 (1977).
30. Milliken v. Bradley, 433 U.S. at 281.
31. Milliken v. Bradley, 433 U.S. at 287.
32. Jones, *Answering the Call*, 164.
33. Gary Orfield, "Still Separate Still Unequal: The Limits of Milliken II's Monetary Compensation to Segregated Schools," in *Dismantling Desegregation: The Quiet Reversal of Brown v. Board of Education*, eds. Gary Orfield and Susan E. Eaton (New York: The New Press, 1999).
34. Orfield, "Still Separate Still Unequal," 146.
35. Orfield, "Still Separate Still Unequal," 174.
36. Later, the Supreme Court would add insult to injury. In a 1995 case called *Missouri v. Jenkins*, it prohibited a federal trial court from requiring the state to continue to fund teacher salary increases and remedial education programs as part of a desegregation order "because student achievement levels were still 'at or below national norms at many grade levels.'" Missouri v. Jenkins, 515 U.S. at 70, 100 (1995). *Jenkins* stood for the proposition that there was no requirement that student achievement levels improve before the federal courts declared that a school district was "unitary," meaning that the constitutional violation was remediated and federal oversight of the school district was removed. 515 U.S. at 101–102. The court wrote that "insistence upon academic goals unrelated to the effects of legal segregation unwarrantably postpones the day when the KCMSD will be able to operate on its own." 515 U.S. at 102. This meant that parties were still free to make a showing that depressed levels of student achievement were the direct result of de jure segregation. This explained why the court remanded the case. It did so to allow the lower court to determine whether segregation in fact had an effect on minority student achievement. But assumptions were off the table; there could be any number of explanations for student achievement levels. "Just as demographic changes independent of de jure segregation will affect the racial composition of student assignments so too will numerous external factors beyond the control of the KCMSD and the State affect minority student achievement," the court warned.
37. Orfield, "Still Separate Still Unequal," 146.
38. Orfield, "Still Separate Still Unequal," 154–55.
39. Orfield, "Still Separate Still Unequal," 155.
40. Orfield, "Still Separate Still Unequal," 156.
41. Email from Paul Dimond to Michelle Adams, Jan. 7, 2021 (on file with the author).
42. Milliken v. Bradley, 418 U.S. at 717, 759–760 (1974).
43. Milliken v. Bradley, 418 U.S. at 760.
44. Milliken v. Bradley, 418 U.S. at 761.
45. Bradley v. Milliken, 540 F.2d at 232.
46. William Grant, "Landmark Integration Case Produced Mostly Frustration," *Detroit Free Press*, May 15, 1979.
47. Ted Goczkowski, "Case in His Name—Won't Be Bussed," *Detroit News*, Jan. 21, 1976.
48. Goczkowski, "Case in His Name—Won't Be Bussed."

49. Cynthia Lee, "Symbol: Boy in Detroit Bus in Case Seeks Return to Anonymity," *Detroit News*, July 16, 1981.
50. Franklin, "Award for Plaintiffs in Desegregation Suit: Frustration, Anger."

23. THE CONSEQUENCES

1. Robert Reinhold, "Impact of the Ruling," *New York Times*, July 26, 1974.
2. Orfield, *Must We Bus?*, 391.
3. Charles T. Clotfelter, *After Brown: The Rise and Retreat of School Desegregation* (Princeton, NJ: Princeton University Press, 2004), 32.
4. Dimond, *Beyond Busing*, 29.
5. Dimond, *Beyond Busing*, 39.
6. Dimond, *Beyond Busing*, 29.
7. Dimond, *Beyond Busing*, 30.
8. Dimond, *Beyond Busing*, 89.
9. Dimond, *Beyond Busing*, 87.
10. Dimond, *Beyond Busing*, 99.
11. Letter from Nick Flannery to Nate Jones, dated Sept. 4, 1970, at 1, NAACP Records, Manuscript Division, Library of Congress, Washington, D.C.
12. Letter from Flannery to Jones, dated Sept. 4, 1970, at 2, NAACP Records, Manuscript Division, Library of Congress, Washington, D.C.
13. As a respondent that was not seeking any change to the judgment in their favor below, the Bradley advocates had the right to "urge any argument . . . in support of the judgment in [their] favor, including contentions not passed on by the court below and even contentions rejected by the court below." Robert L. Stern and Eugene Gressman, *Supreme Court Practice: Jurisdiction, Procedure, Arguing and Briefing Techniques, Forms, Statutes, Rules for Practice in the Supreme Court of the United States* (Washington, D.C.: Bureau of National Affairs, 1969), 314–15.
14. Brief for the Respondents at 1, Milliken v. Bradley, 418 U.S. at 717.
15. Brief for the Respondents at 38, Milliken v. Bradley, 418 U.S. at 717.
16. Dimond, *Beyond Busing*, 101.
17. Dimond, *Beyond Busing*, 103.
18. Wilkinson, *From Brown to Bakke*, 224.
19. William L. Taylor, "The Supreme Court and Urban Reality: A Tactical Analysis of Milliken v. Bradley," *Wayne Law Review* 21 (1975): 751, 753.
20. United States Commission on Civil Rights, "Statement on Metropolitian School Desegregation, A Report of the United States Commission on Civil Rights," Feb. 1977, 93, https:// archive.org/details/eric_ed137490/page/n97/mode/2up.
21. Dimond, *Beyond Busing*, 287; Evans v. Buchanan, 379 F. Supp. 1218, 1220 (1974).
22. Dimond, *Beyond Busing*, 287–88.
23. Evans v. Buchanan, 379 F. Supp. at 1233.
24. Brett Gadsden, "The 'Other Side of the Milliken Coin': The Promise and Pitfalls of Metropolitan School Desegregation," *Journal of Urban History* 36 (2010): 173, 178.
25. Evans v. Buchanan, 393 F. Supp. at 432, 438–39.
26. Evans v. Buchanan, 393 F. Supp. at 432–33; Gadsden, "The 'Other Side of the Milliken Coin,'" 178.
27. Dimond, *Beyond Busing*, 290.
28. Dimond, *Beyond Busing*, 291.
29. Dimond, *Beyond Busing*, 292; Evans v. Buchanan, 393 F. Supp. 428, 445–46 (1975).
30. Evans v. Buchanan, 555 F.2d 373 (1977).
31. Newburg Area Council, Inc. v. Board of Education of Jefferson County, 510 F.2d 1358, 1360 (1974).

32. Although it should be noted that the *Milliken* court effectively ignored what happened in the Carver School District in Royal Oak Township. Milliken v. Bradley, 418 U.S. at 717, 749–50 (1974). And, with respect to the Carver school district, the Sixth Circuit drew a contrast: "In the present cases the disregarding of school district lines in a single county in Kentucky cannot be characterized as a mere isolated incidence as was the case in Milliken with respect to the Carver-Detroit high school situation." Newburg Area Council, Inc. v. Board of Education of Jefferson County, 510 F.2d 1358, 1360–1361 (1974).

33. Jefferson County, 510 F.2d 1358, 1360 (1974).

34. Robert A. Sedler, "The Louisville-Jefferson County School Desegregation Case: A Lawyer's Retrospective," *Register of the Kentucky Historical Society* 105, no. 1 (2007): 3, 19.

35. Orfield, "Milliken, Meredith, and Metropolitan Segregation," 364, 378.

36. Orfield, *Must We Bus?*, 416–17.

37. Orfield, *Must We Bus?*, 417.

38. Myron Orfield and Thomas F. Luce, "America's Racially Diverse Suburbs: Opportunities and Challenges," *Housing Policy Debate* 23 (2013): 395, 421.

39. Orfield, "Milliken, Meredith, and Metropolitan Segregation," 438.

40. Orfield, "Milliken, Meredith, and Metropolitan Segregation," 438.

41. Alison Morantz, "Desegregation at Risk, Threat and Reaffirmation in Charlotte," in *Dismantling Desegregation: The Quiet Reversal of* Brown v. Board of Education, eds. Gary Orfield and Susan E. Eaton (New York: The New Press, 1999), 180.

42. Morantz, "Desegregation at Risk," 180–81.

43. Roslyn Arlin Mickelson, Stephen Samuel Smith, and Amy Hawn Nelson, "Yesterday, Today, and Tomorrow: Structure and Agency in the Resegregation of the Charlotte-Mecklenburg Schools," in *Yesterday, Today, and Tomorrow: School Desegregation and Resegregation in Charlotte*, eds. Roslyn Arlin Mickelson, Stephen Samuel Smith, and Amy Hawn Nelson (Cambridge, MA: Harvard Education Press, 2015), 3.

44. Diana Pearce, "Breaking Down Barriers: New Evidence on the Impact of Metropolitan School Desegregation on Housing," *Center For National Policy Review, Catholic University of America School of Law* (Nov. 1980): 35; Morantz, "Desegregation at Risk," 181–82.

45. *Swann*, 401 U.S. at 1, 21 (1971).

46. Orfield, "Milliken, Meredith, and Metropolitan Segregation," 440.

47. P. R. Lockhart, "Smaller Communities Are 'Seceding' from Larger School Districts. It's Accelerating School Segregation," *Vox*, Sept. 9, 2019, https://www.vox.com/2019/9/6/20853091/school-secession-racial-segregation-louisiana-alabama.

48. Robert A. Sedler, "The Profound Impact of Milliken v. Bradley," *Wayne Law Review* 33 (1987): 1693, 1696.

49. Sedler, "The Profound Impact of Milliken v. Bradley," 1702.

50. Derrick A. Bell Jr., "Serving Two Masters: Integration Ideals and Client Interests in School Desegregation Litigation," *Yale Law Journal* 85 (1976): 470, 471.

51. Bell Jr., "Serving Two Masters," 471.

52. Bell Jr., "Serving Two Masters," 479.

53. Bell Jr., "Serving Two Masters," 482.

54. Bell Jr., "Serving Two Masters," 489.

55. Bell Jr., "Serving Two Masters," 512.

56. Bell Jr., "Serving Two Masters," 505.

57. Nathaniel Jones, "To the Editors, School Desegregation," *Yale Law Journal* 86 (1976): 378.

58. Jones, "To the Editors, School Desegregation," 378.

59. Jones, "To the Editors, School Desegregation," 379–80.

60. Jones, "To the Editors, School Desegregation," 379.

61. Jones, "To the Editors, School Desegregation," 379.

62. Jones, "To the Editors, School Desegregation," 379.
63. Rucker C. Johnson with Alexander Nazaryan, *Children of the Dream: Why School Integration Works* (New York: Basic Books, 2019), 60.
64. Johnson with Nazaryan, *Children of the Dream*, 60–64.
65. Johnson with Nazaryan, *Children of the Dream*, 244–45.
66. Sarah J. Reber, "School Desegregation and Educational Attainment for Blacks," *National Bureau of Economic Research*, Working Paper 12193, 2007, 28, https://www.nber.org/system/files/working_papers/w13193/w13193.pdf.
67. Johnson with Nazaryan, *Children of the Dream*, 58, 81–82.
68. Genevieve Siegel-Hawley, "How Non-Minority Students Also Benefit from Racially Diverse Schools," *National Coalition on School Diversity*, 2012.
69. Garrett Anstreicher, Jason Fletcher, and Owen Thompson, "The Long Run Impacts of Court Ordered Desegregation," National Bureau of Economic Research, Working Paper 29926, 2022, https://www.nber.org/papers/w29926.
70. Anstreicher, Fletcher, and Thompson, "The Long Run Impacts of Court Ordered Desegregation," 1.
71. Anstreicher, Fletcher, and Thompson, "The Long Run Impacts of Court Ordered Desegregation," 23.
72. Anstreicher, Fletcher, and Thompson, "The Long Run Impacts of Court Ordered Desegregation," 23.
73. Anstreicher, Fletcher, and Thompson, "The Long Run Impacts of Court Ordered Desegregation," 23.
74. Johnson with Nazaryan, *Children of the Dream*, 132.
75. Reardon et al., "Is Separate Still Unequal?," 37.
76. Gary Orfield and Danielle Jarvie, "Black Segregation Matters: School Resegregation and Black Educational Opportunity," UCLA Civil Rights Project, 2020, 5, https://www.civilrightsproject.ucla.edu/research/k-12-education/integration-and-diversity/black-segregation-matters-school-resegregation-and-black-educational-opportunity/black-segregation-matters-final-121820.pdf.
77. Ronald P. Formisano, *Boston Against Busing: Race, Class, and Ethnicity in the 1960s and 1970s* (Chapel Hill: University of North Carolina Press, 1991), 223.
78. Nikole Hannah-Jones, "It Was Never About Busing," *New York Times*, July 12, 2019.
79. Board of Education of Oklahoma City Public Schools v. Dowell, 498 U.S. at 237 (1991).
80. *Dowell*, 498 U.S. at 248.
81. Bradley W. Joondeph, "Killing Brown Softly: The Subtle Undermining of Effective Desegregation in Freeman v. Pitts," *Stanford. Law Review* 46 1993): 147, 161.
82. Freeman v. Pitts, 503 U.S. at 467, 494 (1992).
83. Missouri v. Jenkins, 515 U.S. at 70, 101 (1995).
84. Orfield and Jarvie, "Black Segregation Matters," 11.
85. "$23 Billion," EdBuild, https://edbuild.org/content/23-billion.

24. "TRUE INTEGRATION"

1. "About the Detroit Public Schools Community District," Detroit Public Schools Community District, https://www.detroitk12.org/Page/15183.
2. "Child Nutrition Programs Income Eligibility Guidelines (2022–2023)," USDA Food and Nutrition Service, https://www.fns.usda.gov/cn/fr-021622.
3. Heewon Jang, "Racial Economic Segregation Among U.S. Public Schools, 1991–2020," *The Segregation Index*, Working Paper 2022-01, http://socialinnovation.usc.edu/wp-content/uploads/2022/09/SegPaper01.pdf.
4. Jang, "Racial Economic Segregation," 1.

5. Complaint at 1, Gary B. v. Snyder, 329 F. Supp 3d 344 (E.D. Mich 2018).
6. Complaint at 44, Gary B. v. Snyder, 329 F.Supp 3d 344 (E.D. Mich 2018).
7. Complaint at 44, Gary B. v. Snyder, 329 F.Supp 3d 344 (E.D. Mich 2018).
8. Complaint at 84, Gary B. v. Snyder, 329 F.Supp 3d 344 (E.D. Mich 2018).
9. Complaint at 100, Gary B. v. Snyder, 329 F.Supp 3d 344 (E.D. Mich 2018).
10. Complaint at 69, Gary B. v. Snyder, 329 F.Supp 3d 344 (E.D. Mich 2018).
11. Ken Coleman, "Do Michigan Students Have a 'Right to Read?' Activists Await Ruling in Detroit Lawsuit," *Michigan Advance*, Dec. 23, 2019, https://michiganadvance.com/2019/12/23/do-michigan-kids-have-a-right-to-read-activists-await-ruling-in-detroit-lawsuit/.
12. Complaint at 1–2, Gary B. v. Snyder, 329 F.Supp 3d 344 (E.D. Mich 2018).
13. Heewon Jang, "Trends in Racial Economic Segregation and Its Geographic Decomposition, 1990–2020," *The Segregation Index*, Research Brief, Sept. 2020, http://socialinnovation.usc.edu/wp-content/uploads/2022/09/Trends-in-Racial-Economic-Segregation-brief.pdf.
14. Stanford Graduate School of Education, "New 'Segregation Index' Shows American Schools Remain Highly Segregated By Race, Ethnicity and Economic Status," May 17, 2022, https://ed.stanford.edu/news/new-segregation-index-shows-american-schools-remain-highly-segregated-race-ethnicity-and.
15. Jang, "Trends in Racial Economic Segregation."
16. The United States Government Accountability Office, "K-12 Education: Student Population Has Significantly Diversified, But Many Schools Remain Divided Along Racial, Ethnic, and Economic Lines," July 16, 2022, https://www.gao.gov/products/gao-22-104737.
17. GAO Highlights, "K-12 Education, Student Population Has Significantly Diversified, But Many Schools Remained Divided Along Racial, Ethnic, and Economic Lines," June 2022, https://www.gao.gov/assets/gao-22-104737-highlights.pdf.
18. GAO Highlights, "K-12 Education, Student Population."
19. Statement of Mark Rosenbaum, the plaintiffs' attorney.
20. Gary B. v. Whitmer, 957 F.3d 616, 654 (6th Cir. 2020).
21. Christine M. Naassana, "Access to Literacy Under the United States Constitution," *Buffalo Law Review* 68 (2020): 1215, 1218.
22. 6 Cir. R. 35(b), United States Court of Appeals for the Sixth Circuit, Federal Rules of Appellate Procedure, last amended Dec. 1, 2023, available at https://www.ca6.uscourts.gov/sites/ca6/files/documents/rules_procedures/Full%20Rules%20w%20FRAP.pdf. "Effect of Granting the Petition. A decision to grant rehearing on en banc vacates the previous opinion and judgment of the court, stays the mandate, and restores the case on the docket as a pending appeal." Gary B. v. Whitmer, 958 F.3d 1216 (6th Cir. 2020).
23. Typically, when a case is settled, the lawsuit ends, as an actual controversy no longer exists. In this way, the settlement "moots" the case. Given that the parties settled the case, why did the defendants petition the Sixth Circuit for en banc review? The answer is they didn't. Instead, the Sixth Circuit—in an atypical move—did that "sua sponte," or on its own initiative. As the Civil Rights Litigation Clearinghouse described it in its discussion of the procedural history of the case, "On May 19, 2020, after the settlement was announced, the Sixth Circuit took the unusual step of voting sua sponte to rehear the case en banc. This vacated the Sixth Circuit opinion that found a basic minimum right to education." Available at https://clearinghouse.net/case/15474/.
24. Todd Spangler and Meredith Spelbring, "What Whitmer Promised Group of Detroit School Students in Literacy Settlement," *Detroit Free Press*, May 14, 2020.
25. Ethan Bakuli, "Detroit's $94 Million 'Right to Read' Lawsuit Settlement Is Finally Coming Through for DPSCD," *Chalkbeat Detroit*, July 7, 2023, https://www.chalkbeat.org/detroit/2023/7/7/23787399/detroit-public-schools-right-to-read-settlement-whitmer-emergency-management/.
26. "Michigan Schools Will See Big Funding Gains for Neediest Students Under Budget Deal,"

Chalkbeat Detroit, June 28, 2023, https://www.chalkbeat.org/detroit/2023/6/28/23777737/michigan-school-funding-budget-at-risk-low-income-language-learners/.

27. Email from Derek Black to Michelle Adams, Apr. 4, 2024 (on file with the author).
28. Halley Potter, "Student Assignment and Enrollment Policies That Advance School Integration: A National Perspective to Support Planning in the District of Columbia," *Century Foundation*, Mar. 6, 2023.
29. *Parents Involved*, 551 U.S. at 701, 788–89 (2007).
30. U.S. Congress, House of Representatives, Strength in Diversity Act of 2019, Sept. 8, 2020, 5, https://www.congress.gov/116/crpt/hrpt496/CRPT-116hrpt496.pdf.
31. House of Representatives, Strength in Diversity Act of 2019, 18.
32. House of Representatives, Strength in Diversity Act of 2019, 15.
33. U.S Congress, House of Representatives, H.R. 2639—116th Congress (2019–2020) Strength in Diversity Act of 2020, 116th Cong. 2nd sess., https://www.congress.gov/bill/116th-congress/house-bill/2639.
34. House of Representatives, Strength in Diversity Act of 2019, 22.
35. "H.R.2639-Strength in Diversity Act of 2020: All Actions," https://www.congress.gov/bill/116th-congress/house-bill/2639/all-actions?overview=closed#tabs.
36. Congressional Research Service, *The Elementary and Secondary Education Act (ESEA), as Amended by the Every Student Succeeds Act (ESSA): A Primer*, Apr. 20, 2022, https://crsreports.congress.gov/product/pdf/r/r45977.
37. Elementary and Secondary Education Act of 1965, https://www.govinfo.gov/content/pkg/comps-748/pdf/comps-748.pdf.
38. "Final Appropriations, FY 2023," National Education Association, www.nea.org/sites/default/files/2023-01/final-fy23-appropriations-for-education-related-discretionary-programs-with-state-tables.pdf.
39. Derek Black, "The Constitutional Failure to Enforce Equal Protection Through the Elementary and Secondary Education Act," *Boston University Law Review* 90 (2010): 313, 317.
40. The National Coalition on School Diversity, Policy Brief 9, at 3, Nov. 2019, available at https://www.school-diversity.org/pdf/DiversityIssueBriefNo9.pdf.
41. The National Coalition on School Diversity, Policy Brief 9, at 5.
42. The National Coalition on School Diversity, Policy Brief 9, at 5.
43. The National Coalition on School Diversity, Policy Brief 9, at 5.
44. Richard D. Kahlenberg, Halley Potter, and Kimberly Quick, "A Bold Agenda for School Integration," *Century Foundation*, Apr. 8, 2019, https://tcf.org/content/report/bold-agenda-school-integration/.
45. Kahlenberg, Potter, and Quick, "A Bold Agenda for School Integration."
46. "Magnet Schools Assistance Program," Office of Elementary and Secondary Education, https://oese.ed.gov/offices/office-of-discretionary-grants-support-services/school-choice-improvement-programs/magnet-school-assistance-program-msap/.
47. "Magnet School Assistance Program, FY20 23 Grant Competition Applicant Resource," Office of Elementary and Secondary Education, https://oese.ed.gov/files/2023/03/msap-brochure.pdf.
48. Kahlenberg, Potter, and Quick, "A Bold Agenda for School Integration."
49. Janel George, Linda Darling-Hammond, and Sara Plasencia, "Advancing Integration and Equity Through Magnet Schools," Learning Policy Institute, Research Brief, Feb. 15, 2023, https://www.school-diversity.org/wp-content/uploads/Magnet_Schools_brief.pdf.
50. Kendra Taylor, "Exclusionary Policies of the Past and Present: How Single Family Zoning Structures Inequality," Atlanta Department of City Planning, Jan. 6, 2021, https://www.atlcitydesign.com/blog/2021/1/5/exclusionary-policies-of-the-past-and-present-how-single-family-zoning-structures-inequality.
51. Henry Grabar, "Minneapolis Confronts Its History of Housing Segregation," *Slate*, Dec. 7, 2018.
52. Linlin Liang, Alex Horowitz, and Adam Staveski, "Minneapolis Land Use Reforms Offer

a Blueprint for Housing Affordability," Pew Charitable Trusts, Jan. 4, 2024, https://www.pewtrusts.org/en/research-and-analysis/articles/2024/01/04/minneapolis-land-use-reforms-offer-a-blueprint-for-housing-affordability?utm_source=newsletter.

53. Laura Bliss, "Oregon's Single-Family Zoning Ban Was a 'Long Time Coming,'" *Citylab*, July 2, 2019.

54. Randyl Drummer and Richard Lawson, "Washington State Joins National Push to Curb Single-Family Zoning to Increase Housing," *CoStar News*, May 15, 2023, https://www.costar.com/article/707306704/washington-state-joins-national-push-to-curb-single-family-zoning-to-increase-housing#; Press Release, "Governor Gianforte Announces Bold, Transformational Pro-Housing Zoning Reform," Office of the Governor of Montana, May 17, 2023, https://news.mt.gov/Governors-Office/Governor_Gianforte_Announces_Bold_Transformational_Pro-Housing_Zoning_Reform.

55. Stephanie DeLuca, Lawrence F. Katz, and Sarah C. Oppenheimer, "'When Someone Cares About You, It's Priceless': Reducing Administrative Burdens and Boosting Housing Search Confidence to Increase Opportunity Moves for Voucher Holders," *RSF* 9, no. 5 (Sept. 2023): 180.

56. DeLuca, Katz, and Oppenheimer, "'When Someone Cares,'" 180.

57. DeLuca, Katz, and Oppenheimer, "'When Someone Cares,'" 180.

58. Peter Bergman et al., "Creating Moves to Opportunity: Experimental Evidence and Barriers to Neighborhood Choice," June 2023, 1, https://opportunityinsights.org/wp-content/uploads/2019/08/cmto_paper.pdf.

59. Dylan Matthews, "America Has a Housing Segregation Problem. Seattle May Just Have the Solution," *Vox*, Aug. 4, 2019

60. Bergman et al., "Creating Moves to Opportunity," 3.

61. Bergman et al., "Creating Moves to Opportunity," 45.

62. Bergman et al., "Creating Moves to Opportunity," 5.

63. Matthews, "America Has a Housing Segregation Problem."

64. Matthews, "America Has a Housing Segregation Problem."

65. "PRRAC Update (Dec. 19, 2019): 2020 School Integration Conference; New Progress on Housing Mobility; AFFH for PHAs," Poverty and Race Research Action Council, Dec. 19, 2019, https://www.prrac.org/prrac-update-12-19-19/.

66. U.S. Congress, Consolidated Appropriations Act, 2022, 117th Cong. 2nd sess., https://www.congress.gov/117/plaws/publ103/plaw-117publ103.pdf.

67. "Howard County Public Schools," Niche, https://www.niche.com/k12/d/howard-county-public-schools-md/; Michelle Burris, "What Howard County Teaches the Nation about Integration," Century Foundation, Nov. 26, 2019, https://tcf.org/content/commentary/howard-county-teaches-nation-integration.

68. Burris, "What Howard County Teaches the Nation."

69. Emma Britton Miller, "Bridges Collective Member Spotlight: Howard County Public Schools Approach to Redistricting for Integration," Century Foundation, Jan. 12, 2021, https://tcf.org/content/commentary/bridges-collaborative-member-spotlight-howard-county-public-schools-approach-redistricting-integration/.

70. Complaint at 16, Latino Action Network v. New Jersey (L-1076-19), https://d3n8a8pro7vhmx.cloudfront.net/njisj/pages/1077/attachments/original/1526582821/Desegregation_Complaint_-_finalfinal.pdf?1526582821.

71. Order Denying Plaintiffs' Motion for Partial Summary Judgment and Granting in Part Defendants' Motion for Summary Judgment, Latino Action Network (L-1076-19), Oct. 6, 2023, https://www.njcourts.gov/system/files/court-opinions/2023/l-1076-18.pdf.

72. Order Denying Plaintiffs' Motion for Partial Summary Judgment and Granting in Part Defendants' Motion for Summary Judgment at 68–69, Latino Action Network, https://www.njcourts.gov/system/files/court-opinions/2023/l-1076-18.pdf.

73. Mark Walsh, "State Judge Says 'Racially Isolated Districts Persist' in New Jersey," *Edu-*

cation Week, Oct. 17, 2023, https://www.edweek.org/policy-politics/state-judge-says-racially-isolated-districts-persist-in-new-jersey/2023/10.

74. Cruz-Guzman v. State of Minnesota, 998 N.W.2d at 262, 266 (Minn. 2023).
75. *Cruz-Guzman*, 998 N.W.2d at 262, 265.
76. *Cruz-Guzman*, 998 N.W.2d at 262, 265.
77. Email from Myron Orfield to Michelle Adams, Feb. 1, 2024 (on file with the author).
78. "About Us," Integrated Schools, https://integratedschools.org/about/.
79. "What We Do," Diverse Charter Schools Coalition, https://diversecharters.org/what-we-do/.
80. Halley Potter et al., "School Integration Is Popular. We Can Make It More So," Century Foundation, June 3, 2021.
81. Potter et al., "School Integration Is Popular."
82. Potter et al., "School Integration Is Popular."
83. john a. powell, "An 'Integrated' Theory of Integrated Education," UCLA Civil Rights Project, Aug. 1, 2002.

EPILOGUE

1. John Grover and Yvette van der Velde, "A School District in Crisis: Detroit's Public Schools 1842–2015," Regrid, https: //landgrid.com/reports/schools#what-happend.
2. "Clinton Elementary School (Closed 2010)," Public School Review, https://www.publicschoolreview.com/clinton-elementary-school-profile/48238.
3. Miriam Francisco, "Jamon Jordan Teaches the Hidden Black Histories of Detroit," *Detroit Metro Times*, Dec. 10, 2019.
4. Van Dusen, *Detroit's Birwood Wall*.
5. "Detroit, Chicago, Memphis: The 25 Most Segregated Cities in America," *USA Today*, July 20, 2019.
6. Mike Alberti, "Squandered Opportunities Leave Detroit Isolated," *Remapping Debate*, Jan. 11, 2012, http://www.remappingdebate.org/article/squandered-opportunities-leave-detroit-isolated.
7. Heather Ann-Thompson, "Rethinking the Politics of White Flight in the Postwar-City: Detroit, 1945–1980," *Journal of Urban History* 25 (1999): 163, 192.
8. Roger Lane, "Milliken Plan to Aid Detroit Causes Split," *Detroit Free Press*, Jan. 16, 1976, 1A.
9. Lane, "Milliken Plan," 1A.
10. Lane, "Milliken Plan," 5A.
11. Lane, "Milliken Plan," 5A.
12. Malcolm Johnson, "Tax Sharing Plan Sought," *Lansing State Journal*, Jan. 15, 1976, 1.
13. Lane, "Milliken Plan," 1A.
14. Ze'Ev Chafets, "The Tragedy of Detroit," *New York Times*, July 29, 1990.
15. Stanley B. Greenberg, *Middle Class Dreams: The Politics and Power of the New American Majority* (New York: Times Books, 1995), 25.
16. Greenberg, *Middle Class Dreams*, 26.
17. Cohen, *Supreme Inequality*, 122.
18. Orfield, "Milliken, Meredith, and Metropolitan Segregation," 364, 447.
19. Grover and Van der Velde, "A School District in Crisis."
20. Monica Davey and Mary Williams Walsh, "Billions in Debt, Detroit Tumbles into Insolvency," *New York Times*, July 18, 2013.
21. Reynolds Farley, "Chocolate City, Vanilla Suburbs Revisited: The Racial Integration of Detroit Suburbs," *Du Bois Review* 19, no. 1 (2022): 1.
22. Farley, "Chocolate City, Vanilla Suburbs Revisited," 7–9.
23. Orfield, "Milliken, Meredith, and Metropolitan Segregation," 354, 457.
24. Orfield, "Milliken, Meredith, and Metropolitan Segregation," 449.

25. Orfield, "Milliken, Meredith, and Metropolitan Segregation," 367.
26. *Parents Involved*, 551 U.S. at 701, 748 (2007).
27. Orfield, "Milliken, Meredith, and Metropolitan Segregation," 460.
28. Michelle Adams interview with Judge Keith, Nov. 21, 2015 (on file with author).
29. Kalyn Belsha and Koby Levin, "45 Years Later, This Case Is Still Shaping School Segregation in Detroit—and America," *Chalkbeat Detroit*, July 25, 2019, https://www.chalkbeat.org/2019/7/25/21121021/45-years-later-this-case-is-still-shaping-school-segregation-in-detroit-and-america/.
30. Siegel-Hawley, "How Non-Minority Students Also Benefit," 2.
31. Siegel-Hawley, "How Non-Minority Students Also Benefit," 2–3.
32. Siegel-Hawley, "How Non-Minority Students Also Benefit," 3.
33. Siegel-Hawley, "How Non-Minority Students Also Benefit," 3.
34. Sherrilyn Ifill, "It's Time to Face the Facts: Racism Is a National Security Issue," *Washington Post*, Dec. 18, 2018.
35. William H. Frey, "The US Will Become 'Minority White' in 2045, Census Projects; Youthful Minorities Are the Engine of Future Growth," Brookings, Mar. 14, 2018, https://www.brookings.edu/articles/the-us-will-become-minority-white-in-2045-census-projects/.
36. Text message from Janai Nelson to Michelle Adams, July 18, 2024.
37. Ed Pilkington, "What Is the 'Great Replacement' Theory and How Did Its Racist Lies Spread in the US?," *Guardian*, May 17, 2022.
38. Nicholas Confessore and Karen Yourish, "A Fringe Theory, Fostered Online, Is Refashioned by the G.O.P.," *New York Times*, May 15, 2022.
39. Confessore and Yourish, "A Fringe Theory."
40. Confessore and Yourish, "A Fringe Theory."
41. David Smith, "How Did Republicans Turn Critical Race Theory into a Winning Electoral Issue?," *Guardian*, Nov. 3, 2021.
42. Smith, "How Did Republicans."

ACKNOWLEDGMENTS

I began this project more than ten years ago as a professor at the Benjamin N. Cardozo School of Law. In 2022, I moved to the University of Michigan Law School. Both institutions have been ideal: warm, supportive, and intellectually engaging. I've been extremely fortunate in that both of these great law schools understood my vision and provided the financial support to turn that vision into a reality. Whether I was based in the Northeast or the Midwest, I could not have asked for a better home. Thank you, Cardozo Law. Thank you, Michigan Law.

Educational institutions are the sum total of the communities they bring together. It is the faculty, administration, staff, and students who bring them alive. The faculty of both institutions are outstanding, and I thank my colleagues at both schools. Elise Boddie, Chris Buccafusco (now at Duke), Michael Burstein, Evan Caminker, Myriam Gilles (now at Northwestern), Betsy Ginsberg, Michael Herz, Don Herzog, Melanie Leslie, Ngozi Okidegbe (now at Boston University), Michael Pollack, Alexander Reinert, David Rudenstine, Kate Shaw (now at Penn), Stew Sterk, and Ekow Yankah were particularly instrumental in the creation of this book. You read my drafts, provided comments, and nourished my vision along the way. You were thoughtful, patient, and kind. Thank you.

Thanks as well to all the librarians who have assisted me in this project: Shay Elbaum, Christine George, Keith Lacy, the late Kay Mackey, Virginia Neisler, Kimberly Ronning, and Lynn Wishart. Through you, I was able to take a deep dive into the media of the time, research archival sources, and obtain even the most obscure books, maps, and monographs. I'd also like to recognize two archives that were especially important to my research: The Walter P. Reuther Library, Archives of Labor and Urban Affairs, at Wayne State University houses an extraordinary collection of Detroit-related material, including the papers of the Detroit Public Schools, the Detroit Branch of the NAACP, Remus Robinson, and Coleman Young. The archivist Louis Jones was particularly helpful to me there. The Bentley Historical Library at the University of Michigan houses Judge Roth's *Bradley v. Milliken* case file, which was extremely useful to me during the research process. Janell Byrd-Chichester, Donna Gloeckner, and Kayla Jenkins provided me with access to certain documents held by the NAACP Legal Defense and Educational Fund, Inc., for which I'm very grateful. Thanks to Cheri Fidh for all that you do to make my work a success.

The heart and soul of this book is research, and I want to recognize the many law students at Cardozo and Michigan—and other researchers—who assisted me along the way. Working with each and every one of you has been one of the highlights of my career. I want to express very special thanks to the following people for assisting in researching this book: Stephanie Alvarez-Jones, Geoffrey Andreu, Jake Aronson, Aliza Balis, Julie Bernstein, Sam Breitbart, Kira Brekke, Liam Carbutt, Samuel Clougher, Micah Coffee, Nick Cutz, Jacqueline Diggs, Morgan Fenton, Rachel Fishman, Ciera Foreman, Deborah Frisch, Regina Gerhardt, Colleen Grogan, Yomidalys Guichardo, Jennifer Kim, Benjamin Leb, Elizabeth Lewis, John Ludwig, Jason Nadboy, Lila Nazarian, Marta Poplawski, Jonathan Raz, Joshua Reznik, Renisha Ricks, Stephen Ross, Carlos Salguero, Nicholas Schmitt, Andrew Schreder, Cooper Sirwatka, Keegan Stephan, Nate Sumimoto, Pamela Takefman, Allison Venuti, Kathleen Wahl, and Rayven Young. I want to extend special thanks to Myles Zhang for re-creating the trial exhibits that were so persuasive to Judge Roth.

Scholars and advocates at other institutions and organizations (or in other fields) have also given me valuable insights on my project, comments on the manuscript, and/or provided welcome words of encouragement. I want to thank them here: Joyce Baugh, Derek Black, Kristi Bowman, Guy

Charles, Joshua Civin, Mary Dudziak, Daniel Farbman, Reynolds Farley, Tristin Green, Ed Hartnett, Danielle Holley-Walker, Olati Johnson, Randall Kennedy, Catherine Y. Kim, Gilbert King, Matt Lassiter, Sophia Lee, Nicholas Lemann, John Logan, Myron Orfield, Florence Roisman, Richard Rothstein, Tom Sugrue, Phil Tegeler, and Heather Ann Thompson.

I'm fortunate to work with a fantastic publication team. They have ably shepherded me through this process: my wonderful publicist, Angela Baggetta; my agent, Ryan Harbage, who has provided me with outstanding representation; and my editors, Amanda Katz and Alex Star. Amanda: you are a wizard with respect to structure, organization, and all the rest. Alex: You instantly understood my project and you've invested deeply in it. You've never wavered in your belief in *The Containment*. Thanks as well to Ian Van Wye and the rest of the team at Farrar, Straus and Giroux for everything along the way.

I'd like to thank my friends for providing me with unwavering support throughout this process: Eliza Byard, Nancy Cohen, Lia Epperson, Susana Fried, Rachel Godsil, Suzanne Goldberg, Stephanie Grant, Jill Harris, Robin Lenhardt, Debra Liebowitz, Aviva Michelman-Dumas, Melissa Murray, Janai Nelson, Kimani Paul-Emile, Renee Russak, Jane Sasseen, Nicole Stromberg, Ben Talton, Linda Villarosa, Jana Welch, Juliet Widoff, Jackie Woodson, and Lesley Yulkowski. Thank you for your time, your friendship, your encouragement, your laughter, and your camaraderie. I couldn't have completed this project without you.

To my wife, Laura Nelsen; my daughter, Ella Nelsen-Adams; and my sister, Dawn Adams—in many ways this project is about family. *The Containment* is dedicated to my parents, Bernard and Frederica; so much of my curiosity that lead me to research this book came from trying to understand their world and experiences. Researching this book brought me closer to them and to you. Thank you for creating an environment in which I could thrive. I also want to recognize my extended Long Island family: Artie Nelsen, Laura M. Nelsen, Bryan Gallagher, Christine Gallagher, Brendan Egan, Sharon Egan, and Ellen Gove. Thank you for believing in me and giving me an opportunity to do this work.

Finally, to Thomas Healy, my friend and colleague. There is no *The*

Containment without you. You live your values. From the very beginning, you knew I could write this book. You read multiple iterations of my book proposal and manuscript, asked the right questions, provided encouragement, and pushed me to give my absolute best to this project. Our friendship illustrates the value of integration: individuals of different races coming together under conditions of equality to move forward, individually and collectively. Thank you.

INDEX

A NOTE ABOUT THE AUTHOR

Michelle Adams is the Henry M. Butzel Professor of Law at the University of Michigan. The former codirector of the Floersheimer Center for Constitutional Democracy at the Benjamin N. Cardozo School of Law, she served on the Biden administration's Presidential Commission on the Supreme Court of the United States and as an expert commentator on the Netflix series *Amend: The Fight for America* and the Showtime series *Deadlocked: How America Shaped the Supreme Court*. Her writing has appeared in *The New Yorker, The Yale Law Journal, California Law Review*, and other publications. She was born and grew up in Detroit.